THE
OXFORD DICTIONARY OF
MODERN GREEK

THE
OXFORD DICTIONARY OF
MODERN GREEK
(GREEK–ENGLISH)

COMPILED BY

J. T. PRING

Reader in Phonetics
University College
London

OXFORD
AT THE CLARENDON PRESS

Oxford University Press, Ely House, London W. 1

GLASGOW   NEW YORK   TORONTO   MELBOURNE   WELLINGTON
CAPE TOWN   SALISBURY   IBADAN   NAIROBI   LUSAKA   ADDIS ABABA
BOMBAY   CALCUTTA   MADRAS   KARACHI   LAHORE   DACCA
KUALA LUMPUR   HONG KONG   TOKYO

FIRST PUBLISHED 1965
REPRINTED LITHOGRAPHICALLY IN GREAT BRITAIN
FROM CORRECTED SHEETS OF THE FIRST EDITION
AT THE UNIVERSITY PRESS, OXFORD
BY VIVIAN RIDLER
PRINTER TO THE UNIVERSITY
1968

PREFACE

THE classical age of Greek literature, under the dominating influence of Athens, was followed by a period of great linguistic change after the conquests of Alexander had carried Greek influence far and wide over the Near East. The Greek which came to be used in common throughout this area, not only by Greeks themselves but also by the native peoples, who learnt it as a second language, is known as the Hellenistic Koine, or common Greek. Its main constituent was the Attic-Ionic dialect, which had been perfected as a medium of oratory by Isocrates and Demosthenes, and of philosophical prose by Plato. But this new extension of Greek naturally brought about many changes in vocabulary, grammar, and pronunciation; and various contemporary writings, especially letters preserved in Egyptian papyri, throw enough light on the state of the vernacular to show that it was already developing some of the characteristic features of the present-day language. The age of the Koine, which saw the Roman conquest of Greece and the rise of Christianity, may be set roughly between 300 B.C. and A.D. 300. Outstanding among works representing literary forms of Hellenistic Greek are the History of Polybius and the New Testament. Some academic purists, reacting against the innovations of the Koine, promoted the doctrine of 'Atticism', which set up classical Attic Greek as the only permissible model of prose composition; and this attitude has never ceased to affect Greek writing by inhibiting free expression in the natural idiom of the times.

The spirit of Atticism may be said to prevail through the whole Byzantine period from the establishment of Constantinople in 330 until its capture by the Turks in 1453. Although Greek had replaced Latin as the official language of the Eastern Empire by about 600, the development of the vernacular during the following centuries remains largely a matter for speculation, since almost all writers continued to regard it as unfit for literature. Thus by the middle of the fifteenth century, when western Europe stood poised upon the threshold of the modern world with well-integrated languages and flourishing literatures, Greece was entering upon four hundred years of bondage to the Turks without benefit of either.

Crete, under Venetian administration, held out against the Turks until 1669; and the poetry written in the Cretan dialect of the seventeenth century may be regarded as the beginning of modern demotic literature. Under the Turks, the regional dialects found expression in a body of folk songs reflecting the life of a people deprived of all material and intellectual progress. When Greece won independence in 1830, Athens and the Peloponnese became the political core of the new kingdom, and it is their dialects which form the basis of the standard spoken Greek of today. But the official language of a modern state could not be wrought out of the folklore of a medieval peasantry. Efforts were made to produce a purified form of Greek ('katharevusa'), suitable for modern needs. But they became too deeply influenced by the spirit of Atticism; and the problem of finding a natural prose medium supple enough to provide expression in both formal and colloquial terms was not solved to anybody's satisfaction. Now, after more than a century of independence, Greeks are still frustrated by the 'language question'. But with the spread of education and the growth of journalism and broadcasting, the question begins to solve itself. Demotic and katharevusa cannot be kept apart, and a form of Greek is already emerging which combines features of both.

THE EVOLUTION OF DEMOTIC

The development of some main features of the modern vernacular is outlined below. It should be borne in mind that they do not represent a coherent or exclusive system; and that other, more conservative, forms are also to be found coexisting with them.

Phonology. After the Hellenistic period the distinguishing power of word-accent lay in its position rather than its pitch; and the former distinctions of vowel-length were lost. Certain words now show a stronger tendency to keep the primary stress in their inflected forms. A ϵ ι o have remained more or less unchanged in quality; ov was already u before the end of the classical period; and ω merged with o as a mid back vowel after the first century A.D. $A\iota$ had merged with ϵ by the second century A.D., and the second element of av ϵv ηv had developed into a labial fricative. H and $\epsilon\iota$ had both become i by early Byzantine times. Y and $o\iota$ were being confused as ü in Hellenistic Greek, and both became i by the tenth century.

Double consonants have been reduced to single, except in a few dialects. The aspirated voiceless stops θ ϕ χ had changed to fricatives by the fourth century A.D., and initial h (marked by 'rough breathing') had disappeared. By the same date the voiced stops represented by β δ γ had become replaced by fricatives. But in certain modern forms the labial and dental stops are still preserved after μ ν, being now written as π τ, e.g.: $\gamma\alpha\mu\pi\rho\delta s < \gamma\alpha\mu\beta\rho\delta s$, $\delta\epsilon\nu\tau\rho o < \delta\epsilon\nu\delta\rho o\nu$. The originally voiceless π τ κ following a nasal have changed to voiced stops (which can also occur without the nasal environment, especially in initial position). Among other phonological changes are: (i) Loss of many initial and medial unaccented vowels, including the verbal augment. (ii) Loss of nasals finally and before a continuant consonant. (iii) Dissimilation of voiceless consonant groups, e.g.: $φτερό < πτερόν$, $ὀχτώ < ὀκτώ$, $σκολιό < σχολεῖον$, $ἔκαψα < ἔκαυσα$.

Morphology and Syntax. The dative case, already restricted in New Testament Greek, had fallen out of popular use by the tenth century. Indirect object is now expressed by the accusative (usually after $σέ$) or genitive. Prepositions govern the accusative. A notable feature of nouns is the extension of a simplified first declension having two terminations in each number, with -ς marking nominative singular of masculines and genitive singular of feminines, and a common plural in -ες, -ων. This includes many nouns adapted from the classical third declension, e.g.: $ὁ ἔρωτας$, $ἡ πατρίδα$, $ἡ βρύση$. A new plural inflexion -δες is very common, especially in non-classical words. The neuter second declension form in -ι has developed from diminutives in -ιον since the Koine period.

Dual number had become obsolete in later classical Greek. Optative mood, already rare in the Koine, fell out of use in the Byzantine period; and the infinitive became superseded by $νά$ with subjunctive. Verbs have lost the old future, perfect, and pluperfect tenses. Futurity is expressed by $θά$ with subjunctive, and conditional mood by $θά$ with imperfect. Compounds of $ἔχω$ provide perfect, pluperfect, future perfect, and past conditional tenses. Durative and perfective aspect of verbs are based upon present and aorist stems respectively, and this category is now extended to future time. The indeclinable relative pronoun $πού$ and active participle in -οντας have been in common use since the Byzantine period.

Other basic features of demotic are: (i) Parataxis in preference to subordination. (ii) Formal redundancy of the types $μικρό κοριτσάκι$, $πιό χειρότερος$, $ξανακοιμήθηκα πάλι$. (iii) Great use of diminutives.

VOCABULARY

The nucleus of the modern vocabulary has been handed down from ancient Greek. It is supplemented by several strata of loan-words, of which the chief are: Latin (from the Hellenistic and Byzantine periods); Italian (from the Venetian and Genoese occupation of Greek lands after 1200); Turkish (from the period 1453–1830); French, and, to a lesser degree, English (during the last 130 years). The abundant resources of derivation and composition which Greek possesses have made easy the creation of new words, especially scientific terms, out of the native stock. These include translation-words, such as σιδηρόδρομος (chemin-de-fer), and the reborrowing of Hellenic coinages already current elsewhere, as ἀεροπλάνον (aeroplane).

This book is designed to meet the need for a compact, up-to-date dictionary suitable both for general reference and for the language student. Much of the less useful material of older dictionaries has been eliminated in favour of a more practical selection of words in common use, covering the vocabulary of everyday affairs and general literature. Due attention is paid to both formal and colloquial usage, and there is a fair proportion of foreign loan-words. Great care has been taken to find clear and accurate translations or explanations, and to improve on traditional renderings where it seemed necessary.

Space has been saved by leaving out many straightforward derivatives and compounds. Thus ἄτολμος (timid) is given, but not ἀτόλμως (timidly) or ἀτολμία (timidity); κρυφά (secretly) and βλέπω (look) are given, but not κρυφοβλέπω (look stealthily).

Among common words usually omitted are:

(1) Feminine equivalents of masculine nouns such as γειτόνισσα (from γείτονας), φοιτήτρια (from φοιτητής), μυλωνοῦ (from μυλωνᾶς).

(2) Adverbs in -ως and -α formed from adjectives, e.g.:
σοφῶς (from σοφός), ἄσχημα (from ἄσχημος).

(3) Diminutives and augmentatives ending in -άκι, -ίτσα,
-ούλης, -αρος, etc.

Some common prefixes are shown separately, with an indication
of their range of meaning, e.g.: καλο-, ξε-, παρα-, σιγο-. For the
general rules of derivation and composition a grammar should
be consulted. This is also the best source of information on the
phonetic, orthographic, and morphological differences (a) between puristic and demotic Greek, and (b) within the field of
demotic itself. Variant spellings of words are so numerous that
many alternative forms have had to be omitted from this dictionary. Examples of common types of variant are the following:
βιβλίον or βιβλίο, ἐφημερίς or ἐφημερίδα, βρύσις or βρύσι or βρύση,
δηλῶ or δηλώνω, ἀγαπῶμαι or ἀγαπιέμαι. Often the first letters
of words are affected, and their several forms must be sought
at widely separated points in the dictionary, e.g.: ὀλίγος or
λίγος, εὑρίσκω or βρίσκω, κτίζω or χτίζω. An attempt is made to
show (as older dictionaries often do not) when such pairs are not
identical in meaning, e.g.: δικαιοῦμαι and δικαιώνομαι, ρεῦμα
and ρέμα, αἱ θέρμαι and οἱ θέρμες. The problem of variant forms
makes it impracticable to give the inflexions of verbs, nouns, and
adjectives. A full dictionary should deal comprehensively with
these matters, and present impartially the puristic and demotic
forms of any word liable to such variation. A small dictionary
cannot do so, and must refer readers to the grammarian for an
explanation of much that is here left unsaid.

ARRANGEMENT OF ENTRIES

The headword is in bold type. A swung dash, used in the body
of the article, represents either the headword or that part of it
preceding a vertical line. Certain derivatives are given under
headwords, being shown by the swung dash with termination

in bold type. Other derivatives have been treated as separate
entries where it seemed more convenient to do so. A shift of accent
is usually shown in quotations of the headword: when it is not,
it may be deduced from the general rules of accentuation.

It should be clear from the nature of an entry whether it is
to be read as a translation of the Greek word, or as a definition
or explanation. Thus 'fish' is a translation; but 'sort of fish' is
a definition, and implies that an English equivalent word is not
found, or is too uncommon to be usefully quoted. Words in
Roman type within brackets form part of the translation or
definition. 'Bedroom (suite)' indicates that the word means
both 'bedroom' and 'bedroom suite'. Words in italics within
brackets are explanatory, e.g.: 'diamond (*cards*)', 'demolish
(*building*)'. Common idioms are included; and a short phrase
may be given to illustrate a particular usage. The derivation of
indeclinable loan-words is given in square brackets.

The term (*fam.*) is used, widely but not exhaustively, to show
colloquial expressions that might be better avoided in serious
or formal utterance. It did not seem advisable to try to assess
degrees of informality or acceptability; but the English rendering
of a word or phrase may help the reader to judge its stylistic
value.

Attention is drawn to two conventions governing the entries
for verbs:

(1) γέρνω *v.t.* & *i.* bend down, tilt; half close (*door*); (*v.i.*) lean
    or bend over, stoop; lie down; sink (*of star*).

The above layout indicates that the meanings which precede
(*v.i.*) refer to the transitive function of the verb, and those which
follow (*v.i.*) refer to its intransitive function.

(2) ἀποκαλύπτ|ω *v.t.* unveil, uncover, reveal. ∼ομαι *v.i.* raise
    one's hat.

The passive form of an active verb is quoted in the body of
the entry if it involves an extension of the range of meaning.

In such cases the simple passive inversion of the active meaning
is not necessarily excluded by not being mentioned. In the
above entry it is understood that ἀποκαλύπτομαι also means
'be unveiled, uncovered, *or* revealed'.

PRONUNCIATION

The pronunciation of Greek bears a consistent relation to its
spelling, so that it need not be separately shown in the body
of the dictionary. The phonetic values of the Greek letters
are summarized here.

Vowels

	phonetic symbol	nearest English equivalent
η ι υ ει οι υι	i	b**ea**t
ε αι	ɛ	b**e**t
α	a	b**u**tt
ο ω	ɔ	b**ou**ght
ου	u	b**oo**t
αυ	af	c**uff**
αυ (before voiced sounds)	av	lo**ve**
ευ	ɛf	ch**ef**
ευ (before voiced sounds)	ɛv	**ev**er
ηυ	if	l**eaf**
ηυ (before voiced sounds)	iv	l**ea**ve

Note 1. The vowel-digraphs included above are pronounced as
shown unless the first letter bears an acute accent or the second
a diaeresis. In these two cases each letter has its separate
value, e.g.:

πολλοί	(pɔli)	ρολόι	(rɔlɔi)
ἅρπυια	(arpia)	μυϊκός	(miikɔs)
αἰτία	(ɛtia)	ἀϊτός	(aitɔs)

Note 2. Unstressed i before another vowel is sometimes reduced to a semivowel glide. This is noted in the very rare cases where a distinction of meaning is concerned, e.g.: σκιάζω (-i-) shade, σκιάζω (-j-) frighten.

Consonants

	phonetic symbol	nearest English equivalent
β	v	o*v*er
γ	ɣ	(Spanish fue*g*o)
γ (before i and ε)	j	*y*ield
δ	ð	fa*th*er
ζ	z	la*z*y
θ	θ	au*th*or
κ	k	s*k*in
λ	l	*l*eave
μ	m	*m*ay
ν	n	*n*ot
ξ	ks	bo*x*
π	p	s*p*in
ρ	r	th*r*ee
σ, s	s	*s*ee
σ (before voiced consonants)	z	la*z*y
τ	t	s*t*ick
φ	f	*f*at
χ	x	(Scots lo*ch*)
χ (before i and ε)	ç	*h*ew
ψ	ps	ta*ps*

The following consonant-digraphs have special values:

γγ	ŋg	fi*ng*er
γξ	ŋks	sphi*nx*

	phonetic symbol	*nearest English equivalent*
γχ	ŋx, nç	
γκ (initial)	g	*g*et
γκ (medial)	g, ŋg, ŋk	
μπ (initial)	b	*b*et
μπ (medial)	b, mb, mp	
ντ (initial)	d	*d*o
ντ (medial)	d, nd, nt	
τζ	dz	a*dz*e

Accentuation

Stress-accent coincides with the written accent of a word, and falls upon one of the last three syllables. If the final syllable contains η, ω, ει, or ου, the accent does not fall earlier than the penultimate syllable. (These rules are subject to some modification in demotic usage.) The difference between acute, grave, and circumflex accent does not affect pronunciation. In printed Greek the grave accent of final syllables is sometimes replaced by an acute. Fluctuation of usage in this matter is reflected in the dictionary.

Among books consulted, I have made the most frequent use of these three: *Lexikon tis Ellinikis Glossis* (Proia), *Antilexikon* (Th. Vostandzoglou), and *Lexique Grec moderne Français* (H. Pernot). My greatest debt is to my wife, whose devoted help and constant encouragement have sustained and comforted me in my task.

J. T. P.

ACKNOWLEDGEMENT

PART of the research for this work has been carried out with the aid of grants from the British Academy and the Central Research Fund of the University of London.

ABBREVIATIONS

a., adjective
acc., accusative
adv., adverb
aero., aeronautical
aor., aorist
archit., architecture
biol., biology
bot., botanical
chem., chemistry
conj., conjunction
D., Dutch
dat., dative
E., English
eccl., ecclesiastical
esp., especially
etc., etcetera
F., French
f., feminine
fam., familiar
fig., figurative
G., German
gen., genitive
geom., geometry
Gk., Greek
I., Italian
i., intransitive
imper., imperative
int., interjection

joc., jocular
iron., ironic
lit., literally
m., masculine
math., mathematics
mech., mechanics
med., medical
mil., military
mus., music
n., neuter
naut., nautical
neg., negative
nom., nominative
num., numeral
part., participle
pass., passive
pej., pejorative
phys., physics
pl., plural
prep., preposition
pron., pronoun
s., substantive
sing., singular
sthg., something
T., Turkish
t., transitive
v., verb

ά- (*privative prefix*) un-, in-, -less.
ἀβαθής *a.* shallow.
ἄβαλτος *a.* not placed in position; unworn, new.
ἀβανιά *s.f.* false accusation.
ἀβάντα *s.f.* (*fam.*) profit, advantage; backing.
ἀβάρετος *a.* indefatigable.
ἀβαρία *s.f.* jettison; damage (*to ship or cargo*); (*fig.*) κάνω ~ moderate one's pretensions.
ἀβασάνιστος *a.* not well thought out.
ἀβάσιμος *a.* groundless.
ἀβάστακτος *a.* unbearable; uncontrollable.
ἄβατος *a.* untrodden; inaccessible.
ἄβγαλτος *a.* not having come out *or* off; inexperienced.
ἀβγατίζω *v.t. & i.* increase.
ἀβγό *s.n.* egg.
ἀβγο- *see* αὐγο-.
ἀβέβαιος *a.* uncertain.
ἀβέρτα *adv.* openly.
ἀβίαστος *a.* unforced, easy.
ἀβίωτος *a.* impossibly difficult.
ἀβλαβής *a.* harmless; unharmed; σῶος καὶ ~ safe and sound.
ἀβλεψία *s.f.* oversight.
ἄβολος *a.* inconvenient, awkward.
ἄβουλος *a.* irresolute; weak-willed.
ἄβραστος *a.* uncooked; under-cooked.
ἀβρός *a.* gracious, delicate, gentle.
ἄβροχ|ος *a.* dry (*not wetted*); ~οις ποσί without any trouble.
ἄβυσσος *s.f.* abyss.
ἀγαθ|ός *a.* good, kind; naïve; τὰ ~ά possessions.
ἀγάλια *adv.* slowly, gently.
ἀγαλλίασις *s.f.* exultation.
ἄγαλμα *s.n.* statue.
ἄγαμος *a.* unmarried.
ἄγαν *adv.* too much.
ἀγανακτ|ῶ *v.i.* be exasperated. ~ησις *s.f.* exasperation.
ἀγανός *a.* loosely woven.
ἀγάνωτος *a.* unplated (*metal*).
ἀγάπη *s.f.* love.

ἀγαπημένος *a.* dear, loved; favourite.
ἀγαπητικός *s.m.* lover, sweetheart.
ἀγαπητός *a.* dear, loved.
ἀγαπίζω *v.t. & i.* reconcile; become reconciled.
ἀγαπ|ῶ *v.t. & i.* love; ὅπως ~ᾶτε as you like.
ἄγαρμπος *a.* unshapely, ill-proportioned, inelegant; uncouth.
ἀγᾶς *s.m.* aga; (*fig.*) despot, sybarite.
ἀγγαρ|εία *s.f.* drudgery; chore; (*mil.*) fatigue (-party). ~εύω *v.t.* impose a task on.
ἀγγεῖον *s.n.* vessel; (chamber-) pot; blood-vessel; αἰσχρὸν ~ rascal.
ἀγγειοπλαστική *s.f.* pottery.
ἀγγελία *s.f.* tidings, announcement; small advertisement. ~φόρος *s.m.* messenger.
ἀγγελικός *a.* angel's; angelic.
ἀγγέλλω *v.t.* announce.
ἄγγελμα *s.n.* announcement.
ἄγγελος *s.m.* angel.
ἀγγελτήριον *s.n.* note announcing wedding, *etc.*
ἀγγίζω *v.t. see* ἐγγίζω.
ἄγγιχτος *a.* untouched.
ἀγγλικός *a.* English.
Ἄγγλος *s.m.* Englishman.
ἀγγούρι *s.n.* cucumber.
ἄγδαρτος *a.* not skinned *or* grazed.
ἀγελάδα *s.f.* cow.
ἀγελαῖος *a.* gregarious (*animal*); (*fig.*) vulgar, commonplace.
ἀγέλαστος *a.* unsmiling, sullen; not taken in.
ἀγέλη *s.f.* herd, flock. ~δόν *adv.* in a herd.
ἀγένεια *s.f.* rudeness.
ἀγένειος *a.* beardless.
ἀγενής *a.* ill-mannered.
ἀγέννητος *a.* unborn; not having given birth.
ἀγέρας *s.m. see* ἀέρας.
ἀγέραστος *a.* ageless.
ἀγέρωχος *a.* haughty.
ἄγημα *s.n.* detachment; (*naut.*) landing-party.

άγια adv. (fam.) well; ~ έκανες κι' ήρθες you did very well to come; καλά καί ~ that is all very well (but ...).
άγιάζι s.n. frost, cold.
άγιάζω v.t. & i. sanctify; asperse; become a saint.
άγίασμα s.n. holy water.
άγιασμός s.m. (blessing with) holy water.
άγιάτρευτος n. incurable; not cured.
άγίνωτος a. unripe, not done; impossible.
άγιογδύτης s.m. robber of churches; (fig.) usurer.
άγιογραφία s.f. sacred painting, ikon.
άγιόκλημα s.n. honeysuckle.
άγιος a. & s.m. holy, sacred; saint.
άγκαζάρω v.t. engage (artist); book, reserve; invite pressingly.
άγκαζέ 1. a. occupied, engaged, booked. 2. adv. arm-in-arm. [F. engagé]
άγκάθι s.n. thorn.
άγκαλά conj. although.
άγκάλη s.f. 1. embrace; arms, bosom. 2. bay, inlet.
άγκαλιά s.f. embrace; arms, bosom, lap; armful; (adv.) in one's arms, on one's lap. ~ζω v.t. embrace.
άγκίδ|α s.f. splinter, prickle. ~ωτός a. barbed.
άγκινάρα s.f. globe artichoke.
άγκίστρι s.n. fish-hook.
άγκλίτσα s.f. shepherd's crook.
άγκομαχῶ v.i. pant; be in the throes of death.
άγκύλαι s.f.pl. square brackets.
άγκύλ|ι s.n. prickle, splinter. ~ ώνω v.t. prick, sting.
άγκύλωσις s.f. (med.) anchylosis.
άγκυλωτός a. bent.
άγκυρ|α s.f. anchor. ~οβολῶ v.t. anchor.
άγκών s.m. elbow; bend.
άγκωνάρι s.n. corner-stone.
άγκωνή s.f. corner; crust.
άγλαΐζω v.t. adorn.
άγναντεύω v.t. see from afar.
άγνοια s.f. ignorance.
άγνός a. pure, chaste.
άγνοῶ v.t. ignore; not to know.
άγνώμ|ων a. ungrateful. ~οσύνη s.f. ingratitude.
άγνώριστος a. unrecognizable.
άγνωστος a. unknown.
άγονος a. sterile, barren; (fig.) fruitless; ~ γραμμή unprofitable line (shipping).

άγορά s.f. market; buying, purchase.
άγοράζω v.t. buy.
άγοραῖος a. market; for hire; (fig.) low-class.
άγορανομία s.f. market inspectorate.
άγοραπωλησία s.f. buying and selling.
άγοραστής s.m. buyer.
άγορ|εύω v.i. speak in public. ~ευσις s.f. speech, address.
άγόρι s.n. boy.
άγουρίδα s.f. unripe grape.
άγουρόλαδο s.n. oil from unripe olives; virgin oil.
άγουρος a. unripe.
άγρα s.f. hunt, pursuit.
άγραβανιά s.f. Judas-tree.
άγράμματ|ος a. illiterate. ~ωσύνη s.f. illiteracy.
άγραφος a. unwritten; ~ χάρτης blank paper, worthless document.
άγριάδα s.f. wildness, fierceness; couch-grass.
άγριεύω v.t. & i. make or become wild or fierce; scare; become scared.
άγρίμι s.n. wild animal, game; (fig.) shy, unsociable person.
άγριος a. wild, fierce.
άγριόχορτο s.n. weed.
άγροικία s.f. country property; boorishness.
άγροῖκος a. coarse, boorish.
άγρόκτημα s.n. country property.
άγρονομία s.f. rural economy; overseeing of land.
άγρ|ός s.m. field. ~ότης s.m. countryman, farmer. ~οτικός a. agrarian, rural.
άγροφυλακή s.f. rural police.
άγρυπν|ῶ v.i. stay awake, keep watch. ~ία s.f. sleeplessness; keeping awake; vigil.
άγυάλιστος a. unpolished.
άγυιόπαις s.m. street-urchin.
άγύμναστος a. untrained.
άγύρευτος a. unsought, not in demand.
άγύριστ|ος a. not traversed; from which there is no return; not given back; ~ο κεφάλι stubborn person.
άγύρτης s.m. charlatan, quack.
άγχίνους a. intelligent.
άγχιστεία s.f. relationship by marriage.
άγχόνη s.f. gibbet, gallows.
άγχος s.n. pathological anxiety.
άγω v.t. & i. lead, bring; be in (year of one's age, etc.); ~ καὶ φέρω lead by the nose; ~μεν let us go.

ἀγωγή s.f. upbringing; training; (med.) regimen; (law) suit, action.

ἀγώγι s.n. load, fare; cost of transport.

ἀγωγιάτης s.m. muleteer.

ἀγωγός s.m. conduit; conductor (of heat, etc.).

ἀγών s.m. struggle, exertion, contest, ~ες (pl.) athletic games.

ἀγωνία s.f. agony, anguish; anxiety.

ἀγων|ίζομαι v.i. struggle, contend. ~ιστής s.m. contender, fighter.

ἀγωνιῶ v.i. be in (death) agony; (fig.) struggle, strive.

ἀδαής a. unfamiliar (not expert) (with gen. or σέ).

ἀδαμάντινος a. diamond; firm, unflinching.

ἀδάμας s.m. diamond.

ἀδάμαστος a. untamed; untameable; indomitable.

ἀδαμιαῖ|ος a. Adam's; ἐν ~α περιβολῆ in the nude.

ἀδάπανος a. costing nothing.

ἄδεια s.f. permission; permit, licence; leave (of absence).

ἀδειάζω v.t. & i. empty; have time to spare.

ἀδειανός a. empty, vacant; unoccupied.

ἄδειος a. empty, vacant.

ἀδεκαρία s.f. pennilessness.

ἀδέκαστος a. incorruptible; impartial.

ἀδελφή s.f. sister.

ἀδέλφια s.n.pl. brothers, brother(s) and sister(s).

ἀδελφικός a. fraternal, brotherly.

ἀδελφός s.m. brother.

ἄδενδρος a. treeless.

ἀδέξιος a. clumsy, maladroit.

ἀδερφ- see ἀδελφ-.

ἀδέσποτος a. without an owner or master.

ἄδετος a. unbound; unmounted; loose.

ἄδηλος a. uncertain, unknown.

ἀδημονῶ v.i. be anxiously impatient.

ἀδήν s.m. gland.

ἄδης s.m. Hades; hell.

ἀδηφάγος a. gluttonous.

ἀδιάβαστος a. unreadable; unread; unprepared (in lessons).

ἀδιάβατος a. impassable.

ἀδιάβροχ|ος a. watertight, waterproof. ~ο s.n. raincoat.

ἀδιάθετος a. indisposed (in health); not disposed of; (law) intestate.

ἀδιαίρετος a. undivided; indivisible.

ἀδιάκοπος a. uninterrupted.

ἀδιά|κριτος a. 1. imperceptible. 2. prying. ~κρίτως adv. irrespectively; indiscriminately; importunately.

ἀδιάλειπτος a. incessant.

ἀδιάλλακτος a. intransigent.

ἀδιάλυτος a. indissoluble; not broken up.

ἀδιάντροπος a. shameless.

ἀδιαπέραστος a. impenetrable, impermeable.

ἀδιάπτωτος a. sustained, unfailing.

ἀδιάρρηκτος a. unbreakable; unbroken.

ἀδιάσπαστος a. indissoluble, unbroken.

ἀδιάφθορος a. incorruptible.

ἀδιάφορετα adv. without profit; to no purpose.

ἀδιάφορ|ος a. indifferent, without interest. ~ία s.f. indifference.

ἀδιαχώρητον s.n. (phys.) impenetrability.

ἀδιαχώριστος a. indivisible; undivided.

ἀδίδακτος a. untaught.

ἀδιέξοδ|ος a. having no outlet; blind (road). ~ον s.n. impasse, cul-de-sac.

ἀδικαιολόγητος a. unjustified; unjustifiable.

ἀδίκημα s.n. wrongful act.

ἀδικία s.f. injustice, wrong.

ἄδικ|ος a. unjust, wrong; vain, fruitless; ἔχω ~ο be wrong. ~ον s.n. injustice, wrong. ~α adv. wrongly; in vain.

ἀδικῶ v.t. & i. wrong; do wrong.

ἀδιόρατος a. hardly perceptible.

ἀδιόρθωτος a. uncorrected; irreparable; incorrigible.

ἀδίστακτος a. unhesitating.

ἄδολος a. without guile; pure, unadulterated.

ἀδόξαστ|ος a. unsung; (fam.) θά σοῦ ἀλλάξω τόν ~ο I'll give you what for!

ἀδούλευτος a. unworked, uncultivated.

ἀδράν|εια s.f. inertia; inactivity. ~ής a. inert; sluggish.

ἀδράχνω v.t. seize, grasp.

ἀδράχτι s.n. spindle.

ἀδρός a. sizeable, generous.

ἀδυναμία s.f. weakness; addiction; leanness.

ἀδυνατίζω v.t. & i. weaken; make thin; lose weight.

ἀδύνατ|ος a. weak; lean; impossible. ~ῶ v.i. be unable.

ἀδυσώπητος d. inexorable.

ἄδυτ|ος a. inaccessible. ~ον s.n. (eccl.) sanctuary. ~α s.n.pl. depths.

ἄδω *v.t. & i.* sing.

ἀεί *adv.* always.

ἀειθαλής *a.* evergreen.

ἀεικίνητον *s.n.* perpetual motion.

ἀείμνηστος *a.* ever-remembered.

ἀέναος *a.* perpetual.

ἀεράμυνα *s.f.* anti-aircraft defence.

ἀέρ|ας *s.m.* air, wind; mien; (*fam.*) key-money; πῆρε ὁ νοῦς του ~α he has got above himself; ~α! *battle-cry.*

ἄεργ|ος *a.* out of work. ~ία *s.f.* un-employment.

ἀερίζω *v.t.* fan, ventilate, air.

ἀέρινος *a.* light as air, ethereal.

ἀέρι|ον *s.n.* gas; ~α (*pl.*) (*med.*) wind.

ἀεριοῦχος *a.* aerated.

ἀεριόφως *s.n.* gaslight; (*fam.*) gas.

ἀερισμός *s.m.* ventilation.

ἀεριστήρ *s.m.* ventilator, fan.

ἀεριώδης *a.* gaseous.

ἀεριωθούμενος *a.* jet-propelled.

ἀεροβατῶ *v.i.* (*fig.*) be in the clouds, be dreaming.

ἀεροδρόμιον *s.n.* aerodrome.

ἀεροκοπανίζω *v.i.* chatter; labour in vain.

ἀερόλιθος *s.m.* meteorite.

ἀερολιμήν *s.m.* airport.

ἀερολογῶ *v.i.* talk nonsense.

ἀεροπλάν|ον *s.n.* aeroplane. ~οφόρον *s.n.* (*naut.*) aircraft-carrier.

ἀεροπορία *s.f.* air-force; air-line.

ἀεροπορικῶς *adv.* by air.

ἀεροπόρος *s.m.* flyer, airman.

ἀερόστατον *s.n.* balloon.

ἀεροστεγής *a.* airtight.

ἀέτειος *a.* aquiline.

ἀετός *s.m.* eagle; kite (*toy*).

ἀέτωμα *s.m.* pediment.

ἀζευγάρωτος *a.* unpaired; unploughed.

ἀζημίωτ|ος *a.* without suffering loss; μέ τό ~ο for a consideration.

ἀζήτητος *a.* unclaimed; not in demand.

ἀζύγι(α)στος *a.* unweighed; (*fig.*) un-considered.

ἄζυμος *a.* unleavened.

ἄζωτον *s.n.* nitrogen.

ἅη- (*prefix*) saint.

ἀηδής *a.* disgusting.

ἀηδ|ία *s.f.* disgust; (*fam.*) anything dis-gusting. ~ιάζω *v.t. & i.* disgust; feel disgust.

ἀηδ|ών *s.f.*, ~όνι *s.n.* nightingale.

ἀήρ *s.m.* air.

ἀήττητος *a.* invincible; unbeaten.

ἄηχος *a.* noiseless.

ἀθανασία *s.f.* immortality.

ἀθάνατος *a.* immortal, everlasting; ὁ ~ American aloe.

ἀθέατος *a.* invisible; unseen, secret.

ἄθελα *adv.* unwillingly; unintentionally.

ἀθέλητος *a.* unintentional; unwilling.

ἀθέμιτος *a.* illicit.

ἄθεος *a.* atheistic; an atheist.

ἀθεόφοβος *a.* impious.

ἀθεράπευτος *a.* incurable; uncured.

ἀθέρας *s.m.* awn; cutting edge; (*fig.*) cream (*best part*).

ἀθετ|ῶ *v.t.* break (*word, etc.*). ~ησις *s.f.* breach.

ἀθεώρητος *a.* not officially examined.

ἄθικτος *a.* intact; untouched.

ἀθλητ|ής *s.m.* athlete. ~ικός *a.* ath-letic, athlete's. ~ισμός *s.m.* athletics.

ἄθλιος *a.* miserable; vile.

ἆθλος *s.m.* contest, exploit, task.

ἀθόλωτος *a.* 1. limpid, not turbid. 2. not vaulted.

ἄθραυστος *a.* unbroken; unbreak-able.

ἀθορύβητος *a.* imperturbable.

ἀθόρυβος *a.* noiseless.

ἀθροίζω *v.t.* assemble; add up.

ἄθροισις *s.f.* addition (*adding up*).

ἄθροισμα *s.n.* sum total; group (*cf people*).

ἀθρόος *a.* in a body; numerous.

ἄθυμος *a.* dispirited.

ἄθυρμα *s.n.* plaything.

ἀθυρόστομος *a.* garrulous; impertinent.

ἀθῶ|ος *a.* innocent, not guilty; artless. ~ότης *s.f.* innocence. ~ώνω *v.t.* acquit. ~ωσις *s.f.* acquittal.

ἀϊβασιλιάτικος *a.* of St. Basil's day.

αἴγαγρος *s.m.* chamois.

αἰγιαλός *s.m.* sea-shore.

αἰγίς *s.f.* shield; aegis.

αἴγλη *s.f.* glitter; glory, magnificence.

αἰγόκλημα *s.n.* honeysuckle.

αἰδέσιμος *a.* reverend.

αἰδήμων *a.* modest, bashful.

αἰδοῖον *s.n.* privy parts.

αἰδώς *s.f.* shame, decency.

αἰθέριος *a.* ethereal; volatile (*oil*).

αἰθήρ *s.m.* ether.

αἴθουσα *s.f.* large room, hall.

αἰθρία *s.f.* cloudless weather.

αἴθριος *a.* clear, serene.

αἴλουρος *s.m.* wild cat; member of cat family.

αἷμ|α *s.n.* blood. ~άσσω *v.i.* bleed.

αἱματηρός *a.* bloody.

αἱματοκύλισμα *s.n.* carnage.

αἱματοχυσία *s.f.* bloodshed.

αἱματώδης *a.* sanguine (*complexion*); like blood.

αἱματώνω *v.t. & i. see* ματώνω.

αἱμοβόρος *a.* bloodthirsty.

αἱμοδοσία *s.f.* blood-donation.

αἱμομιξία *s.f.* incest.

αἱμόπτυσις *s.f.* spitting of blood.

αἱμορραγία *s.f.* haemorrhage.

αἱμοσφαίριον *s.n.* blood-corpuscle.

αἱμόφυρτος *a.* covered in blood.

αἴνιγμα *s.n.* enigma, riddle.

αἶνος *s.m.* praise.

ἄιντε *int.* come on!

αἴξ *s.f.* goat.

αἵρ|εσις *s.f.* heresy, sect; option. ~ετικός *a.* heretical; an heretic.

αἱρετός *a.* elected.

αἴρω *v.t.* raise, lift up; raise (*siege*), lift (*embargo*).

αἰσθάνομαι *v.t. & i.* feel (*well, fear, the cold, etc.*); sense.

αἴσθημα *s.n.* sensation, feeling (*physical*); ~τα (*pl.*) feelings (*sympathies*).

αἰσθηματίας *s.m.* person of responsive feelings.

αἰσθηματικ|ός *a.* sentimental. ~ότης *s.f.* sentimentality.

αἴσθησ|ις *s.f.* sense (*bodily faculty*); προκάλεσε ~ιν it made an impression.

αἰσθητικ|ός *a.* of the senses; aesthetic; an aesthete; a beauty specialist. ~ή *s.f.* aesthetics.

αἰσθητός *a.* perceptible.

αἰσιόδοξ|ος *a.* optimistic. ~ία *s.f.* optimism.

αἴσιος *a.* auspicious, favourable.

αἶσχος *s.n.* shame, infamy.

αἰσχροκέρδεια *s.f.* illicit gain; profiteering.

αἰσχρολογία *s.f.* obscene talk.

αἰσχρός *a.* disgraceful; indecent.

αἰσχύν|η *s.f.* shame, disgrace. ~ομαι *v.i.* feel ashamed.

αἴτημα *s.n.* demand (*thing asked for*); postulate.

αἴτησις *s.f.* application, request.

αἰτία *s.f.* cause, reason.

αἰτιατική *s.f.* (*gram.*) accusative.

αἰτιολογία *s.f.* explanation, giving a reason (*for*).

αἴτι|ος *a.* responsible, to blame. ~ον *s.n.* cause, motive. ~ῶμαι *v.t.* hold to blame.

ἀϊτός *s.m.* eagle; kite (*toy*).

αἰτ|ῶ *v.t.* request (*something*). ~οῦμαι *v.t.* beg (*something*).

αἴφνης *adv.* 1. suddenly. 2. for example.

αἰφνιδιασμός *s.m.* sudden attack, surprise.

αἰφνίδιος *a.* sudden, unexpected.

αἰχμάλωτ|ος *s.m.* prisoner, captive. ~ίζω *v.t.* take prisoner; (*fig.*) captivate.

αἰχμή *s.f.* point (*of weapon, etc.*). ~ρός *a.* sharp, pointed.

αἰών *s.m.* age, century, era. ~ιος *a.* eternal. ~όβιος *a.* centuries old.

αἰώρ|α *s.f.* swing. ~οῦμαι *v.i.* swing; (*fig.*) waver.

ἀκαδημ|ία *s.f.* academy. ~αϊκός *a.* academic; an academician.

ἀκαθαρσί|α *s.f.* dirt, dirtiness; ~ες (*pl.*) excrement.

ἀκάθαρτος *a.* dirty, unclean.

ἀκάθεκτος *a.* unrestrainable, unbridled.

ἀκάθιστος *a.* who does not sit down; ~ ὕμνος (*eccl.*) a canticle.

ἀκαθόριστος *a.* undefined; indefinable.

ἄκαιρος *a.* untimely.

ἀκακία *s.f.* 1. acacia. 2. guilelessness.

ἄκακος *a.* harmless, guileless.

ἀκαλαίσθη|τος *a.* lacking in taste. ~σία *s.f.* lack of good taste.

ἀκάλεστος *a.* uninvited.

ἀκαλλιέργητος *a.* uncultivated; uncultured.

ἀκαμάτης *a.* lazy.

ἀκάματος *a.* tireless.

ἄκαμπτος *a.* inflexible.

ἀκάμωτος *a.* not done; unripe.

ἄκανθ|α, ~ος *s.f.* thorn; acanthus.

ἀκανόνιστος *a.* not settled, not cleared up; disproportioned.

ἀκαρεῖ *a.* ἐν ~ instantly.

ἀκαριαῖος *a.* instantaneous.

ἄκαρπος *a.* unfruitful; (*fig.*) fruitless.

ἀκατάβλητος *a.* 1. indomitable. 2. unpaid (*money*).

ἀκατάδεκτος *a.* disdainful.

ἀκαταλαβίστικος *a.* (*fam.*) incomprehensible.

ἀκατάληπτος *a.* incomprehensible.

ἀκατάλληλος *a.* unsuitable.

ἀκαταλόγιστος *a.* not fully responsible (*for one's actions*).

ἀκαταμάχητος *a.* irrefutable; unconquerable; irresistible.

ἀκατανόητος *a.* incomprehensible.

ἀκατάπαυστος *a.* incessant, continuous.

ἀκαταπόνητος *a.* tireless.

ἀκατάρτιστος *a.* not organized; lacking qualifications *or* knowledge.

ἀκατάστα|τος *a.* untidy; variable. ~σία *s.f.* disorder; changeability (*of weather*).

ἀκατάσχετος *a.* that cannot be stanched *or* stemmed; (*law*) not distrained *or* distrainable.

ἀκατάφερτος *a.* who cannot be persuaded; not feasible; unaccomplished.

ἀκατέβατα *adv.* at a fixed price.

ἀκατέργαστος *a.* not wrought *or* refined, crude, raw; uncut (*gem*).

ἀκατοίκητος *a.* uninhabited; uninhabitable.

ἀκατόρθωτος *a.* not feasible; unaccomplished.

ἄκαυ(σ)τος *a.* incombustible; unburnt.

ἀκένωτος *a.* inexhaustible; not emptied.

ἀκέραιος *a.* whole, intact; honest; ~ ἀριθμός integer.

ἀκεφιά *s.f.* low spirits.

ἀκηδής *a.* negligent.

ἀκήρυκτος *a.* unproclaimed, undeclared.

ἀκίνδυνος *a.* not dangerous.

ἀκίνητ|ος *a.* immovable; real (*estate*). ~ον *s.n.* item of real estate, building, property. ~ῶ *v.t. & i.* immobilize; remain motionless.

ἀκκίζομαι *v.i.* assume coquettish airs.

ἀκκισμός *s.m.* coquettish air.

ἀκλείδωτος *a.* unlocked.

ἀκληρονόμητος *a.* without heirs.

ἄκληρος *a.* childless; poor; hapless.

ἀκλήρωτος *a.* unallotted; not drawn (*of lots*); (*mil.*) not yet called up.

ἄκλιτος *a.* indeclinable.

ἀκλόνητος *a.* unshakeable, firm.

ἀκμάζω *v.i.* flourish, prosper; be in one's prime.

ἀκμαῖος *a.* in full vigour.

ἀκμή *s.f.* point, edge; acme, peak; (*med.*) acne.

ἄκμων *s.m.* anvil.

ἀκο|ή *s.f.* hearing; ἐξ ~ῆς by hearsay.

ἀκοίμητος *a.* unable to sleep; vigilant.

ἀκοινώνητος *a.* 1. unsociable. 2. not having received the sacrament.

ἀκολασία *s.f.* excess, debauchery.

ἀκόλαστος *a.* 1. licentious. 2. unpunished.

ἀκολουθ|ία *s.f.* retinue, suite; coherence; church service; κατ' ~ίαν in consequence.

ἀκόλουθος *s.m.* attendant; page; attaché.

ἀκόλουθος *a.* next, following; true (*to one's word, etc.*).

ἀκολουθ|ῶ *v.t. & i.* follow; ~εῖ to be continued.

ἀκολούθως *adv.* next, afterwards; ὡς ~ as follows.

ἀκόμα, ἀκόμη *adv.* still, yet; more; ~ καί even.

ἀκόν|η *s.f.*, ~ι *s.n.* whetstone. ~ίζω *v.t.* sharpen, whet.

ἀκόντιον *s.n.* javelin.

ἄκοπ|ος *a.* not cut; easy, not tiring. ~ως *adv.* without trouble.

ἀκόρεστος *a.* insatiable.

ἄκοσμος *a.* unseemly.

ἀκουμπῶ *v.t. & i.* touch; stand, lean; place (*money in bank, etc.*); (*v.i.*) rest, lean (*for support*).

ἀκούμπωτος *a.* unbuttoned.

ἀκούραστος *a.* untiring, energetic.

ἀκούρδιστος *a.* not tuned; not wound up.

ἀκούσιος *a.* unintentional; against one's will.

ἀκουστικ|ός *a.* acoustic, auditory. ~ή *s.f.* acoustics. ~όν *s.n.* (*telephone*) receiver; hearing-aid; stethoscope.

ἀκουστ|ός *a.* audible; famous; (*fam.*) ἔχω ~ά πώς I have heard that . . . .

ἀκού|ω *v.t. & i.* hear, listen (to); obey; ~ω ἕναν πόνο feel a pain; ~ω μυρωδιά smell a smell; (*fam.*) ἄκου λέει phrase *of assent.* ~ομαι *v.i.* be well known.

ἄκρα *s.f. see* ἄκρη.

ἄκρα *s.n.pl.* limbs.

ἀκράδαντος *a.* steadfast.

ἀκραιφνής *a.* pure, sincere.

ἀκρατ|ής *a.* intemperate. ~εια *s.f.* intemperance; incontinence.

ἀκράτητος *a.* unrestrainable.

ἄκρατος *a.* undiluted; (*fig.*) pure.

ἄκρ|η *s.f.* end, edge, tip, summit; cape; corner; βάζω λεφτά στήν ~η put money aside; ~ες μέσες disjointedly.

ἀκριανός *a. see* ἀκρινός.

ἀκριβά *adv.* dearly, at a high price.

ἀκριβαίνω *v.t. & i.* raise price of; become dearer.

ἀκρίβεια *s.f.* 1. exactness, precision. 2. costliness, expense, high price(s).

ἀκριβής *a.* exact, correct; punctual.

ἀκριβοθώρητος *a.* rarely to be seen.

ἀκριβολόγος *a.* precise in speech.

ἀκριβός *a.* dear, loved; costly; (*with* σέ) sparing of.

ἀκριβῶς *adv.* exactly, precisely.

ἀκρίδα s.f. locust.
ἀκρινός a. at the far end, last.
ἀκριτικός a. of the frontier (ballads).
ἀκριτομυθία s.f. indiscreet talk.
ἄκριτος a. lacking in judgement.
ἀκροάζομαι v.t. & i. listen (to); (med.) auscultate.
ἀκρόασις s.f. hearing, audition; audience, interview; auscultation.
ἀκροατήριον s.n. audience, auditorium.
ἀκροατής s.m. listener.
ἀκρο|βασία s.f. acrobatics. ~βάτης s.m. acrobat.
ἀκροβολισμός s.m. skirmish.
ἀκρογιάλι s.n. sea-shore.
ἀκρογωνιαῖος a. ~ λίθος corner-stone
ἀκροθαλασσιά s.f. sea-shore.
ἄκρ|ον s.n. end, extremity; τῶν ~ων extremist; φθάνω εἰς τὰ ~α go to extremes.
ἀκροποδητί adv. on tip-toe.
ἀκρόπολις s.f. acropolis, citadel.
ἄκρ|ος a. extreme, complete, utmost; last; εἰς ~ον extremely. ~ως adv. extremely.
ἀκροσφαλής a. precarious.
ἀκροῶμαι v.t. & i. listen (to); give audience; auscultate.
ἀκρωτηριάζω v.t. mutilate; perform amputation on.
ἀκρωτήριον s.n. cape, promontory.
ἀκταιωρός s.m.f. coastguard (-vessel).
ἀκτ|ή s.f. shore; ~ές (pl.) coast.
ἀκτήμων a. without property, poor.
ἀκτινοβολία s.f. radiation, shining.
ἀκτινογραφία s.f. X-ray photograph(y).
ἀκτινοθεραπεία s.f. radiotherapy.
ἀκτινοσκοπῶ v.t. X-ray.
ἀκτ|ίς s.f. ray; radius; spoke; ~ῖνες (pl.) X-rays.
ἀκτοπλοΐα s.f. coastal shipping.
ἀκύμαντος a. without waves, calm.
ἄκυρ|ος a. invalid, void. ~ῶ v.t. nullify, cancel.
ἀκωλύτως adv. without hindrance.
ἄκων a. against one's will.
ἀλάβαστρον s.n. alabaster.
ἀλάδωτος a. without oil; (fig.) without bribery; unbaptized.
ἀλαζ|ών a. arrogant. ~ονεία s.f. arrogance.
ἀλάθευτος a. unerring, infallible.
ἀλάθητ|ος a. unerring, infallible. ~ον s.n. infallibility.
ἀλαλάζω v.i. cry, shout (in joy or triumph).

ἀλαλιάζω v.t. & i. daze, stupefy; be dazed.
ἄλαλος a. speechless, dumb, agape.
ἀλαμπουρνέζικ|ος a. (fam.) bizarre, nonsensical; ~α adv. double Dutch.
ἀλάνθαστος a. with no mistakes; (fam.) infallible.
ἀλάνι s.n. vacant plot of ground; street-lounger.
ἀλάργα adv. far off.
ἅλας s.n. salt.
ἁλάτ|ι s.n. salt. ~ιέρα s.f. salt-cellar.
ἁλατίζω v.t. salt.
ἀλαφιάζ|ω, ~ομαι v.i. be startled.
ἀλαφροΐσκιωτος a. who sees the fairies
ἀλαφρός a. see ἐλαφρός.
ἀλγεινός a. painful, grievous.
ἄλγος s.n. pain, grief.
ἀλέθω v.t. grind (corn, etc.).
ἀλείβω v.t. rub, coat, smear, spread.
ἄλειμμα s.n. smearing, greasing; animal fat.
ἀλείφω v.t. see ἀλείβω.
ἄλειωτος a. unmelted, undissolved; not decomposed; that does not wear out.
ἀλέκτωρ s.m. cock.
ἀλεξικέραυνον s.n. lightning-conductor.
ἀλεξίπτωτ|ον s.n. parachute. ~ιστής s.m. parachutist.
ἀλεποῦ s.f. fox.
ἄλεσμα s.n. grinding; grist.
ἀλέστ|ος a. quick, nimble. ~α adv. quickly; εἶμαι ~α be ready.
ἀλέτρι s.n. plough.
ἄλ|ευρον, ~εύρι s.n. flour.
ἀλήθ|εια s.f. truth; (adv.) really, indeed, by the way. ~εύω v.i. come true; be right. ~ής a. true. ~ινός a. true, genuine. ~ῶς, ~ινά adv. truly.
ἀλησμόνητος a. unforgettable; unforgotten.
ἀλήτης s.m. vagabond.
ἀλί int. alas!
ἀλιάνιστος a. not cut up small.
ἁλιεία s.f. fishing, fishery.
ἁλι|εύς s.m. fisherman. ~ευτικός a. of fishing. ~εύω v.t. & i. fish (for).
ἅλικος a. scarlet.
ἀλίμονο int. alas!
ἁλίπαστος a. salted.
ἀλισβερίσι s.n. commercial dealings.
ἀλισίβα s.f. lye.
ἀλιτήριος a. rascally.
ἀλιφασκιά s.f. sage.
ἀλκ|ή s.f. bodily strength. ~ιμος a. strong.

ἀλκο(ο)λικός *a.* alcoholic (*person*); (*fam.*) excessively addicted.

ἀλκυών *s.f.* kingfisher.

ἀλλά *conj.* but.

ἀλλαγή *s.f.* change.

ἀλλά|ζω *v.t. & i.* change; ~ζει that alters things. ~ξιά *s.f.* exchange; set of underwear, suit of clothes.

ἀλλαντικά *s.n.pl.* various kinds of sausage.

ἀλλάσσω *v.t. & i.* see **ἀλλάζω**.

ἀλλαχοῦ *adv.* elsewhere.

ἀλλεπάλληλος *a.* one on top of another, repeated.

ἀλλεργία *s.f.* (*med.*) allergy.

ἀλληγορία *s.f.* allegory.

ἀλληλεγγύη *s.f.* solidarity, mutual aid.

ἀλληλένδετος *a.* linked with each other, interdependent.

ἀλληλογραφ|ία *s.f.* correspondence (*written*). ~ῶ *v.i.* correspond.

ἀλληλοδιάδοχος *a.* one after another, successive.

ἀλληλοπαθής *a.* (*gram.*) reflexive.

ἀλληλοσυγκρούομαι *v.i.* clash, run counter to each other.

ἀλληλοτρώγομαι *v.i.* squabble with each other.

ἀλλήλ|ους *pron. acc. pl.* one another. ~ων (*gen. pl.*) one another's.

ἀλληλουχία *s.f.* sequence.

ἀλλιῶς *adv.* see **ἀλλοιῶς**.

ἀλλοδαπ|ή *s.f.* foreign parts. ~ός *a.* alien, a foreign subject.

ἄλλοθεν *adv.* from elsewhere.

ἄλλοθι *adv.* elsewhere; alibi.

ἀλλόθρησκος *a.* of another creed.

ἀλλοίθωρ|ος *a.* cross-eyed. ~ίζω *v.i.* squint.

ἀλλοίμονο *int.* alas!

ἀλλοῖ|ος *a.* different, not the same. ~ῶς *adv.* differently, otherwise.

ἀλλοι|ώνω *v.t.* alter; falsify. ~ώνομαι *v.i.* deteriorate, go off. ~ωσις *s.f.* deterioration, falsification.

ἀλλοιώτικος *a.* different; odd (*of character*).

ἀλλόκοτος *a.* strange, queer, grotesque.

ἀλλοπρόσαλλος *a.* changeable, fickle.

ἄλλ|ος *pron. & a.* other, else, rest; next; different; more; ~οι . . . ~οι some . . . others; ~η φορά another time; τήν ~η φορά next time; τίς ~ες the other day; χωρίς ~ο without fail; ἐξ ~ου besides; ~α ἀντ' ~ων random talk;

κάθε ~ο anything but! ~ο τίποτα nothing but! κι' ~ο some more; ~α δύο two more.

ἄλλοτε *adv.* formerly; another time; ~ μέν . . . ~ δέ now . . . now.

ἀλλοτινός *a.* of former times.

ἀλλότριος *a.* other people's.

ἀλλοῦ *adv.* elsewhere; (*fam.*) ~ αὐτά don't tell me that!

ἀλλό|φρων *a.* frantic, beside oneself. ~φροσύνη *s.f.* frenzy, violent agitation.

ἀλλόφωνος *a.* speaking another language.

ἄλλως *adv.* otherwise; or else; ~ πως in some other way.

ἄλλωστε *adv.* besides.

ἄλμα *s.n.* jump, leap. ~τώδης *a.* proceeding by leaps and bounds.

ἄλμη *s.f.* brine.

ἀλμπάνης *s.m.* farrier.

ἄλμπουρο *s.n.* mast.

ἀλμύρα *s.f.* saltness.

ἁλμυρός *a.* salt; (*fig.*) expensive.

ἀλόγα *s.f.* mare; (*fam.*) ungainly woman.

ἀλογάριαστος *a.* beyond calculation; with one's accounts unsettled; spending improvidently.

ἀλόγιστος *a.* lacking judgement; thoughtless; beyond calculation.

ἄλογ|ο *s.n.* horse. ~όμυγα *s.f.* horse-fly.

ἄλογος *a.* devoid of reason.

ἀλόη *s.f.* aloe.

ἀλοιφή *s.f.* ointment.

ἀλουμίνιον *s.n.* aluminium.

ἄλουστος *a.* not having washed.

ἀλπακᾶς *s.m.* 1. alpaca. 2. metal resembling silver.

ἄλσος *s.n.* grove, small wooded park.

ἄλτ *int.* halt!

ἀλτῆρες *s.m.pl.* dumb-bells.

ἄλτης *s.m.* jumper (*athletic*).

ἀλτρουισμός *s.m.* altruism.

ἀλύγιστος *a.* unbending, inflexible.

ἀλυκή *s.f.* salt-pan.

ἀλύπητ|ος *a.* pitiless; without sorrow. ~α *adv.* without pity; unsparingly.

ἁλυσίδα *s.f.* chain.

ἅλυσις *s.f.* chain, sequence, succession.

ἀλύτρωτος *a.* unredeemed.

ἄλυτος *a.* not untied; unsolved; unsolvable; (*fig.*) indissoluble.

ἀλυχτῶ *v.i.* bark.

ἄλφα *s.n.* the letter **A**; (*fig.*) beginning, start.

ἀλφάβητ|ον s.n. alphabet. ~άριο s.n. primer. ~ικός a. alphabetic(al).

ἀλφάδι s.n. level, square, plumb-line.

ἀλχημεία s.f. alchemy.

ἀλώβητος a. intact.

ἀλωνάρης s.m. July.

ἀλών|ι s.n. threshing-floor. ~ίζω v.t. & i. thresh; (fig.) scatter; thrash; (v.i.) wander round.

ἀλώπηξ s.f. fox.

ἅλωσις s.f. capture, fall.

ἅμα adv. as soon as, when; if; ἅμ' ἔπος ἅμ' ἔργον no sooner said than done.

ἀμάδα s.f. flat stone used in game like bowls.

ἀμαζών s.f. amazon.

ἀμάθεια s.f. ignorance.

ἀμάθευτος a. that has not become known; not used (to).

ἀμαθής a. ignorant.

ἀμάθητος a. not learnt (of lessons); see also ἀμάθευτος.

ἄμαθος a. not used (to).

ἀμάκα s.f. & adv. (fam.) without paying.

ἀμάλ|αγος, ~ακτος a. not pliable; (fig.) unrelenting, hard.

ἀμάν int. for mercy's sake!

ἀμανάτι s.n. pawn, security; parcel delivered by private individual.

ἀμανές s.m. love song pleading for compassion.

ἅμ|αξα s.f. coach, carriage; horse-cab; (fam.) τὰ ἐξ ~άξης unrestrained abuse. ~αξᾶς s.m. coachman, driver.

ἀμάξι s.n. horse-cab; (motor) car.

ἀμαξιτός a. carriageable.

ἀμαξοστοιχία s.f. train.

ἀμαξωτός a. carriageable.

ἀμάραντος 1. a. unfading. 2. s.m. amaranth.

ἀμαρτάνω v.i. sin, err.

ἁμάρτημα s.n. a sin.

ἁμαρτί|α s.f. sin; ἔχουμε ~ες ἀκόμη we have more troubles in store; λέω τήν ~α μου I make no secret of it; εἶναι ~α (ἀπό τό Θεό) it is a pity.

ἁμαρτωλός a. sinful; a sinner.

ἀμασκάλη s.f. armpit.

ἀμαυρ|ός a. dim, dark. ~ώνω v.t. darken, obscure; (fig.) sully.

ἀμάχη s.f. enmity, hatred.

ἀμαχητί adv. without a fight.

ἄμαχος a. non-combatant.

ἄμβ|ιξ, ~υξ s.m. still, alembic.

ἀμβλ|ύς a. blunt, dull; (geom.) obtuse. ~ύνω v.t. blunt, take the edge off.

ἄμβλωσις s.f. abortion.

ἀμβροσία s.f. ambrosia.

ἄμβων s.m. pulpit, rostrum.

ἀμ' δέ int. not on your life!

ἄμε int. go!

ἀμέ int. see ἀμμέ.

ἀμείβω v.t. reward, recompense.

ἀμείλικτος a. implacable.

ἀμείωτος a. undiminished; without loss of prestige.

ἀμέλγω v.t. milk.

ἀμέλεια s.f. negligence, carelessness; laziness (at lessons).

ἀμελέτητ|ος a. 1. not having prepared (lesson); not prepared or studied. 2. unmentionable; (fam.) ~α (s.n.pl.) testicles.

ἀμελής a. negligent; lazy (pupil).

ἀμελῶ v.t. neglect.

ἄμεμπτος a. irreproachable.

ἀμερικάνικος a. American.

Ἀμερικάνος s.m. Greek from America.

Ἀμερικανός s.m. American.

ἀμέριμνος a. carefree; heedless.

ἀμέριστος a. indivisible; undivided.

ἀμερό|ληπτος a. impartial. ~ληψία s.f. impartiality.

ἄμεσος a. direct, immediate.

ἄμεστος a. unripe.

ἀμέσως adv. at once.

ἀμετάβατος a. (gram.) intransitive.

ἀμετάβλητος a. unchanged; unalterable.

ἀμετάκλητος a. irrevocable.

ἀμετα|μέλητος, ~νόητος a. unrepentant.

ἀμετάπειστος a. unpersuadable, obstinate.

ἀμετάπτωτος a. undiminished.

ἀμεταχείριστος a. not in use; unused, unworn.

ἀμέτοχος a. not taking part (in) (with gen. or εἰς).

ἀμέτρητος a. countless.

ἄμετρος a. measureless.

ἀμήν int. amen!

ἀμηχαν|ία s.f. perplexity, embarrassment. ~ῶ v.i. be at a loss or embarrassed.

ἀμίαντος 1. a. undefiled. 2. s.m. asbestos.

ἀμίλητος a. silent; stand-offish; whose favour has not been solicited.

ἄμιλλ|α s.f. rivalry, emulation. ~ῶμαι v.t. & i. vie with, rival; contend, compete.

ἀμίμητος *a.* inimitable.

ἄμισθ|ος *a.* unpaid. ~ί *adv.* without payment.

ἀμμέ, ἀμμή *int.* well! of course!

ἀμμοκονία *s.f.* mortar, plaster.

ἄμμ|ος *s.m.f.* sand. ~ώδης *a.* sandy.

ἀμμουδιά *s.f.* sandy beach.

ἀμμωνία *s.f.* ammonia.

ἀμνάς *s.f.* ewe-lamb.

ἀμνημόνευτος *a.* unmentioned; immemorial; not commemorated.

ἀμνήμ|ων *a.* forgetful. ~ονῶ *v.i. & t.* be forgetful; forget. ~οσύνη *s.f.* forgetfulness.

ἀμνησία *s.f.* loss of memory.

ἀμνησίκακος *a.* not resentful.

ἀμνηστία *s.f.* amnesty.

ἀμνός *s.m.* lamb.

ἀμοιβάδες *s.f.pl.* amoebic dysentery.

ἀμοιβαῖος *a.* mutual, reciprocal.

ἀμοιβή *s.f.* reward, recompense.

ἄμοιρος *a.* hapless; not provided with (*with gen.*).

ἀμολ(λ)ά(ρ)ω *v.t.* slacken, let loose, release; fly (*kite*). ~ιέμαι *v.i.* hasten, rush.

ἀμόνι *s.n.* anvil.

ἄμορφος *a.* shapeless.

ἀμόρφωτος *a.* uneducated.

ἄμουσος *a.* unmusical.

ἀμπαζούρ *s.n.* lampshade. [F. *abat-jour*]

ἀμπάρα *s.f.* bolt, bar.

ἀμπάρι *s.n.* storehouse; hold (*of ship*).

ἀμπᾶς *s.m.* coarse woollen cloth, drugget.

ἄμπ|ελος *s.f.*, ~έλι *s.n.* vine; vineyard.

ἀμπελουργία *s.f.* viticulture.

ἀμπελοφάσουλο *s.n.* bean of the vine.

ἀμπελών *s.m.* vineyard.

ἀμπέχονον *s.n.* soldier's tunic.

ἄμποτε *adv.* would that!

ἀμπραγιάζ *s.n.* clutch (*of motor*). [F. *embrayage*]

ἀμ' πῶς *int.* of course!

ἄμπωτις *s.f.* ebb-tide.

ἀμυγδαλές *s.f.pl.* tonsils.

ἀμυγδαλῆ *s.f.* almond-tree.

ἀμύγδαλο *s.n.* almond.

ἀμυγδαλωτός *a.* almond-shaped; made with almonds.

ἀμυδρός *a.* dim, faint.

ἀμύητος *a.* uninitiated.

ἀμύθητος *a.* untold, fabulous.

ἄμυλον *s.n.* starch.

ἄμυν|α *s.f.* defence, resistance. ~ομαι

v.t. & i. defend (*with gen.*); resist, defend oneself. ~τικός *a.* defensive.

ἀμυχή *s.f.* scratch.

ἀμφι- *denotes* round, about, both.

ἄμφια *s.n.pl.* (*eccl.*) vestments.

ἀμφιβάλλω *v.i.* doubt.

ἀμφίβιος *a.* amphibious.

ἀμφίβολ|ος *a.* doubtful, uncertain. ~ία *s.f.* doubt.

ἀμφιδέξιος *a.* ambidextrous; dextrous.

ἀμφίεσις *s.f.* dress, attire.

ἀμφιθέατρ|ον *s.n.* amphitheatre. ~ικῶς *adv.* in the form of an amphitheatre.

ἀμφιρρ|έπω *v.i.* waver. ~οπος *a.* undecided.

ἀμφισβητήσιμος *a.* questionable, doubtful.

ἀμφισβητ|ῶ *v.t.* dispute, call in question. ~οῦμαι *v.i.* be in dispute.

ἀμφίστομος *a.* two-edged.

ἀμφιταλαντεύομαι *v.i.* waver, be uncertain.

ἀμφιτρύων *s.m.* host, giver of party.

ἀμφορεύς *s.m.* amphora, jar.

ἀμφότεροι *pron. pl.* both.

ἄμωμος *a.* blameless.

ἄν *conj.* if, whether; ~ καί although.

ἀν- (*privative prefix*) un-, in-, -less.

ἀνά *prep.* 1. (*with acc.*) along, over, throughout, across; ~ χεῖρας in one's hands. 2. (*with nom. & acc.*) (*distributive*) ~ εἷς one by one; ~ εἴκοσι-τετράωρον every 24 hours; ἔλαβον ~ τρεῖς λίρες they received £3 each.

ἀνα- *denotes* up, back, again, intensification.

ἀνάβαθος *a.* shallow.

ἀναβαίνω *v.i. &t.* come *or* go up; ascend, mount, rise (*in level*); (*v.t.*) go up (*stairs, etc.*).

ἀναβάλλω *v.t.* postpone, put off.

ἀνάβασις *s.f.* ascent.

ἀναβατήρ *s.m.* step (*of vehicle*); lift.

ἀναβάτης *s.m.* climber; rider.

ἀναβιβάζω *v.t. see* ἀνεβάζω.

ἀναβιῶ *v.i.* revive.

ἀναβλέπω *v.i.* look up; recover one's sight.

ἀναβλητικός *a.* dilatory, delaying.

ἀναβλύζω *v.i.* well up.

ἀναβολεύς *s.m.* stirrup.

ἀναβολή *s.f.* postponement.

ἀνάβολος *a.* inconvenient.

ἀναβρασμός *s.m.* agitation, state of ferment.

ἀναβροχιά *s.f.* drought.

ἀναβρύω *v.i.* well up.

ἀνάβω *v.t.* & *i.* light (*fire, etc.*); turn on (*light, etc.*); inflame, provoke; (*v.i.*) light, take fire; get inflamed *or* provoked; break out; go bad.

ἀναγαλλιάζω *v.i.* exult.

ἀναγγέλλω *v.t.* announce.

ἀναγέννησις *s.f.* rebirth; renaissance.

ἀναγερτός *a.* half-reclining.

ἀναγινώσκω *v.t.* read.

ἀναγκάζω *v.t.* compel, oblige.

ἀναγκαῖ|ος *a.* necessary. ~ον *s.n.* W.C.

ἀναγκασμός *s.m.* compulsion.

ἀναγκαστικ|ός *a.* compulsory; ~ὰ ἔργα hard labour.

ἀνάγκη *s.f.* need, necessity; ἐν ~ if necessary.

ἀνάγλυφος *a.* in relief.

ἀναγνώρησις *s.f.* recognition; admission; reconnaissance.

ἀναγνωρίζω *v.t.* recognize; admit; reconnoitre.

ἀναγνωριστικός *a.* of reconnaissance.

ἀνάγνωσις *s.f.* (*act of*) reading.

ἀνάγνωσμα *s.n.* reading (*matter*).

ἀναγνωσματάριον *s.n.* primer.

ἀναγνωστήρι *s.n.* lectern.

ἀναγνωστήριον *s.n.* reading-room.

ἀναγνώστης *s.m.* reader.

ἀναγνωστικ|ός *a.* concerned with reading. ~όν *s.n.* primer.

ἀναγορεύω *v.t.* proclaim (*ruler, etc.*).

ἀναγούλα *s.f.* feeling of sickness *or* disgust.

ἀναγράφω *v.t.* inscribe, record, publish.

ἀνάγ|ω *v.t.* raise; (*math.*) reduce; trace back. ~ομαι *v.i.* relate to, go back to, date from; put out (*to sea*).

ἀναγωγεύς *s.m.* (*geom.*) protractor.

ἀναγωγή *s.f.* reduction, conversion.

ἀνάγωγος *a.* ill-mannered, badly brought up.

ἀναδασμός *s.m.* redistribution of land.

ἀναδάσωσις *s.f.* reafforestation.

ἀναδεικνύ|ω *v.t.* show to advantage, mark out. ~ομαι *v.i.* make one's mark.

ἀνα|δεκτός, ~δεξιμιός *s.m.* godson.

ἀναδεύω *v.t.* & *i.* stir, move.

ἀναδέχομαι *v.t.* undertake; stand sponsor to.

ἀναδίδω *v t.* emit, give forth.

ἀναδίνω *v.i.* give off steam, smell, *etc.*

ἀναδιπλασιασμός *s.m.* (*gram.*) reduplication.

ἀναδιφῶ *v.t.* search through, scrutinize (*documents*).

ἀναδουλιά *s.f.* lack of work.

ἀνάδοχος *s.m.* & *f.* sponsor, guarantor; godparent.

ἀναδρομικός *a.* retrospective.

ἀναδύομαι *v.i.* emerge, break surface.

ἀνάερος *a.* light as air, ethereal.

ἀνάζερβη *s.f.* (*fam.*) back-handed slap.

ἀναζητῶ *v.t.* search high and low for.

ἀναζωογονῶ *v.t.* revivify.

ἀναζωπυρῶ *v.t.* rekindle.

ἀναθαρρ|εύω, ~ῶ *v.i.* take fresh courage.

ἀνάθεμα *s.n.* & *int.* curse; (*eccl.*) interdict.

ἀναθεματίζω *v.t.* interdict; curse.

ἀναθέτω *v.t.* charge, entrust (*duty to person*); present (*offering*).

ἀναθεώρ|ησις *s.f.* revision. ~ῶ *v.t.* revise.

ἀνάθημα *s.n.* ex-voto offering.

ἀναθρώσκω *v.i.* rise (*of smoke*); (*fig.*) be kindled (*of hope*).

ἀναθυμίασις *s.f.* (emission of) fumes, bad smell.

ἀναίδ|εια *s.f.* impudence. ~ής *a.* impudent.

ἀναίμακτος *a.* without bloodshed.

ἀναιμία *s.f.* anaemia.

ἀναίρεσις *s.f.* refutation; (*law*) cassation; manslaughter; (*mus.*) natural.

ἀναιρῶ *v.t.* refute; revoke.

ἀναισθησία *s.f.* unconsciousness; (*fig.*) insensibility; heartlessness.

ἀναισθητικόν *s.n.* anaesthetic.

ἀναίσθητος *a.* unconscious; (*fig.*) indifferent, without feeling.

ἀναισχυντία *s.f.* shamelessness.

ἀναίτ|ιος *a.* not responsible, innocent. ~ίως *adv.* without cause.

ἀνακαινίζω *v.t.* renovate, renew.

ἀνακαλ|ύπτω *v.t.* discover, find out. ~υψις *s.f.* discovery.

ἀνακαλῶ *v.t.* recall, revoke, countermand; ~ εἰς τὴν τάξιν call to order.

ἀνάκατα *adv.* without fixed order, indiscriminately.

ἀνακάτευτος *a.* not mixed; not involved.

ἀνακατεύω *v.t. see* ἀνακατώνω.

ἀνακατών|ω *v.t.* mix up, stir; involve; confuse. ~ομαι *v.i.* interfere; feel sick.

ἀνακάτωμα *s.n.* mixing; confusion; nausea.

ἀνακάτωση *s.f.* disturbance; nausea.

ἀνακατωσούρης *s.m.* trouble-maker.

ἀνακεφαλαιώνω *v.t.* recapitulate.

ἀνακηρύσσω *v.t.* declare (*winner, etc.*).

ἀνακινῶ *v.t.* stir up; revive (*an old topic*).

ἀνάκλασις *s.f.* refraction.

ἀνάκλησις *s.f.* recall; revocation.

ἀνακλητήριος *a.* of recall.

ἀνάκλιντρον *s.n.* reclining seat.

ἀνακοινῶ *v.t.* announce. ~ωθέν *s.n.* communiqué.

ἀνακόλουθος *a.* inconsequent.

ἀνακοπή *s.f.* checking; reprieve.

ἀνακούρκουδα *adv.* in crouching position.

ἀνακουφ|ίζω *v.t.* relieve, ease. ~ισις *s.f.* relief.

ἀνακριβής *a.* inaccurate, inexact.

ἀνάκρισις *s.f.* interrogation.

ἀνακριτής *s.m.* examining magistrate.

ἀνάκρουσις *s.f.* recoil (*of gun*); backing water; (*mus.*) performance.

ἀνακρούω *v.t.* thrust back; ~ πρύμναν go astern; (*mus.*) perform.

ἀνάκτορ|ον *s.n.* palatial residence; ~α (*pl.*) king's palace.

ἀνακτῶ *v.t.* regain.

ἀνακύπτω *v.i.* emerge; crop up; recover (*from reverse*).

ἀνακωχή *s.f.* armistice.

ἀναλαμβάνω *v.t. & i.* undertake, take up (again); (*v.i.*) recover. ἀνελήφθη he ascended into heaven; (*fam.*) he has vanished.

ἀναλαμπή *s.f.* flash.

ἀνάλατος *a.* without salt, insipid; lacking charm.

ἀνάλαφρος *a.* light as air, ethereal.

ἀνάλγητος *a.* unfeeling.

ἀναλήθεια *s.f.* untruth.

ἀνάληψις *s.f.* withdrawal (*of money*); undertaking; resumption; (*eccl.*) ascension.

ἀνάλλαγος *a.* not having changed one's linen.

ἀναλλοίωτος *a.* unchanging, fast (*colour*).

ἀναλογία *s.f.* relation, proportion, analogy, ratio.

ἀναλογίζομαι *v.t.* bethink oneself of.

ἀναλογικ|ός *a.* proportionate; ~όν ἐκλογικὸν σύστημα proportional representation.

ἀναλόγιον *s.n.* music-stand; lectern.

ἀνάλογ|ος *a.* in proportion. ~ον, ~οῦν *s.n.* quota.

ἀναλογ|ῶ *v.i.* correspond; τί μοῦ ~εῖ; what is my share?

ἀναλόγως *adv.* proportionately, accordingly; (*prep.*) ~ τῶν περιστάσεων according to circumstances.

ἀνάλυ|σις *s.f.* analysis. ~τικός *a.* analytical; detailed.

ἀναλύ|ω *v..* analyse; melt; ~ομαι εἰς δάκρυα dissolve in tears.

ἀναλφάβητος *a.* illiterate.

ἀναμαλλιασμένος *a.* dishevelled; worn rough (*of material*).

ἀναμασῶ *v.t.* chew well; (*fig.*) keep on repeating.

ἀνάμελος *a.* neglectful.

ἀναμένω *v.t.* wait for, expect.

ἀνάμεσα *adv.* in between; (*prep.*) ~ σέ among; ~ ἀπό between.

ἀναμεταξύ *adv. & prep.* (*with gen.*) between, among; στό ~ in the mean time; ~ μας between ourselves.

ἀναμετρῶ *v.t.* weigh up, take stock of.

ἀναμιγνύ|ω *v.t.* mix; implicate. ~ομαι *v.i.* intervene.

ἀνάμικτος *a.* mixed.

ἀναμιμνήσκω *v.t.* remind.

ἀναμίξ *adv.* mixed together.

ἀνάμιξις *s.f.* mixing; intervention.

ἄναμμα *s.n.* (*act of*) lighting; inflammation; rotting (*of cereals, etc.*).

ἀναμμένος *a.* alight; heated; gone bad.

ἀνάμνησις *s.f.* memory, recollection.

ἀναμονή *s.f.* waiting, expectation.

ἀναμόρφωσις *s.f.* reformation.

ἀναμπουμπούλα *s.f.* bustle, fuss.

ἀναμφιβόλως *adv.* indubitably.

ἀναμφισβήτητος *a.* indisputable.

ἀνανᾶς *s.m.* pineapple.

ἀνανδρία *s.f.* cowardice.

ἀνανεώνω *v.t.* renew, renovate.

ἀνανταπόδοτος *a.* unrequited; unrepaid; unrepayable.

ἀναντικατάστατος *a.* irreplaceable; not replaced.

ἀναντίρρητος *a.* incontrovertible.

ἄναξ *s.m.* king, sovereign.

ἀνα|ξαίνω, ~ξέω *v.t.* (*fig.*) reopen, rekindle (*wound, strife, etc.*).

ἀναξιόλογος *a.* unworthy of note.

ἀναξιοπαθής *a.* suffering undeservedly.

ἀναξιοπρεπής *a.* undignified.

ἀνάξιος *a.* unworthy; unfit, incompetent.

ἀνάπαλιν *adv.* conversely.

ἀναπάντεχος *a.* unexpected.

ἀναπαράγω *v.t.* (*biol.*) reproduce.

ἀναπαραδιά *s.f.* (*fam.*) lack of money.

ἀναπαράστασις *s.f.* representation; re-construction.

ἀνάπαυλα *s.f.* respite.

ἀνάπαυσ|ις *s.f.* rest, repose; ~εις (*pl.*) comfort.

ἀναπαυτικός *a.* comfortable.

ἀναπαύ|ω *v.t.* give repose to. ~ομαι *v.i.* rest; ~θηκε he is at rest (*dead*).

ἀναπέμπω *v.t.* give forth (*smell*); offer up (*thanks*).

ἀναπεπταμένος *a.* open (*not enclosed*); unfurled.

ἀναπηδῶ *v.i.* jump *or* spring *or* shoot up; start, jump.

ἀνάπηρος *a.* disabled, mutilated.

ἀνάπλασις *s.f.* remoulding, reforming; recalling to mind.

ἀναπλάσσω *v.t.* remould; recall to mind.

ἀναπλαστικ|ός *a.* of remoulding *or* re-shaping.

ἀναπληρώνω *v.t.* replace; find *or* act as substitute for.

ἀναπληρω(μα)τικ|ός *a.* substitute, deputy; ~ὲς ἐκλογές by-election.

ἀναπνέω *v.t. & i.* breathe.

ἀναπνευστικός *a.* respiratory.

ἀναπνοή *s.f.* breath, breathing.

ἀνάποδα *adv.* the wrong way round, up-side down, inside out, awry.

ἀναπόδεικτος *a.* unproved; unprovable.

ἀναπόδεκτος *a.* unacceptable.

ἀνάποδη *s.f.* wrong *or* reverse side; back-handed slap.

ἀναποδι|ά *s.f.* hitch, reverse; contrari-ness. ~άζω *v.i.* become contrary *or* difficult.

ἀναποδογυρίζω *v.t. & i.* turn inside out *or* upside down.

ἀνάποδος *a.* the wrong way round; dif-ficult, perverse.

ἀναπόδραστος *a.* unavoidable.

ἀναπολόγητος *a.* without being al-lowed to justify oneself; confounded, at a loss.

ἀναπολῶ *v.t.* recollect.

ἀναπόσπαστος *a.* inseparable; indis-pensable.

ἀναποφάσιστος *a.* irresolute.

ἀναπόφευκτος *a.* inevitable.

ἀναπτήρ *s.m.* (*cigarette*) lighter.

ἀνάπτυξις *s.f.* unfolding; develop-ment.

ἀναπτύσσω *v.t.* unfold; develop, ex-pound.

ἀνάπτω *v.t. & i. see* ἀνάβω.

ἀνάργυρ|ος *a.* without money; Ἅγιοι ~οι SS. Cosmas & Damian.

ἄναρθρος *a.* inarticulate; (*gram.*) with-out the article.

ἀναρίθμητος *a.* countless.

ἀνάριος *a.* sparse, not closely set.

ἀναρμόδιος *a.* not competent (*not authorized officially*).

ἀνάρμοστος *a.* unseemly.

ἀνάρπαστος *a.* snapped up.

ἀνάρρησις *s.f.* accession.

ἀναρριχῶμαι *v.i.* climb up.

ἀνάρρωσις *s.f.* convalescence.

ἀναρτῶ *v.t.* hang up, suspend.

ἀναρχί|α *s.f.* anarchy. ~κός *a.* anarchi-cal; an anarchist.

ἀναρωτιέμαι *v.i.* wonder.

ἀνάσα *s.f.* breath, breathing; respite.

ἀνασαίνω *v.i.* breathe, get one's breath.

ἀνασηκώνω *v.t.* raise slightly.

ἀνασκάπτω *v.t.* dig up, excavate; raze.

ἀνασκαφή *s.f.* excavation.

ἀνάσκελα *adv.* on one's back.

ἀνασκευάζω *v.t.* refute.

ἀνασκοπῶ *v.t.* pass in review, weigh up.

ἀνασκουμπώνομαι *v.i.* roll up one's sleeves; prepare for action.

ἄνασσα *s.f.* queen, sovereign.

ἀνασταίνω *v.t.* revive; rear ('esp. as foster child*).

ἀνασταλτικός *a.* delaying, restraining.

ἀνάστασις *s.f.* resurrection.

ἀνάστατος *a.* in a stir; in disorder.

ἀναστατώνω *v.t.* (*fig.*) upset, turn up-side down.

ἀναστέλλω *v.t.* check, stay, suspend.

ἀναστεν|άζω *v.i.* sigh. ~αγμός *s.m.* sigh.

ἀναστηλών|ω *v.t.* restore (*by rebuilding*). ~ομαι *v.i.* (*fig.*) show a bold front.

ἀναστήλωσις *s.f.* (*archaeological*) restora-tion.

ἀνάστημα *s.n.* height, stature.

ἀναστολή *s.f.* check, stay, suspension.

ἀναστρέφω *v.t.* invert, reverse.

ἀνασυγκρότησις *s.f.* rehabilitation.

ἀνασυνδέω *v.t.* reconnect; (*fig.*) renew (*ties, etc.*).

ἀνασύρω *v.t.* pull up *or* out, raise, draw forth.

ἀνασφάλιστος *a.* not insured.

ἀνασχηματίζω *v.t.* reconstruct.

ἀναταράσσω *v.t.* stir (up).

ἀνάτασις *s.f.* lifting up (*of hands, soul*).

ἀνατείνω *v.t.* extend, hold up.

ἀνατέλλω *v.i.* rise (*of sun, etc.*).

ἀνατέμνω v.t. dissect.

ἀνατίμησις s.f. rise in price.

ἀνατινάζ|ω v.t. shake up; blow up. ~ομαι v.i. explode; jump (from surprise, etc.).

ἀνατίναξις s.f. explosion.

ἀνατοκισμός s.m. compound interest.

ἀνατολή s.f. rising (of sun, etc.); east; orient; Levant.

ἀνατολικ|ός a. east, eastern. ~ῶς adv. to the east.

Ἀνατολίτ|ης s.m. Oriental; (esp.) Greek from Asia Minor. ~ικος a. oriental; (esp.) from Asia Minor.

ἀνατομία s.f. anatomy.

ἀνατρεπτικός a. subversive.

ἀνατρέπ|ω v.t. upset, overthrow. ~ομαι v.i. capsize, overturn.

ἀνατρέφω v.t. rear, bring up.

ἀνατρέχω v.i. refer or go back (to).

ἀνατριχ|ιάζω v.i. shiver, shudder, have goose-flesh. ~ιαστικός a. hair-raising. ~ίλα s.f. shiver.

ἀνατροπή s.f. upset, overthrow.

ἀνατροφή s.f. upbringing.

ἀνάτυπον s.n. off-print.

ἀνατυπώνω v.t. reprint.

ἄναυδος a. speechless.

ἄναυλα adv. without paying a fare; (fam.) ignominiously.

ἀναφαγιά s.f. (fam.) not eating much.

ἀναφαίνομαι v.i. appear, arise.

ἀναφαίρετος a. inalienable.

ἀναφανδόν adv. openly.

ἀναφέρ|ω v.t. mention, quote. ~ομαι v.i. refer, relate.

ἀναφλέγ|ω v.t. inflame. ~ομαι v.i. catch fire.

ἀνάφλεξις s.f. combustion.

ἀναφορά s.f. relation, reference; report; application, petition.

ἀναφορικός a. relative.

ἀναφουφουλιάζω v.t. fluff up or out.

ἀναφυλλητό s.n. sob, sobbing.

ἀναφύομαι v.i. (re)appear, arise.

ἀναφωνῶ v.i. cry out.

ἀναχαιτίζω v.t. check, restrain.

ἀναχρονισμός s.m. anachronism; old-fashioned views.

ἀνάχωμα s.n. mound, bank.

ἀναχώρησις s.f. departure.

ἀναχωρητής s.m. anchorite, hermit.

ἀναχωρῶ v.i. set out, leave.

ἀναψηλάφησις s.f. (law) retrial.

ἀναψυκτικά s.n.pl. refreshments (cold drinks, ices).

ἀναψυχή s.f. recreation, pleasure.

ἀνδρ- see ἀντρ-.

ἀνδραγάθημα s.n. heroic or daring feat.

ἀνδραγαθία s.f. prowess.

ἀνδράδελφος s.m. husband's brother.

ἀνδράποδον s.n. enslaved prisoner; (fig.) servile wretch.

ἀνδρεία s.f. bravery.

ἀνδρείκελον s.n. puppet.

ἀνδρεῖος a. brave.

ἀνδριάς s.m. statue (of person).

ἀνδρικός a. of a man, men's; manly.

ἀνδρόγυνον s.n. married couple.

ἀνδροῦμαι v.i. grow to manhood.

ἀνεβάζω v.t. carry or lift up; put up (price); put on (play); (fig.) ~ στά οὐράνια praise to the skies.

ἀνεβαίνω v.t. & i. see ἀναβαίνω.

ἀνέβασμα s.n. going up, climbing; lifting or carrying up; rise (in price); production (of play).

ἀνεβοκατεβαίνω v.t. & i. go up and down.

ἀνέγγιχτος a. untouched, intact, new.

ἀνεγείρω v.t. raise, erect.

ἀνέγερσις s.f. erection, building (act); getting up.

ἀνεγνωρισμένος a. recognized.

ἀνειλημμένος a. undertaken.

ἀνειλικρινής a. insincere, dissembling.

ἀνέκαθεν adv. ever, always (in the past).

ἀνεκδιήγητος a. beyond description.

ἀνέκδοτ|ος a. unpublished. ~ον s.n. anecdote.

ἀνεκμετάλλευτος a. unexploited.

ἀνεκπλήρωτος a. unfulfilled; unfulfillable.

ἀνεκποίητος a. inalienable; not sold.

ἀνεκτέλεστος a. unaccomplished; that cannot be performed.

ἀνεκτικός a. patient, forbearing.

ἀνεκτίμητος a. inestimable, invaluable.

ἀνεκτός a. bearable; passable.

ἀνέκφραστος a. inexpressible; not expressed; expressionless, inexpressive.

ἀνελεύθερος a. illiberal.

ἀνελκυστήρ s.m. lift, hoist.

ἀνελλιπ|ής a. with nothing missing. ~ῶς adv. without missing (an occasion).

ἀνέλπιστος a. unexpected.

ἀνέμη s.f. winder (in spinning).

ἀνεμίζω v.t. & i. expose to open air; wave in the air; winnow; (v.i.) blow about (of hair, flag, etc.).

ἀνεμιστήρ s.m. fan, ventilator.

ἀνεμοβλογιά s.f. chicken-pox.

ἀνεμογκάστρι s.n. false pregnancy.
ἀνεμοδείκτης s.m. weathercock.
ἀνεμοδέρνω v.i. be storm-tossed.
ἀνεμοδούρα s.f. weathercock; whirl-wind; winder (in spinning); wind-swept spot.
ἀνεμοζάλη s.f. hurricane.
ἀνεμομάζωμα s.n. ill-gotten goods.
ἀνεμόμυλος s.m. windmill.
ἀνεμοπύρωμα s.n. erysipelas.
ἄνεμος s.m. wind.
ἀνεμόσκαλα s.f. rope-ladder.
ἀνεμοστρόβιλος s.m. whirlwind.
ἀνεμπόδιστος a. unhindered, free.
ἀνεμώδης a. windy.
ἀνεμώνη s.f. anemone.
ἀνενδοίαστος a. unhesitating.
ἀνένδοτος a. unyielding; persistent.
ἀνενόχλητος a. undisturbed.
ἀνεξαίρ|ετος a. not excepted or ex-empted. ~έτως adv. without excep-tion.
ἀνεξακρίβωτος a. not confirmed.
ἀνεξάλειπτος a. ineffaceable.
ἀνεξάντλητος a. inexhaustible.
ἀνεξαρτησία s.f. independence.
ἀνεξάρτητος a. independent.
ἀνεξέλεγκτος a. not verified; not sub-ject to scrutiny or control.
ἀνεξέλικτος a. not fully developed (in personality or career).
ἀνεξερεύνητος a. unfathomable; un-explored.
ἀνεξετάστως adv. without inquiry or examination.
ἀνεξήγητος a. inexplicable; not ex-plained.
ἀνεξιθρησκεία s.f. religious tolerance.
ἀνεξίκακος a. forgiving.
ἀνεξίτηλος a. indelible.
ἀνεξιχνίαστος a. untraced; untrace-able; inscrutable.
ἀνέξοδος a. costing nothing.
ἀνεξόφλητος a. not paid (back) (of debt or creditor).
ἀνεπαίσθητος a. imperceptible.
ἀνεπανόρθωτος a. irreparable.
ἀνεπαρκής a. insufficient, inadequate.
ἀνέπαφος a. untouched, intact.
ἀνεπηρέαστος a. not affected, unin-fluenced.
ἀνεπίδεκτος a. not admitting of (with gen.).
ἀνεπιθύμητος a. undesirable; undesired.
ἀνεπίληπτος a. irreproachable.
ἀνεπίσημος a. unofficial, informal.

ἀνεπιτήδειος a. maladroit.
ἀνεπιτήδευτος a. unaffected, simple.
ἀνεπιτυχής a unsuccessful; ill-chosen.
ἀνεπιφύλακτος a. without reserve.
ἀνεπρόκοπος a. good for nothing.
ἀνεπτυγμένος a. cultivated (of persons).
ἄνεργ|ος a. out of work. ~ία s.f. un-employment.
ἀνερεύνητος a. unsearched, uninvesti-gated.
ἀνερευνῶ v.t. investigate.
ἀνερμάτιστος a. without ballast; (fig.) lacking stability; not well versed.
ἀνέρχομαι v.t. & i. ascend, climb; rise; amount.
ἀνέρωτος a. undiluted.
ἄνεσ|ις s.f. relaxation, comfort, ease; μὲ ~ιν at leisure.
ἀνεστραμμένος a. reversed, upside-down.
ἀνέτοιμος a. unready.
ἄν|ετος a. comfortable; convenient. ~έτως adv. in comfort; easily, without constraint.
ἄνευ prep. (with gen.) without; ἐκ τῶν ὦν οὐκ ~ sine qua non.
ἀνεύθυνος a. not responsible.
ἀνευλαβής a. impious; disrespectful.
ἀνεύρεσις s.f. finding.
ἀνεύρετος a. not to be found.
ἀνευρίσκω v.t. find (again), discover.
ἀνευχάριστος a. not satisfied; ungrate-ful.
ἀνεφάρμοστος a. inapplicable; not fit-ting; unrealizable.
ἀνέφελος a. cloudless.
ἀνέφικτος a. unrealizable, unattainable.
ἀνεφοδιάζω v.t. provision.
ἀνεφοδιασμός s.m. provisionment.
ἀνεφοδίαστος a. not provisioned.
ἀνέχεια s.f. indigence.
ἀνέχομαι v.t. tolerate, bear.
ἀνεχόρταγος a. insatiable.
ἀνεψιά s.f. niece.
ἀνεψιός s.m. nephew.
ἀνήθικος a. immoral.
ἄνηθο s.n. dill.
ἀνήκουστος a. unheard of.
ἀνήκω v.i. belong.
ἀνηλεής a. pitiless.
ἀν|ήλικος, ~ῆλιξ a. under age; a minor.
ἀνήλιος a. not sunny.
ἀνήμερα adv. on the actual day.
ἀνήμερος a. wild (beast).
ἀνήμπορος a. indisposed, ill.

ἀνήξερ|ος a. (fam.) κάνω τόν ~ο pretend not to know.

ἀνήρ s.m. man.

ἀνησυχία s.f. uneasiness.

ἀνήσυχος a. uneasy, restless.

ἀνησυχῶ v.t. & i. disquiet; be worried.

ἀνήφορ|ος s.m. uphill slope, acclivity. ~ικός a. uphill.

ἀνθεκτικός a. resistant.

ἀνθηρός a. blooming.

ἄνθ|ησις s.f., ~ισμα s.n. flowering, bloom.

ἀνθίσταμαι v.i. resist.

ἀνθόγαλα s.n. cream.

ἀνθοδέσμη s.f. bunch of flowers.

ἀνθοδοχεῖον s.n. flower-vase.

ἀνθολογ|ῶ v.i. select the best specimens. ~ία s.f. anthology.

ἀνθόνερο s.n. orange-flower water.

ἀνθοπώλης s.m. florist, flower-seller.

ἄνθος s.n. flower.

ἀνθός s.m. flower; flowering.

ἀνθόσπαρτος a. flower-strewn.

ἀνθρακεύω v.i. coal; (fig.) take in supplies.

ἀνθρακιά s.f. glowing fire.

ἀνθρακικός a. carbonic.

ἀνθρακίτης s.m. anthracite; (naut.) stoker.

ἀνθρακωρυχεῖον s.n. coal-mine.

ἀνθρακωρύχος s.m. coal-miner.

ἄνθραξ s.m. coal; carbon; anthrax.

ἀνθρωπεύω v.t. & i. civilize, improve; become civilized or improved.

ἀνθρωπιά s.f. humaneness; civility; (fam.) τῆς ~ς decent.

ἀνθρώπινος a. human.

ἀνθρωπινός a. decent, good enough.

ἀνθρωπισμός s.m. humaneness; humanism; (fam.) civility.

ἀνθρωπιστής s.m. humanist.

ἀνθρωποειδής a. anthropoid.

ἀνθρωποκτονία s.f. homicide.

ἀνθρωπολόγος s.m. anthropologist.

ἀνθρωπόμορφος a. in human shape.

ἄνθρωπος s.m. man, person, human being.

ἀνθρωπότης s.f. mankind.

ἀνθρωποφαγία s.f. cannibalism.

ἀνθρωποφοβία s.f. misanthropy.

ἀνθυγιεινός a. unhealthy, unhygienic.

ἀνθυπασπιστής s.m. (mil.) regimental sergeant-major.

ἀνθυπολοχαγός s.m. (mil.) second lieutenant.

ἀνθυπομοίραρχος s.m. (gendarmerie) sub-lieutenant.

ἀνθυποπλοίαρχος s.m. (navy) sub-lieutenant.

ἀνθῶ v.i. blossom, flourish.

ἀνία s.f. boredom. ~ρός a. boring.

ἀνίατος a. incurable.

ἀνίδεος a. having no idea; unsuspecting.

ἀνιδιοτελής a. disinterested.

ἀνιδρύω v.t. (re)erect.

ἀνίερος a. impious.

ἀνικανοποίητος a. unsatisfied.

ἀνίκανος a. incompetent, unfit; impotent.

ἀνίκητος a. invincible; unbeaten.

ἄνιπτος a. with hands or face unwashed.

ἀνίσκιωτος a. shadeless.

ἀνισόρροπος a. unbalanced.

ἄνισος a. unequal, uneven.

ἀνίσταμαι v.i. rise (esp. of resurrection).

ἀνιστορῶ v.t. recollect, relate; decorate (with sacred scenes).

ἀνίσχυρος a. powerless; not valid.

ἀνίσως 1. adv. unevenly. 2. conj. if by chance; ~ καί in case.

ἀνίχνευσις s.f. tracking; reconnaissance.

ἀνιψ- see ἀνεψ-.

ἀνιῶ v.t. & i. bore; be bored.

ἄνοδος s.f. ascent.

ἀνοησία s.f. nonsense, foolishness, folly.

ἀνόητος a. foolish, silly.

ἀνόθευτος a. unadulterated.

ἄνοιγμα s.n. opening.

ἀνοίγ|ω v.t. & i. open, cut open; cut, dig (road, door, well, etc.); (fam.) burgle; ~ω τό δρόμο widen the road, clear the way (for); ~ω τό βῆμα μου walk faster; turn on (light, tap); let out (garment); (v.i.) begin; brighten (of weather); open up or out; come out (of blossom); get lighter (in colour). ~ομαι v.i. (fig.) be over-confiding; launch out too ambitiously.

ἀνοίκειος a. unbecoming.

ἀνοίκιαστος a. unlet.

ἀνοικοδόμητος a. not built (on).

ἀνοικοδομῶ v.t. (re)build.

ἀνοικονόμητος a. (fam.) impossible to deal with.

ἀνοικτ|ός a. open; light in colour; affable, open-handed; διατηρῶ ~ὲς σχέσεις have a wide circle of acquaintance; στὰ ~ά on the open sea.

ἀνοιξιάτικος a. of spring.

ἄνοιξις s.f. spring (season).

ἀνοιχτόκαρδος *a.* genial.
ἀνοιχτομάτης *a.* wide-awake, sharp.
ἀνοιχτοχέρης *a.* open-handed.
ἀνομβρία *s.f.* drought.
ἀνομοιογενής *a.* heterogeneous; uneven.
ἀνόμοιος *a.* dissimilar, odd.
ἄνομος *a.* lawless; unlawful.
ἀνοξείδωτος *a.* stainless, rustless.
ἀνόργανος *a.* inorganic; without instruments.
ἀνοργάνωτος *a.* unorganized.
ἀνορεξιά *s.f.* lack of appetite; (*fig.*) half-heartedness.
ἀνορθογραφία *s.f.* spelling mistake; (*fam.*) solecism, not the thing.
ἀνορθώνω *v.t.* stand upright, raise; restore.
ἀνοσία *s.f.* immunity (*from disease, etc.*).
ἀνόσιος *a.* unholy; vile.
ἀνοσταίνω *v.t. & i.* make *or* become insipid, vapid *or* unattractive.
ἄνοστος *a.* insipid, vapid, unattractive.
ἀνούσιος *a. see* ἄνοστος.
ἀνοχή *s.f.* patience; tolerance, consent; οἶκος ~ς brothel.
ἀνοχύρωτος *a.* unfortified; (*fig.*) undefended.
ἀντ- *see* ἀντι-.
ἀνταγωνίζομαι *v.t. & i.* rival, conflict (with).
ἀνταγωνισμός *s.m.* rivalry, confliction.
ἀνταλλαγή *s.f.* exchange, barter.
ἀντάλλαγμα *s.n.* thing given in exchange, recompense; εἰς ~ in exchange.
ἀνταλλακτικ|ός *a.* of *or* by exchange. ~όν *s.n.* spare part, refill.
ἀνταλλάξιμ|ος *a.* exchangeable. ~α (*s.n.pl.*) bonds issued to Gk. refugees from Turkey.
ἀνταλλάσσω *v.t.* exchange.
ἀντάμα *adv.* together.
ἀνταμείβω *v.t.* reward.
ἀνταμοιβή *s.f.* reward.
ἀνταμώνω *v.t.* meet.
ἀντάμωση *s.f.* καλή ~ au revoir.
ἀντανάκλασις *s.f.* reflection, reverberation.
ἀντανακλαστικ|ός *a.* reflecting; ~ὸν φαινόμενον reflex action.
ἀντανακλῶ *v.t. & i.* reflect.
ἀντάξιος *a.* corresponding in worth.
ἀνταποδίδω *v.t.* give in return, repay.
ἀνταποκρίνομαι *v.i.* correspond; respond; come up (*to*).

ἀνταπόκρισις *s.f.* correspondence; response; journalist's dispatch.
ἀνταποκριτής *s.m.* correspondent.
ἀντάρα *s.f.* storm; noise, uproar.
ἀνταρκτικός *a.* antarctic.
ἀνταρσία *s.f.* rebellion.
ἀντάρτ|ης *s.m.* rebel, guerrilla. ~ικός *a.* rebel. ~ικο *s.n.* rebel forces.
ἀντασφάλεια *s.f.* reinsurance.
ἀνταύγεια *s.f.* reflection, brightness.
ἄντε *int.* ᵹο! come! come on!
ἀντέγκλησις *s.f.* counter-charge, recrimination.
ἀντεθνικός *a.* against the national interest.
ἀντεκδίκησις *s.f.* reprisal.
ἀντένα *s.f.* aerial.
ἀντενδείκνυμαι *v.i.* be contra-indicated.
ἀντεπανάστασις|*s.f.* counter-revolution.
ἀντεπίθεσις *s.f.* counter-attack.
ἀντεπιστέλλον *a.* ~ μέλος corresponding member.
ἀντεπιτίθεμαι *v.i.* counter-attack.
ἀντεραστής *s.m.* rival in love.
ἄντερο *s.n.* intestine, bowel; (*fam.*) στριμμένο ~ cantankerous person.
ἀντέτι *s.n.* custom.
ἀντέχω *v.i.* resist, endure, hold firm.
ἀντζούγια *s.f.* anchovy.
ἀντηλιά *s.f.* strong reflection of sunlight, glare.
ἀντηχῶ *v.i.* resound.
ἀντί *prep.* (*with gen. or acc.*) instead of, in return for; for (*price*); ~ γιά instead of; ~ πληρωμῆς by way of payment, for pay; ~ νά (*with verb*) instead of.
ἀντι- *denotes* opposition, opposite situation, replacement, reciprocation, equivalence, negation, posteriority.
ἀντιαεροπορικός *a.* anti-aircraft.
ἀντιαισθητικός *a.* offending good taste.
ἀντιαρματικός *a.* (*mil.*) anti-tank.
ἀντιβαίνω *v.i.* (*with εἰς*) go against, be contrary to.
ἀντίβαρον *s.n.* counter-weight.
ἀντιβασιλεύς *s.m.* viceroy, regent.
ἀντιγραφή *s.f.* copying; (*fig.*) copy.
ἀντίγραφον *s.n.* copy, transcript.
ἀντιγράφω *v.t. & i.* copy, copy out, imitate; crib.
ἀντιδημοτικός *a.* unpopular.
ἀντίδι *s.n.* endive.
ἀντιδιαστολή *s.f.* contradistinction.
ἀντίδικος *s.m.* opponent (*at law*).
ἀντίδοτον *s.n.* antidote.
ἀντίδρασις *s.f.* reaction.

ἀντιδραστήριον s.n. (chem.) reagent.
ἀντιδραστικός a. reactionary; reactive.
ἀντιδρῶ v.i. react; be opposed.
ἀντίδωρον s.n. (eccl.) Host.
ἀντίζηλ|ος a. rival. ~ία s.f. rivalry.
ἀντίθεσις s.f. contrast.
ἀντίθετος a. contrary, opposite, reverse.
ἀντιθέτω v.t. set against, oppose.
ἀντίκα s.f. antique.
ἀντικαθιστῶ v.t. replace; relieve (sentry, etc.).
ἀντικαθρέφτισμα s.n. reflection (of image).
ἀντικάμαρα s.f. antechamber; (fam.) κάνω ~ keep people waiting, keep aloof.
ἀντικανονικός a. irregular; against regulations.
ἀντικατασκοπεία s.f. counter-espionage.
ἀντικατάστασις s.f. replacement.
ἀντιακαταστάτης s.m. substitute; successor.
ἀντικατοπτρισμός s.m. reflection; mirage.
ἀντίκειμαι v.i. be opposed.
ἀντικειμενικ|ός a. objective. ~ότης s.f. objectivity.
ἀντικείμενον s.n. thing, object; aim.
ἀντικλείδι s.n. pass-key.
ἀντικοινωνικός a. anti-social.
ἀντικρούω v.t. repulse; refute.
ἀντίκρυ adv. opposite.
ἀντικρύζω v.t. face; behold; meet (debt, etc.).
ἀντικρυνός a. opposite, facing.
ἄντικρυς adv. completely, absolutely.
ἀντίκρυσμα s.n. encounter; (fin.) cover.
ἀντίκτυπος s.m. repercussion.
ἀντιλαϊκός a. against the popular interest; unpopular.
ἀντίλαλος s.m. echo.
ἀντιλαμβάνομαι v.t. & i. understand; perceive, notice; be quick in the uptake.
ἀντιλέγω v.i. object, retort; say the opposite.
ἀντιληπτικός a. perceptive.
ἀντιληπτός a. noticed; understandable.
ἀντίληψις s.f. understanding; opinion; perception, notice; quickness of mind.
ἀντιλογία s.f. contradiction.
ἀντιλυσσικός a. anti-rabies.
ἀντιμάχομαι v.t. fight against; detest.
ἀντιμετωπίζω v.t. face, brave.
ἀντιμέτωπος a. face-to-face.
ἀντιμιλῶ v.i. answer back.
ἀντιμισθία s.f. reward, fee.
ἀντιμόνιον s.n. antimony.

ἀντιναύαρχος s.m. vice-admiral.
ἀντινομία s.f. antinomy.
ἀντίξοος a. unfavourable.
ἀντίο int. good-bye. [It. addio]
ἀντιπάθεια s.f. dislike, aversion.
ἀντιπαθητικός a. provoking dislike.
ἀντιπαθῶ v.t. dislike.
ἀντίπαλος s.m. rival, adversary.
ἀντιπαρατάσσω v.t. array against.
ἀντιπαρέρχομαι v.t. & i. pass (by), get past.
ἀντιπατριωτικός a. unpatriotic.
ἀντιπειθαρχικός a. insubordinate.
ἀντίπερα adv. on the farther side.
ἀντιπερισπασμός s.m. diversion, distraction.
ἀντιπλοίαρχος s.m. (naut.) commander.
ἀντίποδες s.m.pl. antipodes.
ἀντιποιητικός a. unpoetical.
ἀντίποινα s.n.pl. reprisals.
ἀντιπολιτεύομαι v.i. be in opposition.
ἀντιπολίτευσις s.f. (political) opposition.
ἀντίπραξις s.f. counter-activity.
ἀντιπρόεδρος s.m. vice-president.
ἀντιπροσωπεία s.f. representation; delegation.
ἀντιπροσωπεύω v.t. represent.
ἀντιπρόσωπος s.m. representative, delegate.
ἀντίρρησις s.f. objection.
ἀντίρροπον s.n. counterpoise.
ἀντίς prep. see ἀντί.
ἀντισήκωμα s.n. counter-weight; (mil.) buying-out money.
ἀντισηπτικός a. antiseptic.
ἀντίσκηνον s.n. tent.
ἀντισμήναρχος s.m. (aero.) wing-commander.
ἀντισταθμίζω v.t. balance; (mech.) compensate.
ἀντίστασις s.f. resistance.
ἀντιστέκομαι v.i. resist.
ἀντίστιξις s.f. (mus.) counterpoint.
ἀντίστοιχος a. equivalent, corresponding.
ἀντιστοιχῶ v.i. be equivalent.
ἀντιστράτηγος s.m. lieutenant-general.
ἀντιστρέφω v.t. reverse.
ἀντίστροφ|ος a. reverse, inverse. ~ως adv. vice versa.
ἀντισυνταγματάρχης s.m. lieutenant-colonel.
ἀντισυνταγματικός a. unconstitutional.
ἀντισφαίρισις s.f. tennis.
ἀντιτάσσω v.t. array (against); oppose;

~ βίαν εἰς τὴν βίαν meet force with force.
ἀντιτείνω v.i. object (to proposal, etc.).
ἀντιτίθεμαι v.i. be opposed.
ἀντίτιμον s.n. price, value.
ἀντιτορπιλλικόν s.n. (naut.) destroyer.
ἀντίτυπον s.n. copy (of book, etc.).
ἀντιφάρμακον s.n. antidote.
ἀντίφα|σις s.f. discrepancy, contradiction. ~τικός a. contradictory.
ἀντιφάσκω v.i. contradict oneself.
ἀντίφωνον s.n. antiphon, anthem.
ἀντίχειρ s.m. thumb.
ἄντλησις s.f. pumping, drawing of water.
ἀντλία s.f. pump; fire-engine; water-cart.
ἀντλῶ v.t. pump, draw off.
ἀντοχή s.f. resistance; strength.
ἀντρ- see ἀνδρ-.
ἄντρακλας s.m. big man.
ἄντρας s.m. man; husband.
ἀντρειωμένος a. brave, strong.
ἀντρίκιος a. see ἀνδρικός.
ἀντρογυναῖκα s.f. masculine woman; brave woman.
ἀντρόγυνο s.n. married couple.
ἄντρον s.n. cave, den.
ἀντρόπιαστος a. unshamed.
ἄντυτος a. not dressed.
ἀντωνυμία s.f. pronoun.
ἄνυδρος a. waterless.
ἀνύμφευτος a. unmarried.
ἀνύπανδρος a. unmarried.
ἀνύπαρκτος a. non-existent.
ἀνυπαρξία s.f. non-existence; lack.
ἀνυπέρβλητος a. insuperable; unsurpassable.
ἀνυπερθέτως adv. without fail; without delay.
ἀνυπόδητος a. barefooted.
ἀνυπόκριτος a. unfeigned.
ἀνυπόληπτος a. in disrepute.
ἀνυπολόγιστος a. incalculable.
ἀνυπόμον|ος a. impatient. ~ῶ v.i. be impatient.
ἀνύποπτος a. unsuspecting; not suspect.
ἀνυπόστατος a. groundless.
ἀνυπότακτος a. refractory; (mil.) a defaulter.
ἀνυπόφορος a. unbearable.
ἀνυψώνω v.t. raise; (fig.) extol.
ἄνω adv. up, above; ~ κάτω in confusion, upset; ἡ ~ Βουλή Upper Chamber; (prep. with gen.) above, over; ~ ποταμῶν incredible.

ἀνώγι s.n. upper story.
ἀνώδυνος a. painless.
ἀνωμαλία s.f. irregularity, unevenness; anomaly.
ἀνώμαλος a. irregular, uneven; anomalous.
ἀνώνυμος a. anonymous; (fin.) ~ ἑταιρεία limited company.
ἀνώτατος a. supreme, highest.
ἀνώτερ|ος a. superior, higher; (with gen.) above; ~α βία force majeure; κ' εἰς ~α to your continued success!
ἀνωφελής a. fruitless.
ἀνώφλι s.n. lintel.
ἄξαφνος a. see ἔξαφνος.
ἀξέγνοιαστος a. without cares; unconcerned.
ἄξενος a. inhospitable.
ἄξεστος a. rough, uncouth.
ἄξεχαστος a. unforgotten; unforgettable.
ἀξί|α s.f. value, worth, merit; ~αι (pl.) stocks and shares; κατ' ~αν deservedly.
ἀξιαγάπητος a. lovable.
ἀξιέπαινος a. praiseworthy.
ἀξιέραστος a. lovable; charming.
ἀξίζ|ω v.t. & i. be worth, cost; deserve; be of worth; be worth while; ~ει τὸν κόπον it is worth the trouble; μοῦ ~ει I deserve it.
ἀξίνα s.f. pick.
ἀξιο- denotes worthy of.
ἀξιοδάκρυτος a. deplorable.
ἀξιοθαύμαστος a. wonderful.
ἀξιοθέατ|ος a. worth seeing; τὰ ~α the sights.
ἀξιοθρήνητος a. lamentable.
ἀξιοκατάκριτος a. reprehensible.
ἀξιόλογος a. worthy of note; distinguished.
ἀξιόπιστος a. worthy of credit, reliable.
ἀξιόποινος a. punishable; deserving punishment.
ἀξιοπρέπεια s.f. dignity, correctness, seemliness.
ἀξιοπρεπής a. dignified, correct, seemly.
ἄξιος a. capable; deserving, worthy.
ἀξιοσημείωτος a. noteworthy.
ἀξιότιμος a. estimable.
ἀξιόχρεος a. solvent, reliable.
ἀξιῶ v.t. claim, demand.
ἀξίωμα s.n. high office; axiom.
ἀξιωματικός s.m. officer.
ἀξιωμένος a. capable (person).
ἀξιών|ω v.t. vouchsafe to permit. ~ομαι v.i. manage, contrive.

άξίωσις s.f. claim, pretension.
άξόδευτος a. not spent, used up or sold out.
άξύριστος a. unshaven.
άξων s.m. axis, axle, pivot.
άοίδιμος a. of blessed memory.
άοιδός s.m. singer, bard.
άοκνος a. tireless.
άόμματος a. blind.
άοπλος a. unarmed.
άόρατος a. invisible.
άοριστία s.f. uncertainty.
άόριστος a. vague, indefinite; (s.m.) (gram.) aorist.
άοσμος a. odourless.
άπαγγελία s.f. recitation; delivery.
άπάγκιο s.n. spot sheltered from wind.
άπαγορ|εύω v.t. forbid, prohibit. ~ευσις s.f. prohibition.
άπαγχονίζω v.t. hang (person).
άπάγω v.t. abduct, carry off.
άπαγωγή s.f. abduction; έκουσία ~ elopement; είς άτοπον ~ reductio ad absurdum.
άπαθανατίζω v.t. immortalize.
άπάθ|εια s.f. impassivity; indifference, apathy. ~ής a. impassive; indifferent, apathetic.
άπαίδευτος a. uneducated, unskilled.
άπαίρω v.i. set sail.
άπαισιόδοξος a. pessimistic.
άπαίσιος a. unpropitious; frightful.
άπαίτη|σις s.f. claim, demand, requirement. ~τικός a. demanding.
άπαιτ|ῶ v.t. demand, claim, require; τά ~ούμενα what is needful.
άπαλλαγή s.f. deliverance, release, discharge.
άπαλλάσσω v.t. deliver, release, absolve; relieve (of duties).
άπαλλοτριῶ v.t. expropriate.
άπαλός a. soft; gentle.
άπάνεμος a. sheltered from wind.
άπάνθρωπος a. inhuman.
άπαντα s.n.pl. complete works (of author).
άπαντέχω v.t. await.
άπάντημα s.n. meeting, encounter.
άπάντησις s.f. answer.
άπαντοχή s.f. expectation.
άπαντῶ v.t. & i. answer; meet (expenses); (also pass.) occur, be found.
άπάνω adv. up, above, on top; upstairs; ~ ~ superficially; ~ κάτω up-and-down, approximately; άπό ~ (from) above, on top; έως ~ to the top; τό ~

πάτωμα the upper floor; ~ πού at the moment when. (prep.) ~ άπό above, over, more than; ~ σέ upon, in the moment of; έγραψε τό σπίτι ~ στό γιό του he made the house over to his son.
άπανωτός a. one after another.
άπαξ adv. once; inasmuch as.
άπαξιῶ v.t. & i. think unworthy (of); disdain (to).
άπαράβατος a. inviolable; inviolate.
άπαραβίαστον s.n. inviolability.
άπαράδεκτος a. unacceptable.
άπαραίτητος a. indispensable.
άπαράλλακτος a. identical.
άπαράμιλλος a. unrivalled.
άπαράσκευος a. unprepared.
άπαρατήρητος a. unnoticed; unrebuked.
άπαρέγκλιτος a. steady, unswerving.
άπαρέμφατον s.n. (gram.) infinitive.
άπαρέσκεια s.f. displeasure.
άπαρηγόρητος a. inconsolable.
άπαριθμῶ v.t. count, enumerate.
άπαρνοῦμαι v.t. renounce, forsake.
άπαρτία s.f. quorum.
άπαρτίζ|ω v.t. form, compose. ~ομαι v.i. be made up, consist.
άπαρτος a. not received; not captured; impregnable.
άπαρχ|ή s.f. outset; ~αί (pl.) first-fruits.
άπ|ας a. all, whole; έξ ~αντος without fail; τά ~αντα complete works.
άπάστρευτος a. not cleaned, peeled, or shelled.
άπασχόλησις s.f. occupation.
άπασχολ|ῶ v.t. occupy; distract attention of; ~ημένος busy; preoccupied.
άπατεών s.m. swindler, rogue.
άπάτη s.f. deceit; illusion.
άπατηλός a. deceptive, illusory.
άπάτητος a. untrodden, inaccessible.
άπατος a. bottomless.
άπατρις a. without a homeland; unpatriotic.
άπατ|ῶ v.t. deceive, cheat. ~ῶμαι v.i. be mistaken.
άπαυδῶ v.i. & t. tire, become sick (of); (fam.) make fed up.
άπαυτ|ός a. (fam.) so-and-so, what's-his-name. ~ώνω v.t. & i. do (replacing another verb from vagueness or euphemism).
άπαχος a. lacking fat.
άπεγνωσμένος a. desperate.
άπειθαρχ|ῶ v.i. be insubordinate. ~ία s.f. insubordination.

ἀπειθής a. disobedient.

ἀπειλή s.f. threat.

ἀπειθῶ v.i. be disobedient.

ἀπεικάζω v.t. portray; figure, understand.

ἀπεικονίζ|ω v.t. represent, portray. ~ομαι v.i. be reflected.

ἀπειλ|ή s.f. threat. ~ητικός a. threatening.

ἀπειλῶ v.t. threaten.

ἀπείραχτος a. untouched; inoffensive.

ἀπειρία s.f. 1. inexperience. 2. unlimited number.

ἄπειρ|ος a. 1. inexperienced. 2. countless, infinite. ~ον s.n. infinity.

ἀπεκδύομαι v.t. divest oneself of, renounce.

ἀπέλασις s.f. deportation.

ἀπελευθερ|ώνω v.t. set free. ~ωσις s.f. liberation.

ἀπελπίζ|ω v.t. deprive of hope. ~ομαι v.i. give up hope.

ἀπελπισία s.f. despair; (fam.) εἶναι ~ it is hopeless!

ἀπελπισμένος a. in despair.

ἀπέναντι adv. & prep. (with gen.) opposite; compared with, in relation to; towards (in part payment); against (receipt).

ἀπεναντίας adv. on the contrary.

ἀπένταρος a. (fam.) without a penny.

ἀπέραντος a. boundless.

ἀπέραστος a. impassable; unbeatable; not threaded; not entered (in accounts); that has not been suffered (of malady).

ἀπεργ|ία s.f. strike. ~ός s.m. striker. ~ῶ v.i. go on strike.

ἀπερίγραπτος a. indescribable.

ἀπεριόριστος a. unlimited; not under restraint.

ἀπεριποίητος a. neglected, untidy.

ἀπερίσκεπτος a. thoughtless, foolish.

ἀπερίσπαστος a. with undivided attention.

ἀπέριττος a. without superfluity, simple.

ἀπεριφράστως adv. straight out, pointblank (of speech).

ἀπέρχομαι v.i. depart.

ἀπεσταγμένος a. distilled.

ἀπεσταλμένος s.m. envoy, representative, delegate.

ἀπευθύν|ω v.t. address, send. ~ομαι v.i. apply.

ἀπευκταῖος a. untoward.

ἀπεύχομαι v.t. wish not to happen.

ἀπεχθάνομαι v.t. detest.

ἀπεχθής a. odious.

ἀπέχω v.i. be distant; abstain.

ἀπηγορευμένος a. forbidden.

ἀπηλιώτης s.m. east wind.

ἀπηλλαγμένος a. absolved (from); free (of).

ἀπηνής a. pitiless, cruel.

ἀπηρχαιωμένος a. antiquated.

ἀπηχ|ῶ v.t. & i. echo; (fig.) ~ καλῶς produce a good impression. ~ησις s.f. (fig.) repercussion, effect.

ἄπιαστος a. not caught; impossible to catch; in mint condition.

ἀπίδι s.n. pear.

ἀπίθαν|ος a. unlikely. ~ότης s.f. unlikelihood.

ἀπιθώνω v.t. put down.

ἀπίκο adv. (fam.) ready to depart. [It. a picco]

ἄπιον s.n. pear.

ἄπιστος a. undrunk; undrinkable; sober.

ἀπίστευτος a. unbelievable.

ἀπιστία s.f. disbelief; infidelity.

ἀπίστομα adv. face downwards.

ἄπιστος a. unbelieving; unfaithful; faithless.

ἀπιστῶ v.i. (with εἰς) disbelieve; deceive; break one's word.

ἅπλα s.f. roominess.

ἁπλά adv. simply (not elaborately).

ἀπλάγιαστος a. not lying down.

ἀπλανής a. fixed.

ἄπλαστος a. unmoulded; unaffected.

ἄπλετος a. abundant (of lighting).

ἀπλήρωτος a. 1. unfulfilled. 2. unpaid.

ἀπλησίαστος a. unapproachable.

ἄπληστος a. insatiable, grasping.

ἁπλογραφία s.f. single-entry bookkeeping.

ἁπλοϊκός a. naive.

ἁπλοποιῶ v.t. simplify.

ἁπλ|ός a. simple; single. ~ότης s.f. simplicity.

ἁπλ|οῦς a. simple; single. ~ούστατα adv. quite simply.

ἁπλοχέρης a. open-handed.

ἁπλόχωρος a. spacious.

ἁπλυσιά s.f. dirtiness.

ἄπλυτ|ος a. unwashed; (fig.) τά ~α dirty linen.

ἅπλωμα s.n. roominess; spreading or hanging out.

ἁπλών|ω v.t. & i. spread, stretch out;

hang up (washing). ~ομαι v.i. extend one's activities.

ἁπλῶς adv. simply, merely.

ἄπλωτος a. not navigable.

ἁπλωτ|ός a. outspread. ~ή s.f. stroke (in swimming).

ἀπνευστί adv. in one breath; at a gulp.

ἄπνοια s.f. absence of wind; (med.) apnoea.

ἄπνους a. lifeless.

ἀπό prep. (with acc. in demotic, gen. in purist Gk.; also with nom.) 1. (source, origin) from, since; ~ ἀρχῆς from the beginning; ~ πολλοῦ for a long time (since); ~ μικρός from childhood. 2. (agent, cause, means, material) by, from, of, on; πεθαίνω ~ die of; πάσχω ~ suffer from; ζῶ ~ live on or by; ~ χαρτί (made) of paper. 3. (separation, deprivation) from, of. 4. (difference, comparison) from, than. 5. (distributive, partitive) πῆραν ~ δύο κομμάτια they got 2 pieces each; πάρε ~ ἐκεῖνα take one (or some) of those. 6. (content, subject-matter, circumstance) γεμᾶτο ~ full of; ἀνάγκη ~ need of; ξέρω ~ be knowledgeable about; στραβός ~ τό ἕνα μάτι blind in one eye; ~ λεφτά ἔχει πολλά he is well-off for money. 7. (route, direction) along, through, via, past; περνῶ ~ τό γραφεῖο I call at the office. 8. (adverbial phrases) ~ μέσα on the inside, from inside; ~ δῶ over here; ~ δῶ κι ἐμπρός from now on. 9. (prepositional phrases) μέσα ~ out of; πρίν ~ before.

ἀπο- denotes source, restoration, completion, cessation, posteriority, separation, the contrary.

ἀποβάθρα s.f. landing-stage, gangway, railway platform.

ἀποβαίνω v.i. disembark; prove, turn out.

ἀποβάλλω v.t. cast off, dismiss, lose; (v.i.) miscarry.

ἀπόβαρον s.n. tare (weight).

ἀπόβασις s.f. disembarkation, landing.

ἀποβατικός a. of or for landing.

ἀποβδομάδα adv. (fam.) next week.

ἀποβιβάζω v.t. disembark, unload.

ἀποβιῶ v.i. die.

ἀποβλακών|ω v.t. make stupid. ~ομαι v.i. become stupid.

ἀποβλέπω v.i. (with εἰς) aim at, aspire to; look to, rely on.

ἀπόβλητος a. rejected; an outcast.

ἀποβολή s.f. casting off; expulsion; loss; miscarriage; abortion.

ἀποβραδίς adv. yesterday evening; the evening before.

ἀπόβρασμα s.n. scum.

ἀπόγειο s.n. land-breeze.

ἀπόγειον s.n. apogee.

ἀπογει|οῦμαι v.i. take off (in flight). ~ωσις s.f. take-off.

ἀπόγε(υ)μα s.n. afternoon. ~τινή s.f. afternoon; matinée.

ἀπογίν|ομαι v.i. 1. become; τί θά ~ω; what will become of me? 2. get worse and worse. 3. be undone (annulled).

ἀπόγνωσις s.f. desperation.

ἀπογοήτευσις s.f. disappointment, disillusion.

ἀπογοητεύω v.t. disappoint, disillusion.

ἀπόγονος s.m. descendant; offspring.

ἀπογραφή s.f. census, inventory.

ἀπογυμνώνω v.t. strip, plunder; lay bare.

ἀποδάσωσις s.f. deforestation.

ἀποδεικνύω v.t. prove, demonstrate.

ἀποδεικτικόν s.n. certificate.

ἀπόδειξις s.f. proof; receipt.

ἀποδεκατίζω v.t. decimate.

ἀποδέκτης s.m. addressee, consignee; (fin.) drawee.

ἀποδεκτός a. acceptable; accepted.

ἀποδέχομαι v.t. accept; admit.

ἀποδημητικός a. migratory.

ἀποδημία s.f. migration; going or living abroad.

ἀπόδημος a. settled abroad.

ἀποδιδράσκω v.i. escape (of prisoner).

ἀποδίδω v.t. give back, return; yield; attribute; render (pay or perform), represent.

ἀποδιοπομπαῖος a. ~ τράγος scapegoat.

ἀποδοκιμάζω v.t. disapprove; demonstrate against.

ἀπόδοσις s.f. return; yield; performance; (gram.) apodosis.

ἀποδοτικός a. profitable, productive.

ἀποδοχ|ή s.f. acceptance; acceptation; ~αί (pl.) emoluments.

ἀπόδρασις s.f. escape (of prisoner).

ἀποδύομαι v.i. undress; (fig.) ~ εἰς τόν ἀγῶνα strip for the fray.

ἀποδυτήριον s.n. changing-room.

ἀποζημιώνω v.t. compensate, repay.

ἀποζημίωσις s.f. compensation, indemnity.

ἀποζητῶ v.t. miss, feel the loss of.

ἀποζῶ v.i. scrape a living.

ἀποθανών *a.* deceased.

ἀποθαρρυντικός *a.* discouraging.

ἀποθαρρύνω *v.t.* discourage.

ἀπόθεμα *s.n.* deposit; stock, reserve.

ἀποθεραπεία *s.f.* complete cure; completion of cure.

ἀποθετικός *a.* (*gram.*) deponent.

ἀποθέτω *v.t.* put down; (*fig.*) confide; put aside (*savings*).

ἀποθε|ώνω *v.t.* deify; (*fig.*) give a hero's welcome to. ~ωσις *s.f.* apotheosis; (*fig.*) great reception.

ἀποθηκάριος *s.m.* store-keeper.

ἀποθηκεύω *v.t.* place in store.

ἀποθήκη *s.f.* any place for storage; magazine (*of gun*).

ἀποθνήσκω *v.i.* die.

ἀποθρασύνομαι *v.i.* grow impudent.

ἀποθυμῶ *v.t.* miss, feel the loss of; feel desire for.

ἀποικία *s.f.* colony.

ἀποικιακ|ός *a.* colonial. ~ά *s.n.pl.* groceries.

ἄποικος *s.m.* colonist, settler.

ἀποκαθήλωσις *s.f.* Descent from the Cross.

ἀποκαθιστ|ῶ *v.t.* restore, re-establish; set up, marry (*one's children, etc.*). ~αμαι *v.i.* be restored; settle down, marry.

ἀποκαλύπτ|ω *v.t.* unveil, uncover, reveal. ~ομαι *v.i.* raise one's hat.

ἀποκάλυψις *s.f.* revelation; Apocalypse.

ἀποκά(μ)νω 1. *v.i.* get tired. 2. *v.t.* finish off; τί ἀπέκαμες μέ τό σπίτι; what have you done about the house?

ἀποκαμωμένος *a.* exhausted.

ἀποκάρωμα *s.n.* torpor (*from heat*).

ἀποκατάστασις *s.f.* restoration, resettlement; marriage.

ἀποκατινός *a.* lower, underneath, below.

ἀπόκει|μαι *v.i.* be, repose; εἰς σέ ~ται it is up to you.

ἀπόκεντρ|ος *a.* outlying. ~ωσις *s.f.* decentralization.

ἀποκεφαλίζω *v.t.* decapitate.

ἀποκηρ|ύσσω *v.t.* renounce, disavow, disinherit. ~υξις *s.f.* renunciation; disinheritance.

ἀποκλεισμός *s.m.* exclusion; blockade; boycott; lock-out.

ἀποκλειστικός *a.* exclusive.

ἀποκλεί|ω *v.t.* exclude, cut off; ~εται it is an impossibility.

ἀπόκληρος *a.* disinherited; outcast.

ἀποκληρώνω *v.t.* disinherit.

ἀποκλίνω *v.i.* lean, incline; diverge.

ἀπόκλισις *s.f.* deviation, declination.

ἀποκοιμίζω *v.t.* put *or* lull to sleep; (*fig.*) lull suspicions of.

ἀποκοιμοῦμαι *v.i.* go to sleep.

ἀποκομίζω *v.t.* carry away; derive, receive.

ἀπόκομμα *s.n.* bit; press-cutting; weaning.

ἀποκοπή *s.f.* cutting off, amputation; weaning; κατ' ~ν on job-work.

ἀποκόπτω *v.t.* cut off; wean.

ἀποκορύφωμα *s.n.* acme.

ἀπόκοτος *a.* audacious.

ἀποκούμπι *s.n.* prop, support.

ἀπόκρεως *s.f.* carnival.

ἀπόκρημνος *a.* precipitous.

ἀποκριές *s.f.pl.* carnival.

ἀποκρίνομαι *v.i.* answer.

ἀπόκρισις *s.f.* answer.

ἀποκρού|ω *v.t.* repulse, reject. ~στικός *a.* repulsive.

ἀποκρυπτογραφῶ *v.t.* decode.

ἀποκρύπτω *v.t.* conceal.

ἀποκρυσταλλῶ *v.t.* crystallize.

ἀπόκρυφος *a.* secret; (*eccl.*) apocryphal.

ἀπόκτημα *s.n.* acquisition.

ἀποκτηνώνω *v.t.* make brutish.

ἀποκτῶ *v.t.* obtain, acquire; have (*children*).

ἀποκύημα *s.n.* product (*of imagination*).

ἀπολαβ|ή *s.f.* gain; ~αί (*pl.*) emoluments.

ἀπολαμβάνω *v.t. & i.* gain, get; feel enjoyment.

ἀπόλαυσις *s.f.* enjoyment.

ἀπολαυστικός *a.* enjoyable; entertaining.

ἀπολαύω *v.t.* gain, get; enjoy, relish; (*with gen.*) enjoy, experience.

ἀπολείπ|ω *v.i.* be lacking; remain to be done; be left over. ~ομαι *v.i.* be inferior.

ἀπολειφάδι *s.n.* remnant of soap.

ἀπολήγω *v.i.* lead (*to*), end up (*in*).

ἀπολίθωμα *s.n.* fossil.

ἀπολιθώνω *v.t.* petrify.

ἄπολις *a.* stateless.

ἀπολίτιστος *a.* uncivilized.

ἀπολλύω *v.t.* lose; destroy.

ἀπολογία *s.f.* defence, justification.

ἀπολογισμός *s.m.* financial statement; account of office, report.

ἀπολογοῦμαι *v.i.* defend *or* justify oneself.

ἀπολυέμαι *v.i.* hasten.

ἀπολύμανσις s.f. disinfection.

ἀπόλυσις s.f. release, dismissal.

ἀπολυταρχία s.f. absolutism.

ἀπολυτήριον s.n. certificate of discharge; school leaving-certificate.

ἀπόλυτος a. absolute; cardinal (number).

ἀπολυτός a. loose.

ἀπολυτρώνω v.t. ransom; deliver.

ἀπολύτως adv. absolutely.

ἀπολύ|ω v.t. release, let loose; dismiss; (v.i.) ~σε ἡ ἐκκλησία church service is over.

ἀπολωλ|ώς a. lost; ~ὸς πρόβατον lost sheep.

ἀπομαθαίνω v.t. 1. learn thoroughly. 2. teach completely. 3. unlearn.

ἀπομακρ|αίνω, ~ύνω v.t. move away. ~υνσις s.f. removal, going away.

ἀπόμακρος a. far-off.

ἀπομανθάνω v.t. unlearn.

ἀπομάσσ|ω v.t. wipe off; rub down. ~ομαι v.i. wipe one's hands or face.

ἀπόμαχος a. past active service.

ἀπομεινάρι s.n. remains, left-over.

ἀπομένω v.i. remain, be left; be left speechless.

ἀπόμερος a. out-of-the-way.

ἀπομεσήμερο s.n. afternoon.

ἀπομίμησις s.f. imitation (of fabric, etc.).

ἀπομνημονεύματα s.n.pl. memoirs.

ἀπομνημονεύω v.t. memorize.

ἀπομονώνω v.t. isolate; insulate.

ἀπομόνωσις s.f. isolation, insulation.

ἀπομυζῶ v.t. suck (blood, etc.).

ἀπονέμω v.t. award, bestow, deal out.

ἀπονενοημένος a. desperate.

ἀπονήρευτος a. without guile.

ἀπονιά s.f. unfeelingness.

ἀπονομή s.f. award, bestowal.

ἄπονος a. unfeeling.

ἀποξενώνω v.t. alienate, estrange.

ἀπόξεσις s.f. scraping down.

ἀποξεχνιέμαι v.i. become oblivious (of time, one's duties, etc.).

ἀποξηραίνω v.t. dry, drain.

ἀπο|παίδι, ~παιδο s.n. neglected or disowned child, waif.

ἀποπαίρνω v.t. chide, be sharp with.

ἀπόπαππας s.m. ex-priest.

ἀπόπατ|ος s.m. w.c. ~ῶ v.i. go to stool.

ἀπόπειρ|α s.f. attempt. ~ῶμαι v.i. make an attempt.

ἀποπέμπω v.t. send away, dismiss.

ἀποπεράτωσις s.f. completion.

ἀπόπι(ω)μα s.n. heel-tap (liquor).

ἀποπλανῶ v.t. mislead; seduce.

ἀποπληξία s.f. apoplexy.

ἀποπληρώνω v.t. pay off.

ἀπόπλους s.m. sailing, departure.

ἀπόπλυμα s.n. dishwater, slops.

ἀποπλύνω v.t. wash well, rinse; (fig.) wipe out (insult, etc.).

ἀπόπνοια s.f. (emission of) smell.

ἀποποιοῦμαι v.t. refuse, decline.

ἀποπομπή s.f. dismissal.

ἀπόρημα s.n. question, problem (to be solved).

ἀπόρθητος a. impregnable.

ἀπορία s.f. doubt, uncertainty, perplexity, difficulty; indigence.

ἄπορος a. poor, needy.

ἀπορρέω v.i. flow, stem, result (from).

ἀπόρρητ|ος a. secret; ὁ ἐξ ~ων confidant.

ἀπορρίμματα s.n.pl. rubbish, refuse.

ἀπορρίπτω v.t. throw away, cast off; reject, refuse; fail (examinee).

ἀπορρίχνω v.t. & i. miscarry.

ἀπόρροια s.f. consequence.

ἀπορροφ|ῶ v.t. absorb, take up. ~ητικός a. absorbent.

ἀπορρυπαντικόν s.n. detergent.

ἀπορῶ v.i. be at a loss, wonder; be indigent.

ἀποσαρίδια s.n.pl. sweepings.

ἀποσαφηνίζω v.t. elucidate.

ἀπόσβεσις s.f. extinguishing; paying off (debt).

ἀποσβήνω v.t. & i. extinguish, wipe out; be wiped out.

ἀποσβολώνω v.t. confound, abash.

ἀποσείω v.t. shake off.

ἀποσιωπητικά s.n.pl. dots to show omission of word(s).

ἀποσιωπῶ v.t. not to mention; hush up.

ἀποσκευαί s.f.pl. baggage.

ἀποσκίρτησις s.f. defection.

ἀποσκοπῶ v.i. aim, have as object (to).

ἀποσμητικόν s.n. deodorant.

ἀποσοβῶ v.t. avert, keep off.

ἀπόσπασμα s.n. extract, excerpt; detachment.

ἀποσπερίτης s.m. evening star.

ἀποσπ|ῶ v.t. tear away, up or out; detach. ~ασμένος a. seconded (to post).

ἀπόσταγμα s.n. distilled liquid.

ἀποσταίνω v.i. get tired.

ἀπόσταξις s.f. distilling.

ἀποστασία s.f. revolt, defection, apostasy.

ἀπόστασις s.f. distance.

ἀποστάτης s.m. rebel; apostate.

ἀποστειρῶ v.t. sterilize.

ἀποστέλλω v.t. dispatch; depute.

ἀποστέργω v.t. spurn, disdain.

ἀποστερ|ῶ v.t. deprive. ~οῦμαι v.t. be deprived of, lose (with acc. or gen.).

ἀποστηθίζω v.t. learn or say by heart.

ἀπόστημα s.n. abscess.

ἀποστολεύς s.m. sender.

ἀποστολή s.f. dispatch, shipment; mission.

ἀπόστολος s.m. apostle.

ἀποστομώνω s.m. silence.

ἀποστράγγισις s.f. straining, draining.

ἀποστρατεία s.f. retirement (of officers).

ἀποστράτευσις s.f. demobilization.

ἀπόστρατος s.m. retired officer.

ἀποστρέφ|ω v.t. avert (face). ~ομαι v.t. detest.

ἀποστροφή s.f. turning away; aversion, abhorrence; apostrophe (rhetorical).

ἀπόστροφος s.m. (gram.) apostrophe.

ἀποσυμφόρησις s.f. decongestion.

ἀποσύνθεσις s.f. decomposition; disorganization.

ἀποσυντίθεμαι v.i. decompose, rot; become disorganized.

ἀποσύρ|ω v.t. withdraw, take away; retract. ~ομαι v.i. withdraw, retire.

ἀποσχίζομαι v.i. separate, secede (from).

ἀποσώνω v.t. finish up, finish off; make up (deficiency).

ἀπότακτος a. cashiered, dismissed the service.

ἀποταμιεύω v.t. save up, put by.

ἀπόταξις s.f. cashiering, dismissal.

ἀποτάσσω v.t. cashier.

ἀποτείν|ω v.t. address (words). ~ομαι v.i. address oneself, inquire (with πρός).

ἀποτελειώνω v.t. finish off.

ἀποτέλεσις s.f. composition, constitution.

ἀποτέλεσμα s.n. result, consequence. ~τικός a. effective.

ἀποτελ|ῶ v.t. form, constitute. ~οῦμαι v.i. consist.

ἀποτέτιος a. (fam.) what's-his-name.

ἀποτεφρώνω v.t. reduce to ashes.

ἀποτινάσσω v.t. shake off.

ἀποτί(ν)ω v.t. pay (debt, penalty, homage).

ἀπότομος a. steep, sheer; sudden, abrupt; brusque.

ἀποτραβ|ῶ v.t. withdraw, draw off. ~ιέμαι v.i. withdraw.

ἀποτρέπω v.t. avert; dissuade.

ἀποτριχωτικόν s.n. depilatory.

ἀποτρόπαιος a. abominable.

ἀποτροπή s.f. prevention, warding off; dissuasion.

ἀποτροπιάζομαι v.t. abhor.

ἀποτρύγημα s.n. completion of vintage.

ἀποτρώγω v.t. & i. eat up; finish eating.

ἀποτσίγαρο s.n. cigarette-end.

ἀποτυγχάνω v.i. fail, be unsuccessful.

ἀποτυπ|ώνω v.t. impress, imprint, stamp. ~ωμα s.n. impression, print.

ἀποτυφλώνω v.t. blind.

ἀποτυχαίνω v.i. see ἀποτυγχάνω.

ἀποτυχία s.f. failure, lack of success.

ἀπουσ|ία s.f. absence; lack. ~ιάζω v.i. be absent.

ἀποφάγια s.n.pl. remains of food on plate.

ἀποφαγωμένος a. having finished eating; eaten up.

ἀποφαίνομαι v.i. give an opinion; show, be apparent.

ἀποφασί|ζω v.t. & i. decide on; make up one's mind; τόν ~σαν they have no hope of his recovery; ~σμένος determined; despaired of (by doctors).

ἀπόφασ|ις s.f. decision, resolve; verdict; τό παίρνω ~ι accept the inevitable or make up one's mind.

ἀποφασιστικός a. decisive, resolute.

ἀποφέρω v.t. produce, bring in.

ἀποφεύγω v.t. avoid, escape.

ἀποφθέγγομαι v.i. lay down the law.

ἀπόφθεγμα s.n. saying.

ἀπόφοιτος s.m.f. one who has finished school or university etc.

ἀποφορά s.f. stink.

ἀπόφορι s.n. cast-off garment.

ἀποφράς a. ~ ἡμέρα unlucky day.

ἀποφυγή s.f. avoidance.

ἀποφυλακίζω v.t. release from prison.

ἀπόφυσις s.f. excrescence.

ἀποχαιρετισμός s.m. leave-taking, farewell.

ἀποχαιρετῶ v.t. say goodbye to.

ἀποχαλιν|ῶ v.t. unbridle, let loose. ~οῦμαι v.i. lose all restraint.

ἀποχαυνώνω v.t. debilitate, make torpid.

ἀποχέτευσις s.f. draining away.

ἀπόχη s.f. (butterfly or fishing) net.

ἀποχή s.f. abstention; abstinence.

ἀποχρεμπτικόν s.n. expectorant.

ἀποχρωματίζω v.t. take colour out of, fade.

ἀποχρῶν a. sufficient, justifiable.

ἀπόχρωσις s.f. 1. fading, discolouring. 2. shade, nuance.

ἀποχώρησις s.f. withdrawal, resignation.

ἀποχωρητήριον s.n. w.c.

ἀποχωρίζ|ω v.t. separate. ~ομαι v.t. & i. part from; part.

ἀποχωρισμός s.n. separation, parting.

ἀποχωρῶ v.i. withdraw, resign.

ἀπόψε adv. tonight; during the (past) night.

ἀποψιλῶ v.t. depilate; (fig.) denude, strip.

ἀποψινός a. tonight's.

ἄποψις s.f. (point of) view, aspect.

ἀπραγματοποίητος a. unrealizable; not carried out.

ἄπραγος a. unexperienced.

ἄπρακτος a. without achieving one's object; unachieved.

ἀπραξία s.f. inactivity; (business) stagnation.

ἀπρέπεια s.f. breach of good manners.

ἀπρεπής a. improper, unbecoming.

Ἀπρίλ|ης, ~ιος s.m. April.

ἀπρόβλεπτος a. unforeseen; unforeseeable.

ἀπρόθυμος a. reluctant.

ἄπροικ|ος, ~ιστος a. without a dowry.

ἀπροκάλυπτος a. undisguised, open.

ἀπροκατάληπτος a. unbiased.

ἀπρόκλητος a. unprovoked.

ἀπρόκοφτος a. good-for-nothing.

ἀπρομελέτητος a. unpremeditated.

ἀπρονοησία s.f. improvidence; thoughtless act.

ἀπρό|οπτος a. unforeseen; ἐξ ~όπτου unexpectedly.

ἀπρόσβλητος a. unaffected (by); unassailable; not offended.

ἀπροσγείωτος a. not having landed (of aircraft); (fig.) not down-to-earth.

ἀπρόσδεκτος a. unacceptable, undesirable.

ἀπροσδιόριστος a. indeterminate, indefinite.

ἀπροσδόκητος a. unexpected.

ἀπρόσ|εκτος a. inattentive. ~εξία s.f. inattentiveness.

ἀπρόσιτος a. inaccessible; unapproachable; beyond one's means.

ἀπροσ|κάλεστος, ~κλητος a. uninvited.

ἀπρόσκοπτος a. smooth, without stumbling.

ἀπροσπέλαστος a. see ἀπρόσιτος.

ἀπροσποίητος a. unfeigned.

ἀπροστάτευτος a. unprotected.

ἀπροσωπόληπτος a. impartial.

ἀπρόσωπος a. impersonal.

ἀποφύλακτος a. without precaution; exposed.

ἀπροχώρητον s.n. limit, dead end.

ἄπταιστος a. faultless.

ἄπτερος a. without wings.

ἀπτόητος a. intrepid.

ἄπτ|ομαι v.t. touch (with gen.); (fam.) μή μοῦ ~ον touchy; fragile, delicate.

ἁπτός a. tangible.

ἀπύθμενος a. bottomless.

ἀπύλωτ|ος a. without gates; (fig.) ~ον στόμα one who cannot keep his mouth shut.

ἀπύρετος a. without a temperature.

ἄπω adv. ἡ ~ Ἀνατολή Far East.

ἀπωθῶ v.t. thrust away, repel, reject.

ἀπώλεια s.f. loss; perdition.

ἀπώλητος a. unsold; unsaleable.

ἀπών a. absent.

ἀπώτατος a. farthest.

ἀπώτερος a. farther; ~ σκοπός ulterior motive.

ἄρα conj. so, consequently.

ἆρα particle I wonder if, can it be that?

ἀρά s.f. curse.

ἀραβικός a. Arabian, Arabic.

ἀραβόσιτος s.m. maize.

ἀραβούργημα s.n. arabesque.

ἄραγε see ἆρα.

ἄραγμα s.n. harbouring, lying at moorings.

ἀράδα s.f. line, row; turn; τῆς ~ς ordinary, common-or-garden; (adv.) continuously; ~ ~ in a row.

ἀραδιάζω v.t. arrange in line; (fig.) recount, tell.

ἀράζω v.t. & i. moor, tie up, bring or come to rest.

ἀράθυμος a. irascible.

ἀραιός a. thin, sparse, scattered.

ἀραιώνω v.t. & i. thin or spread out, dilute; make or become fewer.

ἀρακᾶς s.m. vetch.

ἀραλίκι s.n. crack, fissure; (fig.) opportunity.

ἀραμπᾶς s.m. cart.

ἀραξοβόλι s.n. anchorage.

ἀράπης s.m. negro; bogyman.

ἀραπίνα s.f. negress; dark girl.

ἄρατος a. (fam.) ἔγινε ~ he vanished.

ἀράχν|η s.f. spider; spider's web. ~ιάζω v.i. get covered with cobwebs.

Άραψ *s.m.* Arab.

Ἀρβανίτης *s.m.* Albanian; Greek of Albanian descent.

ἀρβύλα *s.f.* soldier's boot.

ἀργά *adv.* slowly; late.

ἀργάζω *v.t.* tan.

ἀργαλειός *s.m.* loom.

ἀργάτης *s.m.* (*fam.*) labourer; windlass.

ἄργητα *s.f.* delay.

ἀργία *s.f.* not being at work; holiday, closing (-day); suspension from duty.

ἄργιλλος *s.f.* clay.

ἀργοκίνητ|ος *a.* slow-moving; (*fam.*) ~ο καράβι slowcoach.

ἀργόμισθ|ος *s.m.* one who draws salary without working. ~ία *s.f.* sinecure.

ἀργοπορία *s.f.* slowness, delay.

ἀργός *a.* slow, idle, not at work; suspended from duty.

ἀργόσχολος *a.* doing nothing.

ἀργότερα *adv.* later on.

ἀργυραμοιβός *s.m.* money-changer.

ἀργύριον *s.n.* money.

ἀργυρολογία *s.f.* collection of money (*esp. by dubious means for one's own ends*).

ἄργυρ|ος *s.m.* silver. ~οῦς *a.* silver.

ἀργῶ *v.i.* be late, lose time; not to be working; be closed.

ἄρδευσις *s.f.* irrigation.

ἄρδην *adv.* from top to bottom, completely.

ἀρειμάνιος *a.* warlike, fierce.

Ἄρειος *a.* ~ Πάγος Areopagus; Supreme Court.

ἀρεοπαγίτης *s.m.* judge of Supreme Court.

ἀρέσκεια *s.f.* taste, liking; κατ' ~ν at choice.

ἀρέσκομαι *v.i.* take pleasure (in), like (*with* νά *or* εἰς).

ἀρεστός *a.* pleasing, agreeable.

ἀρέσ|ω *v.i.* please, give pleasure; μοῦ ~ει I like (it).

ἀρετή *s.f.* virtue.

ἀρετσίνωτος *a.* unresinated.

ἀρθρῖτις *s.f.* arthritis.

ἀρθρογράφος *s.m.f.* leader-writer; journalist.

ἄρθρον *s.n.* article, clause.

ἀρθρώνω *v.t.* articulate, utter.

ἄρθρωσις *s.f.* joint, articulation.

ἀριά *adv.* ~ καὶ ποῦ rarely.

ἀρίδα *s.f.* (*fam.*) leg.

ἀρίθμησις *s.f.* counting, numbering.

ἀριθμητής *s.m.* numerator; adding-machine.

ἀριθμητικ|ός *a.* numerical, arithmetical. ~ή *s.f.* arithmetic.

ἀριθμός *s.m.* number, figure.

ἀριθμ|ῶ *v.t.* count, number. ~οῦμαι *v.i.* amount (*to*).

ἄριστα *adv.* excellently.

ἀριστεῖον *s.n.* first prize.

ἀριστερά 1. *s.f.* left hand; left wing. 2. *adv.* on the left.

ἀριστερός *a.* left; left-handed; left-wing.

ἀριστεύω *v.i.* win highest mark; be (among) the best.

ἀριστοκρατία *s.f.* aristocracy.

ἄριστος *a.* best, excellent.

ἀριστοτέχνης *s.m.* virtuoso.

ἀριστούργημα *s.n.* masterpiece.

ἀριστοῦχος *s.m.f.* one who has passed with highest mark.

ἀρκετ|ός *a.* enough; a fair amount of. ~ά *adv.* enough, rather, considerably.

ἀρκοῦδ|α *s.f.* bear. ~ίζω *v.i.* crawl (*of babies*).

ἀρκούντως *adv. see* ἀρκετά.

ἀρκτικός *a.* 1. initial. 2. arctic, northern.

ἄρκτος *s.f.* bear.

ἀρκ|ῶ *v.i.* suffice, be enough; ~εῖ νά provided that. ~οῦμαι *v.i.* confine oneself, be content (*with* νά *or* εἰς).

ἀρλούμπα *s.f.* foolish talk *or* boast.

ἅρμα *s.n.* chariot; (*mil.*) ~ μάχης tank.

ἁρμαθιά *s.f.* bunch, string (*of keys, onions, etc.*).

ἁρμάρι *s.n.* cupboard, wardrobe.

ἅρματα *s.n.pl.* arms, weapons.

ἁρματολός *s.m.* armed Greek having police duties under Turkish occupation.

ἁρματώνω *v.t.* arm; equip (*ship*).

ἁρμέγω *v.t.* milk.

Ἀρμέν|ης, ~ιος *s.m.* Armenian.

ἁρμενίζω *v.i.* make sail; journey.

ἁρμένικ|ος *a.* Armenian; (*fam.*) ~η ἐπίσκεψις (unduly) prolonged visit.

ἄρμεν|ο *s.n.* sail; ship; ~α (*pl.*) rigging.

ἅρμη *s.f.* brine.

ἁρμόδι|ος *a.* propitious; proper, competent. ~ότης *s.f.* competency, province.

ἁρμόζω *v.i.* fit, be suitable.

ἁρμονία *s.f.* harmony.

ἁρμός *s.m.* joint; gap.

ἁρμοστής *s.m.* high commissioner.

ἁρμυρ- *see* ἁλμυρ-.

ἀρνάκ|ι *s.n.* little lamb; (*fam.*) ~ια (*pl.*) white horses (*waves*).

ἀρνησίθρησκος *a.* apostate.
ἀρνησικυρία *s.f.* veto.
ἀρνήσιος *a.* lamb's.
ἄρνησις *s.f.* refusal; denial; negation.
ἀρνητικός *a.* negative.
ἀρνί(ον) *s.n.* lamb.
ἀρνοῦμαι *v.t. & i.* refuse; deny.
ἄρον ἄρον *adv.* in hot haste.
ἀρόσιμος *a.* arable.
ἄροσις *s.f.* ploughing.
ἄροτρ|ον *s.n.* plough. ~ιῶ *v.t.* plough.
ἄρουρ|α *s.f.* ploughed land; (*fig.*) ἄχθος
  ~ης wastrel.
ἀρουραῖος *s.m.* vole.
ἄρπα *s.f.* harp.
ἁρπαγή *s.f.* rapine; seizure, rape.
ἁρπάγη *s.f.* hook, grapnel.
ἅρπαγμα *s.n.* rape, plunder; scuffle.
ἁρπάζ|ω *v.t. & i.* snatch, carry off,
  seize; catch (*illness*); (*v.i.*) catch fire;
  catch (*in cooking*). ~ομαι *v.i.* grab
  hold of (*with ἀπό*); get irritated;
  ἁρπάχτηκαν they came to blows.
ἁρπακτικός *a.* rapacious; of prey.
ἅρπαξ *s.m.* rapacious person.
ἁρπαχτά *adv.* in haste.
ἅρπυια *s.f.* harpy.
ἁρπῶ *v.t. & i. see* ἁρπάζω.
ἀρραβών *s.m.* deposit, earnest; engagement (ring); ~ες (*pl.*) betrothal.
ἀρραβωνιάζ|ω *v.t.* betroth. ~ομαι *v.i.*
  get engaged.
ἀρραβωνιαστικ|ός *s.m.*, ~ιά *s.f.* one's
  betrothed.
ἀρράγιστος *a.* uncracked; unbroken;
  unbreakable.
ἀρρεναγωγεῖον *s.n.* boys' school.
ἄρρεν *s.n.* male child.
ἀρρενωπός *a.* manly.
ἄρρηκτος *a.* unbreakable; unbroken.
ἄρρην *a.* male.
ἄρρητος *a.* inexpressible.
ἀρρωσταίνω *v.t. & i.* make ill; fall ill.
ἀρρώστι|α *s.f.* illness. ~άρης *a.* sickly,
  delicate.
ἄρρωστος *a.* ill.
ἀρρωστῶ *v.t. & i. see* ἀρρωσταίνω.
ἀρσενικός *a.* male; masculine (*gender*).
ἄρσις *s.f.* lifting, removal; (*mus.*) up-
  beat.
ἀρτέμων *s.m.* (*naut.*) jib.
ἀρτηρί|α *s.f.* artery. ~ακός *a.* arterial.
ἄρτι *adv.* recently, newly.
ἀρτιγενής *a.* newly born.
ἀρτιμελής *a.* sound of limb.
ἄρτ|ιος *a.* whole, intact; even (*number*);

εἰς τὸ ~ιον at face value. ~ίως *adv.*
  recently; with nothing missing.
ἀρτοποιεῖον *s.n.* bakery.
ἀρτοπωλεῖον *s.n.* baker's shop.
ἄρτος *s.m.* bread.
ἄρτυμα *s.n.* seasoning.
ἀρτύν|ω *v.t.* season; feed with meat.
  ~ομαι *v.i.* break one's fast, eat meat.
ἀρύομαι *v.t.* draw, derive.
ἀρχαί *s.f.pl.* the authorities.
ἀρχαΐζω *v.i.* adopt old-fashioned ways
  or expressions.
ἀρχαϊκός *a.* archaic.
ἀρχαιοκαπηλία *s.f.* smuggling of an-
  tiques.
ἀρχαιολόγ|ος *s.m.* archaeologist. ~ία
  s.f. archaeology.
ἀρχαῖ|ος *a.* old, ancient; ~ότερος
  senior; ~α (*s.n.pl.*) antiquities.
ἀρχαιότης *s.f.* antiquity; seniority.
ἀρχαιρεσίαι *s.f.pl.* election of officers.
ἀρχάριος *a.* beginner.
ἀρχέγονος *a.* primordial, primitive.
ἀρχεῖον *s.n.* archives.
ἀρχέτυπον *s.n.* archetype.
ἀρχ|ή *s.f.* beginning, origin; principle;
  authority; κατ' ~ήν in principle; κατ'
  ~άς in the beginning.
ἀρχηγεῖον *s.n.* command headquarters.
ἀρχηγία *s.f.* command.
ἀρχηγός *s.m.* commander, leader.
ἀρχι- *denotes* first, chief.
ἀρχιεπίσκοπος *s.m.* archbishop.
ἀρχιεργάτης *s.m.* foreman.
ἀρχιερεύς *s.m.* prelate; chief priest.
ἀρχίζω *v.t. & i.* begin.
ἀρχικελευστής *s.m.* (*naut.*) chief petty
  officer.
ἀρχικός *a.* first, initial.
ἀρχιμανδρίτης *s.m.* archimandrite.
ἀρχιμηνιά *s.f.* first day of month.
ἀρχινῶ *v.t. & i.* begin.
ἀρχιπέλαγος *s.n.* archipelago.
ἀρχιστράτηγος *s.m.* (*mil.*) commander-
  in-chief.
ἀρχισυντάκτης *s.m.* editor-in-chief.
ἀρχιτεκτονική *s.f.* architecture.
ἀρχιτέκτων *s.m.* architect.
ἀρχιφύλαξ *s.m.* sergeant of city police.
ἀρχιχρονιά *s.f.* New Year's Day.
ἄρχομαι *v.i. & t.* (*with gen.*) begin.
ἀρχομανία *s.f.* lust for power.
ἄρχοντας *s.m.* notable, man of substance.
ἀρχοντιά *s.f.* breeding, distinction.
ἀρχοντικό *s.n.* gentleman's house.

ἀρχοντικός *a.* of distinction, fine.

ἀρχοντοξεπεσμένος *s.m.* impoverished gentleman.

ἀρχοντοπιάνομαι *v.i.* give oneself lordly airs.

ἀρχοντόπουλο *s.n.* son of distinguished or well-to-do family.

ἀρχοντοχωριάτης *s.m.* vulgar well-to-do person.

ἀρχύτερα *adv.* earlier; μία ὥρα ~ as soon as possible.

ἄρχω *v.i. & t.* (*with gen.*) rule, reign.

ἄρχων *s.m.* ruler, lord; archon.

ἀρωγή *s.f.* aid.

ἄρωμα *s.n.* scent, aroma; flavour (*of ice-cream, etc.*). ~τικός *a.* scented.

ἄς 1. *particle* (*introducing wishes, suppositions, etc.*) let, may. 2. (*imperative*) allow, let (alone), leave.

ἀσάλευτος *a.* stable, not moving.

ἀσανσέρ *s.n.* lift. [F. *ascenseur*]

ἄσαρκος *a.* fleshless, skinny.

ἀσαφής *a.* not clear.

ἀσβέστης *s.m.* lime.

ἀσβέστιον *s.n.* calcium.

ἀσβεστοκονίαμα *s.n.* plaster, mortar.

ἀσβεστόλιθος *s.m.* limestone.

ἄσβεστος *a.* see ἄσβυστος.

ἄσβεστος *s.f.* lime.

ἀσβεστώνω *v.t.* whitewash.

ἀσβόλη *s.f.* soot.

ἀσβός *s.m.* badger.

ἄσβυστος *a.* that is not or cannot be extinguished or erased.

ἀσέβ|εια *s.f.* disrespect, impiety. ~ής *a.* disrespectful, impious.

ἀσέλγ|εια *s.f.* licentiousness. ~ής *a.* licentious.

ἄσεμνος *a.* obscene, indecent.

ἀσετυλίνη *s.f.* acetylene.

ἀσήκης *s.m.* (*fam.*) ladies' man; fine fellow.

ἀσήκωτος *a.* too heavy to lift; still in bed.

ἀσήμαντος *a.* insignificant.

ἀσημένιος *a.* silver.

ἀσήμι *s.n.* silver.

ἀσημικά *s.n.pl.* silverware.

ἀσημείωτος *a.* unnoted.

ἀσημοκαπνισμένος *a.* silver-plated.

ἄσημος *a.* not well-known, obscure.

ἀσηπτικός *a.* aseptic.

ἀσθένεια *s.f.* illness, weakness (*of will*).

ἀσθενής *a.* ill, weak; a patient.

ἀσθενικός *a.* sickly.

ἀσθενῶ *v.i.* be ill.

ἄσθμα *s.n.* asthma.

ἀσθμαίνω *v.i.* pant.

ἀσίτευτος *a.* not ripened; not hung (*meat*).

ἀσιτία *s.f.* under-nourishment.

ἀσκαρδαμυκτί *adv.* fixedly, without blinking.

ἀσκεπής *a.* uncovered; bare-headed.

ἄσκεπτος *a.* thoughtless.

ἀσκέρι *s.n.* army, crowd.

ἀσκημ- see ἀσχημ-.

ἄσκησις *s.f.* exercise, practice.

ἀσκητής *s.m.* hermit.

ἀσκητικός *a.* ascetic.

ἀσκί *s.n.* skin (*for wine, etc.*).

ἄσκοπος *a.* pointless.

ἀσκός *s.m.* skin (*for wine, etc.*); sac.

ἀσκ|ῶ *v.t.* exercise, practise (*profession*). ~οῦμαι *v.i.* exercise oneself (*with εἰς*).

ᾆσμα *s.n.* song.

ἀσμένως *adv.* gladly.

ἀσουλούπωτος *a.* (*fam.*) badly shaped.

ἀσπάζομαι *v.t.* kiss, embrace; (*fig.*) adopt.

ἀσπασμός *s.m.* kiss, embrace.

ἀσπαστός *a.* acceptable.

ἄσπαστος *a.* unbroken; unbreakable.

ἄσπιλος *a.* immaculate.

ἀσπιρίνη *s.f.* aspirin.

ἀσπίς *s.f.* 1. shield. 2. asp.

ἄσπλαγχνος *a.* without compassion.

ἄσπονδος *a.* irreconcilable.

ἀσπόνδυλος *a.* invertebrate.

ἀσπούδαστος *a.* uneducated.

ἀσπράδα *s.f.* whiteness.

ἀσπράδι *s.n.* white spot; white (*of eye, egg*).

ἀσπρειδερός *a.* whitish.

ἀσπρίζω *v.t. & i.* whiten, distemper; become white; appear as a white shape.

ἀσπρίλα *s.f.* whiteness.

ἀσπρομάλλης *a.* white-haired.

ἀσπροπρόσωπος *a.* without loss of credit.

ἀσπρόρουχα *s.n.pl.* underclothes, linen.

ἄσπρ|ος *a.* white. ~α *s.n.pl.* money.

ἀσπρόχωμα *s.n.* white clay.

ἄσσος *s.m.* ace.

ἀστάθ|εια *s.f.* instability, changeability. ~ής *a.* unsteady, changeable.

ἀστάθμητος *a.* unweighed; (*fig.*) ~ παράγων unknown factor.

ἀστακός *s.m.* lobster.

ἀστάρι *s.n.* lining; undercoating.

ἄστατος *a.* changeable.

ἀστειεύομαι v.i. joke.
ἀστεῖζομαι v.i. joke.
ἀστεῖ|ος a. funny, amusing; trifling (of things). ~o s.n. joke.
ἀστείρευτος a. inexhaustible.
ἀστεϊσμός s.m. joke.
ἀστέρ|ας s.m., ~ι s.n. star.
ἀστερισμός s.m. constellation.
ἀστερό|εις a. starry; ~εσσα (s.f.) Stars and Stripes.
ἀστεροσκοπεῖον s.n. observatory.
ἀστεφάνωτος a. not legally married.
ἀστήρ s.m. star.
ἀστήρικτος a. unsupported; (fig.) untenable.
ἀστιγματισμός s.m. astigmatism.
ἀστικός a. urban; civic.
ἀστοίχειωτος a. not haunted.
ἀστοιχείωτος a. not knowing the rudiments (of).
ἄστοργος a. showing no affection.
ἀστός s.m. townsman, bourgeois.
ἀστόχαστος a. thoughtless.
ἄστοχος a. that misses the target, unsuccessful.
ἀστράγαλος s.m. ankle.
ἀστραπή s.f. lighting. ~δόν adv. like lightning.
ἀστραπιαῖος a. quick as lightning.
ἀστραπόβροντο s.n. thunder and lightning.
ἀστράπτω v.i. lighten; sparkle, gleam.
ἀστράτευτος a. exempt from military service.
ἀστρικ|ός a. stellar. ~ό s.n. one's destiny.
ἄστριφτος a. not twisted.
ἄστρο s.n. star.
ἀστρολόγος s.m. astrologer.
ἀστρονόμ|ος s.m. astronomer. ~ία s.f. astronomy.
ἀστροπελέκι s.n. thunderbolt.
ἀστροφεγγιά s.f. starlight.
ἄστρωτος a. unmade (bed); unlaid (table); unpaved; bare (floor); not saddled; not broken in.
ἄστυ s.n. city.
ἀστυνομ|ία s.f. police. ~ικός a. of the police; a member of the police force.
ἀστυνόμος s.m. police inspector.
ἀστυφιλία s.f. drift of population to cities.
ἀστυφύλαξ s.m. police constable.
ἀσυγκίνητος a. unmoved.
ἀσυγκράτητος a. unrestrainable.
ἀσύγκριτος a. incomparable.

ἀσυγύριστος a. untidy.
ἀσυγχρόνιστος a. not synchronized; unprogressive.
ἀσυγχώρητος a. unforgiven; unforgivable.
ἀσυδοσία s.f. immunity, exemption.
ἀσύδοτος a. immune, exempt.
ἀσυζήτητ|ος a. without being discussed; beyond dispute; out of the question. ~ί adv. without discussion.
ἀσυλία s.f. (right of) asylum; (diplomatic) immunity; privilege.
ἀσύλληπτος a. not caught; difficult to imagine or understand.
ἀσυλλόγιστος a. thoughtless.
ἄσυλον s.n. place of refuge, asylum.
ἀσυμβίβαστος a. incompatible; not having reached agreement; difficult, obstinate.
ἀσύμμετρος a. disproportionate.
ἀσυμπάθ|ητος, ~ιστος a. unlikeable; unforgivable.
ἀσυμπλήρωτος a. not completed; not filled; unfillable.
ἀσύμφορος a. not advantageous.
ἀσυμφώνητος a. with whom one has not made an agreement.
ἀσυναγώνιστος a. defying competition.
ἀσυναίσθητος a. unconscious, involuntary; inconsiderate.
ἀσύνακτος a. not gathered.
ἀσυνάρτητος a. incoherent.
ἀσυνείδητος a. unscrupulous; unconscious, unwitting.
ἀσυνεπής a. inconsistent, inconsequent; not true (to promise, etc.).
ἀσύνετος a. foolish, imprudent.
ἀσυνήθιστος a. unusual; unused (to).
ἀσύντακτος a. unorganized; not yet composed (of speech, etc.); ungrammatical.
ἀσύρματος s.m. wireless.
ἀσύστατος a. unrecommended; unfounded; inconsistent.
ἀσύστολος a. shameless.
ἄσφαιρος a. blank (shot, etc.).
ἀσφάλεια s.f. sureness; safety, security; insurance (company); police; fuse; safety-catch.
ἀσφαλής a. sure, safe, secure.
ἀσφαλίζω v.t. secure; insure.
ἀσφάλισις s.f. insurance, assurance.
ἀσφαλιστήριον s.n. insurance policy.
ἀσφαλιστικός a. of safety; of insurance.
ἀσφάλιστος a. 1. not closed. 2. not insured.

ἀσφάλιστρ|ον *s.n.* safety-catch; ~α (*pl.*) insurance premium.
ἄσφαλτος *a.* unerring.
ἄσφαλτος *s.f.* asphalt; tarred road.
ἀσφαλῶς *adv.* safely; certainly.
ἀσφόδελος *s.m.* asphodel.
ἀσφράγιστος *a.* unsealed, open.
ἀσφυκτιῶ *v.i.* suffocate.
ἀσφυξία *s.f.* suffocation.
ἄσχ|ετος *a.* irrelevant, unrelated. ~έτως *adv.* independently (*of*).
ἀσχημάτιστος *a.* not fully formed.
ἀσχημία *s.f.* ugliness; unseemly act.
ἀσχημίζω *v.t.* & *i* make *or* become ugly.
ἀσχημονῶ *v.i.* commit unseemly acts.
ἄσχημος *a.* ugly; unseemly; bad.
ἀσχημοσύνη *s.f.* impropriety.
ἀσχολία *s.f.* occupation, business.
ἀσχολίαστος *a.* not annotated; not discussed.
ἀσχολοῦμαι *v.i.* be occupied *or* engaged in (*with* μέ *or* εἰς).
ἀσώματ|ος *a.* bodiless; τῶν ~ων Michaelmas.
ἄσωστος *a.* endless; not completed.
ἀσωτία *s.f.* dissoluteness, prodigality.
ἄσωτος *a.* I. dissolute, prodigal. 2. *see* ἄσωστος.
ἀταίριαστος *a.* not matching; incompatible.
ἄτακτος *a.* irregular; disorderly; naughty.
ἀταξία *s.f.* irregularity; disorder; naughty act; (*med.*) ataxy.
ἀταραξία *s.f.* calmness, imperturbability.
ἀτάσθαλος *a.* insolent, unbridled.
ἄταφος *a.* unburied.
ἄτεγκτος *a.* relentless.
ἄτεκνος *a.* childless.
ἀτέλεια *s.f.* defect; exemption.
ἀτελείωτος *a.* endless; unfinished.
ἀτελεσφόρητος *a.* ineffectual.
ἀτελεύτητος *a.* endless.
ἀτελής *a.* incomplete; defective; free of tax.
ἀτελώνιστος *a.* exempt from duty; not cleared through customs.
ἀτενής *a.* intent (*of gaze*).
ἀτενίζω *v.t.* gaze at.
ἀτενῶς *adv.* fixedly.
ἀτέρμων *a.* endless.
ἄτεχνος *a.* badly done; unskilful.
ἀτζαμής *a.* (*fam.*) unskilled.
ἀτζέμ-πιλάφι *s.n.* lamb with rice.
ἀτημέλητος *a.* unkempt; in dishabille.
ἄτι *s.n.* stallion, steed.

ἀτίθασος *a.* untameable.
ἀτιμάζω *v.t.* dishonour.
ἀτίμητος *a.* priceless.
ἀτιμία *s.f.* dishonour, disgrace; disgraceful act.
ἄτιμος *a.* disgraceful, dishonourable.
ἀτιμωρησία *s.f.* impunity.
ἀτίμωσις *s.f.* disgrace, dishonour (*downfall*).
ἀτλάζι *s.n.* satin.
ἀτμάκατος *s.m.* steam-launch.
ἀτμάμαξα *s.f.* locomotive.
ἀτμολέβης *s.m.* boiler.
ἀτμομηχανή *s.f.* steam-engine.
ἀτμοπλοΐα *s.f.* steam navigation (company).
ἀτμόπλοιον *s.n.* steamship.
ἀτμός *s.m.* vapour, steam.
ἀτμόσφαιρα *s.f.* atmosphere.
ἄτοκος *a.* sterile; (*fig.*) (*fin.*) without interest.
ἄτολμος *a.* timid.
ἀτομικιστής *s.m.* egoist.
ἀτομικ|ός *a.* personal; individual; atomic. ~ότης *s.f.* individuality.
ἄτομον *s.n.* atom; person, individual.
ἄτονος *a.* languid; colourless; unaccented.
ἄτοπος *a.* out of place, unbecoming.
ἀτού *s.n.* trump. [F. *atout*]
ἀτόφυος *a.* solid (*silver, etc.*).
ἀτράνταχτος *a.* unshakeable; (*fig.*) solid (*wealth*).
ἀτραπός *s.f.* path.
ἄτριφτος *a.* not rubbed, scrubbed, grated *or* ground.
ἄτριχος *a.* hairless.
ἀτρόμητος *a.* intrepid.
ἀτροφία *s.f.* atrophy.
ἀτρόχιστος *a.* unsharpened.
ἀτρύγητος *a.* unharvested.
ἄτρωτος *a.* unscathed; invulnerable.
ἀτσάλ|ι *s.n.* steel. ~ένιος *a.* of steel.
ἄτσαλος *a.* disorderly, untidy; foul (*of speech*).
ἀτσίγγανος *s.m.* gipsy.
ἀτσίδα *s.f.* (*fam.*) wide-awake person.
ἀτύχημα *s.n.* stroke of ill fortune; accident.
ἀτυχής *a.* unlucky, unfortunate.
ἀτυχία *s.f.* ill fortune, bad luck.
ἄτυχος *a.* *see* ἀτυχής.
ἀτυχῶ *v.i.* suffer bad luck; fail.
αὐγερινός *s.m.* morning star.
αὐγή *s.f.* dawn.
αὐγό *s.n.* egg.

αὐγοθήκη s.f. egg-cup.

αὐγολέμονο s.n. soup or sauce with eggs and lemon.

αὐγοτάραχο s.n. roe preserved in wax, botargo.

αὐγότσουφλο s.n. egg-shell.

αὐγουλᾶτος a. egg-shaped.

αὐγουλιέρα s.f. egg-cup.

Αὔγουστος s.m. August.

αὐθάδ|ης a. impudent, impertinent. ~εια s.f. impudence. ~ιάζω v.i. be impertinent.

αὐθαίρετος a. high-handed.

αὐθέντης s.m. lord, master.

αὐθεντία s.f. authority; seigniory.

αὐθεντικός a. authentic.

αὐθημερόν adv. on the same day.

αὖθις adv. once again.

αὐθομολογούμενος a. self-evident.

αὐθόρμητος a. spontaneous.

αὐθυποβολή s.f. auto-suggestion.

αὐθωρεί adv. forthwith.

αὐλαία s.f. stage curtain.

αὐλάκι s.n. groove, furrow, ditch, irrigation trench.

αὐλακωτός a. grooved, furrowed, rifled.

αὖλαξ s.f. see αὐλάκι.

αὐλάρχης s.m. lord chamberlain.

αὐλή s.f. yard; court.

αὐλητής s.m. piper, flautist.

αὐλίζομαι v.i. give access to, be reached from (of entrance to property).

αὐλικός a. of the court; a courtier.

αὐλόγυρος s.m. enclosure.

αὐλοκόλαξ s.m. fawner.

αὐλός s.m. pipe, flute.

ἄϋλος a. incorporeal.

αὐξάν|ω v.t. & i. increase. ~ομαι v.i. increase.

αὔξησις s.f. increase; (gram.) augment.

αὐξομείωσις s.f. fluctuation.

αὔξων a. increasing; (math.) ~ ἀριθμός serial number.

ἀϋπνία s.f. insomnia.

αὔρα s.f. gentle breeze.

αὐριανός a. of tomorrow.

αὔριον adv. tomorrow.

αὐστηρός a. strict; austere.

αὐτ- denotes self, same.

αὔτανδρος a. with all hands.

αὐταπάρνησις s.f. self-denial.

αὐταπάτη s.f. self-delusion.

αὐτάρεσκος a. complacent.

αὐτάρκης a. self-sufficient; satisfied with little.

αὐταρχικός a. authoritarian.

αὐτεξούσι|ος a. independent. ~ον s.n. free-will.

αὐτί s.n. ear.

αὐτοβιογραφία s.f. autobiography.

αὐτόβουλος a. of one's own volition.

αὐτόγραφος a. autograph.

αὐτόδηλος a. self-evident.

αὐτοδημιούργητος a. self-made.

αὐτοδιάθεσις s.f. self-determination.

αὐτοδίδακτος a. self-taught.

αὐτοδικαίως adv. of right.

αὐτοδικία s.f. taking law into one's own hands.

αὐτοδιοίκησις s.f. self-government.

αὐτοθελῶς adv. of one's own accord.

αὐτόθεν adv. thence.

αὐτόθι adv. in the same place; ibidem.

αὐτοθυσία s.f. self-sacrifice.

αὐτοκαλούμενος a. self-styled.

αὐτοκέφαλος a. independent; (eccl.) autocephalous.

αὐτοκινητάμαξα s.f. rail motor-car.

αὐτοκινητιστής s.m. motorist.

αὐτοκίνητ|ος a. self-propelling. ~ον s.n. motor-car.

αὐτόκλητος a. self-invited; ~ μάρτυς one who volunteers evidence.

αὐτοκράτειρα s.f. empress.

αὐτοκρατορ|ία s.f. empire. ~ικός a. imperial.

αὐτοκράτωρ s.m. emperor.

αὐτοκτονία s.f. suicide.

αὐτοκτονῶ v.i. commit suicide.

αὐτοκυβέρνησις s.f. self-government.

αὐτοκυριαρχία s.f. self-command.

αὐτολεξεί adv. word for word.

αὐτόματ|ος a. automatic. ~ον s.n. automaton.

αὐτομολῶ v.i. desert to the enemy.

αὐτονόητος a. self-explanatory.

αὐτονομία s.f. autonomy.

αὐτοπαθής a. (gram.) reflexive.

αὐτοπεποίθησις s.f. self-confidence.

αὐτοπροαίρετος a. voluntary.

αὐτοπροσώπως adv. in person.

αὐτόπτης s.m. eye-witness.

αὐτ|ός pron. he; this; ὁ ~ός the same; ἡ ~οῦ ὑψηλότης His Highness.

αὐτοστιγμεί adv. immediately.

αὐτοσυντήρησις s.f. self-preservation.

αὐτοσυντήρητος a. self-supporting.

αὐτοσχεδιάζω v.t. improvise.

αὐτοσχέδιος a. impromptu, improvised.

αὐτοτελής a. self-contained.

αὐτοῦ adv. there.

αὐτουργός s.m. perpetrator.

αὐτούσιος *a.* in its original state, intact.

αὐτοφυής *a.* indigenous; wild (*of plants*); native (*of metals, etc.*).

αὐτό|φωρος *a.* (*detected*) in the very act; ἐπ' ~φώρω red-handed. ~φωρο *s.n.* (*fam.*) police-court.

αὐτόχειρ *s.m.* suicide (*person*).

αὐτοχειροτόνητος *a.* self-appointed.

αὐτόχθων *a.* indigenous (*person*).

αὐτόχρημα *adv.* purely and simply.

αὐτοψία *s.f.* post-mortem; (*magistrate's*) investigation on the spot.

αὐχήν *s.m.* nape of neck; (*fig.*) neck, col.

αὐχμηρός *a.* arid.

ἄφαγος *a.* who eats insufficient; not having eaten.

ἀφάγωτος *a.* uneaten; not having eaten; (*fig.*) intact.

ἀφαίμαξις *s.f.* blood-letting.

ἀφαίρεσις *s.f.* taking away; subtraction; abstraction.

ἀφαιρ|ῶ *v.t.* take away, subtract; steal. ~οῦμαι *v.i.* have one's thoughts elsewhere.

ἀφαλοκόβω *v.t.* (*fam.*) weigh down (*with burden*); spificate.

ἀφαλός *s.m.* navel.

ἀφάνα *s.f.* besom.

ἀφαν|ής *a.* invisible; obscure. ~εια *s.f.* obscurity (*being unknown*).

ἀφανίζ|ω *v.t.* annihilate; harass. ~ο-μαι *v.i.* vanish; be destroyed.

ἀφάνταστος *a.* unimaginable.

ἄφαντος *a.* invisible.

ἀφαρπάζομαι *v.i.* flare up (*in anger*).

ἀφασία *s.f.* aphasia.

ἄφατος *a.* ineffable.

ἀφεδρών *s.m.* anus; w.c.

ἀφειδής *a.* lavish.

ἀφέλεια *s.f.* simplicity; naïveté; (*fam.*) fringe (*hair*).

ἀφελής *a.* simple, naïve.

ἀφέντης *s.m.* lord, master; proprietor.

ἀφεντιά *s.f.* nobility; (*fam.*) ἡ ~ σου your honour, you.

ἀφεντικό *s.n.* (*fam.*) boss, governor.

ἀφερέγγυος *a.* insolvent.

ἄφεσις *s.f.* remission, discharge.

ἀφετηρία *s.f.* point of departure.

ἀφέτης *s.m.* starter (*of race*).

ἄφευκτ|ος *a.* inevitable. ~ως *adv.* without fail.

ἀφέψημα *s.n.* decoction.

ἀφ|ή *s.f.* 1. (*sense of*) touch. 2. lighting; περὶ λύχνων ~άς at lighting-up time (*i.e. at dusk*).

ἀφήγησις *s.f.* narration.

ἀφηγοῦμαι *v.t.* narrate.

ἀφηνιάζω *v.i.* bolt; take the bit between one's teeth.

ἀφήνω *v.t.* let, allow; let alone; let go of, let slip; leave; abandon; entrust; emit.

ἀφηρημάδα *s.f.* (act of) absentmindedness.

ἀφηρημένος *a.* absent-minded; abstract.

ἄφθα *s.f.* sore place on gum.

ἀφθαρσία *s.f.* indestructibility.

ἄφθαστος *a.* unrivalled; unsurpassable.

ἄφθον|ος *a.* abundant, plenty of. ~ία *s.f.* abundance. ~ῶ *v.i.* abound.

ἀφίεμαι *v.i.* relax; be released.

ἀφιερ|ώνω *v.t.* dedicate, devote. ~ωμα *s.n.* offering. ~ωσις *s.f.* dedication.

ἀφικνοῦμαι *v.i.* arrive.

ἀφιλοκερδής *a.* disinterested.

ἀφιλότιμος *a.* mean, lacking self-respect.

ἀφίνω *v.t. see* ἀφήνω.

ἄφιξις *s.f.* arrival.

ἀφιόνι *s.n.* poppy; opium.

ἀφιππεύω *v.i.* dismount (*from horse*).

ἀφίσταμαι *v.i.* differ; hold aloof.

ἄφλεκτος *a.* non-inflammable.

ἀφλογιστία *s.f.* misfire.

ἄφοβος *a.* fearless.

ἀφοδεύω *v.i.* go to stool.

ἀφομοι|ώνω *v.t.* assimilate. ~ωσις *s.f.* assimilation.

ἀφόντας *conj. see* ἀφότου.

ἀφοπλίζω *v.t.* disarm.

ἀφοπλισμός *s.m.* disarmament.

ἀφόρετος *a.* unworn, new.

ἀφόρητος *a.* unbearable.

ἀφορία *s.f.* scarcity of crops.

ἀφορίζω *v.t.* excommunicate; delimit.

ἀφορισμός *s.m.* excommunication; aphorism.

ἀφορμή *s.f.* occasion, ground.

ἀφορμίζω *v.i.* fester.

ἀφορολόγητος *a.* untaxed.

ἄφορος *a.* unfruitful.

ἀφορ|ῶ *v.t.* relate to, concern; ὅσον ~ᾶ as regards.

ἀφοσιοῦμαι *v.i.* devote oneself.

ἀφοσίωσις *s.f.* devotion.

ἀφότου *conj.* since (*time*).

ἀφοῦ *conj.* since (*causal*); after, when.

ἀφουγκράζομαι *v.t. & i.* listen (to).

ἄφρακτος *a.* unfenced.

ἀφρᾶτος *a.* light and soft; light and crisp (*bread*); plump and white (*flesh*); puffed, billowy.

ἀφρίζω v.i. foam; (fig.) rage.
ἀφρόγαλα s.n. cream.
ἀφροδισία s.f. sexual instinct.
ἀφροδισιακός a. aphrodisiac.
ἀφροδισιολόγος s.m. specialist in venereal diseases.
ἀφροδίσιος a. venereal.
ἀφρόντιστος a. without caring; not looked after.
ἀφρός s.m. foam, scum; lather; cream.
ἀφροσύνη s.f. foolishness.
ἀφρώδης a. frothy, foaming.
ἄφρων a. foolish, thoughtless.
ἀφτί s.n. ear.
ἀφτιάζομαι v.i. prick up one's ears.
ἄφτιαστος a. not made or done; not made up (of face).
ἄφτρα s.f. sore place on gum.
ἀφυδάτωσις s.f. dehydration.
ἀφυπηρετῶ v.i. complete one's military service.
ἀφύπνισις s.f. awakening.
ἀφύσικος a. unnatural; abnormal.
ἄφωνος a. mute; without a (singing) voice.
ἀφώτιστος a. unlit; unenlightened; (fig.) unbaptized.
ἄχ int. ah! oh!
ἀχαΐρευτος a. good-for-nothing.
ἀχάλαστος a. not destroyed or spoilt; indestructible; not spent or changed (money).
ἀχαλίνωτος a. unbridled.
ἀχαμν|ός a. lean. ~ά s.n.pl. testicles.
ἀχανής a. vast.
ἀχαρακτήριστος a. difficult to describe; unspeakable.
ἄχαρις a. see ἄχαρος.
ἀχάριστος a. ungrateful.
ἄχαρος a. ungraceful; giving no pleasure.
ἄχερο s.n. straw, chaff.
ἀχηβάδα s.f. sea-shell.
ἄχθος s.n. burden.
ἀχθοφόρος s.m. porter.
ἀχίλλειος a. of Achilles.
ἀχινός s.m. sea-urchin.
ἀχλάδι s.n. pear.
ἀχλύς s.f. thin mist; (fig.) melancholy.
ἀχμάκης s.m. dolt.
ἄχνα s.f. mist, vapour; (fam.) μή βγάλης ~ do not utter a sound.
ἀχνάρι s.n. footprint; (fig.) (paper) pattern.
ἄχνη s.f. mist, vapour; finest powder, sublimate.

ἀχνίζω v.t. & i. steam, make misty; give off vapour.
ἀχνός s.m. mist, vapour.
ἀχνός a. pallid.
ἀχόρταγος a. see ἀχόρταστος.
ἀχόρταστος a. insatiable; unsated.
ἀχός s.m. noise, din.
ἄχου int. oh!
ἀχοῦρι s.n. stable.
ἄχραντ|ος a. immaculate; ~α μυστήρια sacraments.
ἀχρείαστος a. not needed.
ἀχρεῖος a. vile, villainous; obscene.
ἀχρησιμοποίητος a. unused; unusable.
ἀχρηστεύ|ω v.t. make useless. ~ομαι v.i. become useless; fall out of use.
ἄχρηστος a. useless; not used.
ἄχρι prep. up to, until.
ἀχρόνι(α)στος a. not yet one year old or dead.
ἀχρονολόγητος a. undated.
ἄχρους a. colourless; (fig.) neutral.
ἀχρωμάτιστος a. not painted; colourless; (fig.) neutral.
ἀχταρμᾶς s.m. transfer from one conveyance to another.
ἄχτι s.n. strong desire (esp. for vengeance); τόν ἔχω ~ I bear him a grudge; βγάζω τό ~ μου let off steam, satisfy a long-felt desire.
ἀχτί|δα, ~να s.f. ray.
ἀχτένιστος a. unkempt; (fig.) not polished up (of speech, etc.).
ἄχυρον s.n. straw, chaff.
ἀχυρών s.m. barn.
ἀχώνευτος a. undigested; (fig.) unbearable.
ἀχώριστος a. unseparated; inseparable.
ἀψεγάδιαστος a. faultless.
ἄψε σβύσε adv. in the twinkling of an eye.
ἄψη(σ)τος a. not (sufficiently) cooked or baked; (fig.) raw.
ἀψήφιστ|ος a. not having voted or been voted for; daring; disregarded. ~α adv. τό πῆρα ~α I treated it lightly.
ἀψηφῶ v.t. defy, brave, ignore.
ἀψιδωτός a. arched.
ἀψίκορος a. quickly tiring of what one has.
ἄψιλος a. (fam.) penniless.
ἀψιμαχία s.f. skirmish.
ἀψίς s.f. arch; apse.
ἄψογος a. impeccable.
ἀψύς a. hot-tempered; sharp, pungent.

αψυχολόγητος *a.* without psychological insight.

άψυχος *a.* lifeless.

αψώνιστος *a.* not bought; not having shopped.

άωρος *a.* unripe; (*fig.*) untimely.

άωτον *s.n.* άκρον ~ acme, ne plus ultra.

B

βαγένι *s.n.* barrel.

βάγια *s.f.* wet-nurse; nursemaid.

βάγια *s.n.pl.* palm branches.

βαγιά *s.f.* laurel.

βαγόνι *s.n.* coach, truck (*railway*).

βάδην *adv.* at walking pace.

βαδίζω *v.i.* walk, march.

βάδισμα *s.n.* gait, walk(ing).

βαζγεστίζω *v.t. & i.* (*fam.*) be fed up (with).

βάζο *s.n.* vase, pot.

βάζω *v.t.* put, apply, place in position; put on (*clothes, radio*); serve with, give (*in shop, at table*); impose (*tax*); hire, employ, get (*person to do sthg.*); ~ τραπέζι lay table; ~ στή μπάντα lay aside, save up; ~ καλό βαθμό give good marks; ~ στοίχημα wager; ~ φωνές start shouting; ~ αὐτί listen; ~ χέρι lay hands (*on*); ~ ἕνα χέρι lend a hand; ~ χρέος contract a debt; ~ ὑποψηφιότητα stand for office; ~ πλώρη set out (*for*); ~ μὲ τρόπο put without being noticed; ~ τὰ δύνατά μου do one's best; τὰ ~ μέ quarrel with; ~ μπρός start (off); τὸν ~ μπροστά or πόστα I reprimand him; ~ μέσα imprison; δὲν τὸ ~ κάτω I will not admit defeat; τὸ ~ στὰ πόδια take to one's heels; τὸν ~ στὸ πόδι μου I leave him in my place; δὲν τὸ βάζει ὁ νοῦς it is inconceivable; βάλε μὲ τὸ νοῦ σου just imagine; βάλε πῶς supposing; βάλθηκε νά μάθη ἀγγλικά he set about learning English.

βαθαίνω *v.t. & i.* deepen.

βαθ|έως, ~ιά *adv.* deeply.

βαθμηδόν *adv.* gradually.

βαθμιαῖος *a.* gradual.

βαθμίς *s.f.* step, rung; (*fig.*) point on a scale.

βαθμολογία *s.f.* marking; graduation.

βαθμός *s.m.* degree; rank; mark (*award*).

βαθμοῦχος *s.m.* (*higher ranking*) officer.

βάθος *s.n.* depth; far end; background; κατὰ ~ thoroughly; at bottom.

βαθουλός *a.* hollow, sunken.

βαθούλωμα *s.n.* hollow place, depression.

βάθρακ|ας, ~ος *s.m.* frog.

βάθρον *s.n.* base, pedestal; bench.

βαθυ- *denotes* deep.

βαθύνοια *s.f.* sagacity.

βαθύνω *v.t. & i.* deepen.

βαθύπλουτος *a.* very rich.

βαθ|ύς *a.* deep, profound. ~ύτης *s.f.* depth, profundity.

βαθύφωνος *a.* (*mus.*) bass; contralto.

βαίνω *v.i.* go; be on the way (*to*).

βά|ϊον *s.n.* palm branch; Κυριακή τῶν ~ίων Palm Sunday.

βάκιλλος *s.m.* bacillus.

βακτηρία *s.f.* stick, crutch.

βακτηρίδιον *s.n.* bacillus.

βακτηριολογία *s.f.* bacteriology

βακχεία *s.f.* orgy.

βάκχ|η, ~ίς *s.f.* bacchante.

βακχικός *a.* bacchic.

βαλανίδ|ι *s.n.* acorn. ~ιά *s.f.* oaktree.

βάλανος *s.f.* acorn.

βαλάντιον *s.n.* purse.

βαλαντώνω *v.i. & t.* be exhausted; exhaust, wear out.

βαλβίς *s.f.* valve; starting-post.

βαλές *s.m.* footman; knave (*cards*).

βαλί|τζα, ~τσα *s.f.* suitcase.

βαλκανικός *a.* Balkan.

βάλλ|ω *v.t. & i.* fire, shoot, throw; (*fig.*) launch (*verbal*) attack. ~ομαι *v.i.* be fired at; ἐβλήθη he was hit.

βαλμένος *a.* 1. worn (*of clothes*). 2. see βαλτός.

βάλς *s.n.* waltz. [F. *valse*]

βάλσαμ|ον *s.n.* balsam, balm. ~ώνω *v.t.* embalm; (*fig.*) console, ease.

βάλσιμο *s.n.* putting (on), placing in position.

βάλτος *s.m.* marsh, bog.

βαλτός *a.* set on, instigated.

βαμβακερός *a.* cotton.

βαμβάκι *s.n.* cotton; cotton-wool.

βαμβακοπυρῖτις *s.f.* gun-cotton.

βάμβαξ *s.m.* cotton; cotton-wool.

βάμμα *s.n.* tincture.

βαμμένος *a.* dyed, painted; (*fig.*) (*fam.*) dyed-in-the-wool.

βάναυσος *a.* rude, rough.

βάνδαλος *s.m.* vandal.

βανίλια *s.f.* vanilla.

βάνω v.t. see βάζω.

βαπόρι s.n. steamer; (fam.) έγινε ~ he got furious or he was off in a flash.

βαπτίζω v.t. baptize, christen; stand sponsor to; (fam.) water (wine, milk).

βάπτισμα s.n. baptism (sacrament).

βάπτισις s.f. christening.

βαπτιστής s.m. baptist.

βαπτιστικ|ός a. baptismal. ~όν s.n. certificate of baptism.

βάπτω v.t. & i. temper (steel); dye, paint; polish (shoes); (v.i.) become stained.

βάραθρον s.n. abyss.

βαραίνω v.t. & i. weigh down; make heavier; be a burden to, weary; (v.i.) weigh, have weight; become heavier; get worse (in health); heel over; dip (of scale).

βαράω v.t. see βαρώ.

βάρβαρος a. barbarous; (a) barbarian.

βαρβαρικός a. barbaric.

βαρβάτ|ος a. not castrated, ruttish; ~ο άλογο stallion; (fig.) competent; considerable.

βαργεστ|ίζω, ~ώ v.t. & i. see βαζγεστίζω.

βάρδα int. (fam.) look out!

βάρδια s.f. watch, guard; shift.

βάρδος s.m. bard.

βαρεία s.f. (gram.) grave accent.

βαρέλι s.n. barrel, cask, drum.

βαρεμένη a. pregnant.

βαρετός a. boring, burdensome.

βαρέως adv. gravely; τὸ φέρω ~ be annoyed or upset by it.

βαρήκοος a. hard of hearing.

βαριά adv. heavily, seriously.

βαρίδι s.n. weight, counterweight.

βαρι|έμαι, ~ούμαι v.i. & t. be bored (with), be tired (of); not want (to); (fam.) δέν ~έσαι never mind about that!

βάριον s.n. barium.

βάρκα s.f. (small) boat, rowing-boat.

βαρκάδα s.f. boat-trip.

βαρκάρης s.m. boatman.

βαρόμετρον s.n. barometer.

βάρος s.n. weight, heaviness; burden, responsibility; εἰς ~ του to his detriment, at his expense.

βαρούλκον s.n. windlass.

βαρυ- denotes heavy.

βαρύθυμος a. dejected.

βαρύν|ω v.t. & i. 1. see βαραίνω. 2. (v.t.) be laid to one's charge, fall

upon (of responsibility, etc.). 3. ~ομαι see βαριέμαι.

βαρυποινίτης s.m. long-term prisoner.

βαρύς a. heavy; hard, severe, extreme; bad for health; strong (wine); deep (in pitch); reserved, distant.

βαρυσήμαντος a. momentous.

βαρύτης s.f. gravity, weight; severity; depth.

βαρύτιμος a. costly, valuable.

βαρύτονος 1. a. bearing grave accent. 2. s.m. (mus.) baritone.

βαρύφωνος a. deep-voiced.

βαρ|ώ v.t. & i. strike, hit; wound, kill (game); play (instrument); sound, strike (of bugle, clock, etc.); (fam.) ~άει ἡ τσέπη του his pocket is well lined.

βαρώνος s.m. baron.

βασάλτης s.m. basalt.

βασανίζ|ω v.t. examine, go into; torture, torment, rack. ~ομαι v.i. have a lot of trouble.

βασανιστήριον s.n. rack, torture; torture-chamber.

βάσανο s.n. torture; trouble, tribulation; (fam.) nuisance; lady-love.

βάσανος s.f. scrutiny, inquiry; torture.

βασίζ|ω v.t. base. ~ομαι v.i. rely.

βασικός a. basic, primary.

βασιλεία s.f. kingship, royalty; reign.

βασίλειον s.n. kingdom.

βασίλεμα s.n. setting (of sun, etc.).

βασιλεύς s.m. king.

βασιλεύω v.i. reign; set (of sun, etc.); close (of eyes).

βασιλιάς s.m. king.

βασιλική s.f. basilica.

βασιλικός a. royal; royalist; regal.

βασιλικός s.n. basil.

βασίλισσα s.f. queen.

βασιλοκτονία s.f. regicide (act).

βασιλομήτωρ s.f. queen mother.

βασιλόπαις s.m.f. king's son or daughter.

βασιλόπηττα s.f. New Year's cake.

βασιλόπουλο s.n. king's son.

βασιλόφρων a. royalist.

βάσιμος a. well-founded, sound.

βάσ|ις s.f. base, basis, foundation; pass-mark; δίνω ~ι σέ attach importance to.

βασκαίνω v.t. & i. cast evil eye (upon).

βάσκα|μα s.n., ~νία s.f. evil eye.

βάσκανος a. jealous; ~ ὀφθαλμός evil eye.

βαστάζω v.t. carry, support.

βαστ|ῶ v.t. & i. carry, support; hold, control; keep, have charge of; (v.i.) last; hold out, endure; originate (from); dare; δέν τοῦ ~άει he does not dare. ~ιέμαι v.i. control oneself; maintain one's position or condition; ~ιέμαι καλά be well or well-off.

βάτα s.f. wadding.

βατεύω v.t. cover (of animals).

βατόμουρο s.n. blackberry.

βάτ|ος s.m.f., ~ο s.n. bramble.

βατός a. passable, fordable.

βάτραχος s.m. frog, toad.

βατσίνα s.f. vaccine.

βαυκαλίζω v.t. rock or lull to sleep; (fig.) lull (with false hopes).

βαφεῖον s.n. dyers'.

βαφή s.f. tempering; dyeing; dye; shoe-polish.

βαφτ- see **βαπτ-**.

βαφτίσια s.n.pl. christening.

βαφτισιμιός s.m. godson.

βαφτιστήρι s.n. godson.

βάφ|ω v.t. see **βάπτω**. ~ομαι v.i. make up.

βάψιμο s.n. tempering; dyeing; painting; make-up.

βγάζω v.t. 1. take, bring, get or draw out; take or get off, remove, extract; dismiss (from job); deduct; ~ τό καπέλλο μου take off one's hat; ἔβγαλα ἕνα δόντι I had a tooth out; ~ τό φίδι ἀπό τήν τρύπα pull the chestnuts out of the fire. 2. give forth, produce; ~ δόντια cut one's teeth; ~ σπυριά come out in spots; ἡ Ἑλλάς βγάζει κρασί Greece produces wine; τί σᾶς ἐβγαλαν; what refreshment did they offer you? ~ λεφτά make money; ~ λόγο make a speech; ~ ὄνομα become known; ~ γλῶσσα answer cheekily; τόν ἔβγαλαν βουλευτή he was returned as deputy; τόν ἔβγαλαν ψεύτη he was proved a liar; τόν ἔβγαλαν Κώστα they named him Costa. 3. work out, make out; τά ἔβγαλα σωστά; did I work it out right? δέν ~ τή γραφή σου I cannot make out your writing; τά ~ πέρα manage, succeed. (v.i.) ποῦ βγάζει ὁ δρόμος; where does the road lead?

βγαίν|ω v.i. go or come out; appear, be produced; come off or out (become detached); diverge, deviate; turn out (good or bad); work or come out (of sum, patience game, etc.); result (from); ~ω δήμαρχος be elected mayor; ~ω

ἀπό τό γυμνάσιο finish one's schooling; δέν τοῦ ~ει κανείς στά χαρτιά none can beat him at cards; δέν ~ει τό ὕφασμα the material is not enough; μοῦ βγῆκε σέ καλό it turned out well for me; βγῆκε λάδι he got off scot free.

βγαλμένος a. taken off or out; graduated; returned (of candidate).

βγάλσιμο s.n. extraction, removal; taking or getting out or off; dislocation.

βδέλλα s.f. leech.

βδέλυγμα s.n. object of disgust, abomination.

βδελυρός a. abominable.

βδομάδα s.f. week.

βέβαι|ος a. sure, certain. ~ότης s.f. certainty. ~ως adv. certainly.

βεβαι|ώνω v.t. assure; confirm, affirm. ~ωσις s.f. assurance; confirmation; certificate. ~ωτικός a. confirmatory; affirmative.

βεβαρημένος a. subject to liabilities; blemished (record); heavy (conscience).

βέβηλ|ος a. profane; sacrilegious. ~ώνω v.t. desecrate, sully.

βεβιασμένος a. forced, unnatural.

βεγγέρα s.f. evening visit.

βεδούρα s.f. wooden bucket (for yogurt).

βεζίρης s.m. vizier.

βέης s.m. bey.

βελάδα s.f. frock-coat.

βελάζω v.i. bleat.

βελανίδι s.n. acorn.

Βέλγος s.m. a Belgian.

βελέντζα s.f. rough blanket.

βέλο s.n. veil.

βελόν|α, ~η s.f., ~ι s.n. needle.

βελονάκι s.n. crochet-needle.

βελονιά s.f. stitch.

βέλος s.n. arrow, shaft.

βελοῦδο s.n. velvet.

βέλτιστος a. best.

βελτί|ων a. better. ~ώνω v.t. improve. ~ωσις s.f. improvement.

Βενετία s.f. Venice.

βενζινάκατος s.f. motor-boat.

βενζίνη s.f. petrol, benzine.

βενζινόπλοιον s.n. motor-assisted caique.

βεντά|για, ~λια s.f. fan.

βεντέτ(τ)α s.f. 1. vendetta. 2. star (actor).

βεντούζα s.f. cupping-glass.

βέρα s.f. wedding or engagement ring.

βεράντα s.f. veranda.

βερβελιά *s.f.* dropping of sheep, rabbits, *etc.*

βερβερίτσα *s.f.* squirrel.

βέργα *s.f.* stick, switch, rod.

βερεσέ *adv.* (*fam.*) on credit, on tick; τ' ἀκούω ~ take it with a grain of salt.

βερίκοκ(κ)ο *s.n.* apricot.

βερμούτ *s.n.* vermouth. [It. *vermuth*].

βερνίκι *s.n.* varnish, polish; (*fig.*) veneer.

βέρος *a.* real, genuine.

βετεράνος *s.m.* veteran.

βέτο *s.n.* veto; (*fam.*) ἔχω τό ~ have the final say.

βῆμα *s.n.* step, pace; rostrum; Ἅγιον ~ (*eccl.*) sanctuary.

βηματίζω *v.i.* pace (*up and down*).

βήξ, βήχας *s.m.* cough.

βῆτα *s.n.* the letter **Β**.

βήχω *v.i.* cough.

βία *s.f.* force, violence; haste, hurry; μετὰ ~ς with difficulty.

βιάζ|ω *v.t.* force; rape; press, urge. ~ομαι *v.i.* be in a hurry.

βιαιοπραγία *s.f.* (*bodily*) assault.

βίαι|ος *a.* violent, forcible. ~ότης *s.f.* violence; ~ότητες (*pl.*) acts of violence.

βιαίως *adv.* violently, forcibly.

βιάσ|η, ~ύνη *s.f.* haste.

βιασμός *s.m.* rape.

βιαστής *s.m.* ravisher.

βιαστικ|ός *a.* in a hurry; pressing, urgent. ~ά *adv.* hurriedly.

βιβλιάριον *s.n.* card, book (*insurance, bank, etc.*).

βιβλικός *a.* biblical.

βιβλιογραφία *s.f.* bibliography.

βιβλιοδέτης *s.m.* bookbinder.

βιβλιοθηκάριος *s.m.* librarian.

βιβλιοθήκη *s.f.* bookcase; library.

βιβλιοκάπηλος *s.m.* publisher of pirated editions.

βιβλιοκρισία *s.f.* book-review.

βιβλίον *s.n.* book.

βιβλιοπώλ|ης *s.m.* bookseller. ~εῖον *s.n.* bookshop.

βίβλος *s.f.* Bible; κυανῆ ~ blue book.

βίγλα *s.f.* look-out post.

βιγλίζω *v.t. & i.* keep a look-out (for).

βίδα *s.f.* screw; (*fam.*) εἶναι or ἔχει ~ he is potty.

βιδάνιο *s.n.* remains of drink in glass.

βιδέλο *s.n.* calf; veal.

βιδολόγος *s.m.* screwdriver.

βιδώνω *v.t. & i.* screw.

βίζα *s.f.* visa.

βίζιτα *s.f.* visit; visitor.

βίλλα *s.f.* villa.

βίντσι *s.n.* winch.

βιογραφία *s.f.* biography.

βιόλα *s.f.* 1. stock (*plant*). 2. (*mus.*) viola.

βιολέττα *s.f.* violet.

βιολί *s.n.* violin; (*fam.*) (same old) tune or game.

βιολι|στής, ~τζῆς *s.m.* violinist.

βιολόγ|ος *s.m.* biologist. ~ία *s.* biology.

βιομηχαν|ία *s.f.* industry, manufacture. ~ικός *a.* industrial.

βιοπαλαιστής *s.m.* one who struggles to earn a living.

βιοπάλη *s.f.* struggle to earn a living.

βιοποριστικός *a.* providing a living.

βί|ος *s.m.* life; διὰ ~ου for life; (*fam.*) ~ος καί πολιτεία one who has had a chequered career.

βι|ός *s.m. & n.*, ~ό *s.n.* wealth, fortune.

βιοτεχνία *s.f.* light manufacture, handicraft.

βιοχημεία *s.f.* biochemistry.

βίρα *int.* (*naut.*) haul! hoist!

βιταμίνη *s.f.* vitamin.

βιτρίνα *s.f.* shop-window; show-case, cabinet.

βίτσα *s.f.* cane, switch.

βίτσιο *s.n.* bad habit, vice.

βιῶ *v.i.* live.

βιώσιμος *a.* viable; livable.

βλαβερός *a.* harmful, injurious, unwholesome.

βλάβη *s.f.* harm, damage, detriment; breakdown.

βλάκας *s.m.* idiot, fool.

βλακεία *s.f.* stupidity; nonsense.

βλακώδης *a.* idiotic, stupid.

βλάξ *s.m.f.* idiot, fool.

βλάπτω *v.t. & i.* harm, hurt, injure; wrong.

βλαστάνω *v.i.* sprout, shoot, grow.

βλαστάρι *s.n.* young shoot; scion.

βλαστημ- *see* **βλασφημ-**.

βλάστησις *s.f.* germination; vegetation.

βλαστός *s.m.* shoot; offspring.

βλασφημ|ία *s.f.* blasphemy; cursing. ~ῶ *v.t. & i.* blaspheme; curse.

βλάφτω *v.t. & i. see* **βλάπτω**.

Βλαχία *s.f.* Wallachia.

βλάχικος *a.* Vlach; (*fig.*) uncouth.

Βλάχος *s.m.* a Vlach; (*fig.*) country bumpkin.

βλέμμα *s.n.* look, glance, expression.

βλέννα *s.f.* mucus.

βλεννόρροια s.f. gonorrhoea.
βλεννώδης a. mucous.
βλέπ|ω v.t. & i. see; look (after); ~ω καί παθαίνω have a hard job (to); ~οντας καί κάνοντας as the case may be; δέ ~ω τήν ώρα νά φύγω I am impatient to leave.
βλεφαρίς s.f. eyelash.
βλέφαρον s.n. eyelid.
βλέψ|ις s.f. sight; ~εις (pl.) aspirations, designs.
βλήμα s.n. missile, projectile.
βλητική s.f. ballistics.
βλογιά s.f. smallpox; disease of vine.
βλογώ v.t. see εὐλογῶ.
βλοσυρός a. fierce (of looks).
βόας s.m. boa (snake).
βογγ|ητό s.n., ~ος s.m. groan(ing), moan(ing).
βογγῶ v.i. groan, moan.
βόδι s.n. ox; ~α (pl.) oxen, cattle.
βοδινό s.n. beef.
βόειος a. bovine.
βοή s.f. confused noise; buzzing, humming, roaring.
βοήθεια s.f. aid, assistance; help (abstract).
βοήθημα s.n. help, aid (concrete).
βοηθητικός a. auxiliary; favourable (wind).
βοηθός s.m. help(er), assistant.
βοηθῶ v.t. & i. help, assist.
βόθρος s.m. cesspool.
βόϊδι s.n. see βόδι.
βολά s.f. time (occasion).
βολάν s.n. 1. steering-wheel. 2. flounce. [F. volant]
βολβός s.m. bulb; sort of onion; eyeball.
βολεῖ v.i. it is convenient.
βολετός a. convenient, feasible.
βολεύ|ω v.t. fit in; cope or manage with; suit, be convenient to; τά ~ω get along, make do. ~ομαι v.i. & t. be comfortable; get settled or fixed up; find convenient or comfortable.
βολή s.f. 1. throwing; firing, fire, shot. 2. comfort, convenience; knack.
βόλι s.n. bullet.
βολιδοσκοπῶ v.t. sound, fathom.
βολικός a. convenient, handy; easy to get on with or to please.
βολίς s.f. bullet; meteor; (naut.) lead.
βόλτα s.f. turn, revolution; stroll, ride; (fam.) τά φέρνω ~ manage, make do; evade the issue; τόν ἔφερα ~ I got round him.

βόμβα s.f. bomb.
βομβαρδίζω v.t. bombard; bomb, shell.
βομβαρδισμός s.m. bombardment, bombing.
βομβαρδιστικ|ός a. of bombardment. ~όν s.n. (aero.) bomber.
βόμβος s.m. buzzing, droning, humming.
βομβυκοτροφία s.f. silkworm breeding.
βόμβυξ s.m. silkworm cocoon.
βομβῶ v.i. buzz, drone, hum.
βορά s.f. prey, food.
βόρβορος s.m. mire.
βορεινός a. see βόρειος.
βορειοανατολικός a. north-east.
βορειοδυτικός a. north-west.
βόρειος a. north, northern, northerly.
βορείως adv. northwards, to the north (of).
βοριᾶς s.m. north (wind).
βορράς s.m. north (wind).
βοσκή s.f. pasture.
βόσκημα s.n. pasturing; pasture-animal.
βοσκοπούλα s.f. shepherdess.
βοσκός s.m. shepherd.
βοσκοτόπι s.n. place of pasture.
βόσκω v.i. & t. graze, browse; (fig.) wander aimlessly; (v.t.) pasture; feed on (of animals).
βόστρυχος s.m. curl.
βοτάν|η s.f., ~ι s.n. herb, simple.
βοτανίζω v.t. & i. weed.
βοτανικ|ός a. botanic(al). ~ή s.f. botany.
βότανο s.n. herb, simple.
βοτανολόγος s.m. botanist.
βότρυς s.m. bunch of grapes.
βότσαλο s.n. pebble.
βουβαίνω v.t. make dumb.
βουβ|άλι s.n., ~αλος s.m. buffalo.
βουβαμάρα s.f. dumbness.
βουβός a. dumb.
βουβών s.m. groin; (med.) bubo. ~ικός a. inguinal; bubonic.
βουδιστής s.m. Buddhist.
βο(υ)ερός a. noisy.
βουή s.f., ~τό s.n. see βοή.
βουίζω v.i. make a confused noise; buzz, hum, roar.
βούκα s.f. mouthful.
βουκόλος s.m. cowherd.
βούλευμα s.n. (law) judicial decision on whether case shall proceed for trial.
βουλεύομαι v.i. deliberate.
βουλευτήριον s.n. parliament house.
βουλευτής s.m. member of Parliament, deputy.

βουλευτικός *a.* parliamentary.

βουλή *s.f.* will, intent; Parliament, Chamber.

βούλησις *s.f.* volition, will-power.

βούλιαγμα *s.n.* sinking; collapse.

βουλιάζω *v.t. & i.* sink; bring down, bash in; (*fig.*) ruin; (*v.i.*) sink; collapse; (*fig.*) be ruined.

βουλιμία *s.f.* voracity.

βοῦλλα *s.f.* seal; spot, dot.

βουλλοκέρι *s.n.* sealing-wax.

βούλλωμα *s.n.* sealing; stopping up, blockage; stopper, cork, plug; filling (*of tooth*).

βουλλώνω *v.t. & i.* seal; stop up, block; close, plug, fasten down; fill (*tooth*); brand (*animals*); (*v.i.*) become stopped up.

βούλ|ομαι *v.i.* wish; (*fam.*) τοῦ ~ήθηκε νά he took it into his head to.

βουλῶ *v.t. & i. see* **βουλιάζω.**

βουνήσιος *a.* of the mountains.

βουνό *s.n.* mountain.

βούρδουλας *s.m.* whip.

βοῦρκος *s.m.* slime, mire, filth.

βουρκώνω *v.i.* brim with tears; threaten rain.

βουρλίζ|ω *v.t.* drive mad. ~ομαι *v.i.* become furious; desire madly.

βοῦρλο *s.n.* bulrush.

βούρτσ|α *s.f.* brush. ~ίζω *v.t.* brush.

βοῦς *s.m.f.* ox; βόες (*pl.*) oxen, cattle.

βουστάσιον *s.n.* byre; milking-shed.

βούτηγμα *s.n.* dipping, plunging; (*fam.*) pilfering.

βούτημα *s.n.* hard biscuit, *etc.*, for dipping in drink.

βουτηχτής *s.m.* diver; (*fam.*) pilferer.

βουτιά *s.f.* dive, plunge; (*fam.*) pilfering.

βουτσί *s.n.* cask.

βουτυράτος *a.* of or like butter.

βούτυρο *s.n.* butter.

βουτ|ῶ *v.t. & i.* dip, plunge; (*fam.*) lay hands on, pilfer, pinch; (*v.i.*) dive; ~ηγμένος covered, loaded (*with*).

βόχα *s.f.* stink.

βοῶ *v.t. & i.* shout, cry aloud (for); *see also* **βουίζω.**

βραβεῖον *s.n.* prize, award.

βραβεύω *v.t.* reward, give prize to.

βράγχια *s.n.pl.* gills.

βραδέως *adv.* slowly.

βραδιά *s.f.* evening, night.

βραδιάζ|ει *v.i.* evening falls. ~ομαι *v.i.* be overtaken by nightfall.

βραδιν|ός *a.* evening. ~ό *s.n.* evening (meal).

βράδυ 1. *s.n.* evening. 2. *adv.* in the evening.

βραδυ- *denotes* slowness.

βραδύνω *v.i.* be slow or late.

βραδύς *a.* slow.

βραδύτης *s.f.* slowness, delay.

βράζ|ω *v.i. & i.* boil; seethe, teem; ferment; wheeze; ~ει τό αἷμα του he is full of vitality; (*fam.*) νά σέ βράσω expression of vexed disappointment.

βράκα *s.f.* breeches; (*fam.*) trousers, underpants.

βρακί *s.n.* (*fam.*) underpants.

βράσιμο *s.n.* boiling; wheezing.

βράσις *s.f.* seething, boiling, fermentation.

βρασμός *s.n.* boiling.

βραστός *a.* boiled.

βραχιόλι *s.n.* bracelet.

βραχίων *s.m.* arm.

βράχν|α, ~άδα *s.f.* hoarseness.

βραχνᾶς *s.m.* nightmare.

βραχνιάζω *v.t. & i.* make or become hoarse.

βραχνός *a.* hoarse.

βράχος *s.m.* rock.

βραχυ- *denotes* shortness.

βραχυκύκλωμα *s.n.* short circuit.

βραχύνω *v.t.* shorten.

βραχυπρόθεσμος *a.* (*fin.*) short-dated.

βραχύτης *s.f.* shortness, brevity.

βραχώδης *a.* rocky.

βρέ *int.* (*fam.*) unceremonious mode of address or cry of surprise, impatience, *etc.*

βρε(γ)μένος *a.* wet, damp.

βρέξιμο *s.n.* making wet or damp.

βρεσ|ίδι, ~ιμο *s.n.* thing found.

βρετίκ|ια, ~ά *s.n.pl.* reward for finding.

βρεφοκομεῖον *s.n.* foundling hospital.

βρέφος *s.n.* infant.

βρέχ|ω *v.t. & i.* wet, moisten; (*v.i.*) ~ει it rains.

βρίζα *s.f.* rye.

βρίζω *v.t. & i.* abuse, revile; swear (at).

βρίθω *v.i.* (*with gen.*) teem (*with*).

βρισι|ά *s.f.* oath, term of abuse; ~ές (*pl.*) abuse.

βρισίδι *s.n.* string of oaths.

βρίσκ|ω *v.t.* find; hit, strike; obtain; consider, judge. ~ομαι *v.i.* be, find oneself.

βρογχῖτις *s.f.* bronchitis.

βρόγχος *s.m.* bronchial tube.
βροντερός *a.* thunderous.
βροντή *s.f.* thunder.
βρόντ|ος *s.m.* loud noise; heavy fall; στό ~ο in vain.
βροντ|ῶ *v.i. & t.* thunder, boom, bang; (*v.t.*) bang on; fell, floor; (*fam.*) ~ῶ κανόνι go bankrupt; τά ~ηξε κάτω he abandoned the job.
βροντώδης *a.* thunderous.
βροτός *a.* mortal.
βροχερός *a.* rainy.
βροχή *s.f.* rain, shower.
βρόχι *s.n.* net, snare.
βρόχιν|ος *a.* ~ο νερό rainwater.
βρόχος *s.m.* noose.
βρυκόλακας *s.m.* vampire.
βρύον *s.n.* moss.
βρύσ|η, ~ις *s.f.* fountain; tap.
βρυχηθμός *s.m.* roar.
βρυχῶμαι *v.i.* roar.
βρύω *v.i.* teem (*with*).
βρῶμα *s.n.* food.
βρῶμα *s.f.* stink; filth; (*fig.*) (*fam.*) bitch, swine.
βρωμερός *a.* dirty; ill-smelling.
βρώμη *s.f.* oats.
βρωμιά *s.f.* filth; (*fig.*) dirty business.
βρωμίζω *v.t. & i.* make *or* get dirty.
βρώμικος *a.* dirty.
βρώμιος *a.* stinking, gone bad.
βρωμο- *denotes* dirtiness.
βρωμῶ *v.i.* stink.
βύζαγμα *s.n.* suckling; sucking.
βυζαίνω *v.t. & i.* suckle; suck; (*fam.*) milk (*person*).
βυζανιάρικο *s.n.* suckling (*child*).
βυζαντινός *a.* Byzantine.
βυζί *s.n.* breast; nipple (*of gun*).
βυθίζ|ω *v.t.* sink, plunge. ~ομαι *v.i.* sink; (*fig.*) be abstracted *or* lethargic.
βύθιση *s.f.* lethargy.
βύθισις *s.f.* sinking.
βύθισμα *s.n.* (*naut.*) draught.
βυθοκόρος *s.f.* dredger.
βυθός *s.m.* bottom, bed (*of sea, etc.*).
βύρσα *s.f.* dressed hide.
βυρσοδεψεῖον *s.n.* tannery.
βύσσιν|ο *s.n.* morello cherry. ~ής *a.* dark-red.
βυσσοδομῶ *v.t. & i.* machinate.
βυτίον *s.n.* large barrel; tank.
βωβός *a.* dumb.
βώδι *s.n. see* βόδι.
βωλοδέρνω *v.i.* break soil; (*fig.*) struggle, wrestle (*with task*).

βωλοκοπῶ *v.t.* harrow.
βῶλ|ος *s.m.* clod, lump; ~οι (*pl.*) marbles (*game*).
βωμολοχία *s.f.* scurrility.
βωμός *s.m.* altar.
βώτριδα *s.f.* moth.

Γ

γαβάθα *s f.* shallow wooden *or* earthen bowl.
γάγγλιον *s.n.* ganglion.
γάγγραινα *s.f.* gangrene, canker.
γάζα *s.f.* gauze.
γαζέτα *s.f.* small change.
γαζί *s.n.* stitch, stitching.
γαζία *s.f.* popinac (*sort of acacia*).
γαζώνω *v.t.* stitch (*by machine*).
γαῖ|α *s.f.* earth; ~αι (*pl.*) land (*cultivable*).
γαιάνθραξ *s.m.* pit-coal.
γάϊδαρος *s.m.* ass, donkey; (*fig.*) boor.
γαϊδουράγκαθο *s.n.* thistle.
γαϊδούρι *s.n. see* γάϊδαρος.
γαϊδουριά *s.f.* boorishness; piece of rudeness.
γαϊδουροκαλόκαιρο *s.n.* (*fam.*) S. Martin's summer.
γαιοκτήμων *s.m.* owner of cultivable land.
γαϊτανάκι *s.n.* maypole-dance.
γαϊτάνι *s.n.* braid.
γάλ|α *s.n.* milk; τοῦ ~ακτος sucking (*pig, etc.*), milk (*chocolate*).
γαλάζιος *a.* blue, azure.
γαλαζοαίματος *a.* blue-blooded.
γαλαζόπετρα *s.f.* turquoise; copper sulphate.
γαλακτερός *a.* made from milk.
γαλακτοκομία *s.f.* dairy-farming.
γαλάκτωμα *s.n.* emulsion.
γαλανόλευκος *a. see* κυανόλευκος.
γαλανός *a.* blue; blue-eyed.
γαλαντόμος *s.m.* generous man.
γαλαξίας *s.m.* Milky Way; milk-tooth.
γαλαρία *s.f.* gallery (*of theatre, mine*).
γαλατάς *s.m.* milkman.
γαλατομπούρεκο *s.n.* sort of cake.
γαλβανίζω *v.t.* galvanize; (*fig.*) rouse to enthusiasm.
γαλέτα *s.f.* hard tack; breadcrumbs.
γαλῆ *s.f.* cat.
γαλήν|η *s.f.* calm. ~εύω *v.t. & i.* make *or* grow calm.

γαλιάνδρα *s.f.* lark (*bird*).
γαλιφιά *s.f.* flattery.
γαλλικός *a.* French.
γαλλόπουλο *s.n.* young turkey.
γάλλος *s.m.* turkey.
Γάλλος *s.m.* Frenchman.
γαλόνι *s.n.* 1. braid; (*mil.*) stripe.
2. gallon (-jar).
γαλότσα *s.f.* galosh; clog.
γαλουχώ *v.t.* suckle; (*fig.*) rear.
γαμ|βρός, ~πρός *s.m.* son-in-law;
brother-in-law (*sister's husband*);
bridegroom; (*fig.*) marriageable man.
γαμήλιος *a.* nuptial, wedding.
γάμμα *s.n.* the letter Γ.
γάμος *s.m.* marriage, wedding.
γάμπα *s.f.* calf, leg.
γαμψός *a.* hooked.
γανιάζω *v.i.* feel dry (*from thirst or talk-ing*).
γάντζος *s.m.* hook, grapple.
γάντι *s.n.* glove.
γανώνω *v.t.* plate with tin.
γαργαλ|εύω, ~ίζω, ~ῶ *v.t.* tickle; (*fig.*)
tempt. ~ιέμαι *v.i.* be ticklish.
γαργαλιστικός *a.* tempting.
γαργάρα *s.f.* gargle, gargling.
γάργαρος *a.* purling; limpid.
γαρίδα *s.f.* shrimp.
γαρμπῆς *s.m.* south-west wind.
γάρμπος *s.n.* line, (*good*) shape.
γαρνίρω *v.t.* garnish, trim.
γαρ(ο)ύφαλλο *s.n.* carnation; clove.
γαστήρ *s.f.* belly.
γάστρα *s.f.* flower-pot.
γαστρικός *a.* gastric.
γάτ|α *s.f.*, ~ί *s.n.*, ~ος *s.m.* cat.
γατάκι *s.n.* kitten.
γαυγίζω *v.i.* bark.
γαυριῶ *v.i.* exult.
γαῦρος *a.* excited.
γαῦρος *s.m.* sort of fish.
γδάρσιμο *s.n.* skinning, barking.
γδέρνω *v.t.* skin, flay; bark; graze; (*fig.*)
fleece.
γδοῦπος *s.m.* thud.
γδυμνός *a. see* γυμνός.
γδύν|ω *v.t.* undress; (*fig.*) rob. ~ομαι
v.i. get undressed.
γδύσιμο *s.n.* undressing; (*fig.*) robbing.
γδυτός *a.* undressed.
γεγονός *s.n.* event; fact.
γειά *s.f.* health; ~ σας *or* ~ χαρά
greeting; μέ ~ good wish to one having
something new.
γεῖσον *s.n.* caves; peak (*of cap*).

γειτ|νιάζω, ~ονεύω *v.i.* be near to-
gether *or* adjoining.
γειτονιά *s.f.* neighbourhood.
γειτονικός *a.* neighbouring.
γείτ|ων, ~ονας *s.m.* neighbour.
γελάδα *s.f.* cow.
γέλασμα *s.n.* deceit; laughing-stock.
γελαστός *a.* smiling, cheerful.
γελέκι *s.n.* waistcoat.
γέλιο *s.n.* laugh, laughter.
γελοιογραφία *s.f.* caricature; cartoon.
γελοιοποι|ῶ *v.t.* make ridiculous.
~οῦμαι *v.i.* make oneself ridiculous.
γελοῖος *a.* ridiculous.
γελ|ῶ *v.i. & t.* laugh; (*with* μέ) laugh
at; cheat, take in. ~ιέμαι *v.i.* be de-
ceived *or* mistaken.
γέλως *s.m.* laugh, laughter.
γελωτοποιός *s.m.* jester.
γέμα *s.n.* (*fam.*) meal; luncheon.
γεμάτος *a.* full, covered (*with*); loaded;
(*fig.*) thick (*in texture*), well-nourished
(*of figure*).
γεμίζω *v.t. & i.* fill, stuff, cover (*with*);
load (*gun*); (*v.i.*) become full *or*
covered (*with*); fill out.
γέμιση *s.f.* stuffing, filling (*of bird,
cushion, etc.*); waxing (*of moon*).
γεμιστός *a.* stuffed (*of food*).
γέμω *v.i.* (*with gen.*) be full (*of*).
Γενάρης *s.m.* January.
γεν|εά, ~ιά *s.f.* race, generation.
γενέθλια *s.n.pl.* birthday.
γένεια *s.n.pl.* beard; ἀφήνω ~ grow a
beard.
γενει|άς, ~άδα *s.f.* long beard.
γένεσις *s.f.* genesis, creation.
γενέτειρα *s.f.* birthplace.
γενετ|ή *s.f. ἐκ ~ῆς* from birth.
γενετήσιος *a.* generative, sexual.
γενετικός *a.* genetic.
γενικεύω *v.t. & i.* make general, spread;
throw open (*discussion*); (*v.i.*) generalize.
γενική *s.f.* (*gram.*) genitive.
γενικός *a.* general.
γενίτσαρος *s.m.* janissary.
γέννα *s.f.* childbirth, confinement;
(*fig.*) breed, spawn.
γενναιόδωρος *a.* generous, liberal.
γενναῖ|ος *a.* brave; ~ο δῶρο generous
gift.
γενναιόφρων *a.* magnanimous, liberal.
γέννημα *s.n.* offspring, product; ~ καὶ
θρέμμα born and bred; ~τα (*pl.*)
cereals.

γέννησις *s.f.* birth.

γεννητικός *a.* genital.

γεννητούρια *s.n.pl.* (*fam.*) birth (*as social event*).

γεννήτρια *s.f.* (*electric*) generator.

γεννήτ|ωρ *s.m.* father; ~ορες (*pl.*) parents.

γενν|ῶ *v.t. & i.* give birth (to), bear; lay eggs; (*fig.*) cause, engender. ~ιέμαι *v.i.* be born.

γέν|ος *s.n.* race, tribe; genus; gender; ἐν ~ει in general.

γερά *adv.* strongly, hard, steadily.

γεράκι *s.n.* hawk.

γεράματα *s.n.pl.* old age.

γερανός *s.m.* crane (*bird, machine*).

γέρας *s.n.* prize, trophy.

γερατειά *s.n.pl.* old age.

γέρικος *a.* old.

γέρνω *v.t. & i.* bend down, tilt; half close (*door*); (*v.i.*) lean *or* bend over, stoop; lie down; sink (*of star*).

γερνῶ *v.t. & i.* make *or* grow old.

γέροντας *s.m.* old man.

γεροντοκόρη *s.f.* old maid.

γεροντοπαλλήκαρο *s.n.* old bachelor.

γέρος *s.m.* old man.

γερός *a.* healthy, hale, strong; whole, undamaged.

γερουσία *s.f.* senate; (*fig.*) old fogies.

γέρων *s.m.* old man.

γεῦμα *s.n.* meal, luncheon.

γεύομαι *v.t.* (*with gen.*) taste.

γεῦσις *s.f.* taste, flavour; tasting.

γευστικός *a.* savoury, tasty.

γέφ|υρα *s.f.*, ~ύρι *s.n.* bridge.

γεω|γραφία *s.f.* geography. ~γράφος *s.m.* geographer.

γεω|λογία *s.f.* geology. ~λόγος *s.m.* geologist.

γεωμετρ|ία *s.f.* geometry. ~ικός *a.* geometric(al).

γεώμηλον *s.n.* potato.

γεωπονία *s.f.* (*science of*) agriculture.

γεωργ|ία *s.f.* farming. ~ός *s.m.* farmer.

γῆ *s.f.* earth, ground, land.

γηγενής *s.f.* indigenous.

γήινος *a.* terrestrial.

γήπεδον *s.n.* piece of ground; sportsground.

γῆρας *s.n.* old age.

γηράσκω *v.t. & i.* make *or* grow old.

γηροκομεῖον *s.n.* old people's home.

γητεύω *v.t.* weave spells over.

γιά I. *prep.* (*with acc.*) for; because of; instead *or* on behalf of; about, concerning; γι᾽ αὐτό therefore; ~ καλά for certain, definitely; ~ τήν ὥρα for the time being, up to now; ~ δέσιμο crazy; ~ ποῦ whither? ~ τό Θεό for God's sake; δέν ἄφησε βουνό ~ βουνό he left not a single mountain (*i.e. unclimbed*). 2. *adv.* as, for; πάει ~ βουλευτής he is standing for Parliament; περνάει ~ ὡραία she passes for beautiful; τό ἔχει ~ γούρι he thinks it a lucky omen. 3. *conj.* ~ νά in order to; ~ νά μήν προσέχῃς ἔπεσες κάτω through not taking care you fell down. 4. *hortatory particle* (*with imperative*) ~ φαντάσου fancy that! ~ πές μου tell me.

γιαγιά *s.f.* grandmother.

γιαίνω *v.t. & i.* heal; make *or* get well.

γιακᾶς *s.m.* collar.

γιαλός *s.m.* sea-shore.

γιάντρες *s.n.* wager on pulling wishbone.

γιαούρτι *s.n.* yogurt.

γιαπί *s.n.* building *or* repairs in progress.

γιαρμᾶς *s.m.* sort of peach.

γιασεμί *s.n.* jasmine.

γιατί *adv.* why.

γιατὶ *conj.* because.

γιατρειά *s.f.* cure.

γιατρεύω *v.t.* cure, heal.

γιατρικό *s.n.* medicine.

γιατρός *s.m.* doctor.

γιατροσόφι *s.n.* nostrum.

γιάτσο *s.n.* (*fam.*) ice-cream.

γιαχνί *s.n.* sort of ragout.

γιγάντειος *a.* gigantic.

γίγας *s.m.* giant.

γιγνώσκω *v.t.* see γινώσκω.

γίδα *s.f.* goat.

γιδοβοσκός *s.m.* goatherd.

γιδοπρόβατα *s.n.pl.* sheep and goats.

γιλέκο *s.n.* waistcoat.

γινάτι *s.n.* obstinacy; spite.

γίν|ομαι *v.i.* become, be done *or* produced; be finished *or* ready; ripen; happen; τί ~εσαι; how are you? τί θά ~ω; what will become of me? ὅ μὴ γένοιτο God forbid! τό ~όμενον (*math.*) product; ~ωμένος ripe.

γινώσκω *v.t.* know.

γιόκας *s.m.* son (*endearing*).

γιομ- *see* γεμ-.

γιορτή *s.f. see* ἑορτή.

γιός *s.m.* son.

γιουβαρλάκια *s.n.pl.* meat-and-rice balls.

γιουρούσι *s.n.* attack, invasion.

γιουχαΐζω *v.t. & i.* hoot, boo.

γιρλάντα *s.f.* garland.

γιώτ *s.n.* yacht. [D. *yacht*]

γιῶτα *s.n.* the letter Ι.

γκ- *see also* κ-.

γκαβός *a.* cross-eyed; blind.

γκάγκαρος *s.m.* (*fam.*) true-born Athenian.

γκάζι *s.n.* gas; paraffin; (*fam.*) πατῶ ~ step on the gas.

γκαζιέρα *s.f.* cooking-stove (*gas or paraffin*).

γκαζόζα *s.f.* bottled lemonade.

γκαμήλα *s.f.* camel.

γκαράζ *s.n.* garage. [F. *garage*]

γκαρδιακός *a.* cordial; bosom (*friend*).

γκαρίζω *v.i.* bray.

γκαρσόν(ι) *s.n.* waiter; bachelor. [F. *garçon*]

γκαρσονιέρα *s.f.* bachelor's apartment.

γκαστρώνω *v.t.* (*fam.*) get with child; (*fig.*) exasperate.

γκάφα *s.f.* blunder, faux pas.

γκέλ *s.n.* bounce; (*fam.*) sex-appeal.

γκέμι *s.n.* bridle.

γκίνια *s.f.* bad luck.

γκιόσα *s.f.* old she-goat.

γκιουβέτσι *s.n.* (vessel for) meat cooked with Italian paste.

γκιώνης *s.m.* screech-owl.

γκλίτσα *s.f.* shepherd's crook.

γκουβερνάντα *s.f.* governess.

γκρέκα *s.f.* meander (*pattern*).

γκρεμίζ|ω *v.t.* cast down (*from height*); demolish; overthrow. ~ομαι *v.i.* fall (*from height*); collapse.

γκρεμ(ν)ός *s.m.* abyss, precipice.

γκρενά *s.n. & a.* colour of garnet. [F. *grenat*]

γκρί(ζος) *a.* grey.

γκρινιάζω *v.i.* grumble, nag; cry, whimper.

γκρινιάρης *a.* grumbling, nagging.

γλάρος *s.m.* seagull.

γλαρώνω *v.i.* close one's eyes in sleep, drowse; (*of eyes*) close.

γλάστρα *s.f.* flower-pot.

γλαυκός *a.* pale blue.

γλαύξ *s.f.* owl.

γλαφυρός *a.* elegant (*of language*).

γλείφ|ω *v.t.* lick. ~ομαι *v.i.* lick one's lips; ἡ γάτα ~εται the cat is washing itself.

γλεντζές *s.m.* pleasure-loving person, reveller; rake.

γλέντι *s.n.* merrymaking, party, beanfeast.

γλεντοκοπῶ *v.i.* go in for riotous living.

γλεντῶ *v.i. & t.* make merry, have a good time; (*v.t.*) dine and wine; enjoy; squander (*money*) on amusement.

γλεῦκος *s.n.* must.

γληγ- *see* γρηγ-.

γλίνα *s.f.* grease (*left from cooking*).

γλιστερός *a.* slippery.

γλιστρῶ *v.i.* slip, slide, glide; (*fig.*) slip away, escape.

γλίσχρος *a.* niggardly, mean.

γλί|τζα, ~τσα *s.f.* dirt, slime.

γλοιώδης *a.* viscous, sticky; (*fig.*) oily (*person*).

γλόμπος *s.m.* globe (*of light*).

γλουτός *s.m.* buttock.

γλύκ|α, ~άδα *s.f.* sweetness; ~ες (*pl.*) caresses, tender looks.

γλυκάδ|ι *s.n.* 1. vinegar. 2. ~ια (*pl.*) sweetbreads.

γλυκαίνω *v.t. & i.* make *or* become sweet *or* mild; alleviate.

γλυκανάλατος *a.* insipid.

γλυκάνισον *s.n.* aniseed.

γλυκερίνη *s.f.* glycerine.

γλύκισμα *s.n.* cake, pudding.

γλυκ|ό *s.n.* sweetmeat; ~ά (*pl.*) pastries, confectionery.

γλυκοαίματος *a.* likeable.

γλυκόζη *s.f.* glucose.

γλυκομίλητος *a.* soft-spoken.

γλυκόξυνος *a.* sweetish-sour.

γλυκόπικρος *a.* bitter-sweet.

γλυκόποτος . *a.* pleasant to drink *or* smoke.

γλυκοπύρουνος *a.* having edible kernel (*esp. apricot*).

γλυκ|ός, ~ύς *a.* sweet; mild; τοῦ ~οῦ νεροῦ fresh-water, (*fig.*) incompetent; (*woman*) no better than she should be.

γλυκοσαλιάζω *v.i.* trifle flirtatiously.

γλυκοχάρα(γ)μα *s.n.* serene daybreak.

γλυκύτης *s.f.* sweetness; mildness.

γλύπτ|ης *s.m.* sculptor. ~ική *s.f.* (*art of*) sculpture.

γλυτ|ώνω *v.t. & i.* save, deliver; (*v.i.*) escape, get away; φτηνά τή ~ωσε he got off cheaply.

γλυφίς *s.f.* chisel.

γλυφός *a.* brackish.

γλύφω *v.t.* carve, sculpt.

γλῶσσα *s.f.* 1. tongue; language. 2. sole (*fish*).

γλωσσεύω *v.i.* answer back impertinently.

γλωσσίδι *s.n.* tongue (*of bell, etc.*).

γλωσσικός *a.* lingual; linguistic.

γλωσσοδέτης *s.m.* impediment of speech; τόν ἔπιασε ~ he was tongue-tied.

γλωσσοκοπάνα *s.f.* talkative and impertinent woman.

γλωσσολογία *s.f.* philology, linguistics.

γλωσσομαθής *s.m.* linguist.

γλωσσοτρώγω *v.t.* bring bad luck to (*by speaking enviously*).

γλωσσοῦ *s.f.* saucily voluble woman.

γλωσσοφαγιά *s.f.* bringing of bad luck (*by envious talk*).

γνάθος *s.m.* jaw.

γνέθω *v.t.* spin.

γνέφω *v.i.* nod, make a sign.

γνέψιμο *s.n.* nod, sign.

γνήσιος *a.* genuine, true.

γνωματεύω *v.i.* deliver one's opinion.

γνώμη *s.f.* opinion, view.

γνωμικόν *s.n.* maxim, adage.

γνωμοδοτῶ *v.i.* deliver one's opinion.

γνώμων *s.m.* T-square, level; (gnomon of) sundial; meter (*for gas, etc.*); (*fig.*) rule, principle.

γνωρίζω *v.t.* know; be *or* get acquainted with; recognize; make known, introduce; ~ ὑμῖν ὅτι I inform you that.

γνωριμία *s.f.* acquaintance; δέν ἔχει ~ he is unrecognizable.

γνώριμος *a.* known; an acquaintance.

γνώρισμα *s.n.* sign, mark (*abstract*).

γνώση *s.f.* good sense; βάζω ~ learn (better) by experience.

γνῶσις, ~η *s.f.* knowledge, cognizance; ~εις (*pl.*) knowledge, learning.

γνώστης *s.m.* expert, connoisseur.

γνωστικός *a.* sensible.

γνωστοποιῶ *v.t.* notify, give notice of (*to someone*).

γνωστός *a.* known; an acquaintance; ὡς ~όν as is known.

γόβα *s.f.* (*woman's*) court shoe. ~άκι *s.n.* slipper.

γογγύζω *v.i.* groan; grumble.

γοερός *a.* loud and poignant.

γόης *s.m.* charmer.

γοητεία *s.f.* charm.

γοητευτικός *a.* charming.

γοητεύω *v.t.* charm.

γόητρον *s.n.* prestige.

γομάρι *s.n.* load; donkey-load; donkey.

γόμμα *s.n.* gum; india-rubber.

γομφίος *s.m.* molar.

γόμφος *s.m.* peg, pin; joint (*of bones*).

γόμωσις *s.f.* loading *or* charge (*of gun*); stuffing.

γόνα *s.n.* (*fam.*) knee.

γονατίζω *v.i. & t.* (make to) kneel; (*fig.*) weigh *or* be weighed down.

γονατιστός *a.* on one's knees.

γόνατο *s.n.* knee.

γον|εύς *s.m.* father; ~εῖς (*pl.*) parents.

γονικός *a.* parental, inherited.

γονιμοποιῶ *v.t.* fecundate.

γόνιμος *a.* fertile, prolific, fruitful.

γονιός *s.m. see* γονεύς.

γόνος *s.m.* (*fig.*) seed, offspring, scion.

γόνυ *s.n.* knee.

γονυκλισία *s.f.* genuflexion.

γονυπετής *a.* on one's knees.

γόος *s.m.* loud cry of pain *or* grief.

γόπα *s.f.* 1. sort of fish. 2. (*fam.*) cigarette-end.

γοργόνα *s.f.* mermaid; (*fig.*) beautiful woman.

γοργός *a.* quick.

γόρδιος *a.* ~ δεσμός Gordian knot.

γορίλλας *s.m.* gorilla.

γοτθικός *a.* Gothic.

γούβα *s.f.* cavity, pothole.

γουδ|ί *s.n.* mortar. ~οχέρι *s.n.* pestle.

γούλα *s.f.* gullet; (*fig.*) greed.

γουλί *s.n.* stalk (*of cabbage, etc.*); (*fam.*) bald.

γουλιά *s.f.* drop, mouthful.

γούνα *s.f.* fur.

γουναρικό *s.n.* fur (*garment*).

γούνινος *a.* made of fur.

γούρι *s.n.* good luck.

γουρλ|ῆς, ~ήδικος *a.* bringing good luck.

γουρλομάτης *a.* with bulging eyes.

γουρλώνω *v.t.* open (*eyes*) wide.

γουρλωτός *a.* bulging (*of eyes*).

γούρνα *s.f.* stone basin *or* trough (*for water*).

γουρούν|ι *s.n.* pig. ~όπουλο *s.n.* sucking-pig.

γουρσούζ|ης *s.m.* unlucky *or* peevish fellow. ~ιά *s.f.* bad luck. ~ικος *a.* bringing bad luck.

γουστάρ|ω *v.t. & i.* desire, feel like; δέν τόν ~ω I do not care for him; ~ω νά *or* μοῦ ~ει νά I enjoy.

γοῦστο *s.n.* taste (*discrimination*); δέν τόν κάνω ~ I do not care for him; κάναμε ~ we had an amusing time; κάνω ~ μιά μπίρα I feel like a beer;

γιά ~ for fun; δέν ἔχει ~ there is no fun in that; ἔχει ~ νά it would be a nice thing if (ironic).
γουστόζικος a. entertaining.
γοφός s.m. hip.
γραβάτα s.f. necktie.
γραβιέρα s.f. gruyère cheese.
γραῖα s.f. old woman.
γραῖγος s.m. north-east wind.
γράμμα s.n. letter.
γραμμάριον s.n. gramme.
γραμματ|εύς s.m.f. secretary. ~εία s.f. secretariat.
γραμματικ|ός a. grammatical; a grammarian; a clerk. ~ή s.f. grammar.
γραμμάτιον s.n. bill of exchange.
γραμματοκιβώτιον s.n. letter-box.
γραμματοκομιστής s.m. postman.
γραμματολογία s.f. history of literature.
γραμματόσημον s.n. postage-stamp.
γραμμένος a. written; (fig.) fated; bold of features).
γραμμή s.f. line; (adv.) straight, in turn; πρώτης ~ς first-class.
γραμμόφωνον s.n. gramophone.
γρανάζι s.n. gear (of motor).
γρανίτα s.f. water-ice.
γρανίτης s.m. granite.
γραπτ|ός a. written. ~ῶς adv. in writing.
γραπώνω v.t. grab.
γρασίδι s.n. grass.
γρατσουν|ίζω, ~ῶ v.t. scratch.
γραφειοκρατία s.f. bureaucracy, red tape.
γραφεῖον s.n. desk; study; office, bureau.
γραφεύς s.m. clerk.
γραφ|ή s.f. writing; reading (of MS.); ~αί (pl.) scriptures; τὸ κάτω κάτω τῆς ~ῆς when all is said and done, if the worst comes to the worst.
γραφικός a. of writing or drawing, clerical; (fig.) picturesque, graphic.
γραφίς s.f. pen.
γραφομηχανή s.f. typewriter.
γραφτός a. written; (fig.) fated.
γράφω v.t. & i. write; enrol; record.
γράψιμο s.n. writing.
γρήγορ|ος a. quick. ~α adv. quickly.
γρηγορῶ v.i. watch, be vigilant.
γριά s.f. old woman.
γριγρί s.n. fishing-boat with lantern.
γρίλλια s.f. grille; slat (of shutter).
γριν- see γκριν-.

γρῖπος s.m. drag-net.
γρίππη s.f. influenza.
γρῖφος s.m. riddle.
γροθιά s.f. fist; punch.
γρό(ν)θος s.m. fist; punch.
γρονθοκοπῶ v.t. punch repeatedly.
γρόσι s.n. piastre; ~α (pl.) (fig.) money.
γρουσ- see γουρσ-.
γρύ adv. (fam.) nothing; not a word.
γρυλλίζω v.i. grunt.
γρύλλος s.m. cricket; jack (tool).
γρυπός a. hooked.
γυάλα s.f. large glass receptacle.
γυαλάδα s.f. shine, gloss.
γυαλένιος a. glass.
γυαλί s.n. glass (substance); mirror; chimney (of lamp); ~ά (pl.) glasses, spectacles.
γυαλίζω v.t. & i. polish; shine.
γυαλικά s.n.pl. glass-ware.
γυάλινος a. glass.
γυάλισμα s.n. polishing.
γυαλιστερός a. glossy.
γυαλόχαρτο s.n. glass-paper.
γυλιός s.m. (mil.) knapsack.
γυμνάζ|ω v.t. train, drill, exercise. ~ομαι v.i. practise, exercise oneself.
γυμνάσια s.n.pl. (mil.) manœuvres.
γυμνάσι|ον s.n. secondary school. ~άρχης s.m.f. head of such school.
γύμνασμα s.n. an exercise.
γυμναστής s.m. instructor, trainer.
γυμναστική s.f. gymnastics.
γύμνια s.f. nakedness.
γυμνισμός s.m. nudism.
γυμνιστής s.m. nudist.
γυμνόπους a. barefoot.
γυμνός a. naked, bare.
γυμνοσάλιαγκος s.m. slug.
γυμνώνω v.t. lay bare, expose; (fig.) strip, rob.
γυναῖκα s.f. woman; wife.
γυναικάδελφος s.m. wife's brother.
γυναικᾶς s.m. man who runs after women.
γυναικεῖος a. woman's.
γυναικολόγος s.m.f. gynaecologist.
γυναικόπαιδα s.n.pl. women and children.
γυναικ|οπρεπής, ~ωτός a. effeminate.
γυναικών, ~ίτης s.m. women's quarters; harem.
γύναιον s.n. hussy, trollop, hag.
γυνή s.f. woman; wife.
γύρα s.f. walk, stroll; (fam.) τά φέρνω ~

make ends meet; βγαίνω στή ~ seek importunately.

γυρεύω *v.t.* seek, look *or* ask for.

γυρίζω *v.t. & i.* turn; give back; take *or* escort around; shoot (*film*); (*v.i.*) turn; return; roam; change (*of weather*); change one's views; sink (*of sun*).

γυρῖνος *s.m.* tadpole.

γύρισμα *s.n.* turn, turning; return (*giving back*); change; sinking (*of sun*).

γυρισμός *s.m.* return (*coming back*).

γυριστός *a.* curved, winding; turned up *or* down.

γυρνῶ *v.t. & i. see* γυρίζω.

γυρολόγος *s.m.* pedlar.

γῦρος *s.m.* circle, circumference; turn, revolution; hem, brim; hoop (*of barrel*); walk, stroll; round (*of boxing, etc.*).

γυρτός *a.* bent, leaning; lying down.

γύρω *adv.* round; (*prep.*) ~ σέ *or* ἀπό round.

γύφτ|ος *s.m.* gipsy; smith; (*fig.*) miser. ~ιά *s.f.* meanness.

γύψ *s.m.* vulture.

γύψος *s.m.* plaster of Paris.

γων|ία, ~ιά *s.f.* angle, corner; square (*instrument*); fireplace; crust of bread.

γωνι|αῖος, ~ακός *a.* corner.

γωνιόλιθος *s.m.* cornerstone.

γωνιόμετρον *s.n.* T-square.

γωνιώδης *a.* angular.

Δ

δά *particle of intensification.*

δάγγειος *s.m.* (*med.*) dengue.

δάγκ|αμα, ~ωμα *s.n.* bite.

δαγκ|ανιά, ~ωματιά *s.f.* bite.

δαγκ|άνω, ~ώνω *v.t. & i.* bite.

δαδί *s.n.* fire-wood (*esp.* pine).

δαίδαλος *a. & s.m.* intricate; a labyrinth.

δαίμονας *s.m. see* δαίμων.

δαιμον|ίζω *v.t.* enrage. ~ίζομαι *v.t.* be possessed of devils; get enraged; ~ισμένος (*fig.*) mischievous, very clever.

δαιμόνι|ον *s.n.* genius; demon; καινά ~α revolutionary ideas.

δαιμόνιος *a.* very clever.

δαίμων *s.m.* demon, devil.

δάκνω *v.t. & i.* bite.

δακρυγόν|ος *a.* lachrymal; ~α ἀέρια tear-gas.

δακρύζω *v.i. see* δακρύω.

δάκρυ(ον) *s.n.* tear; (*fig.*) small drop.

δάκρυσμα *s.n.* exuding of drops, oozing, watering.

δακρυσμένος *a.* tearful; oozing.

δακρύω *v.i.* exude drops, ooze, weep; water (*of eyes*).

δακτυλικ|ός *a.* ~ά ἀποτυπώματα fingerprints (*on record*).

δακτύλιος *s.m.* ring.

δακτυλογράφος *s.m.f.* typist.

δακτυλοδεικτούμενος *a.* in the public eye (*for good or bad*).

δάκτυλος *s.m.* finger; toe; inch; dactyl; (*fig.*) hand, influence.

δαλτωνισμός *s.m.* colour-blindness.

δαμάζω *v.t.* tame.

δαμάλι *s.n.* heifer.

δαμαλισμός *s.m.* vaccination.

δαμάσκηνο *s.n.* prune.

δαμιζάνα *s.m.* demijohn.

δανδής *s.m.* dandy.

δανείζ|ω *v.t.* lend. ~ομαι *v.t.* borrow.

δανεικ|ός *a.* lent; τά ~ά (*pl.*) money borrowed. ~ά *adv.* on loan.

δάνειον *s.n.* loan.

δανειστής *s.m.* lender.

δαντέλλα *s.f.* lace.

δαπάν|η *s.f.* expenditure, expense. ~ηρός *a.* costly; extravagant. ~ ῶ *v.t.* spend, consume.

δάπεδον *s.n.* floor, ground.

δαρ|μός *s.m.*, ~σιμο *s.n.* beating.

δάς *s.f.* torch, brand.

δασεία *s.f.* (*gram.*) rough breathing.

δασικός *a.* of forests *or* forestry.

δασκάλ|α, ~ισσα *s.f.* (*primary*) schoolmistress; (*pej.*) schoolmarm.

δασκαλεύω *v.t.* coach, prime.

δάσκαλος *s.m.* teacher; (*primary*) schoolmaster; (*pej.*) pedant.

δασμολόγιον *s.n.* tariff.

δασμός *s.m.* duty, tax.

δασολογία *s.f.* forestry.

δασονομία *s.f.* conservancy of forests.

δάσος *s.n.* wood, forest.

δασόφυτος *a.* wooded.

δασ|ύς, ~ός *a.* hairy, bushy.

δασώδης *a.* forested.

δαυλ|ί *s.n.*, ~ός *s.m.* torch, brand.

δαῦτος *pron.* this one.

δάφν|η *s.f.* laurel, bay; (*fig.*) δρέπω ~ας triumph, succeed.

δαχτυλήθρα *s.f.* thimble.

δαχτυλιά *s.f.* finger-mark.
δάχτυλο *s.n.* finger; toe.
δαχτυλίδι *s.n.* ring.
δαψιλής *a.* abundant, lavish.
δέ *conj.* and; but; on the other hand.
δέ(ν) *adv.* not (*before verb*).
δεδομέν|ος *a.* given; τά ~α (*pl.*) facts, data; ~ου ὅτι given that.
δέησις *s.f.* prayer.
δεῖ *v.i.* there is need; ὀλίγου ~ν ἔπιπτε he nearly fell; πολλοῦ γε καὶ ~ far from it.
δεῖγμα *s.n.* sample, specimen; token, proof.
δεικνύω *v.t. & i.* show, indicate, demonstrate; (*with* νά) show how to; point (at); seem, appear.
δείκτης *s.m.* forefinger; indicator; pointer, hand.
δεικτικός *a.* (*gram.*) demonstrative.
δείλ|ι, ~ινό *s.n.* late afternoon.
δειλι|άζω, ~ῶ *v.i.* lack *or* lose courage.
δειλός *a.* timorous, cowardly.
δεῖνα(ς) *pron.* ὁ ~ so-and-so.
δειν|ός *a.* terrible; (*fig.*) clever, expert; τά ~ά (*pl.*) sufferings.
δεῖπνον *s.n.* supper, dinner.
δεισιδαιμονία *s.f.* superstition.
δείχνω *v.t. & i.* see δεικνύω.
δέκα *num.* ten.
δεκαδικός *a.* decimal.
δεκαεννέα *num.* nineteen.
δεκαέξ(ι) *num.* sixteen.
δεκαεπτά *num.* seventeen.
δεκαετία *s.f.* decade.
δεκάλογος *s.m.* Ten Commandments.
δεκανεύς *s.m.* (*mil.*) corporal.
δεκανίκι *s.n.* crutch.
δεκαοκτώ *num.* eighteen.
δεκαπενθήμερον *s.n.* fortnight.
δεκαπεντασύλλαβος *s.m.* fifteen-syllable line.
δεκαπέντε *num.* fifteen.
δεκάρα *s.f.* ten-lepta piece.
δεκάρι *s.n.* ten (*esp. at cards*); ten-drachma piece. ~κο *s.n.* ten-drachma piece.
δεκάς *s.f.* group of ten.
δεκασμός *s.m.* bribery.
δεκατέσσερεις *a.* fourteen.
δέκατ|ος *a.* tenth; τά ~α (*pl.*) temperature recurrently above normal.
δεκατρεῖς *a.* thirteen.
Δεκέμβρ|ης, ~ιος *s.m.* December.
δέκτης *s.m.* receiver.
δεκτικός *a.* capable of receiving.

δεκτός *a.* received, accepted; acceptable.
δελεάζω *v.t.* lure, tempt.
δέλεαρ *s.n.* bait.
δελεαστικός *a.* tempting, enticing.
δέλτα *s.n.* the letter Δ; delta.
δελτάριον *s.n.* postcard.
δελτίον *s.n.* bulletin, report; form; card (*ration, identity, etc.*).
δελφίνι *s.n.* dolphin, porpoise.
δέμα *s.n.* cord, lace; parcel, bundle.
δεμάτι *s.n.* bunch, sheaf, truss.
δέ(ν) *adv.* not (*before verb*).
δένδρον *s.n.* tree.
δενδροστοιχία *s.f.* avenue of trees.
δέντρ|ο, ~ί *s.n.* tree.
δεντρολίβανο *s.n.* rosemary.
δένω *v.t. & i.* tie (up), bind; bandage; assemble (*parts*); set (*jewel*); thicken (*sauce, etc.*); render impotent by spell. (*v.i.*) thicken; form (*of fruit*).
δεξαμενή *s.f.* reservoir; (*naut.*) dock, basin.
δεξιά 1. *s.f.* right hand; right wing. 2. *adv.* to the right; propitiously.
δέξιμο *s.n.* welcoming home.
δεξιός *a.* 1. (on the) right; right-hand(ed); right-wing. 2. dextrous.
δεξιοτέχνης *s.m.* virtuoso.
δεξιότης *s.f.* dexterity.
δεξιώνομαι *v.t.* receive (*as guest*).
δεξίωσις *s.f.* reception.
δέομαι 1. *v.t.* (*with gen.*) need. 2. *v.i.* pray.
δέον *s.n.* what is necessary; πλέον τοῦ ~τος too much; τὰ ~τα the needful; respects; ~ νὰ σημειωθῇ it must be noted.
δεόντως *adv.* properly, duly.
δέος *s.n.* awe; apprehension.
δέρας *s.n.* fleece.
δερβέναγας *s.m.* (*fig.*) tyrant.
δερβένι *s.n.* defile.
δερβίσης *s.m.* dervish.
δέρμα *s.n.* skin; hide, leather.
δερματικός *a.* of the skin.
δερμάτινος *a.* leather.
δερματολόγος *s.m.f.* skin specialist.
δέρ|(ν)ω *v.t.* beat; lash, beat down on (*of elements*). ~νομαι *v.i.* beat one's breast; toss and turn.
δές *imperative of* βλέπω.
δέσιμο *s.n.* tying (up), binding, *etc.* (*see* δένω); binding (*of book*); (*fam.*) γιά ~ crazy.
δεσμά *s.n.pl.* fetters; imprisonment.

δεσμεύω *v.t.* bind, make prisoner.
δέσμη *s.f.* bunch, bundle, sheaf.
δέσμιος *a.* captive.
δεσμός *s.m.* bond, tie.
δεσμώτης *s.m.* prisoner.
δεσπόζω *v.t.* (*with gen.*) dominate, command.
δεσποινίς *s.f.* young lady; Miss.
δεσπότης *s.m.* ruler; (*fam.*) bishop.
δεσποτικός *a.* despotic.
Δευτέρα *s.f.* Monday.
δευτερεύων *a.* secondary.
δευτεροβάθμιος *a.* second-grade.
δευτερόλεπτο *s.n.* second (*of time*).
δεύτερ|ος *a.* second; ἐκ ~ου a second time; ~ο πρᾶμα second-rate.
δευτερώνω *v.t. & i.* do or happen a second time.
δέχομαι *v.t.* receive, accept.
δή *particle of intensification.*
δῆγμα *s.n.* bite, sting.
δῆθεν *adv.* as if, supposedly; so-called.
δηκτικός *a.* biting.
δηλαδή *adv.* namely, that is.
δηλητήρι|ον *s.n.* poison, venom. ~άζω *v.t.* poison. ~ώδης *a.* poisonous, venomous.
δηλ|ῶ, ~ώνω *v.t.* declare, return.
δήλωσις *s.f.* declaration, statement.
δημαγωγός *s.m.* demagogue.
δήμαρχ|ος *s.m.* mayor. ~είον *s.n.* town hall.
δημεύω *v.t.* confiscate.
δημηγορῶ *v.i.* speak in public; harangue.
δημητριακά *s.n.pl.* cereals, corn.
δήμιος *s.m.* executioner.
δημιούργημα *s.n.* creation (*thing*).
δημιουργία *s.f.* creation (*act*).
δημιουργικός *a.* creative.
δημιουργός *a. & s.m.* creative; creator.
δημιουργῶ *v.t.* create.
δημογραφία *s.f.* population statistics.
δημοδιδάσκαλος *s.m.* primary school-teacher.
δημοκοπία *s.f.* demagogy.
δημοκράτης *s.m.* democrat.
δημοκρατ|ία *s.f.* democracy; republic. ~ικός *a.* democratic, republican.
δημοπρασία *s.f.* auction.
δήμος *s.n.* municipality, borough.
δημοσιά *s.f.* public highway.
δημοσι|εύω *v.t.* publish, promulgate. ~ευσις *s.f.* publication. ~ευμα *s.n.* newspaper article.
δημοσιογράφος *s.m.* journalist.

δημόσ|ιος *a.* public; ~ιος ὑπάλληλος civil servant; τὸ ~ιον the state, the public. ~ία, ~ίως *adv.* in public.
δημότης *s.m.* citizen of borough.
δημοτικ|ή *s.f.* demotic Greek. ~ιστής *s.m.* partisan of δημοτική.
δημοτικ|ός *a.* municipal; ~ό σχολείο primary school; ~ό τραγούδι folk-song.
δημοτικότης *s.f.* popularity.
δημοφιλής *a.* popular (*of persons*).
δημοψήφισμα *s.n.* plebiscite.
δημώδης *a.* popular (*of the people*), folk-.
δηῶ *v.t.* ravage.
δι- *denotes two.*
διά *prep.* 1. (*with acc.*) for; because of; about, concerning; ~ τοῦτο for this reason; ~ τί why? 2. (*with gen.*) through, across; with, by means of; ~ βίου for life; ~ παντός for ever; ~ βίας by force; ~ μιᾶς at one go; ~ μακρῶν at length (*in detail*).
δια- *denotes passing through; separation; conflict; intensification.*
διαβάζω *v.t. & i.* read, study; coach, prime; hear (*person*) his lesson.
διαβάθμισις *s.f.* grading.
διαβαίνω *v.t. & i.* cross, pass.
διαβάλλω *v.t.* traduce, denigrate slyly.
διάβασις *s.f.* crossing, passage; ford, pass.
διάβασμα *s.n.* reading; studying.
διαβατήριον *s.n.* passport.
διαβάτης *s.m.* passer-by.
διαβατικός *a.* of passage, passing by; ~ δρόμος frequented street.
διαβατός *a.* negotiable, fordable.
διαβεβαι|ώνω *v.t.* assure. ~ωσις *s.f.* assurance.
διάβημα *s.n.* step (*action taken*), démarche.
διαβήτης *s.m.* 1. pair of compasses. 2. (*med.*) diabetes.
διαβιβάζω *v.t.* transmit, convey.
διαβιῶ *v.i.* live, pass one's life.
διαβλέπω *v.t.* discern (*below surface*).
διαβόητος *a.* notorious.
διαβολάνθρωπος *s.m.* very shrewd and active person, live wire; (*fig.*) devil.
διαβολεμένος *a.* very shrewd and active; (*fig.*) devilish (*hunger, etc.*).
διαβολή *s.f.* sly denigration.
διαβολικός *a.* diabolic(al), devilish.
διάβολ|ος *s.m.* devil (*also as mark of admiration*); ~ου κάλτσα very shrewd and able person.

διαβούλιον *s.n.* (secret) meeting, plot.
διάβροχος *a.* soaking wet.
διάβρωσις *s.f.* corrosion, eating away.
διάγγελμα *s.n.* edict, rescript.
διαγι(γ)νώσκω *v.t.* diagnose.
διαγκωνίζομαι *v.i.* elbow one's way.
διάγνωσις *s.f.* diagnosis.
διαγουμίζω *v.t.* pillage; waste.
διάγραμμα *s.n.* diagram, plan.
διαγράφω *v.t.* trace, describe, outline; erase, cross out *or* off.
διάγ|ω *v.i. & t.* live; pass (*time, one's life*); ~ει καλῶς he is well.
διαγωγή *s.f.* behaviour, conduct.
διαγωνίζομαι *v.i.* compete.
διαγώνιος *a.* diagonal.
διαγώνισ|μα *s.n.*, ~μός *s.m.* competition (*for award*), examination.
διαδέχομαι *v.t.* succeed.
διαδήλωσις *s.f.* (*public*) demonstration.
διάδημα *s.n.* diadem, crown.
διαδίδ|ω *v.t.* spread; noise abroad; ~εται ὅτι it is rumoured that.
διαδικασία *s.f.* procedure.
διάδικος *s.m.f.* (*law*) party to action.
διάδοσις *s.f.* spreading; rumour.
διαδοχή *s.f.* succession.
διάδοχος *s.m.* successor; crown prince.
διαδραματίζ|ω *v.t.* play (*role*). ~ομαι *v.i.* be enacted (*occur*).
διαδρομή *s.f.* run, course, distance.
διάδρομος *s.m.* passage, corridor; carpet for this; ~ προσγειώσεως (*aero.*) runway.
διαζευγνύομαι *v.i.* get divorced.
διαζύγιον *s.n.* divorce.
διάζωμα *s.n.* frieze.
διαθέσιμ|ος *a.* available, at one's disposal. ~ότης *s.f.* availability; suspension from duty.
διάθεσ|ις *s.f.* arrangement, disposition; disposal; mood, humour; (*gram.*) voice; ~εις (*pl.*) intentions.
διαθέτ|ω *v.t.* have at one's disposal; dispose, arrange; use; appropriate, devote; bequeath; μὲ ~ει καλά it puts me in a good mood *or* makes me well disposed. *See also* **διατίθεμαι**.
διαθήκη *s.f.* testament; will.
διαθλῶ *v.t.* refract.
διαίρεσις *s.f.* division; dissension.
διαιρετός *a.* divisible.
διαιρῶ *v.t.* divide.
διαίσθησις *s.f.* intuition.
δίαιτα *s.f.* diet.
διαιτησία *s.f.* arbitration.
διαιτητής *s.m.* arbitrator, referee.

διαιτῶμαι *v.i.* eat.
διαιωνίζω *v.t.* perpetuate; protract.
διακαής *a.* ardent.
διακανονίζω *v.t.* regulate, settle.
διάκειμαι *v.i.* be disposed.
διακεκαυμένος *a.* torrid.
διακεκριμένος *a.* distinguished.
διακήρυξις *s.f.* declaration, proclamation.
διάκι *s.n.* tiller, helm.
διακινδυνεύω *v.t. & i.* risk; run risks.
διακλάδωσις *s.f.* branching, fork; branch (*road, line, etc.*).
διακοίνωσις *s.f.* diplomatic note.
διακονιάρης *s.m.* beggar.
διάκονος *s.m.* deacon.
διακοπ|ή *s.f.* suspension, recess; cutting *or* breaking off; interruption, cut; ~ές (*pl.*) vacation, holidays.
διακόπτης *s.m.* switch, stopcock, main tap.
διακόπτω *v.t.* suspend; cut *or* break off; interrupt.
διακορεύω *v.t.* deflower.
διάκος *s.m.* deacon.
διακόσιοι *a.* two hundred.
διακόσμησις *s.f.* decoration; illumination (*of MSS.*).
διάκοσμος *s.m.* decoration (*of room, street, etc.*); décor.
διακοσμῶ *v.t.* decorate, adorn.
διακρίν|ω *v.t. & i.* make out, distinguish; differentiate; (*v.i.*) see. ~ομαι *v.i.* be outstanding *or* visible; distinguish oneself.
διάκρισις *s.f.* distinction, differentiation; discretion (*judgement, pleasure, choice*).
διακριτικός *a.* distinguishing; discreet; discretionary.
διακυβεύω *v.t.* risk, stake.
διακύμανσις *s.f.* fluctuation; undulation.
διακωμωδῶ *v.t.* ridicule.
διαλαλῶ *v.t.* proclaim loudly, cry (*wares*).
διαλαμβάνω *v.t.* deal with, treat of, contain.
διαλανθάνω *v.t. & i.* escape attention of; escape unnoticed.
διαλέγω *v.t.* choose, select.
διάλειμμα *s.n.* interval, break.
διαλείπων *a.* intermittent, occulting.
διαλεκτικός *a.* 1. of dialectic. 2. of dialects.
διάλεκτος *s.f.* dialect.

διάλεξις s.f. lecture.
διαλευκαίνω v.t. elucidate.
διαλεχτός a. choice, exceptional.
διαλλαγή s.f. settlement (of difference).
διαλλακτικός a. conciliatory.
διαλογή s.f. sorting, scrutiny.
διαλογίζομαι v.t. consider, ponder.
διάλογος s.m. dialogue.
διαλύζω v.t. comb.
διάλυμα s.n. (liquid) solution.
διάλυσις s.f. solution, dissolution; liquidation, disbanding, breaking off.
διαλυστήρ|α s.f., ~ι s.n. comb.
διαλυτικ|ός a. dissolvent; ~όν στοιχείον disruptive element. ~ά s.n.pl. diaeresis.
διαλυτός a. soluble.
διαλύω v.t. dissolve, liquidate, disband, break off, dispel.
διαμάντ|ι s.n. diamond. ~ικά s.n.pl. jewellery.
διαμαρτύρ|ομαι v.i. protest. ~όμενος s.m. protestant.
διαμαρτυρώ v.t. protest (bill).
διαμάχη s.f. dispute, struggle.
διαμελίζω v.t. dismember.
διαμένω v.i. reside, sojourn.
διαμέρισμα s.n. region, constituency; compartment; apartment, flat.
διαμερισμός s.m. apportionment.
διαμέσον s.n. (pej.) κάνω τό ~ act as go-between.
διάμεσ|ος a. intermediary; in between. ~ον s.n. interval, space between.
διαμετακόμισις s.f. transit (of goods).
διαμέτρημα s.n. bore, calibre.
διάμετρος s.f. diameter.
διαμονή s.f. (place of) residence, sojourn.
διαμόρφωσις s.f. formation, conformation.
διαμπάξ adv. right through (of wounds).
διαμπερής a. passing right through (of wound).
διαμφισβητώ v.t. call in question, contest.
διάνα s.f. 1. turkey. 2. bull's-eye. 3. reveille.
διανέμω v.t. distribute.
διανόημα s.n. thought (idea).
διανόησις s.f. thought (process).
διανοητικός a. intellectual; profound.
διάνοι|α s.f. intellect; έχω κατά ~αν have in mind.
διανομεύς s.m. distributor; postman.
διανομή s.f. distribution.

διανο|ούμαι v.t. & i. think (of). ~ούμενος s.m. intellectual.
διάνος s.m. turkey.
διανυκτερεύω v.i. spend the night; stay up or open all night.
διανύω v.t. cover (distance); be in the course of (specified period of time).
διαξιφισμός s.m. sword-thrust.
διάολος s.m. see διάβολος.
διαπασῶν s.f.n. (mus.) octave; tuning-fork; (fam.) στή ~ full-blast.
διαπεραιώνω v.t. ferry.
διαπεραστικός a. piercing.
διαπερ(ν)ῶ v.t. pierce; penetrate, pass through.
διαπιστεύ|ω v.t. accredit. ~τήρια s.n.pl. credentials, letters of credence.
διαπιστ|ώνω v.t. confirm, note. ~ωσις s.f. confirmation.
διάπλασις s.f. formation, conformation.
διάπλατος a. wide open.
διαπληκτίζομαι v.i. quarrel; exchange blows.
διάπλους s.m. passage, crossing (of ship).
διαπνέ|ω v.i. blow through; transpire. ~ομαι v.i. be animated (by feeling).
διαπομπεύω v.t. (fig.) pillory.
διαπορθμεύω v.t. ferry.
διαποτίζω v.t. saturate.
διαπραγματεύομαι v.i. negotiate, deal.
διαπράττω v.t. perpetrate.
διαπρεπής a. eminent.
διαπρέπω v.i. excel.
διαπύησις s.f. suppuration.
διάπυρος a. red-hot; (fig.) ardent.
διάρθρωσις s.f. articulation; structure.
διάρκεια s.f. duration.
διαρκής a. continuous; permanent.
διαρκῶ v.i. last.
διαρκῶς adv. continually, always.
διαρπάζω v.t. pillage.
διαρρέω v.i. flow through; leak (of vessel); leak out (of liquid, news, etc.); elapse; fall off (of following).
διαρρηγνύω v.t. tear, burst or break (down, open or off); ~ τά ίμάτιά μου protest one's innocence.
διαρρήδην adv. flatly.
διαρρήκτης s.m. burglar.
διάρρηξις s.f. bursting, rupture; burglary.
διαρροή s.f. leakage.
διάρροια s.f. diarrhoea.
διαρρύθμισις s.f. arrangement, disposition.

διασάλευσις s.f. disturbance; derangement.

διασάφησις s.f. clarification; (customs) declaration.

διάσεισις s.f. concussion.

διάσελο s.n. saddle (of mountain).

διάσημ|ος a. famous. ~α s.n.pl. insignia.

διασκεδάζω v.t. & i. dispel; entertain, amuse; enjoy oneself.

διασκέδασ|ις s.f. dispersion, dispelling; entertainment, amusement. ~τικός a. amusing.

διασκελίζω v.t. step over.

διασκέπτομαι v.i. deliberate.

διασκευάζω v.t. arrange, adapt (book, music, etc.).

διάσκεψις s.f. deliberation; conference.

διασκορπίζω v.t. scatter, disperse; waste.

διασπαθίζω v.t. squander (wealth).

διάσπασις s.f. splitting; distracting (of attention).

διασπείρω v.t. disseminate, scatter.

διασπορά s.f. dissemination; Dispersion.

διασπῶ v.t. split; distract (attention).

διασταλτικός a. expanding, dilating.

διάστασις s.f. separation, disagreement; dimension.

διασταυρ|ώνω v.t. cross; ~ώθηκα μαζί του I passed him. ~ωσις s.f. crossing.

διαστέλλω v.t. distinguish; dilate; expand.

διάστημα s.n. space, interval, distance.

διάστικτος a. spotted, dotted.

διαστολή s.f. distinction; expansion; (med.) diastole; (mus.) bar-line.

διαστρεβλώνω v.t. twist; distort.

διαστρεμμένος a. cantankerous.

διαστρέφω v.t. twist; distort; pervert.

διαστροφή s.f. perversion; deterioration.

διασυμμαχικός a. inter-allied.

διασύρω v.t. denigrate.

διασχίζω v.t. pass through, cross, traverse.

διασώζω v.t. save, preserve.

διαταγή s.f. order, command.

διάταγμα s.n. order (of executive authority).

διατάζω v.t. order; order about.

διατακτική s.f. (written) warrant, authority.

διάταξις s.f. arrangement; provision, stipulation; ἡμερησία ~ order of day.

διαταράσσω v.t. disturb, upset.

διατάσσω v.t. arrange; order.

διατεθειμένος a. disposed.

διατείν|ω v.t. stretch. ~ομαι v.i. assert.

διατελῶ v.i. (continue to) be; ~ πρόθυμος I remain yours truly (formula ending letter).

διατέμνω v.t. divide, intersect.

διατήρησις s.f. maintenance, preservation.

διατηρ|ῶ v.t. keep, maintain, preserve. ~οῦμαι v.i. keep; remain intact.

διατί adv. why.

διατίθεμαι v.i. be disposed.

διατιμῶ v.t. fix price of; tariff.

διατρανώνω v.t. say straightforwardly, make quite clear.

διατρέφω v.t. keep, support (family, etc.).

διατρέχ|ω v.t. run through; cover (distance); be in the course of (period, stage, etc.); ~ω κίνδυνον be in danger; τὰ ~οντα what is going on; τὰ διατρέξαντα what happened.

διάτρησις s.f. perforation, drilling.

διάτρητος a. perforated, riddled.

διατριβή s.f. sojourn; study, treatise, thesis; diatribe.

διατροφή s.f. keep, board; alimony.

διατρυπῶ v.t. pierce, perforate.

διάττων s.m. shooting star.

διατυπώνω v.t. express, formulate, word.

διατύπ|ωσις s.f. formulation, wording; ~ώσεις (pl.) formalities.

διαύγεια s.f. limpidity.

δίαυλος s.m. narrow channel, strait.

διαφαίνομαι v.i. show through, be just visible.

διαφανής a. clear, transparent.

διαφεντεύω v.t. defend; run, manage.

διαφέρω v.i. be different.

διαφεύγ|ω v.i. & t. escape, slip away; μοῦ ~ει it escapes me; ~ω τὸν κίνδυνον become out of danger.

διαφημ|ίζω v.t. make known, advertise, vaunt. ~ισις s.f. advertisement.

διαφθείρω v.t. corrupt, seduce, bribe.

διαφιλονικῶ v.t. dispute (prize, etc.).

διαφορά s.f. difference.

διαφορετικ|ός a. different, dissimilar. ~ά adv. otherwise; differently.

διαφορικός a. differential.

διάφορο s.n. profit, interest.

διάφορος a. different, dissimilar, various, mixed.

διάφραγμα s.n. diaphragm; partition.

διαφυγή s.f. escape; leak; evasion.

διαφυλάσσω v.t. preserve intact, keep.

διαφωνῶ v.i. disagree.

διαφωτίζω v.t. solve, clear up; enlighten.

διαχειμάζω v.i. winter.

διαχείρισις s.f. handling, management; supply department.

δια|χέω, **~χύνω** v.t. spread, give off; **~χύνομαι εἰς** burst into (applause, etc.).

διάχυσις s.f. diffusion; effusive welcome.

διαχυτικός a. cordial, effusive.

διάχυτος a. diffused, spread about.

διαψεύδω v.t. belie, prove false, deny.

διάψευσις s.f. belying, proving false, denial.

διβάνι s.n. divan.

διβάρι s.n. hatchery.

δίγαμος s.m.f. bigamist.

δίγλωσσος a. bilingual.

δίγνωμος a. undecided.

δίδαγμα s.n. teaching, lesson; moral.

διδακτέος a. (material) to be taught.

διδακτικός a. of teaching; didactic; educative.

διδακτορία s.f. doctorate.

διδακτός a. teachable (of subject).

δίδακτρα s.n.pl. tuition fees.

διδάκτωρ s.m.f. doctor (degree title).

διδασκαλεῖον s.n. normal school.

διδασκαλία s.f. teaching; (stage) production.

διδάσκαλος s.m. teacher; (primary) schoolmaster.

διδάσκω v.t. & i. teach; produce (play).

διδόμενον s.n. ground (motive).

δίδραχμον s.n. two-drachma piece.

δίδυμ|ος a. twin; **~α** (s.n.pl.) twins.

δίδω v.t. see **δίνω**.

διέγερσις s.f. stimulation, excitement.

διεγερτικόν s.n. stimulant.

διεθνής a. international.

διεισδύω v.i. slip in, penetrate.

διεκδικῶ v.t. lay claim to; contest.

διεκπεραιώνω v.t. dispatch, forward.

διέλευσις s.f. crossing, passing through.

διελκυστίνδα s.f. tug-of-war.

διένεξις s.f. dispute.

διενεργῶ v.t. hold, conduct.

διεξάγω v.t. hold, conduct; accomplish.

διεξοδικός a. lengthy, prolix.

διέξοδος s.f. way out, issue; outlet.

διέπω v.t. govern.

διερμην|εύς s.m.f. interpreter. **~εύω** v.t. interpret.

διέρχομαι v.t. & i. pass through, cross; spend (time).

διερωτῶμαι v.i. wonder.

δίεσις s.f. (mus.) sharp.

διεστραμμένος a. perverse; perverted.

διετία s.f. period of two years.

διευθετῶ v.t. arrange, settle.

διεύθυνσις s.f. address; direction; management.

διευθυντής s.m. director, principal; (mus.) conductor.

διευθύν|ω v.t. direct, administer; steer, drive, pilot; address, direct (letter, glance, etc.). **~ομαι** v.i. (with πρός) make for.

διευκολύνω v.t. facilitate; assist, oblige (esp. financially).

διευκρινίζω v.t. make clear; clear up; look into.

διευρύνω v.t. widen; enlarge.

διεφθαρμένος a. corrupt; immoral.

διήγημα s.n. story, tale. **~τικός** a. narrative.

διήγησις s.f. narration, narrative.

διηγοῦμαι v.t. & i. relate, tell.

διηθῶ v.t. filter.

διημερεύω v.i. spend the day.

διήμερος a. lasting two days; two days old.

διηνεκής a. continual.

διηρημένος a. divided.

διθύραμβος s.m. dithyramb.

διίσταμαι v.i. disagree.

διισχυρίζομαι v.i. assert.

δικάζω v.t. try, judge.

δικαιοδοσία s.f. jurisdiction.

δικαιολογ|ία s.f. justification, excuse. **~ῶ** v.t. justify; offer excuses for; side with.

δίκαιον s.n. justice, law, right.

δίκαι|ος a. just, fair, right; **ἔχω ~ον** be right. **~ως** adv. justly rightly.

δικαιοσύνη s.f. justice.

δικαιοῦμαι v.i. & t. (with νά or gen.) be entitled (to).

δικαιοῦχος a. entitled.

δικαίωμα s.n. right; **~τα** (pl.) dues, fees.

δικαιωματικῶς adv. of right.

δικαιώνω v.t. decide in favour of, side with; justify, vindicate.

δικαίωσις s.f. justification, vindication.

δίκαννο s.n. double-barrelled shot-gun.

δικαστήρι|ον s.n. law-court; **~α** (pl.) (fam.) litigation.

δικαστής s.m. (law) judge.

δικαστικός a. legal; a member of the judiciary.

δικέλλ|α s.f., **~ι** s.n. two-pronged fork.

δικέφαλος a. two-headed.

δίκη *s.f.* law-suit, trial; θεία ~ divine retribution.

δικηγόρος *s.m.f.* lawyer, solicitor, barrister.

δίκην *prep.* (*with gen.*) like.

δίκιο *s.n.* right; ἔχω ~ be right; παίρνω τό ~ τον I take his part.

δικλίς *s.f.* valve.

δικογραφία *s.f.* (*law*) documents of a case.

δικολάβος *s.m.* unlicensed lawyer.

δίκοπος *a.* two-edged.

δικός *a.* close, related; ~ μον my, mine, my own.

δίκοχον *s.n.* (*mil.*) forage-cap.

δικράνι *s.n.* pitchfork.

δικτατορία *s.f.* dictatorship.

δίκτυον *s.n.* net; network.

δικτυωτόν *s.n.* (wire) netting; lattice, grille; duck-board.

δίλημμα *s.n.* dilemma.

διμερής *a.* bipartite.

διμεταλλισμός *s.m.* bimetallism.

διμοιρία *s.f.* (*mil.*) platoon.

δίνη *s.f.* whirlpool, whirlwind.

δίνω *v.t.* give, grant; offer (*price*); yield, produce; ~ καί παίρνω be influential, be the rage; τον ~ στά νεῦρα I get on his nerves; ~ ἐξετάσεις take examination; τον ~ δίκιο I take his part.

διό *conj.* for which reason.

διόγκωσις *s.f.* swelling.

διόδια *s.n.pl.* toll.

δίοδος *s.f.* passage, pass, crossing; thoroughfare.

διοίκησις *s.f.* administration, command; governing body; province of governor.

διοικητ|ής *s.m.* governor, commandant. ~ικός *a.* administrative.

διοικῶ *v.t.* administer, govern, command.

διόλου *adv.* (not) at all; ὅλως ~ completely.

διομολογήσεις *s.f.pl.* Capitulations.

διονυχίζω *v.t.* examine minutely.

δίοπος *s.m.* (*naut.*) lowest rank of petty officer.

δίοπτρα *s.n.pl.* spectacles.

διόπτρα *s.f.* binoculars.

διορατικός *a.* clear-sighted.

διοργανώνω *v.t.* organize, get up.

διορθώνω *v.t.* correct, put right *or* straight; mend; reform; punish.

διόρθωσις *s.f.* correction; repair.

διορία *s.f.* time allowed, term, delay.

διορίζω *v.t.* appoint, prescribe.

διορύσσω *v.t.* dig through.

διορῶ *v.t.* see διαβλέπω.

διότι *conj.* because.

διοχετεύω *v.t.* conduct (*fluid*), pipe, carry; divert.

δίπατος *a.* two-storied.

δίπλ|α *s.f.* fold, pleat; ~ες (*pl.*) fritters.

δίπλα *adv.* near, by the side, next door; ~ σέ near, beside, next to; (*fam.*) τό κόβω ~ have a nap.

διπλά *adv.* twice as much.

διπλάνον *s.n.* biplane.

διπλανός *a.* near-by, next-door.

διπλαρώνω *v.t. & i.* accost; come alongside.

διπλάσι|ος *a.* double; twice as big. ~άζω *v.t.* double.

διπλογραφία *s.f.* double-entry book-keeping.

διπλοπόδι *adv.* cross-legged.

διπλός *a.* double.

διπλότυπον *s.n.* duplicate (*bill, etc.*).

διπλ|οῦς *a.* double; εἰς ~οῦν in duplicate.

δίπλωμα *s.n.* folding, wrapping; diploma, degree.

διπλωμάτης *s.m.* diplomat; (*fam.*) artful person.

διπλωματ|ία *s.f.* diplomacy; (*fam.*) artfulness. ~ικός *a.* diplomatic; (*fam.*) artful.

διπλωματοῦχος *a.* having diploma *or* degree.

διπλώνω *v.t.* fold, wrap (up).

δίποδον *s.n.* biped.

δίπορτ|ος *a.* (*fam.*) τό ἔχω ~ο have two strings to one's bow.

δίπους *a.* two-legged.

διπρόσωπος *a.* double-faced.

διπυρίτης *s.m.* hard tack.

δίς *adv.* twice.

δισάκκι *s.n.* (saddle) bag.

δισέγγονο *s.n.* great-grandchild.

δισεκατομμύριον *s.n.* billion.

δίσεκτον *s.n.* leap year.

δίσεχτος *a.* unlucky (*year*).

δισκίον *s.n.* (*med.*) tablet.

δισκοβόλος *s.m.* discus-thrower.

δίσκος *s.m.* discus; disk; tray; collection-plate; gramophone-record.

δισταγμός *s.m.* hesitation.

διστάζω *v.i.* hesitate.

διστακτικός *a.* hesitant.

δίστιχον *s.n.* couplet.

δίστομος *a.* two-mouthed; two-edged.

δισυπόστατος *a.* being in two places at once; showing two sides to one's character.

διττός *a.* double.

διυλίζω *v.t.* filter, distil; (*fig.*) scrutinize, screen.

διυλιστήριον *s.n.* refinery.

διφθερῖτις *s.f.* diphtheria.

δίφθογγος *s.f.* diphthong.

διφορούμενος *a.* ambiguous.

δίφραγκο *s.n.* (*fam.*) two-drachma piece.

διχάζω *v.t.* divide, split.

διχάλ|α *s.f.* pitchfork. ~ωτός *a.* forked.

διχασμός *s.m.* division; disagreement.

διχογνωμία *s.f.* difference of opinion.

διχόνοια *s.f.* dissension.

διχοτομῶ *v.t.* bisect.

δίχρονος *a.* for two years; two years old; two-stroke (*engine*).

δίχτυ *s.n.* net.

δίχως *prep.* (*with acc.*) without; μέ ~ without; ~ ἄλλο without fail.

δίψα *s.f.* thirst.

διψ|ῶ *v.i. & t.* be thirsty; thirst for; ~ασμένος thirsty.

διωγμός *s.m.* persecution.

διώκτης *s.m.* persecutor.

διώκω *v.t.* persecute; chase, pursue; dismiss, expel; prosecute.

διώνυμον *s.n.* (*math.*) binomial.

διώξιμο *s.n.* dismissal.

δίωξις *s.f.* pursuit; prosecution.

διώροφος *a.* two-storied.

διῶρυξ *s.f.* canal.

διώχνω *v.t.* send away, dismiss.

δόγης *s.m.* doge.

δόγμα *s.n.* dogma; principle.

δοθιήν *s.m.* boil.

δόκανο *s.n.* trap.

δοκάρι *s.n.* beam, girder.

δοκιμάζ|ω *v.t.* test, try on *or* out; taste, sample; attempt; undergo, suffer. ~ομαι *v.i.* suffer.

δοκιμασία *s.f.* suffering.

δοκιμαστικός *a.* trial, tentative; ~ σωλήν test-tube.

δοκιμή *s.f.* trial, testing; rehearsal; fitting (*of clothes*).

δοκίμιον *s.n.* essay; printer's proof.

δόκιμος I. *a.* of proven worth; classic. 2. *s.m.* (*naut.*) cadet; (*eccl.*) novice.

δοκός *s.f.* beam, girder.

δοκοῦν *s.n.* κατὰ τὸ ~ as one sees fit.

δολιεύομαι *v.t.* trick.

δόλιος [-i-] *a.* wily.

δόλιος [-j-] *a.* poor, unfortunate.

δολιοφθορά *s.f.* sabotage.

δολλάριον *s.n.* dollar.

δολοπλοκία *s.f.* intrigue.

δόλος *s.m.* bait, trap; guile.

δολοφόν|ος *s.m.* murderer. ~ία *s.f.* murder. ~ῶ *v.t.* murder.

δόλ|ωμα *s.n.* bait, decoy. ~ώνω *v.t.* bait.

δόνησις *s.f.* vibration; (*earthquake*) shock.

δόντι *s.n.* tooth, tusk; tine; cog; τοῦ πονεῖ τό ~ γιά αὐτή he is sweet on her; μιλῶ ἔξω ἀπό τά ~α speak straight out *or* severely.

δοντιά *s.f.* mark of a bite.

δον|ῶ *v.t.* cause to vibrate, shake. ~οῦμαι *v.i.* vibrate.

δόξ|α *s.f.* glory. ~άζω *v.t.* glorify, praise; worship, believe in.

δοξάρι *s.n.* rainbow; (*mus.*) bow.

δοξασκία *s.f.* belief.

δοξολογία *s.f.* (*eccl.*) doxology.

δορά *s.f.* skinning; (*animal's*) skin.

δορκάς *s.f.* roebuck.

δόρυ *s.n.* spear. ~φόρος *s.m.* satellite.

δοσίλογος *a.* answerable; (*fam.*) a quisling.

δόσ|ις *s.f.* giving; dose; instalment (*of payment*).

δοσοληψία *s.f.* (business) dealing.

δοτήρ *s.m.* donor.

δοτική *s.f.* (*gram.*) dative.

δούγα *s.f.* stave (*of barrel*).

δουκᾶτον *s.n.* I. duchy. 2. ducat.

δοῦλα *s.f.* maidservant.

δουλεία *s.f.* slavery, bondage.

δουλειά *s.f.* work; job, business; trouble, bother.

δούλεμα *s.n.* running-in (*use*); working up, fashioning; stirring, kneading; digging; leg-pulling.

δουλευτής *s.m.* hard *or* good worker.

δουλεύω *v.i. & t.* work, function; (*v.t.*) work for, serve; work up, fashion; stir, knead; dig (*soil*); pull leg of.

δουλικ|ός *a.* servile. ~ό *s.n.* (*fam.*) skivvy.

δουλοπάροικος *s.m.* serf.

δουλοπρεπής *a.* servile.

δοῦλος *a. & s.m.* enslaved; slave, servant.

δοῦναι *s.n.* (*fin.*) money which one owes; ~ καὶ λαβεῖν debit and credit, (*fig.*) dealings, relations.

δούξ *s.m.* duke.

δοχεῖον *s.n.* receptacle, vessel; chamber.
δραγάτης *s.m.* custodian of vineyard.
δραγουμάνος *s.m.* dragoman.
δρακόντειος *a.* Draconian.
δράκος *s.m.* ogre; dragon; unchristened baby.
δράκων *s.m.* ogre, dragon; (*fig.*) vigilant guard.
δράμα *s.n.* drama; (*fig.*) much ado. ~τικός *a.* dramatic.
δραματολόγιον *s.n.* repertory.
δραματοποιῶ *v.t.* dramatize.
δράμι(ον) *s.n.* dram; (*fig.*) small quantity.
δράξ *s.f.* handful.
δραπέτ|ης *s.m.* fugitive, escaped prisoner. ~εύω *v.i.* escape, get away.
δρᾶσις *s.f.* activity, action; ἄμεσος ~ flying squad.
δρασκελίζω *v.t.* step over.
δραστήριος *a.* active, diligent; effective.
δράστης *s.m.* doer; culprit.
δραστικός *a.* efficacious; drastic.
δράττομαι *v.t.* (*with gen.*) grasp; ~ τῆς εὐκαιρίας take the opportunity.
δραχμή *s.f.* drachma.
δρέπ|ανον, ~άνι *s.n.* sickle.
δρέπω *v.t.* pick, gather.
δριμ|ύς *a.* sharp, biting, harsh. ~έως *adv.* severely.
δρομαῖος *a.* running.
δρομάς *s.f.* dromedary.
δρομεύς *s.m.* runner.
δρομολόγιον *s.n.* itinerary, route.
δρόμ|ος *s.m.* running, race; speed; journey, distance; way, road, street; ~ο! off with you!
δροσερός *a.* cool, fresh.
δροσιά *s.f.* cool, freshness; dew.
δροσίζ|ω *v.t. & i.* cool, refresh; get cool (*of weather, drink*). ~ομαι *v.i.* cool down; quench one's thirst; (*ironic*) suffer a let-down.
δρόσος *s.f.* dew.
δρυάς *s.f.* dryad.
δρύϊνος *a.* of oak.
δρυμός *s.m.* forest.
δρῦς *s.f.* oak.
δρῶ *v.i.* act, be active.
δυαδικός *a.* dual; binary.
δυάρι *s.n.* the figure 2; deuce (*at cards*).
δυϊκός *s.m.* (*gram.*) dual.
δύναμαι *v.i.* be able, can.
δυναμικός *a.* energetic, dynamic.
δύναμ|ις *s.f.* strength, power; ~ει by virtue of; ~εις (*pl.*) (*mil.*) forces.

δυναμῖτις *s.f.* dynamite.
δυνάμωμα *s.n.* intensification; increase in strength, loudness, etc.
δυναμώνω *v.t. & i.* strengthen, intensify; (*v.i.*) gain strength *or* force.
δυναμωτικός *a.* tonic, strengthening.
δυναστεία *s.f.* dynasty; rule, reign.
δυνατά *adv.* strongly, hard; well, ably; loudly, aloud.
δυνατ|ός *a.* strong, powerful, vigorous; good, able; loud; possible; ὅσον τὸ ~όν as far as possible; βάζω τά ~ά μου do one's best.
δυνητική *s.f.* (*gram.*) conditional mood.
δύο, δυό *num.* two; καὶ τὰ ~ both; στὰ ~ in two.
δυόσμος *s.m.* mint (*herb*).
δυσ- *denotes* difficult; bad.
δυσανάβατος *a.* hard to climb.
δυσανάγνωστος *a.* illegible.
δυσανάλογος *a.* disproportionate.
δυσαναπλήρωτος *a.* hard to replace *or* fill.
δυσανασχετῶ *v.i.* fret and fume.
δυσαρέσκεια *s.f.* displeasure; coolness (*between persons*).
δυσάρεστος *a.* unpleasant.
δυσαρεστ|ῶ *v.t.* displease. ~οῦμαι *v.i.* (*with μέ*) grow cool towards.
δυσαρμονία *s.f.* disharmony.
δύσβατος *a.* difficult of passage.
δυσδιάκριτος *a.* hard to discern.
δυσειδής *a.* uncomely.
δυσεντερία *s.f.* dysentery.
δυσεύρετος *a.* hard to find, rare.
δυσθυμία *s.f.* low spirits.
δύσις *s.f.* setting (*of sun, etc.*); west; (*fig.*) decline.
δύσκαμπτος *a.* inflexible, stiff.
δυσκίνητος *a.* moving slowly; sluggish.
δυσκοίλι|ος *a.* constipated; constipating. ~ότης *s.f.* constipation.
δυσκολεύ|ω *v.t. & i.* make difficult; impede; become difficult. ~ομαι *v.i.* have difficulty; hesitate.
δυσκολία *s.f.* difficulty.
δύσκολος *a.* difficult; fussy.
δύσληπτος *a.* hard to catch, take, *or* understand.
δυσμαί *s.f.pl.* west; (*fig.*) decline.
δυσμενής *a.* adverse, unfavourable.
δύσμορφος *a.* uncomely.
δυσνόητος *a.* hard to understand.
δυσοίωνος *a.* inauspicious.
δυσοσμία *s.f.* bad smell.
δυσπεψία *s.f.* indigestion.

δύσπιστος a. incredulous, mistrustful.
δύσπνοια s.f. difficult breathing.
δυσπραγία s.f. slump; straitened circumstances.
δυσπρόσιτος a. difficult of access.
δυστοκία s.f. difficult parturition; (fig.) indecision.
δυστύχημα s.n. accident, (stroke of) misfortune.
δυστυχία s.f. unhappiness; misfortune; poverty.
δυστυχ|ής a. unhappy, unfortunate. ~ῶς adv. unfortunately.
δύστυχος a. unfortunate.
δυστυχ|ῶ v.i. suffer misfortune or poverty; ~ισμένος a. unfortunate.
δυσφημ|ίζω, ~ῶ v.t. defame, vilify. ~ησις s.f. defamation.
δυσφορία s.f. displeasure; indisposition.
δυσχέρεια s.f. difficulty.
δύσχρηστος a. unhandy, awkward (thing); rare (word).
δυσώδης a. foul-smelling.
δύτης s.m. diver.
δυτικ|ός a. west, western. ~ῶς adv. to the west.
δύω v.i. set (of sun, etc.); (fig.) decline.
δυωδία s.f. duet.
δώδεκ|α num. twelve. ~άς, ~άδα s.f. dozen. ~ατος a. twelfth.
δωδεκαδάκτυλον s.n. (med.) duodenum.
δωδεκασύλλαβος s.m. twelve-syllable line.
δῶμα s.n. flat roof; ~τα (pl.) apartments.
δωμάτιον s.n. room.
δωρε|ά s.f. bequest, donation. ~άν adv. gratis; to no purpose.
δωρητής s.m. donor.
δωρ|ίζω, ~ῶ v.t. give (as present).
δωρικός a. Doric.
δωροδοκ|ία s.f. bribery. ~ῶ v.t. bribe.
δῶρον s.n. gift, present; ~ ἄδωρον gift bringing more trouble than profit.
δωσίλογος a. see δοσίλογος.

E

ἔ int. of summons, interrogation, resignation, etc.
ἐάν conj. if.
ἔαρ s.n. spring. ~ινός a. of spring, vernal.
ἑαυτ|ός pron. (one)self; ὁ ~ός μου myself; ἀφ' ~οῦ μου of my own accord;

ὁμιλεῖ καθ' ~όν he talks to himself; καθ' ~οῦ genuinely, absolutely.
ἔβγα 1. s.n. way out; end (of month, etc.). 2. imperative of βγαίνω.
ἐβδομ|άς, ~άδα s.f week; Μεγάλη ~άς Holy Week. ~αδιαῖος a. week's; weekly. ~αδιάτικο s.n. a week's wage.
ἑβδομή|(κο)ντα num. seventy. ~κοστός a. seventieth.
ἔβδομος a. seventh.
ἔβενος s.m.f. ebony.
ἑβραϊκός a. Hebrew, Jewish.
Ἑβραῖος s.m. Jew.
ἔγγαμος a. married.
ἐγγαστρίμυθος s.m. ventriloquist.
ἐγγίζω v.t. & i. touch (upon); offend, hurt; (v.i.) approach.
ἔγγιστα adv. ὡς ~ approximately.
ἐγγλέζικος a. English.
Ἐγγλέζος s.m. Englishman.
ἐγγόνι s.n. grandchild.
ἔγγον|ος, ~ός s.m. grandson.
ἐγγράμματος a. literate, educated.
ἐγγραφή s.f. enrolment, registration.
ἔγγραφ|ος a. written, in writing. ~ον s.n. document, instrument, paper.
ἐγγράφω v.t. enrol, register.
ἐγγύη|σις s.f. guarantee; bail, security, deposit. ~τής s.m. guarantor, surety.
ἐγγύς adv. near; (prep. with gen.) near.
ἐγγυῶμαι v.t. & i. guarantee; stand surety for (with διά or περί).
ἐγείρ|ω v.t. raise, erect; waken, rouse. ~ομαι v.i. get up.
ἔγερσις s.f. erection, raising; awakening.
ἐγερτήριον s.n. reveille.
ἐγκάθετος a. hired (esp. bravo, etc.).
ἐγκαθιστ|ῶ v.t. install, establish, appoint. ~αμαι v.i. settle, establish oneself.
ἐγκαίνια s.n.pl. inauguration.
ἔγκαιρος a. timely, opportune.
ἐγκάρδιος a. cordial.
ἐγκάρσιος a. transversal.
ἐγκαρτερῶ v.i. bear up, persevere.
ἔγκατα s.n.pl. bowels, depths.
ἐγκατα|λείπω v.t. abandon; ~λελειμμένος deserted.
ἐγκατάστασις s.f. installation; settling.
ἔγκαυμα s.n. burn.
ἔγκειται v.i. εἰς ὑμᾶς ~ ἡ ἀπόφασις the decision rests with you.
ἐγκέφαλ|ος s.m. brain. ~ικός a. cerebral.
ἔγκλειστος a. imprisoned.

ἐγκλείστως *adv.* enclosed (herewith).

ἐγκλείω *v.t.* confine, enclose.

ἔγκλημα *s.n.* crime (*criminal act*). ~τίας *s.m.* criminal. ~τικός *a.* criminal. ~τικότης *s.f.* (*commission of*) crime, delinquency.

ἔγκλισις *s.f.* (*gram.*) mood; (*geom.*) inclination.

ἐγκόλπιος *a.* worn on the breast; pocket-size.

ἐγκολποῦμαι *v.t.* pocket, appropriate; take up (*protégé, idea*).

ἐγκοπή *s.f.* incision, notch.

ἐγκόσμιος *a.* worldly, mundane.

ἐγκράτεια *s.f.* sobriety, restraint; abstinence.

ἐγκρίνω *v.t.* approve (of), sanction.

ἔγκρισις *s.f.* approval.

ἔγκριτος *a.* distinguished, notable.

ἐγκύκλιος *a.* general (*education*); circular (*letter*).

ἐγκυκλοπαιδεία *s.f.* encyclopaedia.

ἐγκυμονῶ *v.i.* & *t.* be pregnant; (*fig.*) be fraught with, bode.

ἔγκυος *a.* pregnant.

ἔγκυρος *a.* authoritative; valid.

ἐγκώμιον *s.n.* eulogy.

ἔγνοια *s.f.* care, worry.

ἐγρήγορσις *s.f.* vigilance.

ἐγχείρημα *s.n.* undertaking.

ἐγχείρησις *s.f.* (*med.*) operation.

ἐγχείρισις *s.f.* handing over, delivery.

ἐγχειρίδιον *s.n.* manual; dagger.

ἔγχορδος *a.* (*mus.*) stringed.

ἔγχρωμος *a.* coloured.

ἐγχώριος *a.* native, local, of the country.

ἐγώ *pron.* I; (*s.n.*) ego. ~ισμός *s.m.* egoism; pride; conceit.

ἐδάφιον *s.n.* paragraph; verse (*of Bible*).

ἔδαφος *s.n.* ground, soil; territory. ~ιαῖος *a.* down to the ground.

ἔδεσμα *s.n.* viand, dish.

ἔδρα *s.f.* seat, see, chair; posterior; facet.

ἑδραιώνω *v.t.* strengthen, consolidate.

ἑδρεύω *v.i.* sit, reside, have one's headquarters.

ἐδῶ *adv.* here; ~ καὶ δύο χρόνια two years ago.

ἐδώδιμος *a.* edible; ~α (*s.n.pl.*) provisions.

ἐδώλιον *s.n.* seat, bench; (*naut.*) thwart.

ἐθελοντής *s.m.* volunteer.

ἐθελούσιος *a.* voluntary.

ἔθιμον *s.n.* custom, tradition. ~οτυπία *s.f.* etiquette.

ἐθνάρχης *s.m.* leader of nation.

ἐθνικισμός *s.m.* nationalism.

ἐθνικός *a.* national; gentile, heathen. ~οποιῶ *v.t.* nationalize. ~ότης *s.f.* nationality. ~όφρων *a.* nationalistic; patriotic.

ἔθνος *s.n.* nation.

ἐθνοσυνέλευσις *s.f.* national assembly.

εἰ *conj.* if; ~ δέ if not.

εἰδάλλως, ~ιῶς *adv.* if not, otherwise.

εἰδεμή *adv.* if not, otherwise.

εἰδεχθής *a.* hideous.

εἰδήμων *a.* expert in *or* on (*with* σέ *or* gen.).

εἴδησ|ις *s.f.* knowledge, intimation, notice; news; ~εις (*pl.*) news; παίρνω ~η get wind of, notice.

εἰδικεύομαι *v.i.* specialize.

εἰδικός *a.* special, specific; a specialist.

εἰδοποι|ῶ *v.t.* inform, notify. ~ησις *s.f.* notification, notice.

εἶδ|ος *s.n.* sort, kind; species; article, commodity; ~η (*pl.*) goods, ware.

εἰδότες *s.n.pl.* οἱ ~ those who know.

εἰδύλλιον *s.n.* idyll; love-affair.

εἴδωλ|ον *s.n.* idol; image. ~ολάτρης *s.m.* idolater, pagan.

εἴθε *particle* would that (*with* νά).

εἰθισμέν|ος *a.* κατὰ τὰ ~α as usual.

εἴθισται *v.i.* it is the custom.

εἰκασία *s.f.* conjecture.

εἰκαστικός *a.* 1. conjectural. 2. representative (*of fine arts*).

εἰκῆ *adv.* ~ καὶ ὡς ἔτυχε at random.

εἰκόνα *s.f.* see εἰκών.

εἰκονίζω *v.t.* depict, show.

εἰκονικός *a.* using imagery; illustrative; fictitious (*sale, etc.*).

εἰκόνισμα *s.n.* picture; (*esp.*) icon.

εἰκονογραφ|ῶ *v.t.* illustrate. ~ία *s.f.* illustration.

εἰκονοκλάστης *s.m.* iconoclast.

εἰκονοστάσι(ον) *s.n.* place where icons are hung; (*in church*) screen.

εἴκοσ|ι *num.* twenty. ~τός *a.* twentieth.

εἰκών *s.f.* image, picture; ἁγία ~ icon.

εἰλικριν|ής *a.* sincere, frank. ~εια *s.f.* sincerity, frankness.

εἵλ|ως, ~ωτας *s.m.* helot.

εἶμαι *v.i.* am.

εἱμαρμένη *s.f.* fate, destiny.

εἰμή *adv.* except, but (*after negative*).

εἰμί *v.i.* am.

εἶναι *v.i.* is, are; τὸ ~ being, existence.

εἰρημένος *a.* aforesaid.

εἰρηνεύω *v.t. & i.* pacify, calm; make peace, live in peace.

εἰρήν|η *s.f.* peace. ~ικός *a.* peaceful, peaceable, pacific.

εἰρηνοδικεῖον *s.n.* magistrate's court.

εἱρκτή *s.f.* prison.

εἱρμός *s.m.* train of thought, coherence.

εἰρων|εία *s.f.* irony. ~εύομαι *v.t. & i.* speak ironically (to).

εἰς *a. & article m.* one; a, an.

εἰς, σέ *prep. (with acc.)* at; in, among; within *(time)*; to, into; on, on to; *(oath)* on, by; στῆς Μαρίας to *or* at Mary's; ψόφιος στήν κούρασῃ dog-tired; ἐρωτεύτηκε στά καλά he fell well and truly in love; μέ πέθανε στῆ φλυαρία he wore me out with his chatter.

εἰσαγγελ|εύς *s.m. (law)* public prosecutor. ~ία *s.f.* public prosecutor's office.

εἰσάγω *v.t.* put in; bring *or* usher in, admit; introduce; import.

εἰσαγωγ|ή *s.f.* introduction, admission; import(ation); *(mus.)* overture. ~εύς *s.m.* importer.

εἰσαγωγικ|ός *a.* introductory; of admission *or* importation. ~ά *s.n.pl.* inverted commas.

εἰσβάλλω *v.i. (with* εἰς) invade, burst in; flow into *(of tributary)*.

εἰσβολ|ή *s.f.* invasion, irruption; bout *(of malady)*. ~εύς *s.m.* invader.

εἰσδύω *v.i.* penetrate, get in.

εἰσελαύνω *v.i. (with* εἰς) invade; make triumphal entry.

εἰσέρχ|ομαι *v.i. (with* εἰς) come *or* go in, enter; τά ~όμενα in-tray.

εἰσέτι *adv.* still; *(not)* yet.

εἰσέχω *v.i.* go in, be hollow, open inwards.

εἰσήγη|σις *s.f.* recommendation; report. ~τής *s.m.* proposer, rapporteur.

εἰσηγοῦμαι *v.t.* propose, moot; report on.

εἰσιτήριον *s.n.* ticket.

εἰσιτήριος *a.* of entry *or* admission.

εἰσόδημα *s.n.* revenue, return, income. ~τίας *s.m.* rentier.

εἴσοδος *s.f.* entrance, entry; admission.

εἴσπλους *s.m.* sailing in; mouth *(of harbour, etc.)*.

εἰσπνέω *v.t.* inhale.

εἰσπράκτωρ *s.m.* collector *(of moneys)*; conductor *(of vehicle)*.

εἴσπραξ|ις *s.f.* collecting *(of moneys)*; encashment; ~εις *(pl.)* takings.

εἰσπράττω *v.t.* collect *(moneys)*; cash.

εἰσφέρω *v.t.* contribute.

εἰσφορά *s.f.* contribution.

εἰσχωρῶ *v.i.* penetrate, slip in.

εἶτα *adv.* then, next.

εἴτε *adv.* ~ ... ~ either ... or, whether ... or.

ἐκ, ἐξ *prep. (with gen.)* 1. *(origin)* from. 2. *(composition)* of. 3. *(partitive)* out of, among. 4. *(manner, cause)* ~ τῆς χειρός by the hand; ~ ἀνάγκης of necessity; ~ νέου anew; ~ ἴσου equally.

ἐκ-, ἐξ- *denotes* out, off; completely. *See also* ξε-.

ἕκαστ|ος *pron.* each (one); καθ' ~ην every day; τά καθ' ~α the details.

ἑκάστοτε *adv.* each time; ἡ ~ κυβέρνησις each successive government.

ἑκάτερ|ος *pron.* each, either *(of two)*. ~ωθεν *adv.* on both sides.

ἑκατόμβη *s.f.* hecatomb.

ἑκατομμύρι|ον *s.n.* million. ~οῦχος *s.m.* millionaire.

ἑκατό(ν) *num.* a hundred; τοῖς *or* τά ~ per cent.

ἑκατονταετηρίς *s.f.* century; centenary.

ἑκατονταετής *a.* hundred years'; a centenarian.

ἑκατονταπλάσιος *a.* a hundredfold.

ἑκατόνταρχος *s.m.* centurion.

ἑκατοντούτης *s.m.* centenarian.

ἑκατοστάρ|ι *s.n.* hundred-drachma note; quarter-oka. ~ικο *s.n.* hundred-drachma note.

ἑκατοστ|ός *a.* hundredth. ~όμετρον *s.n.* centimetre.

ἐκβαίνω *v.i. see* βγαίνω.

ἐκβάλλω *v.t. & i.* take off; pull *or* have out; eject, expel; give forth, shed; utter; cast up; *(v.i.) (of rivers, roads)* flow *or* lead out *(into)*.

ἔκβασις *s.f.* outcome, issue.

ἐκβιάζω *v.t.* compel; blackmail; extort; force *(passage, etc.)*.

ἐκβολή *s.f.* ejection; mouth *(of river)*.

ἐκβράζω *v.t.* cast up.

ἐκγυμνάζω *v.t.* train, exercise.

ἐκδέρω *v.t.* flay, skin; graze.

ἔκδηλ|ος *a.* clear, apparent. ~ώνω *v.t.* show, manifest.

ἐκδίδω *v.t.* issue, publish; pronounce *(judgement)*; draw *(bill, etc.)*; extradite.

ἐκδικάζω *v.t. (law)* try *(case)*.

ἐκδίκη|σις *s.f.* revenge, vengeance. ~τής *s.m.* avenger. ~τικός *a.* revengeful, avenging.

ἐκδικοῦμαι *v.t. & i.* avenge; take revenge (on).

ἐκδιώκω *v.t.* expel, dismiss; (*mil.*) dislodge.

ἐκδορ|ά *s.f.* skinning; excoriation; abrasion. ~ιον *s.n.* blistering plaster.

ἔκδοσις *s.f.* issue, publication; edition; version, story; extradition.

ἐκδότ|ης *s.m.* publisher; drawer (*of bill*). ~ικός *a.* publishing; issuing.

ἔκδοτος *a.* addicted; dissolute.

ἐκδούλευσις *s.f.* service, favour.

ἐκδοχή *s.f.* version, interpretation.

ἐκδράμω *v.i.* θὰ ~ *future of* ἐξέδραμον.

ἐκδρομή *s.f.* excursion, outing.

ἐκδύω *v.t.* undress.

ἐκεῖ *adv.* there; ~ πού while, instead of, whereas. ~θεν *adv.* thence.

ἐκεῖνος *pron.* he, that (one).

ἐκεχειρία *s.f.* truce.

ἔκθαμβος *a.* dazzled; enraptured.

ἐκθειάζω *v.t.* praise extravagantly.

ἔκθεμα *s.n.* exhibit.

ἔκθεσις *s.f.* putting out, exposure; abandoning; exhibition; statement, report; essay.

ἐκθέτης *s.m.* exhibitor.

ἔκθετ|ος *a.* exposed. ~ον *s.n.* foundling.

ἐκθέτω *v.t.* put out in the open, expose; abandon (*child*); exhibit; expound, relate; put up to auction; put forward (*candidature*); compromise. (*See* ἐκτίθεμαι).

ἐκθλίβω *v.t.* squeeze (*lemon, etc.*); elide.

ἐκθρονίζω *v.t.* dethrone.

ἔκθυμος *a.* cordial, eager.

ἐκκαθαρίζω *v.t. & i.* settle (*account, etc.*); clarify; conclude; purge, clean up; (*v.i.*) remain as balance in hand.

ἐκκαλῶν *s.m.* (*law*) appellant.

ἐκκεντρικός *a.* eccentric.

ἐκκενῶ *v.t.* empty, clear; leave, evacuate; discharge (*gun*).

ἐκκένωσις *s.f.* emptying; (*electrical*) discharge.

ἐκκίνησις *s.f.* starting off.

ἐκκλησία *s.f.* church.

ἐκκλησιάζομαι *v.i.* go to church.

ἐκκλησίασμα *s.n.* congregation.

ἐκκλησιαστικός *a.* ecclesiastical, religious.

ἔκκλησις *s.f.* appeal.

ἐκκλίνω *v.i.* deviate.

ἐκκοκκίζω *v.t.* remove seeds of; shell; gin.

ἐκκολάπτω *v.t.* hatch.

ἐκκρεμ|ής *a.* pending, unsettled. ~ές *s.n.* pendulum.

ἐκκρίνω *v.t.* secrete (*physiologically*).

ἐκκωφαντικός *a.* deafening.

ἐκλαϊκεύω *v.t.* present in popular form.

ἐκλαμβάνω *v.t.* take, interpret, construe.

ἔκλαμπρος *a.* brilliant, eminent.

ἐκλέγω *v.t.* choose, select; elect.

ἐκλείπω *v.i.* vanish, be in eclipse; ὁ ἐκλιπών the deceased.

ἔκλειψις *s.f.* eclipse.

ἐκλεκτικός *a.* who chooses only the best.

ἐκλεκτ|ός *a.* choice, select, exceptional; elected; οἱ ~οί élite.

ἐκλελυμένος *a.* lax, dissolute.

ἐκλέξιμος *a.* eligible (*for office*).

ἐκλιπαρῶ *v.t.* beseech.

ἐκλογεύς *s.m.* elector.

ἐκλογ|ή *s.f.* choice, selection; ~αί (*pl.*) election(s). ~ικός *a.* electoral; of elections.

ἔκλυσις *s.f.* release; laxity.

ἐκμαγεῖον *s.n.* (plaster) cast.

ἐκμαιεύω *v.t.* extract, worm out (*truth, etc.*).

ἐκμανθάνω *v.t.* learn thoroughly, master.

ἐκμεταλλεύομαι *v.t.* work, exploit.

ἐκμηδενίζω *v.t.* annihilate.

ἐκμισθῶ *v.t.* let out for hire, rent. ~τής *s.m.* lessor.

ἐκμυζῶ *v.t.* suck out, drain; (*fig.*) exploit, milk.

ἐκμυστηρεύομαι *v.t.* confide (*secret*).

ἐκνευρίζω *v.t.* irritate, annoy.

ἔκνομος *a.* unlawful.

ἑκούσιος *a.* voluntary.

ἔκπαγλος *a.* breath-taking, wondrous.

ἐκπαίδευσις *s.f.* education.

ἐκπαιδευτήριον *s.n.* school.

ἐκπαιδευτικός *a.* educational; a school-teacher.

ἐκπαιδεύω *v.t.* educate, train.

ἔκπαλαι *adv.* from time immemorial.

ἐκπαρθενεύω *v.t.* deflower.

ἐκπατρίζω *v.t.* expatriate.

ἐκπέμπω *v.t.* emit, send out; broadcast (*by radio*).

ἐκπίπτω *v.i. & t.* decline in value; ~ θέσεως lose one's position; reduce in value *or* price; deduct.

ἔκπλη|ξις *s.f.* surprise. ~κτικός *a.* surprising.

ἐκπληρῶ *v.t.* fulfil, carry out.

ἐκπλήσσω *v.t.* astonish.

ἔκπλους *s.m.* departure (*of ship*).

ἐκπνέω v.t. & i. exhale; die; terminate, expire.

ἐκποιῶ v.t. sell, dispose of.

ἐκπολιτίζω v.t. civilize.

ἐκπομπή s.f. emission; (radio) broadcast.

ἐκπονῶ v.t. produce, achieve (painstakingly); train (for sports).

ἐκπορεύομαι v.i. come, proceed (from).

ἐκπορθῶ v.t. capture (city, etc.); lay waste.

ἐκπορνεύω v.t. prostitute.

ἐκπρόθεσμος a. not within prescribed time-limit.

ἐκπρόσωπ|ος s.m. representative. ~ῶ v.t. represent, act for.

ἔκπτωσις s.f. decline, fall; loss (of rights, etc.); reduction, rebate.

ἔκπτωτος a. deposed, dispossessed.

ἐκπυρσοκρότησις s.f. detonation.

ἐκρήγνυμαι v.i. explode, burst; erupt; ἐξερράγη πόλεμος war broke out.

ἐκρηκτικός a. explosive.

ἔκρηξις s.f. explosion, eruption, outbreak, outburst.

ἐκριζῶ v.t. uproot, pull out, eradicate.

ἔκρυθμος a. abnormal, irregular.

ἐκσκαφή s.f. excavation.

ἔκστασις s.f. ecstasy, wonderment.

ἐκστομίζω v.t. utter.

ἐκστρατεία s.f. campaign, expedition.

ἐκσφενδονίζω v.t. sling, fling; fire (torpedo, etc.).

ἐκτάδην adv. (lying) at full length.

ἔκτακτ|ος a. temporary, emergency; special, exceptional; excellent. ~ως adv. temporarily; exceptionally.

ἔκτασις s.f. extent, expanse; (gram.) lengthening.

ἐκτεθειμένος a. exposed; committed; compromised.

ἐκτείν|ω v.t. stretch out, extend, enlarge. ~ομαι v.i. extend.

ἐκτέλεσις s.f. execution; performance, perpetration; fulfilment.

ἐκτελεστικ|ός a. executive; ~ὸν ἀπόσπασμα firing-squad.

ἐκτελῶ v.t. execute; perform, carry out.

ἐκτενής a. extended, lengthy.

ἐκτεταμένος a. extensive; lengthy.

ἐκτίθεμαι v.i. be exposed or exhibited; be committed or compromised; ~ (ὑποψήφιος) stand for election. (See ἐκθέτω).

ἐκτιμ|ῶ v.t. esteem, value; appraise, estimate. ~ησις s.f. esteem; valuation, estimate.

ἐκτί(ν)ω v.t. serve (sentence), pay (penalty).

ἐκτομή s.f. cutting off; castration.

ἐκτοξεύω v.t. shoot (arrow); hurl.

ἐκτοπ|ίζω v.t. displace, dislodge; send into political exile. ~ισμα s.n. displacement (of fluid).

ἔκτος a. sixth.

ἐκτός adv. & prep. outside; except; ~ τῆς πόλεως outside the city; ~ τοῦ Γιάννη except John; ~ ἀπό except for, apart from; ~ ἄν unless; ~ ἑαυτοῦ beside oneself; ~ κινδύνου out of danger.

ἔκτοτε adv. from that time.

ἐκτραγωδῶ v.t. dramatize, paint in lurid colours.

ἐκτραχηλίζομαι v.i. become slovenly; let oneself go (too far).

ἐκτραχύνω v.t. (fig.) worsen (relations, etc.).

ἐκτρέπ|ω v.t. divert. ~ομαι v.i. deviate, stray; get drawn into (dispute, etc.).

ἔκτροπ|ος a. improper; ~a (s.n.pl.) unseemly behaviour.

ἐκτροχιάζομαι v.i. become derailed; (fig.) run off the rails.

ἔκτρωμα s.n. abortion, monster.

ἔκτρωσις s.f. abortion, miscarriage.

ἐκτυλίσσ|ω v.t. unwind, unwrap. ~ομαι v.i. unfold, happen.

ἐκτυπώνω v.t. emboss; print.

ἐκτυφλωτικός a. blinding.

ἐκφέρ|ω v.t. utter, express; carry to burial. ~ομαι v.i. (gram.) be construed.

ἐκφοβίζω v.t. intimidate.

ἐκφορά s.f. funeral.

ἐκφορτωτής s.m. unloader, stevedore.

ἐκφράζω v.t. express, declare.

ἔκφρασ|ις s.f. expression. ~τικός a. expressive.

ἐκφυλίζομαι v.i. abate, slacken; degenerate.

ἐκφυλισμός s.m. degeneration, corruption.

ἐκφωνῶ v.t. call (roll); deliver (speech).

ἐκχυδαΐζω v.t. vulgarize.

ἐκχύλισμα s.n. extract, essence.

ἐκχωμάτωσις s.f. clearing away of earth.

ἐκχωρῶ v.t. & i. assign, transfer, concede; make way.

ἐκών a. willingly; ~ ἄκων willy-nilly.

ἔλα v.i. come! (imperative of ἔρχομαι).

ἐλαία s.f. olive (-tree).

ἐλαιογραφία s.f. oil-painting.

ἐλαιόλαδον s.n. olive-oil.

ἔλαιον s.n. olive-oil; oil.

ἐλαιοτριβεῖον s.n. olive-press.

ἐλαιόχρους a. olive-coloured.

ἐλαιόχρωμα s.n. oil-paint.

ἐλαιώδης a. oily; containing oil.

ἐλαιών(ας) s.m. olive-grove.

ἔλασμα s.n. metal plate.

ἐλάσσων a. less, lesser; (mus.) minor.

ἐλαστικ|ός a. elastic, flexible. ~όν s.n. rubber; tyre; elastic.

ἐλ|άτη s.f., ~ατο s.n., ~ατος s.m. fir.

ἐλατήριον s.n. spring (of clock, vehicle); incentive, motive.

ἐλάττωμα s.n. fault, defect.

ἐλάττων a. see ἐλάσσων.

ἐλαττώνω v.t. lessen, reduce.

ἐλάττωσις s.f. lessening, decrease.

ἐλαύνω v.t. & i. drive; (v.i.) ride, press on.

ἐλ|άφι s.n., ~αφος s.f. deer.

ἐλαφρόπετρα s.f. pumice.

ἐλαφρ|ός, ~ύς a. light, slight; trifling; mild, weak (tea, etc.).

ἐλαφρυντικ|ός a. mitigating; ~ά (s.n. pl.) extenuating circumstances.

ἐλαφρώνω v.t. & i. lighten, ease, alleviate; feel eased or relieved; get lighter.

ἐλάχιστ|ος a. least, very small; ~ος ὅρος minimum; τουλάχιστον at least. ~α adv. very little.

Ἐλβετ|ός, ~ικός a. Swiss.

ἐλεγεῖον s.n. elegy.

ἐλεγκτής s.m. inspector.

ἐλεγκτικ|ός a. inspectoral; ~ὸν συνέδριον Audit Board.

ἔλεγχος s.m. inspection, examination; control; audit; censure, criticism; school report; ~ συνειδήσεως remorse.

ἐλέγχω v.t. inspect, examine; audit; censure; show, testify.

ἐλεειν|ός a. wretched, vile; pitiable. ~ολογῶ v.t. pity; deplore.

ἐλεήμ|ων a. merciful, compassionate. ~οσύνη s.f. (giving of) alms.

ἔλ|εος s.n. mercy, charity, compassion; τὰ ~έη τοῦ Θεοῦ wealth; δὲν ἔχω ~εος κρασί I have not a drop of wine.

ἐλευθερία s.f. liberty, freedom.

ἐλευθέριος a. liberal; generous; loose (of morals).

ἐλεύθερος a. free; unmarried.

ἐλευθερόστομος a. outspoken.

ἐλευθερόφρων a. open-minded; free-thinking.

ἐλευθερώνω v.t. set free, release; rid.

ἐλεφάντειος a. elephantine; ivory.

ἐλεφαντόδους s.m. elephant's tusk; ivory.

ἐλεφαντοστοῦν s.n. ivory.

ἐλέφας s.m. elephant.

ἐλε|ῶ v.t. give alms to; show compassion to; Κύριε ~ησον Lord have mercy!

ἐλιά s.f. olive (-tree); mole, beauty-spot.

ἐλιγμός s.m. twisting, winding; manœuvre.

ἐλικοειδής a. spiral, winding.

ἐλικοκίνητος a. propeller-driven.

ἐλικόπτερον s.n. helicopter.

ἕλιξ s.m. & f. coil, spiral; thread (of screw); volute; cochlea; tendril; propeller.

ἐλίσσομαι v.i. wind, coil; whirl round; perform evolutions.

ἕλκηθρον s.n. sledge.

ἕλκος s.n. ulcer; sore.

ἑλκυστικός a. attractive, tempting.

ἑλκύω v.t. attract, charm.

ἕλκω v.t. & i. draw, pull, tow; ~ τὴν καταγωγήν be descended (from). (v.i.) weigh.

ἑλανοδίκης s.m. judge (of contest).

ἔλλειμμα s.n. deficit, deficiency.

ἐλλειπτικός a. elliptic(al); deficient.

ἔλλειψις s.f. lack, deficiency; ellipse.

Ἕλλην(ας) s.m. Greek.

ἑλληνικός a. Greek.

ἑλληνισμός s.m. the Greek people; Hellenism.

ἑλληνιστί adv. in Greek.

ἐλλιπής a. defective, deficient.

ἐλλοχεύω v.i. lie in ambush.

ἕλξις s.f. pull; traction; attraction, charm.

ἑλονοσία s.f. malaria.

ἕλος s.n. marsh, bog.

ἐλπίζω v.i. & t. hope (for), expect.

ἐλπ|ίς s.f. expectation, hope; παρ' ~ίδα contrary to expectation.

ἐλώδ|ης a. marshy; ~εις πυρετοί malaria.

ἐμαυτόν pron. myself.

ἐμβαδόν s.n. area (measurement).

ἐμβαθύνω v.i. delve (mentally).

ἐμβάλλω v.t. insert, introduce; ~ εἰς φόβον inspire with fear; ~ εἰς πειρασμόν lead into temptation.

ἔμβασμα s.n. remittance.

ἐμβατήριον s.n. (mus.) march.

ἔμβλημα s.n. emblem, badge, motto.

ἐμβολή s.f. insertion; embolism; (naut.) collision, ramming.

ἐμβολι|άζω v.t. graft; inoculate. ~ασμός s.m. grafting; inoculation, vaccination.

ἐμβόλιμος a. intercalary.

ἐμβόλιον s.n. see μπόλι.

ἔμβολον s.n. piston; ramrod; ram (of ship); sting.

ἐμβριθής a. erudite, serious, profound.

ἐμβρόντητος a. thunderstruck.

ἔμβρυον s.n. embryo, foetus.

ἐμέ(να) pron. me.

ἐμεῖς pron. we.

ἔμετ|ος, ~ός s.m. vomiting. ~ικός a. emetic.

ἐμμανῶς adv. madly, to distraction.

ἐμμένω v.i. (with εἰς) abide by, adhere to.

ἔμμεσος a. indirect, mediate.

ἔμμετρος a. 1. in moderation. 2. in verse.

ἔμμηνα s.n.pl. menstruation.

ἔμμισθος a. paid, salaried.

ἔμμονος a. persistent, fixed.

ἐμός pron. my, mine.

ἔμπα 1. s.n. way in; beginning (of month, etc.). 2. imperative of μπαίνω.

ἐμπάθεια s.f. animosity, violent feeling.

ἐμπαίζω v.t. mock; deceive.

ἐμπεδῶ v.t. establish, consolidate.

ἐμπειρία s.f. experience, practice.

ἐμπειρικός a. empiric(al); quack.

ἐμπειρογνώμων s.m.f. expert.

ἔμπειρος a. experienced, skilled.

ἐμπεριστατωμένως adv. in detail.

ἐμπιστεύομαι v.t. & i. entrust, trust, confide.

ἐμπιστευτικός a. confidential.

ἔμπιστ|ος a. trustworthy. ~οσύνη s.f. trust, confidence.

ἔμπλαστρον s.n. (med.) plaster.

ἔμπλε|ος, ~ως a. full, replete.

ἐμπλοκή s.f. engagement; jamming (of gun).

ἐμπλουτίζω v.t. enrich; improve quality of.

ἔμπνευσις s.f. inspiration.

ἐμπνέ|ω v.t. insufflate; inspire. ~ομαι v.t. & i. conceive idea of; feel inspired.

ἐμποδίζω v.t. prevent, hinder, obstruct, prohibit.

ἐμπόδιον s.n. hindrance, obstacle.

ἐμποιῶ v.t. cause, inspire.

ἐμπόλεμος a. belligerent, at war; ~ δύναμις war footing; ~ ζώνη zone of hostilities.

ἐμπόρευμα s.n. merchandise.

ἐμπορεύομαι v.i. & t. be in commerce; trade or deal in; traffic in, exploit.

ἐμπορικ|ός a. commercial, mercantile. ~όν s.n. shop selling textiles; clothier's; haberdasher's.

ἐμπόριον s.n. trade, commerce.

ἔμπορος s.m. merchant, tradesman, vendor.

ἐμποροϋπάλληλος s.m.f. shop-assistant.

ἐμποτίζω v.t. impregnate, imbue.

ἔμπρακτος a. real, actual, put into practice.

ἐμπρησ|μός s.m. arson. ~τικός a. incendiary.

ἐμπρόθεσμος a. within prescribed time-limit.

ἐμπρός adv. & prep. forward(s), ahead, in front; ~ σέ in front of, compared with; ~ ἀπό before, in front of; ~ μου in front of me; βάζω ~ start, set in motion, scold; πηγαίνω ~ do well, succeed; τὸ ρολόϊ πάει ~ the clock is fast; ~! hallo! (on telephone); come in!

ἔμπροσθεν adv. & prep. in front; previously; (with gen.) in front of; (as a.) (in) front, previous.

ἐμπρόσθιος a. (in) front, fore.

ἔμπυ|ο s.n. pus. ~άζω v.i. suppurate.

ἐμφαίνω v.t. show, indicate.

ἐμφανής a. manifest; prominent.

ἐμφανίζ|ω v.t. show, reveal; (photography) develop. ~ομαι v.i. appear, present oneself.

ἐμφάνισις s.f. appearance; presentation; (photography) developing.

ἔμφασις s.f. emphasis, stress.

ἐμφιλοχωρῶ v.i. creep in (of errors, etc.).

ἔμφοβος a. frightened.

ἐμφορούμαι v.i. be animated (by).

ἔμφροντις a. pensive, worried.

ἐμφύλιος a. ~ πόλεμος civil war.

ἐμφυσῶ v.t. insufflate; instil.

ἐμφυτεύω v.t. plant, implant.

ἔμφυτ|ος a. innate. ~ον s.n. instinct.

ἐμφωλεύω v.i. nestle; lurk.

ἔμψυχ|ος a. animate, living. ~ώνω v.t. enliven, encourage.

ἐν prep. (with dat.) in; ~ τούτοις however; ~ τάξει all right.

ἕν(α) num. & article n. one; a, an. See also ἕνας.

ἐναγκαλίζομαι v.t. embrace.

ἐνάγ|ω v.t. (law) sue; ~ων plaintiff; ~όμενος defendant.

ἐναγωνίως adv. anxiously, impatiently.

ἐναέριος *a.* aerial, by air, overhead.

ἐνάλιος *a.* found in the sea, marine.

ἐναλλαγή *s.f.* alternation; exchange.

ἐναλλάξ *adv.* alternately.

ἐναλλάσσω *v.t.* alternate.

ἔναντι *prep.* (*with gen.*) towards (*in part payment*); against (*receipt*).

ἐνάντια *adv.* contrarily, adversely; ~ σέ against.

ἐναντίον *adv.* & *prep.* (*with gen.*) against.

ἐναντίον *s.n.* opposite.

ἐνάντ|ιος, ~ίος *a.* contrary, adverse; opposed; ἀπ' ~ίας on the contrary.

ἐναντιοῦμαι *v.t.* & *i.* (*with gen. or* εἰς) oppose, thwart.

ἐναποθέτω *v.t.* place, repose.

ἐναπόκειται *v.i.* σὲ σένα ~ it rests with you.

ἐναργής *a.* clear, lucid; evident.

ἐνάρετος *a.* virtuous.

ἔναρθρος *a.* articulate; (*gram.*) with definite article.

ἐναρκτήριος *a.* inaugural, opening.

ἐναρμονίζω *v.t.* harmonize.

ἔναρξ|ις *s.f.* opening, beginning.

ἔνας *a.* & *article m.* one; a, an; ~ ~ one by one; ~ κι ~ especially good *or* bad; ὁ ~ τὸν ἄλλον one another.

ἐνασχόλησις *s.f.* occupation.

ἔνατος *a.* ninth.

ἔνδακρυς *a.* tearful.

ἔνδεια *s.f.* want, penury.

ἐνδεικν|ύω *v.t.* indicate. ~υμαι, ~ύομαι *v.i.* be called for *or* necessary.

ἐνδεικτικ|ός *a.* indicative. ~όν *s.n.* certificate (*scholastic*).

ἔνδειξις *s.f.* mark, indication.

ἕνδεκα *num.* eleven.

ἐνδελεχής *a.* assiduous.

ἐνδέχ|εται *v.i.* it is likely, there is a possibility; ~όμενον eventuality.

ἐνδημικός *a.* endemic.

ἐνδιαιτῶμαι *v.i.* (*with* εἰς) dwell, inhabit.

ἐνδιάμεσος *a.* in between; intervening.

ἐνδιατρίβω *v.i.* sojourn; dwell *or* insist (*on*).

ἐνδιαφέρον *s.n.* interest, concern.

ἐνδιαφέρ|ω *v.t.* interest, concern. ~ομαι *v.i.* be interested (*with* γιά *or* νά).

ἐνδιαφέρων *a.* interesting.

ἐνδίδω *v.i.* give way, give in.

ἔνδικος *a.* legal.

ἐνδοιάζω *v.i.* hesitate, be undecided.

ἐνδόμυχος *a.* interior, inward.

ἔνδ|ον *adv.* & *prep.* (*with gen.*) within.

~ότερα *s.n.pl.* innermost parts; inside story.

ἔνδοξος *a.* glorious, renowned.

ἐνδοτικός *a.* ready to make concessions; concessive.

ἐνδοχώρα *s.f.* hinterland.

ἔνδυμα *s.n.* garment; dress, attire. ~σία *s.f.* suit, dress; attire.

ἐνδύ|ω *v.t.* dress. ~ομαι *v.i.* & *t.* get dressed; put on.

ἐνέδρ|α *s.f.* ambush. ~εύω *v.t.* & *i.* (lie in) ambush.

ἕνεκ|α, ~εν *prep.* (*with gen.*) on account of.

ἐνενή(κο)ντα *num.* ninety.

ἐνεός *a.* dumbfounded.

ἐνέργεια *s.f.* activity, action, operation; effort; energy.

ἐνεργητικ|ός *a.* energetic; active; (*med.*) laxative. ~όν *s.n.* assets; εἰς τὸ ~όν του to his credit (*morally*). ~ότης *s.f.* activeness.

ἐνεργός *a.* active, operational; effective.

ἐνεργ|ῶ *v.i.* & *t.* act, take steps; hold, carry out; open bowels of. ~οῦμαι *v.i.* take place; pass motion of bowels.

ἔνεσις *s.f.* injection.

ἐνεστώς *a.* present; (*gram.*) ὁ ~ present tense.

ἐνετικός *a.* Venetian.

ἐνέχυρ|ον *s.n.* pawn, pledge. ~οδανειστής *s.m.* pawnbroker.

ἐνέχ|ω *v.t.* contain. ~ομαι *v.i.* be implicated.

ἐνῆλ|ιξ, ~ικος *a.* of age, major. ~ικιοῦμαι *v.i.* come of age.

ἐνήμερ|ος *a.* aware, informed. ~ώνω *v.t.* inform; bring up to date.

ἔνθα *adv.* where.

ἐνθάδε *adv.* here.

ἐνθαρρ|ύνω *v.t.* encourage. ~υνσις *s.f.* encouragement.

ἔνθεν *adv.* hence; ~ καὶ ~ on both sides.

ἔνθερμος *a.* warm, fervent.

ἐνθουσιάζ|ω *v.t.* fill with enthusiasm. ~ομαι *v.i.* become enthusiastic.

ἐνθουσιασμός *s.m.* enthusiasm.

ἐνθουσιαστικός *a.* inspiring enthusiasm.

ἐνθουσιώδης *a.* enthusiastic.

ἐνθυλακώνω *v.t.* pocket.

ἐνθυμίζ|ω *v.t.* bring to mind; μοῦ ~ει τὸν Πέτρο he reminds me of Peter.

ἐνθύμιον *s.n.* reminder, souvenir.

ἐνθυμοῦμαι *v.t.* remember, recall.

ἑνιαῖος *a.* single, unified.

ἐνιαύσιος *a.* annual; lasting one year.

ἐνιαυτός *s.m.* year.

ἑνικός *a.* (*gram.*) singular.

ἔνιοι *pron.* (*pl.*) some.

ἐνίοτε *adv.* sometimes.

ἐνισχ|ύω *v.t.* strengthen, reinforce; confirm. ~υσις *s.f.* strengthening, reinforcement.

ἐννέα *num.* nine. ~κόσιοι *a.* nine hundred.

ἐννιά *num.* nine.

ἐννιάμερα *s.n.pl.* prayers on ninth day after death.

ἔννοια (-ι-) *s.f.* idea, concept; meaning.

ἔννοια (-j-) *s.f.* care; worry; ~ σου take care! (*threat*) *or* don't worry! ἄλλη ~ δὲν ἔχω I couldn't care less.

ἔννομος *a.* legal.

ἐννο|ῶ *v.t.* mean; intend; expect, require; understand; notice; ~εῖται naturally *or* it is understood.

ἐνοικιάζ|ω *v.t.* let, rent, hire (*of either party*); ~εται 'to let'.

ἐνοικιαστήριον *s.n.* lease; 'to let' notice.

ἐνοικιαστής *s.m.* lessee, tenant.

ἐνοίκι|ον *s.n.* hire; rent. ~οστάσιον *s.n.* rent-control.

ἔνοικος *s.m.* occupant, inmate.

ἐνόν *s.n.* what is possible; θὰ φᾶμε ἐκ τῶν ~των we shall take pot luck.

ἔνοπλος *a.* armed.

ἐνοποιῶ *v.t.* unify.

ἐνόρασις *s.f.* intuition.

ἐνόργανος *a.* organic; instrumental; with instruments.

ἐνορία *s.f.* parish.

ἔνορκ|ος *a.* sworn; a juryman. ~ως *adv.* on oath.

ἐνορχήστρωσις *s.f.* orchestration.

ἐνόσω *adv.* while, as long as.

ἑνότης *s.f.* unity.

ἐνοχή *s.f.* guilt, culpability.

ἐνοχλ|ῶ *v.t.* annoy, trouble; molest, pester. ~ησις *s.f.* annoyance, trouble. ~ητικός *a.* annoying, troublesome.

ἔνοχ|ος *a.* guilty, culpable. ~οποιῶ *v.t.* inculpate.

ἐνσάρκωσις *s.f.* incarnation.

ἔνσημ|ος *a.* stamped. ~ον *s.n.* stamp (*for insurance, etc.*).

ἐνσκήπτω *v.i.* break out; appear *or* happen suddenly; burst upon the scene.

ἐνσπείρω *v.t.* sow, spread (*discord, etc.*).

ἐνσταλάζω *v.t.* pour drop by drop; instil.

ἔνστασις *s.f.* objection; (*law*) demurrer.

ἐνστερνίζομαι *v.t.* embrace, adopt.

ἔνστικτ|ος *a.* instinctive. ~ον *s.n.* instinct.

ἔνσφαιρ|ος *a.* with bullets; ~ον φυσίγγιον ball cartridge; ~α πυρά live shots.

ἐνσφράγιστος *a.* under seal.

ἔνταλμα *s.n.* warrant, writ.

ἔντασις *s.f.* stretching, strain; strength, intensity; intensification.

ἐντατικός *a.* strong, intensive; aphrodisiac.

ἐνταῦθα *adv.* here; local (*in postal address*).

ἐνταφιάζω *v.t.* inter.

ἐντείνω *v.t.* stretch; intensify, increase; raise (*voice*).

ἔντεκα *num.* eleven.

ἐντέλεια *s.f.* perfection.

ἐντελ|ής *a.* perfect, complete. ~ῶς *adv.* completely, quite.

ἐντέλλομαι *v.t. & i.* order, bid; be ordered.

ἐντερικ|ός *a.* intestinal. ~ά (*s.n.pl.*) diarrhoea.

ἐντεριώνη *s.f.* pith.

ἔντερον *s.n.* intestine, bowel.

ἐντεταλμένος *a.* charged (*with*), responsible (*for*); a delegate.

ἐντεῦθεν *adv.* hence; (*with gen.*) on this side of.

ἐντευκτήριον *s.n.* club, meeting-place, reception-room.

ἔντεχνος *a.* skilful, adroit.

ἔντιμος *a.* honest, honourable.

ἔντοκος *a.* bearing interest.

ἐντολ|ή *s.f.* order; mandate; authorization; δέκα ~αί Ten Commandments.

ἐντομή *s.f.* incision.

ἔντομ|ον *s.n.* insect. ~οκτόνον *s.n.* insecticide. ~ολόγος *s.m.* entomologist.

ἔντονος *a.* vigorous; strong, vivid, intense.

ἐντοπίζω *v.t.* confine, localize.

ἐντόπιος *a.* local, native.

ἐντός *adv. & prep.* inside, within; ~ τῆς πόλεως inside the city; ~ ὀλίγου shortly; ἡ ~ ἐπιφάνεια the inner surface.

ἐντόσθια *s.n.pl.* entrails.

ἐντράδα *s.f.* dish of meat with vegetables.

ἐντρ- *see also* ντρ-.

ἐντριβή *s.f.* friction, massage.

ἐντριβής *a.* versed, experienced.

ἐντρυφῶ *v.i.* (*with εἰς*) take delight in.

ἔντυπ|ος *a.* printed. ~ον *s.n.* printed matter; form.

ἐντύπωσ|ις *s.f.* impression; sensation. ~ιακός *a.* impressive.

ἔνυδρος *a.* aquatic; hydrate.
ἐνυπόθηκος *a.* on mortgage.
ἐνῶ *conj.* while; although.
ἐνωμοτάρχης *s.m.* sergeant of gendarmerie.
ἐνωμοτία *s.f.* squad.
ἐνώνω *v.t.* join, unite.
ἐνώπιον *prep.* (*with gen.*) before, in presence of.
ἐνωρίς *adv.* early.
ἔνωσις *s.f.* union, combination; short circuit.
ἐξ *prep. see* ἐκ.
ἕξ *num.* six.
ἐξαγόμενον *s.n.* conclusion; (*math.*) product, result.
ἐξαγοράζω *v.t.* avoid by payment, buy off; acquire by payment; redeem, ransom; secure by bribery.
ἐξαγριώνω *v.t.* make fierce, infuriate.
ἐξάγω *v.t.* take *or* bring out, extract; export; deduce, infer.
ἐξαγωγή|ή *s.f.* export(ation); extraction. ~εύς *s.m.* exporter.
ἐξάδελφος *s.m.* cousin.
ἐξαερίζω *v.t.* ventilate.
ἐξαερῶ *v.t.* vaporize; gasify.
ἐξαίρεσ|ις *s.f.* exception; exemption; extraction; κατ' ~ιν by way of exception.
ἐξαιρετικ|ός *a.* exceptional; beyond the usual degree; special, excellent. ~ά *adv.* very, exceptionally.
ἐξαίρ|ετος *a.* excellent, specially good. ~ετα *adv.* very well, famously. ~έτως *adv.* particularly (*of good qualities*).
ἐξαίρω *v.t.* stress, bring out; sing praises of.
ἐξαιρῶ *v.t.* except; exempt.
ἐξαίσιος *a.* superb.
ἐξαίφνης *adv.* suddenly.
ἐξακολουθῶ *v.t.* & *i.* continue.
ἐξακοντίζω *v.t.* hurl, fling.
ἐξακόσιοι *a.* six hundred.
ἐξακριβώνω *v.t.* verify, ascertain.
ἐξαλείφω *v.t.* efface, erase, remove.
ἔξαλλος *a.* beside oneself.
ἐξάμβλωμα *s.n.* abortion, monstrosity.
ἐξάμετρον *s.n.* hexameter.
ἐξάμην|ον *s.n.*, ~ία *s.f.* six months; rent *or* pay for such period.
ἐξαναγκάζω *v.t.* compel.
ἐξανδραποδίζω *v.t.* enslave, subdue.
ἐξάνθημα *s.n.* eruption (*on skin*).
ἐξανίσταμαι *v.i.* revolt, protest.
ἐξαντλῶ *v.t.* use up, exhaust.

ἐξάπαντος *adv.* for a certainty, without fail.
ἐξαπατῶ *v.t.* cheat, delude, deceive.
ἐξαπίνης *adv.* unawares.
ἐξάπλωσις *s.f.* spread(ing).
ἐξαποδῶ(ς) *s.m.* (*fam.*) the devil.
ἐξαπολύω *v.t.* unleash.
ἐξάπτω *v.t.* excite, inflame.
ἐξαργυρώνω *v.t.* cash.
ἐξάρθρωσις *s.f.* dislocation.
ἐξάρτημα *s.n.* attachment; ~τα (*pl.*) gear, tackle.
ἐξάρτησις *s.f.* dependence.
ἐξάρτια *s.n.pl.* (*naut.*) shrouds.
ἐξάρτυσις *s.f.* (*mil.*) soldier's equipment.
ἐξαρτῶμαι *v.i.* depend.
ἔξαρχος *s.m.* exarch.
ἐξασθένησις *s.f.* enfeeblement, weakening.
ἐξασκ|ῶ *v.t.* exercise, drill; discharge (*function*); practise (*profession*); exert (*pressure, etc.*). ~ησις *s.f.* exercise, practice.
ἐξασφαλίζω *v.t.* make certain of, assure; book, reserve.
ἐξατμίζ|ω *v.t.* evaporate; (*v.i.*) give off steam. ~ομαι *v.i.* evaporate.
ἐξάτμισις *s.f.* evaporation; exhaust (*of motor*).
ἐξαϋλῶ *v.t.* render incorporeal; reduce to a shadow.
ἐξαφαν|ίζω *v.t.* make disappear; wipe out, eliminate. ~ίζομαι *v.i.* disappear; ~ισθέντες (*pl.*) (*mil.*) missing.
ἔξαφν|ος *a.* sudden, unexpected. ~α *adv.* suddenly; for instance.
ἐξαχνίζω *v.t.* sublimate.
ἐξαχρειώνω *v.t.* corrupt, deprave.
ἔξαψις *s.f.* heat, fit of anger *or* excitement; flushing.
ἐξεγείρ|ω *v.t.* rouse. ~ομαι *v.i.* rise, revolt.
ἐξέδρα *s.f.* (*spectators'*) stand; pier.
ἐξέδραμον *v.i.* (*aorist*) went for an outing.
ἐξεζητημένος *a.* far-fetched, recherché.
ἐξε(ι)λιγμένος *a.* developed, advanced.
ἐξελικτικός *a.* evolutionary; capable of developing.
ἐξέλιξις *s.f.* evolution, development.
ἐξελίσσομαι *v.i.* evolve, develop, unfold.
ἐξελληνίζω *v.t.* hellenize; translate into Greek.
ἐξεμῶ *v.t.* vomit.
ἐξεπίτηδες *adv.* on purpose.
ἐξερευν|ῶ *v.t.* explore, investigate. ~ητής *s.m.* explorer.

ἐξέρχ|ομαι v.i. go or come out, leave : τὰ ∼όμενα out-tray.

ἐξετάζω v.t. examine, interrogate.

ἐξέτασις s.f. examination, interrogation.

ἐξέταστρα s.n.pl. examination fees.

ἐξευγενίζω v.t. ennoble; improve (stock).

ἐξευμενίζω v.t. propitiate.

ἐξευρ|ίσκω v.t. manage to find. ∼εσις s.f. finding.

ἐξευτελίζω v.t. cheapen, lower.

ἐξέχ|ω v.i. stand out. ∼ων a. prominent.

ἐξήγησις s.f. explanation, exposition; translation.

ἐξηγ|ῶ v.t. explain, interpret. ∼οῦμαι v.i. make oneself clear, explain.

ἐξή(κο)ντα num. sixty.

ἐξημερῶ v.t. tame, civilize.

ἐξημμένος a. heated; conceited.

ἐξηνταβελόνης s.m. miser.

ἐξηντλημένος a. used up, exhausted.

ἐξῆς adv. ὡς ∼ as follows; τὰ ∼ the following; εἰς τὸ ∼ from now on; καὶ οὕτω καθ' ∼ and so on.

ἐξιδανικεύω v.t. idealize.

ἐξιλεών|ω v.t. appease. ∼ομαι v.i. find forgiveness.

ἕξις s.f. habit.

ἐξίσταμαι v.i. be filled with wonder.

ἐξίσωσις s.f. equalizing, balancing; (math.) equation.

ἐξιχνιάζω v.t. ferret out, discover.

ἐξοβελίζω v.t. strike out, reject; get rid of.

ἐξόγκωμα s.n. swelling; protuberance.

ἐξογκώνω v.t. swell; exaggerate.

ἐξόγκωσις s.f. swelling; exaggeration.

ἐξοδεύ|ω v.t. spend, consume, use (up); sell (of shops); waste. ∼ομαι v.i. be put to expense.

ἔξοδον s.n. expense.

ἔξοδος s.f. going out; way out, exit; sortie; retirement.

ἐξοικειώνω v.t. accustom, familiarize.

ἐξοικονομ|ῶ v.t. manage to find; fix up (person); meet (situation). ∼οῦμαι v.i. make do.

ἐξοκέλλω v.i. run aground; go astray.

ἐξολοθρεύω v.t. exterminate.

ἐξομαλύνω v.t. make level; smooth down.

ἐξομοιώνω v.t. liken, compare.

ἐξομολόγησις s.f. confession.

ἐξομολογ|ῶ v.t. confess (penitent). ∼οῦμαι v.t. & i. acknowledge, confess.

ἐξόν prep. except; ∼ ἂν unless.

ἐξοντῶ v.t. annihilate.

ἐξονυχίζω v.t. examine minutely.

ἐξοπλίζω v.t. arm.

ἐξοργίζω v.t. anger.

ἐξορ|ία s.f. banishment, exile. ∼ίζω v.t. banish, exile.

ἐξορκίζω v.t. conjure; exorcise.

ἐξορμῶ v.i. rush forth; make a sortie.

ἐξορύσσω v.t. dig up; pluck out.

ἐξοστρακίζω v.t. ostracize; get rid of.

ἐξουδετερῶ v.t. neutralize.

ἐξουθενίζω v.t. defeat or exhaust utterly.

ἐξουσία s.f. power, authority, right.

ἐξουσιάζω v.i. & t. be in authority (over).

ἐξουσιοδοτῶ v.t. authorize, charge.

ἐξόφθαλμος a. with protuberant eyes; clear as daylight.

ἐξοφλ|ῶ v.t. & i. pay off, discharge (debt); (v.i.) have done (with); be finished, have exhausted one's talent. ∼ησις s.f. payment of debt, settlement.

ἐξοχ|ή s.f. 1. country(side), rural spot or resort. 2. protrusion; κατ' ∼ήν preeminently.

ἐξοχικός a. country, rural.

ἔξ|οχος a. eminent; excellent. ∼όχως adv. particularly, very.

ἐξοχότης s.f. excellence; leading light; ἡ αὐτοῦ ∼ His Excellency.

ἐξύβρισις s.f. abuse.

ἐξυγιαίνω v.t. cleanse; restore to healthy condition.

ἐξυμνῶ v.t. glorify, sing praises of.

ἐξυπακούεται v.i. it is understood (supplied mentally).

ἐξυπηρέτ|ησις s.f. service, assistance. ∼ικός a. helpful, of service.

ἐξυπηρετῶ v.t. serve, assist, be of service to.

ἔξυπν|ος a. wide-awake, smart, clever, intelligent. ∼άδα s.f. cleverness.

ἐξυπνῶ v.t. & i. wake up.

ἐξυφαίνω v.t. weave; (fig.) hatch (plot).

ἐξυψώνω v.t. elevate; exalt.

ἔξω adv. & prep. out, outside; abroad; ἀπ' ∼ (from) outside, by heart; ἀπ' ∼ ἀπ' ∼ in a roundabout way; ∼ τῆς πόλεως outside the city; ∼ ἀπό outside, except for; μιὰ κι' ∼ in one go; ∼ νοῦ away with cares!

ἐξώγαμος a. illegitimate, bastard.

ἐξώδικος a. unofficial.

ἔξωθεν adv. from outside or abroad; outward(ly).

ἐξώθυρα s.f. outside door.

ἐξωθῶ v.t. push, drive (to action).

ἐξωκκλήσιον s.n. country chapel.

ἐξώλης a. depraved; (fam.) ~ καὶ προώλης a thoroughly bad lot.

ἔξωμος a. décolleté.

ἐξωμότης s.m. renegade.

ἐξώπορτα s.f. outside door.

ἐξωραΐζω v.t. beautify.

ἐξώρας adv. late.

ἔξωσις s.f. expulsion, eviction.

ἐξώστης s.m. balcony.

ἐξωτερικεύ|ω v.t. reveal (thoughts, feelings). ~ομαι v.i. reveal one's thoughts or feelings.

ἐξωτερικ|ός a. external, exterior; foreign. ~όν s.n. exterior; outward appearance; foreign parts.

ἐξωτικ|ός a. exotic; (eccl.) lay. ~ό s.n. supernatural being.

ἐξωφρενικός a. mad, crazy; maddening; inconceivable.

ἐξωφρενισμός s.m. extravagance, eccentricity.

ἐξώφυλλον s.n. cover (of book); outside shutter.

ἑορτάζω v.t. & i. celebrate; celebrate one's name-day or patronal festival.

ἑορτάσιμος a. observed as a holiday; festive.

ἑορτή s.f. festival, holiday; name-day.

ἐπαγγελία s.f. promise.

ἐπαγγέλλομαι v.t. promise; be by profession; profess to be.

ἐπάγγελμα s.n. profession, trade, calling.

ἐπαγγελματίας s.m. one who plys a trade or profession (not as employee); professional.

ἐπαγρυπνῶ v.i. (with ἐπί) watch over, look after.

ἐπαγωγ|ή s.f. induction. ~ικός a. 1. inductive. 2. charming.

ἔπαθλον s.n. prize, reward.

ἔπαιν|ος s.m. praise; honourable mention. ~ῶ v.t. praise, commend.

ἐπαίρομαι v.i. be puffed up, swagger.

ἐπαισθητός a. perceptible, appreciable.

ἐπαίσχυντος a. shameful.

ἐπαίτης s.m. beggar.

ἐπακόλουθα s.n.pl. consequences.

ἐπακολουθῶ v.t. & i. follow; ensue.

ἔπακρον s.n. εἰς τὸ ~ in the highest degree.

ἐπάκτιος a. coastal.

ἐπαλείφω v.t. rub or paint (with medicament).

ἐπαληθεύω v.i. & t. come true; verify.

ἐπάλληλος a. successive.

ἔπαλξ|ις s.f. battlement; ἐπὶ τῶν ~εων in the forefront of battle.

ἐπαμφοτερίζω v.i. waver; be ambiguous.

ἐπαν(α)- denotes again, back, upon.

ἐπάναγκες a. necessary.

ἐπανάγω v.t. bring back.

ἐπανακάμπτω v.i. return.

ἐπανακτῶ v.t. get back.

ἐπαναλαμβάνω v.t. & i. resume; repeat.

ἐπανάληψ|ις s.f. resumption; repetition; κατ' ~ιν repeatedly.

ἐπαναπαύομαι v.i. rest (on one's laurels); rely or count (on).

ἐπανάστασις s.f. revolution.

ἐπαναστάτ|ης s.m. insurgent; revolutionary. ~ικός a. revolutionary.

ἐπαναστατῶ v.i. & t. rebel, revolt; rouse to rebellion; upset.

ἐπανασυνδέω v.t. re-establish (connexion), join together again.

ἐπαναφέρω v.t. bring back, restore; recall (to mind).

ἐπανειλημμέν|ος a. repeated. ~ως adv. repeatedly.

ἐπανέρχομαι v.i. come back.

ἐπάνοδος s.f. return.

ἐπανορθ|ώνω v.t. redress, rectify. ~ωσις s.f. reparation.

ἐπάνω adv. see ἀπάνω.

ἐπανωφόρι s.n. overcoat.

ἐπαξίως adv. fittingly, deservedly.

ἐπαπειλ|ῶ v.t. threaten; ~εῖται (v.i.) it threatens.

ἐπάρατος a. accursed.

ἐπάργυρος a. silver-plated.

ἐπάρκεια s.f. sufficiency.

ἔπαρσις s.f. hoisting; conceit.

ἐπαρχί|α s.f. eparchy (administrative division); (fig.) the provinces. ~ώτης s.m. provincial; ~ώτικος a. provincial.

ἔπαυλις s.f. villa.

ἐπαύριον adv. ἡ ~ the next day, tomorrow.

ἐπαφή s.f. touch, contact.

ἐπαχθής a. burdensome.

ἐπείγ|ω v.i. be urgent. ~ομαι v.i. be in a hurry.

ἐπείγ|ων a. urgent. ~όντως adv. urgently, hurriedly.

ἐπειδή conj. since, because.

ἐπεισόδιον s.n. incident, episode; scene, row.

ἔπειτα adv. then, next; besides; ~ ἀπό after.

ἐπέκτασις *s.f.* extension; spreading.

ἐπεκτείνω *v.t.* extend; spread.

ἐπεμβαίνω *v.i.* intervene; interfere.

ἐπέμβασις *s.f.* intervention; interference; (*med.*) operation.

ἐπένδυσις *s.f.* facing, lining, covering; (*fin.*) investment.

ἐπενεργῶ *v.i.* act, produce an effect (on).

ἐπεξεργασία *s.f.* polishing up (*of speech, etc.*); processing (*of materials*).

ἐπεξήγησις *s.f.* elucidation.

ἐπέρχομαι *v.i.* come on suddenly, occur; (*with κατά*) attack.

ἐπερώτησις *s.f.* interpellation.

ἐπέτειος *s.f.* anniversary.

ἐπετηρίς *s.f.* anniversary; year-book; (*army, etc.*) list.

ἐπευφημῶ *v.t.* cheer, acclaim.

ἐπήκο|ος *a.* εἰς ~ον πάντων in everyone's hearing.

ἐπηρεάζω *v.t.* influence; have (bad) effect on.

ἐπήρεια *s.f.* influence.

ἐπηρμένος *a.* puffed up with pride.

ἐπί *prep.* 1. (*with acc.*) towards; for (*duration*); ~ πλέον in addition; ~ τὰ βελτίω for the better. 2. (*with gen.*) on; in the time of, under; ~ τέλους at last; ~ κεφαλῆς at the head. 3. (*with dat.*) (*occasion, circumstance*) ~ τῇ εὐκαιρίᾳ by the way, on the occasion of; ~ κλοπῇ (*charge*) of theft.

ἐπίατρος *s.m.* (*mil.*) army doctor.

ἐπιβαίνω *v.t.* (*with gen.*) mount; go aboard; (*of animals*) cover.

ἐπιβάλλον *s.n.* air of authority.

ἐπιβάλλ|ω *v.t.* impose, inflict. ~ομαι *v.i.* impose one's authority, command respect.

ἐπιβαρύνω *v.t.* aggravate, burden.

ἐπιβάτ|ης *s.m.* passenger. ~ηγόν *s.n.* passenger ship. ~ικόν *s.n.* passenger vehicle *or* ship.

ἐπιβεβαιώνω *v.t.* confirm.

ἐπιβεβλημένος *a.* imperative, bounden.

ἐπιβήτωρ *s.m.* stud-animal; usurper.

ἐπιβιβάζ|ω *v.t.* embark, put aboard. ~ομαι *v.i.* embark, go aboard.

ἐπιβλαβής *a.* injurious.

ἐπιβλέπω *v.t. & i.* supervise, invigilate.

ἐπιβλητικός *a.* imposing.

ἐπιβολή *s.f.* imposition, infliction; authority, imposingness.

ἐπιβουλεύομαι *v.t.* plot against; wish ill to.

ἐπίβουλος *a.* insidious.

ἐπιβραδύνω *v.t.* retard; slow down.

ἐπιγαμία *s.f.* intermarriage.

ἐπίγειος *a.* earthly.

ἐπίγνωσις *s.f.* knowledge, realization.

ἐπίγονος *s.m.* descendant.

ἐπίγραμμα *s.n.* epigram.

ἐπιγραφ|ή *s.f.* inscription; shop-sign; heading, title (*of book*); address (*of letter*). ~ική *s.f.* epigraphy.

ἐπιδαψιλεύω *v.t.* lavish.

ἐπιδεικνύ|ω *v.t.* display, exhibit; show off. ~ομαι *v.i.* show off.

ἐπιδεικτικός *a.* ostentatious; showy.

ἐπιδεινῶ *v.t.* make worse.

ἐπίδειξις *s.f.* display; showing off; (*mil.*) diversion.

ἐπιδέξιος *a.* adroit.

ἐπιδερμίς *s.f.* epidermis; (*fam.*) complexion.

ἐπίδεσμος *s.m.* bandage.

ἐπιδέχομαι *v.t.* admit of; put up with.

ἐπιδημία *s.f.* epidemic.

ἐπιδίδ|ω *v.t.* hand over, present. ~ομαι *v.i.* apply oneself.

ἐπιδιορθ|ώνω *v.t.* repair. ~ωσις *s.f.* repair(ing).

ἐπιδιώκω *v.t.* be ambitious of, aim at.

ἐπιδοκιμάζω *v.t.* approve of.

ἐπίδομα *s.n.* extra payment, allowance.

ἐπίδοξος *a.* presumptive, to be.

ἐπιδόρπια *s.n.pl.* dessert.

ἐπίδοσις *s.f.* presentation, delivery; applying oneself; proficiency; record (*in performance*).

ἐπίδρασις *s.f.* effect; influence.

ἐπιδρομή *s.f.* incursion, raid.

ἐπιδρῶ *v.i.* (*with ἐπί*) influence, have an effect on.

ἐπιεικής *a.* lenient.

ἐπίζηλος *a.* enviable.

ἐπιζήμιος *a.* harmful.

ἐπιζητῶ *v.t.* be ambitious of, hope for.

ἐπιζῶ *v.i.* survive.

ἐπίθεσις *s.f.* affixing, application; attack.

ἐπιθετικός *a.* 1. aggressive, offensive. 2. adjectival.

ἐπίθετον *s.n.* epithet; adjective; surname.

ἐπιθανάτιος *a.* death (*bed, agony, etc.*).

ἐπιθεώρησις *s.f.* inspection; inspectorate; review; revue.

ἐπιθυμία *s.f.* desire.

ἐπιθυμ|ῶ *v.t.* desire, wish for; τὴν ~ησα I miss her.

ἐπίκαιρ|ος a. timely; well-placed; topical; τὰ ~α current events.

ἐπικαλ|οῦμαι v.t. invoke, appeal to; ~ούμενος called, nicknamed.

ἐπικαρπία s.f. enjoyment; (law) usufruct.

ἐπίκειμαι v.i. be imminent.

ἐπικερδής a. lucrative.

ἐπικεφαλίς s.f. heading.

ἐπικήδειος a. funeral.

ἐπικήρυξις s.f. setting a price on person's head.

ἐπικίνδυνος a. dangerous.

ἐπίκλησις s.f. invocation; nickname, personal epithet.

ἐπικλινής a. sloping.

ἐπικοινων|ία s.f. intercourse, contact, communication. ~ ῶ v.i. communicate.

ἐπικός a. epic; an epic poet.

ἐπικουρία s.f. aid; (mil.) relief.

ἐπικράτεια s.f. state, land.

ἐπικρατῶ v.i. & t. prevail, predominate, reign; (with gen.) prevail against.

ἐπικρέμαμαι v.i. threaten, be imminent.

ἐπικρίνω v.t. criticize, censure.

ἐπικροτῶ v.t. approve, applaud.

ἐπίκτητος a. acquired.

ἐπικυριαρχία s.f. suzerainty.

ἐπικυρώνω v.t. ratify, confirm.

ἐπιλαμβάνομαι v.t. (with gen.) broach (subject); address oneself to (task).

ἐπιλαχών s.m. runner-up (of candidates).

ἐπίλεκτος a. picked, outstanding (of persons).

ἐπιληψία s.f. epilepsy.

ἐπιλήψιμος a. reprehensible.

ἐπιλογή s.f. selection.

ἐπίλογος s.m. epilogue; conclusion.

ἐπίλοιπος a. remaining.

ἐπιλοχίας s.m. (mil.) sergeant-major.

ἐπίμαχος a. contested, disputed; controversial.

ἐπιμέλ|εια s.f. care, diligence. ~ής a. diligent.

ἐπιμελητεία s.f. (mil.) commissariat.

ἐπιμελητήριον s.n. board, chamber; ἐμπορικὸν ~ Chamber of Commerce.

ἐπιμελητής s.m. keeper, superintendent; university tutor.

ἐπιμελοῦμαι v.t. look after, care for.

ἐπιμένω v.i. persist, insist.

ἐπίμετρον s.n. εἰς ~ to boot, for good measure.

ἐπιμήκης a. oblong.

ἐπιμιξία s.f. inter-marriaჳe; cross-breeding; intercourse.

ἐπιμίσθιον s.n. extra pay.

ἐπίμον|ος a. persistent; stubborn; pressing, urgent. ~ή s.f. perseverance; obstinacy.

ἐπίμοχθος a. toilsome.

ἐπιμύθιον s.n. moral (of tale).

ἐπίνειον s.n. port serving inland town.

ἐπινίκι|ος a. of victory; τὰ ~α celebration of victory.

ἐπινοῶ v.t. invent, devise; fabricate.

ἐπίορκος s.m. breaker of oaths.

ἐπιοῦσα s.f. next day, morrow.

ἐπιούσιος a. ~ ἄρτος daily bread.

ἐπίπαγος s.m. crust (on soft or liquid substance).

ἐπίπεδον s.n. level; (geom.) plane.

ἐπίπεδος a. plane, level, flat.

ἐπιπίπτω v.i. (with κατά) fall upon.

ἐπίπλαστος a. feigned.

ἐπιπλέω v.i. float; (fig.) be among the successful.

ἐπίπληξις s.f. reprimand.

ἐπιπλήττω v.t. reprimand.

ἐπιπλοκή s.f. complication.

ἔπιπλ|ον s.n. piece of furniture; ~α (pl.) furniture.

ἐπιπλώνω v.t. furnish.

ἐπίπλωσις s.f. furnishing.

ἐπιπόλαιος a. superficial.

ἐπίπονος a. hard, laborious.

ἐπιπροσθέτως adv. in addition.

ἐπιρρεπής a. inclined, prone (to).

ἐπίρρημα s.n. adverb.

ἐπιρρίπτω v.t. impute.

ἐπιρροή s.f. influence.

ἐπισημαίνω v.t. stamp; mark (position, etc.).

ἐπίσημ|ος a. official; formal; marking a special occasion; οἱ ~οι official personalities.

ἐπίσης adv. too, likewise.

ἐπισιτισμός s.m. food supply.

ἐπισκεπτήριον s.n. visiting-card.

ἐπισκέπτης s.m. visitor.

ἐπισκέπτομαι v.t. visit.

ἐπισκευ|άζω v.t. repair. ~ή s.f. repair(ing).

ἐπίσκεψις s.f. visit.

ἐπισκιάζω v.t. overshadow, eclipse.

ἐπίσκοπ|ος s.m. bishop. ~ή s.f. bishopric; diocese; bishop's palace.

ἐπισκοπῶ v.t. survey, inspect.

ἐπισμηναγός s.m. (aero.) squadron-leader.

ἐπισπεύδω v.t. hasten, advance date of.

ἐπισταμένως adv. with expert attention.

ἐπιστασία s.f. supervision.

ἐπιστάτης s.m. custodian, janitor, overseer.

ἐπιστατῶ v.t. & i. superintend; be in charge.

ἐπιστεγάζω v.t. roof; (fig.) crown, cap.

ἐπιστήθιος a. ~ φίλος bosom friend.

ἐπιστήμη s.f. branch of learning; science.

ἐπιστημονικός a. scientific.

ἐπιστήμων s.m.f. professionally qualified person; scientist.

ἐπιστολή s.f. letter.

ἐπιστόμιον s.n. mouthpiece; valve.

ἐπιστρατεύω v.t. call up, mobilize.

ἐπιστρέφω v.t. & i. give back; come back.

ἐπιστροφή s.f. return.

ἐπίστρωμα s.n. covering, layer.

ἐπιστύλιον s.n. architrave.

ἐπισύρω v.t. draw upon or attract to oneself.

ἐπισφαλής a. precarious.

ἐπισφραγίζω v.t. set seal on, confirm; crown, round off.

ἐπισωρεύω v.t. pile up, accumulate.

ἐπιταγή s.f. order; cheque.

ἐπιτακτικός a. imperative.

ἐπίτακτος a. requisitioned.

ἐπίταξις s.f. requisition.

ἐπιτάσσω v.t. enjoin; requisition.

ἐπιτάφιος a. funeral; (s.m.) Good Friday procession and office.

ἐπιταχύνω v.t. increase speed of; advance date of.

ἐπιτείνω v.t. intensify.

ἐπιτελάρχης s.m. (mil.) chief of staff.

ἐπιτελεῖον s.n. chief collaborators or staff; (mil.) general staff.

ἐπιτελής s.m. member of general staff.

ἐπιτέλους adv. at last.

ἐπιτετραμμένος s.m. chargé d'affaires.

ἐπίτευγμα s.n. achievement, success.

ἐπίτευξις s.f. attainment, securing.

ἐπιτήδειος a. suitable (for); clever, smart; deft; crafty.

ἐπίτηδες adv. on purpose.

ἐπιτήδευμα s.n. trade, occupation; tax on this.

ἐπιτηδεύ|ομαι v.t. & i. feign, affect; (with εἰς) be skilled in; ~μένος affected.

ἐπιτηρῶ v.t. supervise, keep watch on, invigilate.

ἐπιτίθεμαι v.i. & t. attack, assault (with κατά or ἐναντίον or gen.).

ἐπίτιμος a. honorary.

ἐπιτιμῶ v.t. reprimand.

ἐπιτόκιον s.n. compound interest.

ἐπίτοκος a. about to give birth.

ἐπιτομή s.f. summary; abridgement.

ἐπίτομος a. short, concise; abridged.

ἐπιτόπιος a. local; on the spot.

ἐπιτραπέζιος a. for or on the table.

ἐπιτρέπω v.t. permit.

ἐπιτροπή s.f. committee; commission.

ἐπίτροπος s.m. guardian, trustee; churchwarden; commissioner, agent; commissar.

ἐπιτυγχάνω v.t. & i. attain, get; hit, get right; bring off; meet, find (by chance or design); be successful.

ἐπιτυχής a. successful.

ἐπιτυχία s.f. success.

ἐπιφάνεια s.f. surface; κατ' ~ν in appearance (but not reality).

ἐπιφανής a. distinguished.

Ἐπιφάνια s.n.pl. Epiphany.

ἐπίφασις s.f. external appearance.

ἐπιφέρω v.t. bring about, occasion; ὁ ~ν bearer (of letter, etc.).

ἐπίφοβος a. dangerous, to be avoided.

ἐπιφοίτησις s.f. divine inspiration.

ἐπιφορτίζω v.t. charge, entrust (duty to person).

ἐπιφυλακή s.f. ἐν ~ at the ready.

ἐπιφυλακτικός a. circumspect.

ἐπιφύλαξις s.f. reserve; reservation (of rights).

ἐπιφυλάσσ|ω v.t. hold in store. ~ομαι v.i. behave with reserve, wait for a suitable occasion.

ἐπιφυλλίς s.f. newspaper serial.

ἐπιφώνημα s.n. exclamation; (gram.) interjection.

ἐπιχαρίτως adv. graciously.

ἐπίχειρα s.n.pl. deserts, just recompense (of badness).

ἐπιχείρημα s.n. argument; attempt.

ἐπιχειρηματίας s.m. businessman, entrepreneur.

ἐπιχειρηματικός a. enterprising.

ἐπιχείρησις s.f. undertaking, (business) enterprise; (strategic) operation.

ἐπιχειρῶ v.t. undertake; attempt.

ἐπιχορήγησις s.f. subvention; civil list.

ἐπιχρίω v.t. coat, paint.

ἐπιχρυσώνω v.t. gild.

ἐπιχωματώνω v.t. level up, embank.

ἐπιχωριάζω v.i. be in use, be found (in locality).

ἐπιψηφίζω v.t. sanction by vote.

ἐποίκησις s.f. settlement (abroad).

ἐποίκ|ισις *s.f.* ~ισμός *s.m.* settlement (*at home*).

ἐποικοδομητικός *a.* edifying.

ἔπομαι *v.i.* follow.

ἐπό|μενος *a.* following, next; τὴν ~μένην on the next day; ὡς ἦτο ~μενον as was to be expected. ~μένως *adv.* consequently.

ἐπονείδιστος *a.* shameful, ignominious.

ἐπονομάζω *v.t.* call, surname.

ἐποποιία *s.f.* epic (poetry).

ἐποπτεύω *v.t.* supervise, oversee.

ἔπος *s.n.* epic poem; ἅμ' ~ ἅμ' ἔργον no sooner said than done.

ἐπουλώνω *v.t.* heal (*wound*).

ἐπουσιώδης *a.* of slight importance, unessential.

ἐποφθαλμιῶ *v.t.* covet, have one's eye on.

ἐποχή *s.f.* epoch, era, age; season, time; ἀφίνω ~ leave one's mark, cause a stir.

ἔποψις *s.f.* point of view.

ἑπτά *num.* seven. ~κόσιοι *a.* seven hundred.

ἐπωάζω *v.t.* incubate.

ἐπῳδός *s.f.* refrain.

ἐπώδυνος *a.* painful.

ἐπωμίζομαι *v.t.* shoulder (*burden*).

ἐπωμίς *s.f.* epaulette.

ἐπωνυμία *s.f.* nickname, name; title (*of company, etc.*).

ἐπώνυμον *s.n.* surname.

ἐπωφελής *a.* useful, profitable.

ἐπωφελοῦμαι *v.t.* (*with gen. or acc.*) take advantage of.

ἔρανος *s.m.* fund, collection; contribution.

ἐρασιτέχνης *s.m.* amateur.

ἐρασμι(α)κός *a.* Erasmian.

ἐράσμιος *a.* charming, amiable.

ἐραστής *s.m.* lover.

ἐργάζομαι *v.i.* work; function, go.

ἐργαλεῖον *s.n.* tool, implement.

ἐργασία *s.f.* work, employment; workmansl ip.

ἐργάσιμος *a.* that can be wrought *or* tilled, *etc.*; working (*hours, day*).

ἐργαστήριον *s.n.* workshop; studio; laboratory.

ἐργάτης *s.m.* worker, workman, labourer; (*naut.*) windlass.

ἐργατιά *s.f.* working class.

ἐργατικ|ός *a.* of *or* for workers; industrious; a. working-class man. ~ά *s.n.pl.* wages.

ἐργένης *s.m.* bachelor.

ἐργοδηγός *s.m.* foreman.

ἐργοδότης *s.m.* employer.

ἐργολάβος *s.m.* 1. contractor. 2. beau, lover. 3. kind of macaroon.

ἐργοληψία *s.f.* (*building, etc.*) contract.

ἔργ|ον *s.n.* (piece of) work, thing done; book, play, film, musical work; ~α (*pl.*) building, *etc.*, operations.

ἐργοστάσιον *s.n.* factory, works.

ἐργόχειρον *s.n.* needlework.

ἔρεβος *s.n.* Erebus; pitch darkness.

ἐρεθίζω *v.t.* irritate, excite.

ἐρεθισμός *s.m.* irritation, excitation.

ἐρείπιον *s.n.* ruin, wreck.

ἐρειπώνω *v.t.* reduce to ruins.

ἔρεισμα *s.n.* prop, support.

ἔρευνα *s.f.* search, research, investigation.

ἐρευνητής *s.m.* researcher.

ἐρευνῶ *v.t. & i.* search, examine.

ἐρήμην *adv.* (*law*) by default.

ἐρημ|ία *s.f.* solitude; wilderness. ~ικός *a.* solitary, lonely.

ἐρημίτης *s.m.* hermit.

ἐρημοκκλήσι *s.n.* isolated country chapel.

ἐρημονήσι *s.n.* uninhabited island.

ἔρημος 1. *a.* desolate, deserted, lonely. 2. *s.f.* desert.

ἐρημώνω *v.t.* lay waste.

ἐρίζω *v.i.* dispute, quarrel.

Ἐρινvύς *s.f.* Fury.

ἔρι|ον *s.n.* wool. ~ουργία *s.f.* wool industry. ~οῦχον *s.n.* woollen material.

ἔρις *s.f.* contention, quarrel.

ἐρίτιμος *a.* valuable; esteemed.

ἐρίφης *s.m.* (*fam.*) poor devil.

ἐρίφιον *s.n.* baby kid.

ἕρμα *s.n.* ballast.

ἕρμαιον *s.n.* thing tossed by waves; prey, victim.

ἑρμάριον *s.n.* cupboard, wardrobe.

ἑρμηνεία *s.f.* interpretation, expounding.

ἑρμηνεύω *v.t.* interpret, expound.

ἑρμητικός *a.* hermetic.

ἕρμος *a.* poor, unfortunate, left to one's fate.

ἑρπετόν *s.n.* reptile.

ἑρπύστρι|α *s.f.* track (*of tractor, tank*). ~οφόρον *s.n.* tracked vehicle.

ἕρπω *v.i.* crawl.

ἔρρινος *a.* nasal (*sound*).

ἐρύθημα *s.n.* blush(ing).

ἐρυθριῶ *v.i.* blush.

ἐρυθρόδερμος *s.m.* redskin.

ἐρυθρός a. red.

ἐρυθρωπός a. reddish.

ἔρχ|ομαι v.i. come; μοῦ ~εται νά I feel a desire to; σᾶς ~εται καλά it suits you; δὲν ~εται βολικά it is not convenient; ~εται σὲ λογαριασμό it will just about do or he is amenable to reason.

ἐρχόμενος a. coming, next.

ἐρχομός s.m. coming, arrival.

ἐρῶμαι v.t. (with gen.) fall in love with.

ἐρωμένη s.f. mistress, leman.

ἐρωμένος s.m. lover, paramour.

ἔρ|ως, ~ωτας s.m. love, passion.

ἐρωτεύ|ομαι v.t. & i. fall in love (with); ~μένος in love.

ἐρώτημα s.n. question, query; problem requiring solution.

ἐρωτηματικ|ός a. interrogative. ~όν s.n. question-mark.

ἐρωτηματολόγιον s.n. questionnaire.

ἐρώτησις s.f. question, inquiry; interrogative sentence.

ἐρωτικ|ός a. erotic; amatory; ~ὸν ποίημα love-poem; ~ὸν ζεῦγος pair of lovers.

ἐρωτοδουλειά s.f. love-affair; intrigue, adventure.

ἐρωτοτροπί|α s.f. flirtation; ~ες (pl.) amorous behaviour.

ἐρωτύλος a. amorous, flirtatious.

ἐρωτῶ v.t. & i. ask, question (person); ask (a question); inquire.

ἐσκεμμένος a. premeditated.

ἐσοδεία s.f. crop, harvest.

ἐσοδεύω v.t. gather in, harvest.

ἔσοδον s.n. income, revenue.

ἐσοχή s.f. recess, indentation.

ἑσπέρα s.f. evening.

Ἑσπερία s.f. western Europe.

ἑσπεριδοειδῆ s.n.pl. citrus fruits.

ἑσπερινός a. evening; (s.m.) vespers.

ἑσπερίς s.f. evening party.

ἕσπερος s.m. evening star.

ἐσπευσμένως adv. hastily, in a hurry.

Ἐσταυρωμένος s.m. Christ crucified.

ἐστί(ν) v.i. is.

ἑστία s.f. hearth, fireplace; home; origin, cradle; focus; burner (of stove).

ἑστιατόριον s.n. restaurant.

ἔστω v.i. so be it; ~ καί even.

ἐσύ pron. thou, you.

ἐσχάρα s.f. grill, gridiron.

ἐσχατιά s.f. furthest point, extremity.

ἔσχ|ατος a. extreme; furthest, last; worst; ~άτη προδοσία high treason. ~άτως adv. recently.

ἔσω adv. inside, within; ὁ ~ κόσμος inner self.

ἐσώγαμβρος s.m. man living with and supported by wife's parents.

ἐσωκλείω v.t. inclose (in letter).

ἐσώρρουχα s.n.pl. underclothes.

ἐσωτερικός a. interior, internal; domestic (not foreign); intrinsic.

ἑταίρα s.f. courtesan.

ἑταιρ(ε)ία s.f. society, company, firm.

ἑταῖρος s.m. companion, associate.

ἑτερο- denotes other, different.

ἑτερογενής a. heterogeneous.

ἑτεροθαλής a. with one parent in common.

ἕτερ|ος pron. (an)other; ὁ ~ος one or the other (of two); ἀφ' ~ου besides.

ἑτερόφωτος a. borrowing one's ideas from others.

ἐτήσ|ιος a. annual; lasting one year; ~ίαι (s.f.pl.) etesian winds.

ἔτι adv. still; moreover.

ἐτικέττα s.f. 1. label. 2. etiquette.

ἑτοιμάζ|ω v.t. prepare. ~ομαι v.i. get ready.

ἑτοιμασία s.f. preparation.

ἑτοιμόρροπος a. tumbledown.

ἕτοιμ|ος a. ready; (fam.) τρώω ἀπ' τὰ ~α live on capital.

ἑτοιμότης s.f. readiness of wit.

ἔτος s.n. year.

ἔτσι adv. so, thus, like this; τὸ δίνουν ~ it is given away free; ~ (νὰ) κουνηθῇς if you so much as stir . . .; ~ κι' ~ so so, middling, in any case; ~ κι' ἀλλοιῶς in any case.

ἐτυμηγορία s.f. verdict.

ἐτυμολογία s.f. etymology.

εὖ adv. well.

εὐ- denotes well, easily.

εὐαγγέλιον s.n. gospel.

Εὐαγγελισμός s.m. Annunciation.

εὐαγής a. pure; philanthropic (of institutions).

εὐάγωγος a. well brought up; docile.

εὐάερος a. well-ventilated.

εὐαισθησία s.f. sensitiveness.

εὐαίσθητος a. sensitive.

εὐάλωτος a. easily captured; corruptible.

εὐανάγνωστος a. legible.

εὐαρέσκεια s.f. satisfaction, pleasure.

εὐάρεστος a. agreeable, pleasant.

εὐαρεστοῦμαι v.i. be pleased, deign.

εὐάρμοστος a. well-matched.

εὖγε int. bravo!

εὐγένεια *s.f.* nobility; politeness, courtesy.

εὐγεν|ής, **~ικός** *a.* noble; polite, courteous.

εὔγευστος *a.* palatable.

εὐγλωττία *s.f.* eloquence.

εὐγνωμονῶ *v.t.* be grateful to.

εὐγνώμ|ων *a.* grateful. **~οσύνη** *s.f.* gratitude.

εὐδαιμονία *s.f.* felicity; prosperity.

εὐδία *s.f.* fine weather.

εὐδιάθετος *a.* in good mood; (well) disposed.

εὐδιάκριτος *a.* discernible.

εὔδιος *a.* fair (*of weather*).

εὐδοκιμῶ *v.i.* succeed, get on; thrive.

εὐδοκῶ *v.i.* be pleased, deign.

εὔδρομον *s.n.* (*naut.*) cruiser.

εὐειδής *a.* good-looking.

εὔελπις *a.* hopeful, promising; (*mil.*) a cadet.

εὐέξαπτος *a.* irritable.

εὐεξία *s.f.* healthy condition, well-being.

εὐεργέτ|ης *s.m.* benefactor. **~ικός** *a.* beneficial; beneficent. **~ῶ** *v.t.* make benefaction to.

εὐερέθιστος *a.* irritable.

εὐζωία *s.f.* comfortable living.

εὔζωνος *s.m.* (*mil.*) evzone (*soldier of kilted Gk. regiment*).

εὐήθης *a.* a simpleton.

εὐήλιος *a.* sunny (*that gets the sun*).

εὐημερῶ *v.i.* enjoy prosperity.

εὔηχος *a.* melodious.

εὐθαλής *a.* luxuriant (*of vegetation*).

εὐθανασία *s.f.* easy death; euthanasia.

εὐθεί|α *s.f.* straight line; κατ' ~αν, ἀπ' ~ας (*adv.*) straight, direct.

εὔθετος *a.* suitable, proper.

εὐθην- *see* **φτην**-.

εὔθικτος *a.* touchy.

εὔθραυστος *a.* fragile, delicate.

εὔθρυπτος *a.* friable.

εὐθυβολία *s.f.* marksmanship; accuracy (*of firearm*).

εὐθύγραμμος *a.* rectilinear, straight.

εὐθυκρισία *s.f.* right judgement.

εὐθυμογράφημα *s.n.* humorous article (*in paper*).

εὔθυμ|ος *a.* merry, gay. **~ία** *s.f.* merriment, gaiety.

εὐθύνη *s.f.* responsibility; ἔχω τὴν ~ (*with gen.*) be in charge of.

εὐθύνομαι *v.i.* be responsible *or* answerable.

εὐθύς *adv.* immediately.

εὐθύς *a.* straight, upright; honest.

εὐθυτενής *a.* erect (*of carriage*).

εὐκαιρία *s.f.* opportunity, chance; (*available*) time; (*good*) bargain; σημαία ~ς flag of convenience.

εὔκαιρος *a.* opportune; free, available.

εὐκάλυπτος *s.m.* eucalyptus.

εὔκαμπτος *a.* supple, flexible.

εὐκατάστατος *a.* well-to-do.

εὐκαταφρόνητος *a.* negligible.

εὐκίνητος *a.* nimble, agile.

εὐκοίλι|ος *a.* laxative; whose bowels work easily. **~ότης** *s.f.* diarrhoea.

εὐκολία *s.f.* ease, convenience; service, good turn.

εὐκολόπιστος *a.* credulous.

εὔκολος *a.* easy; easy-going.

εὐκολύν|ω *v.t.* facilitate; help financially. **~ομαι** *v.i.* be in a position (*to pay, etc.*).

εὐκοσμία *s.f.* decorum, propriety.

εὔκρατ|ος, **~ής** *a.* temperate.

εὐκρινής *a.* clear, distinct.

εὐκταῖος *a.* to be wished for.

εὐκτική *s.f.* (*gram.*) optative.

εὐλαβ|ής *a.* devout. **~οῦμαι** *v.t.* show respect for, revere.

εὔληπτος *a.* easy to catch, understand *or* take.

εὐλογημένος *a.* blessed; (*fam.*) epithet of mild reproach.

εὐλογία *s.f.* blessing, benediction.

εὐλογι|ά *s.f.* smallpox. **~οκομμένος** *a.* pock-marked.

εὔλογος *a.* proper, reasonable; plausible.

εὐλογῶ *v.t.* bless.

εὐλύγιστος *a.* supple, flexible.

εὐμάρεια *s.f.* luxurious living, opulence.

εὐμελής *a.* 1. melodious. 2. well-built (*of persons*).

εὐμενής *a.* favourably disposed.

εὐμετά|βλητος, **~βολος** *a.* changeable.

εὔμορφος *a.* see **ὄμορφος**.

εὐνή *s.f.* bed.

εὐνόητ|ος *a.* understandable; intelligible; αὐτὸ εἶναι ~ον that is understood.

εὔνοια *s.f.* favour, goodwill.

εὐνοϊκός *a.* favourable, propitious.

εὐνομία *s.f.* law and order.

εὐνοούμενος *a.* favourite.

εὐνοῦχος *s.m.* eunuch.

εὐνοῶ *v.t.* favour; show favours to.

εὐοδ|ῶ *v.t.* bring to successful conclusion. **~οῦμαι** *v.i.* go well, succeed.

εὐοίωνος *a.* auspicious.

εὔοσμος *a.* having a pleasant smell.
εὐπάθ|εια *s.f.* sensitiveness; proneness (*to ailment*). ~ής *a.* sensitive, delicate.
εὐπαρουσίαστος *a.* presentable.
εὐπατρίδης *s.m.* patrician.
εὐπειθής *a.* obedient.
εὔπεπτος *a.* digestible.
εὔπιστος *a.* credulous.
εὔπλαστος *a.* plastic; shapely (*of body*).
εὔπορος *a.* well-off.
εὐπρέπεια *s.f.* decorum, propriety.
εὐπρεπίζω *v.t.* tidy, smarten.
εὐπρόσβλητος *a.* susceptible (*to ailment*); vulnerable.
εὐπρόσδεκτος *a.* acceptable, welcome.
εὐπροσήγορος *a.* affable.
εὐπρόσιτος *a.* accessible, approachable.
εὐπρόσωπος *a.* presentable.
εὕρεσις *s.f.* finding.
εὑρεσιτεχνί|α *s.f.* δίπλωμα ~ας patent.
εὑρετήριον *s.n.* index, catalogue.
εὑρέως *adv.* widely.
εὕρημα *s.n.* find; original touch.
εὑρίσκ|ω *v.t.* find; hit, strike; obtain; consider, judge. ~ομαι *v.i.* be, find oneself.
εὐρύνω *v.t.* widen.
εὐρ|ύς *a.* wide, broad, extended. ~ύτης *s.f.* breadth.
εὐρύχωρος *a.* spacious, roomy.
εὐρωπαϊκός *a.* (west) European.
εὔρωστος *a.* robust.
εὔσαρκος *a.* fat, corpulent.
εὐσέβεια *s.f.* piety.
εὐσεβής *a.* pious.
εὐσπλαγχνία *s.f.* compassion.
εὐστάθεια *s.f.* stability, steadiness.
εὐσταλής *a.* smart and upstanding.
εὔστοχος *a.* well-aimed; to the point, happy.
εὔστροφος *a.* agile; quick (*of mind*).
εὐσυγκίνητος *a.* easily moved (*emotionally*).
εὐσυνείδητος *a.* conscientious, scrupulous.
εὔσχημος *a.* decent; specious; without giving offence.
εὔσωμος *a.* well-built; large (*of body*).
εὔτακτος *a.* orderly, quiet.
εὐτέλεια *s.f.* bad quality; baseness.
εὐτελής *a.* cheap and nasty; base, mean.
εὐτράπελος *a.* humorous.
εὐτραφής *a.* well-nourished, plump.
εὐτρεπίζω *a.* tidy, smarten.
εὐτύχημα *s.n.* stroke of good fortune.

εὐτυχ|ής *a.* lucky, fortunate; happy. ~ῶς *adv.* luckily, happily.
εὐτυχία *s.f.* happiness; good fortune.
εὐτυχισμένος *a. see* εὐτυχής.
εὐυπόληπτος *a.* reputable.
εὐφάνταστος *a.* over-imaginative.
εὐφημισμός *s.m.* praise; euphemism.
εὔφημος *a.* ~ μνεία favourable mention.
εὔφλεκτος *a.* inflammable.
εὐφορία *s.f.* fruitfulness; euphoria.
εὐφραδής *a.* eloquent, fluent.
εὐφραίνω *v.t.* rejoice, delight.
εὐφραντικός *a.* delectable.
εὐφρόσυνος *a.* giving joy *or* pleasure.
εὐφυ|ής *a.* intelligent; witty. ~ΐα *s.f.* intelligence, wit.
εὔχαρις *a.* graceful, charming; pleasant.
εὐχαρίστησις *s.f.* pleasure, satisfaction.
εὐχαριστί|α *s.f.* Eucharist. ~ες (*pl.*) thanks.
εὐχάριστ|ος *a.* pleasant. ~ως *adv.* with pleasure, gladly.
εὐχαριστ|ῶ *v.t.* thank; please, gratify. ~οῦμαι *v.i.* be pleased, enjoy oneself; ~ημένος pleased, satisfied.
εὐχέρεια *s.f.* ease, facility; fluency.
εὐχή *s.f.* prayer, wish; blessing.
εὔχομαι *v.t.* wish; give blessing *or* good wishes to.
εὔχρηστος *a.* easy to use; in common use (*of word*).
εὔχυμος *a.* juicy.
εὐψυχία *s.f.* bravery.
εὐώδης *a.* fragrant.
εὐωχία *s.f.* feasting.
ἐφ' *prep. see* ἐπί.
ἐφάμιλλος *a.* (*with gen.*) equal to, a match for.
ἐφάπαξ *adv.* once only; (in) a lump sum.
ἐφάπτ|ομαι *v.i.* touch, be in contact. ~ομένη *s.f.* tangent.
ἐφαρμογή *s.f.* fit, fitting; application, carrying out.
ἐφαρμόζω *v.t. & i.* fit, apply, put into effect; (*v.i.*) fit.
ἔφεδρ|ος *s.m.* (*mil.*) reservist. ~εία *s.f.* (*mil.*) reserve.
ἐφεκτικός *a.* reserved, cautious.
ἐφεξῆς *adv.* henceforth.
ἔφεσις *s.f.* 1. (*law*) appeal. 2. inclination.
ἐφετεῖον *s.n.* Court of Appeal.
ἐφέτ|ος *adv.* this year. ~ινός *a.* this year's.
ἐφεύρεσις *s.f.* invention.
ἐφευρετικός *a.* inventive.

εφευρίσκω v.t. invent; contrive.
έφηβος s.m. youth, young man.
εφηβικ|ός a. youth's; ~ή ηλικία adolescence.
εφημερεύω v.i. be on duty.
εφημέριος s.m. officiating priest.
εφημερ|ίς, ~ίδα s.f. newspaper, gazette.
εφήμερος a. ephemeral.
εφιάλτης s.m. nightmare.
εφίδρωσις s.f. sweating.
εφικτός a. attainable, possible.
έφιππος a. on horseback; a horseman.
εφιστώ v.t. ~ την προσοχήν (with gen.) draw (person's) attention.
εφόδι|α s.n.pl. supplies, equipment: requirements. ~άζω v.t. supply, equip.
εφοδιοπομπή s.f. supply convoy.
έφοδος s.f. charge, assault; snap inspection.
εφοπλίζω v.t. arm; equip (ship).
εφοπλιστής s.m. ship-owner.
εφορ(ε)ία s.f. supervision; board of governors; revenue department; tax office.
εφορμώ v.i. 1. attack. 2. be at anchor.
έφορος s.m. inspector, director, keeper (in various public services).
εφτά num. seven. ~κόσιοι a. seven hundred.
εφτάζυμο s.n. unleavened bread.
εφταμηνίτ|ης, ~ικος a. a seven months' child; underdeveloped physically.
εφτάψυχος a. having seven lives.
εχέγγυον s.n. pledge, guarantee.
έχει(ν) s.n. possessions.
εχεμύθεια s.f. discretion; υπό ~ν under pledge of secrecy, (iron.) inaudibly.
εχθές adv. yesterday.
έχθρα s.f. enmity.
εχθρεύομαι v.t. hate.
εχθρικ|ός a. of the enemy; hostile. ~ότης s.f. hostility.
εχθροπραξί|α s.f. hostile act; ~ες (pl.) hostilities.
εχθρός s.m. enemy.
έχιδνα s.f. viper, adder.
εχίνος s.m. sea-urchin; hedgehog.
εχτ- see εχθ- or εκτ-.
έχ|ω v.t. & i. have; keep, hold; consider, regard; cost, be worth; ~ει there is or are; είχε there was or were; ~ει καλώς all right; τί ~εις; what is the matter with you? ~ω δίκιο I am right; τό ~ω σε καλό I think it lucky; καλύτερα ~ω νά I prefer to; τα ~ομε καλά we are on good terms; τα ~ει

τετρακόσα he has his head screwed on the right way; τα ~ω μαζί της I am annoyed with her or I am having an affair with her; ~ει νά κάνει it makes a difference; ~ει ο Θεός God will provide; πόσες ~ει ο μήνας; what day of the month is it? ~ει ως εξής it goes as follows.
εψές adv. yesterday (evening).
έψιλον s.n. the letter E.
εωθιν|ός a. morning. ~όν s.n. reveille.
έως 1. prep. (time & place) until, up to, as far as; (with acc.) ~ την αυγή until dawn; (with gen.) ~ θανάτου unto death. 2. conj. (with ου or ότου & νά) until. 3. adv. (with numbers) about.
Εωσφόρος s.m. Lucifer.

Z

ζαβάδα s.f. stupidity.
ζαβλακώνω v.t. stupefy.
ζαβολιά s.f. cheating (esp. at play).
ζαβός a. crooked, perverse; clumsy, stupid.
ζαγάρι s.n. hound.
ζακέτα s.f. jacket.
ζάλ|η, ~άδα s.f. giddiness; ~ες, ~άδες (pl.) fits of giddiness; (fig.) worries.
ζαλίζ|ω v.t. make dizzy or tipsy, confuse, daze. ~ομαι v.i. become dizzy, tipsy or confused.
ζαμπόν(ι) s.n. ham.
ζάντα s.f. rim (of wheel).
ζάπλουτος a. very rich.
ζάρα s.f. crease, wrinkle.
ζαργάνα s.f. sort of fish.
ζαρετιέρα s.f. suspender.
ζαρζαβάτι s.n. vegetable(s).
ζάρι s.n. die; ~α (pl.) dice.
ζαρίφης a. (fam.) elegant.
ζαρκάδι s.n. roebuck.
ζάρωμα s.n. creasing, wrinkling; crease, wrinkle. ~τιά s.f. crease, wrinkle.
ζαρώνω v.t. & i. crease, wrinkle; (fig.) huddle oneself up.
ζατρίκι s.n. chess.
ζαφείρι s.n. sapphire.
ζάχαρ|η s.f. sugar. ~άτος a. sweet (having sugar). ~ένιος a. sweet; (fig.) honeyed; η ~ένια (iron.) dear life.
ζαχαριέρα s.f. sugar-bowl.
ζαχαροκάλαμον s.n. sugar-cane.
ζαχαροπλαστείον s.n. confectioner's.

ζαχαρώνω *v.t. & i.* cover with sugar; (*v.i.*) candy; (*fig.*) flirt.

ζαχαρωτά *s.n.pl.* sweets.

ζεϊμπέκικος *s.m.* sort of dance.

ζεματ|ίζω, ~ώ *v.t. & i.* scald; be very hot; (*fam.*) rook (*charge too much*), punish severely. ~ίζομαι *v.i.* get a nasty shock.

ζεμπίλι *s.n.* flat straw basket.

ζενίθ *s.n.* zenith.

ζερβ|ός *a.* left-handed; left. ~ά *adv.* to the left; (*fig.*) awry, wrong.

ζέρσεϋ *s.n.* jersey (*material*). [E. *jersey*]

ζέσις *s.f.* boiling; (*fig.*) ardour.

ζεσταίν|ω *v.t. & i.* heat, warm; get hot. ~ομαι *v.i.* get or feel hot.

ζέσταμα *s.n.* heating (*making hot*).

ζεστασιά *s.f.* (right degree of) warmth.

ζέστη *s.f.* heat; fever; κάνει ~ it is hot.

ζεστ|ός *a.* hot, warm. ~ό *s.n.* hot drink.

ζευγαράκι *s.n.* (*fam.*) pair of lovers.

ζευγάρι *s.n.* pair, couple, brace; yoke (*of oxen, land*); ploughing.

ζευγαρώνω *v.t. & i.* match, mate; (*v.i.*) mate; plough.

ζευγάς *s.m.* ploughman.

ζευγνύω *v.t.* yoke, harness, join; bridge.

ζεῦγος *s.n.* pair, couple, brace.

ζευξέκης *a.* silly and superficial.

ζεῦξις *s.f.* yoking; bridging.

ζεύω *v.t.* yoke, harness; put horse, *etc.*, to (*cart*).

ζέφυρος *s.m.* zephyr.

ζέω *v.i.* boil.

ζήλ(ε)ια *s.f.* envy, jealousy.

ζηλεμένος *a.* attractive.

ζηλευτός *a.* enviable, attractive, excellent.

ζηλεύω *v.t. & i.* envy; be jealous (of).

ζηλιάρης *a.* envious, jealous.

ζήλος *s.m.* zeal.

ζηλότυπος *a.* jealous.

ζηλοφθονία *s.f.* (*malicious*) envy.

ζημί|α *s.f.* damage, loss. ~ώνω *v.t. & i.* inflict loss on; suffer loss.

ζήση *s.f.* life; livelihood.

ζήτα *s.n.* the letter Z.

ζήτεια *s.f.* begging.

ζήτημα *s.n.* question, problem, issue, matter; εἶναι ~ it is doubtful.

ζήτησις *s.f.* demand (*for commodity*); quest (*for truth, etc.*).

ζητιάν|ος *s.m.* beggar. ~εύω *v.t. & i.* beg for; go begging.

ζήτω *int.* long live, hurrah for!

ζητ|ῶ *v.t.* seek, look or ask for; demand; (*v.i.*) beg. ~ιέμαι *v.i.* be in demand.

ζητωκραυγ|ή *s.f.* cheer, acclamation. ~άζω *v.t. & i.* cheer.

ζιζάνιον *s.n.* tare, weed; (*fig.*) dissension; mischievous person.

ζόρ|ι *s.n.* force; trouble, difficulty; με τό ~ι by force. ~ίζω *v.t.* force, put pressure on.

ζόρικος *a.* difficult, troublesome.

ζούγκλα *s.f.* jungle.

ζουζούνι *s.n.* (*small*) insect.

ζουλεύω *v.t. & i.* see ζηλεύω.

ζούλ|ημα, ~ισμα *s.n.* squeezing.

ζουλῶ *v.t.* crush, squeeze, squash, mash.

ζουμ|ί *s.n.* juice; broth. ~ερός *a.* juicy.

ζουμπούλι *s.n.* hyacinth.

ζουπῶ *v.t.* see ζουλῶ.

ζουριάζω *v.t. & i.* shrink, shrivel.

ζούρλα *s.f.* madness.

ζουρλομανδύας *s.m.* straitjacket.

ζουρλός *a.* mad; a madcap.

ζοφερός *a.* dark.

ζοχάδ|α *s.f.* (*fam., fig.*) peevishness; peevish person; ~ες (*pl.*) piles.

ζυγαριά *s.f.* pair of scales.

ζύγι *s.n.* weighing; μὲ τό ~ by weight; ~α (*pl.*) weights.

ζυγιάζω *v.t. & i.* see ζυγίζω.

ζυγίζ|ω *v.t. & i.* weigh; balance; arrange (*soldiers*) in line. ~ομαι *v.i.* poise, hover.

ζυγός *s.m.* yoke; (beam of) balance; mountain peak; (*mil.*) rank, row.

ζυγ|ός *a.* even (*number*); μονά ~ά odd or even.

ζυγούρι *s.n.* two-year-old lamb.

ζυγῶ *v.i.* (*mil.*) dress.

ζύγωμα *s.n.* 1. approach. 2. cross-bar.

ζυγώνω *v.t. & i.* bring or come near.

ζύθ|ος *s.m.* beer. ~οποιία *s.f.* brewing.

ζυμάρ|ι *s.n.* dough, paste. ~ικά *s.n.pl.* Italian paste (*macaroni, etc.*).

ζύμη *s.f.* leaven; dough; (*fig.*) stuff, quality (*of character*).

ζύμωμα *s.n.* kneading.

ζυμών|ω *v.t. & i.* knead; ferment; (*v.i.*) make bread. ~ομαι *v.i.* ferment.

ζύμωσις *s.f.* fermentation.

ζῶ *v.i. & t.* live; (*v.t.*) live through, experience; keep, support (*family*).

ζωάριον *s.n.* small animal.

ζωγραφιά *s.f.* picture.

ζωγραφίζω *v.t.* paint, draw, depict.

ζωγραφική *s.f.* (*art of*) painting.

ζωγραφιστός *a.* painted; (*fig.*) beautiful.

ζωγράφος s.m. painter, artist.

ζώδι|ον s.n. sign of zodiac; (fig.) destiny; ~ακός κύκλος zodiac.

ζωέμπορος s.m. cattle dealer.

ζωή s.f. life; vitality; livelihood.

ζωηρεύω v.t. & i. make or get livelier; get brighter (of colour).

ζωηρ|ός a. lively, energetic; warm, animated; bright (of colour). ~ότης s.f. vivacity, warmth.

ζωικ|ός a. 1. pertaining to life. 2. animal; ~ὴ μέταξα pure silk.

ζωμός s.m. broth.

ζωνάρι s.n. belt, waistband; (fam.) κρεμῶ τὸ ~ μου seek a quarrel.

ζώνη s.f. girdle, belt; cordon; zone.

ζωντανεύω v.t. & i. revive; bring back or come back to life.

ζωντάνια s.f. vitality.

ζωνταν|ός a. living, alive; vivid; underdone (of food). ~ά s.n.pl. animals (esp. cattle).

ζωντόβολο s.n. beast; (fig.) dolt.

ζωντοχήρα s.f. divorced woman.

ζωντοχήρος s.m. divorced man.

ζών|ω v.t. gird (on); encircle, surround. ~ομαι v.t. put on (sword, lifebelt, etc.).

ζωογονῶ v.t. invigorate, brace.

ζωοδότης s.m. giver of life.

ζωοδόχος a. ~ πηγή life-giving spring.

ζωοκλοπή s.f. cattle-thieving.

ζωολογία s.f. zoology.

ζῶον s.n. animal; (fig.) dolt.

ζωοτομία s.f. vivisection.

ζωοτροφίαι s.f.pl. victuals.

ζωόφιλος a. fond of animals.

ζωοφόρος s.f. frieze (of temple).

ζωπυρῶ v.t. rekindle.

ζωστήρ s.m. belt, baldric; (med.) shingles.

ζωτικ|ός a. vital. ~ότης s.f. vitality; (fig.) vital importance.

ζωύφιον s.n. small insect; louse.

ζωώδης a. brutish.

H

ἡ article f. the.

ἤ conj. 1. or; ἤ . . . ἤ either . . . or. 2. than.

ἤ pron. f. who (see ὅς).

ἥβη s.f. puberty; pubes.

ἡγεμ|ών s.m. prince, sovereign. ~ονία s.f. hegemony, sovereignty; principality. ~ονικός a. princely.

ἡγεσία s.f. leadership.

ἡγ|έτης, ~ήτωρ s.m. leader.

ἡγοῦμαι v.i. & t. (with gen.) lead, be in command (of).

ἡγούμενος s.m. abbot.

ἤγουν adv. namely.

ἤδη adv. already.

ἡδον|ή s.f. pleasure (esp. sensual). ~ικός a. sweet, voluptuous.

ἡδύνω v.t. sweeten; delight; (fig.) alleviate (pain).

ἡδυπαθής a. sensual; a voluptuary.

ἡδύποτον s.n. liqueur.

ἡδ|ύς a. sweet. ~έως adv. sweetly.

ἠθική s.f. ethics, morals; morality.

ἠθικολογῶ v.i. moralize.

ἠθικόν s.n. morale; morality.

ἠθικ|ός a. ethical, moral; virtuous; ~ὸς αὐτουργός instigator (of crime). ~ότης s.f. morality, virtue.

ἠθμός s.m. filter.

ἠθογραφία s.f. description of local customs.

ἠθοπλαστικός a. (morally) uplifting.

ἠθοποι|ία s.f. acting. ~ός s.m.f. actor, actress.

ἦθ|ος s.n. character, nature; air, manner; ~η (pl.) manners, habits; morals.

ἥκιστα adv. very little; not at all.

ἠλεκτρίζω v.t. charge with electricity; (fig.) rouse to enthusiasm.

ἠλεκτρικ|ός a. electric. ~ό s.n. electricity (supply).

ἠλεκτρισμός s.m. electricity.

ἠλεκτροκίνητος a. driven by electricity.

ἠλεκτρολόγος s.m. electrician.

ἤλεκτρον s.n. amber.

ἠλεκτρονική s.f. electronics.

ἠλεκτρόνιον s.n. electron.

ἠλεκτροπληξία s.f. electric shock.

ἠλεκτροφωτίζω v.t. light by electricity, lay on electricity to.

ἡλιακός a. sun's, solar.

ἡλίασις s.f. sunstroke.

ἠλίθιος a. idiotic; an idiot.

ἡλικία s.f. age (length of life); (mil.) class.

ἡλικιωμένος a. elderly.

ἡλιοβασίλεμα s.n. sunset.

ἡλιοθεραπεία s.f. sunbathing.

ἡλιοκαμένος a. sunburnt.

ἡλιόλουστος a. bathed in sunshine.

ἥλι|ος s.m. sun; sunflower. ~οστάσιον s.n. solstice.

ἧλος s.m. nail; corn, callus.

ἡμαρτημένα s.n.pl. errata.

ἥμαρτον *v.i.* forgive me! (*see* ἁμαρτάνω).

ἡμεῖς *pron.* we.

ἡμέρα *s.f.* day; τῆς ~ς laid, caught, *etc.* the same day.

ἡμερεύω *v.t. & i.* tame, calm; become tame *or* calm.

ἡμερήσιος *a.* daily; a day's.

ἡμερολόγιον *s.n.* calendar, almanac; diary, log-book.

ἡμερομηνία *s.f.* date.

ἡμερομίσθιον *s.n.* day's wage.

ἥμερος *a.* domesticated; cultivated (*plant, ground*); tame, gentle, peaceable.

ἡμερώνω *v.t. & i.* tame; cultivate (*wild plant*); (*fig.*) civilize; (*v.i.*) calm down.

ἡμέτερος *a.* our, ours.

ἡμι- *denotes* half.

ἡμιαργία *s.f.* half-day's holiday.

ἡμιεπίσημος *a.* semi-official.

ἡμιθανής *a.* half-dead.

ἡμίθεος *s.m.* demigod.

ἡμίκοσμος *s.m.* demi-monde.

ἡμικρανία *s.f.* migraine.

ἡμικύκλιον *s.n.* semicircle.

ἡμιμάθεια *s.f.* smattering of knowledge.

ἡμίμετρα *s.n.pl.* half-measures.

ἡμίονος *s.m.f.* mule.

ἡμιπληγία *s.f.* (*med.*) paralysis of one side.

ἡμίρρευστος *a.* half-liquid.

ἡμισέληνος *s.f.* half-moon; crescent.

ἥμισ|υς *a.* half; ἐξ ~είας half-and-half.

ἡμισφαίριον *s.n.* hemisphere.

ἡμιτελής *a.* half-finished; unfinished.

ἡμιτόνιον *s.n.* (*mus.*) semitone.

ἡμίτροφος *s.m.f.* half-boarder.

ἡμίφωνον *s.n.* (*gram.*) semivowel.

ἡμίφως *s.n.* dim light; twilight.

ἡμιχρόνιον *s.n.* half-time (*in games*).

ἡμίωρον *s.n.* half-hour.

ἡμπορῶ *v.i. see* μπορῶ.

ἡνί|ον *s.n.* rein. ~οχος *s.m.* charioteer.

ἡνωμένος *a.* united.

ἡξεύρω *v.t. & i. see* ξέρω.

ἥπ|αρ *s.n.* liver; ~ατα (*pl.*) strength; (*fam.*) τοῦ κόπηκαν τά ~ατα he had quite a turn.

ἤπειρ|ος *s.f.* mainland; continent; Epirus. ~ωτικός *a.* continental. ~ώτικος *a.* Epirot.

ἤπιος *a.* mild.

ἠρέμ|α, ~ως *adv.* calmly, quietly.

ἤρεμ|ος *a.* calm, quiet. ~ία *s.f.* calm, quiet. ~ῶ *v.i.* be calm, quiet *or* at rest.

ἡρωικός *a.* heroic.

ἡρωίνη *s.f.* heroin.

ἡρῶον *s.n.* war memorial.

ἥρ|ως, ~ωας *s.m.* hero. ~ωίς *s.f.* heroine. ~ωισμός *s.m.* heroism.

ἤσκα *s.f.* tinder.

ἡσυχάζω *v.i. & t.* grow *or* make calm *or* quiet; rest, sleep; be reassured.

ἥσυχ|ος *a.* quiet, peaceful, free from worry. ~ία *s.f.* quietness, peace.

ἦτα *s.n.* the letter Η.

ἤτοι *adv.* namely.

ἥττ|α *s.f.* defeat. ~οπάθεια *s.f.* defeatism.

ἧττον *adv.* less; οὐχ ~ none the less.

ἡττῶμαι *v.i.* be defeated.

ἡφαίστειον *s.n.* volcano.

ἠχηρός *a.* resonant, loud; (*gram.*) sonant.

ἠχητικός *a.* producing *or* employing sound.

ἠχοβόλισις *s.f.* echo-sounding.

ἦχος *s.m.* sound.

ἠχώ *s.f.* echo.

ἠχῶ *v.i.* sound, ring.

ἠώς *s.f.* dawn.

Θ

θά *particle introducing future, conditional, etc., verbs.*

θάβω *v.t.* bury.

θαλαμηγός *s.f.* yacht.

θαλαμηπόλος *s.m.f.* manservant; housemaid.

θάλαμος *s.m.* room, chamber, ward.

θάλασσα *s.f.* sea; (*fam.*) τὰ κάνω ~ make a mess of it.

θαλασσιν|ός *a.* of *or* from the sea; a seafarer; ~ά (*s.n.pl.*) shell-fish.

θαλάσσιος *a.* of *or* from the sea, maritime.

θαλασσόβιος *a.* living in *or* frequenting the sea.

θαλασσοδάνειον *s.n.* bottomry; (*fig.*) risky loan.

θαλασσοδέρν|ω *v.t.* buffet. ~ω, ~ομαι *v.i.* be buffeted by waves *or* (*fig.*) by adversity.

θαλασσοκρατ|ία, ~ορία *s.f.* mastery of the seas.

θαλασσόλυκος *s.m.* sea-dog, old salt.

θαλασσοπνίγομαι *v.i.* suffer hardship at sea; (*fig.*) be in difficulties.

θαλασσοπόρος *s.m.* voyager, navigator.
θαλασσώνω *v.t.* τὰ ∼ make a mess of it.
θαλερός *a.* verdant; (*fig.*) youthful.
θάλλω *v.i.* blossom, flourish.
θαλπωρή *s.f.* pleasant warmth.
θάμβος *s.n.* dazzlement; amazement.
θάμνος *s.m.* bush, shrub.
θαμπάδα *s.f.* dullness, mistiness (*of sight, polished surface*).
θαμπός *a.* dim, dull; turbid, clouded.
θάμπωμα *s.n.* dazzlement; amazement; clouding, tarnishing.
θαμπώνω *v.t. & i.* dazzle; make *or* become dull *or* clouded. ∼ομαι *v.i.* be dazzled.
θαμών *s.m.* habitué (*of café, etc.*).
θανάσιμος *a.* deadly.
θανατηφόρος *a.* deadly.
θανατικ|ός *a.* capital. ∼ό *s.n.* deadly epidemic.
θάνατ|ος *s.m.* death. ∼ώνω *v.t.* put to death; (*fig.*) grievously afflict.
θανή *s.f.* death; funeral.
θάπτω *v.t.* bury.
θαρραλέος *a.* bold.
θαρρετός *a.* bold; assured (*not shy*).
θαρρεύ|ω *v.i.* take courage. ∼ομαι *v.t.* trust.
θάρρος *s.n.* boldness, courage; assurance.
θαρρ|ῶ *v.i. & t.* think, believe; (*v.t.*) τὸν ∼εψα γιά I took him for.
θαῦμα *s.n.* miracle, marvel, wonder.
θαυμάζω *v.t. & i.* wonder at, admire; be surprised.
θαυμάσιος *a.* wonderful, marvellous.
θαυμασμός *s.m.* wonder, admiration.
θαυμαστής *s.m.* admirer.
θαυμαστικ|ός *a.* admiring. ∼όν *s.n.* (*gram.*) exclamation mark.
θαυμαστός *a.* admirable, deserving praise.
θαυματοποιός *s.m.* juggler.
θαυματουργός *a.* miracle-working.
θάψιμο *s.n.* burial.
θεά *s.f.* goddess.
θέα *s.f.* sight, view, prospect.
θεαθῆναι *v.i.* see θεῶμαι.
θέαμα *s.n.* spectacle, show. ∼τικός *a.* spectacular.
θεάρεστος *a.* meritorious (*of good works*).
θεατής *s.m.* spectator.
θεατός *a.* visible.
θεατρικός *a.* for the theatre; theatrical.
θεατρίνος *s.m.* actor.
θέατρο *s.n.* theatre; γίνομαι ∼ become a laughing-stock.

θεατρώνης *s.m.* impresario.
θεία *s.f.* aunt.
θειάφι *s.n.* su¹phur.
θειικός *a.* sulphuric.
θεϊκός *a.* divine.
θείον *s.n.* sulphur.
θείος *s.m.* uncle.
θείος *a.* divine.
θέλγ|ω *v.t.* charm. ∼ητρον *s.n.* charm, fascination.
θέλημα *s.n.* will (*thing intended*); errand. ∼τικός *a.* voluntary.
θέλησις *s.f.* will (*faculty*), volition; willpower; wish (*thing intended*).
θελκτικός *a.* charming, alluring.
θέλ|ω *v.t. & i.* want, need, require; owe; (*v.i.*) be willing; attempt. ∼ω νά πῶ I mean to say; ∼εις . . . ∼εις either . . . or; ∼ει δὲ ∼ει willy-nilly; λίγο ἤθελε νὰ πέση he nearly fell.
θέμα *s.n.* subject, topic, theme; (*gram.*) stem; τὸ ∼ εἶναι the thing is.
θεματοφύλαξ *s.m.* depositary, guardian.
θεμέλιον *s.n.* foundation, basis.
θέμ|ις *s.f.* justice (*personified*). ∼ιτός *a.* lawful.
θεο- *denotes* 1. of God. 2. extremely, utterly.
θεογνωσία *s.f.* religiousness; (*fig.*) τὸν ἔφερα σὲ ∼ I brought him to his senses.
θεόγυμνος *a.* stark naked.
θεόθεν *adv.* from God.
θεοκατάρατος *a.* accursed.
θεοκρατία *s.f.* theocracy.
θεολόγ|ος *s.m.* theologian. ∼ία *s.f.* theology. ∼ικός *a.* theological.
θεομηνία *s.f.* natural disaster.
Θεομήτωρ *s.m.* Mother of God.
θεομπαίχτης *s.m.* pious humbug (*person*).
θεοποιῶ *v.t.* deify; (*fig.*) idolize.
θεόρατος *a.* huge (*esp. in height*).
θεός *s.m.* god.
θεοσεβής *a.* godly.
θεοσκότεινος *a.* pitch-dark.
θεότης *s.f.* deity.
Θεοτόκος *s.f.* Mother of God.
θεοφάν(ε)ια *s.n.pl.* Epiphany.
θεοφιλής *a.* dear to God.
θεοφοβούμενος *a.* god-fearing.
θεραπεία *s.f.* cure, treatment, remedy; cultivation (*of arts*).
θεραπευτήριον *s.n.* sanatorium.
θεραπευτικ|ός *a.* curative. ∼ή *s.f.* therapeutics.
θεραπεύω *v.t.* cure, treat, remedy; cultivate (*arts*).

θεράπων *s.m.* servant, devotee; ~ ἰατρός medical attendant.

θέρετρον *s.n.* summer resort *or* residence.

θεριακλῆς *s.m.* avid consumer of coffee *or* tobacco.

θεριεύω *v.i.* grow bigger, shoot up.

θερίζω *v.t.* harvest, reap, mow; mow down; (*fig.*) torment (*of pain, cold, etc.*).

θερινός *a.* of summer; summery.

θεριό *s.n.* wild beast.

θέρ|ισμα *s.n.*, ~ισμός *s.m.* harvest, reaping, mowing.

θεριστής *s.m.* reaper; June.

θεριστικός *a.* for reaping *or* mowing.

θέρμαι *s.f.pl.* hot springs.

θερμαίν|ω *v.t.* heat, warm. ~ομαι *v.i.* get a fever.

θέρμανσις *s.f.* heating.

θερμαντικός *a.* imparting warmth.

θερμαστής *s.m.* stoker.

θερμάστρα *s.f.* (*heating*) stove.

θέρμ|η *s.f.* fever (*also* ~ες); (*fig.*) fervour. ~αι *s.f.pl.* hot springs.

θερμίς *s.f.* calorie.

θερμόαιμος *a.* warm-blooded; quick to anger.

θερμογόνος *a.* calorific.

θερμοκήπιον *s.n.* hot-house.

θερμοκρασία *s.f.* temperature.

θερμόμετρον *s.n.* thermometer.

θέρμ|ος *s.m.*, ~ός *s.n.* thermos flask.

θερμός *a.* hot, warm; (*fig.*) warm, ardent; expansive.

θερμοσίφων *s.m.* water-heater, geyser.

θερμοστάτης *s.m.* thermostat.

θερμότης *s.f.* heat, warmth; (*fig.*) ardour; expansiveness.

θερμοφόρος *s.f.* hot-water bottle.

θέρος *s.m.* harvest.

θέρος *s.n.* summer; harvest.

θεσιθήρας *s.m.* place-seeker.

θέσις *s.f.* position, place, situation; post, employment; seat; room (*available space*); class (*of travel*); thesis; (*mus.*) down-beat.

θεσμός *s.m.* institution, law.

θεσπέσιος *a.* divine, superb.

θεσπίζω *v.t.* decree, enact.

θέσπισμα *s.n.* decree.

θετικισμός *s.m.* positivism.

θετικ|ός *a.* positive; definite, down-to-earth; ~ὲς ἐπιστήμες natural science.

θετός *a.* adoptive.

θέτω *v.t.* put, set; impose, submit.

θεῶμαι *v.t. & i.* look at; be seen; πρός τὸ θεαθῆναι for appearance sake.

θεωρεῖον *s.n.* (*theatre*) box; (*press, etc.*) gallery.

θεώρημα *s.n.* theorem.

θεώρησις *s.f.* official scrutiny (*of document*); visa.

θεωρητικός *a.* 1. theoretical; a theoretician. 2. of imposing appearance.

θεωρία *s.f.* 1. theory. 2. imposing appearance.

θεωρῶ *v.t.* consider, regard; scrutinize (*document*), visa; submit for visa, *etc.*

θηκάρι *s.n.* scabbard, sheath.

θήκη *s.f.* box, case, receptacle.

θηλάζω *v.t. & i.* suckle.

θηλασμός *s.m.* suckling (*process*).

θηλαστικόν *s.n.* mammal.

θήλαστρον *s.n.* baby's feeding-bottle.

θηλ(ε)ιά *s.f.* noose, slip-knot, loop; stitch (*in knitting*).

θηλή *s.f.* nipple; papilla.

θῆλ|υ, ~υκό *s.n.* female.

θηλυκ|ός *a.* female; feminine. ~ότης *s.f.* femininity.

θηλυκώνω *v.t.* button, do up.

θηλυπρεπής *a.* womanish, effeminate.

θῆλυς *a.* female.

θημωνιά *s.f.* stack (*of hay, corn*).

θήρα *s.f.* chase, pursuit; hunting, shooting; game, quarry.

θήραμα *s.n.* game, quarry.

θηρεύω *v.t.* pursue, hunt.

θηριοδαμαστής *s.m.* animal-tamer.

θηρίον *s.n.* wild beast; (*fig.*) monster.

θηριοτροφεῖον *s.n.* menagerie.

θηριώδης *a.* ferocious.

θησαυρίζω *v.t. & i.* amass (*riches*); grow rich.

θησαυρός *s.m.* treasure; (*fig.*) store, storehouse; thesaurus.

θησαυροφυλάκιον *s.n.* treasury; strong-room.

θῆτα *s.n.* the letter Θ.

θητεία *s.f.* military service; term of office.

θιασάρχης *s.m.* head of theatrical company.

θίασος *s.m.* theatrical company; cast.

θιασώτης *s.m.* votary, supporter.

θίγω *v.t.* touch (upon); (*fig.*) offend.

θλάσις *s.f.* breaking; (*med.*) contusion.

θλιβερός *a.* grievous, piteous.

θλίβω *v.t.* squeeze; (*fig.*) afflict, grieve.

θλιμμένος *a.* sad, sorrowful; in mourning.

θλίψις *s.f.* squeezing; (*fig.*) affliction, sorrow, mourning.

θνησιμότης *s.f.* death-rate.
θνήσκω *v.i.* die.
θνητ|ός *a.* mortal. ~ότης *s.f.* mortality.
θόλος *s.m.* dome, cupola, vault.
θολός *a.* dull, lustreless; blurred, clouded; turbid; confused.
θολ|ώνω *v.t. & i.* make *or* become dull, blurred, turbid *or* confused; ~ωσε τό μάτι του he was seized with anger *or* desire, *etc.*
θολωτός *a.* vaulted, domed.
θόρυβος *s.m.* noise, row; sensation, fuss.
θορυβ|ῶ *v.i. & t.* make a noise; disturb, worry. ~οῦμαι *v.i.* get worried.
θορυβώδης *a.* noisy, rowdy.
θούριον *s.n.* martial song.
θράκα *s.f.* embers.
θρανίον *s.n.* (*pupil's*) desk.
θράσος *s.n.* effrontery, cheek.
θρασύδειλος *a.* blustering but cowardly.
θρασύς *a.* impudent, cheeky.
θραῦσις *s.f.* fracture, breaking; havoc.
θραῦσμα *s.n.* splinter, fragment.
θραύω *v.t.* break, shatter.
θρεμμένος *a.* well-nourished.
θρεπτικός *a.* nourishing; alimentary.
θρεφτάρι *s.n.* fattened animal.
θρέφω *v.t.* nourish.
θρέψις *s.f.* nutrition.
θρῆν|ος *s.m.* lamentation, dirge. ~ητικός *a.* plaintive, mournful. ~ῶ *v.i. & t.* lament, mourn.
θρηνώδ|ης *a.* plaintive, mournful. ~ία *s.f.* lament.
θρησκεία *s.f.* religion.
θρησκευτικός *a.* religious, of religion.
θρησκόληπτος *a.* obsessed with religion.
θρῆσκος *a.* religious, god-fearing.
θριαμβεύ|ω *v.i.* triumph. ~τής *s.m.* triumphant one, victor. ~τικός *a.* triumphal, triumphant.
θρίαμβος *s.m.* triumph.
θρίξ *s.f.* a hair, bristle.
θρόϊσμα *s.n.* rustle.
θρόμβ|ος *s.m.* clot; bead (*of sweat*). ~ωσις *s.f.* (*med.*) thrombosis.
θρονιάζομαι *v.i.* settle comfortably, install oneself.
θρόνος *s.m.* throne.
θρούμπα *s.f.* ripe olive (*fallen from tree*).
θρυαλλίς *s.f.* wick, fuse.
θρύβω *v.t. & i.* crumble.
θρυλεῖται *v.i.* it is rumoured.
θρῦλ|ος *s.m.* legend, tale; rumour. ~ικός *a.* legendary, heroic.

θρύμμα *s.n.* fragment, crumb. ~τίζω *v.t.* break into fragments.
θρύψαλο *s.n.* fragment (*of glass, china*).
θυγάτηρ *s.f.* daughter.
θύελλα|α *s.f.* storm. ~ώδης *a.* stormy, tempestuous.
θυλάκιον *s.n.* pocket.
θύλαξ *s.m.* pouch.
θῦμα *s.n.* victim.
θυμᾶμαι *v.t. & i. see* θυμοῦμαι.
θυμάρι *s.n.* thyme.
θυμηδία *s.f.* mirth (*esp. ironic*).
θύμηση *s.f.* memory.
θυμητικό *s.n.* memory.
θυμίαμα *s.n.* incense; (*fig.*) adulation.
θυμιατ|ήριον, ~ό *s.n.* censer.
θυμιατίζω *v.t.* cense; (*fig.*) adulate.
θυμίζω *v.t.* remind (*one*) of, recall.
θυμ|ός *s.m.* anger. ~ώδης *a.* irascible.
θυμοῦμαι *v.t. & i.* remember, recall.
θυμώνω *v.t. & i.* make *or* get angry.
θύρα *s.f.* door.
θυρεοειδής *a.* thyroid.
θυρεός *s.m.* escutcheon.
θυρίς *s.f.* small window; ticket-office window, guichet.
θυρόφυλλον *s.n.* leaf of door.
θυρωρός *s.m.f.* door-keeper, hall-porter.
θύσανος *s.m.* tassel, tuft.
θυσί|α *s.f.* sacrifice. ~άζω *v.t.* sacrifice.
θύω *v.t. & i.* sacrifice; (*fig.*) ~ καὶ ἀπολλύω run riot.
θωπεία *s.f.* caress.
θωπεύω *v.t.* caress; (*fig.*) flatter.
θωρακίζω *v.t.* protect with armour-plate.
θώραξ *s.m.* breastplate; thorax.
θωρηκτόν *s.n.* battleship.
θωριά *s.f.* look, appearance; colour.
θωρῶ *v.t.* see, look at.

I

ἰαίνω *v.t.* cure, heal.
ἰαματικός *a.* curative, medicinal.
ἴαμβ|ος *s.m.* iambus. ~ικός *a.* iambic.
'Ιανουάριος *s.m.* January.
'Ιάπων *s.m.* a Japanese.
ἰαπωνικός *a.* Japanese.
ἰάσιμος *a.* curable.
ἴασις *s.f.* cure, healing.
ἰατρεῖον *s.n.* surgery, consulting-room, clinic.
ἰατρεύω *v.t.* cure, heal.

ἰατρική *s.f.* (*science of*) medicine.
ἰατρικόν *s.n.* medicine, medicament.
ἰατρικός *a.* medical.
ἰατροδικαστής *s.m.* (*law*) medical expert.
ἰατρός *s.m.f.* doctor.
ἰατροσυμβούλιον *s.n.* consultation between doctors.
ἰαχή *s.f.* war-cry.
ἰβίσκος *s.m.* hibiscus.
ἰδανικ|ός *a.* ideal. ~όν *s.n.* ideal.
ἴδε, ἰδέ *v.t.* see! lo!
ἰδέα *s.f.* idea; opinion.
ἰδεαλιστής *s.m.* idealist.
ἰδεατός *a.* in one's imagination.
ἰδεολογία *s.f.* ideology; utopian idea.
ἰδεολόγος *s.m.f.* idealist.
ἰδεώδ|ης *a.* ideal. ~ες *s.n.* ideal.
ἰδία *adv.* in particular, above all.
ἰδιάζ|ων *a.* characteristic, peculiar. ~όντως *adv.* in particular.
ἰδιαίτερ|ος *a.* special, particular; ὁ ~ος private secretary; τὰ ~α private affairs.
ἰδιαιτέρως *adv.* especially; privately.
ἰδικός *a.* see δικός.
ἰδιοκτησία *s.f.* ownership; property.
ἰδιοκτήτης *s.m.* owner, proprietor.
ἰδιόκτητος *a.* of one's own, private.
ἰδιοποιοῦμαι *v.t.* appropriate.
ἰδιόρρυθμος *a.* peculiar, eccentric; (*eccl.*) idiorhythmic.
ἴδι|ος *a.* (of) one's own; (*one*)self, ἐγὼ ὁ ~ος I myself; same, ~ος μέ the same as. ~α *adv.* ~α μέ the same as, like.
ἰδιοσυγκρασία *s.f.* temperament; constitution.
ἰδιοτέλ|εια *s.f.* self-interest. ~ής *a.* self-seeking.
ἰδιότης *s.f.* property, quality, peculiarity.
ἰδιότροπος *a.* unusual; fussy.
ἰδιοφυ|ΐα *s.f.* talent. ~ής *a.* talented.
ἰδιόχειρος *a.* with *or* into one's own hand.
ἰδίωμα *s.n.* characteristic; habit; dialect. ~τικός *a.* dialectal.
ἰδιω(μα)τισμός *s.m.* idiom (*form of expression*).
ἰδίως *adv.* in particular, above all.
ἰδιωτεύω *v.i.* live as a private citizen.
ἰδιώτ|ης *s.m.* individual, private citizen. ~ικός *a.* private.
ἰδού *int.* see! behold!
ἴδρυμα *s.n.* foundation, institution (*thing*).

ἴδρυσις *s.f.* founding, establishment (*act*).
ἱδρυτής *s.m.* founder.
ἱδρύω *v.t.* found, establish.
ἱδρώ|νω *v.i.* & *t.* sweat; (*fig.*) toil; cause to sweat; ~μένος sweating.
ἱδρ|ώς, ~ώτας *s.m.* sweat.
ἱδῶ *v.t.* aorist subjunctive of βλέπω.
ἱέραξ *s.m.* falcon, hawk.
ἱεραπόστολος *s.f.* missionary.
ἱεράρχ|ης *s.m.* prelate. ~ία *s.f.* hierarchy.
ἱερατικ|ός *a.* priestly; ~ὴ σχολή seminary.
ἱέρεια *s.f.* priestess.
ἱερεμιάς *s.f.* jeremiad.
ἱερεύς *s.m.* priest.
ἱερογλυφικά *s.n.pl.* hieroglyphics.
ἱερόδουλος *s.f.* prostitute.
ἱερ(ο)εξεταστής *s.m.* inquisitor.
ἱεροκήρυξ *s.m.* preacher.
ἱερομάρτυς *s.m.f.* holy martyr.
ἱερομόναχος *s.m.* monk in holy orders.
ἱερόν *s.n.* (*eccl.*) sanctuary.
ἱερ|ός *a.* sacred, holy; ~ὸν ὀστοῦν (*anat.*) sacrum.
ἱεροσυλία *s.f.* sacrilege.
ἱεροτελεστία *s.f.* sacred rite, divine office.
ἱερουργῶ *v.i.* officiate at church service.
ἱεροφάντης *s.m.* hierophant.
ἴζημα *s.n.* sediment.
ἰησουίτης *s.m.* Jesuit.
ἰθαγέν|εια *s.f.* nationality, citizenship. ~ής *a.* native.
ἰθύνω *v.t.* direct, govern, rule.
ἱκανοποι|ῶ *v.t.* satisfy, please. ~ησις *s.f.* satisfaction. ~ητικός *a.* satisfactory, satisfying.
ἱκαν|ός *a.* capable, competent; sufficient; a fair amount of; (*mil.*) fit. ~ότης *s.f.* capability, competence.
ἱκεσία *s.f.* entreaty.
ἱκετεύω *v.t.* entreat.
ἱκέτης *s.m.* suppliant.
ἰκμάς *s.f.* sap; (*fig.*) vitality.
ἰκρίωμα *s.n.* scaffolding; scaffold.
ἴκτερος *s.m.* jaundice.
ἰκτίς *s.f.* animal of weasel tribe.
ἱλαρά *s.f.* measles; (*fam.*) βγάζω τήν ~ feel very hot.
ἱλαρότης *s.f.* merriment.
ἵλεως *a.* clement.
ἴλη *s.f.* (*mil.*) troop of cavalry.
ἴλιγγ|ος *s.m.* giddiness, vertigo. ~ιῶ *v.i.* become giddy *or* dizzy. ~ιώδης *a.* (*causing one to feel*) giddy *or* dizzy.

ἰλύς *s.f.* sediment, mud, slime.

ἰμάμ|ης *s.m.* imam (*Moslem priest*) ; ~ μπαϊλντί dish of aubergines with oil.

ἱμάς *s.m.* strap, thong ; belt (*in machinery*).

ἱματιοθήκη *s.f.* wardrobe ; linen-room ; cloak-room.

ἱμάτιον *s.n.* garment.

ἱματιοφυλάκιον *s.n.* cloak-room.

ἱματισμός *s.m.* (outfit of) clothing.

ἵνα *s.f.* fibre, filament.

ἵνα *conj.* in order to.

ἴνδαλμα *s.n.* ideal, idol (*admired person*).

ἰνδιάνος *s.m.* turkey ; red-indian.

ἰνδικ|ός *a.* Indian ; ~όν χοιρίδιον guinea-pig ; ~όν κάρυον coconut.

ἰνδοκάλαμος *s.m.* bamboo.

ἰνιακός *a.* occipital.

ἰνστιτοῦτον *s.n.* institute ; ~ καλλονῆς beauty-parlour.

ἴντσα *s.f.* inch.

ἰνώδης *a.* fibrous, stringy.

ἰξώδης *a.* glutinous.

ἰοβόλος *a.* venomous.

ἴον *s.n.* violet.

'Ιόνιος *a.* of the Ionian Sea *or* Islands.

ἰός *s.m.* venom ; (*med.*) virus.

'Ιουδαῖος *s.m.* Jew.

'Ιούλιος *s.m.* July.

'Ιούνιος *s.m.* June.

ἰόχρους *a.* violet.

ἱππασία *s.f.* riding ; horsemanship.

ἱππεύς *s.m.* rider ; cavalryman ; knight (*chess*).

ἱππεύω *v.i. & t.* ride ; mount, sit astride.

ἱππικόν *s.n.* cavalry.

ἱπποδρομίες *s.f.pl.* races.

ἱπποδρόμιον *s.n.* racecourse ; circus.

ἱπποκόμος *s.m.* groom.

ἱπποπόταμος *s.m.* hippopotamus.

ἵππ|ος *s.m.* horse ; δέκα ~ων 10-horse-power.

ἱπποσκευή *s.f.* harness.

ἱππότ|ης *s.m.* knight ; (*fig.*) chivalrous man. ~ικός *a.* knightly, chivalrous. ~ισμός *s.m.* chivalry.

ἱπποφορβεῖον *s.n.* stud farm.

ἵπτ|αμαι *v.i.* fly. ~αμένη *s.f.* air-hostess. ~άμενος *s.m.* flyer, airman.

ἰριδ|ίζω *v.i.* be iridescent. ~ισμός *s.m.* iridescence.

ἶρις *s.f.* rainbow ; iris (*of eye*) ; iris (*plant*).

ἶς *s.f.* fibre, filament.

ἴσα *adv.* equally, evenly ; straight, directly ; in a straight line ; ~ ~ exactly, precisely ; ~ μέ up to, as far as, until.

ἰσάδα *s.f.* straightness.

ἰσάζω *v.t.* straighten ; make even.

ἴσαλος *s.f.* (*naut.*) water-line.

ἴσαμε *prep.* (*with acc.*) up to, as far as, until.

ἰσάξιος *a.* equal in worth *or* ability.

ἰσάριθμος *a.* equal in number.

ἰσημερία *s.f.* equinox.

ἰσημερινός 1. *a.* equinoctial. 2. *s.m.* equator.

ἰσθμός *s.m.* isthmus.

ἴσια *adv. see* ἴσα.

ἴσι|ος *a.* straight, level, upright ; honest ; equal (*to*), the same (*as*) (*with μέ*) ; τό ~ο justice, right.

ἰσ(ι)|ώνω *v.t.* straighten ; make even. ~ωμα *s.n.* straightening, levelling ; level road.

ἴσκιος *s.m.* shade.

ἰσο- *denotes* equality ; level.

ἰσόβιος *a.* for life, lifelong.

ἰσόγειον *s.n.* ground floor.

ἰσοδύναμ|ος *a.* equivalent. ~ῶ *v.i.* be equivalent.

ἰσοζύγιον *s.n.* balancing ; ἐμπορικόν ~ balance of trade.

ἰσολογισμός *s.m.* balance-sheet.

ἴσον *adv.* (*math.*) equals.

ἰσόπαλ|ος *a.* equally matched ; βγῆκαν ~οι the result was a draw.

ἰσοπεδώνω *v.t.* make level.

ἰσόπλευρος *a.* equilateral.

ἰσορροπ|ία *s.f.* balance. ~ῶ *v.i. & t.* balance ; ~ημένος well-balanced (*mentally*).

ἴσ|ος *a.* equal (*to*), the same (*as*) ; ἐξ ~ου equally ; τό ~ο justice, right ; κρατῶ τό ~ο sustain the same note ; (*fig.*) play up (*to*), support.

ἰσοσκελής *a.* balanced (*of budget*) ; (*geom.*) isosceles.

ἰσότης *s.f.* equality.

ἰσότιμος *a.* equal in rights, rank, *or* value.

ἰσοφαρίζω *v.t. & i.* equal (*quantitatively*) ; become equal.

ἰσόχρονος *a.* isochronous ; simultaneous.

ἰσοψηφ|ία *s.f.* equal division of votes. ~ῶ *v.i.* obtain same number of votes.

ἰσπανικός *a.* Spanish.

'Ισπανός *s.m.* Spaniard.

ἵσταμαι *v.i.* stand.

ἰστιοδρομία *s.f.* yacht-racing.

ἰστίον *s.n.* sail.

ἰστιοπλοΐα *s.f.* sailing.

ἰστιοφόρον *s.n.* sailing-vessel.

ἱστολογία *s.f.* histology.

ἱστόρημα *s.n.* story.
ἱστορί|α *s.f.* history; story; ~ες (*pl.*) (*prolonged*) trouble, bother.
ἱστορικ|ός *a.* historical; historic; an historian. ~όν *s.n.* story, account (*of event*).
ἱστοριοδίφης *s.m.* historical researcher.
ἱστορῶ *v.t.* relate, tell.
ἱστός *s.m.* 1. mast. 2. loom. 3. web; (*biol.*) tissue.
ἰσχί|ον *s.n.* hip. ~αλγία *s.f.* sciatica.
ἰσχν|ός *a.* lean, thin, meagre. ~αίνω *v.t. & i.* make *or* become lean, thin *or* meagre.
ἰσχυρ|ίζομαι *v.i.* assert, claim. ~ισμός *s.m.* assertion, claim.
ἰσχυρογνώμων *a.* obstinate.
ἰσχυρός *a.* strong; intense; loud.
ἰσχ|ύς *s.f.* strength; force, validity; ἐν ~ύϊ in force.
ἰσχύω *v.i.* have weight *or* validity; be in force.
ἰσ|ῶ *v.t.* equalize. ~οῦμαι *v.i.* (*with* μέ) be equal to.
ἴσ|ωμα, ~ώνω *see* ἴσιω-.
ἴσως *adv.* perhaps; ~ (νὰ) ἔρθη perhaps he will come.
ἰταλικός *a.* Italian.
'Ιταλ|ός, ~ιάνος *s.m.* an Italian.
ἰταμός *a.* defiantly impertinent.
ἰτ|έα, ~ιά *s.f.* willow.
ἰχθυοπωλεῖον *s.n.* fishmonger's.
ἰχθυοτροφεῖον *s.n.* hatchery.
ἰχθύς *s.m.* fish.
ἰχνηλατῶ *v.t.* track down.
ἰχνογράφημα *s.n.* sketch.
ἰχνογραφία *s.f.* sketching.
ἴχνος *s.n.* footprint, track; trace, vestige.
ἰώβειος *a.* of Job.
ἰωβηλαῖον *s.n.* jubilee.
ἰώδιον *s.n.* iodine.
ἰῶμαι *v.i.* be cured.
ἰωνικός *a.* Ionic.
ἰῶτα *s.n.* the letter Ι.
ἰωτακισμός *s.m.* iotacism.

K

κάβα *s.f.* wine-cellar; pool (*in cards*).
καβάκι *s.n.* black poplar.
καβαλιέρος *s.m.* escort, partner.
καβάλλα *adv.* on horseback; astride; (*fam.*) ψωνίζω ~ be taken in (*by seller*).

καβαλλάρης *s.m.* horseman; (*mus.*) bridge (*of violin*).
καβαλλέτο *s.n.* easel.
καβαλλικεύω *v.t. & i.* ride, mount, sit astride; (*fig.*) dominate.
καβαλλίνα *s.f.* dung of horses.
καβάλλ|ος *s.m.*, ~ο *s.n.* fork of trousers.
καβαλλῶ *v.t. & i. see* καβαλλικεύω.
καβα(ν)τζάρω *v.t.* round, double (*cape*).
καβγ|ᾶς *s.m.* quarrel, row. ~αδίζω *v.i.* quarrel. ~ατζῆς *s.m.* quarrelsome person.
κάβ|ος *s.m.* cape, headland; (*naut.*) hawser; (*fam.*) παίρνω ~ο get an inkling.
καβούκι *s.n.* shell (*of tortoise, etc.*).
κάβουρας *s.m.* crab.
καβουρδίζω *v.t.* roast (*beans, etc.*); fry lightly, brown.
καβούρι *s.n.* crab.
καγκάγια *s.f.* (*fam.*) hag.
καγκελάριος *s.m.* chancellor.
κάγκελο *s.n.* banister, rail, railing, grille.
καγκελόπορτα *s.f.* garden gate.
καγχάζω *v.i.* laugh loudly *or* scornfully.
καδένα *s.f.* (watch) chain.
κάδος *s.m.* bucket, tub.
κάδρο *s.n.* framed picture; frame.
καδρόνι *s.n.* beam (*timber*).
καζάνι *s.n.* boiler; cauldron, copper.
καήλα *s.f.* feeling *or* smell of burning; (*fig.*) ardent desire.
καημέν|ος *a.* burnt; (*fig.*) poor, unfortunate; (*fam.*) ~ε καὶ σύ *phrase of mild remonstration.*
καημός *s.m.* sorrow; yearning.
καθ' *see* κατά.
καθά(περ) *adv.* as, according to (*with verb*).
καθαίρεσις *s.f.* deposition, dismissal.
καθαίρω *v.t.* cleanse, purge.
καθαιρῶ *v.t.* depose, dismiss.
καθάπτομαι *v.t.* (*with gen.*) offend (*honour, etc.*).
καθαρεύουσ|α *s.f.* purified (*i.e.* formal) language. ~ιάνος *s.m.* user *or* advocate of this.
καθαρίζω *v.t. & i.* clean, clear; peel, shell, gut; burnish; refine; clarify (*explain*); settle (*account*); (*fam.*) clean out, polish off, kill off. (*v.i.*) become clean *or* clear.
καθαριότης *s.f.* cleanness, cleanliness.
καθάρισμα *s.n.* cleaning, etc. (*see* καθαρίζω).

καθαριστήριον *s.n.* (*dry*) cleaners'.
καθαρίστρ(ι)α *s.f.* charwoman.
κάθαρμα *s.n.* refuse, riffraff, scum.
καθαρόαιμος *a.* thoroughbred.
καθαρογράφω *v.t.* make fair copy of.
καθαρ|ός *a.* clean; clear, distinct, plain; straightforward; pure, unmixed; sheer; net; ~ό μυαλό lucid mind; τό μέτωπό του είναι ~ό he has nothing to be ashamed of; ~ ά 'Εβδομάς first week of Lent.
καθαρότης *s.f.* purity; clarity.
καθάρσιον *s.n.* (*med.*) purgative.
κάθαρσις *s.f.* purification; catharsis; quarantine.
καθαρτήριον *s.n.* purgatory.
καθαρτικός *a.* purgative.
καθ|αυτό, ~εαυτοῦ *adv. & a.* real(ly), genuine(ly).
κάθε *a.* every, each; ~ άλλο far from it; τό ~ τί everything; ~ πού whenever.
κάθειρξις *s.f.* imprisonment.
καθ|είς, ~ένας *pron.* each one; anyone, the first comer.
καθέκαστα *s.n.pl.* details.
καθέκλα *s.f.* chair.
καθελκύω *v.t.* launch.
καθεστώς *a.* established; τό ~ régime, status quo.
κάθετος *a.* vertical; at right-angles.
καθεύδω *v.i.* sleep.
καθηγητής *s.m.* professor; master, teacher.
καθήκι *s.n.* chamber-pot; (*fam.*) riffraff.
καθήκον *s.n.* duty; ~τα (*pl.*) functions.
καθηλώνω *v.t.* nail *or* pin down; immobilize.
καθημαγμένος *a.* bloodstained.
κάθημαι *v.i. see* κάθομαι.
καθημερ(ι)ν|ός *a.* daily, everyday. ~ή *s.f.* working day. ~ό *s.n.* daily bread. ~ῶς *adv.* daily.
καθησυχάζω *v.t. & i.* calm, reassure, allay; become calm *or* quiet; be allayed.
κάθιδρος *a.* bathed in sweat.
καθιερώ|νω *v.t.* consecrate; establish, countenance (*a practice*); είναι ~μένο it is customary.
καθίζησις *s.f.* subsidence; (*chem.*) precipitate.
καθίζω *v.t.* seat, place; strand (*ship*).
καθίκι *s.n. see* καθήκι.
καθισιά *s.f.* sitting (*interval of time*).
καθισιό *s.n.* not working, doing nothing.

κάθισμα *s.n.* manner of sitting; seat; subsidence; running aground.
καθίσταμαι *v.i.* become, turn out to be, prove.
καθιστικός *a.* sedentary.
καθιστός *a.* seated.
καθιστῶ *v.t.* make, appoint, set up.
καθό *adv.* as, qua.
καθοδηγητής *s.m.* political indoctrinator.
καθοδηγῶ *v.t.* give guidance to.
κάθοδος *s.f.* descent, alighting; invasion; (*phys.*) cathode.
καθολικεύω *v.t. & i.* generalize.
καθολικ|ός *a.* universal, general; catholic. ~όν *s.n.* 1. (*eccl.*) nave. 2. ledger.
καθόλου *adv.* in general; (not) at all.
κάθομαι *v.i.* be seated; sit (down); settle, sink; remain; spend time (*doing sthg.*); be without work.
καθομιλουμένη *s.f.* spoken language, everyday speech.
καθορ|ίζω *v.t.* determine, fix, state precisely. ~ισμός *s.m.* fixing, settling.
καθοσίωσ|ις *s.f.* consecration; έγκλημα ~εως high treason, outrage.
καθόσον *adv.* (in) so far as; as (*causal*).
καθούμεν|ος *a.* seated; στά καλά ~α out of the blue.
καθρέπτης *s.m.* mirror.
καθρεφτίζ|ω *v.t.* mirror, reflect. ~ομαι *v.i.* look in the mirror, be reflected.
κάθυγρος *a.* wet, sodden.
καθυστέρησις *s.f.* delay; retardation.
καθυστερ|ῶ *v.t. & i.* delay, withhold; be behind *or* late; ~ημένος backward; ~ούμενα arrears.
καθώς 1. *conj.* as, when. 2. *adv.* as, such as; ~ πρέπει proper, respectable.
καί *conj.* and, also, too, even; ~ . . . ~ both . . . and; ~ νά even if; ~ νά . . . ~ νά μή whether . . . or not; θέλει ~ δὲ θέλει whether he likes it or not. *Also functions like* νά, ὅτι, πώς, πού, διότι.
καΐκ|ι *s.n.* caique. ~τσῆς *s.m.* captain *or* owner of caique.
καΐλα *s.f. see* καήλα.
καϊμάκι *s.n.* thick cream; froth on coffee.
καινός *a.* new.
καινοτομία *s.f.* innovation.
καινουργ|ής, ~ιος *a.* new.
καίπερ *conj.* although.
καιρικός *a.* of the weather, atmospheric.
καίριος *a.* timely; telling; mortal (*wound*); vital (*spot*).

καιρ|ός *s.m.* time, period; weather, wind; μὲ τὸν ~ό eventually; στὸν ~ό του in (its) season.

καιρο|σκοπῶ, ~φυλακτῶ *v.i.* bide one's time.

καισαρικός *a.* Caesarean.

καϊσί *s.n.* (*sweet-kernelled*) apricot.

καίτοι *conj.* although.

καί|ω *v.t. & i.* burn, shrivel; smart; be hot *or* alight. ~ομαι *v.i.* be on fire; get burned *or* shrivelled; fuse; κάηκα (*fam.*) I got caught out.

κακά *adv.* badly.

κακάο *s.n.* cocoa.

κακαρίζω *v.i.* cackle.

κακαρ|ώνω *v.t. & i.* (*fam.*) perish from cold; τὰ ~ωσε he kicked the bucket.

κακεντρέχεια *s.f.* malevolence.

κακία *s.f.* vice; malice, ill-will.

κακίζω *v.t.* censure, find fault with.

κακιώνω *v.i.* get angry; become on bad terms.

κακο- denotes bad, difficult.

κακοανατεθραμμένος *a.* ill-bred.

κακοβάζω *v.i.* form suspicions; imagine the worst.

κακόβουλος *a.* malevolent.

κακογερνῶ *v.i.* suffer unhappy old age; age prematurely; become ugly in old age.

κακογλωσσιά *s.f.* scandalous gossip.

κακοδαιμονία *s.f.* misfortune, distress.

κακοήθης *a.* evil, immoral; (*med.*) malignant, pernicious.

κακόηχος *a.* ill-sounding.

κακοκαιρία *s.f.* bad weather.

κακοκαρδίζω *v.t. & i.* disappoint, distress; suffer disappointment *or* distress.

κακοκεφαλιά *s.f.* folly, ill-considered action.

κακοκεφιά *s.f.* bad mood.

κακολογία *s.f.* casting aspersions.

κακομαθ|αίνω *v.t. & i.* learn badly; spoil (*child, etc.*); get into bad habits; ~ημένος ill-behaved, spoiled.

κακομελετῶ *v.t. & i.* bring bad luck (on) (*with inauspicious words*).

κακομεταχειρίζομαι *v.t.* ill-treat.

κακό|μοιρος, ~μοίρης *a.* unfortunate, poor (*commiserative*).

κακ|ό(ν) *s.n.* evil; harm; wrong; ill fortune; uproar; παίρνω ἀπὸ ~ό take a dislike to; τὸ ἔχω σὲ ~ό I think it a bad omen; ψάρια καὶ ~ό fish galore; τοῦ κάκου in vain; σκάει ἀπ' τὸ ~ό του he is bursting with rage.

κακοπαίρνω *v.t.* take amiss; speak roughly to.

κακοπέραση *s.f.* hardship.

κακοπερνῶ *v.i.* suffer hardship; have a hard life.

κακοπέφτω *v.i.* make a bad marriage.

κακοπιστία *s.f.* bad faith.

κακοπόδαρος *a.* bringing ill luck.

κακοποι|ός *a.* injurious; a malefactor. ~ῶ *v.t.* ill-treat; rape.

κακο(ρ)ρίζικος *a.* unlucky; (*fam.*) wretched, cussed.

κακός *a.* bad, evil; ill-natured.

κακοσμία *s.f.* bad smell.

κακοσυνηθίζω *v.t. & i.* spoil (*child, etc.*); get into bad habits.

κακοσυσταίνω *v.t.* bring into discredit; speak ill of.

κακοτοπιά *s.f.* rough ground; (*fig.*) awkward situation.

κακοτυχία *s.f.* mischance, ill fortune.

κακοτυχίζω *v.t.* express pity for.

κακοτυχῶ *v.i.* suffer ill fortune.

κακούργημα *s.n.* felony, crime.

κακουργ(ι)οδικεῖον *s.n.* criminal court.

κακοῦργος 1. *a.* criminal. 2. *s.m.* felon, criminal; (*fig.*) cruel person.

κακουχία *s.f.* hardship.

κακοφαίν|ομαι *v.i.* μοῦ ~εται it offends me, I take exception to it; κακοφανισμένος offended, piqued.

κακοφέρνομαι *v.i.* behave rudely.

κακοφορμίζω *v.t. & i.* (cause to) fester.

κακοφτιαγμένος *a.* badly done *or* made; ill-shaped.

κακόφωνος *a.* cacophonous.

κάκτος *s.f.* cactus.

κακῶς *adv.* badly.

κάκωσις *s.f.* maltreatment; hardship.

καλά *adv.* well; properly; all right; γιὰ (τὰ) ~ seriously, definitely; πάει ~ all right! τὰ ἔχω ~ μέ be on good terms with; σώνει (*or* ναί) καὶ ~ with obstinate insistence; τὸν κάνω ~ I cure him *or* (*fig.*) I can handle him.

κάλ|αθος *s.m.,* ~άθι *s.n.* basket; ~αθος ἀχρήστων waste-bin.

καλάϊ *s.n.* solder.

καλαισθησία *s.f.* good taste.

καλαϊτζῆς *s.m.* tinker.

καλαμαρᾶς *s.m.* scribe; (*fam.*) pen-pusher.

καλαμάρι *s.n.* 1. inkstand. 2. cuttle-fish.

καλαματιανός *a.* (dance) of Kalamata.

καλάμι s.n. reed, cane; fishing-rod; bobbin; shin-bone.

κάλαμος s.m. reed, cane; pen.

καλαμοσάκχαρον s.n. cane sugar.

καλαμπαλίκι s.n. (fam.) mass of people or things; ~α (pl.) paraphernalia; testicles.

καλαμπόκι s.n. maize.

καλαμπούρι s.n. pun.

κάλαντα s.n.pl. Christmas and New Year carols.

καλαντάρι s.n. calendar.

καλαπόδι s.n. shoemaker's last.

καλαφατίζω v.t. caulk.

καλέμι s.n. pen; chisel.

κάλεσμα s.n. invitation; ~τα (pl.) guests.

καλεσμένος a. invited; a guest.

καλή s.f. ή ~ του (poetic) his bride or beloved; see also **καλός**.

καλημαύκι s.n. Orthodox priest's headgear.

καλημέρα int. & s.f. good-morning.

καληνύχτα int. & s.f. good-night.

καλησπέρα int. & s.f. good-afternoon, good-evening.

κάλι s.n. potash.

καλιακούδα s.f. crow.

καλιγώνω v.t. shoe (horse).

κάλλια adv. better.

καλλιέπεια s.f. fine language.

καλλιέργεια s.f. cultivation, culture.

καλλιεργήσιμος a. cultivable.

καλλιεργητής s.m. cultivator.

καλλιεργώ v.t. cultivate; foster, develop.

καλλικάντζαρος s.m. goblin.

κάλλι|ος a. better, superior. ~ο adv. better.

καλλιστεί|ον s.n. prize for beauty; ~α (pl.) beauty contest.

κάλλιστ|ος a. most beautiful; best. ~α adv. very well.

καλλιτερ- see **καλυτερ-**.

καλλιτέχνημά s.n. work of art.

καλλιτέχνης s.m. artist.

καλλιτεχνία s.f. art (esp. fine arts); artistry.

καλλιτεχνικός a. of art or arti ts; artistic.

καλλονή s.f. beauty.

κάλλος s.n. beauty.

καλλυντικός a. cosmetic.

καλλωπίζω v.t. beautify, embellish.

καλμάρω v.t. & i. make or become calm.

καλντερίμι s.n. cobbles, cobbled street.

καλο- denotes good, well.

καλοαναθρεμμένος a. well-bred.

καλόβαθρον s.n. stilt.

καλοβαλμένος a. well appointed or turned out.

καλοβλέπω v.i. & t. have good sight; look well at; look favourably on; covet, ogle.

καλόβολος a. easy-going, obliging.

καλόγερος s.m. monk; boil; clothes-horse; hat-stand; hopscotch; μπῆκε ό ~ στὸ φαΐ the food is burnt.

καλόγηρος s.m. monk.

καλόγνωμος a. well-disposed.

καλόγρια s.f. nun.

καλοδεμένος a. well bound or tied; well set (ring); well set-up (man).

καλοδεχούμενος a. welcome; welcoming.

καλοζῶ v.i. & t. live well; maintain in comfort.

καλοήθης a. moral; (med.) benign.

καλοθελητής s.m. (ironic) well-wisher.

καλοθρεμμένος a. well-nourished.

καλοκάγαθος a. exceptionally good and kind (person).

καλοκαίρ|ι s.n. summer; summery weather. ~ία s.f. fine weather. ~ινός a. of summer; summery.

καλοκαμωμένος a. well prepared or finished; shapely, handsome.

καλοκαρδίζω v.t. & i. cheer, gladden; be cheered or gladdened.

καλόκαρδος a. kindly, jovial.

καλοκοιτάζω v.t. look carefully at; look after well; covet, ogle.

καλομαθ|αίνω v.t. & i. learn well; pamper; become pampered; ~ημένος well-behaved; pampered.

καλομελετῶ v.t. & i. bring good luck (to) (with auspicious words).

καλό|μοιρος, ~μοίρης a. fortunate.

καλ|ό(ν) s.n. good; ~ά (pl.) benefits, riches; στὸ ~ό so long! μὲ τὸ ~ό safely, with God's help; ~οῦ κακοῦ or (γιὰ) ~ὸ κακό for better for worse; τὸ ~ὸ πού σοῦ θέλω take my advice; παίρνω μὲ τὸ ~ ὁ wheedle; τὸν πῆρα ἀπὸ ~ό I regard him favourably; ~ὸ νάχεις formula of entreaty; σὲ ~ό σου expression of mild disapproval; βάζω τὰ ~ά μου put on one's best clothes; δὲν εἶναι στὰ ~ά του he is not in good form or health or a good mood or his right mind.

καλοντυμένος a. well-dressed.

καλοπέραση s.f. comfort, well-being.

καλοπερνῶ v.i. have an easy life; have a good time.

καλοπιάνω v.t. wheedle, get round.

καλοπόδαρος a. bringing good luck.

καλοπροαίρετος a. well-intentioned.

καλοριφέρ s.n. central-heating (radiator); heater. [F. *calorifère*]

καλο(ρ)ρίζικος a. lucky, auspicious.

καλόρχεται v.i. it fits (*of clothes*); it is welcome.

κάλος s.m. corn, callus.

καλ|ός a. good; kind; ~αἱ τέχναι fine arts; ὥρα~ή greeting or farewell; μιὰ καὶ ~ή once and for all; ἡ ~ή the right side (*of cloth, etc.*); τὸν ξέρω ἀπ' τὴν ~ή του I know his real character; τοῦ τὰ εἶπα ἀπ' τὴν ~ή I gave him a piece of my mind; ὁ ~ός της (*poetic*) her good man or lover; ~έ familiar mode of address.

καλοσυνηθ|ίζω v.t. & i. pamper; become pampered; ~ισμένος well-behaved, pampered.

καλοσυσταίνω v.t. do credit to; speak well of, recommend.

καλόττα s.f. crown (*of hat*).

καλότυχ|ος a. fortunate. ~ίζω v.t. envy, consider fortunate.

καλούπ|ι s.n. form, mould. ~ώνω v.t. put into moulds; (*fig.*) deceive.

καλούτσικος a. fair, passable, goodish.

καλοφαίν|ομαι v.i. μοῦ ~εται I am pleased.

καλοφτιασμένος a. well made or built.

καλπάζω v.t. gallop.

καλπάκι s.n. fur cap.

καλπασμός s.m. gallop.

κάλπη s.f. ballot-box; βάζω ~ stand for election.

κάλπικος a. counterfeit.

καλπονόθευσις s.f. electoral fraud.

καλπουζάνος s.m. counterfeiter; (*fig.*) dishonest person.

κάλτσα s.f. sock, stocking; τοῦ διαβόλου ~ sly fox.

καλτσοδέτα s.f. garter.

καλύβ|α, ~η s.f., ~ι s.n. hut.

κάλυμμα s.n. cover, covering; headgear.

κάλυξ s.m. (*bot.*) calyx, bud; (*mil.*) cartridge case; (*anat.*) calix.

καλύπτω v.t. cover; conceal.

καλυτερεύω v.t. & i. improve.

καλύτερ|ος a. better. ~α adv. better.

κάλυψις s.f. (act of) covering.

κάλφας s.m. foreman mason; apprentice.

καλῶ v.t. call, name; summon; invite.

καλώδιον s.n. rope; (*electric*) cable.

κάλως s.m. thick rope, hawser.

καλῶς adv. well; ἔχει ~ good, agreed; ~ ὡρίσατε welcome; ~ τονε welcome to him; ~ ἐχόντων τῶν πραγμάτων all being well.

καλωσορίζω v.t. welcome.

καλωσυνεύω v.i. clear up, brighten.

καλωσύνη s.f. goodness, kindness; fine weather.

κάμα s.f. sort of dagger.

καμάκι s.n. harpoon.

κάμαρα s.f. room.

καμάρα s.f. arch, vault.

καμάρι s.n. air of pride, jaunty air; object of pride.

καμαριέρα s.f. chamber-maid.

καμαρίνι s.n. (*stage*) dressing-room.

καμαρότος s.m. (*ship's*) steward.

καμαρώνω v.i. & t. wear a proud air; take pride (in).

καμαρωτ|ός a. 1. arched. 2. with an air of pride. ~ά adv. proudly, jauntily.

κάματος s.m. fatigue; tilling.

καμβάς s.m. canvas (*for embroidery*).

καμήλα s.f. camel.

καμηλοπάρδαλις s.f. giraffe.

καμηλαύκι s.n. see καλημαύκι.

καμινάδα s.f. chimney, funnel.

καμινέτο s.n. spirit-lamp.

καμινεύω v.t. smelt; burn (*in kiln*).

κάμ|ινος s.f., ~ίνι s.n. furnace, kiln.

καμιόνι s.n. lorry.

καμμιά pron. f. see κανένας.

καμμύω v.t. half close (*eyes*).

κάμνω v.t. see κάνω.

καμουτσί(κι) s.n. whip.

καμουφλάρω v.t. camouflage.

καμπάνα s.f. (*church, etc.*) bell; (*fam.*) scolding.

καμπαναρειό s.n. belfry.

καμπανιά s.f. bell-ringing; stroke of bell; (*fam.*) unpleasant hint.

καμπάνια s.f. newspaper campaign.

καμπανίτης s.m. champagne.

κα(μ)παρ(ν)τίνα s.f. gabardine.

κάμπ|η, ~ια s.f. caterpillar.

καμπή s.f. bend, turn.

καμπήσιος a. of the plain.

καμπίνα s.f. cabin.

καμπινές s.m. W.C.

κάμπος s.m. plain, open country.

κάμ|ποσος, ~πόσος pron. some, a fair number (of); κάνω τὸν ~πόσο talk big or blusteringly.

καμπούρα s.f. hump, boss.

καμπούρης *s.m.* a hunchback.

καμπουριάζω *v.t. & i.* hunch, bend; stoop, become bent.

καμπουρωτός *a.* humped, bent, curved.

κάμπτ|ω *v.t. & i.* bend; round (*bend, cape*); (*v.i.*) turn. ∼ομαι *v.i.* bend, give way; drop (*of prices*).

καμπύλη *s.f.* curve.

καμπύλος *a.* curved, convex, rounded.

καμτσίκι *s.n.* whip.

καμφορά *s.f.* camphor.

κάμψις *s.f.* bending, giving way; lessening, fall.

κάμωμα *s.n.* making; ripening; ∼τα (*pl.*) coquettish airs, affectation of reluctance.

καμωμένος *a.* done, made; ripe.

καμώνομαι *v.i.* pretend; affect reluctance.

κἄν *conj.* at least; οὔτε ∼ not even; ∼ ... ∼ either ... or; ∼ καὶ ∼ a lot (of).

κανάγιας *s.m.* rascal.

κανακάρης *a.* petted, one-and-only; a darling only son.

κανάλι *s.n.* channel, strait.

καναπές *s.m.* sofa, settee.

καναρίνι *s.n.* canary.

κανάτα *s.f.* jug.

κανάτι *s.n.* 1. pitcher. 2. shutter.

κανδήλα *s.f.* votive lamp.

κανείς *pron. see* **κανένας.**

κανέλλα *s.f.* cinnamon.

κανένας *pron.* any, anyone, one; some; (*after neg.*) no, no one; καμμιά ὥρα about an hour; καμμιά φορά some time, sometimes.

κάνθαρος *s.m.* beetle.

κανθός *s.m.* corner of eye.

κανιά *s.n.pl.* (*fam.*) (*spindly*) legs.

κάνν|α, ∼η *s.f.* barrel (*of gun*).

κανναβάτσο|α *s.f.,* ∼ο *s.n.* pack-cloth.

καννάβ|ι *s.n.* hemp. ∼ούρι *s.n.* hempseed.

καννίβαλος *s.m.* cannibal.

κανόνας *s.m.* rule (*measure, principle*).

κανόνι *s.n.* cannon; (*fam.*) ρίχνω or σκάζω∼ go bankrupt; τὸ σκάζω ∼ play truant.

κανονιά *s.f.* cannon-shot.

κανονίζω *v.t.* arrange, regulate, settle.

κανονικός *a.* regular, ordinary, usual; (*eccl.*) canonical.

κανονιοφόρος *s.f.* gunboat.

κανονισμός *s.m.* settlement, regulation(s).

κάνουλα *s.f.* faucet, tap for barrel.

καντάδα *s.f.* serenade.

καντάρι *s.n.* steelyard; hundredweight.

καντήλα *s.f.* (votive) (*olive-oil*) lamp; blister.

καντήλι *s.n.* small (*olive-oil*) light.

καντίνα *s.f.* canteen (*shop*).

κάν|ω *v.t. & i.* 1. do, make, perform; have (*sthg.*) done *or* made; ∼ω μαθήματα have *or* give lessons; ∼ω κοστούμι have a suit made; ∼ω μπάνιο have a bath *or* bathe; τὸν ∼ω καλά I cure him *or* (*fig.*) I can handle him; τοῦ ∼ω καλό I do him good; τὸν ἔ∼α γιά I mistook him for; τὰ ∼ω θάλασσα (*or* σαλάτα) make a mess of it; ∼ω χωρίς do without; ∼ω πίσω move back; δὲν ∼ω μέ I do not get on with; δὲν ∼ει (*νά*) it is not right *or* proper (to); δὲν ∼ει γιά it is not suitable for; ἔχει νὰ ∼ει it makes a difference; τὸ ἴδιο μοῦ ∼ει it is all the same to me; ∼ει ἀέρα it is windy. 2. produce; ∼ω παιδί have a child; ἡ Ἑλλάδα ∼ει κρασί Greece produces wine; ∼ω νερά leak, (*fig.*) hedge. 3. behave, be occupied; spend *or* take time; ∼ω σὰν τρελλός (*γιά*) behave like a madman, be madly keen (on); ∼ω τὸν τρελλό pretend to be mad; ∼ω τὸ γιατρό be a doctor; ∼ω πώς pretend that; ∼ω νά make an effort to; ἔ∼ε καιρό νὰ μᾶς γράψει he took a long time to write to us; ἔ∼ε στὴν Ἀμερική he has been in America; ἔ∼ε γιατρός he was a doctor; ∼ε γρήγορα make haste! 4. τί ∼ετε; how are you? πόσο ∼ει; how much does it cost? ∼ει νὰ πάρω κι' ἄλλα λεφτά there is still some money due to me.

κανών *s.m.* rule (*measure, principle*); (*eccl. & mus.*) canon.

καούρα *s.f.* burning (*sensation*).

κάπα *s.f.* shepherd's cloak.

καπάκι *s.n.* cover, lid, cap.

καπάντζα *s.f.* trap-door; mouse-trap.

καπάρ|ο *s.n.* earnest, deposit. ∼ώνω *v.t.* pay deposit on; book.

καπαρτίνα *s.f.* gabardine.

καπάτσος *a.* clever at getting things done.

κάπελας *s.m.* wine-shop keeper.

καπέλλο *s.n.* hat.

καπετάνιος *s.m.* captain (*of ship or irregulars*).

καπηλ|εία *s.f.* exploitation (*for base ends*). ∼εύομαι *v.t.* exploit thus.

καπηλειό s.n. wine-shop.
καπηλικός a. gross, vulgar.
καπίστρι s.n. halter.
καπλαμάς s.m. veneer.
καπλαντίζω v.t. veneer; (fig.) put protective cover on (quilt, book).
καπνέμπορος s.m. tobacco-merchant.
καπνιά s.f. soot.
καπν|ίζω v.t. & i. smoke; τοῦ ∼ισε νά he took it into his head to.
κάπνισμα s.n. smoking.
καπνιστής s.m. smoker.
καπνιστός a. smoked.
καπνοδόχ|η, ∼ος s.f. chimney, smokestack.
καπνοπώλης s.m. tobacconist.
καπν|ός s.m. 1. (pl. ∼οί) smoke; (pl.) fumes; (fig.) ἔγινε ∼ός he vanished. 2. (pl. τὰ ∼ά) tobacco-plant, tobacco.
κάποιος pron. somebody; some, a certain.
καπόνι s.n. capon.
καπότα s. f. shepherd's cloak.
κάποτε adv. sometimes; some time; once.
κάπου adv. somewhere; ∼ ∼ now and then; ∼ δέκα about ten.
καπούλια s.n.pl. hindquarters.
κάππα s.n. the letter Κ.
κάππαρη s.f. caper (edible).
καπρίτσιο s.n. caprice; (mus.) capriccio.
κάπρος s.m. boar.
κάπως adv. somewhat.
κάρα s.f. head.
καραβάν|α s.f. mess-tin; λόγια τῆς ∼ας nonsense. ∼ᾶς s.m. (pej.) (boorish) officer.
καραβάνι s.n. caravan, company of travellers.
καράβ|ι s.n. ship. ∼ιά s.f. shipload.
καραβίδα s.f. crayfish.
καραβοκύρης s.m. owner or skipper of vessel.
καραβόπανο s.n. sailcloth.
καραβοτσακισμένος a. shipwrecked.
καραγκιόζ|ης s.m. (chief character of) shadow-theatre; (fig.) comical person. ∼λίκι s.n. crudely comical behaviour.
καραδοκῶ v.t. lie in wait for; be on look-out for.
καρακάξα s.f. magpie; (fam.) ugly, talkative woman.
καραμέλα s.f. sweet, bon-bon; lumpsugar.
καραμούζα s.f. toy flute; motor-horn.

καραμπίνα s.f. carbine.
καραμπογιά s.f. green vitriol; jet-black.
καραντίνα s.f. quarantine.
καραούλι s.n. watch, guard; sentinel; look-out post.
καράτι(ον) s.n. carat.
καρατομῶ v.t. behead.
καράφα s.f. carafe, decanter.
καράφλα s.f. see φαλάκρα.
καρβέλι s.n. round loaf.
κάρβουν|ο s.n. charcoal; coal. ∼ιάζω v.t. & i. char. ∼ιάρης s.m. charcoalburner; coal-merchant; coal-man.
κάργα adv. (full) to the brim; tightly.
κάρδαμον s.n. cress.
καρδαμώνω v.i. & t. become invigorated; invigorate.
καρδιά s.f. heart; κάνω ∼ take courage; δὲν βαστᾶ ἡ ∼ μου I have not the courage or the heart (to); (fam.) ἔχω ∼ ἀγγινάρα have many love affairs.
καρδιακός a. cardiac; suffering from heart trouble.
καρδιολόγος s.m. heart specialist.
καρδιοχτύπι s.n. palpitation; (fig.) anxiety.
καρ|έκλα, ∼έγλα s.f. chair.
καρικώνω v.t. darn, mend.
καρίνα s.f. keel.
καρκινοβατῶ v.i. (fig.) go crabwise, hence make no progress.
καρκίνος s.m. crab; cancer; palindrome.
καρκινώδης a. cancerous.
καρκίνωμα s.n. cancerous growth; (fig.) affliction, worrying circumstance.
καρμανιόλα s.f. guillotine; (fig.) danger spot; dishonest card-game; extortionate shop, etc.
καρμίρης s.m. miser.
καρμπόν s.n. carbon-paper. [F. carbone]
καρναβάλι s.n. carnival.
καρντάν s.n. universal joint (of engine). [F. cardan]
καρότο s.n. carrot.
καρ|ούλα s.f., ∼ούμπαλο s.n. bump (on head).
καρούλι s.n. pulley; caster; roller; reel.
καρπαζιά s.f. slap on the head.
καρπερός a. prolific.
καρπίζ|ω v.i. fruit. ∼ομαι v.t. enjoy fruits of.
καρπ|ός s.m. 1. fruit; ξηροὶ ∼οί dried fruit and nuts. 2. wrist.
καρπούζι s.n. watermelon.

καρποῦμαι *v.t.* enjoy fruits of.
καρποφορῶ *v.i.* bear fruit.
καρποφόρος *a.* fruit (*tree*); fruitful; effective; profitable.
καρραγωγεύς *s.m.* cart-driver.
καρρέ I. *s.n.* foursome (*at cards*); open neck (*of dress*); neck so exposed; (*naut.*) ward-room. 2. *a.* square. [F. *carré*]
καρρό *s.n.* diamond (*cards*); check (*pattern*). [F. *carreau*]
κάρρο *s.n.* cart.
καρροτσάκι *s.n.* hand-cart, barrow; pram, push-cart.
καρσί *adv.* opposite.
κάρτα *s.f.* picture postcard; greeting-card; visiting-card.
καρτέρι *s.n.* ambush.
καρτερία *s.f.* patient endurance.
καρτερῶ *v.i. & t.* show patient endurance; wait (for).
κάρτο *s.n.* quarter (*of hour*).
καρυά *s.f.* walnut-tree.
καρύδι *s.n.* walnut; Adam's apple; κάθε καρυδιᾶς ∼ all sorts and conditions of men.
καρυδιά *s.f.* walnut-tree; walnut (*wood*).
καρύκευμα *s.n.* seasoning, sauce.
καρυοθραύστης *s.m.* nutcracker.
καρυοφύλλι *s.n.* I. clove. 2. flint-lock.
καρφ|ί *s.n.* nail; ∼ιά (*pl.*) pedestrian crossing; ∼ὶ δὲν μοῦ καίγεται I do not care a pin; κόβω ∼ιά shiver with cold; τοῦ βάζω τά ἑφτά ∼ιά I tease him.
καρφίτσα *s.f.* pin; brooch.
καρφιτσώνω *v.t.* pin (*on, together*).
κάρφωμα *s.n.* nailing.
καρφ|ώνω *v.t.* nail (up, down, *etc.*); (*fig.*) fix, transfix; τοῦ ∼ώθηκε ἡ ἰδέα he is possessed with the idea; (*fam.*) inform against.
καρχαρίας *s.m.* shark.
κά(σ)σα *s.f.* packing-case; safe; cash-desk; door *or* window frame; (*fam.*) coffin.
κα(σ)σέλλα *s.f.* wooden chest.
κα(σ)σέρι *s.n.* sort of cheese.
κα(σ)σίδα *s.f.* (*fam.*) balding, scurvy head.
κασκαβάλι *s.n. see* κασέρι.
κασκέτο *s.n.* cap.
κασμήρι *s.n.* wool suiting material.
κα(σ)σόνι *s.n.* packing-case.
κασσίτερος *s.m.* tin.
καστανιά *s.f.* I. chestnut-tree; chestnut (*wood*). 2. collapsible picnic-box.

κάστανο *s.n.* chestnut.
καστανός *a.* chestnut (*colour*).
καστόρι *s.n.* beaver (*fur*); felt (*for hats*); sort of leather.
κάστρο *s.n.* fortress.
κάστωρ *s.m.* beaver.
κατά *prep.* I. (*with acc.*) (*place*) towards, by, in the direction of; ∼ ξηρὰν καὶ θάλασσαν by land and sea; καθ' ὁδόν on the way; ∼ κεῖ in that direction; ∼ μέρος aside. (*time*) at, about, during; ∼ αὐτάς these days; καθ' ἥν στιγμήν at the moment when. (*relation*) according to; ∼ τύχην by chance; ∼ βάθος at bottom, thoroughly; τὸ κατ' ἐμέ as for me. (*distribution*) ∼ ἔτος every year, per year; καθ' ἑκάστην every day. 2. (*with gen.*) against; ∼ γῆς to *or* on the ground; φέρομαι ∼ κρημνῶν be heading for destruction; ∼ διαβόλου to the devil.
κατα- denotes down; against; very, completely.
καταβαίνω *v.t. & i. see* κατεβαίνω.
καταβάλλω *v.t.* lay low, exhaust; pay, put down (*money*); ∼ προσπάθειαν make an effort.
κατάβασις *s.f.* descent.
καταβεβλημένος *a.* run-down, done-up.
καταβιβάζω *v.t. see* κατεβάζω.
καταβόθρα *s.f.* swallow-hole; covered drain; (*fig.*) insatiable person.
καταβολάδα *s.f.* layer (*horticulture*).
καταβολ|ή *s.f.* payment; ἀπὸ ∼ῆς κόσμου since the world began.
καταβρεκτήρ *s.m.* water-cart.
καταβρέχω *v.t.* sprinkle, spray, soak.
καταβροχθίζω *v.t.* devour.
καταβυθίζω *v.t.* sink (*in liquid*).
καταγγελία *s.f.* (*law*) charge, complaint; annulment.
καταγέλαστος *a.* an object of ridicule.
καταγῆς *adv.* on *or* to the ground.
καταγίνομαι *v.i.* be busy *or* engaged (*in*).
κάταγμα *s.n.* (*med.*) fracture.
κατάγ|ω *v.t.* win (*victory*). ∼ομαι *v.i.* be descended *or* come (*from*).
καταγωγή *s.f.* origin, descent.
καταγώγιον *s.n.* den of thieves; sink of iniquity.
καταδεικνύω *v.t.* prove, demonstrate.
καταδέχομαι *v.t. & i.* deign to accept; take notice of, be nice to (*inferiors*); deign, condescend, permit oneself (*to*).
κατάδηλος *a.* obvious.
καταδίδω *v.t.* betray, give away.

καταδικάζω *v.t.* condemn; sentence.
κατάδικος *s.m.f.* convict, prisoner.
καταδιωκτικ|ός *a.* of pursuit. ~όν *s.n.* (*aero.*) fighter plane.
καταδιώκω *v.t.* pursue, chase; persecute.
κατάδοσις *s.f.* betrayal.
καταδρομή *s.f.* pursuit; (*naut.*) privateering; ~ τῆς τύχης persistent ill fortune.
καταδρομικόν *s.n.* (*naut.*) cruiser.
καταδυναστεύω *v.t.* oppress.
καταδύομαι *v.i.* dive.
καταθέτω *v.t.* lay (down), deposit; give (*evidence*); lay down (*arms*).
καταθλιπτικ|ός *a.* oppressive, crushing; ~ή ἀντλία compression pump.
καταιγ|ίς, ~ίδα *s.f.* violent storm.
καταιγισμός *s.m.* (*mil.*) concentrated artillery-fire.
καταΐφι *s.n.* sort of oriental cake.
κατακάθ|ι *s.n.* dregs, residue. ~ίζω *v.i.* sink, settle, subside.
κατάκαρδα *adv.* seriously, to heart.
κατακέφαλ|α *adv.* on the head; headlong. ~ιά *s.f.* blow on the head.
κατακλ|είς *s.f.* conclusion, end; ἐν ~είδι in conclusion.
κατακλίνομαι *v.i.* lie down.
κατακλύζω *v.t.* inundate, flood.
κατακλυσμ|ός *s.m.* deluge; (*fig.*) abundance; φέρνω τὸι ~ό make difficulties about trifles.
κατάκοιτος *a.* confined to bed.
κατακόμβη *s.f.* catacomb.
κατάκοπος *a.* tired out, exhausted.
κατακόβ|ω *v.t.* cut deeply *or* in many places *or* on a large scale; cut to pieces. ~ομαι *v.i.* get exhausted; make great efforts.
κατακόρυφ|ος *a.* vertical. ~ον *s.n.* zenith; (*fig.*) extreme degree.
κατακρατῶ *v.t.* withhold unlawfully.
κατακραυγή *s.f.* outcry.
κατακρεουργῶ *v.t.* butcher.
κατακρίνω *v.t.* censure, blame.
κατάκτησις *s.f.* conquest.
κατακτῶ *v.t.* conquer, win.
κατακυρώνω *v.t.* award (*judicially*); knock down (*at auction*); give (*contract*).
καταλαβαίνω *v.t. & i.* understand; notice.
καταλαγιάζω *v.t. & i.* calm (down).
καταλαμβάνω *v.t. & i.* seize, possess oneself of; detect (*wrongdoer*); take up (*space*); understand; notice.

καταλείπω *v.t.* leave (behind).
καταλεπτῶς *adv.* in detail.
καταλήγω *v.i.* end up (*in, as*); lead up (*to*).
κατάληξις *s.f.* termination, end(ing).
καταληπτός *a.* comprehensible.
κατάληψις *s.f.* seizure, occupation; comprehension.
κατάλληλος *a.* suitable.
καταλογίζω *v.t.* impute; charge up.
κατάλογος *s.m.* list; directory; menu; catalogue (*of exhibition, etc.*).
κατάλυμα *s.n.* billet, lodging.
κατάλυσις *s.f.* abolition; billeting; (*chem.*) catalysis.
καταλύω *v.t.* abolish; billet.
καταλῶ *v.t.* wear out, use up; digest.
κατάματα *adv.* straight in the eye.
καταμερίζω *v.t.* apportion.
καταμεσῆς *adv.* right in the middle.
κατάμεστος *a.* very full.
καταμετρῶ *v.t.* measure, count; survey (*land*).
κατάμουτρα *adv.* to *or* in one's face.
καταναλίσκω *v.t.* consume, spend, use up.
κατανάλωσις *s.f.* consumption, using up.
καταναλωτής *s.m.* consumer.
κατανέμω *v.t.* divide up; allot, assign.
κατανεύω *v.i.* nod assent.
κατανο|ῶ *v.t. & i.* fully understand. ~ησις *s.f.* understanding.
κατάντ|ημα, ~ι *s.n.*, ~ια *s.f.* sorry state (*that one is reduced to*).
καταντῶ *v.i. & t.* be reduced (*to*), end up (*in, as, by*); reduce, bring (*to*).
κατάνυξις *s.f.* devout concentration.
καταπακτή *s.f.* trap-door.
καταπάτι *s.n.* dregs, residue.
καταπατῶ *v.t.* trample on; violate; encroach upon.
κατάπαυσις *s.f.* cessation, ending.
καταπέλτης *s.m.* catapult; (*fig.*) bolt from the blue.
καταπέτασμα *s.n.* curtain; (*fam.*) τρώω τὸ ~ eat one's bellyful.
καταπιάνομαι *v.i.* (*with μέ*) start work on, take up.
καταπιέζω *v.t.* oppress.
καταπίνω *v.t.* swallow (up).
καταπίπτω *v.i.* fall, collapse; subside; decline.
καταπλακώνω *v.t.* flatten, squash.
κατάπλασμα *s.n.* poultice.
κατάπλατα *adv.* in the middle of the back.

καταπλέω v.i. & t. sail in; (v.t.) sail down (river).

καταπληκτικός a. amazing.

κατάπληξις s.f. amazement.

καταπλήσσω v.t. amaze.

κατάπλους s.m. sailing in.

καταπνίγω v.t. stifle; suppress.

καταπόδι adv. close behind, on one's heels.

καταπολεμῶ v.t. combat.

καταποντίζ|ω v.t. sink (in sea). ~ομαι v.i. sink, founder.

καταπονάω v.t. & i. hurt badly; suffer great pain.

καταπον|ῶ v.t. tire out, exhaust. ~οῦμαι v.i. get exhausted.

καταπότι(ον) s.n. pill.

καταπραΰνω v.t. assuage, mollify.

κατάπτυστος a. despicable.

κατάπτωσις s.f. collapse, fall; decline.

κατάρα s.f. curse.

καταραμένος a. cursed; the devil.

καταργῶ v.t. abolish, abrogate.

καταριέμαι v.t. & i. curse.

καταρράκτης s.m. waterfall; cataract.

καταρρακώνω v.t. tear or wear to shreds.

καταρρέω v.i. crumble, collapse.

καταρρίπτω v.t. fell, shoot down; demolish; beat (record).

κατάρ|ρους s.m., ~ροή s.f. catarrh.

κατάρρυτος a. well-watered.

κατάρτι s.n. mast.

καταρτίζω v.t. form, put together; prepare, equip.

καταρῶμαι v.t. & i. curse.

κατάσαρκα adv. next to the skin.

κατάσβεσις s.f. quenching, quelling.

κατασκευάζω v.t. make, manufacture, construct; concoct.

κατασκεύασμα s.n. thing made, construction; concoction.

κατασκευή s.f. making, construction; manufacture, make; way a thing is made or shaped.

κατασκήνωσις s.f. camp.

κατάσκοπ|ος s.m. spy. ~εία s.f. espionage.

κατασκοτών|ω v.t. beat unmercifully. ~ομαι v.i. get tired or bruised; make a great effort.

κατασπαράσσω v.t. tear to pieces.

κάτασπρος a. very white.

κατασταλάζω v.i. settle (of sediment); (fig.) reach a decision.

κατασταλτικός a. repressive.

κατάστασις s.f. state (of affairs), condition, situation; status; return (in accountancy); list, register; goods, wealth.

καταστατικόν s.n. charter, statutes.

καταστέλλω v.t. repress, curb.

κατάστηθα adv. full on the chest.

κατάστημα s.n. establishment, institution, office; shop. ~τάρχης s.m. shopkeeper.

κατάστικτος a. spotted, dotted.

κατάστιχον s.n. ledger, register.

καταστολή s.f. repression.

καταστρατηγῶ v.t. get round (law).

καταστρεπτικός a. destructive.

καταστρέφω v.t. destroy, ruin; spoil; deflower.

καταστροφή s.f. destruction, ruin; damage; catastrophe.

κατάστρωμα s.n. deck.

καταστρώνω v.t. draw up, frame.

κατάσχεσις s.f. (law) attachment, distraint.

κατατάσσ|ω v.t. classify, count, rank (among). ~ομαι v.i. enlist.

κατατομή s.f. vertical section; profile.

κατατόπια s.n.pl. (fam.) ins-and-outs (of a place).

κατατοπίζ|ω v.t. direct, give guidance to, brief. ~ομαι v.i. get one's bearings.

κατατρέχω v.t. persecute.

κατατρίβ|ω v.t. wear down. ~ομαι v.i. waste one's time.

κατατροπώνω v.t. rout.

κατατρύχω v.t. torment.

καταυλίζομαι v.i. bivouac.

καταφανής a. evident, clear; conspicuous.

καταφατικός a. affirmative.

κατα|φέρνω v.t. persuade, win over; beat (at sthg.); τὰ ~φέρνω succeed, manage; μοῦ τὴν ~φερε he played me a trick.

καταφερτζῆς s.m. (fam.) one with a knack of succeeding.

καταφέρ|ω v.t. deal (blow); μοῦ ~ε μιά he fetched me a blow. ~ομαι v.i. (with κατά or ἐναντίον) speak against, attack.

καταφεύγω v.i. (with εἰς) take refuge in, have recourse to.

καταφθάνω v.i. arrive (unexpectedly).

κατάφορτος a. (over)loaded.

καταφρονῶ v.t. disdain.

καταφυγή s.f. refuge (abstract).

καταφύγιον s.n. (place of) refuge, shelter.

κατάφυτος a. rich in vegetation.

κατάφωρος *a.* flagrant, obvious (*of misdeed*).

κατάφωτος *a.* brightly lit.

κατάχαμα *adv.* on the ground.

καταχερίζω *v.t.* smack.

καταχθόνιος *a.* infernal; (*fig.*) darkly secretive, deep-laid.

καταχνιά *s.f.* mist.

καταχραστής *s.m.* embezzler.

κατάχρεως *a.* sunk in debt.

κατάχρησ|ις *s.f.* excessive use, abuse; embezzlement; ~εις (*pl.*) excess (*sensual*).

καταχρηστικῶς *adv.* improperly; against regulations; as an exception.

καταχρῶμαι *v.t.* abuse, take undue advantage of; embezzle.

καταχωνιάζω *v.t.* swallow up; hide away.

καταχωρῶ *v.t.* enter (*in register*); insert (*in newspaper*).

καταψηφίζω *v.t.* vote against.

κατάψυξις *s.f.* deep refrigeration.

κατεβάζω *v.t.* bring *or* carry *or* take *or* let down; lower; (*fam.*) devour; ~ μιά strike a blow; τά ~ pull a long face.

κατεβαίν|ω *v.i. & t.* come *or* go *or* get down, descend; dismount; fall (*in level*); μοῦ ~ει I take it into my head (*to*). (*v.t.*) go down (*street, etc.*).

κατεβασιά *s.f.* flood, downpour; cold in the head; cataract (*of eyes*).

κατέβασμα *s.n.* descent, lowering, taking *or* going down; hernia.

κατεβασμένος *a.* downcast; reduced (*in price*).

κατεβατό *s.n.* page (*paper*).

κατεδαφίζω *v.t.* demolish (*building*).

κατειλημμένος *a.* occupied, taken.

κάτεργα *s.n.pl.* galleys (*as punishment*).

κατεργάζομαι *v.t.* work, fashion; plot.

κατεργάρ|ης *s.m.* rascal. ~ιά *s.f.* cunning (act), trick, trickery.

κατέρχομαι *v.t. & i.* descend, come down; fall; ~ εἰς τάς ἐκλογάς take part in elections.

κατεσπευσμένως *adv.* in hot haste.

κατεύθυνσις *s.f.* direction, course.

κατευθύν|ω *v.t.* direct, turn. ~ομαι *v.i.* turn, go.

κατευνάζω *v.t.* appease, calm, assuage.

κατευόδιον *s.n.* good journey (*wish*).

κατέχω *v.t.* have, hold, occupy; know.

κατεψυγμένος *a.* frozen; frigid (*zone*).

κατηγορηματικός *a.* categorical; (*gram.*) attributive.

κατηγορητήριον *s.n.* (*law*) indictment.

κατηγορία *s.f.* 1. accusation. 2. category.

κατήγορος *s.m.* (*law*) plaintiff; δημόσιος ~ prosecutor.

κατηγορούμεν|ος *a.* accused; (*law*) defendant. ~ον *s.n.* (*gram.*) complement.

κατηγορῶ *v.t.* accuse, charge; criticize.

κατηφής *a.* downcast.

κατήφορος *s.m.* downward slope, declivity.

κατηχ|ῶ *v.t.* catechize, initiate, admonish. ~ησις *s.f.* catechism.

κάτι *pron.* something; some, certain; (*adv.*) somewhat; νά ~ μῆλα there are (*beautiful*) apples for you!

κάτι *s.n.* fold; strand (*of thread*).

κατισχύω *v.i. & t.* (*with gen.*) prevail (over).

κατι|ών *a.* descending; ~όντες (*s.m.pl.*) descendants.

κατμᾶς *s.m.* makeweight (*of meat*).

κατοικία *s.f.* habitation, residence.

κατοικίδιος *a.* domestic (*animal*).

κάτοικος *s.m.f.* inhabitant, resident.

κατοικῶ *v.i. & t.* (*with acc. or* εἰς) live, dwell (in), inhabit.

κατολίσθησις *s.f.* landslip.

κατόπιν *adv.* behind; afterwards; ~ ἀπό after; τὸν πῆρα τὸ ~ I followed him closely.

κατοπτεύω *v.t.* keep watch on, observe. (*from above*).

κατοπτρίζω *v.t. see* καθρεφτίζω.

κάτοπτρον *s.n.* mirror.

κατόρθωμα *s.n.* feat, exploit.

κατορθώνω *v.t.* accomplish, succeed in.

κατορθωτός *a.* feasible.

κάτουρ|ο, ~λιό *s.n.* (*fam.*) urine.

κατουρ|ῶ *v.i. & t.* make water (on). ~ιέμαι *v.i.* desire to make water; wet oneself; (*fam.*) be in a funk.

κατοχή *s.f.* possession, keeping; (*mil.*) occupation.

κάτοχος *s.m.* possessor; ~ τῆς Ἀγγλικῆς having a command of English.

κατοχυρώνω *v.t.* fortify; (*fig.*) safeguard.

κατρακυλῶ *v.t. & i.* bring *or* come tumbling down.

κατράμι *s.n.* tar.

κατραπακιά *s.f.* slap on the head.

κατσαβίδι *s.n.* screwdriver.

κατσάβραχα *s.n.pl.* rocky ground.

κατσάδα *s.f.* scolding.

κατσαμάκι *s.n.* affectation of reluctance; evasion.

κατσαρίδα *s.f.* cockroach.

κατσαρόλα *s.f.* saucepan.

κατσαρ|ός *a.* curly. ~ό *s.n.* curl.

κατσ(ι)άζω *v.t. & i.* (cause to) waste away.

κατσίβελος *s.m.* gipsy; sloven.

κατσίκα *s.f.* she-goat.

κατσικήσιος *a.* goat's.

κατσίκι *s.n.* kid; goat.

κατσουφιάζω *v.i.* frown, look sullen.

κάτω *adv.* down, below, underneath; on the ground; τὸ ~ ~ when all is said and done; ἀπάνω ~ up-and-down, approximately; ἀπὸ ~ (from) below, underneath; ἄνω ~ upside down (*in confusion*), upset; ἡ ~ Βουλή Lower Chamber; τὰ ρίχνω ~ give up, throw in one's hand; βάζω ~ defeat (*person*); παίρνω τὴν ~ βόλτα get worse; ~ τὰ χέρια hands off! ~ ἡ κυβέρνησις down with the government! (*prep. with ἀπὸ or gen.*) below, under, less than; ~ τοῦ μηδενός below zero.

κατώγ|ειον, ~ι *s.n.* (lower) ground-floor.

κάτωθεν *adv.* (from) below.

κατώτατος *a.* lowest; minimum.

κατώτερος *a.* lower; inferior.

κατωφέρεια *s.f.* downward slope.

κατώφλι *s.n.* threshold.

καυγᾶς *s.m. see* καβγᾶς.

καύκαλο *s.n.* skull; shell (*of crab, etc.*).

καυκί *s.n.* shell (*of crab, etc.*).

καϋμ- *see* καημ-.

καῦμα *s.n.* heat; burn; κυνικά ~τα dog-days.

καύσιμ|ος *a.* combustible; ~α (*s.n.pl.*) fuel.

καῦσις *s.f.* burning; combustion.

καυστικός *a.* caustic.

καύσων *s.m.* heat-wave.

καυτερός *a.* hot, peppery; (*fig.*) scathing.

καυτηριάζω *v.t.* cauterize; brand (*animals*); (*fig.*) reprobate.

καυτός *a.* burning hot, boiling.

καύχημα *s.n.* boast, object of pride.

καυχηματίας *s.m.* boaster.

καυχησιά *s.f.* boast, boasting.

καυχ|ιέμαι, ~ῶμαι *v.i. & t.* boast (of).

καφάσι *s.n.* lattice; crate (*for fruit*).

καφεκοπτεῖον *s.n.* shop where coffee is ground.

καφενεῖον *s.n.* coffee-house, café.

καφές *s.m.* coffee.

καφετζῆς *s.m.* café-keeper.

καφετής *a.* coffee-coloured.

καφωδεῖον *s.n.* café chantant.

καχεκτικός *a.* sickly, stunted.

καχεξία *s.f.* (*med.*) cachexy.

καχύποπτος *a.* mistrustful.

κάψα *s.f.* 1. great heat. 2. crucible.

καψαλίζω *v.t.* singe; toast.

καψερός *a.* (*fam.*) poor, unfortunate.

κάψιμο *s.n.* burning (*act or sensation*); burn.

καψοῦλες *s.f.pl.* eyelets for shoelaces.

καψ|οῦλι, ~ύλλιον *s.n.* percussion-cap; (*med.*) capsule.

καψώνω *v.i.* feel very hot.

κβάντουμ *s.n.* (*physics*) quantum.

κέδρος *s.f.* cedar.

κεῖμαι *v.i.* lie; be found.

κείμεν|ος *a.* existing, prevailing (*laws, etc.*). ~ον *s.n.* text.

κειμήλιον *s.n.* precious object, relic, heirloom.

κεῖνος *pron. see* ἐκεῖνος.

κέκ *s.n.* cake. [E. *cake*]

κεκοιμημένοι *s.m.pl.* οἱ ~ the departed.

κεκορεσμένος *a.* charged, saturated.

κέκτημαι *v.t.* have, possess.

κελα(ϊ)δῶ *v.i.* sing (*of birds*), warble.

κελαρύζω *v.i.* purl (*of stream*).

κελεπούρι *s.n.* find, bargain.

κέλευσμα *s.n.* command, bidding.

κελευστής *s.m.* (*naut.*) chief petty officer.

κέλης *s.m.* (*riding*) horse; (*naut.*) captain's launch.

κελλάρι *s.n.* larder.

κελλί(ον) *s.n.* cell.

κέλυφος *s.n.* shell (*of nut, egg, etc.*).

κεμέρι *s.n.* money-belt.

κενόδοξος *a.* vain, conceited.

κενόν *s.n.* void, empty space; vacuum; gap; vacancy.

κενός *a.* empty, vacant; vain, idle.

κέντημα *s.n.* sting, prick; needlework, embroidery.

κεντητός *a.* embroidered.

κεντιά *s.f.* sting, bite, prick; (*fig.*) cutting remark.

κεντράδι *s.n.* graft.

κεντρί *s.n.* sting (*organ*).

κεντρίζω *v.t.* sting; graft.

κεντρικός *a.* central.

κεντρομόλος *a.* centripetal.

κέντρον s.n. 1. sting, prick, goad. 2. centre; τηλεφωνικὸν ~ telephone exchange. 3. place of entertainment or refreshment.

κεντρόφυξ a. centrifugal.

κέντρωμα s.n. sting (wound); grafting.

κεντρώνω v.t. sting; graft.

κεντῶ v.t. & i. sting, prick, goad; rouse, provoke; embroider.

κενώνω v.t. empty; serve up (dish).

κένωσις s.f. emptying; evacuation (of bowels); serving up (of dish).

κεραία s.f. antenna; wire, aerial; trolley (of tram); minus-sign, dash.

κεραμεῖον s.n. tile-works, pottery.

κεραμίδα s.f. tile; (fam.) μοῦ ἦρθε ~ it was a bombshell to me.

κεραμίδι s.n. tile; peak (of cap).

κεραμική s.f. ceramics.

κέραμος s.m.f. tile.

κέρας s.n. horn; wing (of army, etc.); ~ τῆς Ἀμαλθείας horn of plenty.

κεράσ|ι s.n. cherry. ~ένιος a. cherry-like; of cherry-wood. ~ιά s.f. cherry-tree.

κέρασμα s.n. treating (to drink, etc.); tip.

κερατᾶς s.m. (fam.) cuckold; (as term of abuse, also joc.) bastard.

κερατένιος a. (fam.) bloody, confounded.

κέρατο s.n. horn; (fam.) ~ (βερνικωμένο) cross-grained person.

κερατώνω v.t. (fam.) cuckold.

κεραυνοβόλος a. like lightning; sudden and dire; ~ ἔρως love at first sight.

κεραυνοβολῶ v.i. & t. hurl thunderbolts (at); (fig.) dumbfound.

κεραυνός s.m. thunderbolt.

κερδ|ίζω, ~αίνω v.t. & i. earn, gain, win; appear in better light; ~ίζει τὸ βράδυ it looks better at night.

κέρδος s.n. gain, profit.

κερδοσκοπῶ v.i. profiteer.

κερένιος a. waxen.

κερί s.n. wax; candle.

κερκίς s.f. shuttle; wedge-shaped tier of seats.

κέρμα s.n. fragment; small coin; token for slot-machine.

κερνῶ v.t. treat, stand, buy (with double acc.).

κερώνω v.t. & i. polish with wax; become pale as wax.

κεσάτι s.n. lack of business.

κεσές s.m. shallow bowl (for jam, etc.).

κετσές s.m. coarse felt.

κεφάλα s.f. big head.

κεφαλαιοκρατία s.f. capitalism.

κεφάλαι|ον s.n. 1. (fin.) capital; ~α (pl.) funds; (fig.) asset to community (person). 2. chapter.

κεφαλαῖον s.n. capital letter.

κεφαλαλγία s.f. headache.

κεφαλάρι s.n. fountainhead; cornerstone; capital (of column); bolster; bed head.

κεφάλας s.m. big-headed or thick-headed person.

κεφαλ|ή s.f. head; leader; ἐπὶ ~ῆς in charge.

κεφάλι s.n. head; (fig.) brains, driving-force; κάνω τοῦ ~οῦ μου go one's own way; πέφτω μὲ τὸ ~ apply oneself avidly; βάζω τὸ ~ μου warrant, wager; κατεβάζει τὸ ~ του he is inventive.

κεφαλικός a. of the head; capital; ~ φόρος poll-tax.

κεφαλόδεσμος s.m. head-scarf; bandeau.

κέφαλος s.m. sort of mullet.

κεφαλοτύρι s.n. hard cheese (for grating).

κεφάτος a. in good spirits.

κέφι s.n. good mood, gaiety, gusto; στὸ ~ slightly tipsy, merry; κάνω τὸ ~ μου do as one pleases; κάνω ~ make merry.

κεφτές s.m. rissole.

κεχρί s.n. millet.

κεχριμπάρι s.n. amber.

κηδεία s.f. funeral.

κηδεμών s.m.f. guardian (of minor).

κηλεπίδεσμος s.m. (med.) truss.

κήλη s.f. hernia.

κηλ|ίς s.f. stain. ~ιδώνω v.t. stain, sully.

κῆπος s.m. garden.

κηπουρ|ός s.m. gardener. ~ική s.f. gardening.

κηρήθρα s.f. honeycomb.

κηρίον s.n. candle; candle-power.

κηροπήγιον s.n. candlestick.

κηρός s.m. wax.

κήρυγμα s.n. preaching, sermon.

κήρ|υξ, ~υκας s.m. herald, crier; (fig.) partisan, advocate (of).

κηρύσσω v.t. & i. proclaim, declare; preach.

κῆτος s.n. cetacean; sea-monster.

κηφήν s.m. drone (bee, also fig.).

κι conj. see καί.

κιαλάρω v.t. look at through binoculars; espy; have one's eye on.

κιάλια s.n.pl. binoculars.

κίβδηλος *a.* debased, counterfeit (*of money*); (*fig.*) false.

κιβώτιον *s.n.* large box; ~ *ταχυτήτων* gear-box.

κιβωτός *s.f.* Ark.

κιγκλίδωμα *s.n.* balustrade, banisters, railings, iron bars.

κιθάρα *s.f.* guitar.

κιλίμι *s.n.* pileless carpet.

κιλλίβας *s.m.* gun-carriage.

κιλό *s.n.* kilo(gram).

κιμ|ᾶς *s.m.* minced meat; (*fam.*) *κάνω* ~ᾶ make mincemeat of.

κιμωλία *s.f.* chalk.

κινά *s.f.* henna.

κίναιδος *s.m.* sodomite.

κινδυν|εύω *v.i. & t.* be in danger, risk, endanger; ~εψε *νὰ πνιγῇ* he nearly got drowned.

κίνδυνος *s.m.* danger, risk.

κινέζικα *s.n.pl.* Chinese (*language*); (*fam.*) anything unintelligible.

κίνημα *s.n.* movement (*action*); (*fig.*) step, measure; uprising.

κινηματογράφος *s.m.* cinema.

κίνησις *s.f.* movement, motion (*action or abstract*); flow of traffic *or* passers-by; activity (*social, business, etc.*).

κινητήρ *s.m.* motor.

κινητοποιῶ *v.t.* mobilize.

κινητ|ός *a.* movable, mobile. ~ά *s.n.pl.* movable property, estate.

κίνητρον *s.n.* motive.

κινίν|η *s.f.*, ~ο *s.n.* quinine; ~ο (*fig.*) anything bitter.

κιν|ῶ *v.t. & i.* set in movement, work; move, rouse; start (*war, lawsuit*). (*v.i.*) set out. ~οῦμαι *v.i.* move; bestir oneself.

κιόλα(ς) *adv.* already; as well.

κιονόκρανον *s.n.* capital (*of column*).

κιονοστοιχία *s.f.* colonnade.

κιόσκι *s.n.* kiosk; pavilion.

κιούγκι *s.n.* drain-pipe.

κιούπι *s.n.* clay storage-jar.

κιρσός *s.m.* varicose vein.

κίσσα *s.f.* magpie.

κισσός *s.m.* ivy.

κιτάπι *s.n.* (*fam.*) notebook.

κιτρινάδα *s.f.* yellowness; paleness.

κιτρινάδι *s.n.* yolk of egg; yellow spot.

κιτριν|ίζω, ~ιάζω *v.i. & t.* turn yellow *or* pale.

κίτρινος *a.* yellow; pale.

κίτρον *s.n.* citron.

κίχ *pron.* (*fam.*) *δὲν βγάζω* ~ not utter a sound.

κίων *s.m.* column, pillar.

κλαγγή *s.f.* clank (*of arms*).

κλαδευτήρι *s.n.* pruning-hook.

κλαδεύω *v.t.* prune, lop.

κλαδί *s.n.* branch of tree.

κλάδος *s.m.* branch (*lit. & fig.*); (season of) pruning.

κλαδωτός *a.* with foliage pattern.

κλαί(γ)|ω *v.t. & i.* weep *or* lament (for); pity. ~ομαι *v.i.* grumble, moan.

κλάμα *s.n.* crying, lamentation.

κλάνω *v.i. & t.* (*fam.*) break wind (at).

κλαουρίζω *v.i.* whimper.

κλαρί *s.n.* branch of tree; (*fig.*) *βγαίνω στὸ* ~ take to the hills (*as outlaw*); make one's debut; (*of woman*) adopt free-and-easy mode of life.

κλάσιμο *s.n.* (*fam.*) breaking wind.

κλάσις *s.f.* class, age-group.

κλάσμα *s.n.* (*math.*) fraction.

κλασσέρ *s.n.* folder, portfolio (*for papers*). [F. *classeur*]

κλασσικός *a.* classic, classical; (*fam.*) monumental (*liar, etc.*).

κλαυθμηρός *a.* plaintive, whimpering.

κλάψ|α *s.f.*, ~ιμο *s.n.* crying; grumbling, moaning.

κλαψιάρης *a.* given to crying *or* complaining.

κλαψιάρικος *a.* plaintive, whining.

κλέβω *v.t.* steal; rob; cheat; abduct; *κλέφτηκαν* they eloped.

κλειδαριά *s.f.* lock.

κλειδαρότρυπα *s.f.* keyhole.

κλειδί *s.n.* key; (*railway*) switch.

κλειδοκύμβαλον *s.n.* piano.

κλειδοῦχος *s.m.* turnkey; (*railway*) pointsman.

κλείδωμα *s.n.* locking.

κλειδώνω *v.t. & i.* lock (up).

κλείδωσις *s.f.* (*anat.*) joint.

κλεῖθρον *s.n.* lock.

κλεινός *a.* renowned.

κλείνω *v.t. & i.* shut, close, ~ *τὸ μάτι* wink; shut up, put away; turn off (*tap, switch*); stop up, block (*crack, road, view*); conclude, arrange (*treaty, meeting*); book (*seats*); *ἔκλεισε τὸ σπίτι* he agreed to take the house; *ἔκλεισε τὰ πενήντα* he has turned fifty. (*v.i.*) shut, close; become blocked; be concluded *or* reached; *ἔκλεισε ἡ πληγή μου* my wound has healed; *ἔκλεισε ἡ φωνή μου* I have lost my voice.

κλείς *s.f. see* **κλειδί**.

κλείσιμο *s.n.* shutting, closing; conclusion, agreement; healing (*of wound*).

κλεισούρα *s.f.* pass, defile; confinement within doors.

κλειστός *a.* shut, closed.

κλείω *v.t. & i.* see **κλείνω**.

κλέος *s.n.* renown.

κλεπταποδόχος *s.m.f.* receiver of stolen goods.

κλέπτης *s.m.* thief.

κλέπτω *v.t.* see **κλέβω**.

κλεφτά *adv.* hurriedly, furtively.

κλέφτης *s.m.* thief; (*fig.*) klepht (*Gk. irregular fighter against Turks*).

κλέφτικος *a.* 1. of the klephts. 2. thieving (*cat, etc.*).

κλεφτοπόλεμος *s.m.* guerrilla warfare.

κλεφτός *a.* stolen; furtive.

κλεφτουριά *s.f.* the klephts.

κλεφτοφάναρο *s.n.* small torch *or* lantern.

κλεψιά *s.f.* theft.

κλεψιγαμία *s.f.* illicit sexual union.

κλεψιμαίικος *a.* stolen.

κλέψιμο *s.n.* theft.

κλεψιτυπία *s.f.* piracy (*of books*).

κλεψύδρα *s.f.* water-clock.

κλήδονας *s.m.* fortune-telling done on St. John's day.

κλήθρα *s.f.* alder.

κλήμα *s.n.* vine. ~**ταριά** *s.f.* climbing vine; vine-arbour. ~**τόφυλλο** *s.n.* vine-leaf.

κλήρα *s.f.* child, heir; (*fig.*) luck.

κληρικός *a.* clerical; a clergyman.

κληροδότημα *s.n.* bequest, legacy.

κληρονομία *s.f.* inheritance, heritage.

κληρονομικ|ός *a.* of inheritance; hereditary, inherited. ~**ότης** *s.f.* heredity.

κληρονόμος *s.m.f.* heir, heiress.

κληρονομώ *v.t.* inherit.

κλήρ|ος *s.m.* 1. lot, portion; fate, destiny; ρίχνω ~**ον** draw lots. 2. clergy.

κλήρωσις *s.f.* election by lot; drawing of lots *or* numbers in lottery.

κληρωτός *a.* conscript.

κλήσις *s.f.* summons, call.

κλητήρ(ας) *s.m.* usher; bailiff.

κλητική *s.f.* (*gram.*) vocative.

κλίβανος *s.m.* oven.

κλίμα *s.n.* climate.

κλιμάκιον *s.n.* detachment, group, party (*of larger organization*).

κλιμακωτός *a.* graduated; stepped.

κλίμαξ *s.f.* staircase, ladder; scale.

κλιματισμός *s.m.* air-conditioning.

κλινάμαξα *s.f.* sleeping-car.

κλίνη *s.f.* bed.

κλινήρης *a.* confined to bed.

κλινικ|ός *a.* clinical. ~**ή** *s.f.* nursing-home, clinic.

κλινοσκέπασμα *s.n.* bed-covering.

κλίνω *v.t. & i.* lean, bend, bow; bear, tend (*towards*); (*gram.*) inflect, decline, conjugate.

κλίσις *s.f.* bending, inclination; list; slope, gradient; change of direction; tendency; (*gram.*) inflexion, declension, conjugation.

κλιτός *a.* inflected.

κλιτύς *s.f.* slope (*of mountain*).

κλίφι *s.n.* pillow-case, mattress-cover.

κλοιός *s.m.* iron ring; (*fig.*) ring (*that closes round quarry*).

κλονίζ|ω *v.t.* shake, rock; unsettle; impair (*health*). ~**ομαι** *v.i.* totter; waver, have doubts.

κλονισμός *s.m.* shaking, shock; impairment (*of health*).

κλοπή *s.f.* theft.

κλοπιμαίος *a.* stolen.

κλούβα *s.f.* dog-catcher's van; (*fam.*) black Maria.

κλουβί *s.n.* cage.

κλούβι|ος *a.* addle. ~**αίνω** *v.i. & t.* become *or* make addle.

κλυδονίζομαι *v.i.* be storm-tossed.

κλύσμα *s.n.* enema.

κλωβός *s.m.* cage.

κλωθογυρίζω *v.t. & i.* (*fam.*) hang around; τὰ ~ prevaricate.

κλώθω *v.t.* spin.

κλῶν|ος *s.m.*, ~**άρι**, ~**ί** *s.n.* branch.

κλῶσ|ις *s.f.*, ~**ιμο** *s.n.* spinning.

κλῶσσα *s.f.* brooding hen.

κλωσσόπουλο *s.n.* new-born chick.

κλωσσώ *v.t. & i.* incubate; (*fig.*) be sickening for (*ailment*).

κλωστή *s.f.* thread.

κλωστική *s.f.* spinning.

κλώτσ|ημα *s.n.*, ~**ιά** *s.f.* kick.

κλωτσοκούφι *s.n.* (*fig.*) one who gets kicked around.

κλωτσώ *v.t. & i.* kick; recoil (*of gun*).

κνήμη *s.f.* shin, lower part of leg.

κνίσα *s.f.* fume of roasting meat.

κνώδαλον *s.n.* (*fig.*) nonentity.

κοάζω *v.i.* croak (*of frog*).

κόβ|ω *v.t. & i.* 1. cut (up *or* out); grind (*corn, etc.*); carve (*joint*); pick (*flower*); slaughter; ~**ω** τὰ μαλλιά μου get one's hair cut; ~ω κοστούμι buy material for suit; (*fig.*) ~ω μονέδα make money; ~ω δρόμο hasten *or* take short cut; (*fam.*) ~ω εἰσιτήριο take *or* issue ticket; τὸ ~ω δίπλα have a nap; τὸ ~ω λάσπη make off, bolt; ~ει καὶ ράβει he has influence *or* he talks incessantly; τοῦ κόψανε ἕνα μισθό they fixed him a salary. 2. cut off (*supply*); break off (*relations*); bar (*way, view*); reduce (*wages, etc.*); take away (*appetite*); give up (*smoking, etc.*); κόψαμε τὴν καλημέρα we are no longer on speaking terms; μοῦ ἔκοψες τὸ αἷμα you gave me a fright. 3. tire, hurt; μὲ ~ουν τὰ παπούτσια my shoes hurt; (*fig.*) μοῦ ~ει τὰ χέρια I feel the loss of it; (*fam.*) τὸν ἔκοψα I tricked him. 4. (*v.i.*) cut; abate (*of wind, fever, etc.*); fade (*of colour*); turn sour; ~ω δεξιά turn right; (*fam.*) ~ει τὸ κεφάλι του he is intelligent; ἔκοψε τὸ αἷμα μου my heart stood still; δὲ μούκοψε it did not occur to me (*to*). 5. ~ομαι *v.i.* cut oneself; (*fig.*) take great trouble, put oneself out (*for*); exhaust oneself; μοῦ κόπηκαν τὰ ἥπατα *or* τὰ γόνατα I felt stunned *or* upset.

κόγχη *s.f.* shell, conch; (*anat.*) eye-socket, conch of ear; (*archit.*) niche.

κογχύλι|η *s.f.*, ~ιον *s.n.* sea-shell.

κόθορνος *s.m.* buskin.

κοιλαίνω *v.t.* hollow out.

κοιλαράς *s.m.* pot-bellied person.

κοιλ|άς, ~άδα *s.f.* valley.

κοιλία *s.f.* belly.

κοιλιόδουλος *s.m.* glutton.

κοιλόπονος *s.m.* belly-ache; pangs of parturition.

κοῖλ|ος *a.* hollow, concave. ~ότης *s.f.* hollowness; hollow, cavity.

κοιμᾶμαι *v.i. see* κοιμοῦμαι.

κοίμησις *s.f.* (*eccl.*) Assumption.

κοιμητήριον *s.n.* cemetery.

κοιμ|ίζω *v.t.* put to sleep, lull; ~ισμένος asleep, (*fig.*) dull-witted.

κοιμ|οῦμαι, ~ῶμαι *v.i.* sleep, go to bed.

κοινόβι|ον *s.n.* coenobitic monastery. ~ακός *a.* coenobitic.

κοινοβουλευτικός *a.* parliamentary.

κοινοβούλιον *s.n.* parliament.

κοινοκτημοσύνη *s.f.* community of wealth.

κοινολογῶ *v.t.* divulge.

κοιν|όν *s.n.* public; ~ά (*pl.*) public affairs.

κοινοποιῶ *v.t.* make known, give notice (of).

κοινοπολιτεία *s.f.* commonwealth.

κοινοπραξία *s.f.* cooperative.

κοιν|ός *a.* common; (*held*) in common; ordinary, commonplace; ~ὴ γνώμη public opinion; ἀπὸ ~οῦ in common.

κοινότ|ης *s.f.* community; commune (*unit of local government*); Βουλὴ τῶν ~ήτων House of Commons.

κοινοτοπία *s.f.* commonplace.

κοινόχρηστος *a.* used in common.

κοινωνία *s.f.* 1. society, social community. 2. Holy Communion.

κοινωνικός *a.* social, sociable.

κοινωνῶ 1. *v.i. & t.* receive Holy Communion *or* administer this to. 2. *v.i.* participate.

κοινωφελής *a.* for the public benefit.

κοίταγμα *s.n.* look; minding; examination.

κοιτάζ|ω *v.t.* look at, examine; take notice of; mind, look after. ~ομαι *v.i.* look at oneself; be examined (*by doctor*).

κοίτασμα *s.n.* layer, deposit, bed.

κοίτη *s.f.* bed; lair, nest.

κοιτίς *s.f.* cradle.

κοίτομαι *v.i.* be lying down; be bedridden.

κοιτών *s.m.* bedroom.

κοκέτα *s.f.* (*naut.*) berth.

κοκεταρία *s.f.* smartness, stylishness; coquetry.

κοκέτης *a.* smart, stylish (*person*).

κοκκαλιάζω *v.i.* become stiff (*of limbs*).

κόκκαλο *s.n.* bone; ivory (*of piano-key*); shoe-horn; (*fam.*) ἔμεινε ~ he was thunderstruck.

κοκκαλώνω *v.i.* become stiff; (*fig.*) be thunderstruck.

κοκκινάδα *s.f.* redness.

κοκκινάδι *s.n.* red spot; rouge.

κοκκινέλι *s.n.* red resinated wine.

κοκκινίζω *v.t. & i.* make *or* become red *or* brown; flush, blush.

κοκκινίλα *s.f.* redness.

κοκκινογούλι *s.n.* beetroot.

κοκκινομάλλης *a.* red-haired.

κόκκινος *a.* red.

κοκκινωπός *a.* reddish.

κόκκος *s.m.* grain, particle; (*coffee*) bean; bead (*on string*).

κοκκοφοίνιξ *s.m.* coconut-palm.

κοκκύτης *s.m.* whooping-cough.

κόκορας *s.m.* cock.

κοκορέτσι *s.n.* grilled sheep's entrails.
κοκορεύομαι *v.i.* show off like a cock.
κοκώνα *s.f.* lady; (*iron.*) ή ~ her ladyship.
κολάζ|ω *v.t.* 1. punish. 2. lessen bad effect of, explain away. 3. tempt. ~ομαι *v.i.* fall into temptation, do wrong.
κολάϊ *s.n.* knack.
κολακεία *s.f.* flattery.
κολακευτικός *a.* complimentary.
κολακεύω *v.t.* flatter.
κόλ|αξ, ~ακας *s.m.* flatterer.
κόλασις *s.f.* hell, damnation.
κολασμένος *a.* damned.
κολατσιό *s.n.* snack.
κόλαφος *s.m.* slap in the face.
κολεός *s.m.* sheath, scabbard; (*anat.*) vagina.
κολικός *s.m.* colic.
κολιός *s.m.* sort of mackerel.
κόλλα *s.f.* 1. glue, paste; starch. 2. sheet of paper.
κολλάρο *s.n.* collar; (*fam.*) head (*on beer*).
κολλάρ|ω, ~ίζω *v.t.* starch.
κολλέγιον *s.n.* college.
κολλήγας *s.m.* share-cropper.
κόλλημα *s.n.* sticking (on, together), soldering; piece stuck on.
κολλητήρι *s.n.* solder, soldering iron.
κολλητικός *a.* contagious.
κολλητ|ός *a.* stuck, soldered; close-fitting; contiguous, adjoining. ~ά *adv.* side-by-side.
κολλιέ *s.n.* necklace. [F. *collier*]
κολλιτσίδα *s.f.* burr.
κόλλυβα *s.f.* boiled wheat (*offered at memorial service*).
κολλυβογράμματα *s.n.pl.* smattering of education.
κολ|λῶ, ~νῶ *v.t. & i.* glue, stick, solder (on, together); attach, fix; catch or give (*malady*). (*v.i.*) stick; fasten or attach oneself (*to*); (*fam.*) δέν ~λάει that's a likely tale!
κολοβός *a.* crop-tailed; truncated.
κολοκύθι *s.n.* vegetable marrow; (*fam.*) ~α (*pl.*) nonsense.
κολόνα *s.f.* column, pillar; block (*of ice*).
κολόνια *s.f.* eau-de-Cologne.
κολοσσ|ός *s.m.* colossus. ~ιαίος *a.* colossal.
κολοφών *s.m.* summit, pinnacle.
κολοφώνιον *s.n.* colophony.

κόλπο *s.n.* trick, ruse; knack.
κόλπος *s.m.* bosom; gulf, bay; apoplectic fit.
κολυμβήθρα *s.f.* font.
κολυμβητής *s.m.* swimmer.
κολυμ|βῶ, ~πῶ, *v.i.* swim.
κολύμπι *s.n.* swimming, swim.
κολώνια *s.f.* eau-de-Cologne.
κομβί|ον *s.n.* button. ~οδόχη *s.f.* buttonhole.
κομβολόγιον *s.n.* string of beads; rosary; (*fig.*) string, stream (*of lies, people, etc.*).
κόμβος *s.m.* knot (*tied or in wood*); junction; traffic roundabout; (*naut.*) knot.
κόμη *s.f.* (*head of*) hair.
κόμης *s.m.* count, earl.
κομητεία *s.f.* county.
κομήτης *s.m.* comet.
κομίζω *v.t.* bring, bear.
κομιστής *s.m.* bearer.
κόμιστρα *s.n.pl.* transport charges.
κομιτατζῆς *s.m.* comitadji.
κομιτᾶτον *s.n.* committee (*esp. revolutionary*).
κόμμα *s.n.* 1. (*political*) party. 2. comma, decimal point.
κομμάρα *s.f.* lassitude.
κομματάρχης *s.m.* (*political*) party-organizer.
κομμάτι *s.n.* piece, bit; (*adv.*) a little, a bit; (*fam.*) ~α νὰ γίνη never mind! στὰ ~α go to hell!
κομματιάζ|ω *v.t.* break or cut or tear into pieces. ~ομαι *v.i.* make great efforts.
κομματίζομαι *v.i.* go in for party politics.
κόμματος *s.m.* (*fam.*) fine bouncing girl or woman.
κομμένος *a.* cut, ground; tired out.
κομ(μ)ό *s.n.* chest-of-drawers. [F. *commode*]
κομ(μ)οδίνο *s.n.* night-table.
κομμουνιστής *s.m.* communist.
κόμμωσις *s.f.* coiffure.
κομμωτήριον *s.n.* hairdresser's.
κομπάζω *v.i.* boast.
κομπιάζω *v.i.* choke; (*fig.*) hum and haw, falter.
κομπίνα *s.f.* (*fam.*) profitable scheme.
κομπιναιζόν *s.n.* slip, petticoat. [F. *combinaison*]
κομπογιαννίτης *s.m.* quack, charlatan.
κομπόδεμα *s.n.* hoard, nest-egg.
κομπολόγι *s.n.* conversation chaplet.
κόμπος *s.m.* knot (*tied or in wood*); bunion; drop, small quantity; lump

in one's throat; ἔφτασε ὁ ~ στὸ χτένι things are coming to a head.

κομπόστα *s.f.* stewed fruit.

κομπρέσσα *s.f.* (*med.*) compress.

κομπριμέ *a.* & *s.n.* compressed; a tablet. [F. *comprimé*]

κομφόρ *s.n.pl.* comfort, conveniences (*in home, etc.*). [F. *confort*]

κομψευόμενος *a.* dandified.

κομψός *a.* smart, elegant.

κομψοτέχνημα *s.n.* bibelot.

κονάκι *s.n.* lodging.

κονδύλιον *s.n.* slate-pencil; item (*of expenditure*).

κόνδυλος *s.m.* knuckle.

κονδυλοφόρος *s.m.* pen-holder.

κονιάκ *s.n.* brandy. [F. *cognac*]

κονίαμα *s.n.* mortar; plaster.

κόνιδα *s.f.* nit.

κόνικλος *s.m.* rabbit.

κονιορτός *s.m.* dust.

κόνις *s.f.* powder, dust.

κονίστρα *s.f.* arena.

κονκάρδα *s.f.* cockade, badge.

κονσέρβα *s.f.* tinned food.

κονσέρτο *s.n.* concert, concerto.

κοντά *adv.* near; nearly; (*prep.*) ~ σέ near, compared with; ~ στὰ ἄλλα in addition; ~ στὸ νοῦ it goes without saying.

κονταίνω *v.t.* & *i.* shorten; get shorter.

κοντάκι *s.n.* butt (*of gun*).

κοντακιανός *a.* a shortish person.

κοντάκιον *s.n.* (*eccl.*) a hymn.

κοντάρι *s.n.* pole, lance; gaff.

κοντεύ|ω *v.i.* be almost finished *or* ready *or* completed; draw near; be about (*to*); κόντεψα νὰ χαθῶ I nearly got lost; ~ει μεσημέρι it is almost midday.

κόντ|ημα, ~εμα *s.n.* shortening.

κοντινός *a.* close, near, near-by; direct (*route*); to happen shortly.

κοντο- *denotes* short, near.

κοντόγεμος *a.* nearly full.

κοντολογῆς *adv.* briefly.

κοντομάνικος *a.* short-sleeved.

κοντοπίθαρος *a.* a dumpy person.

κόντος *s.n.* shortness.

κοντός *s.m.* pole.

κοντός *a.* short; ~ ψαλμός ἀλληλούια that's that!

κοντοστέκ|ω|, ~ομαι *v.i.* stop short.

κοντούλα *s.f.* sort of pear.

κοντούλης *a.* of small stature.

κοντόφθαλμος *a.* short-sighted; obtuse.

κόντρα *adv.* counter; in the opposite direction.

κοντυλένιος *a.* slim, graceful (*of bodily features*).

κοντύλι *s.n.* see **κονδύλιον.**

κοπάδι *s.n.* flock, herd.

κοπάζω *v.i.* abate.

κοπαν|άω, ~ίζω *v.t.* beat, pound; (*fig.*) τὰ ἴδια ~άω keep repeating the same thing; ~ίζω ἀέρα talk nonsense; (*fam.*) τά ~άω drink.

κόπανος *s.m.* pestle, beater; butt (*of gun*); (*fig.*) blockhead.

κοπέλλα *s.f.* young woman, girl.

κοπέλλι *s.n.* lad; apprentice.

κοπετός *s.m.* lamentation.

κοπή *s.f.* cutting.

κόπια *s.f.* copy.

κοπι|άζω *v.i.* work hard, toil; take the trouble (*to*); ~άστε μέσα please come in.

κοπιαστικός *a.* laborious, toilsome.

κοπίδι *s.n.* cutting-tool.

κόπιτσα *s.f.* hook-and-eye fastener.

κόπ|ος *s.m.* pains, trouble; hard work; (*pl.* ~οι *and* ~ια) reward (*for labour*).

κόπρανα *s.n.pl.* excrement.

κοπριά *s.f.* dung, manure.

κοπρίζω *v.t.* & *i.* manure; defecate (on).

κόπρος *s.f.* dung, manure.

κοπρόσκυλο *s.n.* scavenging mongrel; (*fig.*) wastrel.

κοπρών *s.m.* midden, dunghill.

κοπτήρ *s.m.* cutter; incisor.

κοπτική *s.f.* cutting (*in tailoring*).

κόπτ|ω *v.t.* see **κόβω.** ~ομαι *v.i.* (*fig.*) beat one's breast.

κόπωσις *s.f.* fatigue.

κόρα *s.f.* crust.

κόρακας *s.m.* crow.

κορακιστικά *s.n.pl.* secret language; double-dutch.

κορακοζώητος *a.* long-lived (*person*).

κοράλλ|ινος, ~ένιος *a.* coral.

κοράλλι(ον) *s.n.* coral.

κόραξ *s.m.* crow; hook.

κοράσ|ιον *s.n.*, ~ίς *s.f.* girl (*not yet adolescent*).

κόρδα *s.f.* string, sinew.

κορδέλλα *s.f.* ribbon, tape (-measure); tape-worm; hairpin-bend.

κορδόνι *s.n.* cord; lanyard; boot-lace; (*adv.*) in succession; πάει ~ it is going well.

κορδών|ω *v.t.* tighten. ~ομαι *v.i.* puff oneself out.

κορεννύω *v.t.* stuff, satiate.

κορεσμός *s.m.* satiation.

κόρη *s.f.* maiden, girl; virgin; daughter; pupil (*of eye*).

κορινθιακ|ός *a.* Corinthian; ~ή σταφίς (grapes producing) currants.

κοριός *s.m.* bed-bug.

κορίτσι *s.n.* girl; virgin.

κορκός *s.m.* yolk (*of egg*).

κορμί *s.n.* body.

κορμός *s.m.* trunk (*of tree, body, or structure*); sort of cake.

κορμοστασιά *s.f.* carriage, bearing.

κορνάρω *v.i.* sound one's (*motor*) horn.

κορνίζα *s.f.* picture-frame; cornice.

κόρνο *s.n.* (motor-) horn.

κοροϊδ|ο *s.n.* laughing-stock; dupe. ~εύω *v.t.* make fun of, mock; fool.

κορόμηλο *s.n.* plum.

κόρ|ος *s.m.* satiety; κατά ~ον to repletion.

κορσές *s.m.* corset.

κορτ|άρω, ~ετζάρω *v.t.* & *i.* flirt (with).

κόρτε *s.n.* flirting.

κορυδαλλός *s.m.* skylark.

κορυφαίος *a.* & *s.m.* leading, pre-eminent; leader of chorus.

κορυφή *s.f.* top of the head; summit, peak; cream (*on milk*); (*fig.*) leading light.

κορυφοῦμαι *v.i.* reach culmination.

κορύφωμα *s.n.* culmination, height.

κορφή *s.f.* top of the head; summit peak; top shoot (*of plant*).

κόρφος *s.m.* bosom; gulf, bay.

κορώνα *s.f.* crown; ~ γράμματα heads or tails.

κορώνω *v.t.* & *i.* heat, inflame; get hot or inflamed.

κόσκιν|ο *s.n.* sieve; ~ο ἀπὸ τὶς σφαῖρες riddled with bullets. ~ίζω *v.t.* sift.

κοσμάκης *s.m.* common people, man in the street.

κόσμημα *s.n.* ornament; jewel; ~τα (*pl.*) jewellery.

κοσμήτωρ *s.m.* dean (*of faculty*); steward (*of meeting*).

κοσμικ|ός *a.* 1. cosmic. 2. lay, temporal; worldly. 3. social (*event*), society (*man or woman*); ~ή κίνησις social activity.

κόσμιος *a.* seemly, modest.

κοσμογυρισμένος *a.* travelled.

κοσμοθεωρία *s.f.* Weltanschauung.

κοσμοϊστορικός *a.* of historic significance.

κοσμοπολιτικός *a.* cosmopolitan.

κόσμ|ος *s.m.* world; people; ὅλος ὁ ~ος everybody; τοῦ ~ου τὰ λεφτά a great deal of money.

κοσμοχαλασιά *s.f.* upheaval; hubbub.

κοσμῶ *v.t.* decorate, adorn.

κοστίζω *v.i.* cost; (*fig.*) be a grievous blow.

κόστος *s.n.* cost; cost price.

κοστούμι *s.n.* (*man's*) suit.

κότα *s.f. see* κόττα.

κότερο *s.n.* (*naut.*) cutter; pleasure-boat.

κοτέτσι *s.n.* chicken-coop.

κοτζάμ *prefix denoting largeness (often with contrasting defect).*

κότινος *s.m.* wild olive; (*fig.*) prize.

κοτολέττα *s.f.* cutlet.

κοτρώνι *s.n.* large stone.

κοτσάνι *s.n.* stem.

κοτσάρω *v.t.* (*fam.*) put, shove, stick; give, land with; impute.

κότσι *s.n.* ankle; bunion; δὲ βαστοῦν τὰ ~α μου it is beyond my strength.

κοτσίδα *s.f.* plait, pigtail.

κότσος *s.m.* chignon, bun.

κότσ|υφας *s.m.*, ~ύφι *s.n.* blackbird.

κότ(τ)|α *s.f.* hen, chicken. ~όπουλο *s.n.* (young) chicken.

κοτῶ *v.i.* (*fam.*) dare.

κουβαλ|ῶ *v.t.* & *i.* carry, bring; move house. ~ιέμαι *v.i.* pay unexpected *or* unwelcome visit.

κουβάρι *s.n.* ball (*of wool, etc.*); μαλλιὰ ~α topsy-turvy, at loggerheads.

κουβαριάζ|ω *v.t.* roll into a ball; crumple; (*fig.*) swindle. ~ομαι *v.i.* curl oneself up; shrink; fall in a heap.

κουβαρίστρα *s.f.* reel, spool.

κουβαρντᾶς *s.m.* (*fam.*) open-handed person.

κουβᾶς *s.m.* bucket.

κουβέντ|α *s.f.* talk, conversation. ~ιάζω *v.i.* & *t.* converse; discuss, criticize.

κουβέρ *s.n.* place laid at table; service charge. [F. *couvert*]

κουβερνάντα *s.f.* governess.

κουβέρνο *s.n.* government.

κουβέρτα *s.f.* blanket; (*naut.*) deck.

κουβούκλι *s.n.* canopy (*over bier, etc.*).

κουδουνᾶτος *s.m.* one in fancy dress.

κουδούνι *s.n.* bell; (*fam.*) εἶναι ~ he is drunk.

κουδουνίζω *v.i.* ring; (*v.t.*) make known.

κουδουνίστρα *s.f.* (*baby's*) rattle.

κουζίνα *s.f.* kitchen; style of cooking; kitchen-stove.

κουζουλός *a.* (*fam.*) dotty.

κουκέτα *s.f.* (*naut.*) berth.

κουκί *s.n.* broad bean; berry, bean.

κουκίδα *s.f.* spot, dot.

κούκλα *s.f.* doll; tailor's dummy; skein (*of wool*); (*head of*) maize; (*fig.*) beautiful child *or* woman.

κούκ(κ)ος *s.m.* 1. cap. 2. cuckoo;(*fam.*) ἀπόμεινε ~ he was left on his own; τρεῖς κι' ὁ ~ (*iron.*) very few; τοῦ κόστισε ὁ ~ ἀηδόνι he paid through the nose for it.

κουκουβάγια *s.f.* owl.

κουκούδι *s.n.* pimple.

κουκούλα *s.f.* hood, cowl; tea-cosy.

κουκουλάρικος *a.* of unspun silk.

κουκούλι *s.n.* silk-worm cocoon.

κουκουλώνω *v.t.* muffle up; bury; hush up; trick *or* force into marriage.

κουκουνάρι *s.n.* pine cone *or* kernel.

κουκούτσι *s.n.* pip, stone; οὔτε ~ not a scrap.

κουλός *a.* one-armed; armless.

κουλούρα *s.f.* ring-shaped loaf; (*fam.*) lifebelt; nought (*no marks*); lavatory-seat.

κουλούρι *s.n.* small ring-shaped biscuit *or* bread.

κουλουριάζω *v.t.* coil, roll up.

κουμάντο *s.n.* command, control.

κουμάρι *s.n.* jug.

κουμάσι *s.n.* hen-coop; (*fam.*) καλό ~ a bad lot.

κουμπάρα *s.f.* godmother of one's child.

κουμπαράς *s.m.* money-box.

κουμπάρος *s.m.* godfather of one's child; best man (*at wedding*).

κουμπ|ί *s.n.* button, stud, link; switch; τοῦ βρῆκα τό ~ί I found his weak spot. ~ότρυπα *s.f.* button-hole.

κουμπούρα *s.f.* pistol.

κουμπώνω *v.t.* button, do up.

κουμπωτήρι *s.n.* button-hook.

κουνά|βι, ~**δι** *s.n.* marten.

κουνέλι *s.n.* rabbit.

κούνημα *s.n.* movement, swaying, swinging, rocking.

κούνια *s.f.* cradle; swing.

κουνιάδα *s.f.* sister-in-law (*spouse's sister*).

κουνιάδος *s.m.* brother-in-law (*spouse's brother*).

κουνιστός *a.* rocking, swaying.

κουνούπι *s.n.* mosquito.

κουνουπίδι *s.n.* cauliflower.

κουνουπιέρα *s.f.* mosquito-net.

κουντῶ *v.t.* push.

κουν|ῶ *v.t. & i.* move, rock, shake, swing; δέν τό ~άω ἀπό δῶ I won't budge from here. ~ ιέμαι *v.i.* move, rock, shake, swing; bestir oneself, get a move on.

κούπα *s.f.* cup, glass; heart (*cards*).

κουπαστή *s.f.* (*naut.*) gunwale.

κουπί *s.n.* oar; κάνω *or* τραβῶ ~ row.

κουπόνι *s.n.* remnant (*of cloth*); coupon.

κούρα *s.f.* cure, treatment; doctor's visit.

κουράγιο *s.n.* courage.

κουράδα *s.f.* (*fam.*) turd.

κουράζ|ω *v.t.* tire, weary. ~ομαι *v.i.* become tired.

κουραμάνα *s.f.* army bread.

κουραμπιές *s.m.* sort of cake; (*fam.*) soldier who dodges front-line service.

κουράντες *s.m.* medical attendant.

κουράρω *v.t.* attend, treat (*of doctor*).

κούραση *s.f.* fatigue.

κουρασμένος *a.* tired.

κουραστικός *a.* tiring, trying.

κουραφέξαλα *s.n.pl.* (*fam.*) nonsense.

κούρβουλο *s.n.* (dried) stem of vine.

κουρδίζω *v.t.* tune; wind up; (*fig.*) provoke, work (*person*) up.

κουρέας *s.m.* barber.

κουρεῖον *s.n.* barber's shop.

κουρελαρία *s.f.* old rags; (*fig.*) ragtag and bobtail.

κουρελ|ής, ~**ιάρης** *s.m.* ragged person.

κουρέλι *s.n.* rag; (*fam.*) τόν κάνω ~ I abuse him.

κούρε(υ)μα *s.n.* haircut; shearing.

κουρεύω *v.t.* cut hair of; shear.

κούρκος *s.m.* turkey.

κουρκούτι *s.n.* batter; pap.

κουρνιάζω *v.i.* perch, roost.

κουρούνα *s.f.* rook.

κούρσα *s.f.* horse-race; errand, trip; racing *or* touring motor-car.

κουρσάρος *s.m.* corsair.

κουρσεύω *v.t.* pillage.

κουρτίνα *s.f.* curtain.

κουσκουσούρης *s.m.* a gossip.

κουσούρι *s.n.* fault, blemish.

κουτάβι *s.n.* puppy, cub; simpleton.

κουτάλι *s.n.* spoon.

κουταμάρα *s.f.* stupidity.

κούτελο *s.n.* forehead.

κουτί *s.n.* box, tin; τοῦ ~οῦ tinned, (*fig.*) spick-and-span; μοῦρθε ~ it was a godsend to me *or* it fitted me to a T.

κουτ|ός *a.* stupid, silly. ~**ιαίνω** *v.t. & i.* make *or* become stupid.
κουτουλώ *v.t. & i.* butt; nod (*drowsily*).
κουτουροῦ *adv.* at random, casually.
κούτρα *s.f.* (*fam.*) head.
κουτρουβάλα *s.f.* somersault.
κουτρούλ|ης *a.* bald; τοῦ ~η ὁ γάμος hullabaloo.
κούτσα *s.f.* lameness; (*adv.*) ~ ~ limpingly.
κουτσαβάκης *s.m.* bully, fire-eater.
κουτσαίνω *v.t. & i.* lame; limp.
κουτσαμάρα *s.f.* lameness.
κουτσο- *denotes* deficiency.
κουτσομπολ|ιό *s.n.*, ~ιά (*pl.*) gossip.
κουτσοπίνω *v.i.* drink (*alcohol*) slowly.
κουτσ|ός *a.* lame; ~ὰ στραβά after a fashion.
κουτσούβελο *s.n.* (*small*) child.
κουτσουλιά *s.f.* bird's droppings.
κουτσουρεύω *v.t.* truncate; cut down drastically.
κούτσουρο *s.n.* tree-trunk, log; (*fig.*) blockhead.
κουφαίν|ω *v.t.* deafen. ~ομαι *v.i.* become deaf.
κουφάλα *s.f.* cavity (*in tree-trunk or tooth*).
κουφαμάρα *s.f.* deafness.
κουφάρι *s.n.* corpse.
κουφέτο *s.n.* pill; sugared almond.
κουφιαίνω *v.t. & i.* make *or* become hollow.
κουφίζω *v.i.* be hard of hearing.
κούφι|ος *a.* hollow; decayed, rotten (*tooth, nut, etc.*); muffled (*sound*); (*fig.*) lacking seriousness (*person*); στὰ ~α without result *or* without noise.
κουφόβραση *s.f.* dull, sultry weather.
κοῦφος *a.* lightweight, not serious; empty (*hope, etc.*).
κουφός *a.* deaf.
κούφταλο *s.n.* bent old woman *or* man.
κούφωμα *s.n.* hollow (*in mountainside*); aperture (*of door or window*).
κόφ|α *s.f.*, ~ίνι *s.n.* deep basket, hamper.
κοφτά *adv.* ὀρθὰ ~ flatly, straight out.
κοφτερός *a.* sharp (*knife, etc.*).
κοφτήριο *s.n.* (*fam.*) place where one gets swindled.
κόφτρα *s.f.* (*fam.*) gold-digger.
κόφτ|ω *v.t. see* **κόβω**; τί μὲ ~ει; what do I care?
κοχλάδι *s.n.* pebble.
κοχλάζω *v.i.* boil, seethe, bubble up.
κοχλιάριον *s.n.* spoon.
κοχλίας *s.m.* snail; screw; cochlea.

κοχύλι *s.n.* sea-shell.
κόψη *s.f.* cutting edge.
κοψιά *s.f.* cut (*wound*).
κόψιμ|ο *s.n.* cutting; style, cut; ~ατα (*pl.*) (*fam.*) the gripes.
κοψομεσιάζομαι *v.i.* (*fig.*) break one's back, exhaust oneself.
κραγιόν(ι) *s.n.* crayon; lipstick.
κραδαίνω *v.t.* brandish; vibrate.
κράζω *v.i. & t.* crow, caw; cry out loud; call, summon.
κραιπάλη *s.f.* debauch.
κρᾶμα *s.n.* mixture; alloy.
κράμβη *s.f.* cabbage, kale.
κρανίον *s.n.* cranium, skull.
κράνος *s.n.* helmet.
κράξιμο *s.n.* crowing, cawing.
κρασᾶτος *a.* wine-coloured; cooked in wine.
κρασί *s.n.* wine.
κρᾶσις *s.f.* (*bodily*) constitution; (*gram.*) crasis.
κράσπεδον *s.n.* hem; kerb; foot (*of hill*); edge (*of shore*).
κραταιός *a.* powerful.
κράτημα *s.n.* (*act of*) holding (back).
κρατήρ *s.m.* 1. crater. 2. ancient wine-bowl.
κράτησις *s.f.* detention, arrest; deduction (*from pay*).
κρατητήριον *s.n.* detention-cell.
κρατικοποίησις *s.f.* nationalization.
κρατικός *a.* of *or* by the state.
κράτος *s.n.* power, rule; the state; κατὰ ~ totally (*of defeat*).
κρατ|ῶ *v.i. & t.* rule, prevail; last, keep (*of time or durability*); come, be descended (*from*); (*v.t.*) have, hold, keep; detain, withhold; book, reserve; ~ιέμαι καλά be well off *or* well preserved; κάνε καὶ λίγο ~ει have a little restraint.
κραυγ|ή *s.f.* shout, cry. ~άζω *v.i.* shout, cry out.
κράχ *s.n.* (*financial*) crash. [G. *Krach*]
κρέας *s.n.* flesh, meat.
κρεατόμυγα *s.f.* bluebottle.
κρεββάτι *s.n.* bed.
κρεββατίνα *s.f.* vine-arbour.
κρεββατοκάμαρα *s.f.* bedroom (suite).
κρεββατώνω *v.t.* confine to bed.
κρέμα *s.f.* cream.
κρεμάζω *v.t.* hang (up).
κρεμάλα *s.f.* gallows.
κρεμανταλᾶς *s.m.* lanky fellow.
κρέμασμα *s.n.* hanging (up).

κρεμαστ|ός *a.* hanging; ~ή γέφυρα suspension-bridge.

κρεμάστ|ρα *s.f.*, ~άρι *s.n.* clotheshanger; hat-stand.

κρεμμύδι *s.n.* onion; bulb; (*fam.*) turnip (*watch*).

κρεμ|(ν)ῶ *v.t. & i.* hang (up); ~ῶ hang (*execute*); (*v.i.*) hang down. ~ομαι *v.i.* hang (*be suspended*). ~ ιέμαι *v.i.* hang (*from trapeze, etc.*); hang *or* lean (*out of window, etc.*); lean (*for support*); (*fig.*) place all one's hopes (*in*); ~άστηκε he hanged himself *or* was hanged.

κρεοπώλης *s.m.* butcher.

κρεουργῶ *v.t.* butcher.

κρεοφάγος *a.* eating meat.

κρέπ *s.n.* crape; crêpe rubber. [F. *crêpe*]

κρεπάρω *v.i.* burst, split.

κρημνίζ|ω *v.t.* cast down (*from height*) demolish; overthrow. ~ομαι *v.i.* fall (*from height*); collapse.

κρημνός *s.m.* precipice, abyss.

κρήνη *s.f.* fountain, spring.

κρηπίδωμα *s.n.* foundation, base; quay; railway platform.

κρησάρα *s.f.* sieve.

κρησφύγετον *s.n.* hiding-place.

κριάρι *s.n.* ram.

κριθαράκι *s.n.* 1. barley-shaped paste (*in soup*). 2. (*med.*) sty.

κριθ|ή *s.f.*, ~άρι *s.n.* barley.

κρίκος *s.m.* ring, link; (*lifting*) jack.

κρῖμα *s.n. & int.* sin; a pity; τό ~ στό λαιμό σου on your head be it; ~ (σ)τά λεφτά what a waste of money!

κρίνος *s.m.* lily.

κρίνω *v.t. & i.* judge, deem, consider; decide.

κριός *s.m.* ram; battering-ram.

κρίσιμος *a.* critical, decisive, serious.

κρίσις *s.f.* judgement, opinion; critical faculty; piece of criticism; crisis, depression; (*med.*) fit, attack.

κριτήριον *s.n.* criterion.

κριτής *s.m.* judge.

κριτική *s.f.* criticism.

κριτικός *a.* critical (*pertaining to criticism*); a critic.

Κροῖσος *s.m.* Croesus; (*fig.*) multimillionaire.

κροκάδι *s.n.* yolk (*of egg*).

κροκόδειλος *s.m.* crocodile.

κρόκος *s.m.* crocus; yolk (*of egg*).

κρομμύδι *s.n.* onion; bulb.

κρόμμυον *s.n.* onion.

κρονόληρος *s.m.* dotard.

κρόσσι *s.n.* fringe.

κρόταλον *s.n.* rattle, castanet.

κρόταφος *s.m.* (*anat.*) temple.

κρότος *s.m.* loud noise; (*fig.*) stir.

κρουαζιέρα *s.f.* pleasure-cruise.

κρουνηδόν *adv.* in torrents.

κρουνός *s.m.* spring; tap; (*fig.*) torrent.

κροῦσις *s.f.* striking; playing (*of instrument*); exploratory attack.

κροῦσμα *s.n.* case (*of theft, typhus, etc.*).

κρούστα *s.f.* crust; scab.

κρούσταλλο *s.n.* (*transparent*) ice; icicle.

κρουστός *a.* 1. thickly woven. 2. percussion (*instrument*).

κρούω *v.t.* strike, knock (on); ring (*bell*); play (*instrument*).

κρυάδ|α *s.f.* coldness; ~ες (*pl.*) shivers.

κρύβ|ω *v.t.* hide. ~ ομαι *v.i.* hide.

κρυμμένος *a.* hidden.

κρύο *s.n.* cold.

κρυολόγημα *s.n.* a cold.

κρυοπάγημα *s.n.* frost-bite.

κρύος *a.* cold, chilly; unresponsive; expressionless, insipid.

κρυπτογραφῶ *v.i. & t.* write in code.

κρύπτω *v.t. see* κρύβω.

κρυστάλλ|ινος, ~ένιος *a.* of *or* like crystal.

κρύσταλλον *s.n.* crystal (*glass*); icicle.

κρύσταλλος *s.m.f.* (*chem.*) crystal.

κρυφά *adv.* secretly.

κρύφ|ιος, ~ός *a.* secret.

κρυφτός *a.* hidden.

κρύφτω *v.t. see* κρύβω.

κρύψιμο *s.n.* (*act of*) hiding.

κρυψίνους *a.* secretive.

κρυψώνας *s.m.* hiding-place.

κρυώνω *v.t. & i.* make, get *or* feel cold.

κρωγμός *s.m.* croaking (*of birds*).

κτέν|ι(ον) *s.n.* comb; rake. ~ίζω *v.t.* comb. ~ισμα *s.n.* combing; coiffure.

κτῆμα *s.n.* (*landed*) property. ~τίας *s.m.* land-owner.

κτηνίατρος *s.m.* veterinary surgeon.

κτῆνος *s.n.* beast, brute.

κτηνοτροφία *s.f.* stock-breeding.

κτηνώδης *a.* bestial, brutish.

κτῆσις *s.f.* (*territorial*) possession.

κτητικός *a.* (*gram.*) possessive.

κτίζω *v.t.* build; found (*city*); wall in *or* up.

κτίριον *s.n.* building.

κτίσιμον *s.n.* (*act of*) building.

κτίστης *s.m.* bricklayer; the Creator.

κτυπ- *see* χτυπ-.

κύαμος *s.m.* broad bean.

κυάνιον s.n. cyanide.

κυανόλευκος a. blue-and-white; ἡ ~ the Greek flag.

κυανοῦς a. blue, azure.

κυβέρνησις s.f. command, government.

κυβερνήτης s.m. commander, governor.

κυβερνητικός a. of or by the government.

κυβερνῶ v.t. command, govern.

κύβ|ος s.m. cube; die. **~ικός** a. cubic.

κυδώνι s.n. quince; sort of shellfish.

κύησις s.f. gestation.

κυκεών s.m. disorder, confusion.

κυκλάμινο s.n. cyclamen.

κυκλικός a. circular; cyclic.

κύκλος s.m. circle; cycle; circuit; ~ ἐργασιῶν business turnover; ~ μαθημάτων course of lessons.

κυκλοτερής a. circular.

κυκλοφορ|ῶ v.t. & i. circulate. **~ία** s.f. circulation; currency; flow of traffic or passers-by.

κύκλωμα s.n. (electric) circuit.

κυκλών s.m. cyclone.

κυκλώνω v.t. encircle.

κυκλωτικός a. encircling.

κύκνει|ος a. swan's; **~ον ᾆσμα** swan-song.

κύκνος s.m. swan.

κυλικεῖον s.n. buffet.

κύλινδρος s.m. cylinder, roller.

κυλί|ω v.t. roll (over, along). **~ομαι** v.i. roll, wallow; **~ομένη κλῖμαξ** moving staircase.

κυλότα s.f. breeches; underpants.

κυλ|ῶ v.t. & i. roll (over, along); (v.i.) roll along or by. **~ιέμαι** v.i. roll, wallow.

κῦμα s.n. wave.

κυμαίνομαι v.i. fluctuate, waver.

κυματίζω v.i. wave, flutter.

κυματοθραύστης s.m. breakwater.

κύμινον s.n. cummin.

κυνήγη|μα, **~τό** s.n. chase, pursuit, search.

κυνήγι s.n. pursuit; hunting, shooting; game, quarry.

κυνηγός s.m. hunter, sportsman.

κυνηγῶ v.t. & i. chase, pursue, hunt; go shooting.

κυνικ|ός a. 1. cynical; a cynic. 2. **~ὰ καύματα** dog-days.

κυνισμός s.m. cynicism.

κυνόδους s.m. canine tooth.

κυοφορῶ v.i. & t. be pregnant, breed; (fig.) meditate, plan.

κυπαρίσσι s.n. cypress.

κύπελλον s.n. cup.

κυπρῖνος s.m. carp.

κύπτω v.t. & i. bend, lean, stoop.

κύρ (prefix to Christian name or title) mister (in provincial usage).

κυρά 1. f. equivalent of **κύρ**. 2. s.f. missus.

κύρης s.m. father; master.

κυρία s.f. lady, mistress; Mrs.; madam.

κυριακάτικ|ος a. of Sunday; **~α** (s.n.pl.) Sunday clothes. **~α** adv. on Sunday.

κυριακή s.f. Sunday.

κυριαρχ|ῶ v.i. & t. (with gen.) be master of; prevail, be paramount. **~ία** s.f. sovereignty, mastery.

κυριεύω v.t. seize control of, take.

κυριολεκτικῶς adv. literally.

κύρι|ος s.m. lord, master; gentleman; mister; **~ε** sir.

κύρι|ος a. main, principal, chief; **~ον ὄνομα** proper name; **~ον ἄρθρον** leading article.

κυριότης s.f. (right of) ownership.

κυρίως adv. chiefly, above all; ~ εἰπεῖν properly speaking.

κῦρος s.n. weight, authority; validity.

κυρτ|ός a. bent; curved, hooked; convex, bulged; **~ὰ στοιχεῖα** italics.

κυρώνω v.t. ratify, authenticate, confirm.

κύρωσις s.f. ratification; penalty, sanction.

κύστις s.f. (anat.) bladder, cyst.

κυτίον s.n. box.

κύτος s.n. hold (of ship).

κυττάζω v.t. see **κοιτάζω**.

κύτταρον s.n. (biol.) cell.

κυφός a. hunchbacked.

κυψέλη s.f. bee-hive; ear-wax.

κύων s.m.f. dog.

κῶδιξ s.m. codex; code.

κώδων s.m. bell.

κωδωνοκρουσία s.f. ringing of bells.

κωδωνοστάσιον s.n. belfry.

κωθώνι s.n. raw recruit, greenhorn.

κώκ s.n. 1. coke. 2. sort of cream bun.

κωλαρᾶς s.m. (fam.) one broad in the beam.

κωλο- (fam.) epithet of opprobrium.

κῶλον s.n. limb; colon (punctuation).

κῶλος s.m. (fam.) bottom, arse; seat (of pants); (fig.) bottom; ~ καὶ βρακί hand-in-glove.

κωλοφωτιά s.f. glow-worm.

κώλυμα s.n. obstacle, hindrance.

κωλυσιεργῶ v.i. be obstructive; filibuster.

κωλύω v.t. hinder, prevent.

κωλώνω *v.i.* come to a halt.
κῶμα *s.n.* coma.
κώμη *s.f.* large village.
κωμικός *a.* comic, funny; a comedian.
κωμόπολις *s.f.* small country town.
κωμωδία *s.f.* comedy; anything comical; *παίζω* ~ play a trick.
κώνειον *s.n.* hemlock.
κῶνος *s.m.* cone.
κώνωψ *s.m.* mosquito.
κώπη *s.f.* oar. ~**λασία** *s.f.* rowing.
κωφάλαλος *a.* deaf-and-dumb.
κωφεύω *v.i.* turn a deaf ear.
κωφός *a.* deaf.
κώχη *s.f.* corner; crease (*of trousers*).

Λ

λάβα *s.f.* lava.
λαβαίνω *v.t. see* λαμβάνω.
λάβαρον *s.n.* banner.
λαβεῖν *s.n.* (*fin.*) credit (*money owed to one*).
λαβή *s.f.* handle, hilt; hold (*in wrestling*); *δίδω* ~ν afford a pretext.
λαβίς *s.f.* tweezers, pincers, tongs, forceps.
λαβομάνο *s.n.* wash-basin.
λάβρα *s.f.* great heat; *φωτιὰ καὶ* ~ (*fig.*) strong passion, (*fam.*) exorbitant price.
λαβράκι *s.n.* bass (*fish*).
λάβρος *a.* vehement, ardent, eager.
λαβύρινθος *s.m.* labyrinth, maze.
λάβωμα *s.n.* wounding; wound. ~**τιά** *s.f.* wound.
λαβώνω *v.t.* wound.
λαγάνα *s.f.* unleavened bread (*for first day of Lent*).
λαγαρός *a.* clear, limpid; pure (*gold, etc.*).
λαγήν|α *s.f.*, ~**ι** *s.n.* pitcher, jug.
λαγκάδ|ι *s.n.*, ~**ιά** *s.f.* narrow valley.
λαγκεμένος *a.* languishing (*look*).
λάγν|ος *a.* lascivious. ~**εία** *s.f.* lasciviousness.
λαγοκοιμοῦμαι *v.i.* sleep with one eye open, nap.
λαγόνες *s.f.pl.* loins.
λαγ|ός *s.m.* hare; (*fig.*) *τάζω* ~**οὺς μὲ** *πετραχήλια* make wonderful but empty promises.
λαγούμι *s.n.* underground run, passage *or* drain.
λαγωνικό *s.n.* harrier; hunting-dog.

λαδ|ᾶς, ~**έμπορος** *s.m.* oil merchant.
λαδερό *s.n.* oil-cruet; oil-can.
λαδερός *a.* oily; (*vegetable dish*) cooked with oil.
λαδής *a.* olive-coloured.
λάδι *s.n.* olive-oil; oil; (*fig.*) *τοῦ βγάζω* ~ I drive him hard; *βγῆκε* ~ he got off scot-free.
λαδιά *s.f.* 1. oil *or* grease stain. 2. olive crop.
λαδικό *s.n.* oil-cruet; oil-can; (*fig.*) gossiping old woman.
λαδομπογιά *s.f.* oil-colour paint.
λαδόχαρτο *s.n.* greaseproof paper.
λαδώνω *v.t.* oil; make oily *or* greasy; (*fam.*) bribe.
λαζαρέτο *s.n.* quarantine station.
λάθ|ος *s.n.* error, mistake. ~**εύω** *v.i. & t.* be mistaken; mislead.
λαθραῖ|ος *a.* clandestine, smuggled. ~**ως** *adv.* secretly.
λαθρέμπ|ορος *s.m.* smuggler. ~**όριο** *s.n.* smuggling.
λαθρεπιβάτης *s.m.* stowaway.
λαθρόβιος *a.* underground (*press*); one with no known means of support.
λαθροθήρας *s.m.* poacher.
λαθροχειρία *s.f.* pilfering.
λαΐδη *s.f.* lady (*of title*).
λαϊκός *a.* popular, of the people; working-class; lay.
λαῖλαψ *s.f.* hurricane.
λαίμαργ|ος *a.* gluttonous. ~**ία** *s.f.* gluttony.
λαιμητόμος *s.f.* guillotine.
λαιμοδέτης *s.m.* necktie.
λαιμ|ός *s.m.* neck, throat; neckline (*of garment*); *τὸν παίρνω στὸ* ~**ό** *μου* I am responsible for his ill fortune.
λακέρδα *s.f.* salted tunny-fish.
λακές *s.m.* lackey.
λάκ(κ)α *s.f.* lacquer.
λάκκα *s.f.* hole (*in ground*); clearing (*in forest*).
λακκάκι *s.n.* small hole; dimple.
λάκκ|ος *s.m.* hole (*in ground*); grave; den; *κάτι* ~**ον** *ἔχει ἡ φάβα* something queer is afoot.
λακκούβα *s.f.* hole, cavity.
λακτίζω *v.t. & i.* kick.
λακωνικός *a.* laconic.
λαλές *s.m.* poppy.
λάλημα *s.n.* singing, crowing (*of birds*).
λαλιά *s.f.* speech, talk.
λάλος *a.* talkative.
λαλούμενα *s.n.pl.* (*rustic*) fiddles.

λαλῶ *v.t. & i.* talk, speak; play (*the drum, fife, etc.*); (*v.i.*) sing (*of birds*); play (*of instruments*).

λάμα *s.f.* 1. thin sheet of metal. 2. blade (*of knife, razor*). 3. llama.

λαμαρίνα *s.f.* sheet-iron; baking-pan.

λάμας *s.m.* lama.

λαμβάνω *v.t.* take; receive, get; ~ τὴν τιμήν I have the honour; ~ μέρος take part; ~ χώραν take place.

λάμβδα *s.n.* the letter Λ.

λάμια *s.f.* ogress; glutton.

λάμνω *v.t. & i.* row; fly with slow flaps of wings.

λάμπα *s.f.* lamp; bulb.

λαμπάδα *s.f.* torch; large candle.

λαμπερός *a.* shining.

λαμπίκ|ος *s.m.* still, alembic; (*fig.*) anything clear and transparent. **~άρω** *v.t.* distil; filter.

λαμπιόνι *s.n.* electric bulb.

λαμποκοπῶ *v.i.* shine (*from cleanness*).

Λαμπρή *s.f.* Easter.

λαμπρ|ός *a.* bright, brilliant. **~ά** *adv.* admirably. **~ῶς** *adv.* brilliantly, splendidly.

λαμπρύνω *v.t.* add lustre to.

λαμπτήρ *s.m.* lamp; bulb.

λαμπυρίδα *s.f.* glow-worm.

λαμπυρίζω *v.i.* twinkle.

λάμπω *v.i.* shine.

λάμψις *s.f.* brilliance; flash.

λανθ|άνω *v.i.* be latent. **~άνομαι** *v.i.* be mistaken; **~ασμένος** wrong.

λανσάρω *v.t.* bring out, launch (*débutante, new fashion*).

λαντζιέρης *s.m.* scullion.

λαξεύω *v.t.* carve, sculpt.

λαογραφία *s.f.* folklore.

λαός *s.m.* people (*race, nation, body of citizens*); common people.

λάου-λάου *adv.* cautiously and cunningly.

λαοῦτο *s.n.* lute.

λαοφιλής *a.* popular (*of persons*).

λαπᾶς *s.m.* rice boiled to pap; poultice; (*fig.*) spineless person.

λαρδί *s.n.* lard.

λάρ|υγγας *s.m.,* **~ύγγι** *s.n.* larynx, throat.

λαρυγγισμός *s.m.* (*mus.*) roulade.

λαρυγγῖτις *s.f.* laryngitis.

λαρυγγολόγος *s.m.* throat specialist.

λάρυγξ *s.m.* larynx.

λασκάρω *v.t. & i.* loosen, slacken (*of rope, etc.*).

λάσπη *s.f.* mud; mortar; ~ ἡ δουλειά μας our efforts have failed; (*fam.*) τὅκοψε ~ he cleared out.

λασπώνω *v.t. & i.* make or become muddy; become mushy; (*fig.*) make a mess of; be a failure.

λαστιχένιος *a.* made of rubber or elastic; (*fig.*) supple.

λάστιχ|ο *s.n.* rubber; elastic; rubber band; india-rubber; tyre; (*boy's*) catapult; **~α** (*pl.*) galoshes.

λατέρνα *s.f.* barrel-organ.

λατινικός *a.* Latin.

λατομεῖον *s.n.* quarry.

λάτρα *s.f.* housework.

λατρεία *s.f.* adoration, worship.

λατρευτός *a.* adored.

λατρεύω *v.t.* adore, worship; look after.

λάτρης *s.m.* devotee, admirer.

λάφυρ|ον *s.n.* booty, spoil. **~αγωγῶ** *v.t.* plunder.

λαχαίνω *v.t. & i.* (*with acc.*) meet by chance; (*with gen.*) befall, fall to the lot of; ἔλαχα ἐκεῖ I happened to be there; ἔλαχε νὰ τὸν δῶ I happened to see him.

λαχαναγορά *s.f.* (fruit and) vegetable market.

λαχανιάζω *v.i.* pant.

λαχανικόν *s.n.* vegetable.

λάχαν|ον *s.n.* cabbage. **~όκηπος** *s.m.* vegetable-garden. **~οπωλεῖον** *s.n.* greengrocer's.

λαχεῖον *s.n.* lottery; (*fig.*) stroke of luck.

λαχνός *s.m.* lot (*drawn*).

λαχτάρα *s.f.* longing, strong desire or emotion; shock.

λαχταρῶ *v.i. & t.* palpitate; be anxious; long (for); make anxious.

λέαινα *s.f.* lioness.

λεβάντα *s.f.* lavender.

λεβάντες *s.m.* east wind.

λεβαντίνος *s.m.* levantine.

λεβέντης *s.m.* fine upstanding fellow; brave or generous man.

λεβεντιά *s.f.* manliness; upstanding appearance; generosity.

λέβης *s.m.* cauldron; boiler.

λεβιέ *s.n.* lever. [F. *levier*]

λεγάμενος *a.* (*fam.*) ὁ ~ (*pej.*) you know who, his nibs.

λεγεών *s.m.* legion.

λέ|(γ)ω *v.t. & i.* say, tell; recite, sing; call, name; δὲν μοῦ ~ει τίποτα it does not impress me; **~ω** νὰ ταξιδέψω I have in mind to travel; δὲν **~ει** νὰ σταματήσῃ it shows no sign of stopping; κοίταξε τί ~ει ὁ καιρός look and see what the weather is like; πόλεγες αὐτό; would you have imagined it? δὲν σοῦ ~ω I do not deny it (*but* . . .); δὲν ~γεται it is beyond description; τὸ ~ει ἡ καρδιά του he is brave; τί ~s fancy that! ~s καί as if; ποὺ ~s well (*resumptive*); ~ει *parenthetic phrase to support narrative*; δὲν μοῦ ~τε *phrase introducing inquiry*; τὸ ~γειν eloquence; θὰ τὰ ποῦμε we will have a talk; πὲς πῶς κέρδισα supposing I won; πὲς . . . πὲς either (*because*) . . . or (*because*); τί θὰ πῆ τοῦτο; what does this mean? νὰ σοῦ πῶ I say, look here (*also as qualified rejoinder or guarded response*).

λεηλασία *s.f.* pillage.

λεηλατῶ *v.t.* pillage.

λεία *s.f.* booty; prey.

λειαίνω *v.t.* make smooth.

λειβάδι *s.n.* pasture (*land*).

λείβομαι *v.i.* be insufficient; be lacking; μοῦ λείφτηκε μία ὑάρδα I was a yard short (*of material*).

λειμών *s.m.* pasture (*land*).

λείξα *s.f.* gluttony.

λεῖος *a.* smooth.

λείπ|ω *v.i.* be absent *or* away; be missing *or* lacking; run out; μοῦ ~ει I miss it *or* feel the lack of it; μᾶς ἔλειπες we missed you; λίγο ἔλειψε νὰ πέση he nearly fell.

λειρί *s.n.* cock's comb.

λειτουργία *s.f.* working, functioning; (*eccl.*) service.

λειτουργιά *s.f.* bread offered for Holy Communion.

λειτουργός *s.m.f.* functionary, official.

λειτουργ|ῶ *v.i.* work, function, go; (*eccl.*) officiate. ~ιέμαι *v.i.* go to church.

λειχήν *s.m.* 1. lichen. 2. (*med.*) herpes.

λείχω *v.t.* lick.

λειψανδρία *s.f.* lack of men.

λείψαν|ο *s.n.* mortal remains; ~α (*pl.*) remains, debris; relics, bones.

λειψός *a.* deficient.

λειψυδρία *s.f.* shortage of water.

λειῶμα *s.n.* pap, pulp; worn-out object.

λειώνω *v.t. & i.* melt, dissolve, reduce to *or* become pulp; wear out, exhaust; get worn out *or* exhausted.

λεκάνη *s.f.* basin, bowl; lavatory-pan; (*anat.*) pelvis.

λεκ|ές *s.m.* stain, spot. ~ιάζω *v.t. & i.* stain; become stained.

λελέκι *s.n.* stork.

λελογισμένος *a.* wise, sensible.

λεμβοδρομία *s.f.* boat-race.

λέμβος *s.f.* small rowing *or* sailing boat.

λεμβοῦχ|ος *s.m.* boatman. ~ικά *s.n.pl.* boatman's charges.

λεμονάδα *s.f.* lemonade.

λεμόν|ι *s.n.* lemon. ~ιά *s.f.* lemon-tree. ~όκουπα *s.f.* empty half of squeezed lemon.

λεξικ|όν *s.n.* dictionary. ~ογραφία *s.f.* lexicography.

λεξιλόγιον *s.n.* vocabulary; glossary.

λέξ|ις *s.f.* word; κατὰ ~ιν, ~ιν πρὸς ~ιν word for word.

λέοντ|ας *s.m.*, ~άρι *s.n.* lion.

λεοντῆ *s.f.* lion's skin.

λεοντιδεύς *s.m.* lion cub; (*fig.*) dandified youth.

λεοπάρδαλις *s.f.* leopard.

λέπι *s.n.* scale (*of fish, reptile*).

λεπ|ίς, ~ίδα *s.f.*, ~ίδι *s.n.* (*cutting*) blade.

λέπρα *s.f.* leprosy.

λεπρ|ός *a.* leprous; a leper. ~οκομεῖον *s.n.* leper-colony.

λεπτά *s.n.pl.* money.

λεπταίνω *v.t. & i.* make *or* become thin *or* refined.

λεπτεπίλεπτος *a.* very refined *or* delicate.

λεπτοδείκτης *s.m.* minute-hand.

λεπτοκαμωμένος *a.* fine, slender, delicate.

λεπτολογῶ *v.t. & i.* examine minutely; split hairs.

λεπτομέρεια *s.f.* detail. ~κός *a.* (*a matter*) of detail.

λεπτομερ|ής *a.* detailed. ~ῶς *adv.* in detail.

λεπτ|όν *s.n.* 1. minute. 2. lepton (*money*); ~ά (*pl.*) money.

λεπτ|ός *a.* thin, slim, lean; fine; delicate, fragile; light (*of clothing*); refined, well-mannered; subtle; keen (*of senses*). ~ότης *s.f.* delicacy, tact, finesse.

λεπτουργός *s.m.* cabinet-maker.

λεπτοφυής *a.* slender, fine.

λέρα *s.f.* dirt; (*fam.*) dirty dog.

λερωμένος *a.* dirty, soiled.

λερών|ω *v.t. & i.* make *or* become dirty; sully. ~ομαι *v.i.* get dirty.

λέσι *s.n.* rotting carcase; stink.

λέσχη *s.f.* club (*institution*).
λέτσος *s.m.* ragamuffin.
λεύκ|α, ~η *s.f.* poplar.
λευκαίνω *v.t.* make white; bleach.
λευκοκύτταρον *s.n.* (*biol.*) white corpuscle.
λευκόλιθος *s.m.* magnesite.
λευκός *a.* white; (*fig.*) pure.
λευκοσίδηρος *s.m.* tin-plate.
λευκόχρυσος *s.m.* platinum.
λεύκωμα *s.n.* 1. album. 2. white of egg; albumen.
λευτεριά *s.f.* (*fam.*) freedom; delivery (*in childbirth*).
λεφτά *s.n.pl.* money.
λεφτό *s.n.* minute.
λεχούδι *s.n.* newly born child.
λεχ|ούσα, ~ώ, ~ώνα *s.f.* mother of newly born child.
λέω *v.t. & i.* see λέγω.
λέων *s.m.* lion.
λεωφορεῖον *s.n.* omnibus.
λεωφόρος *s.f.* avenue, boulevard.
λήγουσα *s.f.* (*gram.*) final syllable.
λήγω *v.i.* terminate, expire; (*gram.*) end.
λήθαργος *s.m.* lethargy.
λήθη *s.f.* oblivion.
λημέρι *s.n.* den, lair; retreat, refuge.
ληξιαρχ|εῖον *s.n.* register-office. ~ικός *a.* relating to registry of births, marriages and deaths.
ληξιπρόθεσμος *a.* (*fin.*) mature.
λῆξις *s.f.* cessation, expiry.
λησμο|νῶ *v.t. & i.* forget, be forgetful. ~σύνη *s.f.* forgetfulness.
λησταρχεῖον *s.n.* nest of brigands.
ληστ|ής *s.m.* brigand, robber. ~εία *s.f.* brigandage, robbery. ~εύω *v.t.* rob.
ληστρικός *a.* robber's; predatory, extortionate.
λῆψις *s.f.* receipt (*act*).
λιάζ|ω *v.t.* put out in the sun. ~ομαι *v.i.* bask in the sun.
λιακάδα *s.f.* sunshine.
λιακωτό *s.n.* sunny balcony or flat roof.
λίαν *adv.* very, too.
λιανίζ|ω *v.t.* cut up small. ~ομαι *v.i.* hover.
λιανικός *a.* retail.
λιαν|ός *a.* thin, slim; νὰ μοῦ τὰ κάνῃς ~ά explain it clearly to me. ~ά *s.n.pl.* small change.
λιανοτούφεκο *s.n.* sporadic rifle-fire.
λιανοτράγουδο *s.n.* couplet of popular verse.

λιαστ|ός *a.* dried in the sun; κρασὶ ~ό wine made from such grapes.
λιβάδι *s.n.* see λειβάδι.
λιβάν|ι *s.n.*, ~ωτός *s.m.* incense.
λιβανίζω *v.t.* cense; (*fig.*) adulate.
λιβάρι *s.n.* hatchery.
λίβας *s.m.* dry, hot wind.
λίβελλος *s.m.* libel.
λίβρα *s.f.* pound (*weight*).
λιβρέα *s.f.* livery.
λιγάκι *adv.* a little.
λίγδα *s f.* grease; grease-stain.
λιγνεύω *v.t. & i.* make or get thin.
λιγνίτης *s.m.* lignite.
λιγνός *a.* thin, slender.
λιγοθυμῶ *v.i.* see λιποθυμῶ.
λίγο *adv.* (a) little; ~ πολύ more or less.
λίγ|ος *a.* small in amount; (a) little, (a) few; ~ο ~ο little by little; σὲ ~ο shortly; παρὰ ~ο (*νά*) nearly. See ὀλίγος.
λιγοστεύω *v.t. & i.* lessen, reduce; grow less.
λιγοστός *a.* scant, barely sufficient.
λιγότερ|ος *a.* less, least. ~ο *adv.* less, least.
λιγούρ|α *s.f.* nausea; feeling of emptiness (*in stomach*); hungry desire.
λιγουρεύ|ω, ~ομαι *v.t.* desire greatly (*esp. food*).
λιγοψυχία *s.f.* faint-heartedness.
λιγώ|νω *v.t. & i.* fill with nausea, cloy; make faint; feel cloyed or faint. ~νομαι *v.i.* feel cloyed or faint; ~μένα μάτια languishing look.
λιθάνθραξ *s.m.* pit-coal.
λιθάρι *s.n.* stone.
λιθίασις *s.f.* (*med.*) calculus.
λίθινος *a.* stone.
λιθοβολῶ *v.t.* throw stones at; stone (*to death*).
λιθογραφία *s.f.* lithography; lithograph.
λιθόδμητος *a.* built of stone.
λιθοκόπος *s.m.* stone-breaker.
λιθόκτιστος *a.* built of stone.
λιθοξόος *s.m.* stone-mason.
λίθος *s.m.f.* stone.
λιθόστρωτ|ος *a.* paved with stones. ~ον *s.n.* paved way, pavement.
λικέρ *s.n.* liqueur. [F. *liqueur*]
λίκν|ον *s.n.* cradle. ~ίζω *v.t.* rock.
λιλά *a.* lilac-coloured. [F. *lilas*]
λιλλιπούτειος *a.* lilliputian.
λίμα *s.f.* 1. file (*tool*); (*fig.*) boring chatter. 2. great hunger.
λιμάζω *v.i. & t.* be famished (for).

λιμάνι *s.n.* port, harbour.
λιμάρης *a.* gluttonous.
λιμάρω *v.t. & i.* file; (*fig.*) (bore with) chatter.
λιμενάρχης *s.m.* harbour-master.
λιμενικός *a.* of port *or* harbour.
λιμήν *s.m.* port, harbour, haven.
λιμνάζω *v.i.* be stagnant; stagnate.
λίμν|η *s.f.* lake. ~ούλα *s.f.* pond.
λιμνοθάλασσα *s.f.* lagoon.
λιμοκοντόρος *s.m.* (*fam.*) toff, nut.
λιμοκτονῶ *v.i.* starve to death.
λιμός *s.m.* famine.
λιμπίζομαι *v.t.* desire greatly; look fondly on.
λινάρι *s.n* flax.
λινάτσα *s.f.* sacking.
λινέλαιον *s.n.* linseed-oil.
λίνον *s.n.* flax.
λιν|ός *a.* linen. ~όν *s.n.* linen.
λιο- *denotes* 1. sun. 2. olive.
λιοντάρι *s.n.* lion.
λιοπύρι *s.n.* great heat of sun.
λιοτριβιό *s.n.* oil-press.
λιπαίνω *v.t.* lubricate, oil; manure.
λιπαρός *a.* greasy.
λίπασμα *s.n.* manure, fertilizer.
λιποβαρής *a.* under-weight.
λιποθυμ|ῶ *v.i.* faint. ~ία *s.f.* fainting-fit.
λίπος *s.n.* fat, grease; lard.
λιπόσαρκος *a.* spare, skinny.
λιποτάκτης *s.m.* deserter.
λιποψυχία *s.f.* faint-heartedness.
λίρα *s.f.* sovereign, pound.
λιρέττα *s.f.* (*Italian*) lira.
λίστα *s.f.* list, menu.
λιτανεία *s.f.* (*eccl.*) procession with icon (*for intercession*).
λιτ|ός *a.* frugal; plain, simple. ~ότης *s.f.* frugality; simplicity.
λίτρα *s.f.* pound (*weight*); litre.
λιχνίζω *v.t.* winnow.
λιχούδ|ης *a.* greedy (*for food*). ~ιά *s.f.* greediness; a titbit.
λοβιτούρα *s.f.* (*fam.*) trick, roguery.
λοβός *s.m.* lobe; pod.
λογαριάζ|ω *v.t. & i.* count up, reckon; regard; take into account; take notice of, pay attention to; intend, expect (*to*). ~ομαι *v.i.* settle one's account.
λογαριασμός *s.m.* calculation, reckoning, account; bill.
λογάριθμος *s.m.* logarithm.
λογᾶς *s.m.* chatterbox; maker of empty promises.

λόγγος *s.m.* thicket.
λογ|ή *s.f.* τί ~ῆς; what sort of? ~ιῶν ~ιῶν all sorts of.
λόγια *s.n.pl.* words.
λογιάζω *v.t.* consider, think of.
λογιέμαι *v.i.* be considered.
λογίζομαι *v.t. & i.* take account of; consider oneself; be considered.
λογικεύομαι *v.i.* think sensibly; become sensible.
λογική *s.f.* logic; way of thinking.
λογικ|ό *s.n.*, ~ά (*pl.*) senses, reason (*sanity*).
λογικός *a.* rational, logical; reasonable.
λόγιον *s.n.* saying, maxim.
λόγι|ος *a.* learned; ~ώτατος a pedant.
λογισμός *s.m.* thought; (*math.*) calculus.
λογιστήριον *s.n.* counting-house; purser's office.
λογιστής *s.m.* accountant, book-keeper; purser.
λογιστική *s.f.* accountancy, book-keeping.
λογογράφος *s.m.* writer, man of letters.
λογοδιάρροια *s.f.* garrulity.
λογοδοτῶ *v.i.* render an account.
λογοκλοπία *s.f.* plagiarism.
λογοκρισία *s.f.* censorship.
λογομαχία *s.f.* exchange of abusive words, row.
λογοπαίγνιον *s.n.* play on words.
λόγ|ος *s.m.* 1. speech (*faculty*); speech, address; talk, mention, question (*of*); saying; word (*pl.* τὰ ~ια); ἔχει ~ο he is a man of his word; ~ου χάριν for example; ἐν ~ῳ in question; ἄξιος ~ου worthy of note; δὲν σοῦ πέφτει ~ος you have no say; μοῦ ἔδωσε τὸν ~ο he called on me to speak; δὲν παίρνει ἀπὸ ~ια he will not listen to reason; τῆς πῆρα ~ια I wormed it out of her; ὁ ~ος τὸ λέει in a manner of speaking; ποὺ λέει ὁ ~ος as it were. 2. reason, ground; account, reckoning; ~ῳ by reason of; ὀρθὸς ~ος good sense. κατὰ μείζονα ~ον with all the more reason; κατ' οὐδένα ~ον on no account. 3. (*fam.*) (τοῦ) ~ου του *or* σου he, him *or* you, *etc.*
λογοτέχν|ης *s.m.* writer, man of letters. ~ία *s.f.* writing; literature.
λογοφέρνω *v.i.* have a row, exchange insults.
λόγχη *s.f.* lance; bayonet.
λοιδορῶ *v.t.* revile, mock.

λοιμ|ός s.m. pestilence, plague. ~ώδης a. pestilential, infectious. ~ωξις s.f. infection.

λοιπόν conj. & int. then, so, well (then).

λοιπ|ός a. the rest (of); καὶ τὰ ~ά etcetera; τοῦ ~οῦ in future.

λοίσθι|ος a. πνέω τὰ ~α breathe one's last.

λοκάντα s.f. small restaurant.

λόξα s.f. 1. slant; piece of material cut on bias. 2. craze, fad.

λοξοδρομῶ v.i. deviate, shift one's course; (naut.) tack.

λοξ|ός a. 1. slanting, oblique, at an angle. 2. a faddist. ~ά adv. slantwise, at an angle.

λόξυγγας s.m. hiccup.

λόπια s.n.pl. sort of kidney-beans.

λόρδα s.f. (fam.) great hunger.

λόρδος s.m. lord.

λοσιόν s.f. lotion (cosmetic). [F. lotion]

λοστός s.m. crowbar.

λοστρόμος s.m. (naut.) boatswain.

λούζ|ω v.t. wash (body, hair); (fam.) scold, revile. ~ομαι v.i. have a bath, wash one's hair.

λουκάνικο s.f. sausage.

λουκέτο s.n. padlock.

λούκι s.n. drainpipe; gutter; bias fold (dressmaking).

λουκούλλειος a. Lucullan.

λουκουμάς s.m. sort of doughnut fried in oil.

λουκούμι s.n. Turkish delight (sweetmeat); (fig.) tender as chicken; μοῦρθε ~ it was a godsend to me.

λουλάκι s.n. indigo, blue (in laundering).

λουλούδι s.n. flower.

λουμίνι s.n. small wick.

λούξ s.n. luxury. [F. luxe]

λουρί s.n. strap, belt.

λουρίδα s.f. strip, belt.

λουσάρ|ω, ~ίζω v.t. (fam.) give a touch of luxury to. ~ομαι v.i. dress up.

λούσιμο s.n. washing (of body, hair); (fam.) scolding.

λούσ|ο s.n. smart clothes; luxury; (fam.) ἄς τά ~α come off it!

λουστράρω v.t. polish.

λουστρίνι s.n. patent-leather; ~α (pl.) patent-leather shoes.

λοῦστρο s.n. polish; (fig.) smattering.

λοῦστρος s.m. shoeblack.

λουτρικό s.n. bath-robe.

λουτρ|όν s.n. bath, bathe; bathroom; ~ά (pl.) mineral springs, spa, waters;

ἔμεινε στὰ κρύα τοῦ ~οῦ he was let down.

λουτρόπολις s.f. spa (town).

λούτσα s.f. (fam.) γίνομαι ~ get drenched.

λουφάζω v.i. lie low, shrink back.

λούω v.t. wash, bathe (body).

λοφίον s.n. (bird's) crest; (mil.) pompon.

λόφος s.m. hill.

λοχαγός s.m. (mil.) captain.

λοχίας s.m. (mil.) sergeant.

λόχμη s.f. clump of dense undergrowth.

λόχος s.m. (mil.) company.

λυγαριά s.f. osier.

λυγερ|ός a. lithe, svelte. ~ή s.f. damsel, beautiful girl.

λυγ|ίζω, ~ῶ v.t. & i. bend; σειέμαι καὶ ~ιέμαι assume coquettish airs.

λυγμός s.m. sob.

λύγξ s.m. lynx.

λυθρίνι s.n. sort of fish.

λυκαυγές s.n. half-light of dawn.

λύκειον s.n. secondary school (esp. private).

λύκος s.m. wolf; cock (of gun).

λυκόσκυλο s.n. wolf-hound.

λυκόφως s.n. dusk.

λυμαίνομαι v.t. ravage, prey on.

λυντσάρω v.t. lynch.

λύνω v.t. see λύω.

λυπᾶμαι v.i. & t. regret, be sorry (for); (fig.) be stingy with.

λύπη s.f. regret, sorrow, grief; mourning; pity.

λυπημένος a. sad; in mourning.

λυποῦμαι v.i. & t. see λυπᾶμαι.

λυσικόμος a. dishevelled.

λύσιμο s.n. loosening, untying; solving; dismantling.

λύσις s.f. termination, dissolution (of partnership, etc.); solving, settling; solution, answer; denouement, ending.

λυσιτέλεια s.f. utility.

λύσσα s.f. rabies; (fig.) fury, frenzy; (fam.) anything very salt.

λυσσ(ι)άζω v.i. & t. get rabies; (fig.) be mad (with anger, desire); madden; (fam.) thrash; ~ τὸ φαγητό make the food like brine.

λυσσιατρεῖον s.n. rabies hospital.

λυσσομανῶ v.i. rage.

λυσσῶ v.i. get rabies; (fig.) be mad (with anger, desire).

λυσσώδης a. furious, fierce.

λύτης *s.m.* solver.

λυτ|ός *a.* not tied up, loose; βάζω ~ούς καὶ δεμένους leave no stone unturned.

λύτρα *s.n.pl.* ransom.

λυτρώνω *v.t.* ransom; set free.

λυτρωτής *s.m.* redeemer.

λυχνάρι *s.n.* see λύχνος.

λυχνία *s.f.* (*any sort of*) lamp; (*electric*) bulb, valve.

λύχνος *s.m.* small olive-oil lamp.

λύ|ω *v.t.* loosen, untie, set free; dismantle; solve, settle; terminate, dissolve. ~ομαι *v.i.* come undone; ~θηκα στὰ γέλια I split my sides with laughing.

λυώνω *v.t. & i.* see λειώνω.

λώβ|α *s.f.* leprosy. ~ός *a.* leprous; a leper.

λωλ|ός *a.* mad, crazy. ~άδα *s.f.* madness; mad action. ~αίνω *v.t.* send crazy.

λωποδύτης *s.m.* thief, pickpocket.

λωρίον *s.n.* see λουρί.

λωρίς *s.f.* see λουρίδα.

λωτός *s.m.* lotus.

M

μά 1. *conj.* but. 2. *particle* (*with acc.*) by; ~ τὸ Θεό by God!

μαβής *a.* dark blue.

μαγαζ|ί *s.n.* shop. ~άτορας *s.m.* shopkeeper.

μαγάρ|α *s.f.* dirt, dung; (*fig.*) dirty beast. ~ίζω *v.t. & i.* pollute, foul; make dirt.

μαγγανεία *s.f.* sorcery.

μαγγ|άνι, ~ανο *s.n.* calendar, vice (*tool*); loom; wheel (*of well, etc.*).

μαγγάνιον *s.n.* manganese.

μαγγανοπήγαδο *s.n.* wheel-well.

μάγγας *s.m.* see μάγκας.

μαγγώνω *v.t.* crush, squeeze.

μαγεία *s.f.* magic, sorcery; enchantment; anything delightful.

μαγειρεῖον *s.n.* kitchen; cook-shop.

μαγείρε(υ)μα *s.n.* cooking.

μαγειρεύω *v.t. & i.* cook; prepare food.

μαγειρικ|ός *a.* culinary; for cooking. ~ή *s.f.* cookery (-book).

μαγειρίτσα *s.f.* soup eaten at Easter.

μάγειρος *s.m.* cook.

μάγερας *s.m.* cook.

μαγερειό *s.n.* kitchen; cook-shop.

μαγεριά *s.f.* (quantity sufficient for) one cooking.

μαγέρικο *s.n.* cook-shop.

μαγευτικός *a.* enchanting, delightful.

μαγεύω *v.t.* bewitch, enchant, charm.

μάγια *s.n.pl.* (*sorcerer's*) spell, charm.

μαγιά *s.f.* yeast, leaven; (*fam.*) initia small capital in business enterprise.

μαγιάτικος *a.* of May.

μαγικός *a.* magic; (*fig.*) magical, enchanting.

μαγιό *s.n.* bathing-dress. [F. *maillot*]

μαγιονέζα *s.f.* mayonnaise.

μάγισσα *s.f.* witch, enchantress.

μαγκάλι *s.n.* brazier.

μάγκ|ας *s.m.* one who has learnt the seamy side of life; street-urchin; sharper, spiv; clever fellow. ~ικα *s.n. pl.* slangy talk of μάγκας.

μαγκλαράς *s.m.* tall, gawky fellow.

μαγκούρα *s.f.* crook, staff, cudgel.

μαγκούφης *s.m.* solitary *or* wretched person; ownerless animal.

μαγνησία *s.f.* magnesia.

μαγνήσιον *s.n.* magnesium.

μαγνήτ|ης *s.m.* magnet. ~ίζω *v.t.* magnetize. ~ικός *a.* magnetic. ~ισμός *s.m.* magnetism.

μαγνητόφωνον *s.n.* tape-recorder.

μάγ|ος *s.m.* magician; ~οι (*pl.*) Magi.

μαγουλήθρα *s.f.* mumps.

μάγουλο *s.n.* cheek.

μαδέρι *s.n.* joist; scaffold-pole.

μάδημα *s.n.* plucking, moulting.

μαδῶ *v.t. & i.* pluck; moult, shed hair, leaves, *etc.*; fall, come out (*of hair, leaves, etc.*); (*fam.*) pluck, swindle.

μαέστρος *s.m.* musical conductor; (*fig.*) expert.

μάζα *s.f.* mass.

μάζεμα *s.n.* gathering, collecting. ~τα (*pl.*) trash, riff-raff.

μαζεμένος *a.* unassuming, wellbehaved; crouching, nestling.

μαζεύ|ω *v.t. & i.* gather, collect; pick up; strike (*sail, flag, etc.*); take in, reduce compass of; wind (*wool*) into ball; curb, restrain; (*v.i.*) shrink (*of cloth*); become purulent. ~ομαι *v.i.* assemble, collect; crouch, nestle; behave with restraint, settle down; ~εται νωρίς he goes home early.

μαζί *adv.* together; (*prep.*) ~ του with him.

μαζικός *a.* 1. of the masses; mass. 2. held in common.

μαζοχισμός *s.m.* masochism.
μαζώνω *v.t. see* **μαζεύω**.
Μάης *s.m.* May.
μαθαίνω *v.t. & i.* learn; become aware; ascertain; teach; ~ σέ get used to.
μαθέ(ς) *adv.* certainly, apparently; by any chance?
μάθημα *s.n.* lesson.
μαθηματικ|ά *s.n.pl.*, ~ή *s.f.* mathematics.
μαθηματικός *a.* mathematical; a mathematician.
μαθημένος *a.* learnt; used, accustomed (*to*).
μάθησις *s.f.* learning.
μαθητεία *s.f.* years of study; apprenticeship.
μαθητεύ|ω *v.i.* be a learner *or* apprentice; ~όμενος an apprentice, tiro.
μαθητής *s.m.* pupil, schoolboy; disciple.
μαθητικ|ός *a.* studious; pupil's; ~ò θρανίο school-desk.
μαῖα *s.f.* midwife.
μαίανδρος *s.m.* meander (*pattern*).
μαιευτήρ *s.m.* obstetrician.
μαιευτήριον *s.n.* lying-in hospital.
μαιευτική *s.f.* obstetrics.
μαϊμοῦ *s.f.* monkey; (*fig.*) ugly *or* cunning person. ~δίζω *v.t.* ape, imitate.
μαινάς *s.f.* maenad.
μαίνομαι *v.i.* rage.
μαϊντανός *s.m.* parsley; (*fam.*) meddlesome person.
Μάϊος *s.m.* May.
μαΐστρος *s.m.* north-west wind.
μαιτρέσσα *s.f.* mistress, concubine.
μακάβριος *a.* macabre.
μακάρι *adv.* would that! ~ καί even.
μακαρίζω *v.t.* hold fortunate, envy (*without malice*).
μακάριος *a.* blessed; blissful, serene.
μακαρίτης *a.* late, deceased.
μακαρόνια *s.n.pl.* macaroni.
μακελλάρης *s.m.* butcher.
μακελλειό *s.n.* butcher's shop; slaughterhouse; (*fig.*) carnage.
μακέττα *s.f.* sketch, model.
μακρ- *denotes* length.
μακραίνω *v.t. & i.* lengthen, extend; grow longer *or* taller; drag on.
μακράν *adv.* far, afar.
μακριά *adv.* far, afar.
μακρινάρι *s.n.* long passage; any elongated object.
μακρινός *a.* distant, far-off.
μακριός *a.* long.

μακρόβιος *a.* long-lived.
μακροβούτι *s.n.* under-water swimming.
μακρόθεν *adv.* from afar.
μακρόθυμος *a.* patient, forbearing; forgiving.
μάκρος *s.n.* length.
μακρ|ός *a.* long; διὰ ~ῶν at length, in detail.
μακροσκελής *a.* (*fig.*) long-winded.
μακρύνω *v.t. & i. see* **μακραίνω**.
μακρύς *a.* long; tall.
μάκτρον *s.n.* towel, napkin.
μαλαγάνας *s.m.* (*fam.*) artful dodger.
μαλ|άζω, ~άσσω *v.t.* knead, massage; soften.
μαλάκιον *s.n.* mollusc.
μαλακ|ός *a.* soft; mild. ~ώνω *v.t. & i.* soften; get milder.
μαλακτικός *a.* emollient.
μαλάκυνσις *s.f.* softening.
μάλαμα *s.n.* gold; (*fig.*) kind-hearted person.
μάλ|η *s.f.* ὑπὸ ~ης under the arm.
μαλθακός *a.* soft, unused to hardship.
μάλιστα *adv.* especially; indeed; even; yes.
μαλλί *s.n.* wool; hair (*collective*).
μαλλιά *s.n.pl.* hair (*of head*); ~ κουβάρια topsy-turvy; ἔγιναν ~ κουβάρια they quarrelled.
μαλλιαρή *s.f.* (*fam.*) extreme form of demotic Gk.
μαλλιαρός *a.* hairy; an advocate of μαλλιαρή.
μάλλινος *a.* woollen.
μᾶλλον *adv.* more, rather; to some extent; κατὰ τὸ ~ ἢ ἧττον more or less.
μάλωμα *s.n.* scolding; quarrelling.
μαλώνω *v.t. & i.* scold; quarrel.
μαμά *s.f.* mother, mamma.
μάμμη *s.f.* grandmother.
μαμμή *s.f.* midwife.
μαμμόθρεπτος *a.* coddled.
μαμμούνι *s.n.* insect.
μάνα *s.f. see* **μάν(ν)α**.
μανάβης *s.m.* greengrocer.
μανδ- *see* **μαντ-**.
μανδύας *s.m.* cloak; cope.
μανθάνω *v.t. & i. see* **μαθαίνω**.
μάνι μάνι *adv.* quickly.
μανία *s.f.* madness; rage; passion; mania; ἔχω ~ μέ be mad on.
μανιάζω *v.i.* become enraged.
μανιακός *a.* maniac(al).
μανιβέλλα *s.f.* lever; starting handle.

μανίκ|ι s.n. sleeve; handle (of implement); (fam.) tricky job. ~έτι s.n. cuff.

μανιτάρι s.n. mushroom.

μανιώδης a. furious; passionately addicted.

μάννα s.n. manna.

μάν(ν)α s.f. mother; (fig.) spring (water); original copy; (fam.) dab, expert.

μαν(ν)ούλα s.f. (fam.) mother; also term of endearment.

μανουάλιον s.n. church candelabrum.

μανούβρα s.f. manœuvre; shunting.

μανούρι s.n. sort of white cheese.

μανταλάκι s.n. clothes-peg.

μάνταλ|ο s.n. bolt, latch. ~ώνω v.t. bolt, latch.

μαντάρα s.f. (fam.) wreck, shambles.

μανταρίνι s.n. tangerine.

μαντάρ|ω v.t. darn. ~ισμα s.n. darning.

μαντάτο s.n. news.

μαντεία s.f. divination; a prophecy, oracle.

μαντείον s.n. oracle (place).

μαντέκα s.f. wax for moustaches.

μαντεύω v.t. divine, guess.

μαντήλι s.n. kerchief; handkerchief.

μαντινάδα s.f. rhyming couplet (esp. humorous).

μάντις s.m. soothsayer.

μαντολάτο s.n. nougat.

μάντρα s.f. stall, fold, pen, sty; (enclosing) wall, fence; storage yard.

μαντράχαλος s.m. tall, gawky fellow.

μαντρόσκυλο s.n. shepherd's dog.

μαντρώνω v.t. pen, fold (animals); wall, fence.

μαξιλλάρι s.n. pillow, cushion.

μαξούλι s.n. crop (esp. grapes).

μαούν|α s.f. lighter (boat). ~ιέρης s.m. lighterman.

μάπ(π)α s.f. cabbage.

μάππας s.m. silly fellow.

μαραγκιάζω v.i. shrivel.

μαραγκός s.m. joiner; carpenter.

μαράζι s.n. pining.

μάραθ(ρ)ο s.n. fennel.

μαραίν|ω v.t. wither. ~ομαι v.i. wither, fade.

μαρασμός s.m. decline, decay.

μαραφέτι s.n. (fam.) thing, thingummy.

μαργαρίνη s.f. margarine.

μαργαρίτα s.f. daisy.

μαργαριτάρι s.n. pearl.

μαργαρίτης s.m. pearl; (fam.) howler.

μαργιολιά s.f. exercise of wiles, coquettishness.

μαρίδα s.f. whitebait; (fam.) crowd of small children.

μάρκα s.f. brand, trade-mark; monogram; counter, token; (fam.) slippery customer.

μάρμαρ|ον s.n. marble; (fam.) έμεινε ~ο he was dumbfounded. ~ένιος, ~ινος a. marble. ~ώνω v.t. & i. turn to marble.

μαρμελάδα s.f. jam, marmalade.

μαρούλι s.n. lettuce.

μαρσιποφόρος a. marsupial.

Μάρτ|ης, ~ιος s.m. March.

μαρτυρία s.f. testimony, evidence.

μαρτυρικός a. evidential; martyr's; full of suffering.

μαρτύριον s.n. token; martyrdom; torment.

μαρτυρῶ v.t. & i. testify, give evidence; indicate; inform against; suffer martyrdom.

μάρτυς s.m. witness; martyr.

μᾶς, μας pron. us; our.

μασέλλα s.f. jaw; set of (false) teeth.

μασιά s.f. tongs.

μάσκα s.f. mask; fancy dress. ~ρᾶς s.m. masker; (fam.) blighter; scamp.

μασόνος s.m. freemason.

μασουλ|ίζω, ~ῶ v.t. chew, munch.

μασούρι s.n. bobbin, spool, reel; stick (of sulphur, etc.).

μαστάρι s.n. udder.

μαστίγιον s.n. horsewhip, switch.

μαστιγώνω v.t. whip.

μαστίζω v.t. scourge, plague.

μάστιξ s.f. whip; scourge.

μαστίχα s.f. mastic; sweet or liqueur from this.

μάστορ|ας, ~ης s.m. (skilled) workman; handyman; (fig.) expert.

μαστορεύω v.t. & i. make; mend; do a job (with tools).

μαστός s.m. breast; udder.

μαστροπός s.m. pimp.

μαστροχαλαστής s.m. (iron.) bungler.

μασχάλη s.f. armpit; arm-hole.

μασῶ v.t. & i. chew; eat.

ματαιόδοξος a. conceited.

ματαιοπονῶ v.i. labour in vain.

μάταιος a. vain, fruitless; conceited.

ματαιώνω v.t. thwart, prevent; cancel.

μάτην adv. in vain.

μάτι s.n. eye; evil eye; bud (leaf or shoot); ~ τῆς θάλασσας whirlpool; αὐγὸ ~ fried egg; ἔχω στὸ ~ covet *or* have a down on; βάζω στὸ ~ set one's heart on; μοῦ μπῆκε στὸ ~ it tickles my fancy; θὰ σοῦ φάω τὸ ~ I will take revenge on you; κλείνω (*or* κάνω) τὸ ~ wink; κλείνω τὰ ~α σέ overlook, be tolerant of; κάνω στραβὰ ~α pretend not to see; βγάζω τὰ ~α μου ruin oneself; παίρνω τὰ ~α (*or* τῶν ὀματιῶν) μου go away in despair; γιὰ τὰ (μαῦρα) ~α for politeness' sake; γιὰ τὰ ~α τοῦ κόσμου for appearance' sake; τὰ ~α σου τέσσερα keep your eyes skinned! ~α μου my dearest!

ματι|ά *s.f.* glance, look; ogle. ~άζω *v.t.* espy; covet, set one's heart on; take aim at; bewitch, bring bad luck to.

ματίζω *v.t.* splice, add piece on to.

ματογυάλια *s.n.pl.* eyeglasses.

ματόκλαδο *s.n.* eyelash.

ματόφυλλο *s.n.* eyelid.

ματσαράγκα *s.f.* cheating.

μάτς μούτς (*onomatopoeia*) (sound of) kisses.

μάτσο *s.n.* bunch, bundle; skein.

ματσούκα *s.f.* club, cudgel.

ματώνω *v.t. & i.* stain with blood; bleed.

μαυρ- *denotes* black.

μαυραγορίτης *s.m.* black-marketeer.

μαυράδι *s.n.* black spot; pupil (*of eye*).

μαυρειδερός *a.* darkish.

μαυρ|ίζω *v.t. & i.* darken; vote against; become brown *or* dark; appear darkly, loom; ~ισε τὸ μάτι μου I am driven to desperation (*by poverty, etc.*).

μαυρίλα *s.f.* blackness, darkness; dark colour, tan.

μαυροδάφνη *s.f.* sort of sweet wine.

μαυροπίναξ *s.m.* blackboard; black-list.

μαυροπούλι *s.n.* starling.

μαῦρ|ος *a.* black; dark; negro; wretched; gloomy; ἔκανα ~α μάτια νὰ τὸν δῶ I have not seen him for ages; τὸν ἔκανα ~ο στὸ ξύλο I gave him a good hiding; ~ο κρασί red wine.

μαυσωλεῖον *s.n.* mausoleum.

μάχ|αιρα *s.f.*, ~αίρι *s.n.* knife; στὰ ~αίρια at daggers drawn.

μαιχαιριά *s.f.* stab.

μαχαιροβγάλτης *s.m.* one quick on the draw; cutthroat.

μαχαιροπήρουνα *s.n.* cutlery.

μαχαλᾶς *s.m.* quarter, district.

μάχη *s.f.* battle. ~τής *s.m.* fighter.

μαχητικός *a.* combative.

μάχιμος *a.* combatant; in fighting trim.

μαχμουρλῆς *a.* still heavy with sleep.

μάχ|ομαι *v.t. & i.* fight; μὲ ~εται he hates me.

μέ *prep.* (*with acc.*) 1. (*in company of, among*) with. 2. (*having, characterized by*) with. 3. (*means, instrument, method*) with, by; ~ τὰ πόδια on foot. 4. (*material, content*) of. 5. (*manner, circumstance*) with; ~ τὸ καλὸ God willing; without mishap; ~ τέτοια χάλια in such a (*bad*) state. 6. (*rate, measure, price*) ~ τὸ μῆνα by the month; ~ κέρδος at a profit; ~ τόσα λίγα δέν ἀγοράζεται it can not be bought for so little; δύο ~ τρία 2 by 3 (metres). 7. (*time*) ~ τὸν καιρό in the course of time; ~ τῆ σειρά in turn; δύο ~ τρεῖς between 2 and 3 o'clock. 8. (*in regard to*) τί μ' αὐτό; what of it? ἔχω μανία ~ to be mad on; σχετικά ~ regarding. 9. (*despite*) μ' ὅλο πού although. 10. (*cause*) γελῶ ~ laugh at. 11. (*proximity*) πλάτη ~ πλάτη back to back. 12. (*exchange*) ἀλλάζω λίρες ~ δραχμές exchange pounds for drachmas. 13. (*after words denoting similarity, contact, agreement, & opposites*) παντρεύομαι ~ get married to; χωρίζω ~ part from; ὁμοιότητα ~ resemblance to; συγγενής ~ related to; ἀναλόγως ~ in proportion to; ἴδια ~ μένα the same as me.

μέ, με *pron.* me.

μέγαιρα *s.f.* shrew, hag.

μεγαλ- *denotes* great, large.

μεγαλεῖ|ον *s.n.* grandeur, magnificence; ~α (*pl.*) honours and wealth; (*fam.*) ~ο first-rate!

μεγαλειότης *s.f.* majesty; ἡ Αὐτοῦ ~ His Majesty.

μεγαλειώδης *a.* grand, grandiose.

μεγαλέμπορος *s.m.* large-scale (wholesale) merchant.

μεγαλεπήβολος *a.* enterprising on a grand scale.

μεγαλόδωρος *a.* liberal, generous.

μεγαλοπιάνομαι *v.i.* put on lordly airs.

μεγαλοποιῶ *v.t.* exaggerate.

μεγαλοπρεπ|ής *a.* majestic, imposing, grand. ~εια *s.f.* grandeur, imposingness.

μεγάλ|ος *a.* great, grand; large, big; long (*duration*); grown up; elder; ~η Ἑβδομάδα Holy Week.

μεγαλόσχημος *a.* eminent, important (*person*); one who pretends to be so.

μεγαλουργώ *v.i.* accomplish great things.

μεγαλο(υ)σιάνος *s.m.* (*esp. iron.*) big shot.

μεγαλόφρων *a.* magnanimous; conceited.

μεγαλοφυ|ής *a.* endowed with genius. ~ΐα *s.f.* genius.

μεγαλόχαρη *a.* (*the Virgin*) full of grace.

μεγαλόψυχος *a.* magnanimous.

μεγαλύνω *v.t.* glorify, extol.

μεγαλώνω *v.t. & i.* enlarge, make bigger; bring up (*children*); exaggerate; grow in size; grow up.

μέγαρον *s.n.* large, imposing building.

μέγας *a.* see μεγάλος.

μεγάφωνον *s.n.* megaphone; loudspeaker.

μέγγενη *s.f.* vice (*tool*).

μέγεθ|ος *s.n.* size, greatness, extent. ~υνσις *s.f.* magnification, enlargement. ~υντικός *a.* magnifying.

μεγιστάν *s.m.* grandee, magnate.

μέγιστ|ος *a.* greatest, largest. ~ον *s.n.* maximum.

μεδούλι *s.n.* marrow (*of bones*).

μέδουσα *s.f.* sort of jellyfish.

μεζές *s.m.* bit of food as appetizer; titbit.

μεζούρα *s.f.* tape-measure.

μεθαύριον *adv.* the day after tomorrow.

μέθη *s.f.* intoxication.

μέθοδ|ος *s.f.* method; course, handbook. ~ικός *a.* methodical.

μεθόριος *a. & s.f.* (of the) frontier.

μεθύσι *s.n.* intoxication.

μεθύσκ|ω *v.t.* intoxicate. ~ομαι *v.i.* get intoxicated.

μεθυσμένος *a.* drunk.

μεθυστικός *a.* intoxicating.

μεθύω *v.i.* become inebriated.

μεθώ *v.t. & i.* intoxicate; get drunk.

μειδι|ώ *v.i.* smile. ~αμα *s.n.* smile.

μείζ|ων *a.* greater; κατὰ·~ονα λόγον all the more so; (*mus.*) major.

μειλίχιος *a.* mild (*of manner*).

μειοδοτώ *v.i.* make lowest tender.

μείον *adv.* less; minus.

μειονέκτημα *s.n.* failing, disadvantage, drawback.

μειονότης *s.f.* minority.

μειο(νο)ψηφία *s.f.* minority.

μείων *a.* lesser.

μειώνω *v.t.* lessen, reduce.

μείωσις *s.f.* lessening, reduction; loss of moral stature.

μελαγχολ|ία *s.f.* melancholy, sadness. ~ικός *a.* melancholy, sad. ~ώ *v.i.* feel sad.

μελάν|η *s.f.*, ~ι *s.n.* ink. ~ιά *s.f.* inkstain; bruise. ~ιάζω *v.t. & i.* bruise; get bruised; turn blue (*with cold*).

μελανοδοχεῖον *s.n.* ink-well, ink-stand.

μέλας *a.* black.

μελᾶτος *a.* 1. like honey. 2. soft-boiled (*egg*). 3. loose-fitting.

μελαχροινός *a.* dark-complexioned; brunette.

μελαψός *a.* swarthy.

μέλει *v.i.* μὲ ~ I mind it, I care about it.

μελένιος *a.* of *or* like honey.

μελέτη *s.f.* study; practice; treatise; plan, design (*for building, etc.*).

μελετηρός *a.* studious.

μελετῶ *v.t. & i.* study; practise; contemplate, have in mind; mention.

μέλημα *s.n.* (*object of*) care *or* concern.

μέλι *s.n.* honey; μὴν τοῦ ~τος honeymoon.

μελίγγι *s.n.* temple (*of head*).

μέλισσα *s.f.* bee.

μελίσσι *s.n.* swarm of bees; (*fig.*) swarm; (*fam.*) ἔχω ~(α) keep bees.

μελισσο|κομία, ~τροφία *s.f.* apiculture.

μελιτζάνα *s.f.* egg-plant, aubergine.

μελλοθάνατος *a.* on the point of death.

μέλλον *s.n.* future.

μελλόνυμφος *a.* about to be married.

μέλλ|ω *v.i.* be about to, be going to; τοῦ ~ει (*or* ~εται) νά he is fated to.

μέλλ|ων *a.* future, elect, to be; ὁ ~ων (*gram.*) future tense.

μελόδραμα *s.n.* opera. ~τικός *a.* (*fig.*) melodramatic.

μέλος *s.n.* 1. limb. 2. member. 3. melody.

μελτέμι *s.n.* north wind in summer.

μελωδί|α *s.f.* melody; tune. ~κός *a.* melodious.

μεμβράνη *s.f.* membrane; parchment.

μεμονωμένος *a.* isolated.

μέμφομαι *v.t.* blame, reproach.

μεμψιμοιρῶ *v.i.* grumble, complain.

μέν *conj.* on the one hand; οἱ ~ . . . οἱ δέ some . . . others.

μενεξές *s.m.* violet.

μέν|ος *s.n.* ardour, fury; ~εα πνέω be wrathful.

μέντα *s.f.* peppermint.

μέντιουμ *s.n.* medium (*spiritualistic*). [F. *médium*]

μένω *v.i.* stay, remain; live, reside; be left over; stop, be suspended; be (*of states*); ἔμεινα I was dumbfounded; ἔμεινε ἔγκυος she is pregnant; ἔμεινε ξερός he was dumbfounded *or* he fell dead; ἔμεινε στόν τόπο he died on the spot; αὐτό μόνο ἔμενε that is the last straw; ~ ἀπό run out of.

μέρα *s.f.* day.

μεράκι *s.n.* yearning, passion; sorrow (*for thing unaccomplished*); τὰ ~ια sentimental mood; καμωμένο μὲ ~ι made with loving care.

μερακλήδικος *a.* done with loving care; fit for a μερακλῆς; charged with passion (*song, etc.*).

μερακλῆς *s.m.* one who demands and relishes the best; one who loves to do a job well.

μεραρχία *s.f.* (*mil.*) division. ~αρχος *s.m.* divisional commander.

μερδικό *s.n.* share, portion.

μερεμέτι *s.n.* (*household*) repair.

μερί *s.n.* thigh.

μεριά *s.f.* place; part; side.

μεριάζω *v.t. & i.* move aside; make way.

μερίδα *s.f. see* μερίς.

μερίδιον *s.n.* share, portion.

μερικεύω *v.t.* particularize.

μερικός *a. & pron.* partial (*not complete*); particular (*not general*); (*pl.*) some, certain.

μέριμνα *s.f.* care, concern. ~ῶ *v.i.* have care *or* concern (*for*).

μερίς *s.f.* portion; helping; ration; political party; περᾶστε το στή ~ίδα μου charge it to my account.

μέρισμα *s.n.* dividend.

μερμήγκι *s.n.* ant.

μεροδούλι *s.n.* a day's work; wages for this; ~ μεροφάϊ from hand to mouth.

μεροκάματο *s.n. see* μεροδούλι.

μεροληπτῶ *v.i.* take sides; show partiality.

μέρος *s.n.* part; role; party (*to contract*); place; w.c.; κατὰ ~ος aside; παίρνω τὸ ~ος του I take his part; ἐκ ~ους του on his behalf.

μέσα *adv.* inside, within; indoors; τὸν ἔβαλαν ~ he was put in prison *or* he was made to lose his money; (*prep.*) ~ σέ in, into, inside; ~ μου within me.

μεσάζω 1. *v.i.* act as intermediary. 2. *v.t.* consume half of.

μεσαῖος *a.* middle, in between; average.

μεσαίων, ~ών *s.m.* middle ages. ~ωνικός *a.* medieval.

μεσάνυχτα *s.n.pl.* midnight; ἔχει ~ he is ignorant *or* in the dark.

μέση *s.f.* middle; waist; ἀφίνω στή ~ leave unfinished; βάζω στή ~ surround; βγάζω στή ~ bring into the open, reveal; βγάζω ἀπ' τή ~ get rid of.

μεσῆλιξ *a.* middle-aged.

μεσημβρία *s.f.* south; noon. ~νός *a.* south, southerly; facing south; midday; meridian.

μεσημέρι *s.n.* noon, midday; μέρα ~ in broad daylight. ~άζω *v.i.* go on till midday. ~ανός *a.* midday; ~ανός ὕπνος siesta.

μεσιάζω *v.i.* be half-consumed.

μεσιακός *a.* shared, held in common.

μεσιανός *a.* middle, in between.

μεσίστιος *a.* at half-mast.

μεσιτεία *s.f.* intervention, mediation, agency; brokerage; commission.

μεσιτεύω *v.i.* intervene, mediate; act as agent or go-between.

μεσίτης *s.m.* broker, (estate) agent; go-between.

μεσιτικός *a.* broker's, agent's; ~ὁ γραφεῖο house-agent's; ~ά (*s.n.pl.*) brokerage, commission.

μεσόγειος *a.* inland; ἡ ~ος the Mediterranean. ~ακός *a.* Mediterranean.

μεσόκοπος *a.* middle-aged.

μεσολαβῶ *v.i.* intervene, mediate; come between (*in space or time*).

μέσον 1. *s.n.* middle; way, means; ~α (*pl.*) middle; means, resources; (*fam.*) pull, influence. 2. ~ον, ~ω *prep.* (*with gen.*) through, via.

μέσος *a.* middle, mid; medium; average.

μεσοτοιχία *s.f.* (sharing of) party wall.

μεσουράνησις *s.f.* zenith, peak.

μεσοφόρι *s.n.* petticoat.

μεσόφωνος *a.* mezzo-soprano.

μεστός *a.* full, well-filled; ripe. ~ώνω *v.i.* ripen, mature.

μετά 1. *adv.* afterwards. 2. *prep.* (*with acc.*) after; (*with gen.*) with.

μεταβαίνω *v.i.* go, proceed.

μεταβάλλω *v.t.* change, alter.

μετάβασις *s.f.* going.

μεταβατικός *a.* transitory; transitional; (*gram.*) transitive.

μεταβιβάζω *v.t.* convey; make over.

μεταβλητός *a.* variable.

μεταβολή *s.f.* change; about turn.
μεταβολισμός *s.m.* metabolism.
μετάγγισις *s.f.* decanting; transfusion.
μεταγενέστερ|ος *a.* later, subsequent; οἱ ~οι posterity.
μεταγωγικ|ός *a.* of transport. ~όν *s.n.* (*mil.*) army service corps; (*naut.*) transport ship.
μεταδίδω *v.t.* transmit; spread (*infection, etc.*).
μετάδο|σις *s.f.* transmission; spreading (*of infection, etc.*); ἁγία ~σις Holy Communion. ~τικός *a.* contagious; able to expound. ~τικόν *s.n.* gift of exposition.
μετάθεσις *s.f.* transposition, transfer.
μεταθέτω *v.t.* transpose; transfer (*employee*).
μεταίχμιον *s.n.* (*mil.*) no-man's-land; (*fig.*) midway point.
μετακαλῶ *v.t.* call in (*expert, esp. from abroad*).
μετακινῶ *v.t.* shift, change position of.
μετακομίζω *v.t. & i.* convey (*objects*) from one place to another; move house.
μεταλαμβάνω *v.i. & t.* receive Holy Communion; administer this to; (*with gen.*) participate in.
μεταλλεῖον *s.n.* mine.
μετάλλευμα *s.n.* ore.
μεταλλικός *a.* of *or* like metal, metallic; mineral.
μετάλλινος *a.* made of metal.
μετάλλιον *s.n.* medal.
μέταλλον *s.n.* metal.
μεταμέλ|ομαι *v.i.* be repentant. ~εια *s.f.* repentance.
μεταμεσημβρινός *a.* afternoon.
μεταμορφ|ώνω *v.t.* transform. ~ωσις *s.f.* transformation.
μεταμόσχευσις *s.f.* grafting; (*med.*) transplantation.
μεταμφι|έζω *v.t.* disguise. ~έζομαι *v.i.* dress up, wear fancy dress. ~εσις *s.f.* disguise.
μεταναστ|εύω *v.i.* migrate, emigrate, immigrate. ~ευσις *s.f.* migration, emigration, immigration. ~ης *s.m.* migrant, emigrant, immigrant.
μετάνοια *s.f.* change of mind; repentance; penitence; prostration.
μετα|νοιώνω, ~νοῶ *v.i.* change one's mind; repent.
μέτ|αξα *s.f.*, ~άξι *s.n.* silk. ~αξένιος *a.* silky.

μεταξοσκώληξ *s.m.* silkworm.
μεταξύ *adv. & prep.* (*with gen.*) between; among; ~ μας between ourselves; ἐν τῷ ~ in the mean time.
μεταξωτ|ός *a.* silk. ~όν *s.n.* silk material.
μεταπείθω *v.t.* dissuade.
μετάπλασις *s.f.* renewal (*of growth, tissue, etc.*).
μεταποιῶ *v.t.* refashion, change style *or* shape of.
μεταπολεμικός *a.* post-war.
μετάπτωσις *s.f.* (sudden) change (*of condition*).
μεταπωλῶ *v.t.* resell.
μεταρρυθμίζω *v.t.* reform, reorganize.
μεταστάς *a.* deceased.
μετάστασις *s.f.* change of place; (*med.*) metastasis.
μετασχηματιστής *s.m.* transformer (*electrical*).
μετατοπ|ίζω *v.t.* shift. ~ισις *s.f.* shifting.
μετατρέπω *v.t.* turn, change, convert.
μεταφέρω *v.t. & i.* carry, transport, convey; transfer; carry over (*in accounts*); move house.
μεταφορ|ά *s.f.* transport, conveyance; removal; amount carried forward; metaphor. ~ικός *a.* of transport; metaphorical; τὰ ~ά transport charges.
μετα|φράζω *v.t.* translate. ~φρασις *s.f.* translation. ~φραστής *s.m.* translator.
μεταφυτεύω *v.t.* transplant.
μεταχειρ|ίζομαι *v.t.* use; treat, behave to (*person*). ~ισμένος *a.* used; worn (*not new*); second-hand.
μετεκπαίδευσις *s.f.* further education; post-graduate study.
μετεξεταστέος *a.* referred (*in examination*).
μετέπειτα *adv.* afterwards; οἱ ~ posterity.
μετέρχομαι *v.t.* practise (*profession*); use (*means*).
μετέχω *v.t.* (*with gen.*) take part in; partake of.
μετέωρον *s.n.* meteor.
μετέωρος *a.* (hanging) in the air; (*fig.*) in suspense; undecided.
μετζεσόλα *s.f.* sole (*of shoe*).
μετημφιεσμένος *a.* in fancy dress; disguised.
μετοικῶ *v.i.* change one's residence; emigrate.
μετόπη *s.f.* metope.
μετόπισθεν *adv.* (*mil.*) τὰ ~ the rear.

μετοχή *s.f.* (*fin.*) share; (*gram.*) participle.

μετόχι *s.n.* farm belonging to monastery.

μετοχικ|ός *a.* (*fin.*) relating to joint stock; (*gram.*) participial.

μέτοχος *s.m.* participant; shareholder.

μέτρη|μα *s.n.* measuring, counting; ~μὸ δὲν ἔχουν they are without number.

μετρημένος *a.* limited; temperate, measured.

μετρητής *s.m.* meter.

μετρητ|ός *a.* measurable; τὰ ~ά cash, ready money; τοῖς ~οῖς in cash.

μετριάζω *v.t.* moderate.

μετρικ|ός *a.* metrical; metric. ~ή *s.f.* prosody, versification.

μετριοπάθ|εια *s.f.* moderation. ~ής *a.* moderate.

μέτριος *a.* moderate; medium; mediocre, indifferent.

μετριό|φρων *a.* modest, unassuming. ~φροσύνη *s.f.* modesty.

μέτρ|ον *s.n.* measure; rule; metre; bar (*music*); moderation; ~α (*pl.*) measurements; measures, steps; παίρνω ~ο (τὰ ~α) take measurements; λαμβάνω ~α take measures.

μετρ|ῶ *v.t.* measure, count; go over (*ground*); pay over (*money*); (*fig.*) calculate, weigh (*words, etc.*); θὰ ~ηθῶ μαζί του I shall match myself against him.

μέτωπον *s.n.* forehead; (*mil.*) front; ἔχει ~ πρός it faces on to.

μέχρι(ς) *prep.* (*with acc. or gen.*) as far as, up to; until, by; about (*in measuring*); ~ ἑνός to the last man; ~ τοῦδε up to now.

μή 1. *adv.* not; don't! οἱ ~ καπνισταί non-smokers. 2. *conj.* lest; (if) by any chance.

μηδαμινός *a.* of no account, worthless.

μηδέ, μηδείς *see* οὐδ-.

μηδέν *s.n.* nothing; zero; nought, cipher. ~ικό *s.n.* nought, cipher.

μηδενίζω *v.t.* give no marks to.

μηδενιστής *s.m.* nihilist.

μήκ|ος *s.n.* length; longitude. ~ύνω *v.t.* lengthen.

μηκῶμαι *v.i.* bellow, moo.

μηλίγγι *s.n. see* μηνίγγι.

μήλ|ον *s.n.* apple; cheekbone. ~ίτης *s.m.* cider.

μή(ν) *see* μή.

μήν, μήνας *s.m.* month.

μηνιαῖος *a.* monthly; month's.

μηνιάτικο *s.n.* month's wages *or* rent.

μηνίγγ|ι *s.n.* temple (*of head*). ~ίτις *s.f.* meningitis.

μήν|ις *s.f.* wrath. ~ίω *v.i.* be enraged.

μήνυμα *s.n.* message.

μην|ύω *v.t.* (*law*) lodge complaint against, summons. ~υσις *s.f.* summons. ~υτής *s.m.* complainant.

μηνῶ *v.t.* & *i.* send word (to *or* of); ~ τὸ γιατρό send for the doctor.

μήπως *adv.* (I wonder) if; lest.

μηρός *s.m.* thigh.

μηρυκ|άζω, ~ῶμαι *v.t.* & *i.* chew (the cud).

μήτε *see* οὔτε.

μήτ|ηρ, ~έρα *s.f.* mother.

μήτρα *s.f.* womb, uterus; matrix, mould.

μητρικ|ός *a.* 1. maternal; ~ὴ γλῶσσα mother tongue. 2. uterine; τὰ ~ά ailments of the womb.

μητρομανής *a.* nymphomaniac.

μητρόπολ|ις *s.f.* metropolis, capital; cathedral; see of metropolitan bishop. ~ιτικός *a.* metropolitan.

μητροπολίτης *s.m.* (*eccl.*) metropolitan bishop.

μητρότης *s.f.* motherhood.

μητρυιά *s.f.* stepmother.

μητρυιός *s.m.* stepfather.

μητρῶον *s.n.* register, roll, official list (*of names*).

μητρῷος *a.* (inherited) from the mother.

μηχανεύομαι *v.t.* contrive, engineer, think up.

μηχανή *s.f.* machine, machinery; engine, works; (*fam.*) typewriter, camera *etc.*; μοῦ στησε μιὰ ~ he played me a trick.

μηχάνημα *s.n.* mechanical appliance.

μηχανικός *a.* mechanical; an engineer *or* mechanic *or* architect. ~ή *s.f.* engineering, mechanics. ~όν *s.n.* (*mil.*) corps of engineers.

μηχανισμός *s.m.* mechanism.

μηχανοδηγός *s.m.* engine-driver.

μηχανοκίνητος *a.* worked by machinery; (*mil.*) motorized.

μηχανοποιῶ *v.t.* mechanize.

μηχανορραφῶ *v.i.* hatch plots, intrigue.

μία, μιά *num.* & *article f.* one; a, an; ~ καί *or* ~ πού as, since, seeing that; ~ καὶ καλή *or* ~ γιὰ πάντα once for all; ~ ἐδῶ ~ ἐκεῖ now here now there; διὰ μιᾶς *or* μὲ μιᾶς (all) at once, suddenly;

έφαγε ~ he suffered a blow *or* shock, etc.

μιαίνω *v.t.* pollute, defile.

μιαρός *a.* foul, vile.

μίασμα *s.n.* miasma; (*fig.*) noxious influence.

μιγάς *s.m.* half-caste; mongrel; hybrid.

μίγμα *s.n.* mixture, blend, alloy, amalgam.

μίζα *s.f* 1. stake (*money*); rake-off. 2. self-starter.

μιζέρια *s.f.* state of poverty; miserliness.

μικραίνω *v.t. & i.* diminish, make *or* become smaller *or* shorter.

μικράτα *s.n.pl.* childhood.

μικρο- *denotes* small.

μικροαστός *s.m.* petit bourgeois.

μικρόβιον *s.n.* microbe.

μικρογραφία *s.f.* miniature.

μικροδουλειά *s.f.* trifle, small dealing.

μικρόκοσμος *s.m.* 1. microcosm. 2. children.

μικρολόγος *a.* cavilling.

μικροπρά(γ)ματα *s.n.pl.* trifles.

μικροπρεπής *a.* mean, petty.

μικρ|ός *a.* small, little; short (*duration*); young; younger; a young servant *or* employee; mean, petty; ~οῦ δεῖν nearly.

μικροσκόπι|ον *s.n.* microscope. ~κός *a.* microscopic, minute.

μικρόφωνον *s.n.* microphone.

μικρόψυχος *a.* pusillanimous.

μικρύνω *v.t. & i. see* **μικραίνω**.

μικτ|ός *a.* mixed; ~ὸν βάρος gross weight.

μιλιά *s.f.* (manner of) speech; δὲν ἔβγαλε ~ he did not utter a word; ~ ! not a word!

μίλι(ον) *s.n.* mile.

μιλ|ῶ *v.t. & i.* speak; δὲν ~ιοῦνται they are not on speaking terms; ~ημένος one whose favour has been solicited; ~ῶ μὲ τὴν τύχη μου be smiled on by fortune.

μίμησις *s.f.* imitation.

μιμητ|ής *s.m.* imitator. ~ικός *a.* imitative.

μιμόζα *s.f.* mimosa.

μίμος *s.m.* mimic.

μιμοῦμαι *v.t.* imitate, copy.

μιναρές *s.m.* minaret.

μινιατούρα *s.f.* miniature.

μίνιο *s.n.* red lead.

μινωικός *a.* Minoan.

μίξις *s.f.* mixing.

μίς *s.f.* (fam.) beauty queen; [E. *Miss*]. πάω γιά ~ compete for such title.

μισαλλόδοξος *a.* intolerant (*esp. in religion*).

μισάνθρωπος *a.* misanthropic.

μισερός *a.* deficient (*physically or mentally*); skimpy.

μισεύω *v.i.* leave one's country.

μισητός *a.* hated, hateful.

μίσθαρνος *a.* mercenary, venal.

μίσθιος *a.* hired, rented.

μισθοδοτῶ *v.t.* pay wages to.

μισθολόγιον *s.n.* payroll; rate of pay.

μισθ|ός *s.m.* wages, salary. ~οφόρος *s.m.* mercenary.

μισθ|ῶ, ~ώνω *v.t.* hire, rent (*from owner*).

μισθωτής *s.m.* hirer, tenant.

μισθωτός *a.* employed; a wage-earner.

μισ|ό *s.n.* half; τὰ ~ά (*pl.*) half, the middle; στὰ ~ά half-way, in the middle.

μισο- *denotes* half.

μισογύνης *s.m.* misogynist.

μῖσος *s.n.* hate, hatred.

μισός *a.* half; incompleted; deficient in health; βλάκας καὶ ~ a perfect fool. *See* **μισό**.

μισοτιμής *adv.* at half price.

μισότριβη *s.f.* middle-aged woman; (*fig.*) one who has knocked around.

μισοφόρι *see* **μεσοφόρι**.

μισσεύω *see* **μισεύω**.

μισύ *a.* half.

μίσχος *s.m.* stalk; (*fig.*) tall, slim person.

μισῶ *v.t.* hate.

μίτος *s.m.* thread, yarn; clew (*of Ariadne*).

μίτρα *s.f.* mitre; cowl (*of chimney*).

μνεία *s.f.* mention; reminding.

μνήμα *s.n.* grave, tomb.

μνημεῖον *s.n.* monument.

μνήμη *s.f.* memory; remembrance.

μνημονεύω *v.t.* mention; commemorate; learn by heart.

μνημονικόν *s.n.* memory.

μνημόσυνον *s.n.* requiem; commemorative meeting.

μνήμων *a.* mindful.

μνησίκακ|ος *a.* rancorous. ~ῶ *v.i.* be resentful, bear a grudge.

μνηστ|εία *s.f.* betrothal. ~εύω *v.t.* betrothe. ~ εύομαι *v.i.* become engaged.

μνηστή *s.f.* fiancée.

μνηστήρ *s.m.* fiancé; (*fig.*) suitor, pretender.

μόδ|α *s.f.* fashion; τῆs ~as in fashion. ~ίστρα *s.f.* dressmaker.

μοιάζ|ω *v.t. & i.* resemble (*with acc. or gen.*); look alike; δὲν τοῦ ~ει νά it ill becomes him to.

μοιασίδι *s.n.* resemblance.

μοῖρα *s.f.* 1. fate, lot. 2. squadron. 3. (*geom.*) degree.

μοιράζ|ω *v.t.* share out, distribute; deliver (*of roundsman*); deal (*cards*); ~ω τὴ διαφορά split the difference. ~ομαι *v.t.* share (*as recipient*).

μοιραῖ|ος *a.* preordained; inevitable; fatal; ~α γυναῖκα femme fatale. ~ως *adv.* inevitably.

μοίραρχος *s.m.* captain of gendarmerie.

μοιρασιά *s.f.* distribution, sharing.

μοιρολατρεία *s.f.* fatalism.

μοιρολόγ|ι *s.n.* dirge. ~ῶ *v.i. & t.* lament (*the dead*).

μοιχεία *s.f.* adultery.

μολαταῦτα *adv.* nevertheless.

μόλις 1. *adv.* just now, only just; hardly, scarcely. 2. *conj.* as soon as.

μολονότι *adv.* although.

μολοσσός *s.m.* large watch-dog.

μόλυβδος *s.m.* lead (*metal*).

μολύβ|ι *s.n.* lead; pencil. ~ιά *s.f.* pencil-stroke.

μόλυνσις *s.f.* infection, contamination.

μολύνω *v.t.* infect, contaminate; defile.

μόλυσμα *s.n.* infectious germ *or* ailment.

μομφή *s.f.* blame.

μοναδικός *a.* unique, sole.

μονάζω *v.i.* live in solitude; be a monk.

μονάκριβος *a.* cherished and only.

μοναξιά *s.f.* solitude; loneliness; lonely place.

μονάρχ|ης *s.m.* monarch. ~ία *s.f.* monarchy. ~ικός *a.* monarchical; a monarchist.

μονάς *s.f.* unit; monad.

μοναστήρι *s.n.* monastery.

μον|άχα, ~αχά *adv.* only.

μοναχικ|ός *a.* 1. monastic. 2. standing alone, isolated. 3. to oneself (*unshared*); δωμάτιο ~ό a room of one's own.

μοναχοπαίδι *s.n.* only child.

μον|άχος, ~αχός *a.* only; alone; ~αχός του by himself *or* on his own; χρυσάφι ~αχό real gold.

μοναχός *s.m.* monk.

μονέδα *s.f.* money; (*fig.*) κόβω ~ coin money.

μονή *s.f.* monastery.

μονήρης *a.* solitary, isolated.

μόνιμ|ος *a.* permanent. ~οποιῶ *v.t.* make permanent.

μονο- *denotes* single.

μονογενής *a.* only (*child*); one and only.

μονόγραμμα *s.n.* monogram.

μονογραφή *s.f.* initials, paraph.

μονογραφία *s.f.* monograph.

μονόδρομος *s.m.* one-way street.

μονόζυγον *s.n.* horizontal bar.

μονοιάζω *v.i. & t.* agree, get on well together; make up a quarrel; reconcile.

μονοκατοικία *s.f.* private house.

μονοκόμματος *a.* in one piece; rigid; forthright.

μονομανία *s.f.* obsession.

μονομαχία *s.f.* duel.

μονομερής *a.* one-sided.

μονομιᾶς *adv.* all at once; immediately.

μόνο(ν) *adv.* only; ~ πού except that; ~ νά provided that; ~ νὰ τὸ σκεφθῶ at the mere thought of it.

μονόξυλον *s.n.* dug-out canoe.

μονοπάτι *s.n.* footpath.

μονόπατος *a.* one-storied.

μονόπλευρος *a.* one-sided.

μονοπώλ|ιον *s.n.* monopoly. ~ῶ *v.t.* enjoy monopoly of; monopolize.

μόν|ος *a.* only; alone; ~ος μου by myself, of my own accord; κατὰ ~ας (*live*) on one's own, (*talk*) to oneself.

μονός *a.* simple (*not compound*); single (*not double*); odd (*not even*).

μονότονος *a.* monotonous.

μονόφθαλμος *a.* one-eyed.

μονόχνωτος *a.* unsociable.

μοντέλο *s.n.* model.

μοντέρνος *a.* modern.

μονύελος *s.m.* monocle.

μον|ώνω *v.t.* isolate; insulate. ~ωσις *s.f.* insulation. ~ωτικός *a.* insulating.

μόριον *s.n.* particle; molecule.

μόρτης *s.m.* hooligan, tough.

μορφ|άζω *v.i.* make faces, grimace. ~ασμός *s.m.* grimace.

μορφή *s.f.* form; face; appearance; aspect; phase.

μορφολογία *s.f.* morphology.

μορφώνω *v.t.* form; train, educate.

μόρφ|ωσις *s.f.* education, culture. ~τικός *a.* educative, educational, cultural.

μόστρα *s.f.* (*fam.*) shop-window.

μοσχάρι *s.n.* calf; veal.

μοσχάτο *s.n.* muscatel grape *or* wine.

μοσχοβολῶ *v.i.* smell sweetly.

μοσχοκάρυδο *s.n.* nutmeg.

μοσχοκάρφι *s.n.* clove.

μοσχολίβανο *s.n.* frankincense.

μόσχος *s.m.* 1. calf; veal. 2. musk.

μοτοσυκλέτα *s.f.* motor-bicycle.

μοῦ, μου *pron.* me; my.

μουγγός *a.* dumb.

μουγγρίζω *v.i.* bellow, roar, moo, moan.

μουδιάζω *v.t. & i.* numb; be numb.

μουλάρι *s.n.* mule.

μοῦλος *s.m.* bastard.

μουλώ(χ)νω *v.i.* conceal one's thoughts, keep silent; lie low.

μούμια *s.f.* mummy.

μουνουχίζω *v.t.* castrate.

μούντζ|α *s.f.* opprobrious gesture with open palm. ~ώνω *v.t.* make μούντζα at; renounce in disgust.

μουντζούρα *s.f.* smudge; moral stain.

μουντός *a.* dull, dark *(not bright)*.

μούργα *s.f.* sediment, lees *(of wine, oil)*.

μοῦργος *s.m.* fierce watch-dog; *(fig.)* fierce *or* ugly fellow.

μούρη *s.f.* *(fam.)* face, mug.

μούρλια *s.f.* madness; *(fam.)* εἶναι ~ it's a dream! *(eulogistic)*.

μουρλός *a.* mad, crazy; over-excited.

μουρμουρ|ίζω *v.i. & t.* murmur; grumble. ~ητό *s.n.* murmuring; grumbling.

μουρντάρης *a.* filthy; *(fig.)* a dirty dog.

μοῦρο *s.n.* mulberry.

μοῦσα *s.f.* muse.

μουσακᾶς *s.m.* dish of minced meat, vegetable, *etc.*

μουσαμᾶς *s.m.* oilcloth, linoleum; rain-coat.

μουσαφίρης *s.m.* visitor, guest.

μουσεῖον *s.n.* museum.

μούσι *s.n.* small pointed beard.

μουσικ|ή *s.f.* music; band. ~ός *a.* musical; a musician.

μούσκεμα *s.n.* soaking; γίνομαι ~ get soaking wet; *(fam.)* τὰ κάνω ~ make a mess of it.

μουσκεύω *v.t. & i.* soak; get soaked; τὰ ~ make a mess of it.

μουσκίδι *s.n.* γίνομαι ~ get soaking wet.

μούσμουλο *s.n.* loquat.

μουσουργός *s.m.f.* composer.

μουστάκι *s.n.* moustache.

μουσταλευριά *s.f.* jelly made with must.

μουστάρδα *s.f.* mustard.

μουστερῆς *s.m.* regular customer, buyer.

μοῦστος *s.m.* must, new wine.

μούτρ|ο *s.n.*, ~α *(pl.)* face; κάνω ~α adopt an injured air; ἔχω ~α νὰ have the cheek to; πέφτω μὲ τὰ ~ apply oneself avidly; *(pej.)* εἶναι ~ο he's a crook.

μουτρωμένος *a.* sulky.

μοῦτσος *s.m.* ship's boy.

μούχλ|α *s.f.* mould; *(mental)* stagnation. ~ιάζω *v.i. & t.* moulder, go mouldy; make mouldy.

μοχθηρός *a.* malicious.

μόχθος *s.m.* toil.

μοχλός *s.m.* lever, bar; *(fig.)* promoter, ringleader.

μπ- *see also* π-.

μπᾶ *int.* expression of surprise, rejection, negation, or assent.

μπαγιατ|εύω *v.i.* get stale. ~ικος *a.* stale.

μπάγκα *s.f.* bank.

μπαγκέτα *s.f.* conductor's baton; drum-stick; clock *(of stocking)*.

μπάγκος *s.m.* bench; counter.

μπάζα *s.f.* trick *(at cards)*; profit from sharp practice.

μπάζ(ι)α *s.n.pl.* rubble.

μπάζω *v.t. & i.* admit, usher in; *(v.i.)* shrink *(of clothes)*.

μπαϊλντίζω *v.i.* swoon.

μπαίν|ω *v.i.* enter, go in; shrink *(of cloth)*; ~ω μέσα incur loss *(in business, cards)*; ~ω σὲ μιὰ σειρά settle down; ~ω σὲ ἰδέα become suspicious; μοῦ ~ει ἡ ἰδέα it occurs to me; μπῆκα στὸ νόημα I grasped the idea.

μπαϊράκι *s.n.* banner; *(fig.)* σηκώνω ~ revolt.

μπακάλ|ης *s.m.* grocer. ~ικο *s.n.* grocer's shop.

μπακαλιάρος *s.m.* cod *(esp. dried)*.

μπακίρι *s.n.* copper.

μπακλαβᾶς *s.m.* cake of almonds and honey.

μπαλαντέρ *s.m.* joker *(cards)*. [F. *baladeur*]

μπαλάντζα *s.f.* balance *(for weighing)*.

μπαλκόνι *s.n.* balcony.

μπάλλα *s.f.* ball; bullet; bale.

μπαλλέτο *s.n.* ballet.

μπαλλόνι *s.n.* balloon.

μπαλ(ν)τᾶς *s.m.* axe.

μπάλωμα *s.n.* patching, mending; patch.

μπαλών|ω *v.t.* patch, mend; *(fig.)* τὰ ~ω make excuses. ~ομαι *v.i.* find what one wants.

μπάμιες s.f.pl. okra, lady's fingers (vegetable).

μπαμπάκ|ι s.n. cotton; cotton wool. ~ερός a. cotton.

μπαμπάς s.m. papa.

μπαμπέσης a. treacherous.

μπαμπόγρια s.f. crone.

μπαμπούλας s.m. bogyman.

μπάμπουρας s.m. hornet.

μπανάνα s.f. banana.

μπανέλα s.f. whalebone (stiffener).

μπανιέρα s.f. bath (tub); bathing-hut.

μπανιερό s.n. bathing-dress.

μπανίζω v.t. eye, ogle. ~ιστήρι s.n. (fam.) watching (esp. through spy-hole).

μπάνιο s.n. bath, bathe; bath (tub); bathroom.

μπάντα s.f. 1. side; corner (quiet spot); βάζω στή ~ put aside (money); κάνε στή ~ stand aside. 2. band (music, robbers).

μπαντιέρα s.f. banner.

μπαξές s.m. garden.

μπαούλο s.n. trunk, chest.

μπαρκάρω v.t. & i. embark.

μπάρμπας s.m.(fam.) uncle; old man.

μπαρμπέρης s.m. barber.

μπαρμπούνι s.n. red mullet.

μπαρούτι s.n. gunpowder; (fam.) έγινε ~ he got furiously angry; βρωμάει ~ there is danger in the air.

μπάς καί adv. see μήπως.

μπασμένος a. knowledgeable; in the know; stunted.

μπάσταρδος s.m. bastard.

μπαστούνι s.n. stick; club (cards); τά βρῆκε ~α he met with difficulties.

μπατάλικος a. large, unwieldy (person).

μπατανία s.f. woollen blanket.

μπαταρία s.f. battery (electric).

μπαταριά s.f. salvo, volley.

μπατάρω v.t. & i. capsize; be quits.

μπατζάκι s.n. trouser-leg; (fam.) ~α (pl.) legs, pins.

μπατζανάκης s.m. brother-in-law (relationship between husbands of sisters).

μπάτης s.m. breeze from the sea.

μπάτσο|α s.f., ~ος s.m. slap; blow. ~ίζω v.t. slap.

μπαχαρικό s.n. spice.

μπέζ a. beige. [F.]

μπέ|ης s.m. bey; (fig.) περνῶ ~ικα live in luxury.

μπεκάτσα s.f. woodcock.

μπεκιάρης s.m. bachelor.

μπεκρής s.m. drunkard.

μπελ|άς s.m. nuisance, trouble; βρῆκα τό ~ᾶ μου I got involved (in trouble). ~αλίδικος a. troublesome.

μπελ(ν)τές s.m. (preserved) tomato purée; jelly (of fruit).

μπέμπης s.m. (fam.) baby.

μπενζίνα s.f. petrol; motorboat.

μπέρδεμα s.n. confusion, muddle.

μπερδεύ|ω v.t. entangle; embroil, involve; confuse; muddle, get wrong; τά ~ω be confused (in one's words). ~ομαι v.i. get entangled, involved, or confused.

μπερντές s.m. curtain.

μπέσα s.f. trustworthiness.

μπετόν s.n. concrete. [F. béton]

μπετούγια s.f. latch.

μπή|γω, ~ζω v.t. drive or push in, pin on; ~ζω τά γέλια burst out laughing.

μπηχτή s.f. (fig.) shrewd thrust.

μπιζέλι s.n. pea.

μπιμπελό s.n. bibelot. [F.]

μπίρα s.f. beer.

μπιρμπάντης s.m. rascal.

μπισκότο s.n. biscuit.

μπίτ(ι) adv. (fam.) completely; not at all.

μπιφτέκι s.n. steak.

μπλάστρι s.n. plaster (curative).

μπλέ, μπλού a. blue. [F. bleu]

μπλέκω v.t. & i. entangle; involve; get entangled or involved.

μπλέξιμο s.n. entanglement; amour.

μπλούζα s.f. blouse.

μπλόφα s.f. bluff.

μπογιά s.f. paint, dye, colouring-matter; boot-polish.

μπογιαντίζω v.t. paint, colour, dye.

μπόγιας s.m. executioner; dog-catcher.

μπογιατζῆς s.m. painter, decorator.

μπόγος s.m. large, soft bundle (esp. clothes).

μποϊ s.n stature; ρίχνω ~ grow taller.

μπόλι s.n. graft; vaccine. ~άζω v.t. graft; inoculate.

μπόλικος a. abundant, plenty of; loose-fitting.

μπόμπα s.f. bomb; cylinder (of gas).

μπομπότα s.f. maize flour or bread.

μποναμάς s.m. new year's gift.

μποξάς s.m. bundle; shawl.

μπόρ s.n. brim (of hat). [F. bord]

μπόρα s.f. squall of rain.

μπορετός a. possible.

μπορ|ῶ v.i. be able, can; ~εῖ it may be, perhaps; δὲν ~ῶ I cannot or I am not well.

μπόσικος a. loose, slack; (fig.) shallow, unreliable; yielding.

μποστάνι s.n. melon-bed; vegetable garden.

μποτίλι|α s.f. bottle. ~άρω v.t. bottle; (fig.) bottle up, block.

μπόττα s.f. boot.

μπουγάδα s.f. (doing of) washing.

μπουγάζι s.n. narrow passage.

μπουγάτσα s.f. confection of flaky pastry.

μπούγιο s.n. κάνω ~ (fig.) make an (unmerited) impression.

μπούζι s.n. 1. (cold as) ice; (fig.) feeble (of jokes). 2. herbage resembling grass.

μπουζί s.n. sparking-plug. [F. bougie]

μπουζούκι s.n. sort of mandoline.

μπούκα s.f. (fig.) mouth; mouthful.

μπουκάλα s.f. large bottle; (fam.) ἔμεινε ~ he was left high and dry.

μπουκάλι s.n. bottle.

μπουκάρω v.i. swarm or pour in; enter (channel, etc.).

μπουκιά s.f. mouthful; (fam.) ~ καὶ συχώριο bit of all-right.

μπούκλα s.f. curl.

μποϋκοτάρω v.t. boycott.

μπουκώνω v.t. & i. stuff with food; be gorged; (fig.) grease the palm of.

μπουλούκι s.n. mass, crowd.

μπουλρῦκος s.m. plump dog; (fam.) plump person.

μπουμπούκι s.n. bud.

μπουμπουνητό s.n. rumble of thunder.

μπουνάτσα s.f. calm, fine weather at sea.

μπούνια s.n.pl. (naut.) scuppers; (fig.) ὡς τὰ ~ over head and ears.

μπουνιά s.f. (blow of) fist.

μπουνταλᾶς s.m. clumsy blockhead.

μπουντρούμι s.n. dungeon.

μπούρδα s.f. (fam.) hot air, nonsense.

μπουρέκι s.n. sort of patty or cream cake.

μπουρί s.n. chimney (of stove).

μπουρ|ί, ~ίνι s.n. squall of wind; (fig.) fit of temper.

μπουρμπουλήθρα s.f. bubble.

μπουρνέλα s.f. mirabelle plum.

μπούσουλ|ας s.m. compass; (fig.) χάνω τὸν ~α be all at sea.

μπουσουλῶ v.i. go on all fours.

μποῦστος s.m. bust; bodice.

μπούτι s.n. thigh.

μπουφές s.m. sideboard; buffet.

μποῦφος s.m. horned owl; dolt (fig.).

μπουχτίζω v.i. & t. become satiated; (fig.) get fed up; make fed up.

μπόχα s.f. stink.

μπράβο int. bravo! good!

μπράβος s.m. bravo.

μπράτσο s.n. arm.

μπρέ int. see βρέ.

μπριάμι s.n. sort of ratatouille.

μπριγιαντίνη s.f. brilliantine.

μπριζόλα s.f. chop, cutlet.

μπρίκ 1. s.n. (preserved) salmon-roe. 2. a. tile-red.

μπρίκι s.n. 1. pot for boiling coffee. 2. (naut.) brig.

μπρός, μπροστά adv. forward(s), ahead, in front (see ἐμπρός).

μπροστινός a. (in) front.

μπρούμυτα adv. face downwards.

μπροῦτζ|ος s.m. bronze. ~ινος a. bronze.

μπρούσκ|ος a. ~ο κρασί dry wine.

μπύρα s.f. beer.

μῦ s.n. the letter Μ.

μυαλ|ό s.n. marrow (of bone); brain(s); mind, sense; πῆραν τὰ ~ά του ἀέρα success has gone to his head.

μυαλωμένος a. wise, prudent.

μῦγα s.f. fly.

μυγιάγγιχτος a. touchy.

μυγι|άζομαι v.i. be touchy, take umbrage.

μύδι s.n. mussel.

μυδραλλιοβόλον s.n. (mil.) machine-gun.

μύδρος s.m. (mil.) shell.

μυελός s.m. marrow (of bone); brain.

μυζήθρα s.f. sort of soft white cheese.

μυζῶ v.t. suck.

μυθικός a. mythical; legendary, fabulous.

μυθιστόρημα s.n. fiction; novel.

μυθιστοριογράφος s.m. novelist.

μυθολογία s.f. mythology.

μῦθος s.m. fable; myth; fairy story.

μυθώδης a. untrue; fabulous.

μυῖα μυῖγα s.f. see μῦγα.

μυϊκός a. muscular.

μυκηθμός s.m. bellowing, mooing.

μύκης s.m. fungus.

μυκτηρίζω v.t. mock.

μυκῶμαι v.i. bellow, roar, moo.

μύλ|ος s.m. mill. ~όπετρα s.f. millstone.

μυλωθρός *s.m.* miller.

μυλωνᾶς *s.m.* miller.

μύξα *s.f.* (*fam.*) snot.

μυρ|ίζω *v.t. & i.* smell (of); δὲν ~ισα τὰ δάχτυλά μου I could not foresee. ~ίζομαι *v.t.* smell; (*fig.*) get wind of, suspect.

μύριοι *a.* ten thousand; (*fig.*) countless.

μυρμήγκι *s.n.* ant. ~άζω *v.i.* have pins and needles.

μύρμηξ *s.m.* ant.

μυροβόλος *a.* fragrant.

μύρον *s.n.* essential oil; ἅγιον ~ chrism.

μυροπωλεῖον *s.n.* perfumery (*shop*).

μυρτιά *s.f.* myrtle.

μυρτόν *s.n.* myrtle-bough.

μυρωδᾶτος *a.* having a sweet smell.

μυρωδιά *s.f.* smell; perfume; flavour; tit-bit from thing being cooked; παίρνω ~ get wind of, suspect.

μυρωδικό *s.n.* (*liquid*) perfume; spice.

μυρώνω *v.t.* anoint (*esp. ritually*).

μῦς *s.m.* 1. muscle. 2. mouse.

μυσαρός *a.* heinous.

μυσταγωγία *s.f.* initiation.

μύσταξ *s.m.* moustache.

μυστήρι|ον *s.n.* mystery; act of charity. ~ος *a.* mysterious. ~ώδης *a.* mysterious.

μύστης *s.m.* initiate; (*fig.*) one deeply versed.

μυστικιστής *s.m.* mystic.

μυστικόν *s.n.* secret.

μυστικός *a.* secret; secretive; discreet; a secret policeman; ~ δεῖπνος Last Supper.

μυστικοσύμβουλος *s.m.* privy councillor; (*fig.*) confidant.

μυστικότης *s.f.* secrecy.

μυστρί *s.n.* trowel.

μυταρᾶς *s.m.* big-nosed man.

μυτερός *a.* pointed, sharp.

μύτη *s.f.* nose; tip, point.

μύχι|ος *a.* inmost; τὰ ~α inmost part, depths.

μυχός *s.m.* inmost part (*esp. of bay, etc.*).

μυῶ *v.t.* initiate.

μυ|ών *s.m.* muscle. ~ώδης *a.* muscular.

μύωψ *a.* myopic.

μωαμεθανός *s.m.* a Mohammedan.

μώβ *a.* mauve. [F. *mauve*]

μῶλος *s.m.* mole, breakwater.

μώλ|ωψ *s.m.* bruise. ~ωπίζω *v.t.* bruise.

μωραίνω *v.t.* make dull or stupid.

μωρ|έ, ~ή *int.* unceremonious mode of address.

μωρία *s.f.* foolishness.

μωρό *s.n.* baby; ingenuous person.

μωρός *a.* foolish, silly.

μωσαϊκόν *s.n.* mosaic.

N

νά 1. *particle of subordination* to, that, in order to, let, may, if, *etc.* 2. *prep.* there! there is, there are (*with nom. or acc.*); νά τος or τον there he is; νά ἡ Μαρία here's Mary; νάμαστε here we are. 3. *int. of imprecation*.

νάζι *s.n.*, ~α (*pl.*) coquettish air; κάνω ~α affect reluctance.

ναί *adv.* yes; ~ καὶ καλά with obstinate insistence.

ναϊάς *s.f.* naiad.

νάϊλον *s.n.* nylon. [E. *nylon*]

νᾶμα *s.n.* spring (*water*).

νάνι *s.n.* (*fam.*) sleep (*childish term*).

νάνος *s.m.* dwarf.

νανουρ|ίζω *v.t.* rock or lull to sleep. ~ισμα *s.n.* rocking, lulling; lullaby.

ναός *s.m.* temple, church.

ναργιλές *s.m.* hookah.

νάρθηξ *s.m.* 1. (*eccl.*) narthex. 2. (*med.*) splint.

ναρκαλιευτικόν *s.n.* (*naut.*) minesweeper.

νάρκη *s.f.* numbness, torpor; electric ray (*fish*); mine (*weapon*).

νάρκισσος *s.m.* narcissus.

ναρκοθέτις *s.f.* (*naut.*) mine-layer.

ναρκ|ώνω *v.t.* make numb, torpid or dull. ~ωσις *s.f.* torpor; (*med.*) narcosis.

ναρκωτικ|ός *a.* narcotic; ~ά (*s.n.pl.*) drugs.

νάτριον *s.n.* sodium.

ναυάγιον *s.n.* shipwreck; (*fig.*) wreck.

ναυαγ|ός *s.m.* shipwrecked sailor, castaway. ~ῶ *v.i.* be shipwrecked.

ναύαρχ|ος *s.m.* admiral. ~εῖον *s.n.* admiralty. ~ίς *s.f.* flag-ship.

ναύκληρος *s.m.* boatswain.

ναῦλα *s.n.pl.* fare (*for any journey*).

ναῦλος *s.m.* freight, passage-money (*esp. by ship*).

ναυλώνω *v.t.* freight, charter (*vessel*).

ναυμαχία *s.f.* sea-battle.

ναυπηγ|είον *s.n.* shipyard. ~ός *s.m.* shipbuilder.

ναῦς *s.f.* ship.

ναυσιπλοΐα *s.f.* shipping; navigation.

ναύσταθμος *s.m.* naval dockyard.

ναύτης *s.m.* sailor, seaman.

ναυτία(σις) *s.f.* seasickness; nausea.

ναυτική *s.f.* seamanship.

ναυτικόν *s.n.* navy.

ναυτικ|ός *a.* maritime, seafaring; nautical, naval, of shipping; a seafaring man (*sailor, officer, fisherman*).

ναυτιλία *s.f.* shipping; navigation; merchant marine. ~κός *a.* marine.

ναυτιῶ *v.i.* be seasick; feel nausea.

ναυτοδικεῖον *s.n.* (*law*) court of Admiralty.

ναυτολογῶ *v.t.* enlist (*crew*).

ναυτόπαις *s.m.* ship-boy.

νέα 1. *s.f.* girl. 2. *s.n.pl.* news.

νεάζω *v.i.* appear young; remain young in outlook.

νεαν|ίας *s.m.* young man. ~ικός *a.* youthful.

νεᾶνις *s.f.* girl.

νεαρός *a.* young.

νέγρος *s.m.* negro.

νειᾶτα *s.n.pl.* see νιᾶτα.

νέκρα *s.f.* complete absence of noise *or* activity; deadness.

νεκρανάστασις *s.f.* resurrection.

νεκρικός *a.* deathly; of death, funeral.

νεκροθάπτης *s.m.* grave-digger.

νεκροκεφαλή *s.f.* skull.

νεκρολογία *s.f.* obituary.

νεκρόπομπός *s.m.* undertaker's mute.

νεκρ|ός *a.* dead; a dead person; ~ὰ φύσις still life.

νεκροταφεῖον *s.n.* cemetery.

νεκροτομεῖον *s.n.* mortuary.

νεκροφάνεια *s.f.* appearance of death.

νεκροφόρα *s.f.* hearse.

νεκροψία *s.f.* (*med.*) post-mortem.

νεκρώνω *v.t.* & *i.* deaden; become deadened; go deathly pale (*from fear*).

νεκρώσιμος *a.* funeral.

νέκταρ *s.n.* nectar.

νέμεσις *s.f.* nemesis.

νέμομαι *v.t.* enjoy use *or* fruits of, hold in usufruct.

νενέ *s.f.* (*fam.*) grandmamma.

νενομισμένος *a.* prescribed, necessary.

νεο- *denotes* new, young.

νεογέννητος *a.* newly born.

νεογνόν *s.n.* newly born baby *or* animal.

νεόδμητος *a.* newly built.

νεοελλαδίτης *s.m.* person from 'new' provinces of Greece (*esp. Macedonia & Thrace*).

νεοελληνικ|ός *a.* of modern Greece. ~ή *s.f.*, ~ά *s.n.pl.* modern Greek language.

νεόκτιστος *a.* newly built.

νεολαία *s.f.* youth (*young people*).

νεόνυμφος *a.* newly married.

νεόπλουτος *a.* newly rich.

νέ|ος *a.* new, modern; young; a young man. ~ο *s.n.* piece of news.

νεοσσός *s.m.* nestling.

νεοσύλλεκτος *s.m.* recruit.

νεοσύστατος *a.* newly established.

νεότης *s.f.* youth.

νεόφυτος *a.* newly planted; a neophyte.

νεοφώτιστος *a.* newly baptized; (*fig.*) a recent convert (*to ideology*).

νεράιδα *s.f.* sort of fairy; (*fig.*) beautiful woman.

νεράντζι *s.n.* bitter orange.

νερ|ό *s.n.* water; rain; μετάξι μὲ ~ά watered silk; χάνω τὰ ~ά μου feel lost; αὐτὸ σηκώνει ~ό it is not quite true; ξέρω τὸ μάθημα ~ό know the lesson by heart.

νερόβραστος *a.* boiled in water; (*fig.*) insipid, ineffectual, limp.

νεροκράτης *s.m.* turncock; water-key.

νερομάννα *s.f.* spring (*of water*).

νερομπογιά *s.f.* water-colour.

νερομπούλι *s.n.* watery pap.

νερόμυλος *s.m.* water-mill.

νεροποντή *s.f.* violent rainstorm.

νερουλ|ός *a.* watery, thin. ~ιάζω *v.i.* become watery *or* flabby.

νεροχύτης *s.m.* sink.

νερώνω *v.t.* water (*adulterate*).

νέτα σκέτα *adv.* plainly, frankly.

νέτος *a.* net; (*fam.*) done, finished (*of work*).

νεῦμα *s.n.* nod, sign.

νευραλγία *s.f.* neuralgia.

νευραλγικ|ός *a.* (*fig.*) ~ὸν σημεῖον vital *or* vulnerable spot.

νευριάζω *v.t.* & *i.* make *or* become exasperated.

νευρικός *a.* of the nerves, nervous; highly strung; irritable.

νεῦρ|ον *s.n.* nerve, sinew; (*fig.*) nervous energy; ἔχω ~α be in irritable mood.

νευροπάθεια *s.f.* nervous disease.

νευρόσπαστον *s.n.* marionette, puppet.

νευρώδης *a.* sinewy; (*fig.*) vigorous (*of speech*).

νευρώνω *v.i. see* **νευριάζω**.

νευρωτικός *a.* neurotic.

νεύω *v.i.* nod, make a sign.

νεφέλ|η *s.f.* cloud. **~ώδης** *a.* cloudy; (*fig.*) vague, obscure. **~ωμα** *s.n.* nebula.

νεφελοκοκκυγία *s.f.* cloud-cuckoo-land.

νέφος *s.n.* cloud.

νεφρ|ός *s.m.*, **~ό** *s.n.* kidney. **~ικός** *a.* renal.

νέφτι *s.n.* turpentine.

νεωκόρος *s.m.* sacristan.

νεώριον *s.n.* dockyard.

νεωστί *adv.* lately.

νεωτερισμ|ός *s.m.* novelty, innovation, new trend; **~οί** (*pl.*) fancy goods.

νεώτερ|ος *a.* newer; younger. **~α** *s.n. pl.* news.

νήμα *s.n.* (cotton) thread.

νηνεμία *s.f.* calm weather.

νηοπομπή *s.f.* (*naut.*) convoy.

νηοψία *s.f.* searching of ships (*for contraband of war*).

νηπιαγωγείον *s.n.* kindergarten.

νήπι|ον *s.n.* infant. **~όθεν** *adv.* from infancy.

νηπιώδης *a.* infantile; (*fig.*) undeveloped, in its infancy.

νηρηίς *s.f.* nereid.

νησί *s.n.* island.

νησιώτ|ης *s.m.* islander. **~ικος** *a.* islander's, of the islands.

νήσος *s.f.* island.

νήσσα *s.f.* duck.

νηστεία *s.f.* fasting; lack of food; τὸν ἄφησαν ~ he was kept in (*at school*).

νηστεύω *v.i.* fast.

νηστήσιμος *a.* lenten (*food*).

νηστικός *a.* not having eaten.

νηφάλιος *a.* sober; calm, collected.

νιανιά *s.f.* (*fam.*) pap.

νιαουρίζω *v.i.* mew, miaow.

νιᾶτα *s.n.pl.* youth.

νίβω *v.t.* wash (*face, hands*).

νίκη *s.f.* victory.

νικητήρια *s.n.pl.* victory celebration.

νικητής *s.m.* victor.

νικηφόρος *a.* victorious.

νικῶ *v.t. & i.* conquer, defeat, beat; overcome; (*v.i.*) be victorious, win.

νίλα *s.f.* (*fam.*) nasty trick, practical joke.

νιο- *see* **νεο-**.

νιπτήρ *s.m.* wash basin.

νίπτω *v.t. see* **νίβω**.

νισάφι *s.n.* mercy, respite.

νίτρον *s.n.* nitre, saltpetre.

νιφάς *s.f.* snowflake.

Νοέμβρ|ιος, **~ης** *s.m.* November.

νοερός *a.* mental.

νόημα *s.n.* thought (*faculty*); sense, meaning, point; nod, sign.

νοήμ|ων *a.* intelligent. **~οσύνη** *s.f.* intelligence.

νόησις *s.f.* intellect.

νοητός *a.* intelligible; imaginary, notional.

νοθ|εία, **~ευσις** *s.f.* adulteration; falsification.

νοθεύω *v.t.* adulterate, falsify.

νόθος *a.* bastard; forged; irregular (*state of affairs*).

νοιάζει *v.t.* μὲ ~ I mind, I care.

νοιάζομαι *v.t. & i.* look after, care about; be worried.

νοῖκ|ι *s.n.* rent. **~ιάζω** *v.t.* let, rent, hire. **~άρης** *s.m.* tenant.

νοικοκυρά *s.f.* housewife; landlady; (*fig.*) housewifely woman.

νοικοκύρης *s.m.* householder; landlord; master; (*fig.*) provident *or* orderly man.

νοικοκυριό *s.n.* household; house-keeping.

νοιώθω *v.t.* understand; notice; feel.

νομαδικός *a.* nomadic.

νομάρχ|ης *s.m.* nomarch (*prefect of department*). **~εῖον** *s.n.* nomarch's office (*premises*).

νομάς *s.m.* nomad.

νομάτ|οι, **~αῖοι** *s.m.pl.* persons.

νομή *s.f.* pasture, pasturage; (*law*) usufruct.

νομίζω *v.i. & t.* think, consider .

νομικ|ός *a.* legal (*of the law*); a member of the legal profession. **~ά** *s.n.pl.* (*study of*) law. **~ή** *s.f.* (*science of*) law.

νόμιμ|ος *a.* legal, lawful. **~ότης** *s.f.* legality; law-abidingness.

νομιμοποιῶ *v.t.* legalize, legitimize.

νομιμόφρων *a.* law-abiding.

νόμισμα *s.n.* coin, specie; currency, money.

νομισματολογία *s.f.* numismatics.

νομοθεσία *s.f.* legislation.

νομοθέτ|ης *s.m.* law-giver. **~ῶ** *v.i.* make laws.

νομομαθής *s.m.* jurist.

νομομηχανικός *s.m.* county engineer.

νομός *s.m.* department, prefecture.

νόμος *s.m.* law, statute.

νομοσχέδιον *s.n.* parliamentary bill.

νομοταγής *a.* law-abiding.

νονά *s.f.* godmother.

νονός *s.m.* godfather.

νοοτροπία *s.f.* mentality.

νοσηλ|εία *s.f.* nursing (*of patient*). ~εύω *v.t.* treat (*sick person*).

νόσημα *s.n.* malady.

νοσηρός *a.* unhealthy.

νοσοκόμ|ος *s.m.f.* nurse. ~είον *s.n.* hospital.

νόσος *s.f.* malady.

νοσταλγ|ία *s.f.* nostalgia. ~ικός *a.* nostalgic. ~ῶ *v.i. & t.* feel nostalgic (for).

νοστιμ|άδα, ~ιά *s.f.* nice flavour, tastiness; piquancy, attractiveness; funniness.

νοστιμ|εύω, ~ίζω *v.t. & i.* make *or* become tasty *or* attractive. ~εύομαι *v.t.* find to one's taste, have appetite for.

νόστιμος *a.* tasty, nice; piquant, attractive; funny.

νοσῶ *v.i.* be ill.

νότ|α *s.f.* (*diplomatic*) note; (*mus.*) note; ~ες (*pl.*) (*written*) music.

νοτι|ά *s.f.* south; south wind; humidity. ~ᾶς *s.m.* south wind.

νοτίζω *v.t. & i.* make *or* become damp.

νότι|ος *a.* south, southern. ~οανατολικός *a.* south-east(ern). ~οδυτικός *a.* south-west(ern).

νότος *s.m.* south; south wind.

νουθε|σία *s.f.* admonition. ~τῶ *v.t.* admonish.

νούλα *s.f.* nought; (*fig.*) cipher.

νούμερο *s.n.* number; (*music-hall*) turn; (*fam.*) droll character, card.

νουνεχής *a.* prudent, sensible.

νουνός *s.m. see* νονός.

νοῦς *s.m.* intellect, mind; sense, wit; βάζω μὲ τὸ νοῦ μου imagine, fancy; δὲν τὸ βάζει ὁ ~ του he cannot imagine it; λέω μὲ τὸ νοῦ μου say to oneself; δὲν εἶσαι μὲ τὸ νοῦ σου you must be mad; (ἔχε) τὸ νοῦ σου take care, keep an eye open; κοντὰ στὸ νοῦ it goes without saying.

νούφαρο *s.n.* water-lily.

νοῶ *v.t. & i.* understand; think.

ντ- *see also* τ-.

νταβ|ᾶς *s.m.* sort of baking-tin. ~ατζῆς *s.m.* (*fam.*) ponce; fence.

νταγιαντίζω *v.t.* bear, endure.

νταγλαρᾶς *s.m.* (*fam.*) lanky fellow.

νταῆς *s.m.* bully, tough.

ντάλα *adv.* ~ μεσημέρι at high noon.

ντάλια *s.f.* dahlia.

ντάμα *s.f.* lady, partner; queen (*cards*); draughts.

νταμάρι *s.n.* quarry; (*fig.*) καλό ~ of good stock (*physically*).

νταμιτζάνα *s.f.* demijohn.

νταμπλᾶς *s.m.* apoplexy; (*fig.*) great astonishment.

νταντά *s.f.* (*child's*) nurse.

νταντέλλα *s.f.* lace.

νταούλι *s.n.* drum.

ντάρα *s.f.* tare (*weight*).

νταραβέρι *s.n.* (business) dealing; trouble (*quarrels*).

νταρί *s.n.* maize.

ντέ *int.* ἔλα ~ come on!

ντελάλης *s.m.* public crier.

ντελβές *s.m.* coffee grounds.

ντεπόζιτο *s.n.* tank, cistern.

ντερβ- *see* **δερβ-**.

ντέρτι *s.n.* sorrow, yearning (*esp. lover's*).

ντιβάνι *s.n.* divan.

ντίπ *adv. see* μπίτ.

ντολμᾶς *s.m.* stuffed vine *or* cabbage leaf.

ντολμές *s.m.* renegade Jew.

ντομάτα *s.f.* tomato.

ντόμπρος *a.* straight, sincere, frank.

ντόπιος *a.* local, native.

ντορβᾶς *s.m.* peasant's bag; nose-bag.

ντόρος *s.m.* noise, row; (*fig.*) sensation.

ντουβάρι *s.n.* wall; (*fig.*) blockhead.

ντούγια *s.f.* stave (*of cask*).

ντουέτο *s.n.* duet.

ντουζίνα *s.f.* dozen.

ντουλάπα *s.f.* wardrobe.

ντουλάπι *s.n.* cupboard.

ντουνιᾶς *s.m.* people, mankind; world.

ντοῦρος *a.* hard, firm (*in substance*); unbending, erect (*in carriage*).

ντούς *s.n.* showerbath. [F. *douche*]

ντρέπομαι *v.i. & t.* be shy; be ashamed (of).

ντροπαλός *a.* shy.

ντροπή *s.f.* shyness; shame.

ντροπιάζω *v.t.* put to shame.

ντυμένος *a.* dressed.

ντύν|ω *v.t.* dress; cover upholster, line. ~ομαι *v.i.* get dressed.

ντύσιμο *s.n.* dressing; dress, attire.

νῦ *s.n.* the letter **Ν**.

νυγμ|ός *s.m.* prick, sting; (*fig.*) hint; ~οὶ τοῦ στομάχου pangs of hunger.

νυκτ- *see* **νυχτ-**.

νυκτεριν|ός *a.* of night, nocturnal. ~όν *s.n.* nocturne.

νυκτόβιος *a.* of nocturnal habits.

νύκτωρ *adv.* by night.

νυμφεύω *v.t. & i. see* παντρεύω.

νύμφη *s.f.* 1. nymph. 2. larva. 3. *see* νύφη.

νυμφίος *s.m.* bridegroom.

νῦν *adv.* now.

νύξ *s.f.* night.

νύξις *s.f.* prick, sting; *(fig.)* hint, allusion.

νύστ|α *s.f.*, ~αγμός *s.m.* sleepiness.

νυστάζω *v.i.* feel sleepy.

νυσταλέος *a.* sleepy, drowsy.

νυστέρι *s.n.* lancet.

νύφη *s.f.* bride; daughter-in-law; sister-in-law *(brother's wife)*.

νυφικός *a.* bridal.

νυφίτσα *s.f.* weasel.

νυχθημερόν *adv.* day and night.

νύχι *s.n.* nail, claw, talon; hoof; *(fig.)* ~α *(pl.)* clutches; περπατῶ στὰ ~α μου walk on tiptoe; ~ καὶ κρέας hand-in-glove.

νυχι|ά *s.f.* scratch. ~άζω *v.t.* scratch.

νύχτα *s.f.* night; *(adv.)* at night.

νυχτέρι *s.n.* work done at night.

νυχτερίδα *s.f.* bat *(animal)*.

νυχτικ|ιά *s.f.*, ~ό *s.n.* nightgown.

νυχτοπούλι *s.n.* night-bird.

νυχτών|ω, ~ομαι *v.i.* be overtaken by night; ~ει night falls.

νωθρός *a.* sluggish, indolent.

νωματάρχης *s.m.* sergeant of gendarmerie.

νωμίτης *s.m.* yoke *(in dressmaking)*.

νωπός *a.* fresh *(not stale or dried up)*; still damp *(of washing)*.

νωρίς *adv.* early.

νῶτ|α *s.n.pl.* back; *(mil.)* rear. ~ιαῖος *a.* vertebral.

νωχελ|ής *a.* nonchalant. ~εια *s.f.* nonchalance.

Ξ

ξάγναντο *s.n.* view-point.

ξαγοράρης *s.m.* confessor.

ξαγορεύ|ω *v.t.* confess *(penitent)*. ~ομαι *v.i.* confess *(to priest)*.

ξαγρυπνῶ *v.i. & t.* stay awake; keep watch (over).

ξαδέρφη *s.f.* cousin.

ξαδέρφια *s.n.pl.* cousins.

ξάδερφος *s.m.* cousin.

ξαίρω *v.t. & i. see* ξέρω.

ξακουσ|μένος, ~τός *a.* renowned.

ξαλαφρώνω *v.t. & i.* relieve, allay; be relieved; relieve oneself.

ξαλλάζω *v.t.* change *(clothes)*.

ξανά *adv.* again.

ξανα- *denotes* again, back.

ξανάβω *v.t. & i.* inflame, irritate; get hot *or* inflamed *or* irritated.

ξαναγεννιέμαι *v.i.* be reborn.

ξαναγυρίζω *v.i. & t.* return back; give back.

ξαναδίνω *v.t.* give back; retake *(exam.)*.

ξανακάνω *v.t.* do *or* make again.

ξανακυλῶ *v.i.* have a relapse.

ξαναλέω *v.t.* repeat, say again.

ξάναμα *s.n.* inflammation *(of wound)*.

ξανανιώνω *v.t. & i.* rejuvenate; be rejuvenated.

ξαναπαίρνω *v.t.* take *or* get back; re-employ; buy again; catch *(ailment)* again; recapture; τὸν ~ go to sleep again.

ξαναρχῆς *adv.* from the beginning.

ξανάρχομαι *v.i.* come again *or* back.

ξανασαίνω *v.i.* rest, relax.

ξανάστροφη *s.f.* wrong *or* reverse side; back-handed slap.

ξανθ|αίνω, ~ίζω *v.t. & i.* make *or* become lighter *(of hair)*.

ξανθ|ός *a.* blond, fair. ~ομάλλης *a.* fair-haired. ~ωπός *a.* on the fair side.

ξάνοιγμα *s.n.* becoming lighter *or* brighter; launching out; clearing *(in forest)*.

ξανοίγ|ω *v.t. & i.* make *or* become lighter *(in colour)*; become brighter *(of weather)*; look at. ~ ομαι *v.i.* unbosom oneself; launch out too ambitiously.

ξαντό *s.n.* lint.

ξάπλα *s.f. (fam.)* lounging about.

ξάπλωμα *s.n.* lying down; spreading.

ξαπλών|ω *v.t. & i.* spread (out); lie down. ~ομαι *v.i.* spread; lie down.

ξαπλωτός *a.* lying down.

ξαποσταίνω *v.i.* rest.

ξαποστέλνω *v.t.* dispatch; *(fam.)* send packing.

ξασπρίζω *v.t. & i.* whiten, bleach; fade.

ξάστερ|ος *a.* starry, clear. ~α *adv.* clearly, plainly. ~ιά *s.f.* starry sky.

ξαφν|ιάζω, ~ίζω *v.t.* surprise, scare. ~ιάζομαι, ~ίζομαι *v.i.* be scared *or* taken aback.

ξαφνικό s.n. surprise (incident); accident, fatality.

ξαφνικ|ός a. sudden, unexpected. ~ά adv. suddenly.

ξάφνου adv. suddenly.

ξαφρίζω v.t. skim; (fam.) sneak, steal.

ξε- see ἐκ or ἐξ.

ξεβάφω v.t. & i. (cause to) lose colour, fade.

ξεβγάζω v.t. rinse; see off; get rid of; kill; initiate into loose ways.

ξεβρακώνω v.t. remove trousers or pants of; (fig.) show up.

ξεβράκωτος a. trouserless; (fig.) penniless; a sans-culotte.

ξεγδέρνω v.t. flay, skin; scratch, graze.

ξεγελῶ v.t. deceive, gull; seduce.

ξεγεννῶ v.t. deliver (woman in parturition).

ξε(γ)νοιάζω v.i. become free from care.

ξεγράφω v.t. (fig.) write off.

ξεδιαλέγω v.t. pick out (the best).

ξεδιαλύνω v.t. & i. clear up, unravel; come true.

ξεδιάντροπος a. shameless.

ξεδίνω v.i. do something to take one's mind off one's worries.

ξεδιπλώνω v.t. unfold.

ξεδιψῶ v.t. & i. quench thirst of; quench one's thirst.

ξεδοντιάρης a. toothless.

ξεθαρρεύ|ω, ~ομαι v.i. grow (too) bold.

ξεθεώνω v.t. (fam.) wear out, exhaust.

ξεθυμαίνω v.i. evaporate; lose strength or pungency; leak (of fumes, gas-pipe, etc.); (fig.) relieve one's feelings.

ξεθωριάζω v.i. fade.

ξεκαθαρίζω v.t. & i. settle (account); clarify; become settled or clarified; (fam.) kill off.

ξεκάνω v.t. dispose of, sell off; (fam.) kill off.

ξεκαρδίζομαι v.i. die of laughing.

ξεκάρφωτος a. unnailed; (fig.) disjointed.

ξεκινῶ v.i. start off, set out.

ξεκλέβω v.t. (fig.) steal, snatch (a moment etc.).

ξεκληρίζ|ω v.t. wipe out (family). ~ω, ~ομαι v.i. die out (of family).

ξεκοιλιάζω v.t. disembowel.

ξεκοκκαλίζω v.t. bone; devour to the bone; (fig.) squander.

ξεκομμέν|ος a. τιμή ~η fixed price. ~α adv. bluntly, straight out.

ξεκουμπίζομαι v.i. (fam.) clear out, depart.

ξεκουμπ|ώνω v.t. unbutton. ~ωτος a. unbuttoned.

ξεκουράζ|ω v.t. rest, relieve, refresh. ~ομαι v.i. rest, repose.

ξεκουτιαίνω v.t. & i. make or grow soft-witted (esp. from old age).

ξεκουφαίνω v.t. deafen.

ξεκόφτω v.t. & i. detach; say straight out; ~ ἀπό give up (doing sthg.).

ξελαρυγγίζομαι v.i. shout oneself hoarse.

ξελιγώ|νω v.t. cloy; (fig.) tire, exhaust (esp. with waiting); ~μένος γιά avid for.

ξελογιάζω v.t. inveigle; turn head of, monopolize interest of.

ξεμαλλι|άζω v.t. pull hair of; ~ασμένος dishevelled.

ξεμοναχιάζω v.t. draw (person) aside; find (person) alone.

ξεμπαρκάρω v.t. & i. unload, land; (v.i.) land.

ξεμπερδεύω v.t. & i. disentangle, sort out; have done with; kill; (v.i.) have done with it.

ξεμπλέκω v.t. & i. disentangle (oneself); ~ ἀπό get rid or free of.

ξεμπουκάρω v.i. come out, issue (as from narrow opening).

ξεμπράτσωτος a. with bare arms.

ξεμυαλίζω v.t. inveigle; seduce; turn head of, monopolize interest of.

ξεμυτίζω v.i. (fig.) show one's nose.

ξεμωραίνομαι v.i. become childish.

ξένα s.n.pl. foreign parts.

ξεναγός s.m.f. (tourists') guide.

ξενηλασία s.f. expulsion of foreigners.

ξενητειά s.f. (sojourning in) foreign parts.

ξενητεύομαι v.i. go to live abroad.

ξενίζ|ω v.t. 1. entertain (guest). 2. surprise, seem strange to. ~ομαι v.i. be surprised.

ξενικός a. foreign.

ξε(ν)νοιάζω v.i. become free from care.

ξενοδουλεύω v.i. go out to work.

ξενοδοχεῖον s.n. hotel; (fam.) restaurant.

ξενοδόχος s.m. hotel-keeper.

ξενοικιάζομαι v.i. become vacant (of property).

ξένος 1. a. foreign; strange; somebody else's; (with πρός) not concerned with. 2. s.m. foreigner, stranger; guest.

ξενοφοβία s.f. xenophobia.

ξενόφωνος a. foreign-speaking.

ξεντύνω v.t. undress.

ξενυχιάζω v.t. trample on toes of.

ξενύχτης s.m. one who stays up late.

ξενυχτώ v.i. & t. stay up late or all night; (v.t.) keep awake at night; sit up with (sick case).

ξενών s.m. guest-room; guest-house.

ξεπαγιάζω v.i. & t. freeze; get chilblains.

ξεπαραδιάζω v.t. leave without a penny.

ξεπαστρεύω v.t. clean up; exterminate.

ξεπατώνω v.t. wear out or remove bottom or floor of; tire to death; exterminate.

ξεπεζεύω v.i. dismount (from horse).

ξεπερ|νῶ v.t. unthread; surpass; ἔλα νὰ ~αστοῦμε let us compete together; ~ασμένος out-of-date, passé.

ξεπεσμός s.m. decline, falling off; reduction (of price).

ξεπετ|άω v.t. finish (job) quickly; (fig.) see (one's children) fledged. ~ιέμαι v.i. shoot up (in stature); fly or jump out suddenly; butt in.

ξεπέφτω v.i. & t. fall off, decline in value or status; reduce in value or price, deduct.

ξεπηδῶ v.i. fly or jump out suddenly.

ξέπλεκος a. loose, let down (of hair).

ξεπλένω v.t. rinse.

ξεπληρώνω v.t. pay off (creditor or debt).

ξέπλυμα s.n. rinsing; (fig.) insipid person or thing.

ξεποδαριάζω v.t. walk the feet off.

ξεπορτίζω v.i. & t. go or slip out (of doors); send (person) out.

ξεπούλημα s.n. sale, selling off.

ξεπουλῶ v.t. & i. sell off; (v.i.) sell out.

ξεπροβοδ|ίζω, ~ῶ v.t. see off.

ξέρα s.f. 1. reef (in sea). 2. drought.

ξεράδι s.n. dead wood; (fig.) dry crust; (fam.) κάτω τὰ ~α σου hands (or feet) off!

ξεραΐλα s.f. aridity.

ξεραίν|ω v.t. dry (up), parch. ~ομαι v.i. dry up; die (of plants); (fig.) ξεράθηκε he was dumbfounded; ξεράθηκε στὰ γέλια he died of laughing.

ξερακιανός a. lean, spare (of body).

ξέρ|ασμα, ~ατό s.n. vomit; vomiting.

ξερικός a. (plant) grown without watering.

ξερνῶ v.t. & i. vomit, spew.

ξερόβηχας s.m. dry cough.

ξερόβόρι s.n. dry, cold north wind.

ξεροβούνι s.n. barren mountain.

ξερογλείφομαι v.i. lick one's lips (in anticipation).

ξεροκαταπίνω v.i. gulp (with embarrassment).

ξεροκέφαλος a. thick-headed; obdurate.

ξεροκοκκαλίζω v.t. (fig.) nibble away, waste (money).

ξερολιθιά s.f. rubble-masonry.

ξερονήσι s.n. barren or desert island.

ξεροπόταμο s.n. dry torrent-bed.

ξερ|ός a. dry, dried; curt; ἔμεινε ~ός he was dumbfounded or fell dead; ἔπεσε ~ὸς στὸν ὕπνο he slept like a log; (fam.) μάζεψε τὰ ~ά σου hands (or feet) off!

ξεροσταλιάζω v.i. become exhausted with standing.

ξεροψωμίζω v.i. live on dry bread.

ξε(ρ)ριζώνω v.t. uproot, pull off; eradicate.

ξέρω v.t. & i. know (how to).

ξεσηκώνω v.t. rouse; disturb; trace, copy; imitate.

ξεσκ|άζω, ~ῶ v.i. relax (in recreation).

ξεσκεπάζω v.t. uncover, lay bare; show up.

ξέσκεπος a. uncovered; (fig.) frank.

ξεσκ|ίζω v.t. tear to pieces; (fig.) ~ισμένος profligate.

ξεσκολ|ίζω v.i. finish one's schooling; (fig.) ~ισμένος practised.

ξεσκονίζω v.t. (clear of) dust.

ξεσκονόπανο s.n. duster.

ξέσκουρα adv. on the surface (of injuries).

ξεσκούφωτος a. hatless.

ξεσπ|άζω, ~άνω, ~ῶ v.i. overflow, burst out.

ξεσπαθώνω v.i. draw one's sword; (fig.) take up cudgels.

ξεστομίζω v.t. utter.

ξεστραβώνω v.t. & i. straighten; (fig.) open eyes of, educate; become straight.

ξεστρώνω v.t. take up, remove; clear (table); ~ τὸ σπίτι take up the carpets.

ξέστρωτ|ος a. unmade (bed); uncarpeted; unpaved; unsaddled; (fam.) ~ο γαϊδούρι extremely rude person.

ξεσυνερίζομαι v.t. see συνερίζομαι.

ξεσχίζω v.t. see ξεσκίζω.

ξετινάζω v.t. shake (violently); leave in weak condition; (fig.) reduce to poverty.

ξετρελλαίνω v.t. drive mad.

ξετρυπώνω v.t. & i. unearth; remove basting from (in dressmaking); pop up.

ξετσιπωσιά s.f. (act of) brazen impudence.

ξετσίπωτος a. without sense of shame, brazen.

ξεύρω v.t. & i. see ξέρω.

ξεφαντώνω v.i. make merry.

ξεφεύγω v.t. & i. escape, avoid; (v.i.) slip out.

ξεφλουδίζω v.t. & i. peel; remove bark or shell of; (v.i.) peel.

ξεφορτ|ώνω v.t. & i. unburden, unload. ~ώνομαι v.t. get rid of; ~ωνέ με or ~ώσου με leave me in peace!

ξεφτέρι s.n. (fig.) quick and intelligent person, adept.

ξέφτ|ι s.n. loose thread, ravel. ~ίζω, ~ῶ v.i. & t. become frayed; get past one's prime; pull out (thread).

ξεφυλλίζω v.t. & i. leaf through (book); pluck leaves of; shed leaves.

ξεφυσῶ v.i. let off steam; puff and blow; break wind.

ξεφυτρώνω v.i. sprout, spring up.

ξεφωνητό s.n. yell, shriek, shout(ing).

ξεφωνίζω v.i. shriek, shout.

ξεχαρβαλώ|νω v.t. make rickety; ~μένος rickety, disorganized.

ξεχασιάρης a. forgetful.

ξεχασμένος a. forgetful; forgotten.

ξεχειλίζω v.t. & i. fill too full; overflow.

ξέχειλος a. full to the brim.

ξεχειλώνω v.i. become misshapen (at the edge) (of garments).

ξεχειμων|ιάζω v.i. spend the winter; ~ίασε the winter is over.

ξεχνῶ v.t. & i. forget.

ξεχρεών|ω v.t. pay off (debt, creditor); complete payment for. ~ω, ~ομαι v.i. discharge one's debts.

ξεχύν|ω v.t. pour forth; break out in (rash, etc.). ~ομαι v.i. pour forth, overflow.

ξέχωρα adv. separately; ~ ἀπό apart from, as well as.

ξεχωρίζω v.t. & i. set apart; single out; distinguish, tell apart; be different, stand out.

ξεχωριστ|ός a. separate; exceptional (pre-eminent); special (peculiar). ~ά adv. separately, apart.

ξεψαχνίζω v.t. investigate closely; sound (person); (fam.) sponge on, soak.

ξεψυχ|ῶ v.i. & t. die; (fig.) feel ardent desire; ~ισμένος γιὰ τσιγάρο dying for a cigarette. (v.t.) worry the life out of.

ξέω v.t. scratch, scrape; scratch out.

ξηλώνω v.t. take apart; unmake, unstitch.

ξημεροβραδιάζομαι v.i spend all day long.

ξημέρωμα s.n., ~τα (pl.) daybreak; (fam.) staying up all night.

ξημερών|ει v.i. day breaks. ~ομαι v.i. wake up or find oneself next morning; stay up or be kept awake till morning.

ξηρά s.f. (dry) land.

ξηραίν|ω v.t. dry (up), parch. ~ομαι v.i. dry up; die (of plants).

ξηρασία s.f. dryness; drought.

ξηρ|ός a. dry, dried; curt; ~οὶ καρποί dried fruit and nuts.

ξῑ s.n. the letter Ξ.

ξιδ- see ξυδ-.

ξίκικος a. underweight.

ξινάρι s.n. pickaxe.

ξινίζω v.t. & i. make or become sour.

ξινίλα s.f. sourness, acidity.

ξινό s.n. citric acid.

ξιν|ός a. sour, acid; μοῦ βγῆκε ~ό it turned out a disappointment after all; μ' ἀρέσουν τὰ ~ά have a weakness for amorous adventures.

ξιππ|άζω v.t. frighten; astonish, impress. ~άζομαι v.i. become puffed up with pride; ~ασμένος vainglorious.

ξιφασκία s.f. fencing.

ξιφήρης a. sword in hand.

ξιφίας s.m. swordfish.

ξιφισμός s.m. sword-thrust.

ξιφολόγχη s.f. bayonet.

ξίφος s.n. sword.

ξιφουλκῶ v.i. draw one's sword.

ξόανον s.n. wooden statue; (fig.) dolt.

ξόβεργα s.f. lime-twig.

ξοδεύ|ω v.t. spend, consume, use (up); sell (of shops); waste. ~ομαι v.i. be put to expense.

ξόδεψη s.f. sale, demand (for commodity).

ξόδι s.n. funeral.

ξοδιάζω v.t. see ξοδεύω.

ξόμπλι s.n. pattern for embroidery; (fig.) malicious gossip.

ξοπίσω adv. (from) behind; again.

ξόρκι s.n. exorcism.

ξουρ|ίζω v.t. shave; (fig.) bore (with loquacity); tell tall stories to; ὁ βοριᾶς μᾶς ~ισε the north wind froze us.

ξύγκι s.n. fat, tallow, grease; groin; βγάζω ἀπὸ τὴ μῦγα ~ squeeze blood from a stone.

ξυδâτος a. pickled; vinegary.

ξύδι s.n. vinegar.
ξυλάδικο s.n. timber-yard; firewood-shop.
ξυλάνθραξ s.m. charcoal.
ξυλεία s.f. timber.
ξυλένιος a. wooden.
ξυλεύομαι v.i. cut or obtain wood.
ξυλιά s.f. blow (with stick).
ξυλιάζω v.t. & i. make or become stiff (with cold) or like wood.
ξυλίζω v.t. beat, cudgel.
ξύλινος a. wooden.
ξύλ|ο s.n. (piece of) wood; ~a (pl.) firewood; (fam.) τρώω ~ο get a beating; έπεσε ~ο blows were struck; τὸ ~ο βγῆκε ἀπ' τὸν παράδεισο spare the rod and spoil the child.
ξυλογράφημα s.n. woodcut.
ξυλοδεσιά s.f. wooden frame (of building).
ξυλοκάρβουνο s.n. charcoal.
ξυλοκόπος s.m. woodcutter.
ξυλοκοπ|ῶ v.t. beat, thrash. ~ημα s.n. beating, thrashing.
ξυλοκρέββατο s.n. wooden bed; coffin.
ξυλοπόδαρο s.n. stilt.
ξυλοστάτης s.m. jamb.
ξυλοσχίστης s.m. chopper of wood; (fam.) one who is no good at his job.
ξυλουργ|ός s.m. joiner. ~ική s.f. joinery.
ξυλοφορτώνω v.t. beat, thrash.
ξυν- see ξιν-.
ξύν|ω v.t. scratch, scrape, grate; sharpen (pencil); scratch out; (fig.) sack (dismiss). ~ομαι v.i. scratch.
ξυπάζω v.i. see ξιππάζω.
ξύπνημα s.n. awakening.
ξυπνητήρι s.n. alarm-clock.
ξυπν|ητός, ~ιος, ~ός a. awake; (fig.) wide-awake, smart.
ξυπνῶ v.t. & i. wake up.
ξυπόλυτος a. bare-footed.
ξυράφ|ι s.n. (cut-throat) razor. ~άκι s.n. razor-blade.
ξυρίζ|ω v.t. shave. ~ομαι v.i. shave, get shaved.
ξύρισμα s.n. shave, shaving.
ξυριστικ|ός a. of or for shaving; ~ὴ μηχανή safety razor.
ξύσιμο s.n. scratching, scraping, grating; sharpening (of pencil); scratching out.
ξύσματα s.n.pl. scrapings.
ξυστ|ός a. scraped, grated. ~ά adv. (almost) grazing the surface.

ξύστρα s.f. scraper; currycomb; (pencil) sharpener.
ξύω v.t. see ξύνω.
ξώδερμα adv. see ξυστά.
ξωκκλήσι s.n. country chapel.
ξώλαμπρα adv. after Easter.
ξωμερίτης s.m. stranger.
ξώπετσα adv. see ξυστά.
ξωτικιά s.f. fairy.
ξωτικό s.n. ghost.
ξώφαρσα adv. see ξυστά.
ξώφυλλο s.n. cover (of book); outside shutter.

O

ὁ article m. the.
ὅ pron. neuter of ὅς.
ὄασις s.f. oasis.
ὀβελίσκος s.m. obelisk.
ὀβελ|ός s.m. spit, skewer. ~ίας s.m. spit-roasted lamb.
ὀβ|ίς, ~ίδα s.f. shell (projectile).
ὀβολός s.m. obol; (fig.) modest contribution, mite.
'Οβριός s.m. (fam.) Jew.
ὀγδόη s.f. (mus.) octave.
ὀγδοή(κο)ντα num. eighty.
ὀγδόντα num. eighty.
ὄγδοος a. eighth.
ὀγκανίζω v.i. bray.
ὀγκόλιθος s.m. large block of stone.
ὄγκος s.m. mass, bulk, volume; great quantity; (med.) swelling, tumour.
ὀγκοῦμαι v.i. swell.
ὀγκώδης a. massive, bulky.
ὀδαλίσκη s.f. odalisque.
ὅδε pron. this; μέχρι τοῦδε up to now.
ὀδεύω v.i. go, proceed.
ὁδηγία s.f. guidance, direction, instruction.
ὁδηγός s.m.f. guide; girl-guide; guide-book; driver.
ὁδηγῶ v.t. guide, direct, lead; instruct, show how (to); drive, steer (vehicle).
ὀδογέφυρα s.f. viaduct.
ὀδοιπορία s.f. journey (esp. on foot).
ὀδοιπορικά s.n.pl. journey-money.
ὀδοιπόρος s.m. wayfarer.
ὀδοκαθαριστής s.m. crossing-sweeper.
ὀδονταλγία s.f. toothache.
ὀδοντίατρος s.m.f. dentist.
ὀδοντόβουρτσα s.f. toothbrush.
ὀδοντο(γ)ιατρός s.m.f. dentist.

όδοντογλυφίδα *s.f.* toothpick.

όδοντόπαστα *s.f.* toothpaste.

όδοντοστοιχία *s.f.* set of (false) teeth.

όδοντοφυΐα *s.f.* cutting of teeth.

όδοντόφωνος *a.* (*gram.*) dental.

όδοντωτός *a.* having teeth *or* cogs; ~ σιδηρόδρομος rack-and-pinion railway.

όδοποιΐα *s.f.* road-construction.

όδ|ός *s.f.* street, thoroughfare, way; (*fig.*) way, path, method; καθ' ~όν on the way.

όδοστρωτήρ *s.m.* steam-roller.

όδούς *s.m.* tooth; cog.

όδόφραγμα *s.n.* barricade.

όδύν|η *s.f.* pain, grief. ~ηρός *a.* painful, grievous.

όδυρμός *s.m.* lamentation.

όδύρομαι *v.i.* lament, wail.

όδύσσεια *s.f.* odyssey.

όζον *s.n.* ozone.

όζω *v.i.* stink.

όζώδης *a.* gnarled.

όθεν *adv.* whence; therefore.

όθόνη *s.f.* sheet, cloth; (*cinema*) screen.

'Οθωμανός *s.m.* Ottoman, Turk.

οί *article m.f.pl.* the.

οίαξ *s.m.* tiller; helm.

οίδ|α *v.i.* know; Κύριος ~ε Lord knows.

οίδημα *s.n.* swelling.

οίησις *s.f.* conceit, presumptuousness.

οίκαδε *adv.* homeward, home.

οίκειοθελώς *adv.* of one's own free will.

οίκειοποιούμαι *v.t.* appropriate.

οίκεί|ος *a.* own, proper; familiar, intimate; ~οι (*pl.*) relatives, intimates. ~ότης *s.f.* intimacy, familiarity.

οίκημα *s.n.* dwelling, habitation.

οίκ|ία *s.f.* house. ~ιακός *a.* domestic.

οίκογένει|α *s.f.* family. ~ακός *a.* family. ~άρχης *s.m.* head of family.

οίκοδέσποινα *s.f.* mistress of house, hostess.

οίκοδεσπότης *s.m.* master of house, host; landlord.

οίκοδομή *s.f.* (*act of*) building; a building (*under construction*).

οίκοδόμημα *s.n.* building, edifice.

οίκοδόμησις *s.f.* (*act of*) building.

οίκοδομώ *v.t.* build.

οίκοθεν *adv.* ~ έννοείται it is self-evident.

οίκοκύρ|ης *s.m.* householder; landlord; master. ~ική *s.f.* domestic science.

οίκονομ|ία *s.f.* economy; ~ίες (*pl.*) savings.

οίκονομικ|ός *a.* economic, financial; not expensive; ~ά (*s.n.pl.*) finances. ~ά *adv.* inexpensively.

οίκονομολόγ|ος *s.m.* economist; (*fam.*) thrifty person. ~ία *s.f.* economics.

οίκονόμος *s.m.f.* steward; (*fig.*) thrifty person.

οίκονομ|ώ, ~άω *v.t.* save, husband (*resources*); find, get hold of (*with some effort*); fix (*someone*) up; τὰ ~άω make ends meet. ~ιέμαι, ~ιούμαι *v.i.* get fixed up.

οίκόπεδον *s.n.* building-plot.

οίκ|ος *s.m.* house; business-house; κατ' ~ον in the home.

οίκόσημον *s.n.* coat of arms.

οίκόσιτος *a.* (*animal*) kept in the home; a boarder.

οίκότροφ|ος *s.m.f.* boarder. ~είον *s.n.* boarding-school, hostel.

οίκουμέν|η *s.f.* world, universe. ~ικός *a.* oecumenical; ~ική κυβέρνησις coalition government.

οίκουρώ *v.i.* be confined to the house (*by illness*).

οίκτ(ε)ίρω *v.t.* pity; despise.

οίκτιρμός *s.m.* pity.

οίκτίρμων *a.* merciful, compassionate.

οίκτος *s.m.* pity; contempt.

οίκτρός *a.* pitiable; wretched, mean.

οίμοι, όϊμέ *int.* alas!

οίμωγή *s.f.* wailing, groaning.

οίνοβαρής *a.* intoxicated.

οίνολογία *s.f.* oenology.

οίνομαγειρείον *s.n.* cheap tavern.

οίνόπνευμ|α *s.n.* alcohol. ~ατώδης *a.* alcoholic.

οίνοποιΐα *s.f.* wine-making.

οίνοποσία *s.f.* (excessive) wine-drinking.

οίνος *s.m.* wine.

οίνοχόος *s.m.* cup-bearer.

οίον *adv.* such as.

οίονεί *adv.* as if.

οίος *pron.* such as, of the kind which.

οίοσδήποτε *pron.* anybody, any; any kind of; whoever, whichever.

οίσοφάγος *s.m.* oesophagus.

οίστρ|ος *s.m.* gadfly; (*fig.*) oestrum, inspiration; high spirits. ~ηλατούμαι *v.i.* be inspired.

οίων|ός *s.m.* omen, presage. ~οσκόπος *s.m.* augur.

όκά *s.f.* oka (*measure of weight*).

όκλαδόν *adv.* squatting, cross-legged.

όκνηρός *a.* lazy.

ὀκνός *a.* slow, sluggish; indolent.
ὀκρίβας *s.m.* easel.
ὀκτάγωνος *a.* octagonal.
ὀκτακόσιοι *a.* eight hundred.
ὀκτά|πους *s.m.* ~πόδι *s.n.* octopus.
ὀκτώ *num.* eight.
Ὀκτώβριος *s.m.* October.
ὅλα *s.n. pl.* everything (*see* ὅλος).
ὁλάκερος *a.* whole, entire.
ὁλάνοικτος *a.* wide *or* fully open.
ὄλβιος *a.* wealthy; blessed, blissful.
ὀλέθριος *a.* disastrous, ruinous.
ὄλεθρος *s.m.* calamity, ruin.
ὁλημερίς *adv.* all day long.
ὀλιγ- *denotes* little, few.
ὀλιγάριθμος *a.* few in number.
ὀλιγαρκής *a.* satisfied with little.
ὀλιγαρχία *s.f.* oligarchy.
ὀλιγοδάπανος *a.* thrifty; inexpensive.
ὀλιγόλογος *a.* taciturn; laconic.
ὀλίγον *adv.* (a) little.
ὀλιγόπιστος *a.* unbelieving.
ὀλίγ|ος *a.* small in amount, (a) little, (a) few; ~ον κατ' ~ον little by little; ἐντὸς ~ον soon; παρ' ~ον (νά), ~ου δεῖν (νά) nearly.
ὀλιγοστεύω *v.t. & i.* lessen, reduce; grow less.
ὀλιγοστός *a.* scant, barely sufficient.
ὀλιγοψυχία *s.f.* faint-heartedness.
ὀλιγωρία *s.f.* negligence, indifference.
ὁλικός *a.* total.
ὀλισθαίνω *v.i.* slip.
ὀλίσθημα *s.n.* slip, slipping; blunder; lapse (*from rectitude*).
ὀλισθηρός *a.* slippery (*not affording foothold*).
ὁλκή *s.f.* pull, weight; calibre.
ὅλμος *s.m.* (*mil.*) mortar.
ὁλο- *denotes* all, completely.
ὅλο *adv.* all (*wholly*); all the time; ~ καὶ περισσότερο more and more.
ὁλό|γεμος, ~γιομος *a.* quite full.
ὁλόγερος *a.* in sound *or* healthy condition; undamaged.
ὁλογράφως *adv.* (*written out*) in full.
ὁλόγυρα *adv.* all round.
ὁλοέν(α) *adv.* all the time.
ὁλοήμερος *a.* lasting all day.
ὁλοΐδιος *a.* exactly the same.
ὁλόϊσ(ι)ος *a.* quite straight.
ὁλοκαύτωμα *s.n.* thing completely burnt, holocaust; sacrifice, offering.
ὁλόκλ|ηρος *a.* whole, entire; ἐξ ~ήρου entirely.
ὁλοκληρ|ῶ *v.t.* bring to completion;

(*math.*) integrate. ~ωτικός *a.* complete; totalitarian; (*math.*) integral.
ὀλολύζω *v.i.* wail, lament.
ὁλόμαλλος *a.* all wool.
ὁλομέλεια *s.f.* total membership.
ὁλομέταξος *a.* all silk.
ὁλομόναχος *a.* all alone.
ὁλονέν *adv.* all the time.
ὁλονυκτία *s.f.* all-night service *or* revelry.
ὁλονυχτίς *adv.* all night long.
ὁλόρθος *a.* upright, erect.
ὅλ|ος *a.* all, the whole; ~οι everybody; ~α everything; ~οι μας all of us; ~α ~α altogether (*in sum*); ~α κι' ~α anything else (*but not that*); ~ος κι' ~ος the selfsame (*person*); μ' ~ο πού although.
ὁλοσηρικόν *s.n.* satin.
ὁλοσχερής *a.* utter, total.
ὁλοταχώς *adv.* at full speed.
ὁλότελ|α, ~ῶς *adv.* completely.
ὁλότης *s.f.* whole, entirety.
ὁλούθε *adv.* from all sides.
ὁλοφάνερος *a.* obvious, evident.
ὁλόφτυστος *a.* the very spit of.
ὁλοφύρομαι *v.i.* wail, lament.
ὁλόφωτος *a.* all lit up.
ὁλόχαρος *a.* full of joy.
ὁλοχρονίς *adv.* all the year round.
ὁλόχρυσος *a.* all gold.
ὁλόψυχος *a.* with all one's heart.
Ὀλύμπι|α *s.n.pl.* Olympic games. ~ακός *a.* Olympic. ~ονίκης *s.m.* Olympic victor.
ὀλύμπιος *a.* olympian; godlike.
ὅλως *adv.* wholly, quite; ~ διόλου completely; ~ ὑμέτερος yours truly.
ὁμάδα *s.f. see* ὁμάς.
ὁμάδ|ι *adv.* together. ~ικός *a.* (in) mass. ~ικῶς *adv.* in a body.
ὁμαλ|ός *a.* level, even, smooth; usual, normal; (*gram.*) regular. ~ότης *s.f.* evenness; normality, order.
ὁμάς *s.f.* body, group; team, (*racing*) crew; (*mil.*) unit.
ὄμβρι|ος *a.* ~α ὕδατα rain-water.
ὀμελέτα *s.f.* omelet.
ὁμήγυρις *s.f.* assembly, gathering.
ὁμῆλιξ *s.m.f.* (*person*) of the same age.
ὁμηρικός *a.* Homeric.
ὅμηρος *s.m.* hostage.
ὄμικρον *s.n.* the letter Ο.
ὁμιλητής *s.m.* speaker.
ὁμιλητικός *a.* talkative; chatty, friendly.
ὁμιλία *s.f.* (*faculty or manner of*) speech;

homily, talk, address; converse; mention.

ὅμιλος s.m. group, circle, club.

ὁμιλῶ v.t. & i. speak.

ὁμίχλη s.f. fog, mist.

ὅμμα s.n. eye.

ὀμματοϋάλια s.n.pl. spectacles.

ὀμνύω v.t. & i. swear, vow.

ὁμο- denotes same, together.

ὁμοβροντία s.f. salvo, volley.

ὁμογάλακτος a. foster-brother or sister.

ὁμογενής a. of the same race; an expatriate Greek.

ὁμοεθνής a. a fellow countryman.

ὁμοειδής a. of the same species.

ὁμόθρησκος a. a co-religionist.

ὁμόθυμος a. unanimous.

ὁμοιάζω v.i. resemble (with πρός); look alike.

ὁμοϊδεάτης a. of the same way of thinking (esp. politically).

ὁμοιο- denotes similarity.

ὁμοιογενής a. homogeneous; even.

ὁμοιοκαταληξία s.f. rhyme.

ὁμοιόμορφος a. uniform.

ὁμοιοπαθ|ής a. a fellow sufferer. **~ητική** s.f. (med.) homoeopathy.

ὅμοι|ος a. similar, alike, like, same. **~ότης** s.f. similarity, resemblance.

ὁμοίωμα s.n. likeness, image.

ὁμοιωματικά s.n.pl. ditto-marks.

ὁμόκεντρος a. concentric.

ὁμολογία s.f. confession, admission; (fin.) debenture.

ὁμόλογον s.n. promissory note, bond.

ὁμολογουμένως adv. admittedly, by common consent.

ὁμολογῶ v.t. confess, acknowledge.

ὁμόνοια s.f. concord, harmony (between persons).

ὅμορος a. with common frontier.

ὁμόρρυθμος a. ~ ἑταιρία business partnership.

ὁμορφαίνω v.t. & i. embellish; become beautiful.

ὀμορφιά s.f. beauty, good looks.

ὀμορφονιός s.m. (ironic) foppish youth.

ὄμορφος a. good-looking, handsome, attractive.

ὁμόσπονδ|ος a. confederate. **~ία** s.f. federation, confederacy.

ὁμοταξία s.f. class (in natural history).

ὁμότιμος a. equivalent in rank or value; a peer; ~ καθηγητής professor emeritus.

ὁμοῦ adv. together.

ὁμόφρων a. having the same opinions.

ὁμοφυλοφιλία s.f. homosexuality.

ὁμοφωνία s.f. unanimity.

ὀμπρέλλα s.f. umbrella, sunshade.

ὀμφαλ|ός s.m. navel. **~ικός** a. umbilical.

ὄμφ|αξ s.m. unripe grape; **~ακες εἰσίν** sour grapes.

ὁμώνυμος a. having the same name.

ὅμως adv. but, nevertheless.

ὄν s.n. being, creature.

ὄναγρος s.m. wild ass, zebra.

ὄναρ s.n. dream.

ὄνειδος s.n. shame, disgrace.

ὀνειρεύομαι v.i. & t. dream (of).

ὀνειρευτός a. dreamlike; dreamed of.

ὀνειροκρίτης s.m. dream-book.

ὄνειρον s.n. dream.

ὀνειροπολῶ v.i. & t. day-dream; dream of, desire.

ὀνειρώδης a. like a dream (in excellence).

ὀνηλάτης s.m. donkey-driver.

ὄνομα s.n. name; (gram.) noun; βγάζω ~ acquire a reputation; ἔχει τὸ ~ του it is his name-day; ~ καὶ πρᾶμα in very truth; ~τι by the name of.

ὀνομάζω v.t. name, call; appoint, nominate.

ὀνομασία s.f. naming; nomination; name; name-day.

ὀνομαστί adv. by name.

ὀνομαστικ|ός a. nominal; **~ὴ ἑορτή** name-day. **~ή** s.f. (gram.) nominative.

ὀνομαστός a. renowned.

ὀνοματεπώνυμον s.n. Christian name and surname.

ὀνοματολογία s.f. terminology.

ὄνος s.m.f. ass.

ὀντότης s.f. entity, being; individuality.

ὄντως adv. indeed, really.

ὄν|υξ s.m. 1. nail, claw, talon; ἐξ ἁπαλῶν **~ύχων** from earliest childhood. 2. onyx. 3. flange (of wheel).

ὀξαλικός a. oxalic.

ὀξαποδῶ(ς) s.m. (fam.) the devil.

ὀξεῖα s.f. (gram.) acute accent.

ὀξείδ|ιον s.n. oxide. **~ωσις** s.f. oxidization.

ὀξικός a. acetic.

ὄξινος a. sour, acid.

ὄξος s.n. vinegar.

ὀξύ s.n. acid.

ὀξυά s.f. beech.

ὀξυγονοκόλλησις s.f. oxy-acetylene welding.

ὀξυγόνον s.n. oxygen.

ὀξυγονοῦχ|ος *a.* containing oxygen; ~ον ὕδωρ peroxide of hydrogen.

ὀξυδέρκεια *s.f.* keen sight; (*fig.*) discernment.

ὀξύθυμος *a.* irascible.

ὀξύνους *a.* shrewd.

ὀξύνω *v.t.* make pointed; sharpen (*wits, etc.*); intensify, exacerbate (*feelings*); (*gram.*) mark with acute accent.

ὀξύς *a.* sharp, acute, piercing.

ὀξύτονος *a.* (*gram.*) with acute accent on last syllable.

ὀξύφωνος *s.m.* (*mus.*) tenor.

ὄξω *adv.* see ἔξω.

ὀπαδός *s.m.f.* follower, adherent.

ὅπερ *pron.* which.

ὅπερα *s.f.* opera.

ὀπή *s.f.* hole, opening, cavity.

ὅπιον *s.n.* opium.

ὄπισθεν *adv.* behind; κάνω ~ go backwards; (*prep.*) ~ μου behind me.

ὀπίσθι|ος *a.* rear, back; τὰ ~α back, hindquarters.

ὀπισθοβουλία *s.f.* ulterior motive.

ὀπισθογραφῶ *v.t.* endorse (*cheque, etc.*).

ὀπισθοδρόμ|ησις *s.f.* retrogression. ~ικός *a.* retrograde; old-fashioned (*in outlook*).

ὀπισθοφυλακή *s.f.* rearguard.

ὀπισθοχώρησις *s.f.* retreat, giving way.

ὀπίσω *adv.* see πίσω.

ὀπλαρχηγός *s.m.* leader of irregular soldiers.

ὁπλή *s.f.* hoof.

ὁπλίζω *v.t.* arm; (*fig.*) strengthen.

ὁπλισμός *s.m.* armament, equipment; armature (*of magnet*); (*mus.*) key-signature.

ὁπλίτ|ης *s.m.* infantry soldier. ~αγωγόν troop-ship.

ὅπλ|ον *s.n.* weapon; rifle; branch of army; ~α (*pl.*) arms. ~οπολυβόλον *s.n.* light machine-gun.

ὁπλοστάσιον *s.n.* armoury, arsenal.

ὁπλοφορία *s.f.* carrying of arms (*by civilians*).

ὁπόθεν *adv.* whence; ~ διῆλθον whichever way I passed.

ὅποιος *pron.* whoever, whichever; ~ κι᾽ ~ anybody (*the first comer*).

ὁποιοσδήποτε *pron.* whosoever, whatsoever; any . . . at all.

ὁποῖος *pron.* of what kind; what (*exclamatory*); ὁ ~ who, which.

ὀπός *s.m.* sap, juice.

ὅποτε *adv.* whenever.

ὁπότε *adv.* when (*at which time*).

ὅπου *adv.* where, wherever; ~ καὶ νᾶναι at any moment *or* wherever he may be.

ὅ|που, ~πού *pron.* he who; whom, which.

ὁπουδήποτε *adv.* wheresoever.

ὀπτασία *s.f.* a vision.

ὀπτικ|ός *a.* optical, optic; an optician. ~ή *s.f.* optics.

ὀπτ|ός *a.* roast; ~ὴ γῆ terracotta.

ὀπωρικά *s.n.pl.* fruit.

ὀπωροπωλεῖον *s.n.* fruiterer's.

ὀπωροφόρ|ος *a.* ~α δένδρα fruit-trees.

ὅπως 1. *adv.* as, like; ~ ~ somehow or other, by hook or by crook, after a fashion. 2. *conj.* (in order) to.

ὁπωσδήποτε *adv.* in any case; definitely; ~ σωστά more or less correctly.

ὁπωσοῦν *adv.* somewhat, fairly.

ὅραμα *s.n.* a vision. ~τίζομαι *v.i.* have visions.

ὅρασις *s.f.* (*sense of*) sight, vision.

ὁρατ|ός *a.* visible. ~ότης *s.f.* visibility.

ὀργανέτο *s.n.* barrel-organ; (*fig.*) paid supporter, tool.

ὀργανικός *a.* organic; instrumental.

ὀργανισμός *s.m.* organism; (*bodily*) constitution; organization.

ὄργανον *s.n.* organ, instrument, agent.

ὀργανώνω *v.t.* organize.

ὀργάνωσις *s.f.* organization.

ὀργασμός *s.m.* rut, heat; (*fig.*) feverish activity.

ὀργή *s.f.* rage; (*fam.*) νά πάρη ἡ ~ damn it! δίνω τόπο στήν ~ give way, not insist.

ὄργι|α *s.n.pl.* orgies; (*fig.*) corrupt practices. ~άζω *v.i.* hold orgies; (*fig.*) run riot.

ὀργίζω *v.t.* anger.

ὀργίλος *a.* angry; irascible.

ὀργ(υ)ιά *s.f.* fathom.

ὀργῶ *v.i.* be in rut; (*fig.*) be avid.

ὄργ|ωμα *s.n.* ploughing. ~ώνω *v.t.* plough.

ὀρδή *s.f.* horde.

ὀρδινάντσα *s.f.* batman.

ὀρέγομαι *v.t.* feel desire for.

ὀρειβασία *s.f.* mountaineering.

ὀρειβάτης *s.m.* climber.

ὀρειβατικ|ός *a.* of *or* for climbing; ~ὸν πυροβολικόν mountain artillery.

ὀρεινός *a.* of the mountains; mountainous.

ὀρείχαλκος *s.m.* brass.

ὀρεκτικ|ός *a.* appetizing; tempting. ~ὸν *s.n.* appetizer; hors-d'œuvre.

ὄρεξις s.f. appetite; desire.
ὀρεσίβιος a. mountain-dwelling.
ὀρθά adv. upright; right, correctly; ~ κοφτά plainly, frankly.
ὀρθάνοιχτος a. wide open.
ὄρθιος a. upright, erect, standing.
ὀρθογραφία s.f. spelling, orthography.
ὀρθογώνι|ος a. rectangular, right-angled. ~ον s.n. rectangle.
ὀρθόδοξ|ος a. orthodox. ~ία s.f. orthodoxy; Orthodox Christianity.
ὀρθολογισμός s.m. rationalism.
ὀρθοπεδ|ία, ~ική s.f. orthopedics.
ὀρθοποδῶ v.i. stand erect; (fig.) prosper again.
ὀρθ|ός a. upright, erect; straight; right, correct; ~ή γωνία right-angle. ~ῶς adv. right, correctly.
ὀρθοστασία s.f. standing.
ὀρθότης s.f. rightness.
ὀρθοφροσύνη s.f. right thinking.
ὄρθρος s.m. (eccl.) matins.
ὀρθών|ω v.t. raise. ~ομαι v.i. rise up, stand on end; rebel.
ὀριζόντιος a. horizontal.
ὀρ|ίζω v.t. & i. bound, delimit; fix, define; rule, control; give orders (to); ~ίστε invitation to do, say, accept, or contemplate something; ~ίστε; I beg your pardon? καλῶς ~ίσατε welcome! ἂς ~ίση let him come in; τί ~ίζετε; what is your pleasure?
ὀρίζων s.m. horizon.
ὅριον s.n. boundary, limit.
ὁρισμένος a. fixed, appointed; certain (unspecified).
ὁρισμός s.m. fixing, appointing; definition; order, command.
ὁριστικ|ός a. definite, decisive. ~ή s.f. (gram.) indicative.
ὁρκίζ|ω v.t. put on oath. ~ομαι v.i. swear.
ὅρκος s.m. oath.
ὁρκωμοσία s.f. taking of oath.
ὁρκωτ|ός a. sworn; ~ὸν δικαστήριον jury court.
ὁρμαθός s.m. bunch, string (of keys, onions, etc.).
ὁρμέμφυτ|ος a. instinctive. ~ον s.n. instinct.
ὁρμή s.f. onrush, violence; impetuousness, passion.
ὁρμηνεύω v.t. advise, instruct.
ὁρμητήριον s.n. base, starting-point.
ὁρμητικός a. violent, impetuous.
ὁρμιά s.f. fishing-line.

ὁρμόνη s.f. hormone.
ὅρμος s.m. bay.
ὁρμ|ῶ v.i. rush. ~ῶμαι v.i. be motivated (by); originate (from).
ὄρνεον s.n. bird of prey.
ὄρνιθα s.f. hen.
ὀρνίθι s.n. pullet; bird.
ὀρνιθοσκαλίσματα s.n.pl. (fig.) scrawl.
ὀρνιθοτροφεῖον s.n. poultry-farm.
ὀρνιθών s.m. chicken-coop.
ὄρνιο s.n. bird of prey, vulture; (fig.) blockhead.
ὀρνιός s.m. wild fig.
ὄρνις s.f. hen.
ὁροθεσία s.f. demarcation of boundaries.
ὁρολογία s.f. terminology.
ὁροπέδιον s.n. plateau.
ὄρος s.n. mountain.
ὅρ|ος s.m. term (limit, word); condition, stipulation; ~οι (pl.) conditions (terms, circumstances); ἐφ' ~ου ζωῆς for life; φθάνω εἰς τὸ πρὸς ὃν ~ον reach one's destination; κατὰ μέσον ~ον on the average; ἀνώτατος ~ος maximum.
ὀρ(ρ)ός s.m. whey, serum.
ὀροσειρά s.f. mountain-range.
ὀρόσημον s.n. boundary-mark.
ὀροφή s.f. ceiling, roof.
ὄροφος s.m. floor, story.
ὄρτ|υξ s.m., ~ύκι s.n. quail.
ὄρυγμα s.n. trench, pit.
ὄρυζα s.f. rice.
ὀρυκτέλαιον s.n. petroleum; lubricating oil.
ὀρυκτ|ός a. mineral. ~ολογία s.f. mineralogy. ~όν s.n. mineral.
ὀρύσσω v.t. dig, excavate.
ὀρυχεῖον s.n. mine, quarry.
ὀρφανεύω v.i. become an orphan.
ὀρφαν|ός a. orphan. ~οτροφεῖον s.n. orphanage.
ὀρχήστρα s.f. orchestra.
ὄρχις s.f. 1. testicle. 2. orchid.
ὄρχος s.m. (mil.) park.
ὀρχοῦμαι v.i. dance.
ὁρῶ v.t. see.
ὅς pron. who, whom, which; ὃ ἐστί that is to say; ἀφ' ἧς since (the time when); δι' ὃ for which reason; καθ' ὃ as, qua; καθ' ἣν στιγμήν at the moment when.
ὁσάκις adv. as often as, whenever.
ὅσ|ιος a. holy, blessed; (fam.) ~ία Μαρία person affecting prudishness or innocence.
ὀσμή s.f. odour.

ὅσ|ο(ν) *adv.* as much *or* long as; ~ο ...
τόσο the more ... the more; ~ο τὸ
δυνατὸν νωρίτερα as early as possible;
~ο γιά as for; ἐφ' ~ον inasmuch as, as
long as; ~ον ἀφορᾶ as regards; ~ο
νἄρθη until *or* by the time he comes;
~ο νἄναι for all that; ~ο καὶ νὰ βρέχη
however much it may rain.

ὁσονούπω *adv.* soon, shortly.

ὅσ|ος *pron.* as much *or* many as, all;
πουλῶ ~α ~α sell at any price.

ὄσπριον *s.n.* pulse (*legume*).

ὀστεοφυλάκιον *s.n.* ossuary.

ὀστεώδης *a.* bony.

ὅστια *s.f.* 1. (*eccl.*) Host. 2. (*med.*)
cachet.

ὅστις *pron.* who, whoever.

ὀστοῦν *s.n.* bone.

ὀστρακιά *s.f.* scarlet fever.

ὄστρακ|ον *s.n.* shell; potsherd. ~όδερ-
μος *a.* crustacean.

ὄστρια *s.f.* south wind.

ὀσφραίνομαι *v.t.* smell.

ὄσφρησις *s.f.* (*sense of*) smell; keen nose.

ὀσφύς *s.f.* waist, loins.

ὅταν *conj.* when.

ὅτε *conj.* when.

ὁτέ *adv.* ~ μὲν ... ~ δέ sometimes ...
sometimes.

ὅτι 1. *conj.* that. 2. *adv.* as soon as;
just (*a moment ago*).

ὅ τι, ὅτι *pron.* what, whatever.

ὁτιδήποτε *pron.* whatsoever; anything at
all.

ὅτου *pron.* ἕως ~ *or* μέχρις ~ until; ἀφ' ~
since.

ὀτρά *s.f.* needleful of thread.

οὐ *adv.* not.

οὐγγιά *s.f.* ounce.

οὔγια *s.f.* selvage.

οὐδαμοῦ *adv.* nowhere.

οὐδαμῶς *adv.* not at all.

οὐδέ *adv. & conj.* not even; ~ ... ~
neither ... nor.

οὐδείς *pron.* no, nobody.

οὐδέποτε *adv.* never.

οὐδέτερος 1. *pron.* neither. 2. *a.*
neutral; (*gram.*) neuter.

οὐδόλως *adv.* by no means.

οὐζερί *s.n.* place where ouzo, *etc.*, is sold.

οὔζο *s.n.* spirit flavoured with aniseed;
cocktail party.

οὐκ *adv.* not.

οὐλαμός *s.m.* (*mil.*) troop (*artillery*).

οὐλή *s.f.* scar.

οὖλον *s.n.* gum (*of mouth*).

οὖρα *s.n.pl.* urine.

οὐρά *s.f.* tail; train (*of dress*); queue;
(*fam.*) λεφτά μέ ~ a lot of money.

οὐραγός *s.m.* one who brings up the
rear.

οὐρανής *a.* sky-blue.

οὐράνιον *s.n.* uranium.

οὐράνι|ος *a.* heavenly; ~ον τόξον rain-
bow.

οὐρανίσκ|ος *s.m.* palate. ~όφωνος *a.*
(*gram.*) palatal.

οὐρανοκατέβατος *a.* heaven-sent.

οὐρανοξύστης *s.m.* skyscraper.

οὐραν|ός *s.m.* sky, heaven; canopy.
~όθεν *adv.* from heaven.

οὐρητήριον *s.n.* urinal.

οὐρικός *a.* uric.

οὔριος *a.* favourable (*wind*).

οὐρλ|ιάζω *v.i.* howl. ~ιασμα *s.n.* howl,
howling.

οὐροδοχεῖον *s.n.* chamber-pot.

οὐρῶ *v.i.* urinate.

οὖς *s.n.* ear.

οὐσία *s.f.* substance; essence; flavour.

οὐσιαστικ|ός *a.* substantial. ~όν *s.n.*
(*gram.*) substantive.

οὐσιώδης *a.* essential, vital.

οὔτε *adv. & conj.* not even; ~ ... ~
neither ... nor.

οὐτιδανός *a.* worthless (*person*).

οὐτοπία *s.f.* utopia.

οὗτος *pron.* he, this (one).

οὕτω(ς) *adv.* so, thus; ~ ὥστε in such a
way as to.

οὐχ *adv.* not; ~ ἧττον none the less.

οὐχί *adv.* not.

ὀφειλέτης *s.m.* debtor.

ὀφειλή *s.f.* debt.

ὀφείλ|ω *v.t. & i.* owe; ~ω νὰ πάω
I ought to go. ~ομαι *v.i.* be due (*owed,
caused*).

ὄφελος *s.n.* profit, advantage.

ὀφθαλμαπάτη *s.f.* optical illusion.

ὀφθαλμίατρος *s.m.f.* eye-specialist.

ὀφθαλμοπορνεία *s.f.* lascivious glances.

ὀφθαλμός *s.m.* eye; bud.

ὀφθαλμοφανής *a.* obvious.

ὄφ|ις *s.m.* snake, serpent. ~ιοειδής *a.*
snaky, serpentine.

ὀφρύς *s.f.* brow, eyebrow; crest (*of hill*).

ὀφφίς *s.n.* domestic office. [F. *office*]

ὄχεντρα *s.f.* viper.

ὀχετ|ός *s.m.* drain. ~ευσις *s.f.* drain-
age.

ὄχημα *s.n.* vehicle, carriage.

ὄχθη *s.f.* bank (*of river*), shore (*of lake*).

ὄχι *adv. & particle* not; no (*negative response*).

ὀχιά *s.f.* viper.

ὀχλαγωγία *s.f.* disturbance, hubbub.

ὀχληρός *a.* tiresome.

ὀχλοβοή *s.f.* disturbance, hubbub.

ὀχλοκρατία *s.f.* ochlocracy.

ὄχλος *s.m.* populace, mob.

ὀχτ- *see* **ὀκτ-**.

ὀχυρ|ός *a.* strong (*proof against attack*). **~όν** *s.n.* strongpoint, fort.

ὀχυρών|ω *v.t.* fortify. **~ομαι** *v.i.* occupy strong defensive position; (*fig.*) arm oneself with excuse *or* pretext.

ὄψη *s.f. see* **ὄψις**.

ὀψιγενής *a.* posthumous (*child*); late (*in maturing*).

ὄψιμος *a.* late (*in maturing*).

ὀψίπλουτος *a.* nouveau riche.

ὄψ|ις *s.f.* appearance, look; sight; face, right side, obverse; ἐν **~ει** in view; ἐξ **~εως** by sight; λαμβάνω ὑπ᾽ **~ιν** take into consideration.

ὀψοφυλάκιον *s.n.* larder.

ὀψώνιον *s.n.* purchase (*item*).

Π

παγάν|α, ~ιά *s.f.* battue.

παγερός *a.* icy, frigid.

παγετός *s.m.* frost.

παγετών *s.m.* glacier.

παγίδ|α *s.f.* trap, snare. **~εύω** *v.t.* trap, ensnare.

παγίδ|ι *s.n.* rib. **~άκι** *s.n. see* **παϊδάκι**.

πάγιος *a.* fixed, permanent; (*fin.*) consolidated.

παγίς *s.f. see* **παγίδα**.

παγκάρι *s.n.* stall for candles in church.

πάγκος *s.m.* bench.

παγκόσμιος *a.* world-wide.

πάγκρεας *s.n.* (*anat.*) pancreas.

παγόβουνο *s.n.* iceberg.

παγοδρομία *s.f.* skating.

παγοπέδιλον *s.n.* skate.

παγοποιεῖον *s.n.* ice-factory.

πάγος *s.m.* ice; frost.

παγούρι *s.n.* soldier's water-bottle.

παγώνι *s.n.* peacock.

παγωνιά *s.f.* frost.

παγωνιέρα *s.f.* ice-box.

παγώ|νω *v.t. & i.* freeze; make *or* get cold; **~μένος** frozen; iced.

παγωτό *s.n.* ice-cream.

παζαρεύω *v.i. & t.* bargain (about).

παζάρι *s.n.* bazaar, market; bargaining.

παθαίν|ω *v.i. & t.* suffer; καλὰ νὰ πάθει it serves him right; τήν ἔπαθε (*fam.*) he got caught out, he copped it. **~ομαι** *v.i.* be moved, get carried away.

πάθημα *s.n.* setback, misfortune.

πάθησις *s.f.* malady.

παθητικόν *s.n.* (*fin.*) liabilities; (*fig.*) discredit.

παθητικός *a.* passive, charged with passion.

παθιασμένος *a.* ailing; (*fig.*) fanatical.

παθο|λογία *s.f.* pathology. **~λόγος** *s.m.* general practitioner.

πάθ|ος *s.n.* illness; passion; animosity; vice; **~η** (*pl.*) sufferings, Passion (*of Christ*).

παθών *s.m.* ὁ **~** the victim.

παιάν *s.m.* paean. **~ίζω** *v.t. & i.* play (*of band*).

παιγνίδι *s.n.* game, sport; toy, plaything; trick; gambling; **~α** (*pl.*) rustic orchestra. **~άρης** *a.* playful; coquettish.

παίγνιον *s.n.* game, sport; toy.

παιγνιόχαρτον *s.n.* playing-card.

παιδαγωγική *s.f.* pedagogy.

παιδάκι *s.n.* little child.

παϊδάκι *s.n.* cutlet.

παιδάρι|ον *s.n.* boy (*about 12–15*). **~ώδης** *a.* puerile.

παιδεία *s.f.* education; learning.

παίδεμ|α *s.n., ~ός* *s.m.* torment.

παιδεραστής *s.m.* paederast.

παιδεύ|ω *v.t.* torment. **~ομαι** *v.i.* strive hard.

παιδί(ον) *s.n.* child; boy; (*fam.*) fellow, chap.

παιδιά *s.f.* game (*play*).

παιδιαρίζω *v.i.* behave like a child.

παιδίατρος *s.m.* (*med.*) child specialist.

παιδικός *a.* of children, child's; childish.

παιδίσκη *s.f.* girl (*about 12–15*).

παιδομάζωμα *s.n.* forced levy of children; crowd of children.

παιζογελῶ *v.t.* (*fam.*) lead up the garden path.

παίζω *v.i. & t.* play; gamble; τὰ **~** μέ flirt with; τοῦ τίς ἔπαιξα I struck him.

παίκτης *s.m.* player; gambler.

παίνεμα *s.n.* praise.

παινεύ|ω *v.t.* praise. **~ομαι** *v.i.* boast.

παίξιμο *s.n.* play, playing; performance; gambling.

παίρν|ω v.t. & i. receive, get; take; contain, hold; marry; beat (at game); begin (to); τὸν ~ω fall asleep; ~ω καὶ δίνω have influence; ~ω πόδι make off; ~ω ἀέρα become cheeky; ~ω μπρός start (of motor); ~ω ἀπὸ πίσω follow closely; ~ω στὸ μεζέ make a fool of; ~ω ἀπάνω μου recover (in health); τὸ ~ω ἀπάνω μου give oneself airs or undertake the job; τὸν ~ω στὸ λαιμό μου I am the cause of his ill fortune; δὲν ~ει ἀπὸ λόγια he won't listen to reason; μᾶς ~ει ἡ ὥρα we have time; πῆρε ἀέρας the wind has risen; μοῦ πῆρε τὸ κεφάλι he drove me distracted; πῆραν τὰ μυαλά του ἀέρα he is too big for his boots; ἔχω πάρε δῶσε μέ have contact with; πάρθηκαν they got married.

παῖς s.m.f. child; boy.

παιχνίδι s.n. see παιγνίδι.

πακέτο s.n. packet, package.

παλαβός a. foolhardy, crazy.

παλάβρα s.f. talking big.

πάλαι, ~ά adv. of old.

παλαιικός a. of the old school.

παλαίμαχος s.m. veteran.

παλαιοελλαδίτης s.m. native of 'Old Greece'.

παλαιοημερολογίτης s.m. supporter of Old Calendar.

παλαιόθεν adv. from ancient times.

παλαιοπώλης s.m. second-hand dealer.

παλαιός a. old (not new); former.

παλαιστής s.m. wrestler.

παλαίστρα s.f. arena.

παλαμάκια s.n.pl. hand-clapping.

παλαμάρι s.n. (naut.) cable.

παλάμη s.f. palm (of hand); span.

παλαμίδα s.f. sort of fish.

παλαμίζω v.t. caulk.

παλάσκα s.f. cartridge-pouch.

παλάτι s.n. palace.

παλεύω v.i. wrestle, strive.

πάλη s.f. wrestling; struggle, conflict.

παληός a. see παλαιός.

πάλι adv. again, once more; on the other hand; back; ~ καλά it's not so bad (as it might have been); ἄλλο ~ there we go again!

παλιάνθρωπος s.m. (fam.) rascal, bounder, scoundrel.

παλιατζῆς s.m. rag-and-bone man.

παλιάτσα s.f. old, worn-out object.

παλιάτσος s.m. clown.

παλιγγενεσία s.f. regeneration.

πάλιν adv. see πάλι.

παλινδρομικός a. reciprocating (movement).

παλινόρθωσις s.f. restoration (of régime).

παλινόστησις s.f. return to one's homeland.

παλινωδῶ v.i. change one's tune.

παλιο- 1. denotes old. 2. pejorative epithet.

παλιογυναῖκα s.f. (pej.) woman; tart.

παλιολλαδίτης s.m. native of 'Old Greece'.

παλιόπαιδο s.n. bad boy.

παλιός a. see παλαιός.

παλίρροια s.f. tide; ebb and flow.

παλιώνω v.t. & i. wear out.

παλλαϊκός a. of all the people.

παλλακεία s.f. concubinage.

πάλλευκος a. pure white.

παλ(λ)ηκάρ|ι s.n. young man; brave person; bachelor. ~ᾶς s.m. ruffian. ~ιά s.f. bravery.

πάλλω v.t. & i. vibrate; throb.

παλμός s.m. pulsation, vibration; enthusiasm, feeling; rhythmic spring or throw (in athletics).

παλούκι s.n. stake, post; (fig.) difficulty; τοῦ σκοινιοῦ καὶ τοῦ ~οῦ (fam.) a thoroughly bad lot.

παλτό s.n. overcoat.

παμ- see παν-.

παμπάλαιος a. very old.

πάμπλουτος a. very rich.

παμφάγος a. omnivorous; voracious.

πάμφθηνος a. dirt cheap.

παμψηφία s.f. unanimous vote.

παν- denotes all, very.

πᾶν s.n. everything; the whole world (see also πᾶς).

Παναγία s.f. the Virgin Mary.

πανάγιος a. very holy.

πανάδα s.f. brown patch (on skin).

πανάκεια s.f. panacea.

πανάκριβος a. very expensive.

παναμᾶς s.m. panama hat.

πανδαιμόνιον s.n. pandemonium.

πανδαισία s.f. sumptuous feast.

πάνδημος a. of all the people.

πανδοχεῖον s.n. inn.

πανελλήνι|ος a. panhellenic. ~ον s.n. the whole of Greece.

πανεπιστήμιον s.n. university.

πανέρι s.n. wide basket.

πανηγύρι s.n. patronal festival; fair; beanfeast; (fam.) row, commotion; a perfect scream (of persons); εἶναι γιὰ τὰ ~α he is quite crazy.

πανηγυρίζω *v.t. & i.* celebrate (*feast day*).

πανηγυρικός I. *a.* festive, with rejoicing. 2. *s.m.* oration; panegyric.

πανήγυρις *s.f.* patronal festival; fair.

πάνθεον *s.n.* pantheon.

πάνθηρ *s.m.* panther.

πανθομολογούμενος *a.* universally acknowledged.

πανικ|ός *s.m.* panic. ~όβλητος *a.* panic-stricken.

παν(ν)ί *s.n.* cloth; sail; baby's napkin; ~ μὲ ~ without a penny; ἕνα ~ tarred with the same brush.

παννιάζω *v.i.* become pale *or* flabby.

παν(ν)ικά *s.n.pl.* drapery, linen.

παννυχίς *s.f.* all-night service *or* revelry.

πανομοιότυπον *s.n.* facsimile.

πανοπλία *s.f.* arms, armour.

πανόραμα *s.n.* panorama.

πανούκλα *s.f.* plague; (*fam.*) harridan.

πανοῦργος *a.* cunning, crafty.

πανσέληνος *s.f.* full moon.

πανσές *s.m.* pansy.

πανσπερμία *s.f.* mixture of races.

πανστρατιά *s.f.* (mobilization of) all available forces.

πάντα *adv.* always; in any case.

πάντα I. *s.n.pl.* everything (*see also* πᾶς). 2. *s.f. see* μπάντα.

πανταλόνι *s.n.* trousers; drawers.

πανταχόθεν *adv.* from all parts.

πανταχοῦ *adv.* everywhere.

πανταχοῦσα *s.f.* encyclical; (*fam.*) long string of reproaches.

παντελής *a.* complete, utter.

παντελόνι *s.n.* trousers; drawers.

παντέρ(η)μος *a.* lone, abandoned.

παντεσπάνι *s.n.* sponge-cake.

παντζάρι *s.n.* beetroot.

παντζούρι *s.n.* shutter.

παντιέρα *s.f.* banner, flag.

παντογνώστης *a.* omniscient.

παντοδύναμος *a.* omnipotent.

παντοειδ|ής *a.* of all kinds. ~ῶς *adv.* in every way.

παντοκράτωρ *s.m.* lord of all, Almighty.

παντομίμα *s.f.* dumb show.

παντοπώλ|ης *s.m.* grocer. ~εῖον *s.n.* grocer's.

πάντοτε *adv.* always.

παντοτινός *a.* eternal.

παντοῦ *adv.* everywhere.

παντόφλα *s.f.* slipper.

παντρειά *s.f.* marriage, wedlock.

παντρεύ|ομαι *v.t.* marry (*of priest, parent, sponsor*). ~ομαι *v.t. & i.* marry (*spouse*); get married.

παντρολογῶ *v.t.* seek a mate for.

πάντως *adv.* in any case, anyhow.

πάνω *adv. see* ἀπάνω.

πανωλεθρία *s.f.* heavy loss *or* destruction.

πανώλης *s.f.* plague.

πανώριος *a.* very beautiful.

πανωφόρι *s.n.* overcoat.

παξιμάδα *s.f.* (*fam.*) light woman.

παξιμάδι *s.n.* I. rusk. 2. nut (*for bolt*).

παπαγαλίζω *v.t.* repeat parrot-fashion.

παπαγάλος *s.m.* I. parrot. 2. spanner.

παπαδιά *s.f.* priest's wife.

παπαδίστικος *a.* priest's.

παπαδίτσα *s.f.* ladybird.

παπάκι *s.n.* duckling.

παπάρα *s.f.* panada, pap; (*fam.*) dressing-down.

παπαρούνα *s.f.* poppy.

πάπας *s.m.* pope.

παπᾶς *s.m.* priest; king (*cards*); (*fam.*) three-card trick.

παπατρέχας *s.m.* hasty person.

παπί *s.n.* young duck; γίνομαι ~ get soaking wet.

πάπια *s.f.* I. duck; κάνω τὴν ~ play dumb. 2. bedpan.

παπιγιόν *s.n.* bow-tie. [F. *papillon*]

παπικός *a.* papal.

πάπλωμα *s.n.* cotton quilt.

παπούτσ|ι *s.n.* shoe. ~ῆς *s.m.* shoemaker *or* -seller.

παππᾶς *s.m. see* παπᾶς.

πάππ|ος, ~οῦς *s.m.* grandfather.

πάπυρος *s.m.* papyrus.

παρά I. *conj.* than; but. 2. *prep.* (*with acc.*) near, beside; contrary to, despite; except, less; μία ~ τέταρτο a quarter to one; μέρα ~ μέρα every other day; παρ' ἀξίαν undeservedly; ~ τρίχα by a hairsbreadth; ~ λίγο (νά) nearly; παρ' ὅλο πού even though. (*with gen.*) from, on the part of; by. (*with dat.*) in, among, with, attached to.

πάρα *adv.* (*of intensity*) ~ πέρα farther off; ~ πολύς very *or* too much.

παρα- *denotes* near, beyond, contrary, excess, *etc.*

παραβαίνω *v.t.* break, infringe.

παραβάλλω *v.t.* compare.

παραβάν *s.n.* screen. [F. *paravent*]

παραβαρύνω *v.t. & t.* overload; be a burden to; become overweight, lose one's mobility.

παράβασις *s.f.* infringement.

παραβάτης *s.m.* contravener, transgressor.

παραβγαίνω *v.i. & t.* compete; (*with gen.*) rival.

παραβιάζομαι (-j-) *v.i.* be in too much of a hurry.

παραβιάζω (-i-) *v.t.* force (*entry, door, etc.*), break open; infringe.

παραβλέπω *v.t. & i.* neglect, overlook; turn a blind eye.

παραβολή *s.f.* comparison; parable; (*math.*) parabola.

παράβολον *s.n.* fee, deposit (*in elections, etc.*).

παραγάδι *s.n.* sort of fishing-net.

παραγγελία *s.f.* instruction, order; message; ἐπὶ ~a made to order. ~οδόχος *s.m.* (*commercial*) agent.

παραγγέλλω *v.t. & i.* order, prescribe; send word.

παράγγελμα *s.n.* (word of) command.

παραγεμίζω *v.t. & i.* overfill; become too full; (*cooking*) stuff.

παραγίνομαι *v.i.* become to excess; go too far; get overripe; ~ χοντρός grow too fat.

παραγιός *s.m.* apprentice, boy.

παράγκα *s.f.* wooden hut.

παραγκωνίζω *v.t.* elbow, thrust aside; ~ισμένος overlooked, left out of things (*at gathering*).

παραγνωρίζω *v.t. & i.* 1. know (*person*) very well. 2. fail to appreciate; mistake identity of; be mistaken (*as to identity*).

παραγραφή *s.f.* (*law*) lapse of right or penalty.

παράγραφος *s.m.* paragraph.

παράγω *v.t.* yield, produce. ~ομαι *v.i.* (*gram.*) be derived.

παραγωγή *s.f.* yield; production; (*gram.*) derivation. ~ικός *a.* productive. ~ός *s.m.* producer, grower.

παράγωγον *s.n.* derivative, by-product.

παράγων *s.m.* factor; leading figure.

παραδάκι *s.n.* (*fam.*) money.

παράδειγμα *s.n.* example; ~τος χάριν for example.

παραδειγματίζω *v.t.* make an example of (*punish*); warn by example. ~ομαι *v.i.* learn by experience; (*with ἀπό*) model oneself on.

παράδεισος *s.m.* paradise.

παραδεκτός *a.* accepted; acceptable, admissible.

παραδέρνω *v.i.* toss, struggle. ~δαρμένη *s.f.* (*fam.*) belly.

παραδέχομαι *v.t.* admit, acknowledge.

παραδίδω *v.t.* hand over; surrender; give (*lessons*), teach. ~ομαι *v.i.* surrender, give oneself up.

παραδοξολογία *s.f.* paradox (*figure of speech*).

παράδοξος *a.* strange, odd, paradoxical.

παραδόπιστος *a.* worshipping money.

παράδοσις *s.f.* handing over; surrender; teaching; tradition.

παραδοτέος *a.* due for delivery.

παραδουλεύτρα *s.f.* charwoman.

παραδρομή *s.f.* inadvertence.

παραείμαι *v.i.* be exceedingly *or* too much.

παραέχω *v.t.* have a great deal *or* too much of.

παραζάλη *s.f.* disorder, bustle.

παραθαλάσσιος *a.* by the sea.

παραθερίζω *v.i.* spend the summer. ~ιστής *s.m.* summer visitor.

παραθετικός *a.* comparative.

παραθέτω *v.t.* juxtapose; compare; cite, quote; serve, offer (*food, drink*).

παράθυρο, ~θύρι *s.n.* window.

παραθυρόφυλλο *s.n.* shutter.

παραίνεσις *s.f.* advice.

παραίσθησις *s.f.* hallucination.

παραίτησις *s.f.* (*act of*) resignation.

παραιτῶ *v.t.* give up, let go, forsake. ~οῦμαι *v.i. & t.* resign, abdicate; (*with gen.*) desist from.

παρακάθημαι *v.i.* attend (*as guest, etc.*).

παρακάθομαι *v.i.* stay too long; eavesdrop.

παράκαιρος *a.* at the wrong time.

παρακαλε(σ)τός *a.* whose favour has to be sought.

παρακάλια *s.n.pl.* entreaties.

παρακαλῶ *v.t.* ask, request (*someone*); ~! please, don't mention it.

παρακά(μ)νω *v.t.* overdo; ~ει κρύο it is very cold.

παρακάμπτω *v.t.* get round.

παρακαταθήκη *s.f.* deposit; stock; heritage.

παρακάτω *adv.* farther down. ~ιανός *a.* of inferior quality; low-class.

παρακεῖ *adv. see* παρέκει.

παρακείμενος *a.* adjacent; (*gram.*) ὁ ~ perfect tense.

παρακεντές *s.m.* (*fig.*) parasite.

παρακέντησις *s.f.* (*med.*) puncture, tapping.

παρακινῶ v.t. incite.

παρακλάδι s.n. branch, offshoot.

παράκλησις s.f. entreaty; (ritual) prayer.

παρακμή s.f. decline, decadence.

παρακοή s.f. disobedience.

παρακολουθῶ v.t. follow, keep up with; grasp meaning of.

παρακόρη s.f. adopted daughter; maid.

παρακούω v.t. & i. mishear; disobey.

παρακρατικός a. unofficial (but connived at by government).

παρακρατῶ v.t. & i. retain, hold back (produce); last too long.

παράκρουσις s.f. mental derangement.

παράκτιος a. coastal.

παραλαβή s.f. receipt (act of receiving).

παραλαμβάνω v.t. take delivery of; take over; take (partner, etc.).

παραλείπω v.t. omit.

παράλειψις s.f. omission.

παραλέω v.t. exaggerate.

παραλήγουσα s.f. penultimate syllable.

παραλήπτης s.m. recipient, addressee.

παραλήρημα s.n. delirium.

παραλί|α s.f. sea-shore, sea-front. ~ακός a. by the sea-shore.

παραλῆς a. (fam.) rich.

παραλλαγή s.f. variation, variant.

παράλληλος a. parallel.

παραλογιάζω v.t. & i. drive or become mad.

παραλογίζομαι v.i. talk nonsense.

παράλογος a. unreasonable.

παραλυσία s.f. profligacy; paralysis.

παράλυσις s.f. paralysis; shakiness.

παραλυτικός a. paralytic.

παράλυτος a. loose, shaky; paralysed; profligate.

παραλύ|ω v.t. & i. make loose or shaky; paralyse; become shaky or paralysed or profligate; ~μένος profligate.

παραμάννα s.f. 1. wet-nurse, nanny. 2. safety-pin.

παραμελῶ v.t. neglect.

παραμένω v.i. stay, remain, continue to be.

παράμερα adv. aside, out of the way.

παραμερίζω v.t. & i. thrust aside; ward off; put or get out of the way.

παραμικρός a. slightest.

παραμιλῶ v.i. talk too much; rave; talk in one's sleep.

παραμονεύω v.t. lie in wait for; spy on.

παραμονή s.f. sojourn; eve.

παραμορφώνω v.t. disfigure, distort.

παραμπαίν|ω v.i. go in too far or too often; μοῦ ~ει (fam.) he gets my goat.

παραμύθι s.n. fairy-tale.

παραμυθία s.f. consolation.

παρανόησις s.f. misinterpretation.

παράνομ|ος a. illegal, illicit. ~ία s.f. illegality; unlawful act. ~ῶ v.i. break the law.

παρανοῶ v.t. misinterpret.

παράνυμφος s.m.f. sponsor (at wedding).

παρανυχίδα s.f. agnail.

παραξενεύ|ω v.t. & i. seem strange to; become fussy. ~ομαι v.i. find it strange.

παράξενος a. strange, peculiar; fussy.

παραξηλώνω v.t. unstitch; (fam.) τὸ ~ overdo it.

παραπαίω v.i. stagger; (fig.) say or do first one thing then another.

παραπάν|ω adv. higher up; in addition; μὲ τὸ ~ω very much; ~ω ἀπό over, more than. ~ήσιος a. to spare, superfluous; excess (charge, etc.).

παραπατῶ v.i. take a false step, slip.

παραπείθω v.t. persuade (to wrong course); dissuade (from right course).

παραπέμπω v.t. refer; send on; (naut.) convoy.

παραπέρα adv. farther on.

παραπέτασμα s.n. curtain.

παραπετῶ v.t. cast aside, leave uncared for.

παραπέφτω v.i. get mislaid.

παράπηγμα s.n. wooden hut; ~τα (pl.) hutment.

παραπλανῶ v.t. lead astray; seduce.

παραπλεύρως adv. next door; at the side.

παραπλήσιος a. similar; neighbouring.

παραποιῶ v.t. counterfeit; falsify.

πάραπολυ adv. very much; too much.

παραπομπή s.f. reference (to book, etc.); referring (sending on).

παραπονετικός a. plaintive.

παραπονιάρ|ης a. complaining. ~ικος a. plaintive.

παράπον|ον s.n. complaint, grievance. ~ιέμαι v.i. complain.

παραπόρτι s.n. wicket-gate.

παραποτάμιος a. riparian.

παραπόταμος s.m. tributary (river).

παράρτωμα s.n. breach, infringement.

παράρτημα s.n. branch (of bank, etc.); annexe, supplement; special edition (of paper).

παρ|ᾶς s.m., ~ᾶδες (pl.) (fam.) money.

παράσημον s.n. decoration, order.

παράσιτ|ον s.n. parasite; ~α (pl.) atmospherics.

παράσιτος s.m. parasite (human).

παρασιωπῶ v.t. avoid mentioning.

παρασκευ|άζω v.t. prepare. ~ασμα s.n. preparation (substance).

παρασκευή s.f. 1. preparing. 2. Friday.

παρασκήνια s.n.pl. wings (theatre). ~κός a. behind-the-scenes.

παρασπονδῶ v.i. break an agreement.

παρασταίνω v.t. see **παριστάνω**.

παράστασ|ις s.f. representation, depiction; presence, bearing; performance (of play, etc.); (law) appearance; ~εις (pl.) representations.

παραστάτης s.m. 1. one who stands by you. 2. jamb.

παραστατικός a. graphic, vivid.

παραστέκ|ω, ~ομαι v.t. (with gen.) stand by; look after.

παράστημα s.n. presence, bearing.

παραστράτημα s.n. going astray (morally).

παρασύνθημα s.n. countersign.

παρασύρω v.t. sweep away (by force); run over; lead on (into error).

παράταιρος a. odd, not matching.

παράταξ|ις s.f. array, order, parade; μάχη ἐκ ~εως pitched battle; (political) party; (gram.) parataxis.

παράτασις s.f. prolongation, extension (in time); respite.

παρατάσσω v.t. range in line, set out.

παρατατικός s.m. (gram.) imperfect tense.

παρατείνω v.t. prolong.

παρατήρησις s.f. observation; remark; reproof.

παρατηρητ|ής s.m. observer. ~ικός a. observant; reproving. ~ικότης s.f. power of observation.

παρατηρῶ v.t. & i. observe, remark, notice; reprove.

παράτολμος a. rash.

παράτονος a. out of tune.

παρατραβῶ v.t. & i. drag out, prolong; last too long; (fig.) go too far.

παρατράγουδο s.n. (untoward) incident.

παρατρέχω v.t. & i. skip, omit; run a race; hasten hither and thither.

παρατσούκλι s.n. nickname.

παρατυγχάνω v.i. happen to be present.

παρατυπία s.f. breach of etiquette.

παρατῶ v.t. see **παραιτῶ**.

πάραυτα adv. at once.

παραφέρνω v.t. & i. bring too much; see a resemblance in; bear a resemblance.

παραφέρ|ω v.t. rouse to passion. ~ομαι v.i. be carried away.

παραφορά s.f. passion.

παραφορτών|ω v.t. overload. ~ομαι v.i. & t. become overloaded; pester.

παράφρασις s.f. paraphrase.

παράφρ|ων a. mad. ~ονῶ v.i. go mad. ~οσύνη s.f. madness.

παραφυάς s.f. sucker, shoot; scion.

παραφυλ|άττω, ~άω v.t. & i. lie in wait (for).

παραφωνία s.f. wrong or jarring note.

παραχαράκτης s.m. counterfeiter.

παραχειμάζω v.t. spend the winter.

παραχρήμα adv. at once.

παραχώνω v.t. bury, hide away; stuff (into).

παραχωρῶ v.t. grant, concede; relinquish.

παρδαλ|ός a. spotted; many-coloured, gaudy; ~ή γυναῖκα light woman.

παρέα s.f. company, party; κάνε μου ~ keep me company.

πάρεδρος s.m. (law) assessor.

παρειά s.f. cheek.

παρείσακτος a. an intruder.

παρεκβαίνω v.i. digress.

παρέκει adv. farther on.

παρεκκλήσι(ον) s.n. chapel.

παρεκκλίνω v.i. deviate.

παρεκτός prep. (with gen.) except.

παρεκτροπή s.f. deviation; moral aberration.

παρέλασις s.f. parade, march-past.

παρέλευσις s.f. lapse, passage (of time).

παρελθ|ών a. past; τὸ ~όν the past.

παρέλκει v.i. it is superfluous.

παρελκύω v.t. protract, draw out.

παρεμβαίνω v.i. intervene, step in.

παρεμβάλλω v.t. interpose.

παρέμβασις s.f. intervention.

παρεμπιπτόντως adv. incidentally.

παρεμφερής a. similar.

παρενέργεια s.f. side-effect.

παρεν|θέτω v.t. insert. ~θεσις s.f. insertion; parenthesis.

παρενοχλῶ v.t. harass, annoy.

παρεξηγ|ῶ v.t. misunderstand. ~ησις s.f. misunderstanding.

παρεπιδημῶ v.i. be staying temporarily (abroad).

παρεπόμενα s.n.pl. consequences.

πάρεργον s.n. side-line, parergon.

παρερμηνεία s.f. wrong interpretation.

παρέρχομαι v.i. & t. pass, go by (of time) ; come to an end ; pass over, skip.

παρεστ|ώς a. present; οἱ ~ῶτες those present.

παρευθύς adv. immediately.

παρευρίσκομαι v.i. be present.

παρεφθαρμένος a. debased, corrupt (linguistically).

παρέχω v.t. afford, provide ; occasion.

παρηγορ|ία s.f. consolation. ~ῶ v.t. console.

παρήκοος a. disobedient.

παρῆλιξ a. advanced in years.

παρθεναγωγεῖον s.n. girls' school.

παρθενι|α s.f. virginity. ~κός a. virginal; (fig.) maiden, first.

παρθένος s.f. & a. virgin.

Παρθενών s.m. Parthenon.

παρίας s.m. outcast.

παρίσταμαι v.i. be present.

παριστ|άνω, ~ῶ v.t. represent, depict; perform (role, play) ; pretend to be.

πάρκο s.n. park.

παρντόν int. excuse me! [F. pardon]

πάροδ|ος s.f. side-street; passing (of time, illness, etc.). ~ικός a. passing, transient.

παροικία s.f. (foreign) colony, quarter.

παροιμί|α s.f. proverb. ~ώδης a. proverbial.

παρομοιάζω v.t. & i. liken; mistake (for) ; resemble (with μέ).

παρόμ|οιος a. similar, of the sort. ~οίωσις s.f. simile.

παρονομασία s.f. pun ; nickname.

παρονομαστής s.m. (math.) denominator.

παροξύτονος a. accented on penultimate syllable.

παρόραμα s.n. oversight; erratum.

παροργίζω v.t. provoke, anger.

παρόρμησις s.f. instigation ; urge.

παροτρύνω v.t. incite, urge.

παρουσία s.f. presence, attendance; δευτέρα ~ second coming.

παρουσιάζ|ω v.t. present, produce. ~ομαι v.i. appear.

παρουσιάσιμος a. presentable.

παρουσιαστικόν s.n. (person's) appearance.

παροχή s.f. allocation, contribution, supplying.

παρρησία s.f. outspokenness.

πάρσιμο s.n. taking; trimming (reducing).

πάρτέρι s.n. flower-bed.

παρτίδα s.f. part (not whole) ; (completed) game (of cards, etc.).

παρτσαδιάζω v.t. cut up.

πάρτυ s.n. (social) party. [E. party]

παρυφή s.f. hem, selvage ; edge.

παρωδία s.f. parody.

παρ|ών a. present; τὸ ~όν the present.

παρωνυχίς s.f. agnail ; (fig.) trifling matter.

παρωπίς s.f. blinker.

πάρωρα adv. late at night.

παρωχημένος a. past.

πᾶς a. all, every; διὰ παντός for ever ; οἱ πάντες everybody.

πασαλεί|βω, ~φω v.t. smear, daub. ~βομαι v.i. become smeared ; get a smattering.

πασαμέντο s.n. skirting.

πασαπόρτι s.n. passport.

πασᾶς s.m. pasha.

πασατέμπο s.n. thing done to kill time. ~s s.m. roasted pumpkin seeds.

πασίγνωστος a. well-known.

πασιέντζα s.f. patience (cards).

πασπαλίζω v.t. cover, sprinkle (with powder, etc.).

πασπατεύω v.t. finger, feel, handle.

πάσσαλος s.m. stake, post.

πάσσ|ο s.n. step, pace; μὲ τὸ ~o unhurriedly; πάω ~o pass (at cards, etc.) ; κάνω ~a assume coquettish airs.

πάστα s.f. Italian paste; a pastry, cake ; (fig.) stuff, quality (of character).

παστέλι s.n. sweet of honey and sesame.

παστίτσιο s.n. baked macaroni.

παστός a. salted.

παστουρμᾶς s.m. highly seasoned cured meat.

πάστρ|α s.f. cleanness. ~εύω v.t. clean.

παστρικός a. clean; (iron.) dubious (character).

Πάσχ|α s.n. Easter. ~άζω v.i. & t. break a fast ; eat (as) one's first fruit, etc., of season.

πασχαλιά s.f. Easter; lilac.

πασχαλι|άτικος, ~νός a. of Easter.

πασχίζω v.i. try hard.

πάσχ|ω v.i. & t. suffer; ὁ ~ων the patient; ὁ παθών the victim.

πάταγ|ος s.m. bang, loud noise; (fig.) stir. ~ώδης a. noisy, resounding.

πατάρι s.n. loft.

πατάσσω v.t. punish severely, crush.

πατάτα s.f. potato.

πατατούκα s.f. thick rustic overcoat.

πατέρας *s.m.* father.

πατερίτσα *s.f.* pastoral staff; crutch.

πατηκώνω *v.t.* press down *or* in, squash; τήν ~ (*fam.*) gorge oneself.

πάτημα *s.n.* step, footstep; footprint; foothold; treading, pressing; pretext.

πατημασιά *s.f.* footprint.

πατήρ *s.m.* father.

πατινάδα *s.f.* serenade.

πατινάρω *v.i.* skate.

πατόκορφα *adv.* from top to toe.

πάτος *s.m.* bottom, base; sole, sock (*of shoe*).

πατούσα *s.f.* sole (*of foot*).

πατριάρχης *s.m.* patriarch.

πατρίδα *s.f.* native country *or* place.

πατρίκιος *a.* patrician.

πατρικός *a.* father's; fatherly.

πάτριος *a.* ancestral; native.

πατρίς *s.f. see* πατρίδα.

πατριώτ|ης *s.m.* fellow countryman; patriot. **~ικός** *a.* patriotic. **~ισμός** *s.m.* patriotism.

πατρογονικός *a.* paternal, ancestral.

πατρόν *s.n.* pattern (*dressmaking*). [F. *patron*]

πατροπαράδοτος *a.* traditional; hereditary.

πατρυιός *s.m.* stepfather.

πατσαβούρα *s.f.* dishcloth, rag; (*fig.*) rag (*newspaper*); slut.

πατσᾶς *s.m.* (soup from) tripe.

πάτσ|ι *adv.* (*fam.*) quits. **~ίζω** *v.i.* become quits.

πατσουρός *a.* flat-nosed.

πατ|ῶ *v.t. & i.* tread on; press (*bell, pen, etc.*); press down; raid; run over; (*v.i.*) tread, step, touch bottom; **~ῶ πόδι** set foot, put one's foot down; **~εῖς με ~ῶ σε** a crush *or* scrimmage.

πάτωμα *s.n.* floor, ground; story.

πατώνω *v.t. & i.* fix floor *or* bottom to; touch bottom.

παῦλα *s.f.* dash (*punctuation*).

παῦσ|ις *s.f.* cessation; dismissal; (*mus.*) rest; **~εις** (*pl.*) vacation.

παύω *v.t. & i.* stop, cease doing; cause to cease; dismiss; (*v.i.*) stop, leave off.

παφλασμός *s.m.* surging *or* swashing noise (*of waves*).

πάφυλας *s.m.* thin sheet of brass *or* tin.

παχαίνω *v.t. & i.* fatten; grow fat.

πάχνη *s.f.* hoar-frost.

παχνί *s.n.* manger.

πάχος *s.n.* thickness, fatness; fat.

παχουλός *a.* plump.

παχύδερμος *a.* thick-skinned; a pachyderm.

παχυλός *a.* gross, crass; fat (*salary*).

παχύνω *v.t. & i. see* παχαίνω.

παχ|ύς *a.* thick, fat; rich in fat; **~ιά λόγια** extravagant promises.

παχύσαρκος *a.* obese.

πά|ω *v.i. & t.* go; take (*convey*); **~ω γιά** stand *or* be candidate for; **~ει** it suits, it is fitting; **~ει αὐτό** it is past *or* done for *or* dead; **~ει νά πεῖ** it means; **~ει μεσημέρι** it is just on midday; **~ει καί ἔρχεται** it will do; **τά ~με καλά** we get on well; (*fam.*) **~ει περίπατο** it is a washout *or* done for *or* gone; **~ω νά σκάσω** I am nearly bursting.

πεδι|άς, **~άδα** *s.f.* plain.

πεδικλών|ω *v.t.* hobble; trip up. **~ομαι** *v.i.* stumble.

πέδιλον *s.n.* sandal.

πεδιν|ός *a.* of the plain; flat; (*mil.*) **~όν πυροβολικόν** field-artillery.

πεδίον *s.n.* plain; ground, field (*of battle, research, etc.*).

πεζῆ *adv.* on foot.

πεζικόν *s.n.* infantry.

πεζογραφία *s.f.* prose.

πεζοδρόμιον *s.n.* pavement.

πεζοναύτης *s.m.* (*mil.*) marine.

πεζοπορία *s.f.* walking.

πεζός *a.* on foot, pedestrian; in prose; (*fig.*) prosaic.

πεζούλι *s.n.* stone sill, parapet; low wall (*esp. as seat*); terrace (*on hillside*).

πεθαίνω *v.i. & t.* die; (*fam.*) be the death of, kill.

πεθαμός *s.m.* death; (*fig.*) purgatory.

πεθερ|ός *s.m.* father-in-law. **~ά** *s.f.* mother-in-law. **~ικά** *s.n.pl.* parents-in-law.

πειθαναγκάζω *v.t.* coerce.

πειθαρχ|ία *s.f.* discipline. **~ικός** *a.* disciplinary; obedient. **~ῶ** *v.i.* be obedient.

πειθήνιος *a.* docile.

πείθω *v.t.* persuade.

πειθώ *s.f.* persuasion.

πεῖνα *s.f.* hunger, starvation. **~λέος** *a.* starving.

πειν|ῶ *v.i.* be hungry *or* starving; **~ασμένος** hungry.

πεῖρα *s.f.* experience, practice.

πείραγμα *s.n.* annoying, teasing; affection (*malady*).

πειρ|άζω *v.t.* vex, annoy; tease; upset, be bad for; disturb, disarrange;

τεmpt; ~αγμένος hurt, offended, affected (in mind), tainted (of meat). (v.i.) ~άζει; does it matter?

πειρακτικός a. vexatious, wounding.

πείραμα s.n. experiment. ~τικός a. experimental.

πειρασμός s.m. temptation.

πειρατής s.m. pirate.

πεῖσμα s.n. obstinacy; στὸ ~ ὅλων in despite of everyone; τὸ βάζω ~ νά firmly resolve to.

πεισματάρης a. obstinate, obdurate.

πεισματώδης a. dogged, stubborn.

πεισματών|ω v.t. & i. make or become obstinately resolved. ~ομαι v.i. become obstinate.

πείσμων a. obstinate.

πειστήριον s.n. (material) proof.

πειστικός a. persuasive.

πεκούνια s.n.pl. (fam.) money.

πέλαγ|ος s.n. (open) sea. ~οδρομῶ v.i. sail the seas; (fig.) dither. ~ώνω v.i. (fig.) feel lost or swamped.

πελαργός s.m. stork.

πελάτ|ης s.m. customer, client, patient. ~εία s.f. clientele.

πελεκούδι s.n. chip, shaving.

πέλεκυς s.m. axe.

πελεκῶ v.t. cut into shape, carve (wood, stone); (fig.) beat, thrash.

πελιδνός a. livid.

πέλμα sole (of foot, shoe); sock (of shoe).

πελτές s.m. see μπελτές.

πελώριος a. huge.

πέμπτ|ος a. fifth; ~η (s.f.) Thursday.

πέμπω v.t. send.

πενήντα num. fifty.

πένης s.m. indigent person.

πενθερός s.m. see πεθερός.

πένθιμος a. sad, mournful; mourning, funeral.

πένθ|ος s.n. grief; mourning. ~ῶ v.i. mourn; be in mourning.

πενία s.f. indigence.

πενιχρός a. meagre, paltry, mean.

πέννα s.f. 1. pen. 2. plectrum. 3. penny.

πένομαι v.i. be indigent.

πένσα s.f. tweezers, forceps; dart (dressmaking).

πεντ- denotes fivefold, extremely.

πεντάγραμμον s.n. (mus.) stave.

πεντακόσιοι a. five hundred.

πεντάμορφος a. very beautiful.

πεντάρα s.f. (fig.) farthing.

πεντάρι s.n. figure 5; five (cards).

πέντε num. five; τὸν πῆγε ~ ~ (fam.) he got the wind up.

πεντήκοντα num. fifty.

Πεντηκοστή s.f. Whit Sunday.

πεντοζάλης s.m. a Cretan dance.

πέος s.n. penis.

πεπαιδευμένος a. educated.

πεπειραμένος a. experienced.

πεπεισμένος a. convinced, sure.

πέπλ|ος s.m., ~ον s.n. veil.

πεποίθησις s.f. conviction, confidence.

πεπόνι s.n. melon.

πεπρωμένον s.n. destiny.

πεπτικός a. digestive (organs).

πέρα adv. over, far, on the other side; ἐκεῖ ~ over there; ἐδῶ ~ over here; ~ (γιὰ) ~ through and through, completely; ~ ἀπό beyond, across; τὰ βγάζω ~ manage; ~ βρέχει (fam.) couldn't care less.

περαιτέρω adv. further.

πέραμα s.n. ford; ferry.

πέραν adv. & prep. over, on the other side; (with gen.) beyond, across.

πέρας s.n. end, term, conclusion.

πέραση s.f. ἔχω ~ be legal tender or valid; be influential or sought after; be frequented (of road, etc.).

πέρασμα s.n. crossing, passage; threading (of needle); passing (of time, illness); much frequented spot.

περασμέν|ος a. past; τὸ ~ο καλοκαίρι last summer.

περαστικ|ός a. passing by; transitory; frequented (road); ~ά may you get well!

περατώνω v.t. finish.

περβάζι s.n. door-frame, skirting, ledge.

περγαμηνή s.f. parchment.

πέρδ|ικα s.f., ~ίκι s.n. partridge; εἶμαι ~ίκι be quite well again.

περδικλώνω v.t. see πεδικλώνω.

πέρδομαι v.i. break wind.

περεχύνω v.t. pour liquid over, drench.

περήφαν|ος a. proud. ~εια s.f. pride. ~εύομαι v.i. grow proud.

περί prep. 1. (with gen.) about, concerning; ~ τίνος πρόκειται; what is in question? ἔχω ~ πολλοῦ think much of. 2. (with acc.) round, near; round about, approximately; (concerned) with.

περι- denotes 1. around. 2. very.

περιαρπάζω v.t. seize; (fam.) pour abuse on.

περιαυτολογῶ v.i. brag.

περιβάλλ|ω *v.t.* surround; clothe. **~ον** *s.n.* surroundings, environment; entourage.

περίβλημα *s.n.* covering, casing.

περιβόητος *a.* famous, notorious.

περιβολή *s.f.* attire, dress; *ἐν ἀδαμιαία* ~ in the nude.

περιβόλ|ι *s.n.* garden, orchard; (*fig.*) *εἶναι ~ι* he is an entertaining person. **~άρης** *s.m.* gardener.

περίβολος *s.m.* enclosed ground, yard; surrounding wall.

περιγελῶ *v.t.* mock, cheat.

περίγελως *s.m.* laughing-stock.

περιγιάλι *s.n.* sea-shore.

περιγράφ|ω *v.t.* describe. **~ή** *s.f.* description.

περιδεής *a.* fearful, alarmed.

περιδέραιον *s.n.* necklace.

περιδιαβάζω *v.i.* stroll.

περίδρομ|ος *s.m.* (*fam.*) *τρώγω τὸν ~ο* eat a bellyful.

περιεκτικός *a.* capacious; substantial (*food*); comprehensive and succinct (*speech*).

περιεργάζομαι *v.t.* scrutinize.

περιέργεια *s.f.* curiosity.

περίεργος *a.* curious, inquisitive, strange.

περιέρχομαι *v.t. & i.* travel through, make the round of; come, reach, be reduced (*to*).

περιέχ|ω *v.t.* contain. **~όμενον** *s.n.* content; import.

περιζήτητος *a.* sought-after.

περιηγητής *s.m.* tourist.

περιηγοῦμαι *v.t.* travel through, tour.

περιθάλπω *v.t.* tend, care for.

περίθαλψις *s.f.* care, relief, welfare work.

περιθώριον *s.n.* margin.

περικάλυμμα *s.n.* covering, casing.

περικεφαλαία *s.f.* helmet.

περικλείω *v.t.* enclose, contain.

περικοκλάδα *s.f.* convolvulus; climbing plant.

περικοπή *s.f.* cutting down, reduction; extract (*from book*).

περικόχλιον *s.n.* nut (*for screw*).

περικυκλώνω *v.t.* encircle.

περιλαίμιον *s.n.* (animal's) collar.

περιλάλητος *a.* famous, notorious.

περιλαμβάνω *v.t.* contain, hold; include.

περιληπτικός *a.* comprehensive; concise; (*gram.*) collective.

περίληψις *s.f.* summary, précis.

περίλυπος *a.* sorrowful.

περιμαζεύω *v.t.* pick up (*scattered objects*); harbour, rescue (*waif or stray*); curb, control.

περιμένω *v.i. & t.* wait; await, expect.

περίμετρος *s.m.* circumference, perimeter.

πέριξ *adv.& prep.* round; *τὰ* ~ environs; (*with gen.*) round.

περιοδεία *s.f.* visit, journey (*on business*).

περιοδικ|ός *a.* periodic. **~όν** *s.n.* magazine.

περίοδος *s.f.* period; season.

περίοικοι *s.m.pl.* *οἱ* ~ the neighbours.

περίοπτος *a.* conspicuous and admired.

περιορίζω *v.t.* confine, restrict; curb, control; reduce.

περιορισμός *s.m.* confinement, restriction; curbing; reduction.

περιουσία *s.f.* property, possessions; estate; wealth.

περιοχή *s.f.* region, area, district.

περιπαθής *a.* full of feeling *or* passion.

περιπαίζω *v.t.* mock; dupe.

περίπατ|ος *s.m.* walk, ride, drive, trip; *πάω ~ο* go for a walk *or* (*fam.*) be a washout *or* done for *or* gone.

περιπατῶ *v.i. & t. see* **περπατῶ**.

περιπέτει|α *s.f.* adventure, misadventure; **~ες** (*pl.*) vicissitudes. **~ώδης** *a.* adventurous (*life, times, etc.*); (*story*) of adventure.

περιπίπτω *v.i.* fall (*into hands, coma, etc.*).

περιπλαν|ῶ *v.t.* take *or* send (a long way) round. **~ῶμαι** *v.i.* wander, roam; lose one's way.

περιπλέκω *v.t.* entangle; complicate, make confused.

περιπλέον *adv.* over and above; *τὸ* ~ surplus.

περιπλέω *v.t.* sail round.

περιπλοκάδα *s.f. see* **περικοκλάδα**.

περίπλοκ|ος *a.* complicated. **~ή** *s.f.* complication.

περίπλους *s.m.* circumnavigation.

περιπόθητος *a.* much desired.

περιποίη|σις *s.f.* attention, looking after; **~σεις** (*pl.*) entertainment, hospitality. **~τικός** *a.* showing attentiveness.

περιποι|οῦμαι *v.t.* look after, tend; nurse; show attentiveness to; **~ημένος** well turned out; fine (*workmanship*).

περίπολος *s.f.* patrol.

περίπου *adv.* about, roughly.

περίπτερον *s.n.* pavilion, lodge, summerhouse, kiosk.

περίπτυξις s.f. embrace.

περίπτωσι|ς s.f. case, circumstance; ἐν πάση ~ει anyhow, in any case.

περισκελίς s.f. trousers (esp. of uniform); pants.

περίσκεψις s.f. circumspection.

περισπασμός s.m. distraction; worry.

περισπῶ v.t. distract (attention).

περισπωμένη s.f. (gram.) circumflex.

περίσσεια s.f. superabundance.

περίσσευμα s.n. surplus.

περισσεύ|ω v.i. be left over; δὲν μοῦ ~ει I have none to spare.

περίσσιος a. enough and to spare.

περισσ|ός a. ὡς ἐκ ~οῦ on top of everything else, into the bargain.

περισσότερ|ος a. more; ὁ ~ος most. ~ον adv. more.

περισταλτικός a. restrictive; (med.) peristaltic.

περίστασις s.f. situation, circumstance, occasion.

περιστατικόν s.n. event, happening.

περιστέλλω v.t. restrict, check, curb.

περιστέρ|ι s.n. pigeon, dove. ~εών(ας) s.m. dove-cot.

περιστοιχίζω v.t. surround.

περιστολή s.f. restriction, curbing.

περιστρέφ|ω v.t. rotate. ~ομαι v.i. rotate.

περιστροφ|ή s.f. rotation; (fig.) ~ές (pl.) beating about the bush.

περίστροφον s.n. revolver.

περισυλλέγω v.t. pick up (scattered objects); harbour, rescue (waif or stray).

περιτοιχίζω v.t. build a wall round.

περιτομή s.f. circumcision.

περιτριγυρίζω v.t. encircle; go round; prowl round; (fig.) court.

περίτρομος a. terrified.

περιτροπ|ή s.f. ἐκ ~ῆς by turns.

περιττός a. superfluous, needless; ~ ἀριθμός odd number.

περιτύλιγμα s.n. wrapping.

περιτυλίσσω v.t. wind (round); wrap up.

περιφέρει|α s.f. periphery, circumference; district; ἔχω ~ες be broad in the beam.

περιφέρ|ω v.t. carry round. ~ομαι v.i. wander about.

περίφημος a. famous; first-rate.

περιφορά s.f. (religious) procession.

περίφραγμα s.n. fence, hedge.

περιφραστικός a. periphrastic.

περιφρόνη|σις s.f. contempt. ~τικός a. contemptuous.

περίφροντις a. concerned, taken up (with).

περιφρονῶ v.t. despise, treat scornfully.

περίχωρα s.n.pl. environs.

περιώνυμος a. renowned, notorious.

περιωπ|ή s.f. high standing or quality; ἀπό ~ῆς with detachment.

περνῶ v.t. & i. 1. (v.t.) pass, go past or through, pierce; make pass through, thread; send or take through or across, cross; excel; go through, experience; spend (time); transfer; put down (on bill, etc.); put on (clothes); coat (with paint); ~ γιά mistake for. 2. (v.i.) pass, go past; go or get through or across; be valid or accepted; fare, get on; ~ ἀπό call at, go via; περᾶστε please come or go in!

περονιάζω v.t. pierce.

περονόσπορος s.m. mildew (on plants).

περούκα s.f. wig.

περπάτημα s.n. walking; gait.

περπατησιά s.f. gait.

περπατῶ v.i. & t. walk; traverse; take for a walk.

πέρ(υ)σι adv. last year. ~νός a. last year's.

πές imperative of λέγω.

πέσιμο s.n. fall, falling.

πεσκέσι s.n. gift (esp. victuals).

πεσκίρι s.n. towel.

πεσμένος a. fallen; impaired, deteriorated.

πέστροφα s.f. trout.

πέταγμα s.n. 1. flight. 2. throwing (away).

πετάγομαι passive of πετῶ.

πετάλι s.n. pedal.

πεταλίδα s.f. limpet.

πέταλ|ο s.n. 1. petal. 2. horseshoe; τινάζω τά ~α (fam.) kick the bucket.

πεταλούδα s.f. butterfly.

πεταλώνω v.t. shoe (horse).

πέταμα s.n. see πέταγμα.

πεταχτ|ός a. 1. protruding. 2. sprightly; στά ~ά on the wing, hurriedly.

πετειν|ός s.m. cock. ~άρι s.n. cockerel.

πετ(ι)μέζι s.n. syrup from must.

πετονιά s.f. fishing-line.

πετούμενο s.n. bird.

πέτρα s.f. (precious) stone; (fig.) ~ τοῦ σκανδάλου cause of the trouble or commotion.

πετράδι s.n. pebble; precious stone.

πετραχήλι s.n. (eccl.) stole.

πετρέλαι|ον s.n. oil, petroleum. ~οκίνητος a. oil-driven. ~οπηγή s.f. oil-well.

πετρελαιοφόρ|ος a. oil-producing. ~ον s.n. tanker.

πετριά s.f. blow with a stone; stone's throw; (fam.) hint; idée fixe.

πέτρινος a. stone.

πετροβολῶ v.t. stone (pelt).

πετρώνω v.t. & i. petrify.

πέτσα s.f. skin, crust; (fig.) shame.

πετσ|ένιος, ~ινος a. leather.

πετσέτα s.f. 1. napkin; towel; (fam.) στρώνω ~ gossip. 2. peseta.

πετσί s.n. skin, hide; leather.

πετσοκόβω v.t. cut to pieces; cut badly.

πέττο s.n. lapel.

πετυχαίνω v.t. & i. see ἐπιτυγχάνω.

πετ|ῶ 1. v.i. fly (off); jump (for joy); twitch (of eyelid). 2. v.t. throw (away); shed; ~ῶ ἔξω dismiss. 3. ~άγομαι, ~ιέμαι v.i. spring or fly up; slip or run (out, round, etc., on errand); butt in (verbally).

πεῦκο s.n. pine.

πέφτ|ω v.i. fall (down or off); drop; come off; fall to the lot of; fall (in date), occur; decline in force or health; ~ω στὸ κρεββάτι go to bed; ~ω στὴ θάλασσα go in for a bathe; ~ω ἔξω run aground, miscalculate; ~ω δίπλα make up (to); ~ω μὲ τὰ μοῦτρα σέ fall upon, take up avidly; δὲν σοῦ ~ει λόγος you have no say; ποῦ ~ει; whereabouts is it? ἔπεσε ξύλο blows were struck.

πεχλιβάνης s.m. wrestler, strong man.

πέψις s.f. digestion.

πῆγα aorist of πάω and πηγαίνω.

πηγάδι s.n. well.

πηγάζω v.i. spring, originate.

πηγαιμός s.m. going, way there.

πηγαιν(ο)έλα s.n. coming and going.

πηγαινοέρχομαι v.i. come and go.

πηγαίνω v.i. & t. go; take (convey). See πάω.

πηγαῖος a. spring (water); (fig.) springing naturally or effortlessly.

πηγή s.f. spring; source.

πηγούνι s.n. chin.

πηδάλι|ον s.n. rudder; helm; steering-wheel. ~οῦχος s.m. helmsman.

πήδημα s.n. jump, jumping.

πηδῶ v.i. & t. jump, leap, bounce; jump over; omit.

πήζω v.t. & i. curdle, thicken.

πηκτ- see πηχτ-.

πηλάλα s.f. running; (adv.) at a run.

πηλαλῶ v.i. run.

πηλήκιον s.n. cap (soldier's or schoolboy's).

πηλίκον s.n. (math.) quotient.

πήλινος a. clay, earthen.

πηλός s.m. clay; mud.

πηνίον s.n. spool, (electric) coil.

πῆξις s.f. curdling, congealing.

πῆρα aorist of παίρνω.

πηρούνι s.n. fork; (fam.) γερό ~ good trencherman.

πήττα s.f. sort of cake or pie.

πήχη s.f. measure of length (2 ft.).

πηχτή s.f. galantine.

πηχτός a. congealed; thick.

πήχτρα s.f. anything very dense.

πῆχυς s.m. 1. fore-arm. 2. see πήχη.

πῖ s.n. the letter Π. στὸ ~ καὶ φῖ in a trice.

πιά adv. (not) any longer; now, definitely, at last (often with nuance of impatience).

πιάνο s.n. piano.

πιάν|ω v.t. & i. (v.t.) 1. catch hold of. 2. catch (quarry); αὐτὸς δὲν ~εται he is not to be caught. 3. occupy, take possession of; ~ω σπίτι take (rent) a house; ~ω τόπο take up space or come in useful. 4. afflict, overtake; τὴν ἔπιασε τὸ κεφάλι της she has a headache; μᾶς ἔπιασε βροχή we got caught in the rain. 5. affect; μὲ ~ει ἡ θάλασσα I am a bad sailor. 6. begin; ~ω κουβέντα get into conversation; ~ω δουλειά start a (new) job. 7. consider, reckon; αὐτὸ δὲν ~εται that does not count. 8. gain, make, get; ~ω τὰ ἔξοδά μου recover one's outlay; ~ω νερό draw water; ~ω κρέας put on flesh. (v.i.) 9. put in, call (of ship). 10. germinate; take effect; stick; (fig.) catch on, come off (of seed, graft, label, play, joke, etc.). 11. burn, catch (of food, saucepan, firewood). 12. come on, break out (of rain, wind, cold, fire, etc.). 13. ~ομαι v.i. be caught or paralysed or busy (doing something else); quarrel. πιάσου ἐπάνω μου lean on me; πιάστηκε ἡ φωνή του he lost his voice; πιάστηκαν (στὰ χέρια) they came to blows; πιάστηκε (ἀπὸ λεφτά) he has made his pile.

πιάσιμο s.n. holding, catching; touch; taking root; thing to hold on by; stiffness, paralysis.

πιασμένος *a.* occupied, taken; paralysed.

πιατάκι *s.n.* small plate; saucer.

πιατέλλα *s.f.* large dish.

πιατικά *s.n.pl.* crockery.

πιάτο *s.n.* plate.

πιάτσα *s.f.* market (*abstract*); (*fam.*) taxi-rank.

πίδαξ *s.m.* jet of water, fountain.

πιέζω *v.t.* press, squeeze, compress; constrain.

πίεσις *s.f.* pressure; blood-pressure.

πιεστήριον *s.n.* press.

πιέτα *s.f.* pleat.

πιθαμή *s.f.* span (*of hand*).

πιθανολογία *s.f.* conjecture.

πιθαν|ός *a.* probable, likely. ~ότης *s.f.* likelihood.

πίθηκος *s.m.* ape.

πίθ|ος *s.m.*, ~άρι *s.n.* large earthen jar.

πίκα *s.f.* 1. pique, offence. 2. spade (*cards*).

πικάντικος *a.* piquant.

πίκρ|α, ~άδα *s.f.* bitterness.

πίκρ|α, ~ία *s.f.* grief, affliction.

πικραίν|ω *v.t. & i.* make *or* become bitter; (*v.t.*) grieve. ~ομαι *v.i.* be grieved.

πικροδάφνη *s.f.* oleander.

πικρ|ός *a.* bitter. ~ότης *s.f.* bitterness.

πικρόχολος *a.* atrabilious.

πιλατεύω *v.t.* torment.

πιλάφι *s.n.* pilaf (*rice dish*).

πίλος *s.m.* hat.

πιλότ|ος *s.m.* pilot. ~ίνα *s.f.* pilot-boat.

πινάκιον *s.n.* plate; roll, list.

πινακίς *s.f.* name-plate, number-plate.

πινακοθήκη *s.f.* picture-gallery.

πίν|αξ, ~ακας *s.m.* list, table; notice-board; blackboard; picture.

πινέζα *s.f.* drawing-pin.

πινέλο *s.n.* (*artist's*) paint-brush.

πίνω *v.t. & i.* drink; (*fam.*) smoke (*cigarette*).

πιό *adv.* more (*with noun, adj., or adv.*).

πιοτό *s.n.* drinking; drink (*esp. alcoholic*).

πίπα *s.f.* tobacco-pipe; cigarette-holder.

πιπεράτος *a.* peppery, sharp, biting.

πιπέρι *s.n.* pepper (*condiment*), peppercorn.

πιπεριά *s.f.* pepper (*vegetable*); pepper-tree.

πιπιλίζω *v.t.* suck.

πίπτω *v.i. see* πέφτω.

πισθάγκωνα *adv.* with hands tied behind one's back.

πισίνα *s.f.* swimming-pool.

πισινός *a.* back, rear; ὁ ~ backside.

πίσσα|α *s.f.* tar, pitch; ~ες (*pl.*) waste oil (*from ships*). ~ώνω *v.t.* tar.

πισσόχαρτο *s.n.* tarred felt.

πίστα *s.f.* ring, track, dance-floor.

πιστευτός *a.* believable.

πιστεύω *v.t. & i.* believe.

πίστις *s.f.* belief, faith, trust; fidelity; (*fin.*) credit; (*fam.*) μοῦ βγῆκε ἡ πίστη (ἀνάποδη) I had great difficulty.

πιστόλ|ι *s.n.* pistol. ~ιά *s.f.* pistol-shot.

πιστοποιητικόν *s.n.* certificate.

πιστοποιῶ *v.t.* certify.

πιστός *a.* faithful, true.

πιστ|ώνω *v.t.* (*fin.*) credit (with). ~ωσις *s.f.* credit. ~ωτής *s.m.* creditor.

πίσω *adv.* behind; back; again; τὸ ρολόϊ πάει ~ the clock loses *or* is slow; κάνω ~ move back; ~ ἀπό (*prep.*) behind; ~ μου behind me.

πίτ|ερο, ~ουρο *s.n.* bran.

πιτσιλάδα *s.f.* freckle.

πιτσιλιά *s.f.* splash (*of mud, etc.*).

πιτσιλ|ίζω, ~ῶ *v.t.* splash, sprinkle.

πιτσιρίκος *s.m.* (*fam.*) small boy.

πιτσούνι *s.n.* young pigeon.

πίττα *s.f. see* πήττα.

πιτυρίδα *s.f.* scurf.

πίτυρον *s.n.* bran.

πιωμένος *a.* drunk.

πλά(γ)ι *s.n.* side.

πλαγιά *s.f.* slope (*of hill*).

πλαγιάζω *v.i. & t.* lie down; put to bed; layer (*plant*).

πλαγιαστ|ός *a.* lying down. ~ά *adv.* (*leaning*) at an angle (*against*).

πλάγ|ιος *a.* oblique; indirect; underhand. ~ίως *adv.* obliquely; next door.

πλαδαρός *a.* flabby.

πλάζ *s.f.* bathing-beach. [F. *plage*]

πλάθω *v.t.* mould, shape, create.

πλάϊ *adv.* at the side, next door; ~ ~ side by side; ~ σέ (*prep.*) next to.

πλαϊνός *a.* adjoining.

πλαίσι|ον *s.n.* frame, framework; chassis. ~ώνω *v.t.* frame, surround.

πλάκα *s.f.* slab, paving-stone; plaque; (*scholar's*) slate; bar (*soap, etc.*); (*gramophone*) record; (*photographic*) plate; σπάσαμε ~ we had fun (*at someone's expense*); ἔχει ~ it makes you laugh.

πλακάκι *s.n.* tile (*on floor or wall*); (*fam.*) τά κάνω ~α hush it up.

πλακί *s.n.* (*fish, vegetables*) cooked with oil and garlic in shallow dish.

πλακόστρωτος *a.* paved, tiled.

πλακοῦς *s.m.* cake; (*med.*) placenta.

πλάκωμα *s.n.* pressing down; sudden arrival; (*feeling of*) oppressive weight.

πλακώνω *v.t. & i.* flatten, press down; run over; appear *or* happen suddenly; (*fam.*) turn up, blow in.

πλακωτός *a.* flat, flattened.

πλανεύω *v.t.* seduce.

πλάνη *s.f.* 1. error. 2. plane (*tool*).

πλανήτης *s.m.* planet.

πλανίζω *v.t.* plane.

πλανόδιος *a.* itinerant.

πλάνος *a.* alluring, deceitful.

πλαντ|άζω, ~ῶ *v.i.* burst, suffocate (*from anger, etc.*).

πλαν|ῶ *v.t.* mislead. ~ῶμαι *v.i.* wander; be mistaken.

πλάξ *s.f.* slab, paving-stone; plaque.

πλασιέ *s.m.* commercial traveller. [F. *placier*]

πλάσις *s.f.* moulding; creation.

πλάσμα *s.n.* (ravishing) creature; creation (*of imagination*).

πλάστης *s.m.* 1. creator. 2. rolling-pin.

πλάστιγξ *s.f.* weighing-machine.

πλαστικός *a.* plastic; shapely.

πλαστογραφῶ *v.t.* forge; falsify.

πλαστός *a.* false, forged, fictitious.

πλαταγίζω *v.t. & i.* smack (*lips*); flap (*of flag*); lap (*of water*).

πλατ|αίνω, ~ύνω *v.t. & i.* make *or* become wider.

πλάτ|ανος *s.m.*, ~άνι *s.n.* plane-tree.

πλατεία *s.f.* square (*of town*); pit (*of theatre*).

πλάτ|η *s.f.* back; (*fam.*) κάνω ~ες give clandestine aid; ἔχω ~ες have friends at court.

πλατιά *adv.* widely.

πλάτος *s.n.* width, breadth; latitude.

πλάττω *v.t.* mould, create, fashion.

πλατύς *a.* wide, broad.

πλατύσκαλο *s.n.* landing (*of staircase*).

πλάτωμα *s.n.* level spot (*in hills*).

πλέγμα *s.n.* anything of woven or plaited structure.

πλειοδοτῶ *v.i.* make highest bid.

πλεῖον *adv.* more.

πλειονότης *s.f.* majority.

πλειο(νο)ψηφία *s.f.* majority of votes.

πλειστηριασμός *s.m.* auction.

πλεῖστ|ος *a.* most, very much; ὡς ἐπὶ τὸ ~ον for the most part.

πλεκτάνη *s.f.* intrigue.

πλεκτός *a.* knitted, plaited, of wicker.

πλέκω 1. *v.t.* plait, knit. 2. *v.i.* swim.

πλεμόνι *s.n.* lung; lights.

πλένω *v.t.* wash.

πλεξ|ίδα, ~ούδα *s.f.* plait, braid.

πλέξιμο *s.n.* knitting; braiding.

πλέον *adv.* more; ἐπὶ ~ in addition; (*not*) any longer; now, definitely, at last (*often with nuance of impatience*).

πλεονάζω *v.i.* be abundant; be found in greater number.

πλεόνασμα *s.n.* surplus.

πλεονέκτημα *s.n.* advantage, good point, merit.

πλεονέκτης *a.* greedy, grasping.

πλεονεκτικός *a.* 1. advantageous. 2. grasping.

πλεονεκτῶ *v.t.* (*with gen.*) be superior to.

πλεονεξία *s.f.* cupidity.

πλεούμενο *s.n.* ship.

πλερ- *see* πληρ-.

πλέριος *a.* full.

πλευρά *s.f.* side; rib.

πλευρίζω *v.i. & t.* (*naut.*) come alongside; (*fig.*) accost.

πλευρῖτις *s.f.* pleurisy.

πλευροκοπῶ *v.t. & i.* make flanking attack (on).

πλευρόν *s.n.* side; rib.

πλεχτό *s.n.* pullover; piece of knitting.

πλέω *v.i.* sail; float; ~ στὸν πλοῦτον be rolling in money.

πληβεῖος *a.* plebeian.

πληγή *s.f.* wound, sore; ʹ(*fig.*) plague, affliction.

πλήγμα *s.n.* blow.

πληγώνω *v.t.* wound; hurt, offend.

πληθ|αίνω, ~ύνω *v.i. & t.* (*v.i.*) multiply; (*v.t.*) augment.

πλήθ|ος *s.n.* crowd; τὰ ~η the masses.

πληθυντικός *s.m.* (*gram.*) plural.

πληθυσμός *s.m.* population.

πληθώρ|α *s.f.* abundance; (*med.*) plethora. ~ισμός *s.m.* (*fin.*) inflation.

πληκτικός *a.* boring, dull, gloomy.

πλῆκτρον *s.n.* key (*of piano, typewriter*); plectrum; drumstick.

πλημμελειοδικεῖον *s.n.* (*law*) criminal court (*intermediate*).

πλημμέλημα *s.n.* (*law*) criminal offence (*of medium gravity*).

πλημμελής *a.* faulty, badly done.

πλημμύρα *s.f.* flood.

πλημμυρ|ίζω, ~ῶ *v.i. & t.* be in flood, overflow; be flooded; (*v.t.*) flood.

πλήν 1. *prep.* (*with gen.*) except, apart

from; ~ τούτου besides. 2. *conj.* but. 3. (*math.*) minus.

πλῆξις *s.f.* boredom.

πληρεξούσιον *s.n.* (*law*) warrant of attorney.

πληρεξούσιος *s.m.f.* plenipotentiary; representative, proxy.

πλήρης *a.* full; complete.

πληροφορ|ία *s.f.* piece of information; ~ίες (*pl.*) information.

πληροφορ|ῶ *v.t.* inform. ~οῦμαι *v.i.* learn, find out.

πληρῶ *v.t.* fill; fulfil.

πλήρωμα *s.n.* crew; ~ τοῦ χρόνου fullness of time.

πληρωμή *s.f.* payment, reward.

πληρώ|νω *v.t.* pay (for); ~νω τὰ σπασμένα pay for others' misdeeds; ~μένος paid, suborned.

πληρωτέος *a.* payable.

πληρωτής *s.m.* payer.

πλησιάζω *v.t. & i.* put *or* bring near, approach, draw near.

πλησιέστερος *a.* nearer; ὁ ~ nearest.

πλησίον *adv. & prep.* near; ~ μου near me; ὁ ~ μου my neighbour; τὸ ~ σχολεῖον the neighbouring school.

πλησίστιος *a.* with all sails set.

πλησμονή *s.f.* abundance, satiety.

πλήττω *v.t. & i.* strike, wound, afflict; be bored.

πλιά *adv. see* πιά.

πλιάτσικο *s.n.* loot; looting.

πλίθ(ρ)α *s.f.* mud-brick; (*fig.*) stodgy food.

πλινθόκτιστος *a.* built o f mud-bricks.

πλίνθος *s.f.* brick.

πλισσές *s.m.* pleating.

πλοηγός *s.m.* pilot.

πλοιάριον *s.n.* small craft.

πλοίαρχος *s.m.* (*naut.*) captain.

πλοῖον *s.n.* ship.

πλόκαμος *s.m.* tress, lock, plait; tentacle.

πλοκή *s.f.* plot (*of book, play*).

πλουμ|ί, ~ίδι *s.n.* design, ornamentation.

πλοῦς *s.m.* voyage, passage.

πλουσιοπάροχος *a.* lavish.

πλούσιος *a.* rich; sumptuous.

πλουταίνω *v.i.* grow rich.

πλουτίζω *v.t. & i.* enrich; grow rich.

πλοῦτ|ος *s.m. & n.* wealth; richness; τὰ ~η riches.

πλυντήριον *s.n.* laundry (-room); washing-machine.

πλύνω *v.t.* wash.

πλύσ|ις *s.f.*, ~ιμο *s.n.* (*act of*) washing.

πλυσταριό *s.n.* laundry-room.

πλύστρα *s.f.* washerwoman; washboard.

πλώρη *s.f.* prow.

πλωτάρχης *s.m.* (*naut.*) lieutenant-commander.

πλωτός *a.* navigable; floating.

πνεῦμα *s.n.* breath of life, ghost; Ἅγιον ~ Holy Ghost; spirit; mind; genius; wit; (*gram.*) breathing.

πνευματικός 1. *a.* spiritual; mental; pneumatic. 2. *s.m.* confessor.

πνευματισμός *s.m.* spiritualism.

πνευματώδης *a.* witty; spirituous.

πνευμονία *s.f.* pneumonia.

πνεύμων *s.m.* lung.

πνευστός *a.* wind (*instrument*).

πνέω *v.i. & t.* blow; ~ τὰ λοίσθια breathe one's last.

πνιγηρός, *a.* suffocating.

πνιγμός *s.m.* drowning; choking.

πνίγω *v.t.* drown; suffocate; choke, strangle.

πνικτικός *a.* suffocating.

πνίξιμο *s.n.* drowning; choking.

πνοή *s.f.* breath, breathing; inspiration.

ποδάγρα *s.f.* gout.

ποδάρι *s.n.* foot, leg.

ποδαρικό *s.n.* κάνω καλὸ ~ bring good luck.

ποδηγετῶ *v.t.* guide.

ποδήλατον *s.n.* bicycle.

ποδήρης *a.* (*dress*) reaching to the feet.

πόδι *s.n.* foot, leg; στὸ ~ standing up *or* on the go; μὲ τὰ ~α on foot; σηκώνω στὸ ~ cause a commotion among; ἔμεινα στὸ ~ του I am acting *or* I acted for him.

ποδιά *s.f.* apron, overall; sill; slope (*of hill*).

ποδίζω *v.i.* (*naut.*) tack; lie up (*in storm*).

ποδοβολητό *s.n.* tramp, thud, clatter (*of feet*).

ποδόγυρος *s.m.* hem; (*fig.*) (*fam.*) skirts, women.

ποδοκρότημα *s.n.* stamping of feet.

ποδοπατῶ *v.t.* stamp *or* trample on.

ποδόσφαιρα *s.f.* a football.

ποδόσφαιρον *s.n.* (*game of*) football.

πόζα *s.f.* pose; κρατῶ ~ be stand-offish.

πόθεν *adv.* whence; τὸ ~ ἔσχες source of one's wealth.

πόθ|ος *s.m.* desire, longing. ~ῶ *v.t.* desire, long for.

ποίημα *s.n.* poem.

ποίησις *s.f.* poetry.

ποιητής *s.m.* poet; maker.

ποιητικός *a.* poetic.

ποικιλία *s.f.* variety, diversity.

ποικίλλω *v.t. & i.* adorn; vary.

ποικίλος *a.* various, variegated, miscellaneous.

ποιμενικός *a.* shepherd's; pastoral.

ποιμήν *s.m.* shepherd; pastor.

ποίμνιον *s.n.* flock, herd.

ποιν|ή *s.f.* penalty, punishment. ~ικός *a.* penal.

ποιόν *s.n.* quality, character.

ποῖ|ος, ~ός *pron. & a.* who? which?

ποιότης *s.f.* quality.

ποι|ῶ *v.t.* make; do; περὶ πολλοῦ ~οῦμαι cherish, value.

πολεμικ|ός *a.* of *or* for war; warlike, aggressive. ~όν *s.n.* (*naut.*) warship.

πολέμιος *a.* hostile; an enemy.

πολεμιστής *s.m.* fighter, warrior.

πόλεμ|ος *s.m.* war. ~οφόδια *s.n.pl.* munitions.

πολεμῶ *v.t. & i.* fight (against), strive.

πολεοδομία *s.f.* town-planning.

πολικός *a.* polar.

πολιορκ|ία *s.f.* siege. ~ῶ *v.t.* besiege.

πόλις *s.f.* city, town.

πολιτεία *s.f.* state; country; town; attitude, line (*of conduct*); (*fam.*) βίος καί ~ chequered career.

πολίτευμα *s.n.* form of government.

πολιτεύομαι *v.i.* go in for politics; handle a situation.

πολιτευ|όμενος, ~τής *s.m.* one who mixes in politics, politician.

πολίτης *s.m.* citizen; civilian.

Πολίτης *s.m.* a Constantinopolitan.

πολιτική *s.f.* politics; policy.

πολιτικ|ός *a.* civil, civilian; political; a politician; τὰ ~ά politics; ~ὸς ἀνήρ statesman; μὲ ~ά in civilian clothes; ~ὸς στίχος 15-syllable verse.

πολιτισμένος *a.* civilized.

πολιτισμός *s.m.* civilization.

πολιτογραφῶ *v.t.* naturalize (*as citizen*).

πολιτοφυλακή *s.f.* militia.

πολίχνη *s.f.* large village.

πολλάκις *adv.* many times.

πολλαπλασιάζω *v.t.* multiply; increase.

πολλαπλασιασμός *s.m.* multiplication.

πολλαπλάσιον *s.n.* multiple.

πολλοί *a. pl.* many.

πόλος *s.m.* pole.

πολτός *s.m.* pap; purée; pulp.

πολύ *adv.* much; very; long; *see* πολύς.

πολυ- *denotes* much, very.

πολυάριθμος *a.* numerous.

πολυάσχολος *a.* very busy.

πολυβόλον *s.n.* machine-gun.

πολυγαμία *s.f.* polygamy.

πολύγλωσσος *a.* polyglot.

πολυέλαιος *s.m.* chandelier.

πολυετής *a.* lasting many years.

πολυθρόνα *s.f.* arm-chair.

πολυκαιρία *s.f.* lapse of time, age.

πολυκατοικία *s.f.* block of flats.

πολυκλινική *s.f.* polyclinic.

πολυκοσμία *s.f.* crowds of people.

πολύκροτον *s.n.* revolver.

πολύκροτος *a.* causing a stir.

πολυκύμαντος *a.* stormy.

πολυλογᾶς *s.m.* chatterbox.

πολυλογία *s.f.* loquacity.

πολυμάθεια *s.f.* learning, erudition.

πολυμελής *a.* with many members.

πολυμερής *a.* many-sided.

πολυμήχανος *a.* ingenious; wily.

πολύνω *v.t. & i.* increase.

πολύξερος *a.* knowledgeable, a mine of information.

πολυπαθής *a.* who has suffered much.

πολύπειρος *a.* very experienced.

πολυπληθής *a.* numerous, crowded.

πολύπλοκος *a.* involved, complicated.

πολύπους *s.m.* octopus; (*med.*) polypus.

πολυπράγμων *a.* interfering, nosey.

πολ|ύς *a.* much, many, great; long (*time*); τὸ ~ύ (~ύ) at the most; πρὸ ~λοῦ long since; ὁ ~ὺς κόσμος most people.

πολύσαρκος *a.* corpulent.

πολυσήμαντος *a.* with different meanings; of great significance.

πολυτέλ|εια *s.f.* luxury. ~ής *a.* luxurious.

πολυτεχνεῖον *s.n.* Polytechnic.

πολύτιμος *a.* valuable, precious.

πολυφαγία *s.f.* gluttony.

πολύφερνος *a.* well-dowered.

πολύφωτον *s.n.* chandelier.

πολυχρονίζω *v.i. & t.* take a long time (over); enjoy a long life; grant *or* wish long life to.

πολύχρωμος *a.* many-coloured.

πολύωρος *a.* long, prolonged.

πόμολο *s.n.* door-knob.

πομπή *s.f.* procession; shame, disgrace.

πομπός *s.m.* transmitter.

πομπώδης *a.* pompous.

πονεμένος *a. see* πονῶ.

πονέντ|ες, ~ης *s.m.* west wind.

πονετικός *a.* sharing sorrows of others.

πονηρεύ|ω *v.t. & i.* make suspicious; become wily. ~ομαι *v.i.* become suspicious.

πονηρ|ία *s.f.* cunning. ~ός *a.* cunning, knowing.

πονόδοντος *s.m.* toothache; (*fam.*) heartache, crush.

πονοκεφαλιάζω *v.t. & i.* weary, distract; rack one's brains.

πονοκέφαλος *s.m.* headache.

πονόλαιμος *s.m.* sore throat.

πόνος *s.m.* pain, ache; compassion.

πονόψυχος *a.* compassionate.

ποντάρω *v.i.& t.* punt (*bet*); back (*horse, etc.*).

ποντίκ|ι *s.n.*, ~ός *s.m.* 1. mouse, rat. 2. muscle.

ποντοπόρος *s.m.* voyager.

πόντ|ος *s.m.* 1. sea. 2. centimetre. 3. point (*in game*). 4. stitch; μούφυγαν ~οι my stocking is laddered *or* I dropped some stitches. 5. ρίχνω ~ο drop a hint.

πον|ῶ *v.i. & t.* feel pain, hurt; (*v.t.*) hurt; be attached to, care for; feel for; δὲν ~άει τὴν τσέπη του he does not spare his purse. ~εμένος *a.* in distress; bad (*injured or ailing*).

ποπός *s.m.* (*fam.*) bottom.

πορδή *s.f.* (*fam.*) fart.

πορεία *s.f.* march; course.

πορεύομαι *v.i.* go, proceed; manage, make do.

πορθμεῖον *s.n.* ferry.

πορθμός *s.m.* strait.

πορθῶ *v.t.* sack, pillage.

πορίζομαι *v.t.* furnish oneself with, get, draw.

πόρισμα *s.n.* inference, conclusion; finding; corollary.

πόρν|η *s.f.* prostitute. ~εῖον *s.n.* brothel.

πόρ|ος *s.m.* 1. ford. 2. pore. 3. ~οι (*pl.*) means, resources.

πόρπη *s.f.* buckle, clasp.

πόρρω *adv.* far.

πορσελάνη *s.f.* china.

πόρτα *s.f.* door, gate.

πορτοκάλ|ι *s.n.* orange. ~άδα *s.f.* orangeade. ~ής *a.* orange-coloured. ~ιά *s.f.* orange-tree.

πορτοφόλ|ι *s.n.* wallet. ~ᾶς *s.m.* pickpocket.

πορτραῖτο *s.n.* portrait.

πορφύρα *s.f.* purple.

πορώδης *a.* porous.

ποσάκις *adv.* how many times.

πόσιμ|ος *a.* fit for drinking; ~ο νερό drinking-water.

ποσόν *s.n.* amount, sum.

πόσο(ν) *adv.* how (much).

πόσος *pron. & a.* how much, how many.

ποσοστόν *s.n.* percentage.

ποσότης *s.f.* quantity.

πόστα *s.f.* post (*mail*); (*fam.*) τόν ἔβαλα ~ I scolded him.

πόστο *s.n.* strategic position; eligible post.

ποσῶς *adv.* (*after neg.*) not at all.

ποταμηδόν *adv.* in torrents.

ποτάμ|ι *s.n.*, ~ός *s.m.* river.

ποταπός *a.* base, dishonourable.

πότε *adv.* when? ~ ~ now and then; ~ ... ~ sometimes ... sometimes.

ποτέ *adv.* once, formerly; ever; (*after neg.*) never.

ποτήρ|ι(ον) *s.n.* a glass; γερὸ ~ι one who likes his liquor.

πότης *s.m.* tippler.

ποτίζω *v.t. & i.* water, give drink to; become damp (*of wall, etc.*).

πότισμα *s.n.* watering.

ποτιστήρι *s.n.* watering-can.

ποτόν *s.n.* drink, beverage.

πότος *s.m.* (heavy) drinking.

ποῦ *adv.* where? γιὰ ~ where are you off to? ~ νὰ ξέρω how should I know? ~ καὶ ~ occasionally.

πού 1. *pron.* who, whom, which, that; when. 2. *conj.* that.

πουγγί *s.n.* purse.

πούδρα *s.f.* powder (*medicinal, cosmetic*).

πουθενά *adv.* anywhere; nowhere.

πουκάμισο *s.n.* shirt; slough (*of snake*).

πουλάδα *s.f.* pullet.

πουλάκι *s.n.* little bird; ~ μου term of endearment.

πουλάρι *s.n.* foal.

πουλερικά *s.n.pl.* poultry.

πούλημα *s.n.* sale.

πουλί *s.n.* bird.

Πούλια *s.f.* Pleiades.

πούλμαν *s.n.* motor-coach. [E. *Pullman*]

πουλῶ *v.t.* sell.

πούντα *s.f.* 1. (-nd-) chill, cold. 2. (-nt-) point (*of promontory*).

πουντιάζω *v.i. & t.* catch a severe cold; (cause to) feel very cold.

πούπουλο *s.n.* down (*plumage*).

πουρές *s.m.* purée.

πουρί *s.n.* porous stone; scale, fur, tartar.

πουρμπουάρ *s.n.* tip. [F. *pourboire*]

πουρνάρι *s.n.* evergreen oak.

πουρνό *s.n.* morning.

πούρο *s.n.* cigar.

πούς *s.m.* foot, leg.

πούσι *s.n.* mist.

πούστης *s.m.* (*fam.*) sodomite.

πουτάνα *s.f.* (*fam.*) whore.

πουτίγγα *s.f.* pudding.

πρᾶγμα *s.n.* thing; matter, affair; merchandise, material (*cloth*); ~τι in fact, indeed.

πραγματεία *s.f.* treatise.

πραγματεύομαι *v.t.* treat of, deal with (*topic*).

πραγματικ|ός *a.* real, actual. ~ότης *s.f.* reality.

πραγματογνώμων *s.m.* valuer, assessor.

πραγματοποιῶ *v.t.* realize, carry out.

πρακτέον *s.n.* what must be done.

πρακτικ|όν *s.n.* written report; ~ά (*pl.*) minutes, proceedings.

πρακτικός *a.* practical; without professional training, quack.

πράκτ|ωρ *s.m.* agent. ~ορεῖον *s.n.* agency.

πρᾶμα *s.n. see* πρᾶγμα.

πραμάτεια *s.f.* merchandise.

πραματευτής *s.m.* pedlar.

πραξικόπημα *s.n.* coup d'état.

πρᾶξ|ις *s.f.* deed, act; practical experience; θέτω εἰς ~ιν put into practice; ἐν τῇ ~ει in practice; registration (*of births, etc.*); (*fin.*) transaction; (*math.*) operation.

πρᾶος *a.* mild, gentle.

πρασιά *s.f.* margin of garden round house.

πρασινάδα *s.f.* green colour; greenery.

πράσιν|ος *a.* green; (*fam.*) ~α ἄλογα nonsense.

πράσο|ο *s.n.* leek; (*fam.*) πιάνω στά ~α catch red-handed.

πρατήριον *s.n.* shop selling single commodity or supplying members of association; ~ βενζίνης petrol-station.

πράττω *v.t. & i.* do; act.

πραΰνω *v.t.* calm, soothe.

πρέζα *s.f.* pinch (*of salt, etc.*).

πρεμούρα *s.f.* anxious eagerness.

πρέπει *v.i.* it is necessary *or* fitting; ~ νὰ πάω I must go; καθὼς ~ respectable, decent, of good manners *or* appearance.

πρέπ|ων *a.* right, fitting, seemly. ~όντως *adv.* properly, suitably.

πρεσβεία *s.f.* embassy, legation.

πρεσβεύω *v.t.* profess, believe in.

πρέσβ|υς, ~ευτής *s.m.* ambassador, minister.

πρεσβύτερος *a.* elder.

πρεσβυωπία *s.f.* (*med.*) long-sightedness.

πρέφα *s.f.* a card game; τὸ πῆρε ~ he got wind of it.

πρήξ|ω *v.t.* (*fig.*) exasperate. ~ομαι *v.i.* become swollen.

πρηνής *a.* (*lying*) prone.

πρήξιμο *s.n.* swelling; (*fig.*) exasperation.

πρήσκω *v.t. see* πρήξω.

πρίγκ|ηψ, ~ιπας *s.m.* prince.

πρίζα *s.f.* (*electric*) plug, socket.

πρίν *adv. & prep.* before; ~ ἀπὸ μένα before me; ~ (ἀπὸ) ἕνα μῆνα a month ago; ~ τοῦ πολέμου *or* ~ τὸν πόλεμο before the war.

πρῖν|ος *s.m.*, ~άρι *s.n.* evergreen oak.

πριόν|ι *s.n.* saw. ~ίζω *v.t.* saw.

πρίσμα *s.n.* prism.

πριχοῦ *adv.* before.

πρό *prep.* (*with gen.*) before, in front of; ~ ἡμερῶν some days ago *or* before; ~ παντός *or* ~ πάντων above all, especially.

προ- *denotes* before.

προάγ|ω *v.t.* advance, promote. ~ωγή *s.f.* advancement, promotion. ~ωγός *s.m.* pimp.

προαίρεσ|ις *s.f.* intent; κατὰ ~ιν optionally.

προαιρετικός *a.* optional; voluntary.

προαίσθη|μα *s.n.*, ~σις *s.f.* presentiment.

προαιώνιος *a.* age-long; belonging to the dim past.

προαλείφομαι *v.i.* prepare the ground (*for self-advancement*).

προάλλες *a.* τὶς ~ the other day.

προανάκρουσμα *s.n.* prelude.

προαναφερθείς *a.* afore-mentioned.

προασπίζω *v.t.* shield, protect.

προάστ(ε)ιον *s.n.* suburb.

προαύλιον *s.n.* forecourt.

πρόβα *s.f.* fitting (*of clothes*); trying out, rehearsal.

προβάδισμα *s.n.* precedence.

προβαίνω v.i. advance, proceed; ~ εἰς do, make, carry out.

προβάλλω v.t. & i. project, extend; cast (shadow); show (film); offer (resistance); raise (objection); put forward (alibi); (v.i.) appear, come into sight.

προβάρω v.t. try on (clothes).

προβατίνα s.f. ewe.

πρόβατον s.n. sheep.

προβιβάζω v.t. promote (in rank).

προβιά s.f. sheep's or other animal's skin.

πρόβιος a. sheep's.

προβλέπω v.t. foresee, anticipate; make provision for.

πρόβλημα s.n. problem.

προβλής s.f. jetty.

προβολεύς s.m. searchlight, headlight; (cinema) projector.

προβολή s.f. projection, etc. (see προβάλλω).

προβοσκίς s.f. trunk, proboscis.

προγάστωρ a. with protuberant belly.

προγενέστερ|ος a. of an earlier time; (pl.) ~οι predecessors.

πρόγευμα s.n. breakfast.

προγεφύρωμα s.n. bridgehead.

πρόγκα s.f. noisy disapproval.

προγκ|άω, ~ίζω v.t. & i. drive (animals) with cries; (fig.) shout down, repulse rudely; (v.i.) shy, start.

προγνωστικόν s.n. forecast, tip.

πρόγονος s.m. ancestor.

προγονός s.m. stepson.

πρόγραμμα s.n. programme.

προγράφ|ω v.t. proscribe. ~ή s.f. proscription.

προγυμνάζω v.t. train; coach (pupil).

πρόδηλος a. obvious, evident.

προδιαγράφω v.t. prearrange.

προδιάθεσις s.f. predisposition.

προδιαθέτω v.t. predispose, influence, prepare.

προδίδω v.t. betray; disclose, give away.

προδοσία s.f. betrayal; treason.

προδότης s.m. betrayer; traitor.

πρόδρομος s.m. forerunner, harbinger; (epithet of John the Baptist).

προεδρ(ε)ία s.f. presidency, chairmanship.

προεδρεῖον s.n. president and his staff.

πρόεδρος s.m.f. president, chairman.

προειδοποι|ῶ v.t. notify in advance; warn. ~ησις s.f. warning.

προεισαγωγή s.f. introduction, preface.

προεκλογικός a. pre-election.

προέκτασις s.f. extension, prolongation (in space).

προέλασις s.f. (mil.) advance.

προσλαύνω v.i. (mil.) advance.

προέλευσις s.f. provenance.

προεξάρχω v.i. stand out (above others).

προεξέχω v.i. stick out, project.

προεξοφλῶ v.t. pay off (debt) in advance; receive (pay) in advance; take for granted, bank on.

προεξοχή s.f. projection.

προεόρτια s.n.pl. eve of or preparations for festival.

προεργασία s.f. preliminary work.

προέρχομαι v.i. originate, spring (from).

προεστώς a. notable, chief.

προετοιμάζω v.t. prepare.

προέχω v.i. project; excel; come first in importance.

πρόζα s.f. prose; θέατρον ~ς prose drama.

προζύμι s.n. leaven.

προηγοῦμαι v.i. & t. come first; (with gen.) precede, come before.

προηγούμεν|ος a. preceding, previous, last. ~ον s.n. precedent; ἔχουν ~α they are on bad terms. ~ως adv. previously, before.

προθάλαμος s.m. ante-room.

πρόθεσις s.f. intention; (gram.) preposition.

προθεσμία s.f. delay, time-limit, term.

προθήκη s.f. shop-window; show-case.

προθυμία s.f. willingness, readiness.

πρόθυμ|ος a. willing, ready; obliging. ~οποιοῦμαι v.i. show readiness, offer.

πρόθυρα s.n.pl. parvis, approach; (fig.) verge, threshold.

προῖκ|α s.f. dowry. ~ίζω v.t. dower, endow.

προικοθήρας s.m. fortune-hunter.

προικιά s.n.pl. effects constituting dowry.

προϊόν s.n. product; ~τα (pl.) produce.

προΐστ|αμαι v.t. (with gen.) be at the head of; ὁ ~άμενος man in charge, superior.

πρόκα s.f. nail, tack.

προκαλύπτω v.t. screen, cover.

προκαλῶ v.t. challenge; provoke, cause.

προκάνω v.t. & i. catch (up with); be or act in time; have enough time (for).

προκαταβάλλω v.t. pay in advance.

προκαταβολ|ή s.f. advance payment; deposit. ~ικῶς adv. in advance.

προκατακλυσμιαῖος a. antediluvian.

ῆροκαταλαμβάνω v.t. occupy before-hand; prepare (for bad news); bias.

προκατάληψις s.f. bias.

προκαταρκτικός a. preliminary.

προκατειλημμένος a. biased.

προκάτοχος s.m. previous occupier; predecessor.

πρόκει|ται v.i. it is a matter or question (of) (with γιά or νά); περὶ τίνος ~ται; what is it about? ~ται νὰ ἔλθη he is supposed to come; ἐ~το νὰ στρίψη he was just going to turn; ~μένου νά seeing that, if; τὸ ~μενον the matter, subject, or point.

προκήρυξις s.f. proclamation.

πρόκλη|σις s.f. challenge; provocation. ~τικός a. provocative.

προκόβω v.i. thrive, progress, do well.

προκομμένος a. industrious, diligent; (iron.) ὁ ~ our fine friend.

προκοπ|ή s.f. industriousness; success; δὲν εἶναι τῆς ~ῆς it is no good.

προκριματικός a. preliminary (of contest leading to finals).

προκρίνω v.t. prefer, favour (plan, solution, etc.).

πρόκριτος a. notable.

προκυμαία s.f. quay.

προκύπτω v.i. arise, crop up; result, follow.

προ|λαβαίνω, ~λαμβάνω v.t. & i. anticipate, forestall; catch (up with); be or act in time; have enough time (for).

προλαλήσας s.m. the previous speaker.

προλέγ|ω v.i. & t. say before; predict. ~όμενα s.n.pl. preface.

προλειαίνω v.t. (fig.) smooth, prepare (way).

προλετάριος a. proletarian.

προληπτικός a. preventive; super-stitious.

πρόληψις s.f. prevention; superstition.

πρόλογος s.m. prologue.

προμάμμη s.f. great-grandmother.

προμαντεύω v.t. prophesy.

πρόμαχος s.m. champion, defender.

προμαχών s.m. bastion, bulwark.

προμελέτη s.f. premeditation; pre-liminary study; ἐκ ~ς deliberate(ly).

προμεσημβρία s.f. forenoon.

προμήθεια s.f. supply, provision; com-mission (percentage).

προμηθευτής s.m. supplier, purveyor.

προμηθεύ|ω v.t. supply, purvey. ~ομαι v.t. get, procure.

προμηνύω v.t. portend.

πρόναος s.m. church porch.

προνοητικός a. having foresight.

πρόνοια s.f. foresight, precaution; provi-dence; Ὑπουργεῖον ~s Ministry of Welfare.

προνόμι|ον s.n. privilege, prerogative; natural gift; ~ον εὑρεσιτεχνίας patent. ~οῦχος a. privileged.

προνοῶ v.i. (with περί) see to, provide for.

προξενεῖον s.n. consulate.

προξενεύω v.t. propose as marriage partner; (fig.) recommend.

προξενητής s.m. go-between (esp. in arranged marriage).

προξενιά s.f. (negotiation of) arranged marriage; (fig.) negotiation.

πρόξενος s.m. 1. author, cause. 2. con-sul.

προξενῶ v.t. cause, bring about.

προοδευτικός a. progressive.

προοδεύω v.i. progress; develop.

πρόοδος s.f. progress; development; progression.

προοίμιον s.n. preamble, prelude.

προοιωνίζομαι v.t. predict.

προοπτική s.f. perspective; prospect in view.

προορατικότης s.f. foresight.

προορί|ζω v.t. destine, intend. ~σμός s.m. appointed end, purpose; destina-tion.

προπαγάνδα s.f. propaganda.

προπαίδεια s.f. primer of arithmetic.

προπαιδευτικός a. preparatory (educa-tion).

πρόπαππος s.m. great-grandfather.

προπαραλήγουσα s.f. antepenultimate syllable.

προπαραμονή s.f. second day before.

προπαρασκευή s.f. preparation; coach-ing.

προπάτορες s.m.pl. forefathers.

προπέλλα s.f. propeller.

προπέμπω v.t. see off.

πρόπερσι adv. the year before last.

προπέτασμα s.n. screen; ~ καπνοῦ smoke-screen.

προπέτεια s.f. impertinence.

προπίνω v.i. drink a toast.

πρόποδες s.m.pl. foot (of hill).

προπολεμικός a. pre-war.

προπόνησις s.f. training, coaching.

πρόποσις s.f. toast (drunk).

προπύλαια s.n.pl. propylaeum.

προπύργιον s.n. bastion, bulwark.

πρόρρησις *s.f.* prediction.

πρός *prep.* 1. (*with acc.*) to, towards (*direction, relation*); for (*use, purpose*); at (*price*); ~ ὄφελός μου to my advantage; ~ τιμήν του in his honour; ~ τὸ παρόν for the present; ἕνα ~ ἕνα one by one; ὡς ~ ἐμέ as for me. 2. (*with gen.*) ~ πατρός on the father's side (*of relatives*); ~ Θεοῦ for God's sake! 3. (*with dat.*) ~ τούτοις in addition. 4. (*adv.*) ~ δέ in addition.

προσαγορεύω *v.t.* address, salute; call.

προσάγω *v.t.* bring forward, produce.

προσάναμμα *s.n.* tinder, kindling.

προσανατολίζ|ω *v.t.* orientate, direct. ~ομαι *v.i.* get one's bearings.

προσάπτω *v.t.* impute.

προσαράσσω *v.i.* run aground.

προσαρμογή *s.f.* fitting, fixing; adaptation, adjustment; adaptability.

προσαρμόζω *v.t.* fit, fix; adapt, adjust.

προσάρτημα *s.n.* thing added, annexe.

προσάρτησις *s.f.* annexation.

προσαρτῶ *v.t.* annex.

προσβάλλω *v.t.* attack; injure (*health*); offend, affront; jar on; contest (*will, etc.*).

πρόσβαρος *a.* over-weight (*of goods sold*).

προσβέλνω *v.t.* offend, affront.

προσβλητικός *a.* offensive, rude.

προσβολή *s.f.* attack; injury (*to health*); offence, affront; contesting (*of will, etc.*).

προσγει|οῦμαι *v.i.* land (*from air*). ~ωσις *s.f.* landing.

προσδίδω *v.t.* lend, impart.

προσδιορίζω *v.t.* determine, fix; ascertain.

προσδοκῶ *v.t.* hope for, expect.

προσεγγίζω *v.t.* & *i.* bring near; approach, draw near; approximate; (*naut.*) put in, call.

προσεκτικός *a.* attentive; careful; circumspect.

προσέλευσις *s.f.* coming.

προσελκύω *v.t.* attract (*attention*); gain (*supporters, etc.*).

προσέρχομαι *v.i.* attend, present oneself.

προσέτι *adv.* besides, also.

προσευχ|ή *s.f.* prayer. ~ομαι *v.i.* pray.

προσεχ|ής *a.* next; approaching. ~ῶς *adv.* shortly, soon.

προσέχω *v.i.* & *t.* pay attention (to), notice; be careful (of), mind; look after.

προσηκόντως *adv.* duly, fittingly.

προσ|ηλιακός, ~ήλιος *a.* sunny (*that gets the sun*).

προσήλυτ|ος *s.m.f.* convert. ~ίζω *v.t.* proselytize, convert.

προσηλ|ώνω *v.t.* nail, fix; ~ωμένος (*fig.*) attached (*to*), engrossed (*in*).

προσηνής *a.* affable.

πρόσθεσις *s.f.* (*process of*) addition.

πρόσθετ|ος *a.* additional; ~α μαλλιά postiche.

προσθέτω *v.t.* add.

προσθήκη *s.f.* addition (*thing added*).

πρόσθιος *a.* front, fore.

προσιτός *a.* accessible; reasonable (*price*).

πρόσκαιρος *a.* temporary.

προσ|καλῶ *v.t.* call, summon; invite. ~κεκλημένος *a.* invited; a guest.

προσκέφαλον *s.n.* pillow, cushion.

προσκήνιον *s.n.* proscenium.

πρόσκλησις *s.f.* call, summons; invitation; complimentary ticket.

προσκλητήριον *s.n.* invitation-card; (*mil.*) call, roll-call.

προσκολλ|ῶ *v.t.* stick, attach. ~ησις *s.f.* sticking, attaching; τῆς ~ήσεως (*one*) who attaches himself unbidden.

προσκομίζω *v.t.* bring forward, produce.

πρόσκομμα *s.n.* obstacle.

πρόσκοπος *s.m.* scout; boy scout.

προσκόπτω *v.i.* stumble; (*with* εἰς) come up against (*obstacle*).

προσκρούω *v.i.* collide; (*with* εἰς) strike against; contravene.

προσκύν|ημα *s.n.* act of worship, respect *or* submission; (place of) pilgrimage. ~ήματα (*pl.*) respects.

προσκυνητής *s.m.* pilgrim.

προσκυνῶ *v.t.* worship; pay respects to; submit to.

προσλαμβάνω *v.t.* take on, engage; assume.

προσμένω *v.t.* wait *or* hope for.

πρόσοδ|ος *s.f.* income, revenue. ~οφόρος *a.* fruitful, profitable.

προσοικειοῦμαι *v.t.* & *i.* gain the support of; (*with* πρός) get used to.

προσόν *s.n.* attribute, qualification; advantage.

προσορμίζομαι *v.i.* put into port.

προσοχή *s.f.* attention, care, caution.

πρόσοψι(ον) *s.n.* towel.

πρόσοψις *s.f.* façade.

προσπάθ|εια *s.f.* attempt, effort. ~ῶ *v.i.* try, attempt.

προσπερνῶ *v.t.* outdistance; pass.
προσπέφτω *v.i.* (*fig.*) bow down, kowtow.
προσποίησις *s.f.* affectation.
προσποιητός *a.* affected; assumed.
προσποιοῦμαι *v.t.* feign, put on; pretend; ~ τὸν ἀδιάφορον feign indifference.
προσπορίζομαι *v.t.* procure, gain.
προσταγή *s.f.* order, command.
προστάζω *v.t.* order, command.
προστακτική *s.f.* (*gram.*) imperative.
προστασία *s.f.* protection.
προστατεύ|ω *v.t.* protect; give patronage to. ~όμενος *s.m.* protégé. ~τικός *a.* protective; patronizing.
προστάτης *s.m.* 1. protector. 2. (*anat.*) prostate.
προστίθεμαι *v.i.* be added.
πρόστιμ|ον *s.n.* fine. ~άρω *v.t.* fine.
προστρέχω *v.i.* hasten (*to assistance*); resort.
προστριβή *s.f.* friction.
προστυχαίνω *v.t. & i.* make vulgar, lower quality of; become vulgar *or* worse in quality.
προστυχιά *s.f.* (piece of) vulgarity *or* bad manners.
πρόστυχος *a.* vulgar, ill-mannered, caddish; cheap; of bad quality.
προσύμφωνον *s.n.* draft agreement.
προσφά(γ)ι *s.n.* food eaten with bread.
πρόσφατος *a.* fresh, recent.
προσφέρ|ω *v.t.* offer, give, present. ~ομαι *v.i.* offer; be suitable.
προσφεύγω *v.i.* resort.
προσφιλής *a.* dear, loved.
προσφορά *s.f.* offer, bid; thing offered; ~ καὶ ζήτησις supply and demand; (*eccl.*) bread offered for Holy Communion.
πρόσφορος *a.* suitable, fit.
πρόσφυγας *s.m.* refugee.
προσφυγή *s.f.* recourse, appeal.
προσφυγικός *a.* of *or* for refugees.
προσφυής *a.* suitable, fit.
πρόσφυξ *s.m.f.* refugee.
προσφωνῶ *v.t.* address, salute.
πρόσχαρος *a.* cheerful, pleasant.
προσχέδιον *s.n.* draft plan.
πρόσχημα *s.n.* pretext, pretence.
προσχωρῶ *v.i.* join, adhere (*to pact, etc.*).
πρόσω *adv.* forwards.
προσωδία *s.f.* prosody.
προσωνυμία *s.f.* nickname, name.
προσωπάρχης *s.m.* personnel officer.
προσωπείον *s.n.* mask.

προσωπικ|ός *a.* personal; ~ά (*s.n. pl.*) private quarrel. ~όν *s.n.* personnel, staff.
προσωπικότης *s.f.* personality.
προσωπίς *s.f.* mask.
προσωπογραφία *s.f.* portrait.
πρόσωπον *s.n.* face; person; part, role.
προσωποποι|ῶ *v.t.* personify. ~ησις *s.f.* personification.
προσωρινός *a.* provisional, temporary.
πρότασις *s.f.* proposal, proposition, motion; (*gram.*) sentence, clause.
προτείνω *v.t. & i.* extend, hold out, put forward; propose, move, suggest.
προτελευταῖος *a.* penultimate.
προτεραία *s.f.* day before.
προτεραιότης *s.f.* priority.
προτέρημα *s.n.* good quality, virtue, advantage.
πρότερ|ος *a.* earlier, previous; ἐκ τῶν ~ων beforehand, in advance.
προτεσταντισμός *s.m.* protestantism.
προτίθεμαι *v.i.* intend.
προτιμ|ῶ *v.t.* prefer. ~ησις *s.f.* preference.
προτιμ|ητέος, ~ότερος *a.* preferable.
προτιν|ός *a.* previous, earlier; τὰ ~ά the past.
προτομή *s.f.* bust (*sculptured*).
προτοῦ *conj. & adv.* before.
προτρέπω *v.t.* urge, instigate.
προτρέχω *v.i. & t.* run ahead; (*with gen.*) outrun.
προτροπάδην *adv.* at full speed (*in retreat*).
προτροπή *s.f.* instigation.
πρότυπ|ος *a.* model. ~ον *s.n.* model, example.
προϋπαντῶ *v.t.* go to meet (*on arrival*).
προϋπάρχω *v.i. & t.* exist previously; (*with gen.*) come before (*in time*).
προϋπο|θέτω *v.t.* presuppose. ~θεσις *s.f.* assumption.
προϋπολογ|ίζω *v.t.* estimate. ~ισμός *s.m.* estimate; budget.
προύχων *s.m.* notable.
προφαν|ής *a.* obvious, evident. ~ῶς *adv.* obviously.
προφαντός *a.* first *or* early to ripen.
πρόφασις *s.f.* pretext, excuse.
προφέρ(ν)ω *v.t.* pronounce, utter (*sounds*).
προφήτ|ης *s.m.* prophet. ~εία *s.f.* prophecy. ~εύω *v.t.* prophesy. ~ικός *a.* prophetic.
προφθάνω *v.t. & i.* see **προφταίνω**.

προφορ|ά *s.f.* pronunciation. **~ικός** *a.* oral, verbal.

προφτ|αίνω, ~άνω *v.t. & i.* anticipate, forestall; catch (up with); be *or* act in time; have time *or* money (for); let out (*secret*); δὲν ~αίνω λάδι I am always needing more oil.

προφυλά(γ)ω *v.t.* see **προφυλάσσω**.

προφυλακή *s.f.* vanguard.

προφυλακίζω *v.t.* detain in custody.

προφυλακτήρ *s.m.* bumper (*of motor*).

προφυλακτικός *a.* cautious; precautionary, preventive.

προφύλαξις *s.f.* precaution, care.

προφυλάσσω|ω *v.t.* protect, guard. **~ομαι** *v.i.* take precautions.

πρόχειρ|ος *a.* ready to hand; improvised; in draft; ~ο βιβλίο notebook; ἐκ τοῦ ~ου without preparation, extempore.

προχθές *adv.* the day before yesterday; the other day.

πρόχωμα *s.n.* earthwork.

προχωρῶ *v.i.* proceed, advance; progress, gain ground.

προωθῶ *v.t.* propel; push forward.

προώλης *a.* depraved; *see* **ἐξώλης**.

πρόωρος *a.* premature.

πρύμα *adv.* with fair wind; successfully.

πρύμ(ν)η *s.f.* stern, poop.

πρύταν|ις *s.m.* head of university *or* college. **~εία** *s.f.* office of πρύτανις. **~εύω** *v.i.* (*fig.*) rule, prevail.

πρώην *adv.* formerly; ~ πρόεδρος ex-president.

πρωθυπουργός *s.m.* prime minister.

πρωί 1. *adv.* in the morning, early. 2. *s.n.* morning.

πρωία *s.f.* morning.

πρώιμος *a.* early, premature; precocious (*of plants*).

πρωινός *a.* morning; rising early.

πρωινό *s.n.* 1. morning. 2. breakfast.

πρωκτός *s.m.* anus.

πρώρα *s.f.* prow, bows.

πρῶτα *adv.* (at) first; before.

πρωταγωνιστής *s.m.* protagonist.

πρωτάθλημα *s.n.* championship.

πρωταίτιος *s.m.* one mainly responsible, ringleader.

πρωτάκουστος *a.* unheard of.

πρωτάρα *s.f.* woman in first child-bed; animal with first litter; tiro.

πρωτάρης *s.m.* tiro.

πρωταρχικός *a.* first in importance.

πρωτεῖα *s.n.pl.* first place, primacy.

πρωτεργάτης *s.m.* moving spirit.

πρωτεύ|ω *v.i.* be the first, lead. **~ουσα** *s.f.* capital (*city*). **~ων** *a.* primary.

πρωτινός *a.* of the old school.

πρωτίστως *adv.* first and foremost.

πρωτο- *denotes* first.

πρωτοβάθμιος *a.* of first instance (*court*); of the first rank.

πρωτόβγαλτος *a.* at the beginning of one's career; inexperienced.

πρωτοβουλία *s.f.* initiative.

πρωτοβρόχια *s.n.pl.* first rain (*of autumn*).

πρωτο|γενής, ~γέννητος *a.* first-born.

πρωτόγονος *a.* primitive.

πρωτοδικεῖον *s.n.* court of first instance.

πρωτοετής *a.* first-year.

πρωτοκαθεδρία *s.f.* place of honour.

πρωτόκολλ|ον *s.n.* 1. register of correspondence. 2. court *or* diplomatic etiquette. **~ῶ** *v.t.* enter (*document*) in register.

Πρωτομαγιά *s.f.* May Day.

πρωτομηνιά *s.f.* first day of month.

πρωτόπειρος *a.* inexperienced.

πρωτοπορ(ε)ία *s.f.* vanguard.

πρωτοπόρος *s.m.* pioneer, avant-gardist.

πρῶτ|ος *a.* first, foremost; prime (*number*); ~αι ὕλαι raw materials; ~αι βοήθειαι first aid. **~α, ~ον** *adv.* (at) first; before.

πρωτοστατῶ *v.i.* play a leading part.

πρωτότοκος *a.* first-born.

πρωτότυπ|ος *a.* original; unusual. **~ία** *s.f.* originality. **~ον** *s.n.* original.

πρωτουργός *s.m.* moving spirit.

πρωτοφανής *a.* unprecedented.

Πρωτοχρονιά *s.f.* New Year's Day.

πρωτύτερα *adv.* earlier, previously.

πτ- *see also* **φτ-**.

πταῖσμα *s.n.* (*law*) minor criminal offence. **~τοδικεῖον** *s.n.* lowest criminal court.

πταίω *v.i.* be to blame.

πτέρνα *s.f.* heel.

πτερνιστήρ *s.m.* spur.

πτερόν *s.n.* feather; wing; blade (*of oar, propeller*).

πτερύγιον *s.n.* fin; aileron.

πτέρυξ *s.f.* wing (*of bird, aeroplane, army, building, political party*).

πτέρωμα *s.n.* plumage.

πτερωτός *a.* winged.

πτην|όν *s.n.* bird, fowl. **~οτροφία** *s.f.* poultry-farming.

πτῆ|σις *s.f.* flight. **~τικός** *a.* 1. designed for flight. 2. volatile (*oil, etc.*).

πτίλον *s.n.* down.

πτοώ *v.t.* terrify.

πτύελον *s.n.* spittle, sputum.

πτυχή *s.f.* fold, pleat; wrinkle.

πτυχί|ον *s.n.* diploma. ~ούχος *a.* holding a diploma.

πτύω *v.t. & i.* spit (on).

πτώμα *s.n.* corpse.

πτώσις *s.f.* fall; collapse; decrease; (*gram.*) case.

πτωχ- *see* φτωχ-.

πτωχ|εύω *v.i.* go bankrupt. ~ευσις *s.f.* bankruptcy.

πτωχοκομείον *s.n.* poor-house.

πυγμαίος *a. & s.m.* pygmy.

πυγμαχία *s.f.* boxing.

πυγμή *s.f.* fist; (*fig.*) drive, determination.

πυγολαμπίς *s.f.* glow-worm.

πυθαγόρειος *a.* Pythagorean; ~ πίναξ multiplication table.

Πυθία *s.f.* Pythoness; (*iron.*) oracle, prophet.

πυθμήν *s.m.* bottom.

πύθων *s.m.* python.

πυκν|ός *a.* thick, dense, compact, close together; in quick succession. ~ά, ~ώς *adv.* thickly, closely.

πυκνότης *s.f.* density, thickness; frequency.

πυκνώνω *v.t. & i.* make or grow thicker or more extensive or more frequent.

πυκνωτής *s.m.* (*electric*) condenser.

πύλη *s. f.* gate (*of city, palace, etc.*); Ὑψηλή ~ Sublime Porte.

πυλών *s.m.* gateway, portal.

πυναίζα *s.f.* drawing-pin.

πυξίς *s.f.* mariner's compass.

πύξ|ος *s.m.*, ~άρι *s.n.* box-tree.

πύον *s.n.* pus.

πῦρ *s.n.* fire.

πύρα *s.f.* heat of fire; (*fig.*) sensation of burning.

πυρά *s.f.* pyre, stake.

πυρακτώνω *v.t.* make red-hot.

πυραμίς *s.f.* pyramid.

πύραυλος *s.m.* rocket.

πύραυνον *s.n.* brazier.

πυργίσκος *s.m.* turret.

πύργος *s.m.* tower; castle; country-house.

πυρείον *s.n.* match (*for lighting*).

πυρέσσω *v.i.* be feverish.

πυρετ|ός *s.m.* fever, high temperature; (*fig.*) great activity. ~ώδης *a.* feverish; feverous.

πυρήν *s.m.* stone, kernel; core; nucleus. ~ικός *a.* nuclear.

πυρηνέλαιον *s.n.* oil from stones or seeds of plants.

πύρινος *a.* burning, fiery.

πυρίτης *s.m.* pyrites.

πυρῖτ|ις *s.f.* gunpowder. ~ιδαποθήκη *s.f.* powder-magazine. ~ιδοποιεῖον *s.n.* powder-factory.

πυρκαϊά *s.f.* (*outbreak of*) fire, conflagration.

πυροβολαρχία *s.f.* (*mil.*) battery.

πυροβολείον *s.n.* gun-emplacement.

πυροβολητής *s.m.* gunner.

πυροβολικόν *s.n.* artillery.

πυροβολισμός *s.m.* firing, shot (*of gun*).

πυροβόλ|ος *a.* ~α ὅπλα firearms.

πυροβολῶ *v.i. & t.* fire; shoot at.

πυρομαχικά *s.n.pl.* munitions; ammunition.

πυροπαθής *a.* victim of fire.

πυροσβέστης *s.m.* fireman.

πυροσβεστικ|ός *a.* ~ὴ ὑπηρεσία fire brigade.

πυροτέχνημα *s.n.* firework.

πυροφάνι *s.n.* grid for lamp (*in bow of fishing-boat*).

πυροπωλητής *s.m.* one who sails a fire-ship.

πυρπολικόν *s.n.* fire-ship.

πυρπολῶ *v.t.* set on fire.

πυρρός *a.* russet; red-haired.

πυρσός *s.m.* torch, brand; beacon.

πυρώνω *v.t. & i.* make or get red hot or warm.

πυτζάμα *s.f.* pyjamas.

πυώδης *a.* purulent.

πῶ *v.t. & i.* aorist subjunctive of λέγω.

πώγων *s.m.* beard; chin.

πώλησις *s.f.* sale.

πωλ|ητής *s.m.* seller; salesman. ~ήτρια *s.f.* seller; saleswoman.

πῶλος *s.m.* foal, colt.

πωλ|ῶ *v.t.* sell; ~εῖται for sale.

πῶμα *s.n.* stopper, cork, bung, plug.

πώ πώ *int.* of surprise or dismay.

πωρόλιθος *s.m.* porous stone.

πωρωμένος *a.* (*fig.*) hardened to wrong-doing.

πώρωσις *s.f.* loss of sense of right and wrong.

πῶς *adv.* how? ~ ὄχι; why not? ~! yes, of course; κάνω ~ καὶ ~ do one's utmost or desire strongly.

πώς *conj.* that.

πως *adv.* (*enclitic*) somehow, somewhat.

Ρ

ραβαῖσι *s.n.* junketing; uproar.

ραβανί *s.n.* sort of cake.

ραβασάκι *s.n.* billet doux.

ραβδί *s.n.* stick, wand.

ραβδ|ίζω *v.t.* beat (*with stick*). ∼ισμός *s.m.* beating; blow.

ραβδο|μάντης, ∼σκόπος *s.m.* diviner.

ράβδος *s.f.* stick, staff, rod, baton, wand; bar (*of gold*); rail (*of track*).

ράβδω|σις *s.f.* stripe; flute, groove; ∼σεις (*pl.*) fluting, rifling ∼τός *a.* striped; fluted.

ράβ|ω *v.t.* sew (on, up); stitch; make or have made (*clothes*); κόβω καὶ ∼ω talk unceasingly or have influence. ∼ομαι *v.i.* have one's clothes made.

ράγα *s.f.* grape; nipple.

ραγάδα *s.f.* chink, crack.

ραγδαῖος *a.* violent, tumultuous, headlong.

ράγια *s.f.* rail (*of railway, etc., track*).

ραγιᾶς *s.m.* rayah, bondsman.

ραγ|ίζω *v.t.& i.* crack. ∼ισμα *s.n.* crack.

ραδίκι *s.n.* dandelion or similar plant.

ραδινός *a.* slender (*of build*).

ραδιογραφία *s.f.* X-ray photograph(y).

ραδιολογία *s.f.* radiology.

ράδιον *s.n.* radium.

ραδιο(τηλε)γράφημα *s.n.* radio-telegram.

ραδιοῦργ|ος *a.* scheming; an intriguer. ∼ία *s.f.* intrigue.

ραδιόφων|ον *s.n.* radio, wireless. ∼ία *s.f.* broadcasting service. ∼ικός *a.* (by) wireless.

ραζακί *s.n.* sort of white grape.

ράθυμος *a.* indolent.

ραιβοσκελής *a.* bow-legged.

ραίνω *v.t.* sprinkle.

ρακένδυτος *a.* dressed in rags.

ρακί *s.n.* sort of spirit.

ράκος *s.n.* rag.

ράμμα *s.n.* stitch; ἔχω ∼τα γιὰ τὴ γοῦνα σου I have a bone to pick with you.

ραμμένος *a.* sewn.

ραμολ|ίρω *v.i.* become soft-witted. ∼ιμέντο *s.n.* soft-witted person.

ράμφ|ος *s.n.* beak; burner, jet (*of light*). ∼ίζω *v.t.* peck.

ρανίς *s.f.* drop.

ραντεβού *s.n.* appointment, engagement; (*fam.*) lovers keeping tryst. [F. *rendezvous*]

ραντιέρης *s.m.* rentier.

ραντίζω *v.t.* sprinkle, shower.

ράν|τζο, ∼τσο *s.n.* camp-bed.

ράξ *s.f.* grape; nipple.

ραπάνι *s.n.* radish.

ραπίζω *v.t.* slap the face of.

ράπτης *s.m.* tailor.

ραπτική *s.f.* sewing, dressmaking.

ραπτομηχανή *s.f.* sewing-machine.

ράπτρια *s.f.* dressmaker.

ράπτω *v.t.* sew (on, up), stitch.

ράσον *s.n.* cassock.

ράτσα *s.f.* breed, race; (*fam.*) rascal; ἀπὸ ∼ thoroughbred.

ραφεῖον *s.n.* tailor's shop.

ραφή *s.f.* making (*of clothes*); seam; stitching (*of wound*).

ράφι *s.n.* shelf; μένω στὸ ∼ be left on the shelf.

ραφινάρω *v.t.* refine.

ραφίς *s.f.* needle.

ράφτ|ης *s.m.* tailor. ∼άδικο *s.n.* tailor's shop.

ραφτικά *s.n.pl.* charge for tailoring or dressmaking.

ραφτός *a.* sewn.

ράφτρα *s.f.* dressmaker.

ράφτω *v.t.* sew (on, up), stitch.

ραχάτ|ι *s.n.* lazing about. ∼ λουκούμ *s.n.* sort of Turkish delight.

ράχη *s.f.* back; spine (*of book*); ridge (*of mountain*).

ραχιτικός *a.* suffering from rickets; malformed.

ραχοκόκκαλ|ο *s.n.*, ∼ιά *s.f.* spine.

ράψιμο *s.n.* sewing (on, up); dressmaking, tailoring.

ραψωδία *s.f.* rhapsody.

ρέ *int. see* βρέ.

ρεαλιστής *s.m.* realist.

ρεβίθι *s.n.* chick-pea.

ρεγάλο *s.n.* present, gift.

ρέγγα *s.f.* herring.

ρέγομαι *v.t.* feel desire for.

ρέγουλα *s.f.* order, moderation.

ρεδιγκότα *s.f.* redingote.

ρεζέρβα *s.f.* reserve (*stock*), spare (*esp. wheel*).

ρεζές *s.m.* hinge.

ρεζιλεύω *v.t.* make ridiculous; humiliate.

ρεζίλ|ι, ∼ίκι *s.n.* (object of) ridicule or shame; γίνομαι ∼ι or παθαίνω ∼ίκι become a laughing-stock, be humiliated.

ρεῖθρον *s.n.* watercourse, gutter.

ρεκλάμα *s.f.* advertisement.

ρέκτης *s.m.* enterprising person.

ρέμα *s.n.*, ~τιά *s.f.* ravine, torrent (-bed).

ρεμβ|άζω *v.i.* muse, dream. ~ασμός *s.m.* reverie.

ρεμούλα *s.f.* plunder; (*fam.*) graft.

ρεμουλκ- *see* ρυμουλκ-.

ρέμπελος *a.* idle and ill-disciplined.

ρεμπέτικο *s.n.* sort of popular song in oriental style.

ρε(μ)πούμπλικα *s.f.* trilby *or* homburg hat.

ρεπάνι *s.n.* radish.

ρεπό *s.n.* time off (*between shifts*). [F. *repos*]

ρέπω *v.i.* lean, incline.

ρέστ|ος *a.* the rest (of). ~α *s.n.pl.* change (*money*).

ρετάλι *s.n.* remnant (*of cloth*).

ρετσέτα *s.f.* prescription, recipe.

ρετσίν|α *s.f.* resin; resinated wine. ~άτο *s.n.* resinated wine.

ρετσίν|ι *s.n.* resin. ~ιά *s.f.* (*fam.*) stigma left by false accusation.

ρετσινόλαδο *s.n.* castor-oil.

ρεῦμα *s.n.* current; draught.

ρευματισμός *s.m.* rheumatism.

ρεύομαι *v.i.* belch.

ρευστ|ός *a.* fluid; liquid (*of assets*); unstable. ~οποιῶ *v.t.* liquefy; turn (*assets*) into cash.

ρεύω *v.i. & t.* fall in, crumble; (*fig.*) waste away. (*v.t.*) wear down, exhaust.

ρεφεν|ές *s.m.* quota, share; (*μέ*) ~έ each paying his share.

ρέψιμο *s.n.* 1. belch, belching. 2. ruin, decay.

ρέω *v.i.* flow.

ρήγας *s.m.* king.

ρήγμα *s.n.* breach, crack, split.

ρηθείς *a.* (afore)said.

ρῆμα *s.n.* verb.

ρημάδι *s.n.* ruin; (*fam.*) derogatory epithet; κλεῖσ' το τό ~ turn the damn thing off (*e.g. radio*); τάκαμες ~ό you have made a mess of it.

ρημάζω *v.t. & i.* ruin, devastate; fall into ruin *or* neglect.

ρηξικέλευθος *a.* pioneering; an innovator.

ρῆξις *s.f.* rupture, breaking; conflict.

ρητίν|η *s.f.* resin. ~ίτης *s.m.* resinated wine.

ρητόν *s.n.* saying.

ρητορεύω *v.i.* hold forth, make speeches.

ρητορική *s.f.* oratory.

ρητός *a.* explicit.

ρήτρα *s.f.* clause.

ρήτωρ *s.m.* orator.

ρηχ|ός *a.* shallow; ~α (*s.n.pl.*) shallows.

ρίγα *s.f.* (*measuring*) rule.

ρίγανη *s.f.* origanum (*herb*); (*fam.*) βάλ' του ~ ironic comment on unfulfilled expectations.

ριγέ *a.* striped. [F. *rayé*]

ρῖγος *s.n.* shiver, shudder.

ριγώ|νω *v.t.* rule *or* make lines. ~τός *a.* striped, lined.

ριγῶ *v.i.* shiver, shudder.

ρίζα *s.f.* root; foot (*of mountain*).

ριζά *s.n.pl.* foot (*of mountain*).

ριζηδόν *adv.* to the roots, radically.

ριζικ|ός *a.* root, original; radical, complete; basic. ~ό *s.n.* fate, destiny.

ριζοβολῶ *v.i.* put out roots, spread.

ριζοβούνι *s.n.* foot of mountain.

ριζοσπάστ|ης *s.m.* radical (*in opinions*). ~ικός *a.* radical.

ριζών|ω, ~ομαι *v.i.* become rooted *or* fixed.

ρικνός *a.* wrinkled, warped.

ρίμα *s.f.* rhyme.

ρίνη *s.f.* file (*tool*).

ρινικός *a.* nasal.

ρινόκερως *s.m.* rhinoceros.

ριξιά *s.f.* charge (*explosive*); shot, throw.

ρίξιμο *s.n.* throwing; dropping; firing; throw, shot; attack.

ριπ|ή *s.f.* burst (*of firing*); gust (*of wind*); ἐν ~ῆ ὀφθαλμοῦ in the twinkling of an eye.

ριπίδιον *s.n.* (*hand*) fan.

ρίπτω *v.t.* throw, cast; overthrow.

ρίς *s.f.* nose.

ρίχν|ω *v.t.* throw, cast; drop, pour (out), sprinkle; knock *or* pull down, overthrow; fire (*shots*); (*fam.*) ~ω κανόνι go bankrupt; ~ω γράμμα post a letter; ~ω τῆ γνώμη μου express one's opinion; ~ω τό παιδί have an abortion; ~ω τά χαρτιά tell fortunes from cards; ~ω τό καράβι ἔξω run the ship aground; τό ~ω ἔξω go on the spree, neglect one's responsibilities; τό ~ω σέ indulge immoderately in (*cards, drink, women, etc.*); ~ει βροχή it is raining. ~ομαι *v.i. & t.* throw oneself; (*with σέ or gen.*) attack; make advances to (*woman*).

ριχτός *a.* (*of clothes*) full, not fitted to figure; worn over shoulders (*with arms not in sleeves*).

ρίψις *s.f. see* ρίξιμο.

ριψοκινδυνεύω *v.i. & t.* take risks; risk, venture.

ροβολῶ v.i. run or roll downhill.

ρόγχος s.m. (bronchial) rattle; death-rattle.

ρόδα s.f. wheel; (fam.) motor-car.

ροδάκινον s.n. peach.

ροδαλός a. rosy (esp. complexion).

ροδάνι s.n. spinning-wheel.

ροδέλαιον s.n. attar of roses.

ροδέλλα s.f. washer (ring); round slice.

ρόδι s.n. pomegranate.

ροδίζω v.i. become rosy; brown (in cooking).

ρόδινος a. rosy; (fig.) rose-coloured.

ροδίτης s.m. sort of pink grape.

ροδοδάφνη s.f. oleander.

ροδοκόκκινος a. ruddy; brown (of cooking food).

ρόδον s.n. rose.

ροδό|στα(γ)μα, **~σταμο** s.n. rose-water.

ροδόχρους a. rosy.

ρόξ a. pink. [F. rose]

ροζάκι s.n. sort of white grape.

ρόζ|ος s.m. knot (in wood); callus. **~ιάρικος** a. knotted, gnarled.

ροή s.f. flow, flux, discharge.

ρόϊδι s.n. pomegranate.

ρόκα s.f. 1. distaff. 2. rocket (plant).

ροκάνα s.f. rattle.

ροκάν|ι s.n. plane (tool). **~ίδι** s.n. wood-shaving.

ροκανίζω v.t. plane; gnaw; (fig.) nibble at, consume.

ρολό s.n. roll (cylindrical); drop-shutter. [F. rouleau]

ρολογάς s.m. watchmaker.

ρολό(γ)ι s.n. clock, watch; meter; (fam.) πάει ~ it goes like clockwork.

ρόλ|ος s.m. roll; role, part; δὲν παίζει ~ο it makes no difference.

ρομάντζο s.n. romance (story, love-affair).

ρομβία s.f. barrel-organ.

ρόμβος s.m. (geom.) rhombus; peg-top.

ρόμπα s.f. dressing-gown; dress.

ρομφαία s.f. two-edged sword.

ρόπαλον s.n. club, cudgel.

ροπή s.f. propensity.

ρούζ s.n. rouge. [F. rouge]

ρουθούν|ι s.n. nostril; (fam.) ~ι δέν ἔμεινε not a soul survived; μοῦ μπῆκε στό ~ι he exasperated me (by pestering). **~ίζω** v.i. snort.

ρουκέτα s.f. rocket; (fam.) vomiting.

ρουλεμάν s.n. ball-bearings. [F. roulement]

Ρούμελη s.f. part of Central Greece.

ρούμι s.n. rum.

ρουμπίνι s.n. ruby.

ρούπι s.n. measure of length (about 3 ins.); (fam.) δέν τό κουνάω ~ I will not budge.

ροῦς s.m. flow; (fig.) current.

ροῦσσος a. red-haired.

ρουσφέτι s.n. illegitimate political favour.

ρουτίνα s.f. routine.

ρούφη(γ)μα s.n. (noisy) sipping, sniffing or sucking in.

ρουφηξιά s.f. sip; sniff; puff, pull (at pipe, etc.).

ρουφήχτρα s.f. whirlpool.

ρουφιάνος s.m. pimp; intriguer.

ρο(υ)φῶ v.t. sip, sniff or suck in (noisily); absorb.

ρουχαλ- see **ροχαλ-**.

ρουχ|ικά s.n.pl., **~ισμός** s.m. clothing.

ροῦχ|ο s.n. cloth, material; garment. **~α** (pl.) clothes, bed-clothes; (fam.) menstrual period; εἶμαι στὰ ~α be confined to bed; τρώγεται μὲ τὰ ~α του he is an inveterate grumbler.

ρόφημα s.n. soup; hot drink.

ροχαλητό s.n. snore, snoring.

ροχαλ|ίζω v.i. snore. **~ισμα** s.n. snore, snoring.

ρόχαλο s.n. phlegm.

ρόχθος s.m. roaring (esp. of waves).

ρύ|αξ s.m., **~άκι** s.n. stream, rivulet.

ρύγχος s.m. snout, muzzle; nozzle.

ρύζ|ι s.n. rice. **~όγαλο** s.n. rice-pudding.

ρυθμίζω v.t. regulate, arrange.

ρυθμικός a. rhythmical.

ρυθμιστ|ήρ, **~ής** s.m. regulator.

ρυθμός s.m. rhythm, proportion; order, style (of architecture, furniture, etc.).

ρύμη s.f. 1. momentum. 2. narrow street.

ρυμοτομία s.f. street-plan.

ρυμούλκα s.f. trailer.

ρυμούλκιον s.n. tow-rope.

ρυμουλκόν s.n. tug-boat; tractor.

ρυμουλκῶ v.t. tow; (fig.) lead by the nose.

ρυπαίνω v.t. make dirty; (fig.) defile, sully.

ρυπαρός a. filthy; vile.

ρύπος s.m. filth; defilement.

ρυτίδ|α s.f. wrinkle; ripple (on water). **~ώνω** v.t. & i. wrinkle, ripple; get wrinkled or rippled.

ρῶ s.n. the letter **Ρ**.

ρώγα s.f. grape; nipple.

ρωγμή s.f. crack, fissure.
ρωγοβύζι s.n. baby's feeding-bottle.
ρώθων s.m. nostril.
ρωμαίικ|ος a. of modern Greece; τὸ ~ο (*pej.*) Greece (*with all her shortcomings*). ~α s.n.pl. Romaic, demotic Greek; μίλα ~α be explicit!
ρωμαϊκός a. Roman.
Ρωμαῖος s.m. a Roman.
ρωμαλέος a. robust, strong.
ρωμανικός a. romanesque; romance (*language*).
ρωμάντζα s.f. romantic scenery or setting; enjoyment of these; (*mus.*) type of song.
ρωμαντικός a. romantic.
ρώμη s.f. robustness, strength.
Ρωμι|ός s.m. a (*modern*) Greek. ~οσύνη s.f. the (*modern*) Greek people.
ρώτημα s.n. question, query.
ρωτῶ v.t. & i. ask, question (*person*); ask (*something*); inquire.

Σ

σ' see **σέ**.
σά conj. see **σάν**.
σάβανον s.n. shroud.
σάββατ|ον s.n. Saturday; Sabbath. ~οκύριακο s.n. week-end.
σαβούρ|α s.f. ballast; trash. ~ώνω v.t. ballast; (τήν) ~ώνω (*fam.*) gorge oneself.
σαγάν|ι, ~άκι s.n. two-handled frying pan; (*fam.*) ~άκι dish of eggs & cheese fried in this.
σαγή s.f. harness.
σαγήν|η s.f. fascination. ~εύω v.t. charm, allure.
σάγμα s.n. pack-saddle.
σαγόνι s.n. jaw, chin.
σαγονιά s.f. jaw, chin; blow on the jaw; (*fam.*) ἔφαγα ~ I was stung (*overcharged*).
σαθρός a. rotten, decayed; ramshackle.
σαΐτα s.f. arrow, dart; shuttle.
σακαράκα s.f. (*fam.*) old motor-car or cycle.
σακάτ|ης s.m. cripple. ~εύω v.t. cripple, maim.
σάκκα s.f. satchel; game-bag; briefcase.
σακκάκι s.n. jacket.
σακκί s.n. sack; (*fam.*) βάζω στό ~ dupe.

σακκίδιον s.n. haversack.
σακκοράφα s.f. sack-needle.
σάκκος s.m. sack, sackful; kitbag; jacket.
σακκούλα s.f. sack, bag; paper or plastic bag; pouch.
σακκούλι s.n. sack, bag. ~άζω v.t. & i. put into sacks; be baggy.
σάκχαρις s.f. see **ζάχαρη**.
σάκχαρον s.n. (*chem.*) sugar.
σάλα s.f. drawing-room.
σάλαγ|ο s.n., ~ος s.m. noise of crowd or herd; herdsman's cry.
σαλαμάνδρα s.f. salamander; slow-combustion stove.
σαλαμούρα s.f. brine.
σαλάτα s.f. salad; τὰ κάνω ~ make a mess of it.
σαλβάρι s.n. Turkish trousers.
σάλεμα s.n. slight movement, stirring.
σαλέπι s.n. salep.
σαλεύω v.t. & i. move, stir.
σάλι s.n. shawl.
σάλιαγκας s.m. snail.
σαλιάζω v.i. make saliva.
σαλιάρα s.f. bib.
σαλιάρης a. a chatterbox.
σαλιαρίζω v.i. chatter, gossip.
σαλιγκάρι s.n. snail.
σάλι|ο s.n. saliva; τρέχουν τὰ ~α μου my mouth waters.
σαλιώνω v.t. lick, moisten.
σαλόνι s.n. drawing-room (suite).
σάλος s.m. swell (*of sea*); rolling (*of ship*); (*fig.*) commotion.
σαλπάρω v.i. (*naut.*) weigh anchor.
σάλπιγξ s.f. trumpet, bugle.
σαλπ|ίζω v.i. & t. blow trumpet; sound (*call*) on trumpet. ~ισμα s.n. trumpet-call.
σαλτάρω v.i. jump.
σαλτιμπάγκος s.m. fair-ground acrobat, etc.
σάλτος s.m. jump.
σάλτσα s.f. gravy, sauce.
σαμάρ|ι s.n. pack-saddle. ~ώνω v.t. saddle.
σαματᾶς s.m. row (*noise*).
σάματι(ς) adv. as if.
σαμιαμίθι s.n. small lizard; (*fig.*) puny fellow.
σαμόλαδο s.n. sesame oil.
σαμούρι s.n. sable.
σαμπάνια s.f. champagne.
σαμποτ|άζ s.n. sabotage. [F.]. ~άρω v.t. sabotage.

σαμπρέλα *s.f.* inner tube (*of tyre*).

σάμπως *adv.* as if; it seems that; *also introduces question.*

σά(ν) *conj. & adv.* when, whenever, as soon as, if; like, as (if) ; ~ *νά* (it seems) as if; ~ *τί* ; what ? ~ *ήλίθιος πού ήταν τόν γέλασαν* being a fool he got cheated; ~ *σήμερα πέρσυ* a year ago today.

σανά *s.n.pl.* hay.

σανδάλιον *s.n.* sandal.

σανίδ|α *s.f.*, ~ι *s.n.* plank, board. ~ώνω *v.t.* board over.

σανιδόσκαλα *s.f.* gang-plank.

σανίς *s.f.* plank, board.

σανός *s.m.* hay.

σαντιγύ *s.n.* chantilly (*cream, lace*). [F. *Chantilly*]

σαντούρι *s.n.* sort of stringed musical instrument.

σαπίζω *v.t. & i.* rot.

σαπίλα *s.f.* decay, rottenness; (*fig.*) corruption.

σάπιος *a.* rotten; corrupt.

σαπουνάδα *s.f.* soapy water; lather.

σαπούν|ι *s.n.* soap. ~ίζω *v.t.* soap.

σαπουνόφουσκα *s.f.* soap-bubble.

σαπρός *a.* rotten; corrupt.

σάπφειρος *s.m.* sapphire.

σάπων *s.m.* soap.

σάρα *s.f.* (*fam.*) *ή* ~ *καί ή μάρα* riff-raff.

σαράβαλο *s.n.* (*fam.*) ruin, wreck.

σαράκι *s.n.* woodworm; (*fig.*) secret sorrow, remorse.

σαρακοστ|ή *s.f.* Lent. ~ιανός *a.* lenten.

σαράντα (*num.*) forty.

σαραντάμερο *s.n.* Advent.

σαρανταποδαρούσα *s.f.* centipede.

σαραντίζω *v.i.* become forty; be forty days old *or* dead *or* delivered of child.

σαράφης *s.m.* money-changer.

σαρδέλλα *s.f.* anchovy; sardine.

σαρδόνιος *a.* sardonic.

σαρίδι *s.n.* sweepings.

σαρίκι *s.n.* turban.

σάρκ|α *s.f.* flesh. ~ικός *a.* carnal.

σαρκασ|μός *s.n.* sarcasm. ~ικός *a.* sarcastic.

σαρκίον *s.n.* (*fam.*) *νά σώσει τό* ~ *του* to save his skin.

σαρκοβόρος *a.* carnivorous.

σαρκοφάγος 1. *a.* carnivorous. 2. *s.f.* sarcophagus.

σαρκώδης *a.* fleshy, corpulent.

σάρκωμα *s.n.* (*med.*) sarcoma.

σάρξ *s.f.* flesh.

σάρπα *s.f.* scarf, shawl.

σάρωθρον *s.n.* broom.

σάρωμα *s.n.* sweeping(s) ; broom.

σαρώνω *v.t.* sweep.

σασ(σ)ί *s.n.* chassis. [F. *chassis*]

σαστίζω *v.t. & i.* disconcert, confuse; get confused.

σατανάς *s.m.* Satan ; (*fig.*) sinister *or* very clever person.

σατανικός *a.* satanic(al), diabolical.

σάτιρ|α *s.f.* satire. ~ίζω *v.t.* satirize. ~ικός *a.* satirical.

σατίρι *s.n.* butcher's chopper.

σατράπης *s.m.* satrap; despot.

σάτυρος *s.m.* satyr.

σαύρα *s.f.* lizard.

σαφήνεια *s.f.* clarity, distinctness.

σαφής *a.* clear, explicit.

σαχάνι *s.n.* see σαγάνι.

σάχης *s.m.* shah.

σάχλα *s.f.* insipidity; silliness. ~μάρα *s.f.* nonsense.

σαχλός *a.* insipid; silly.

σάψαλο *s.n.* see σαράβαλο.

σβάρνα *s.f.* harrow; (*fam.*) *παίρνω* ~ sweep *or* drag along; make the round of.

σβέλτος *a.* quick, nimble.

σβέρκος *s.m.* nape of neck.

σβήνω *v.t. & i.* extinguish, quench, put out; erase; be quenched *or* erased; go out; (*fig.*) die.

σβήσιμο *s.n.* putting out; erasure.

σβηστός *a.* (put) out, erased.

σβίγγος *s.m.* fritter.

σβουνιά *s.f.* cattle-dung.

σβούρα *s.f.* spinning-top.

σβύνω *v.t. & i.* see σβήνω.

σβώλος *s.m.* clod; clot.

σγάρα *s.f.* (*bird's*) crop.

σγουρός *a.* curly, curly-haired.

σέ 1. *pron.* you. 2. *prep.* see εἰς.

σέβ|ας *s.n.* ~ασμός *s.m.* respect, reverence.

σεβ|άσματα, ~η *s.n.pl.* respects.

σεβάσμιος *a.* reverend.

σεβαστός *a.* respected; respectable, not inconsiderable.

σεβντάς *s.m.* love, heart-ache.

σέβομαι *v.t.* respect, revere.

σειρά *s.f.* series, row, line; turn; sequence, order; *μέ τή* ~ in turn; *τῆς* ~*s μας* of our (social) class; *τῆς* ~*s* common, ordinary; *ἔχει τή* ~ *του* he is comfortably off; *μπαίνω σέ* ~ settle down to a steady course.

σειρήν *s.f.* siren, charmer; hooter; motor-horn.

σειρήτι *s.n.* stripe, chevron (*on uniform*).

σεῖς *pron.* you.

σείσιμο *s.n.* shaking, tremor.

σεισμικός *a.* seismic.

σεισμο|παθής, ~πληκτος *a.* stricken by earthquake.

σεισμός *s.m.* earthquake.

σεί|ω *v.t.* shake. ~έμαι *v.i.* shake; affect undulating gait.

σεκλέτι *s.n.* care, worry.

σελαγίζω *v.i.* shine (*of star, lighthouse*).

σέλας *s.n.* βόρειον ~ northern lights.

σελάχι *s.n.* 1. belt for pistols, *etc.* 2. ray (*fish*).

σελέμ|ης *s.m.* sponger, cadger. ~ίζω *v.t.* cadge.

σελήνη *s.f.* moon.

σεληνιασμός *s.m.* epilepsy.

σεληνόφως *s.n.* moonlight.

σελίνι(ον) *s.n.* shilling.

σέλινον *s.n.* celery.

σελ|ίς, ~ίδα *s.f.* page.

σέλλα *s.f.* saddle.

σεμιγδάλι *s.n.* semolina.

σεμνός *a.* decorous, unassuming, modest.

σεμνοπρεπής *a.* decorous, modest.

σεμνότυφος *a.* prudish.

σέμπρος *s.m.* share-cropper.

σένα *pron.* you.

σεντόνι *s.n.* (*bed*) sheet.

σεντούκι *s.n.* linen-chest.

σεξουαλισμός *s.m.* sexual instinct.

Σεπτέμβρ|ης, ~ιος *s.m.* September.

σεπτός *a.* venerated (*of relics, etc.*).

σερβίρω *v.t.* serve (*at table*).

σερβιτόρος *s.m.* waiter.

σερβίτσιο *s.n.* service (*set of plates, etc.*); place-setting.

σεργιάν|ι *s.n.* walk, stroll. ~ίζω *v.t. & i.* take (for) a walk; wander.

σερμαγιά *s.f.* capital, funds.

σερμπέτι *s.n.* sherbet; manure-and-water.

σερνικός *a.* (*fam.*) male.

σέρν|ω *v.t.* draw, pull, drag; lead (*dance*); ~ω φωνή cry out; τί μᾶς ἔσυρε how he abused us! σῦρε στὸ διάολο go to the devil! ~ομαι *v.i.* crawl, drag; drag oneself along; ~εται γρίππη there is an epidemic of flu.

σερπετός *a.* sharp, lively, spry.

σέρρα *s.f.* greenhouse.

σεσημασμένος *a.* (*criminal*) whose particulars are known to police.

σέσουλα *s.f.* scoop; (*naut.*) skeet.

σεφτές *s.m.* first sale of the day.

σήκαλη *s.f.* rye.

σήκωμα *s.n.* lifting; withdrawal.

σηκωμός *s.m.* rising, revolt.

σηκών|ω *v.t.* raise, lift up; carry; remove, withdraw; put up with, take; do with, require; τὸν ~ει τὸ κλίμα the climate is good for him; ~ω τὸ τραπέζι clear away the table; ~ω στὸ πόδι rouse, throw into confusion; ~ω κεφάλι get uppish. ~ομαι *v.i.* rise, get up; revolt; σήκω get up!

σῆμα *s.n.* mark, badge; signal; omen; ~ κατατεθέν trade-mark.

σημαδ|εύω *v.t.* mark; aim at; ~εμένος having physical defects, scarred.

σημάδι *s.n.* mark, scar, birth-mark; target; omen; sign, indication.

σημαδιακός *a.* having physical defects, scarred; exceptional, rare.

σημαδούρα *s.f.* buoy.

σημαία *s.f.* flag, banner.

σημαίν|ω *v.t. & i.* mean, signify; sound, signal (*alarm, etc.*); (*v.i.*) matter, be important; sound, go (*of bells, etc.*); ~ον πρόσωπον leading personality.

σημαιοφόρος *s.m.* standard-bearer; (*naut.*) ensign (*lowest rank of officer*).

σήμανσις *s.f.* stamping; recording of (criminal's) particulars.

σημαντικός *a.* signifying (*with gen.*); important, noteworthy.

σήμαντρον *s.n.* wood or metal bar serving as church bell; stamp, seal.

σημασία *s.f.* meaning; importance.

σηματο|γράφος, ~φόρος *s.m.* semaphore.

σημεῖον *s.n.* sign, indication; point (*place or degree*), stage, pitch; sign, symbol (*maths., etc.*); ~ τοῦ ὁρίζοντος point of the compass.

σημείωμα *s.n.* (*written*) note.

σημειωματάρι(ον) *s.n.* notebook, diary.

σημειώ|νω *v.t.* mark; make a note of; take note of, observe; ~μένος having physical defects, scarred.

σημείωσις *s.f.* (*written*) note.

σημειωτέος *a.* to be noted.

σημειωτ|ός *a.* βῆμα ~όν mark time!

σήμερ|α, ~ον *adv.* today. ~ινός *a.* today's.

σήπομαι *v.i.* rot.

σηπτικός *a.* septic.

σήραγξ *s.f.* tunnel.

σηροτροφία *s.f.* production of raw silk.

σησάμι *s.n.* sesame.

σηψαιμία *s.f.* septicaemia.

σῆψις *s.f.* putrefaction; (*med.*) sepsis.
σθεναρός *a.* strong, vigorous.
σθένος *s.n.* strength.
σιαγών *s.f.* jaw, chin.
σιάζω *v.t. & i.* settle, put straight; get better; τᾶσιαξαν (*fam.*) they have made it up *or* formed an attachment.
σίαλος *s.m.* saliva.
σιάξιμο *s.n.* straightening, arranging; improvement.
σιάχνω *v.t. & i. see* σιάζω.
σιγά *adv.* quietly, gently, slowly; ~ ~ gradually, carefully.
σιγαλός, ~νός *a.* quiet, gentle, slow; ~νό ποτάμι still waters run deep.
σιγανοπαπαδιά *s.f.* person affecting prudishness *or* innocence.
σιγή *s.f.* silence.
σιγηλός *a.* silent; taciturn.
σίγμα *s.n.* the letter Σ.
σιγο- *denotes* quietly, slowly.
σίγουρος *a.* certain, sure, secure. ~α *adv.* for certain.
σιγῶ *v.i.* be silent; subside, abate.
σιδερένιος *a.* iron; (*fig.*) ~! may you enjoy robust health!
σιδερικά *s.n.pl.* things made of iron.
σίδερο *s.n.* iron; flat-iron, curling-tongs. ~α (*pl.*) ironwork; railway-lines; prison; ἔφαγα τὰ ~α I made a superhuman effort.
σιδερώνω *v.t.* iron, press. ~ωμα *s.n.* ironing.
σιδηρόδρομος *s.m.* railway. ~ικός *a.* of railways; a railwayman. ~ικῶς *adv.* by rail.
σίδηρος *s.m.* iron.
σιδηροτροχιά *s.f.* railway-track.
σιδηρουργεῖον *s.n.* forge.
σιδηρουργός *s.m.* blacksmith.
σιδηροῦς *a.* iron.
σιδηροῦχος *a.* ferruginous.
σίελος *s.m.* saliva.
σίκαλις *s.f.* rye.
σιμά *adv.* near.
σιμός *a.* snub-nosed.
σιμώνω *v.t. & i.* approach.
σινάπι *s.n.* mustard.
σινάφι *s.n.* guild, group.
σινδών *s.f.* (*bed*) sheet.
σινιάλο *s.n.* sign, signal.
σιντριβάνι *s.n.* fountain.
σιρόκος *s.m.* south-east wind.
σιρόπι *s.n.* syrup.
σιταράτος *a.* corn-coloured; (*fig.*) clear, to the point (*of speech*).

σιτάρ|ι *s.n.* wheat. ~ένιος *a.* wheaten.
σιτάρκεια *s.f.* self-sufficiency in cereals.
σιτεύω *v.t. & i.* fatten (*livestock*); hang, get tender *or* high (*of meat*).
σιτηρά *s.n.pl.* cereals.
σιτηρέσιον *s.n.* day's ration.
σιτίζω *v.t.* feed.
σιτιστής *s.m.* (*mil.*) quartermaster-sergeant.
σιτοβολών *s.m.* granary.
σιτοδεία *s.f.* failure of wheat crop, famine.
σῖτος *s.m.* wheat.
σιφόνι *s.n.* siphon; S-bend pipe.
σίφουνας *s.m.* water-spout, whirlwind.
σίφων *s.m.* siphon; S-bend pipe; water-spout, whirlwind.
σιχαίνομαι *v.t.* loathe, be disgusted by.
σιχαμάρα *s.f.* (object of) disgust.
σιχαμένος, ~μερός *a.* disgusting.
σιχαμός *s.m.* (object of) disgust.
σιωπή *s.f.* silence.
σιωπηλός *a.* silent, taciturn.
σιωπηρός *a.* tacit.
σιωπῶ *v.i.* be silent; stop talking.
σκ- *see* σχ-.
σκάβω *v.t. & i.* dig; carve, hollow out.
σκάγια *s.n.pl.* small shot.
σκάζω *v.t. & i.* burst; crack, chap; exasperate; be exasperated, maddened, choked (*by heat, jealousy, etc.*); (*fam.*) pay, cough up; τὸ ~ escape, make off; σκάσε shut up! νὰ σκάση damn him!
σκαιός *a.* unmannerly, abrupt, rude.
σκάκι *s.n.* chess.
σκάλα *s.f.* staircase, steps, ladder; stirrup; landing-place, port, harbour; wave (*in hair*); degree; (*mus.*) scale.
σκαλί *s.n.* step, rung; degree.
σκαλίζω *v.t. & i.* hoe, dig over; search, rummage; carve, sculpt; pick (*teeth, nose*).
σκάλισμα *s.n.* hoeing; searching; carving.
σκαλιστήρι *s.n.* hoe.
σκαλιστός *a.* carved, engraved.
σκαλοπάτι *s.n. see* σκαλί.
σκαλώνω *v.i.* climb up; (*fig.*) meet with a hitch, get held *or* caught up.
σκαλωσιά *s.f.* scaffolding.
σκαλωτός *a.* having steps; wavy (*of hair*).
σκαμνί *s.n.* stool.
σκαμπάζω *v.t. & i.* (*fam.*) understand, know.

σκαμπανεβάζω v.i. (naut.) pitch.

σκαμπίλι s.n. 1. slap. 2. a card game.

σκανδάλη s.f. trigger.

σκανδαλ|ίζω v.t. intrigue, tempt; scandalize. ~ιστικός a. tempting.

σκανδαλοθήρας s.m. scandalmonger.

σκάνδαλ|ον s.n. scandal; βάζω ~a sow dissension.

σκανδαλώδης a. scandalous.

σκανταλιάρ|ης, ~ικος a. mischievous, naughty; provocative (sensually).

σκαντζόχοιρος s.m. hedgehog.

σκάνω v.t. & i. see σκάζω.

σκαπανεύς s.m. sapper, pioneer.

σκαπάνη s.f. mattock.

σκαπουλάρω v.t. & i. escape.

σκάπτω v.t. & i. see σκάβω.

σκάρα s.f. grill.

σκαρί s.n. (naut.) στὰ ~ά on the stocks; (of persons) constitution, disposition.

σκαρίφημα s.n. sketch, rough draft.

σκαρπίνι s.n. woman's lace-up shoe.

σκάρτος a. defective, dud.

σκαρφαλώνω v.i. climb up.

σκαρφ|ίζομαι v.t. think up, contrive; τοῦ ~ίστηκε νά he took it into his head to. . . .

σκαρ|ώνω v.t. (fam.) put in hand, put together; organize, lay on; τοῦ ~ωσα μιά I played him a trick.

σκάσ|η, ~ίλα s.f. chagrin, worry, vexation.

σκασιάρχης s.m. truant.

σκάσιμο s.n. bursting, cracking; escaping, playing truant; see also σκάση.

σκασμός s.m. see σκάση. (int.) shut up!

σκαστός a. resounding; in hard cash; truant.

σκατο- opprobrious qualification of sthg.

σκατ|ό s.n. (fam.) excrement; ~ά (pl.) int. of annoyance or defiance.

σκάφανδρον s.n. diving apparatus or suit.

σκάφη s.f. trough; cockle-boat.

σκάφος s.n. hull; ship.

σκάψιμο s.n. digging.

σκάω v.t. & i. see σκάζω.

σκεβρώνω v.t. & i. warp, bend; become bent.

σκέλεθρο s.n. skeleton.

σκελετός s.m. skeleton; framework.

σκέλος s.n. leg; side (of angle, etc.).

σκεπάζω v.t. cover; shelter; conceal.

σκεπάρνι s.n. adze.

σκέπασμα s.n. covering; cover, lid.

σκεπαστ|ός a. covered (in); (fig.) covert. ~ά adv. covertly.

σκέπη s.f. cover; protection.

σκεπή s.f. roof.

σκεπτικισ|μός s.m. scepticism. ~τής s.m. sceptic.

σκεπτικός a. thoughtful, pensive.

σκέπτομαι v.t. & i. think about; think, reflect.

σκέρτσ|ο s.n. charm, coquetry; (mus.) scherzo. ~a (pl.) coquettish mannerisms.

σκερτσόζ|ικ)ος a. coquettish; natty, saucy (of hat, etc.).

σκέτος a. plain, unmixed; unsweetened.

σκευασία s.f. preparation, compound.

σκεῦος s.n. utensil, tool, piece of equipment.

σκευοφόρος s.m. luggage-van.

σκευωρία s.f. machination, trick.

σκέψις s.f. thought, reflexion.

σκηνή s.f. scene; stage; tent.

σκηνικ|ός a. of the stage; τὰ ~ά stage scenery.

σκηνογραφία s.f. (designing of) stage scenery.

σκηνο|θεσία s.f. stage production. ~θέτης s.m. producer.

σκήν|ος, ~ωμα s.n. mortal remains.

σκῆπτρ|ον s.n. sceptre; κατέχω τὰ ~a bear the palm.

σκήτη s.f. small monastery (dependency of a greater).

σκιά s.f. shade, shadow; ghost.

σκιαγραφῶ v.t. sketch.

σκιάδι s.n. straw hat; parasol.

σκιάζω (-i-) v.t. cast shade upon; conceal (sun).

σκιάζ|ω (-j-) v.t. frighten. ~ομαι v.t. & i. be frightened (of).

σκιάχτρο s.n. scarecrow.

σκιερός a. shady.

σκίζα s.f. splinter.

σκίζ|ω v.t. split, tear; (fig.) ~ω τὰ ροῦχα μου protest one's innocence. ~ομαι v.i. make great efforts; protest vehemently.

σκίουρος s.m. squirrel.

σκιόφως s.n. half-light.

σκιρτῶ v.i. jump, leap.

σκίσιμο s.n. tear, tearing.

σκιτζῆς s.m. (fam.) one who is no good at his job.

σκίτσο s.n. sketch.

σκιώδης a. shadowy, unsubstantial.

σκλαβιά s.f. slavery; (fig.) obligation, responsibility.

σκλάβος s.m. slave.

σκλαβώνω v.t. enslave; (fig.) oblige greatly.

σκλήθρα s.f. splinter; alder.

σκλῆθρος s.m. alder.

σκληραγωγῶ v.t. inure to hardship.

σκληρ|αίνω, ~ύνω v.t. & i. harden.

σκληρός a. hard; severe; unmanageable (of child).

σκληροτράχηλος a. opinionated.

σκνίπα s.f. midge; (fam.) very drunk.

σκοινί s.n. rope.

σκολειό s.n. school.

σκόλη s.f. holiday.

σκολιαν|ός a. φορῶ τὰ ~ά μου wear one's Sunday 'best; τοῦ ἔψαλα τὰ ~ά του I called him over the coals.

σκολιός a. crooked; difficult (of persons).

σκολίωσις s.f. (med.) scoliosis.

σκολνῶ v.t. & i. see σχολάζω.

σκολόπενδρα s.f. centipede.

σκόνη s.f. dust, powder.

σκονίζω v.t. cover with dust.

σκοντάφτω v.i. stumble; meet with obstacle.

σκόντο s.n. discount.

σκόπελος s.m. reef (above surface); (fig.) stumbling-block.

σκοπευτήριον s.n. shooting-range.

σκοπεύω v.t. & i. aim at; take aim; intend.

σκοπιά s.f. observation post; sentry-box.

σκόπ|ιμος a. opportune, expedient; intentional. ~ίμως adv. intentionally.

σκοποβολή s.f. target-practice.

σκοπός' s.m. sentry, sentinel; target; aim, intention; tune.

σκοπῶ v.i. intend.

σκορβοῦτον s.n. (med.) scurvy.

σκορδαλιά s.f. sauce of garlic, etc.

σκόρδ|ο s.n. garlic; ~α (pl.) said to avert evil eye after praise.

σκόρ|ος s.m. moth. ~οφαγωμένος a. moth-eaten.

σκορπίζω v.t. & i. scatter, emit; squander; (v.i.) disperse, disintegrate.

σκόρπιος a. scattered.

σκορπιός s.m. scorpion.

σκορπῶ v.t. & i. see σκορπίζω.

σκοτάδι s.n. darkness, dark.

σκοτεινιάζ|ω v.t. & i. darken; ~ει it gets dark. ~ομαι v.i. be overtaken by darkness.

σκοτεινιά s.f. darkness, dark.

σκοτειν|ός a. dark, obscure; unlucky, sinister; ἦταν ~ά it was dark.

σκοτ|ίζω v.t. darken, confuse; worry. ~ίζομαι v.i. worry, care; (fam.) ~ίστηκα I could not care less.

σκότιος a. dark, sinister.

σκοτοδίνη s.f. giddiness.

σκότος s.n. darkness, dark.

σκοτοῦρα s.f. giddiness; (fig.) worry, nuisance.

σκοτωμός s.m. killing; (fig.) jostling for priority in crowd.

σκοτών|ω v.t. kill; harass. ~ομαι v.i. hurt oneself badly; (fig.) slave away; endeavour with zeal.

σκούζω v.i. howl.

σκουλαρίκι s.n. ear-ring.

σκουλήκι s.n. worm.

σκουντουφλῶ v.i. stumble.

σκουντῶ v.t. push.

σκοῦπα s.f. broom.

σκουπιδαρειό s.n. rubbish-dump.

σκουπίδι s.n. rubbish.

σκουπιδιάρης s.m. scavenger, dustman.

σκουπίζω v.t. sweep, wipe.

σκουραίνω v.t. & i. make or become dark; get worse.

σκουρι|ά s.f. rust. ~άζω v.t. & i. rust.

σκοῦρ|ος a. dark; τὰ βρῆκα ~α I met with obstacles. ~α s.n.pl. shutters.

σκουτί s.n. thick woollen cloth.

σκουφ|ί s.n., ~ια s.f., ~ος s.m. cap.

σκύβαλο s.n. siftings of grain; (fig.) sweepings.

σκύβω v.t. & i. bend, lean, stoop.

σκυθρωπός a. sullen, scowling.

σκύλα s.f. bitch.

σκυλεύω v.t. despoil.

σκυλήσιος a. dog's.

σκυλ|ί s.n. dog; ἔγινε ~ί he got mad. ~άζω v.t. & i. enrage; get enraged.

σκυλοβρίζω v.t. revile grossly.

σκυλολόγι s.n. canaille, rabble.

σκυλομούρης a. dog-faced; (fig.) shameless.

σκυλοπνίχτης s.m. (fam.) unseaworthy boat, tub.

σκύλος s.m. dog.

σκυλόψαρο s.n. dogfish; shark.

σκύμνος s.m. cub.

σκύρα s.n.pl. gravel or stones for road-making.

σκυταλοδρομία s.f. relay-race.

σκυφτός a. bent, stooping.

σκωληκόβρωτος a. worm-eaten.

σκωληκοειδῖτις s.f. appendicitis.

σκώληξ s.m. worm, larva.

σκῶμμα s.n. gibe.

σκώπτω v.t. mock, jeer at.
σκωρία s.f. rust.
σκώτι s.n. liver.
σλαυικός a. Slav, Slavonic.
σλέπι s.n. large flat-bottomed river craft.
σμάλτον s.n. enamel.
σμαράγδι s.n. emerald.
σμάρι s.n. swarm.
σμέουρο s.n. raspberry.
σμην|αγός s.m. (aero.) flight-lieutenant. ~αρχος s.m. group-captain.
σμην|ίας s.m. (aero.) sergeant. ~ίτης s.m. aircraftman.
σμήνος s.n. swarm; (aero.) squadron.
σμίγω v.t. & i. mix; meet.
σμίκρυνσις s.f. reduction in size.
σμίλ|η s.f. chisel, scalpel. ~άρι s.n. chisel.
σμίξιμο s.n. mixing, meeting.
σμιχτοφρύδης a. whose eyebrows meet.
σμόκιν s.n. dinner-jacket. [E. smoking]
σμπαράλια s.n.pl. smithereens.
σμπάρο s.n. shot, discharge of gun.
σμύρις s.f. emery.
σνομπαρία s.f. snobbery; (fam.) snob(s).
σοβαρ|ός a. serious; ~όν ποσόν considerable amount. ~εύομαι v.i. become serious, talk seriously.
σοβάς s.m. plaster.
σοβα(ν)τίζω v.t. plaster.
σοβώ v.i. be imminent.
σόδα s.f. (bicarbonate of) soda; soda-water.
σοδειά s.f. crop, harvest.
σόϊ s.n. stock, breed; kind; από ~ of good family.
σοκάκι s.n. (narrow) street.
σοκάρω v.t. (fam.) shock.
σόκιν a. (fam.) risqué. [E. shocking]
σοκολάτα s.f. chocolate.
σόλα s.f. sole (of shoe).
σόλοικος a. ungrammatical; (fig.) wrong, out-of-place.
σολομός s.m. salmon.
σολομονική s.f. book of magic; mumbo-jumbo.
σομμιέ s.n. spring-mattress. [F. sommier]
σόμπα s.f. stove (for room heating).
σορόκος s.m. south-east wind.
σορός s.f. coffin; mortal remains.
σός pron. your, yours.
σοσιαλιστής s.m. socialist.
σου pron. your, to you.

σουβάς s.m. see σοβάς.
σούβλ|α s.f. spit, skewer. ~άκια s.n.pl. skewers of grilled meat.
σουβλερός a. sharp, pointed.
σούβλ|ι s.n. awl; sharp-pointed object. ~ιά s.f. hole or wound from pointed object; twinge.
σουβλίζω v.t. impale, pierce; roast on spit; give twinges to; sew clumsily.
σουγιάς s.m. penknife.
σούζα adv. (of animals) στέκομαι ~ sit up and beg; (fig.) fawn.
σουλατσάρω v.i. stroll about.
σουλούπ|ι s.n. shape, cut; (fam.) cut of one's jib. ~ιάζω, ~ώνω v.t. improve or restore shape of.
σουλτανί s.n. fresh σουλτανίνα.
σουλτανίνα s.f. kind of seedless grape; sultana from this.
σουλτάν|ος s.m. Sultan. ~α s.f. Sultana.
σουμάδα s.f. orgeat of almonds.
σούπα s.f. soup.
σουπιά s.f. cuttlefish; (fig.) sly person.
σούρα s.f. fold, gathering, crease.
σουραύλι s.n. shepherd's pipe.
σουρλουλού s.f. gadabout, light woman.
σουρομαδώ v.t. pull by the hair.
σούρουπ|ο, ~ωμα s.n. dusk. ~ώνει v.i. twilight falls.
σουρτούκης s.m. gadabout.
σουρώ|νω v.t. & i. strain, filter; gather, pucker; (v.i.) crease, shrivel, waste away; τὴ ~σε he is three sheets in the wind; ~μένος (fam.) drunk.
σουρωτήρι s.n. strainer, colander.
σουσάμι s.n. sesame.
σουσουράδα s.f. wagtail; gossip.
σούσουρο s.n. rustle; commotion; covert gossip.
σοῦστα s.f. spring (of seat, etc.); press-fastener; trap, gig; a folk dance.
σούτ int. hush! quiet!
σουτζούκ|ι s.n. kind of sausage; sweet of same shape. ~άκια s.n.pl. kind of meat-balls.
σουτιέν s.n. brassière. [F. soutien]
σούφρα s.f. wrinkle, crease.
σουφρώνω v.t. wrinkle, crease; (fam.) pinch, pilfer.
σοφία s.f. wisdom; erudition.
σοφίζομαι v.t. invent.
σοφιστεία s.f. sophistry.
σοφίτα s.f. attic.
σοφός a. wise; learned; clever.
σπαγγοραμμένος a. miserly.

σπάγγος s.m. string; (fam.) stingy person.

σπάζω v.t. & i. break, smash; ~ τὸ κεφάλι μου rack one's brains; ~ στὸ ξύλο thrash.

σπαθᾶτος a. sword-bearing; (fig.) tall and lithe.

σπάθη s.f. sword, sabre.

σπαθ|ί s.n. sword; club (at cards). ~ιά s.f. stroke or scar of sword.

σπανάκι s.n. spinach.

σπανίζω v.i. be rare or scarce.

σπάν|ιος a. rare; exceptional. ~ίως adv. rarely, seldom.

σπάν|ις, ~ιότης s.f. rarity, scarcity.

σπανός a. hairless, beardless; deficient in hairs, threads, etc.

σπάνω v.t. & i. see σπάζω.

σπαράγγι s.n. asparagus.

σπαραγμός s.m. tearing, rending.

σπαράζω 1. v.t. see σπαράσσω. 2. v.i. see σπαρταρῶ.

σπαρακτικός a. heart-rending.

σπαράσσω v.t. tear, rend; (fig.) distress.

σπάραχνα s.n.pl. gills.

σπάργανα s.n.pl. swaddling-clothes.

σπαρμένος a. scattered; sown.

σπαρταριστός a. freshly caught (fish); blooming (girl); graphic, vivid; that makes you laugh.

σπαρταρ|ῶ, ~ίζω v.i. quiver, palpitate, leap.

σπαρτ|ός a. scattered; sown; τὰ ~ά crops.

σπάσιμο s.n. breaking; fracture; hernia.

σπασμ|ός s.m. spasm. ~ωδικός a. convulsive; ~ωδικὰ μέτρα hastily improvised measures.

σπατ|άλη s.f. waste, wastefulness. ~αλος a. wasteful. ~αλῶ v.t. waste, squander.

σπάτουλα s.f. spatula.

σπεῖρα s.f. coil, spiral; gang.

σπείρω v.t. sow.

σπέρμα s.n. seed, germ; semen; (fig.) offspring.

σπερμολογία s.f. gossip.

σπέρνω v.t. see σπείρω.

σπεύδω v.i. hasten.

σπήλ|αιον, ~ιο s.n., ~ιά s.f. cave.

σπίθ|α s.f. spark. ~οβολῶ v.i. sparkle.

σπιθαμ|ή s.f. span (of hand); ~ὴν πρὸς ~ήν inch by inch. ~ιαῖος a. tiny, dwarfish.

σπιθούρι s.n. pimple.

σπιλ(ι)άδα s.f. gust of wind.

σπιλῶ v.t. sully.

σπινθήρ s.m. see σπίθα.

σπίνος s.m. finch.

σπιοῦνος s.m. spy; calumniator.

σπιρούνι s.n. spur.

σπιρτάδα s.f. pungency, pungent smell; (fig.) quick-wittedness.

σπίρτο s.n. alcohol, spirit; match; (fig.) ~ μονάχο quick-witted person.

σπιτήσιος a. home-made.

σπίτι s.n. house, home; firm; ἀπὸ ~ of good family.

σπιτικ|ός a. home-made; home-loving. ~ό s.n. home.

σπιτονοικοκύρης s.m. householder, landlord.

σπιτώνω v.t. house; (fam.) keep (woman).

σπλά(γ)χν|α s.n.pl. entrails, bowels; (fig.) feelings. ~ο s.n. child, one's own flesh. ~ικός a. compassionate.

σπλήν s.m., ~α s.f. (anat.) spleen.

σπληνάντερο s.n. dish of sheep's intestine with spleen, etc., on spit.

σπληνιάρης a. irritable.

σπογγαλιεία s.f. sponge-fishing.

σπογγίζω v.t. sponge, wipe.

σπόγγ|ος s.m. sponge. ~ώδης a. spongy.

σποδός s.f. ashes.

σπολλάτη int. that explains it; many thanks (ironic).

σπονδή s.f. libation.

σπόνδυλ|ος s.m. vertebra; drum (of column). ~ικός a. vertebral; ~ική στήλη spine, backbone. ~ωτός a. vertebrate.

σπόρ s.n. sport. [E. sport]

σπορά s.f. sowing; seed; (fig.) offspring.

σποράδην adv. here and there.

σποραδικός a. sporadic, sparse.

σπορέλαιον s.n. seed-oil.

σποριάζω v.i. seed; run to seed.

σπόρ|ος s.m. seed, germ; semen; (fam.) ~ια (n.pl.) seeds (of edible fruit, vegetables).

σπουδάζω v.t. & i. study; provide with means to study.

σπουδαῖος a. important; of value, outstanding.

σπουδαστής s.m. student.

σπουδή s.f. 1. haste, eagerness. 2. study.

σπουργίτης s.m. sparrow.

σπρωξ|ιά s.f. push, shove. ~ιμο s.n. push(ing); urging.

σπρώχνω v.t. push, shove; urge.

σπυρ|ί s.n. grain (of corn); bead (of

necklace); grain (weight); spot, pimple.
~ωτός a. granular; (of cooked rice) not reduced to pap.

σπῶ v.t. & i. see σπάζω.

στάβλος s.m. see σταῦλος.

στάγδην adv. drop by drop.

σταγονόμετρον s.n. dropper; μὲ τὸ ~ in driblets.

σταγ|ών, ~όνα s.f. drop.

σταδιοδρομία s.f. career.

στάδιον s.n. stadium; career; stage, phase.

στάζω v.i. & t. drip, leak; drip with.

σταθερ|ός a. stable, steady, steadfast. ~οποίησις s.f. stabilization.

σταθμά s.n.pl. weights; ἔχω δύο μέτρα καὶ δύο ~ apply one standard to others and another to oneself.

σταθμάρχης s.m. station-master; station superintendent (gendarmerie).

σταθ|μεύω v.i. stop, halt, camp, park. ~μευσις s.f. stopping, parking.

στάθμη s.f. level, plumb-line; water-level.

σταθμίζω v.t. weigh; take level of; weigh consequences of.

σταθμός s.m. halt; station; landmark (in history, etc.).

στάλ|α, ~α(γ)ματιά s.f. drop.

σταλάζω v.t. & i. drop, drip.

σταλακτίτης s.m. stalactite.

σταλίζω v.t. & i. repose, rest (of flocks).

στάλος s.m. (place for) repose of flocks.

σταμάτημα s.n. stopping, checking; break.

σταματ|ῶ v.t. & i. stop, break off, cease activity.

στάμν|α s.f., ~ί s.n. pitcher.

στάνη s.f. sheepfold.

στανιό s.n. μὲ τὸ ~ unwillingly, by force.

σταξ|ιά s.f. drop. ~ιμο s.n. dripping.

στάρι s.n. see σιτάρι.

στασιάζω v.i. revolt, mutiny.

στασίδι s.n. pew.

στάσιμος a. stationary (not changing); stagnant; passed over for promotion.

στάσις s.f. stop, stopping-place; suspension, stoppage; posture; behaviour, attitude; revolt, mutiny.

στατήρ s.m. hundredweight.

στατικ|ός a. static. ~ή s.f. statics.

στατιστική s.f. statistics.

σταυλάρχης s.m. Master of the Horse.

σταῦλος s.m. stable; cow-shed.

σταυροδρόμι s.n. crossroads.

σταυροειδής a. cruciform.

σταυροκοπιέμαι v.i. cross oneself (repeatedly).

σταυρόλεξο s.n. crossword puzzle.

σταυροπόδι adv. cross-legged (squatting).

σταυρ|ός s.m. cross, crucifix; κάνω τὸ ~ό μου cross oneself; starfish; part of forehead between brows; τοῦ ~οῦ feast of (esp. Elevation of) Cross (14 Sept.).

σταυροφορία s.f. crusade.

σταυρώ|νω v.t. crucify; place crosswise; make sign of cross over; encounter; tease, badger; exhort; (fam.) δέ ~σα δεκάρα I have not had a penny. (v.i.) cross over (of front of jacket, panel, etc.).

σταυρωτός a. crossed, crosswise; double-breasted.

σταφίδα s.f. raisin; κορινθιακή ~ currant; grapes or vineyard producing these; (fam.) γίνομαι ~ get drunk or shrivelled; τὰ μάτια μου ἔγιναν ~ I cannot keep my eyes open.

σταφιδιάζω v.i. dry up, shrivel.

σταφυλή s.f. grapes; uvula.

σταφύλι s.n. grapes.

στάχι s.n. ear of corn.

στάχτη s.f. ashes.

σταχτής a. ashen, grey.

σταχτόνερο s.n. lye.

Σταχτοπούτα s.f. Cinderella.

σταχ(υ)ολόγημα s.n. gleaning; (fig.) selection, anthology.

στεατοκήριον s.n. tallow-candle.

στεγάζω v.t. roof; shelter.

στεγανόπους a. web-footed.

στεγανός a. air-tight, water-tight.

στέγασις s.f. (act of) roofing or housing.

στέγασμα s.n. roof; see also στέγασις.

στέγη s.f. roof; (fig.) home.

στεγν|ός a. dry. ~ώνω v.t. & i. dry, get dry.

στειλιάρι s.n. helve; cudgel; cudgelling.

στεῖρος a. barren, sterile.

στέκα s.f. billiard-cue; (fam.) tall, thin woman.

στέκομαι v.i. stand up, stand still, stop; be, prove to be; happen; μοῦ στάθηκε he stood by me; δὲ στάθηκε νὰ τὴ φιλήσω she would not let me kiss her.

στέκ|ω v.i. stand up, stand still; δὲ ~ει it is not fitting; σοῦ ~ει τὸ φόρεμα the dress fits or suits you; ~ει καλά he keeps well or is well off.

στέλεχ|ος s.n. stalk, stem; handle; counterfoil; ~η (pl.) (mil.) cadres.

στέλ|λω, ~νω v.t. send.

στέμμα s.n. crown.

στέμφυλον s.n. residue of grapes after pressing.

στέναγ|μα s.n., ~μός s.m. sigh(ing), groan(ing).

στενάζω v.i. sigh, groan.

στεν|εύω v.t. & i. reduce width of; hurt by being tight (of clothes); get narrow, shrink; ~εψαν τὰ πράματα things have worsened.

στενογραφία s.f. shorthand.

στενοδακτυλογράφος s.m.f. shorthand-typist.

στενόκαρδος a. inclined to fuss or worry.

στενοκέφαλος a. narrow-minded.

στενόμακρος a. long and narrow.

στενόν s.n. strait; pass, defile.

στεν|ός a. narrow; tight-fitting; close (friend, etc.); ~ὰ τὰ πράματα (there are) difficulties; περνῶ ~ά live on a shoe-string; βάζω στὰ ~ά press hard.

στενότης s.f. closeness; narrowness; ~ χρήματος shortage of money.

στενοχωρία s.f. lack of space; difficulty, worry, vexation; depression.

στενόχωρος a. narrow, cramped, tight; depressing; see also στενόκαρδος.

στενοχωρ|ῶ v.t. worry, upset, depress; press hard; ~ημένος upset, hard up.

στενωπός s.f. lane.

στέργω v.i. consent, agree (to) (with εἰς).

στερε|ός a. firm, strong, solid; fast (colour); ~ὰ Ἑλλάς central Greece; ~ά (s.f.) mainland.

στερεοποιῶ v.t. solidify.

στερεότυπος a. stereotyped.

στερεύω v.i. run dry; cease to run.

στερέωμα s.n. strengthening; support, prop; firmament.

στερεώνω v.t. & i. strengthen; make fast or firm; ~ σὲ μία δουλειά stick to one job.

στέρ|ησις s.f. deprivation; lack; ~ήσεις (pl.) privation.

στεριά s.f. dry land. ~νός s.m. landsman, mainlander.

στερλίνα s.f. (pound) sterling.

στέρνα s.f. cistern.

στέρνον s.n. (breast)bone.

στερν|ός a. later, last; καλὰ ~ά happy old age.

στερ|ῶ v.t. deprive (of, with gen.). ~οῦμαι v.t. & i. lack, go short of (with gen.); live in want.

στέφανα s.n.pl. marriage wreaths.

στεφάνη s.f. hoop (of barrel); rim (of cup); crown (of tooth).

στεφάνι s.n. hoop (of barrel); child's hoop; wreath (esp. in marriage).

στέφανος s.m. hoop (of barrel); wreath, crown; (fig.) reward.

στεφανών|ω v.t. crown; celebrate marriage of. ~ομαι v.t. & i. marry; get married.

στέψις s.f. coronation, crowning; marriage ceremony.

στηθαῖον s.n. parapet, breastwork.

στηθικός a. of the chest; consumptive.

στηθόδεσμος s.m. brassière.

στῆθ|ος s.n. chest, breast, bosom; ~ια (pl.) breasts.

στηθοσκοπῶ v.t. examine with stethoscope.

στήλη s.f. upright slab, pillar; column; electric battery.

στηλιτεύω v.t. stigmatize.

στηλώνω v.t. shore up, support; give strength to.

στημόνι s.n. warp (weaving).

στήνω v.t. set upright, erect, put up; ~ αὐτί prick up one's ears; ~ παγίδα set a trap.

στήριγμα s.n. prop, support.

στηρίζ|ω v.t. prop, support; base. ~ομαι v.i. lean (for support); be based or grounded (on).

στητός a. firm and erect.

στιβάλι s.n. top-boot.

στιβαρός a. strong, firm.

στίβος s.m. arena (of stadium).

στίγμα s.n. mark, brand, stigma.

στιγμή s.f. moment; point (printing); dot; τελεία ~ full-stop; ἄνω ~ colon.

στιγμιαῖος a. instantaneous; momentary.

στιγμιότυπον s.n. snapshot.

στικτός a. spotted, dotted.

στίλβω v.i. shine, gleam.

στιλβώνω v.t. polish.

στιλβωτήριον s.n. shoe-shine parlour.

στιλπνός a. shining, gleaming.

στίξις s.f. punctuation.

στιφάδο s.n. meat stewed with onions.

στῖφος s.n. swarm, mass.

στιχομυθία s.f. fast-moving dialogue; stichomythia.

στίχ|ος s.m. line, verse. ~ουργός s.m. rhymester.

στοά s.f. portico; arcade, passage; gallery (of mine); masonic lodge.

στοίβ|α *s.f.* pile, heap. **~άζω** *v.t.* pile up; cram, squeeze.

στοιχειό *s.n.* ghost.

στοιχειοθεσία *s.f.* type-setting.

στοιχεῖ|ον *s.n.* element; (piece of) evidence (*law*); letter (*of alphabet*); cell (*electric*); **~α** (*pl.*) rudiments; type (*printing*).

στοιχειώδης *a.* elementary, basic, essential.

στοιχειώ|νω *v.i.* become a ghost; become haunted; **~μένος** haunted.

στοίχημα *s.n.* bet, wager; *βάζω* **~** lay a bet. **~τίζω** *v.t. & i.* bet.

στοιχίζω *v.i.* cost; cause pain *or* grief.

στοῖχος *s.m.* row, file.

στόκος *s.m.* putty.

στολή *s.f.* uniform; costume.

στολίδι *s.n.* piece of finery *or* decoration.

στολίζω *v.t.* adorn, decorate, dress; (*fam.*) abuse.

στολίσκος *s.m.* (*naut.*) flotilla.

στολισμός *s.m.* adornment, decoration.

στόλος *s.m.* navy, fleet.

στόμα *s.n.* mouth; cutting edge.

στόμ|αχος *s.m.*, **~άχι** *s.n.* stomach. **~αχιάζω** *v.i.* get indigestion.

στόμιον *s.n.* orifice, mouth.

στόμφος *s.m.* pompous *or* declamatory way of speaking.

στομώνω *v.t. & i.* temper (*metal*); make *or* get blunt.

στοργή *s.f.* love, tender solicitude.

στουμπίζω *v.t.* pound, crush; stump up.

στουμπώνω *v.t. & i.* stuff full, plug; become stuffed full.

στουπί *s.n.* tow; (*fam.*) blind drunk.

στουπόχαρτο *s.n.* blotting-paper.

στουπώνω *v.t. & i.* stop up (*hole*); blot; become stopped up.

στουρνάρι *s.n.* flint.

στοχάζομαι *v.t. & i.* think, reflect (about).

στόχασ|η *s.f.* considerateness; judgement. **~τικός** *a.* considerate; judicious.

στοχασμός *s.m.* thought.

στόχαστρον *s.n.* foresight (*of gun*).

στόχος *s.m.* target, objective.

στραβά *adv.* awry, askance; wrongly; *τόβαλε* **~** he does not care.

στραβισμός *s.m.* squint, squinting.

στραβο- *denotes* crooked, askance, stubborn.

στραβοκάνης *a.* (*fam.*) bandy-legged.

στραβομάρα *s.f.* blindness; (*fig.*) hitch, reverse.

στραβομουτσουνιάζω *v.i.* make a wry face.

στραβόξυλο *s.n.* (*fam.*) contrary *or* cussed fellow.

στραβοπάτημα *s.n.* false step.

στραβ|ός *a.* crooked, twisted; faulty; blind; *κάνω* **~ά μάτια** pretend not to see; *τά* **~ά** (*fam.*) eyes.

στραβοτιμονιά *s.f.* error in steering; (*fig.*) ill-considered action.

στραβών|ω *v.t. & i.* make crooked, spoil; blind; become bent *or* spoiled. **~ομαι** *v.i.* become blind.

στραγάλια *s.n.pl.* roasted chick-peas.

στραγγαλίζω *v.t.* strangle.

στραγγίζω *v.t. & i.* strain, drain, wring out; become worn out, exhausted.

στραγγιστήρι *s.n.* strainer, colander.

στραγγουλίζω *v.t.* sprain.

στράκ|α *s.f.* crack (*noise*); cracker (*fire-work*); *κάνω* **~ες** make a sensation.

στραμπουλίζω *v.t.* sprain.

στραπατσάρω *v.t.* damage; rumple; humiliate.

στραπάτσο *s.n.* damage, harm.

στράτα *s.f.* way, road.

στρατάρχης *s.m.* field-marshal.

στράτευμα *s.n.* army; **~τα** (*pl.*) troops.

στρατεύομαι *v.i.* (be liable to) serve in the army.

στρατεύσιμος *a.* liable to conscription.

στρατηγεῖον *s.n.* headquarters.

στρατήγημα *s.n.* stratagem.

στρατηγία *s.f.* generalship (*office of general*).

στρατηγικ|ός *a.* strategic. **~ή** *s.f.* strategy.

στρατηγός *s.m.* general.

στρατί *s.n.* road, street.

στρατιά *s.f.* army.

στρατιώτης *s.m.* (private) soldier.

στρατιωτικ|ός *a.* military; **~ός νόμος** martial law. **~ό** *s.n.* military service.

στρατοδικεῖον *s.n.* court-martial.

στρατοκρατία *s.f.* stratocracy; militarism.

στρατολογία *s.f.* recruitment, conscription.

στρατόπεδον *s.n.* camp.

στρατός *s.m.* army.

στρατόσφαιρα *s.f.* stratosphere.

στράτσο *s.n.* thick wrapping-paper.

στρατών|(ας) *s.m.* barracks.

στρεβλός *a.* crooked, distorted.

στρείδι *s.n.* oyster.

στρέμμα *s.n.* quarter of an acre.

στρέφ|ω *v.t. & i.* turn; face about. ~ομαι *v.i.* turn; face about; revolve.

στρεψοδικία *s.f.* chicanery.

στρίβω *v.t. & i.* twist, turn; (*fam.*) τό ~ decamp, bunk; τοῦ ἔστριψε (ἡ βίδα) he is cracked.

στρί(γ)γλ|α *s.f.* witch, shrew, hag. ~ιά *s.f.* shrewishness; shrill discordant cry.

στριμμένος *a.* twisted; maliciously perverse.

στρίποδο *s.n.* trestle, tripod, easel.

στριφογυρίζω *v.t. & i.* whirl round; (*v.i.*) turn hither and thither; τὰ ~ prevaricate.

στρίφωμα *s.n.* hem.

στρίψιμο *s.n.* twist(ing), turn(ing).

στροβιλίζω *v.t. & i.* whirl round; waltz.

στρόβιλος *s.m.* whirlwind, whirlpool; turbine; top; waltz; pine-cone.

στρογγυλ|ός *a.* round, circular; (*fig.*) plain (*of words*). ~εύω *v.t.* make round.

στρούγγα *s.f.* sheepfold; (*fig.*) herd following blindly.

στρουθίον *s.n.* sparrow.

στρουθοκάμηλος *s.f.* ostrich.

στρουμπουλός *a.* small and plump.

στρόφαλος *s.m.* handle (*for turning*).

στροφεῖον *s.n.* winch.

στροφεύς *s.m.* hinge.

στροφή *s.f.* turn, turning; change of direction; stanza; (*mus.*) ritornello.

στρόφιγξ *s.f.* tap, key.

στρυμώ(χ)νω *v.t.* squeeze, squash (*in crowd*); press hard.

στρυφνός *a.* crabbed; hard (*of nut*).

στρῶμα *s.n.* layer, stratum; mattress, bed; στὸ ~ confined to bed.

στρών|ω *v.t.* spread, lay; cover, pave; ~ω τὸ κρεββάτι make the bed; (*v.i.*) settle down, find one's feet; work properly; τὸ φόρεμα ~ει καλά the dress fits well. ~ομαι *v.i.* apply oneself; invite oneself to stay.

στρώση *s.f.* layer; bedding.

στρωσίδι *s.n.* carpet; bedding.

στρωτός *a.* paved; even, regular.

στύβω *v.t.* squeeze, wring; rack (*brains*).

στυγερός *a.* odious, heinous.

στυγνός *a.* scowling, gloomy.

στυλό *s.n.* (*fam.*) fountain-pen. [F. *stylo*]

στυλοβάτης *s.m.* stylobate; (*fig.*) pillar (*supporter*).

στυλογράφος *s.m.* fountain-pen.

στῦλος *s.m.* column, pillar; post, prop, support.

στυλώνω *v.t. see* στηλώνω.

στυπτηρία *s.f.* alum.

στυπτικός *a.* binding, astringent, styptic.

στυφός *a.* having astringent taste.

στύψη *s.f.* alum.

στύψιμο *s.n.* squeezing, wringing.

στωικός *a.* stoic(al).

στωμύλος *a.* talkative, fluent.

σύ *pron.* thou, you.

συβαρίτης *s.m.* sybarite.

συγ- *see* συν-.

σύγγαμβρος *s.m. see* μπατζανάκης.

συγγένεια *s.f.* relationship, affinity.

συγγεν|ής *a.* related; a relation, kinsman. ~ολό(γ)ι *s.n.* all one's relations.

συγγνώμη *s.f.* pardon.

σύγγραμμα *s.n.* work of scholarship, treatise.

συγγραφεύς *s.m.* writer, author.

συγγράφω *v.t.* write (*books, etc.*).

σύγκαιρα *adv.* opportunely; at the same time.

συγκαί|ω, ~ομαι *v.i.* be chafed.

σύγκαλα *s.n.pl.* στὰ ~ μου sane, in normal health.

συγ|καλύπτω *v.t.* conceal, hush up; ~κεκαλυμμένος veiled.

συγκαλῶ *v.t.* convoke.

συγκαταβατικός *a.* reasonable (*price, terms*).

συγκατάθεσις *s.f.* assent, consent.

συγκαταλέγω *v.t.* include, count(*among*).

συγκατανεύω *v.i.* consent, agree.

συγκατατίθεμαι *v.i.* assent, consent.

συγκατοικῶ *v.i.* share the same living quarters.

σύγκειμαι *v.i.* be composed (*of*).

συγκεκαλυμμένος *a.* veiled, indirect.

συγκεκριμέν|ος *a.* concrete. ~ως *adv.* actually, to be precise, in point of fact.

συγκεντρών|ω *v.t.* gather together, concentrate; centralize. ~ομαι *v.i.* concentrate.

συγκέντρωσις *s.f.* gathering, meeting; party; concentration; centralization.

συγκερασμός *s.m.* compromise (*of opinions*).

συγκεφαλαιώνω *v.t.* recapitulate.

συγκεχυμένος *a.* confused, vague.

συγκιν|ῶ *v.t.* move, touch. ~ησις *s.f.* emotion. ~ητικός *a.* moving.

σύγκλησις *s.f.* convocation.

σύγκλητος s.f. senate (university & Roman).

συγκλίνω v.i. converge.

συγκλον|ίζω, ~ῶ v.t. shake, shock.

συγκοινωνία s.f. communication(s); (means of) transport.

συγκοινωνῶ v.i. communicate.

συγκολλῶ v.t. stick together, weld, solder; ~ σαμπρέλα mend a puncture.

συγκομιδή s.f. harvest.

συγκοπή s.f. syncopation; heart-failure.

σύγκορμος a. with one's whole body.

συγκρατ|ῶ v.t. restrain; contain, retain, hold; remember. ~οῦμαι v.i. control oneself.

συγκρίνω v.t. compare.

σύγκρι|σις s.f. comparison. ~τικός a. comparative.

συγκρότ|ημα s.n. group. ~ῶ v.t. form, assemble; ~ῶ μάχην give battle.

συγκρ|ούομαι v.i. collide; clash. ~ουσις s.f. collision, clash.

σύγκρυ|ο s.n., ~α (pl.) shivering.

συγκυρία s.f. coincidence.

συγυρίζω v.t. tidy up; (fam.) scold.

συγχαίρω v.t. congratulate.

συγχαρητήρια s.n.pl. congratulations.

συγχέω v.t. get mixed, confuse.

συγχορδία s.f. (mus.) chord.

σύγχρονος a. simultaneous; contemporary.

συγχρωτίζομαι v.i. associate (with).

συγχύζω v.t. get mixed; worry, upset, confuse.

σύγχυσις s.f. confusion, worry; upset (due to quarrel, etc.).

συγχωνεύω v.t. amalgamate.

συγχώρη|σις s.f. forgiveness. ~τός a. forgivable.

συ(γ)χωρ|ῶ v.t. forgive, pardon; μὲ ~εῖτε excuse me; ~έθηκε he is dead; ~εμένος late lamented.

συδ- see συνδ-.

συζήτησις s.f. discussion, argument; οὔτε ~ it is quite definite.

συζητ|ῶ v.t. & i. discuss, argue about; raise objections; δὲν ~εῖται it is quite definite.

συζυγία s.f. (astr.) conjunction; (gram.) conjugation.

σύζυγ|ος s.m.f. spouse, husband, wife. ~ικός a. conjugal.

συζῶ v.i. cohabit.

σύθαμπο s.n. dusk.

συθέμελα adv. to the very foundations.

σῦκον s.n. fig.

συκοφάντ|ης s.m. slanderer. ~ῶ v.t. slander, defame.

συκώτι s.n. liver; βγάζω τὰ ~α μου be as sick as a dog.

σύλησις s.f. pillage (esp. of churches, etc.).

συλ- see συν-.

συλλαβή s.f. syllable.

συλλαλητήριον s.n. demonstration, public meeting.

συλλαμβάνω v.t. catch, seize, arrest; (v.t. & i.) conceive (child, idea).

συλλέγω v.t. collect.

συλλέκτης s.m. collector.

συλλήβδην adv. collectively.

σύλληψις s.f. capture, seizure; conception.

συλλογή s.f. 1. collection. 2. thought, reflexion.

συλλογί|ζομαι v.t. & i. think, reflect (about), consider; ~σμένος pensive.

συλλογικός a. collective, joint.

συλλογισμός s.m. reflexion; syllogism.

σύλλογος s.m. society, association.

συλλυπητήρια s.n.pl. condolences.

συλλυποῦμαι v.t. condole with.

συλφίς s.f. sylph.

συλῶ v.t. pillage (esp. church, etc.).

συμ-. see συν-.

συμβαδίζω v.i. keep pace; go together.

συμβαίνω v.i. happen, occur.

συμβάλλ|ω v.i. (with εἰς) contribute to; flow into, unite with. ~ομαι v.i. contract, make an agreement.

συμ|βάν, ~βεβηκός s.n. event, happening.

σύμβασις s.f. agreement, pact.

συμβία s.f. wife.

συμβιβά|ζω v.t. reconcile; τὰ ~σαμε we made it up. ~ζομαι v.i. reach agreement or compromise; be compatible.

συμβιβασμός s.m. compromise, settlement.

συμβίωσις s.f. living together.

συμβολαιογράφος s.m. notary (public).

συμβόλαιον s.n. contract.

συμβολή s.f. contribution; confluence.

συμβολίζω v.t. symbolize.

σύμβολον s.n. symbol, emblem; ~ τῆς πίστεως Creed.

συμβουλεύ|ω v.t. advise. ~ομαι v.t. consult.

συμβουλή s.f. advice.

σύμβουλ|ος s.m. counsellor; councillor. ~ιον s.n. council, board.

συμμαζεύω v.t. gather together, tidy; curb, restrain.

σύμμαχ|ος a. allied; an ally. ~ία s.f. alliance.

συμμερίζομαι v.t. share (grief, views, etc.).

συμμετέχω v.i. & t. (with gen.) take part, have share (in).

συμμετοχή s.f. participation.

συμμετρία s.f. symmetry, proportion.

συμμετρικός a. symmetrical; well-shaped.

συμμορία s.f. gang, band.

συμμορφών|ω v.t. conform; bring to heel, make compliant; tidy up. ~ομαι v.i. conform, comply.

συμπαγής a. compact, solid.

συμπάθεια s.f. sympathy; liking, weakness; favourite.

συμπαθής a. likeable.

συμπαθητικός a. likeable; sympathetic (nerve, ink).

συμπάθιο s.n. (fam.) μέ τό ~ begging your pardon.

συμπαθ|ῶ v.t. feel sympathy for; have a liking for; μὲ ~ᾶτε excuse me.

συμπαιγνία s.f. collusion.

σύμπαν s.n. universe; everybody, everything.

συμπατριώτης s.m. compatriot.

συμπεθερι|ά s.f., ~ό s.n. relationship by marriage; negotiation of marriage through third party.

συμπέθεροι s.m.pl. fathers-in-law of couple (in relation to each other); relations by marriage.

συμπεπυκνωμένος a. condensed.

συμπερ|αίνω v.t. & i. conclude, infer. ~ασμα s.n. conclusion, inference.

συμπεριλαμβάνω v.t. include.

συμπερι|φέρομαι v.i. behave. ~φορά s.f. behaviour.

σύμπηξις s.f. coagulation; formation.

συμπίεσις s.f. compression.

συμπίπτω v.i. coincide, converge; befall, so happen.

σύμπλεγμα s.n. complex; cluster, group (esp. sculpture, etc.); network; monogram.

συμπλέκ|ω v.t. interlace; ~ω τὰς χεῖρας clasp one's hands. ~ομαι v.i. come to blows, clash.

συμπλήρωμα s.n. complement; supplement. ~τικός a. complementary.

συμπληρώνω v.t. complete, finish off; fill (post, etc.); fill in (form).

συμπλήρωσις s.f. completion, filling.

συμπλοκή s.f. affray, clash.

σύμπνοια s.f. accord.

συμπολιτεία s.f. confederation.

συμπολίτευ|σις s.f. government party. ~όμενος a. supporting the government.

συμπολίτης s.m. fellow citizen.

συμπονῶ v.t. feel sympathy for.

συμπόσιον s.n. banquet.

συμποσοῦμαι v.i. amount (to).

σύμπραξις s.f. co-operation.

συμπτύσσ|ω v.t. shorten, abbreviate. ~ομαι v.i. fall back (of troops).

σύμπτωμα s.n. symptom.

σύμπτωσις s.f. coincidence.

συμπυκνῶ v.t. condense. ~τήρ, ~τής s.m. condenser.

συμφέρει v.i. it is to one's advantage, it pays.

συμφέρον s.n. interest, advantage. ~τολογία s.f. self-interest.

συμφιλιώνω v.t. reconcile, make friends again.

συμφορά s.f. calamity.

συμφόρησις s.f. congestion; stroke (apoplexy).

σύμφορος a. advantageous.

συμφυής a. innate.

συμφύρ|ω v.t. jumble, confuse. ~ομαι v.i. consort or get mixed up (with).

συμφωνητικόν s.n. (deed of) contract, agreement.

συμφωνία s.f. agreement; stipulation; symphony.

σύμφωνον s.n. consonant; pact.

σύμφων|ος a. in agreement, in accord; ἐκ ~ου with one accord. ~α adv. ~α μέ in accordance with, according to.

συμφωνῶ v.i. & t. agree; match, correspond; (v.t.) agree on; match, engage, hire.

συμφώνως adv. accordingly; ~ πρός in accordance with, according to.

συμψηφίζω v.t. offset, balance.

σύν prep. (with dat.) with; (math.) plus; ~ τῷ χρόνῳ in the course of time; ~ τοῖς ἄλλοις in addition.

συν- denotes together, with, completely.

συναγερμός s.m. alarm, alert; mass-meeting.

συναγρίδα s.f. dentex (sea fish).

συνάγ|ω v.t. & i. bring together, collect; infer; ~εται ὅτι the inference is that . . . .

συναγωγή s.f. (place of) assemblage; collection; synagogue.

συναγωνίζομαι *v.i.* fight together; (*v.t. & i.*) compete (with).

συναγωνιστής *s.m.* brother-in-arms; rival; competitor.

συνάδελφος *s.m.* colleague, confrère.

συνάζω *v.t.* collect (*people, taxes, stamps, etc.*).

συναθροίζω *v.t.* collect, gather (*people, wealth, information, etc.*).

συναινώ *v.i.* consent.

συναίρεσις *s.f.* (*gram.*) contraction.

συναισθάνομαι *v.t.* be conscious of, realize, feel.

συναίσθημα *s.n.* sentiment, feeling; ~τα (*pl.*) emotions. ~τικός *a.* emotional.

συναίσθησις *s.f.* consciousness, realization, feeling, sense.

συναλλαγή *s.f.* business dealing; ἐλευθέρα ~ free trade.

συνάλλαγμα *s.n.* (*fin.*) (bill of) exchange; foreign currency; τιμή ~τος rate of exchange. ~τική *s.f.* bill of exchange.

συναλλάσσομαι *v.i.* deal, do business; mix, associate.

συνάμα *adv.* at the same time, together.

συναναστρέφομαι *v.t.* associate with.

συναναστροφή *s.f.* relations, company; party.

συναντ|ῶ *v.t.* meet. ~ῶμαι *v.i.* meet; be found (*of quotations*). ~ησις *s.f.* meeting, encounter, match.

συναξάρι(ον) *s.n.* book of saints; (*fig.*) long-winded story.

σύναξις *s.f.* meeting; collection.

συναπάντημα *s.n.* (*esp.* unlucky) meeting.

συναπτός *a.* consecutive, on end.

συνάπτω *v.t.* join (*hands, battle*); append; contract (*marriage, debt*); conclude (*agreement, peace*); ~ σχέσεις make friends.

συναρμολογῶ *v.t.* assemble, put together.

συναρπάζω *v.t.* charm, carry away, transport.

συνάρτησις *s.f.* connexion; coherence.

συνασπισμός *s.m.* coalition.

συναυλία *s.f.* concert.

συναφ|ής *a.* touching, related, similar. ~εια *s.f.* contact, intercourse.

συνάφι *s.n.* see σινάφι.

συνάχι *s.n.* cold in the head.

σύναψις *s.f.* joining, concluding, *etc.* (*see* συνάπτω).

συνδαιτυμών *s.m.* fellow diner.

συνδαυλίζω *v.t.* poke (*fire*); (*fig.*) foment.

συνδεδεμένος *a.* (closely) connected; intimate.

σύνδενδρος *a.* wooded.

σύνδεσμος *s.m.* bond, tie; ligament; league, union; (*mil.*) liaison; (*gram.*) conjunction.

συνδετήρ *s.m.* paper-fastener.

συνδετικός *a.* connecting.

συνδέω *v.t.* join, unite, connect.

συνδιαλέγομαι *v.i.* converse.

συνδιαλλαγή *s.f.* reconciliation; compromise.

συνδιάσκεψις *s.f.* conference.

συνδικᾶτον *s.n.* syndicate; union (*of workers*).

συνδράμω *v.t. & i.* support, assist; (*with* εἰς) contribute to, help.

συνδρομή *s.f.* help, succour; subscription. ~τής *s.m.* subscriber.

συνδυάζ|ω *v.t.* combine; put together (& *make inference from*); contrive, arrange. ~ομαι *v.i.* go together, harmonize.

συνδυασμός *s.m.* 1. combination, arrangement; harmonization. 2. (list of) party's candidates at election.

σύνεγγυς *adv.* ἐκ τοῦ ~ very close.

συνεδριάζω *v.i.* meet, be in session.

συνέδριον *s.n.* congress; ἐλεγκτικὸν ~ Audit Board.

σύνεδρος *s.m.* judge of criminal court; member of a congress.

συνείδησις *s.f.* consciousness (*having one's faculties awake*); awareness; conscience.

συνειδητός *a.* conscious, deliberate.

συνειρμός *s.m.* connexion, coherence; ~ παραστάσεων association of ideas.

συνεισφέρω *v.t. & i.* contribute.

συνεκτικός *a.* strong, resistant; cohesive.

συνέλευσις *s.f.* assembly.

συνεννόησις *s.f.* understanding, agreement; exchange of views; conspiracy.

συνεννοοῦμαι *v.i.* reach an understanding; exchange views; conspire.

συνενοχή *s.f.* complicity.

συνέντευξις *s.f.* rendezvous; interview.

συνενῶ *v.t.* join, unite, combine.

συνεπάγομαι *v.t.* entail, have as consequence.

συνεπαίρνω *v.t.* carry away, overwhelm.

συνέπεια *s.f.* consequence; consistency.

συνεπ|ής a. consistent, true to one's word; punctual. ~**ῶς** adv. consequently.

συνεπτυγμένος a. shortened, abridged.

συνεργάζομαι v.i. work together, collaborate.

συνεργάτ|ης s.m. collaborator; contributor. ~**ική** s.f. co-operative.

συνεργεῖον s.n. workshop; repair shop or party; gang, team (on a job).

συνεργία s.f. complicity; (med.) synergy.

σύνεργο s.n. implement.

συνεργός s.m. accomplice, accessary.

συνερίζομαι v.t. insist on being even with; keep up petty rivalry with.

συνέρχομαι v.i. recover, come to one's senses; come together; ~ εἰς γάμον contract marriage.

σύνεσις s.f. good sense.

συνεσταλμένος a. shy, reserved.

συνέταιρος s.m. partner, associate.

συνετός a. judicious, sensible.

συνεφέρνω v.t. & i. revive, bring to; come to.

συνέχεια s.f. continuity; continuation, sequel; (adv.) continuously.

συνεχ|ής a. continuous, continual; successive. ~**ῶς** adv. continually, in succession.

συνεχίζω v.t. & i. continue.

συνέχ|ω v.t. possess, seize (of emotions); restrain. ~**ομαι** v.i. be adjoining or communicating.

συνήγορος s.m. advocate, counsel.

συνήθει|α s.f., ~**ο** s.n. habit, custom.

συνήθ|ης a. usual, customary, ordinary. ~**ως** adv. usually.

συνηθ|ίζω v.t. & i. accustom; get used to (with νά or σέ or acc.); be in the habit of; ~ισε νά μαγειρεύη she has got used to cooking; ~ίζει νά κοιμᾶται νωρίς he usually goes to bed early; ~ίζεται it is the fashion or the usual thing.

συνηθισμένος a. used (to), accustomed; usual, habitual.

συνημμένος a. annexed, enclosed (of papers).

σύνθεσις s.f. composition; collocation; editing; synthesis.

συνθέτης s.m. composer.

συνθετικ|ός a. component; synthetic. ~**όν** s.n. component.

σύνθετ|ος a. compound, composite. ~**ον** s.n. (gram.) compound word.

συνθέτω v.t. compose.

συνθήκ|η s.f. treaty, pact; ~**αι** (pl.) conditions, circumstances.

συνθηκολογῶ v.i. come to terms; (mil.) capitulate.

σύνθημα s.n. signal, pass-word. ~**τικός** a. in code.

συνθλίβω v.t. squeeze, crush.

συνίζησις s.f. subsidence (of soil); (gram.) fusion of i or e with following vowel.

συνίσταμαι v.i. (with ἐκ) consist of.

συνιστῶ v.t. form, set up (committee, etc.); introduce (person); advise, recommend (something to somebody).

συννεφι|ά s.f. cloudy weather. ~**άζω** v.i. cloud over.

σύννεφ|ο s.n. cloud. ~**όκαμα** s.n. sultry and overcast weather.

συννυφάδα s.f. sister-in-law (relationship between wives of brothers).

συνοδεύω v.t. accompany, escort.

συνοδία s.f. suite, escort, convoy, procession; (mus.) accompaniment.

συνοδοιπόρος s.m.f. fellow traveller.

σύνοδος s.f. assembly; synod; session.

συνοδός s.m.f. escort; ἱπταμένη ~ airhostess.

συνοικέσιον s.n. (negotiation of) arranged marriage.

συνοικ|ία s.f. quarter (of town). ~**ιακός** a. local, suburban.

συνοικισμός s.m. settlement (place where people live).

σύν|ολον s.n. total; ἐν ~**όλω** in all. ~**ολικός** a. total.

συνομήλικος a. of the same age.

συνομιλητής s.m. interlocutor.

συνομιλία s.f. conversation.

συνομολογῶ v.t. conclude (agreement).

συνομοταξία s.f. class (natural history).

συνονόματος a. a namesake.

συνοπτικός a. summary, synoptic.

συνορίζομαι v.t. see συνερίζομαι.

σύνορ|ον s.n. boundary; ~**α** (pl.) frontier. ~**εύω** v.i. have common boundary or frontier.

συνουσία s.f. coition.

συνοφρυοῦμαι v.i. frown.

συνοχή s.f. coherence, cohesion.

σύνοψις s.f. summary, synopsis; prayerbook.

συνταγή s.f. prescription; recipe.

σύνταγμα s.n. constitution; (mil.) regiment.

συνταγματάρχης s.m. (mil.) colonel.

συνταγματικός a. constitutional.

συντάκτης *s.m.* editor; author.

συντακτικ|ός *a.* constituent; editorial; syntactic, of syntax. **~όν** *s.n.* (book of) syntax.

συνταξιούχος *s.m.f.* pensioner.

σύνταξις *s.f.* compilation; writing, drawing up; editorial staff; pension; (*gram.*) construction.

συνταράσσω *v.t.* convulse, shake, trouble.

συντάσσ|ω *v.t.* arrange, compile; write, draw up; (*gram.*) construe. **~ομαι** *v.i.* (*with* μετά) side with; (*gram.*) govern.

συνταυτίζω *v.t.* identify (*associate with*).

συντείνω *v.i.* conduce, play a part.

συντέλεια *s.f.* ~ τοῦ κόσμου end of the world.

συντελεστ|ής *s.m.* factor; (*math.*) co-efficient. **~ικός** *a.* contributory.

συντελῶ *v.t. & i.* complete, accomplish; play a part, contribute.

συντέμνω *v.t.* shorten.

συντεταγμένη *s.f.* (*math.*) co-ordinate.

συντετριμμένος *a.* contrite, deeply afflicted.

συντεχνία *s.f.* guild.

συντήρη|σις *s.f.* conservation; maintenance, subsistence. **~τικός** *a.* conservative; cautious.

συντηρῶ *v.t.* conserve; maintain, support.

συντίθεμαι *v.i.* be composed (*of*).

συντομεύω *v.t.* shorten.

συντομία *s.f.* brevity; saving of space *or* time.

σύντομ|ος *a.* short, brief; concise. **~α** *adv.* briefly; quickly, soon.

συντονίζω *v.t.* co-ordinate.

σύντονος *a.* intensive, unrelaxing.

συντρέχ|ω *v.t. & i.* aid; (*v.i.*) meet, coincide; contribute; δὲν **~ει** λόγος there is no reason.

συντρίβ|ω *v.t.* crush, smash; afflict. **~ή** *s.f.* crushing; contrition.

σύντριμμα *s.n.* fragment; **~τα** (*pl.*) debris.

συντριπτικός *a.* (*fig.*) crushing.

συντροφ|ιά *s.f.* companionship, company; party; (*adv.*) together; καὶ **~ία** & Co.

σύντροφος *s.m.f.* companion, comrade; partner.

συντυχαίνω *v.t. & i.* meet by chance; converse with; happen; συνέτυχε νά it happened that . . . .

συνύπαρξις *s.f.* coexistence.

συνυπάρχω *v.i.* coexist.

συνυφαίνω *v.t.* interweave; (*fig.*) hatch, plot.

συνωθοῦμαι *v.i.* jostle.

συνωμο|σία *s.f.* conspiracy (*esp. treasonable*). **~τῶ** *v.i.* conspire.

συνώνυμ|ος *a.* synonymous. **~ον** *s.n.* synonym.

συνωστισμός *s.m.* jostling, crush.

σύξυλ|ος *a.* with all hands (*of shipwreck*); (*fig.*) ἔμεινε **~ος** he was dumbfounded; μ' ἄφησε **~ο** he left me in the lurch.

σύριγξ *s.f.* Pan's pipe; syringe.

συρίζω *v.i. & t.* hiss (at), whistle (at).

σύρμα *s.n.* wire. **~τόπλεγμα** *s.n.* wire netting; barbed wire.

συρμός *s.m.* railway train; fashion.

σύρραξις *s.f.* collision, clash.

συρρέω *v.i.* throng, flock.

σύρριζα *adv.* root and branch; very close.

συρροή *s.f.* throng, influx; abundance.

συρτάρι *s.n.* drawer.

συρτή *s.f.* drag-net.

σύρτης *s.m.* bolt.

σύρτις *s.f.* sandbank.

συρτός 1. *a.* dragging; drawling; sliding (*door*). 2. *s.m.* sort of cyclic dance.

συρφετός *s.m.* mob.

σύρω *v.t.* see **σέρνω**; σῦρ' τα φέρ' τα comings and goings.

συσκέπτομαι *v.i.* confer, deliberate.

συσκευάζω *v.t.* pack, box, put up.

συσκευασία *s.f.* packing; (*pharmaceutical*) preparation.

συσκευή *s.f.* apparatus.

σύσκεψις *s.f.* conference, consultation.

συσκοτ|ίζω *v.t.* darken, black out; *fig.*) confuse. **~ισις** *s.f.* black-out.

σύσπασις *s.f.* contraction (*of brow, etc.*).

συσπειρούμαι *v.i.* coil; (*fig.*) (*with* περί) rally round (*leader, etc.*).

συσσίτιον *s.n.* mess, common table; soup-kitchen.

σύσσωμος *a.* united, in a body.

συσσωρεύ|ω *v.t.* accumulate. **~τής** *s.m.* accumulator.

συστάδην *adv.* ἐκ τοῦ ~ hand-to-hand.

συσταίνω *v.t.* introduce (*person*).

συστάς *s.f.* clump (*trees*).

σύστασ|ις *s.f.* composition (*that of which anything is composed*); consistency (*thickness*); formation, setting up; recommendation; **~εις** (*pl.*) references, advice; introductions; ~η address; ἐπὶ ~ει registered (letter).

συστατικ|ός a. component, constituent; ~ἠ ἐπιστολή letter of introduction; ~ά (pl.) ingredients; references.

συστέλλ|ω v.t. contract; take in (sail). ~ομαι v.i. contract; feel hesitant or shy.

σύστημα s.n. system, method. ~τικός a. systematic.

συστή|νω v.t. see συνιστῶ. ~μένο γράμμα registered letter.

συστολή s.f. contraction; modesty, shame.

συσφίγγω v.t. tighten.

συσχετίζω v.t. correlate, put together.

συφάμελος a. with the whole family.

σύφιλις s.f. syphilis.

συχαρίκια s.n.pl. gift to first bringer of good news.

συχνά, ~κις adv. often; ~ πυκνά very often.

συχνάζω v.t. frequent, be habitué of.

συχν|ός a. frequent. ~ότης s.f. frequency.

συχωράω v.t. see συγχωρῶ.

συχώριο s.n. (fam.) forgiveness of sins (to dead); μπουκιά καὶ ~ piece of all right.

σύψυχος a. body and soul; with all hands.

σφαγεῖον s.n. slaughter-house.

σφαγ|ή s.f. slaughter, carnage. ~ιάζω v.t. slaughter; sacrifice.

σφάγιον s.n. victim, animal (to be) slaughtered.

σφαδάζω v.i. writhe, struggle, jerk.

σφάζω v.t. slaughter, kill.

σφαῖρ|α s.f. sphere; ball; bullet. ~ίδιον s.n. small shot; ballot-ball.

σφαιριστήριον s.n. billiard table or room.

σφαλερός a. erroneous; unsafe, slippery.

σφαλιάρα s.f. hard slap in face.

σφαλ|ίζω, ~(ν)ῶ v.t. & i. shut in; close. ~ιστός a. shut.

σφάλλ|ω, ~ομαι v.i. err, do or be wrong; misfire.

σφάλμα s.n. wrong act, fault; error; misfire.

σφαντῶ v.i. look glamorous.

σφάξιμο s.n. slaughtering.

σφαχτ|άρι, ~ό s.n. animal (to be) slaughtered.

σφάχτης s.m. twinge.

σφενδόνη s.f. sling.

σφερδούκλι s.n. asphodel.

σφετερίζομαι v.t. appropriate dishonestly, embezzle.

σφή(γ)κα s.f. wasp.

σφήν s.m., ~α s.f. wedge. ~ώνω v.t. wedge, thrust in between.

σφήξ s.m. wasp.

σφίγγ|ω v.t. & i. squeeze, clasp; tighten, clench; make or get thick or hard; become tight, stick; get constipated; ~ω τὴν καρδιά μου master one's grief; ἔσφιξε τὸ κρύο it has become intensely cold. ~ομαι v.i. make great efforts, strain; squeeze together.

σφίγξ s.f. sphinx.

σφίξ|η s.f. urgency; urgent desire to relieve oneself; constipation; δὲν εἶναι ~η there is no hurry; ἔχει ~ες he is in difficulties.

σφίξιμο s.n. tightening, squeezing.

σφιχτός a. tight, firm, hard; miserly.

σφόδρα adv. extremely, strongly.

σφοδρ|ός a. strong, violent, intense. ~ότης s.f. violence, intensity.

σφουγγάρ|ι s.n. sponge. ~ᾶς s.m. sponge-fisher or seller.

σφουγγαρόπανο s.n. floor-cloth.

σφουγγᾶτο s.n. omelet.

σφουγγίζω v.t. wipe; (fam.) sweep the board of.

σφραγίζω v.t. seal, stamp; cork; bottle (wine); fill (tooth).

σφραγ|ίς, ~ίδα s.f. seal, stamp.

σφρίγος s.n. youthful exuberance.

σφυγμός s.m. pulse; (fig.) weak point.

σφύζω v.i. pulsate, throb; (fig.) be bursting with vitality.

σφύξις s.f. pulse, pulsation.

σφύρ|α s.f., ~ί s.n. hammer. ~ηλατῶ v.t. hammer, forge.

σφύριγμα s.n. whistling; whistle (noise).

σφυρίδα s.f. sort of fish.

σφυρίζω v.i. hoot, whistle, hiss.

σφυρίχτρα s.f. whistle (instrument).

σφυροκοπῶ v.t. hammer; rain blows on.

σφυρόν s.n. ankle.

σχεδία s.f. raft.

σχεδι|άζω v.t. sketch, design; plan, intend. ~αστής s.m. designer, draughtsman.

σχέδιον s.n. sketch, design, plan, draft, project; ~ πόλεως town-planning authority.

σχεδόν adv. almost, nearly.

σχέσις s.f. relation, connexion.

σχετίζ|ω v.t. connect, associate, compare. ~ομαι v.i. be or get acquainted.

σχετικ|ά, **~ῶς** adv. relatively; **~ὰ** or **~ῶς μέ** regarding, with reference to.

σχετικ|ός a. relative, relevant; on familiar terms. **~ότης** s.f. relativity.

σχετλιασμός s.m. lamenting, complaining.

σχῆμα s.n. form, shape; diagram; (geom.) figure; format; cloth (clerical); salute; gesture; **~ λόγου** figure of speech.

σχηματ|ίζω v.t. form. **~ισμός** s.m. formation, configuration; (gram.) scheme of inflexion.

σχίζα s.f. splinter.

σχίζ|ω v.t. & i. split, cleave; tear. **~ομαι** v.i. split, tear; fork, divide.

σχίνος s.f. lentisk.

σχίσμα s.n. crack; schism.

σχισμ|άδα, **~ή** s.f. crack, fissure, split.

σχιστόλιθος s.m. slate, schist.

σχιστός a. slit, open.

σχοινίον s.n. rope.

σχοινοβάτης s.m. rope-dancer, acrobat.

σχοινοτενής a. long-winded.

σχολάζω v.i. & t. not to be at work; be on vacation; stop work; (v.t.) let out (of school, office, etc.); dismiss (from job).

σχολαστικός a. pedantic.

σχολεῖον s.n. school.

σχολή s.f. leisure; school (esp. of university, painting, etc.).

σχόλη s.f. holiday, feast-day.

σχολι|άζω v.t. comment on, criticize; annotate, edit. **~αστής** s.m. commentator; editor, scholiast.

σχολικός a. of school.

σχόλιον s.n. comment.

σώβρακο s.n. pants.

σώγαμπρος s.m. see ἐσώγαμβρος.

σώζ|ω v.t. save, rescue; preserve. **~ομαι** v.i. be extant, remain in existence.

σωθικά s.n.pl. entrails, bowels.

σωλήν s.m. pipe, tube. **~άριον** s.n. small tube (of medicament, etc.).

σῶμα s.n. body, corps; (mil.) **~ στρατοῦ** army corps; copy (of book).

σωματάρχης s.m. (mil.) commander of army corps.

σωματεῖον s.n. guild.

σωματεμπορία s.f. (white) slave-traffic.

σωματικός a. of the body, bodily, physical.

σωματοφυλακή s.f. bodyguard.

σωματώδης a. corpulent.

σών|ω v.t. & i. save, preserve; finish up, consume; reach (with hand etc.); (v.i.) reach; be enough; **~ει καὶ καλά** with obstinate insistence.

σῶος a. safe, whole, unharmed.

σωπαίνω v.i. & t. stop talking; hush.

σωρεία s.f. pile; abundance of.

σωρηδόν adv. in great quantity.

σωριάζομαι v.i. fall in a heap.

σωρός s.m. heap, pile; lot of.

σωσίας s.m. double, living image.

σωσίβιον s.n. life-belt or jacket.

σώσιμο s.n. saving; finishing up, consuming.

σῶμα s.n. last of wine (in barrel).

σωστ|ός a. correct, right, upright; real, absolute; **μὲ τὰ ~ά του** in his right mind, in earnest; **δύο ~ἐς ὧρες** two whole hours. **~ά** adv. correctly, exactly, right(ly).

σωτήρ s.m. saviour, rescuer. **~ία** s.f. deliverance, rescue, salvation; way out (of dilemma).

σωφ|έρ s.m. chauffeur, driver. [F. chauffeur]. **~άρω** v.t. & i. drive (vehicle).

σωφρον|ίζω v.t. bring to reason, correct, reform. **~ιστήριον** s.n. reformatory.

σωφροσύνη s.f. prudence, sense, moderation.

σώφρων a. prudent, sensible, moderate.

Τ

τά article & pron. n. pl. the; them.

ταβάνι s.n. ceiling.

ταβατούρι s.n. row, noise.

ταβέρνα s.f. tavern, eating-house.

τάβλα s.f. board; low table; (fam.) **~ στὸ μεθύσι** blind drunk.

τάβλι s.n. backgammon.

ταγάρι s.n. peasant's bag; nosebag.

ταγγ|ός a. rancid. **~ίζω** v.i. go rancid.

ταγή s.f. fodder.

ταγιέρ s.n. woman's suit. [F. tailleur]

ταγίζω v.t. feed.

τάγμα s.n. (priestly, etc.) order; (mil.) battalion.

ταγματάρχης s.m. (mil.) major.

ταγμένος a. under a vow.

τάδε pron. such-and-such; **ὁ ~(s)** so-and-so; **~ ἔφη** so (he) spake.

τάζ|ω v.t. vow, promise. **~ομαι** v.i. make a vow.

ταΐζω v.t. feed.

ταινία s.f. band, strip, ribbon; (cinema) film; tape, ribbon (in machines); tapeworm.

ταίρι s.n. one of a pair; companion, mate; match; equal.

ταιρι|άζω v.t. & i. match, assort; (v.i.) match, suit, go (with); δὲν ~άζει it is not fitting; τὰ ~άσαμε we came to an understanding.

ταιριαστός a. well-matched.

τακίμι s.n. set (of implements); shift (of workmen).

τάκος s.m. wooden fixing-block; (fam.) nice 'piece' (woman).

τακούνι s.n. heel.

τάκτ s.n. tact. [F. tact]

τακτική s.f. tactics, policy; method, orderliness.

τακτικ|ός a. regular; orderly; ordinal (number). ~ά, ~ῶς adv. regularly.

τακτοποι|ῶ v.t. arrange, put in order; settle. ~ησις s.f. arranging, settling.

τακτός a. fixed.

ταλαίπωρ|ος a. poor, unfortunate. ~ία s.f. hardship, suffering. ~ῶ v.t. torment. ~οῦμαι v.i. suffer hardship.

ταλαντεύομαι v.i. sway, rock; waver.

τάλαντον s.n. talent (aptitude or money).

τάλας a. poor, unfortunate.

ταλέντο s.n. (person of) talent.

τάλ(λ)ηρον s.n. five-drachma piece.

τάμα s.n. vow; ex-voto offering.

ταμάχι s.n. insatiable greed.

ταμεῖον s.n. treasury, accounts department; cash-desk, booking-office; pension or provident society.

ταμίας s.m. cashier, treasurer.

ταμιευτήριον s.n. savings bank.

ταμπάκικο s.n. tannery.

ταμπάκ|ος s.m. snuff. ~ιέρα s.f. snuffbox; cigarette-box or case.

ταμπέλα s.f. name-plate; registration-plate (of motor).

ταμπλό s.n. picture; dash-board; switchboard. [F. tableau]

ταμπουράς s.m. sort of guitar.

ταμπούρ|ι s.n. (mil.) defensive position. ~ώνομαι v.i. occupy such position.

ταμποῦρλο s.n. side-drum.

τανάλια s.n.pl. pliers (tool).

τανάπαλιν adv. conversely.

τάνκ s.n. (mil.) tank. [E. tank]

τανύ|ω, ~ζω v.t. stretch. ~ομαι, ~έμαι v.i. stretch oneself; strain (at stool).

ταξειδ- see **ταξιδ-**.

ταξί s.n. taxi. [F. taxi]

ταξιάρχης s.m. 1. archangel. 2. commander (of order of chivalry).

ταξιαρχία s.f. (mil.) brigade.

ταξίαρχος s.m. brigadier.

ταξιδεύω v.i. travel.

ταξίδ|ι(ον) s.n. journey; ~ια (pl.) travel.

ταξιδιώτης s.m. traveller.

ταξιθέτις s.f. theatre-attendant.

ταξικός a. class; ~ ἀγών class struggle.

ταξίμετρον s.n. taximeter.

τάξιμο s.n. vow.

ταξινομῶ v.t. classify.

τάξ|ις s.f. 1. order (sequence, tidiness, calm state); ἐν ~ει all right, in order. 2. class, grade; form (school); ~εις (pl.) ranks (of army, etc.); πρώτης ~εως first class.

τάπα s.f. cork, stopper; (fam.) ~ στὸ μεθύσι blind drunk.

ταπειν|ός a. humble; abject. ~οφροσύνη s.f. humility.

ταπεινών|ω v.t. humble, humiliate. ~ομαι v.i. abase oneself; be humbled or humiliated.

ταπέτο s.n. carpet, rug.

ταπετσαρία s.f. wall-covering; upholstery.

τάπ|ης s.m. carpet, rug; ἐτέθη ἐπὶ ~ητος it came up for discussion. ~ητουργία s.f. manufacture of carpets.

ταπίστομα adv. in prone position.

τάραγμα s.n. shaking.

ταρ|άζω, ~άσσω v.t. shake; disturb.

ταραμάς s.m. preserved roe.

ταραξίας s.m. rowdy person.

ταράτσα s.f. flat roof; (fam.) τήν κάνω ~ eat a bellyful.

ταραχ|ή s.f. disturbance, commotion; upset, shock. ~οποιός s.m. rowdy person. ~ώδης a. stormy, disturbed.

ταρίφα s.f. scale of charges.

ταριχεύω v.t. embalm; preserve.

ταρσανάς s.m. boat-builder's yard.

τάρταρα s.n.pl. bowels of the earth.

τασάκι s.n. ashtray.

τάσι s.n. shallow bowl; scale (of balance); cymbal.

τάσις s.f. stretching (of arms in drill); tension (of gas, electricity); tendency, inclination.

τάσσ|ω v.t. place; marshal; set, appoint. ~ομαι v.i. place oneself; (fig.) side (with).

ταῦ s.n. the letter **Τ**.

ταῦρ|ος s.m. bull. ~ομαχία s.f. bull-fight.

ταῦτα pron.n.pl. these.

ταυτίζω v.t. treat as identical, iden-tify.

ταυτόσημος a. having the same import.

ταυτότης s.f. identity (card).

ταυτόχρονος a. simultaneous.

ταφή s.f. burial.

τάφος s.m. grave, tomb; (fig.) one who never betrays a secret.

τάφρος s.m. ditch, trench.

ταφτᾶς s.m. taffeta.

τάχα, ~τε(ς) adv. supposedly; as if; I wonder if, can it be that? μᾶς κάνει τὸν ~ (μου) he puts on airs.

ταχεῖα s.f. express (train).

ταχ|έως adv. quickly; soon; ὡς ~ιστα as soon as possible.

ταχιά adv. tomorrow.

ταχινή s.f. morning.

ταχίνι s.n. ground sesame.

ταχύ adv. & s.n. (tomorrow) morning.

ταχυδακτυλουργία s.f. conjuring (trick).

ταχυδρομεῖον s.n. post, mail; post-office.

ταχυδρόμος s.m. postman.

ταχυδρομικ|ός a. postal; of the post-office ~ά s.n.pl. postage. ~ῶς adv. by post.

ταχυδρομῶ v.t. post (letters).

ταχύνους a. quick-witted.

ταχύνω v.t. quicken.

ταχυπαλμία s.f. (med.) palpitation.

ταχ|ύς a. quick, fast, rapid. ~ύτης s.f. speed, rapidity; gear (of motor).

ταψί s.n. shallow baking-tin.

ταώς s.m. peacock.

τε conj. ~ . . . καί both . . . and . . . .

τέζα adv. stretched, tight; (fam.) ἔμεινε ~ he died; ~ στὸ μεθύσι blind drunk.

τεθλασμέν|ος a. broken. ~η s.f. zigzag line.

τεθλιμμένος a. afflicted, grief-stricken.

τείνω v.t. & i. stretch (out); strain. (v.i.) tend; lead (to), be aimed (at).

τεῖον s.n. tea.

τεῖχος s.n. wall (of city, etc.).

τεκμήριον s.n. token, mark, indication.

τέκνον s.n. child.

τεκταίνομαι v.i. & t. plot, contrive.

τέκτ|ων s.m. mason; freemason. ~ονι-σμός s.m. freemasonry.

τελάρο s.n. tapestry-frame; stretcher (for canvas); frame (of door, etc.)

τελεία s.f. full-stop; ἄνω ~ semicolon.

τελειοποιῶ v.t. perfect.

τέλειος a. perfect, complete.

τελειότης s.f. perfection.

τελειόφοιτος a. final-year student; graduate.

τελειώμ|α s.n., ~ός s.m. finishing; ex-haustion (of supply); ~ό δέν ἔχει it is endless or inexhaustible.

τελειώνω v.t. & i. exhaust, use up; end, finish; (fig.) die.

τελείως adv. perfectly; completely.

τελειωτικός a. decisive, final.

τελεσίγραφον s.n. ultimatum.

τελεσίδικος a. final (without appeal).

τέλεσις s.f. celebration (of rite); per-petration.

τελεσφορῶ v.i. end successfully.

τελετ|ή s.f. ceremony, rite. ~άρχης s.m. master of ceremonies. ~ουργῶ v.i. officiate.

τελευταῖ|ος a. last; latest; σὰν τὸν ~ο βλάκα like an utter fool. ~ως adv. lately, recently.

τελευτή s.f. end; (fig.) death.

τελεύω v.t. & i. see τελειώνω.

τέλι s.n. (thin) wire.

τελικ|ός a. final. ~ά adv. in the end.

τέλμα s.n. swamp.

τέλ|ος s.n. 1. end; ~ος πάντων after all, finally; ἐπὶ ~ους at last; (στὸ) ~ος at last; ἐν ~ει finally. 2. tax.

τελ|ῶ v.t. perform, do. ~οῦμαι v.i. take place.

τελωνεῖον s.n. customs (house).

τελώνης s.m. customs officer.

τεμάχ|ιον s.n. piece. ~ίζω v.t. cut in pieces.

τέμενος s.n. temple, shrine.

τέμν|ω v.t. cut; pass through (of road); ~ουσα (math.) secant.

τεμπέλ|ης a. lazy. ~ιάζω v.i. loaf.

τέμπλο s.n. iconostasis.

τέναγος s.n. fen.

τενεκ|ές s.m. tin (substance); large can or tin; (fam.) ignoramus. ~εδένιος a. tin. ~ετζῆς s.m. tinsmith.

τενόρος s.m. tenor.

τέντα s.f. tent; awning. (adv.) wide open.

τέντζερ|ες, ~ης s.m. (metal) cooking-pot.

τεντ|ώνω v.t. stretch (out); open (door, etc.) wide; (fam.) τὰ ~ωσε he died.

τένων s.m. tendon.

τέρας s.n. monster; freak, phenomenon; fam.) a terror, a caution.

τεράστιος *a.* huge, enormous.

τερατολογία *s.f.* extravagant tale.

τερατόμορφος *a.* hideous.

τερατούργημα *s.n.* monstrosity; outrageous deed.

τερατώδης *a.* monstrous; ugly; phenomenal.

τερεβινθέλαιον *s.n.* turpentine.

τερετίζω *v.i.* chirp, twitter.

τέρμα *s.n.* terminus, end; goal (*sports*). **~τίζω** *v.t. & i.* put an end to, bring to a close. (*v.i.*) finish.

τερματοφύλαξ *s.m.* goalkeeper.

τερπνός *a.* agreeable, enjoyable.

τέρπω *v.t.* give pleasure to.

τερτίπι *s.n.* trick.

τέρψις *s.f.* enjoyment.

τέσσαρα|α *num.* four. **~άκοντα** *num.* forty.

τέσσερ|(ε)ις *a.* four; μὲ τὰ ~α on all fours.

τεταγμένος *a.* placed, fixed; appointed.

τεταμένος *a.* stretched, strained.

τέτανος *s.m.* (*med.*) tetanus.

τεταρταῖος *a.* quartan (*fever*).

Τετάρτη *s.f.* Wednesday.

τέταρτον *s.n.* quarter (of an hour); quarto; (*mus.*) crotchet.

τέταρτος *a.* fourth.

τετελεσμέν|ος *a.* done; ~ον γεγονός fait accompli; (*gram.*) ~ος μέλλων future perfect.

τέτοιος *pron.* such; ὁ ~ what's-his-name.

τετράγωνον *s.n.* (*geom.*) square, quadrangle; block (*between streets*).

τετράγων|ος, **~ικός** *a.* square; (*fig.*) well-grounded, logical.

τετράδιον *s.n.* exercise-book.

τετράκις *adv.* four times.

τετρακόσι|οι *a.* four hundred; τὰ ἔχει ~α he has his wits about him.

τετράπαχος *a.* very plump.

τετραπέρατος *a.* very clever *or* cunning.

τετρα|πλάσιος, **~πλοῦς** *a.* fourfold.

τετράποδο *s.n.* quadruped; (*fig.*) ass; brute.

τετράπους *a.* four-footed.

τετρ|άς *s.f.* set of four; κατὰ ~άδας in fours.

τετράτροχος *a.* four-wheeled.

τετριμμένος *a.* worn; (*fig.*) trite.

τέττιξ *s.m.* cicada.

τεῦτλον *s.n.* beetroot.

τεῦχος *s.n.* instalment, part, issue.

τέφρα *s.f.* ashes.

τεφρ|ός, **~όχρους** *a.* ashen; grey.

τεφτέρι *s.n.* notebook.

τεχνάζομαι *v.t.* contrive, think up, invent.

τέχνασμα *s.n.* artifice, ruse.

τέχν|η *s.f.* art, craft, skill; skilled occupation; trick, dodge; καλαὶ ~αι fine arts.

τεχνηέντως *adv.* adroitly, artfully.

τεχνητός *a.* artificial; forced, feigned.

τεχνική *s.f.* technique.

τεχνικός *a.* technical; skilful; skilled (*in mechanical arts*); a technician.

τεχνίτης *s.m.* craftsman; technician, mechanic; (*fam.*) expert.

τεχνοκρίτης *s.m.* art critic.

τεχνολογία *s.f.* technology; (*gram.*) parsing.

τεχνοτροπία *s.f.* (*artistic*) style.

τέως *adv.* formerly; ~ βουλευτής ex-M.P.

τζάκι *s.n.* hearth, fireplace; range; ἀπὸ ~ of distinguished family.

τζαμ|αρία *s.f.*, **~λίκι** *s.n.* glass panelling *or* partition; space enclosed by this; conservatory.

τζάμι *s.n.* window-pane.

τζαμί *s.n.* mosque.

τζαμόπορτα *s.f.* glazed door.

τζάμπα *adv.* (*fam.*) for nothing (*free, to no purpose*). **~τζῆς** *s.m.* one who gets things for nothing.

τζαναμπέτης *s.m.* crabbed person, sourpuss.

τζάνερο *s.n.* mirabelle plum.

τζελατίνα *s.f.* 1. gelatine. 2. celluloid holder (*for identity card, etc.*).

τζερεμές *s.m.* fine *or* cost of damage (*incurred undeservedly*).

τζίβα *s.f.* vegetable fibre.

τζίγκος *s.m.* zinc.

τζιριτζάντζουλες *s.f.pl.* (*fam.*) evasiveness; coquettish airs.

τζίρος *s.m.* (*business*) turnover.

τζίτζικας *s.m.* cicada.

τζιτζιφιά *s.f.* jujube-tree.

τζίφος *s.m.* vain effort.

τζίφρα *s.f.* paraph; initials (*as signature*).

τζόγος *s.m.* card-playing.

τζόκεϋ *s.m.* jockey. [E. *jockey*]

τζούτα *s.f.* jute.

τζουτζές *s.m.* dwarf; (*fig.*) clown.

τζούτζης *s.m.* (*fam.*) cheat, equivocator.

τήβεννος *s.f.* toga, gown.

τηγανητός *a.* fried.

τηγάν|ι s.n. frying-pan. ~ίζω v.t. fry. ~ίτα s.f. fritter.

τήκ|ω v.t. melt. ~ομαι v.i. melt; pine, languish.

τηλεβόας s.m. loud-hailer.

τηλεβόλον s.n. cannon.

τηλεγραφείον s.n. telegraph-office.

τηλεγράφημα s.n. telegram, cable.

τηλέγραφ|ος s.m. telegraph. ~ώ v.i. & t. telegraph, wire.

τηλεόρασις s.f. television.

τηλεπάθεια s.f. telepathy.

τηλεπικοινωνία s.f. telecommunication(s).

τηλεσκόπιον s.n. telescope.

τηλεφώνημα s.n. telephone-call.

τηλεφωνητής s.m. telephone-operator.

τηλέφων|ον s.n. telephone. ~ώ v.i. & t. telephone.

τήξις s.f. melting; pining.

τήρησις s.f. observance.

τηρώ v.t. keep (up), observe.

τηρ|ώ, ~άω v.t. & i. look at; take care.

τί pron. (interrogative) what; (exclamatory) what, how.

τι pron. something; a little.

τίγκα adv. (fam.) full to overflowing.

τίγρις s.f. tiger.

τιθασ(σ)εύω v.t. tame.

τίθεμαι v.i. be put, set or imposed.

τίκτω v.t. give birth to; bring forth.

τίλιο s.n. (infusion of) lime flowers.

τίλλω v.t. pull out (hair, etc.); card (wool).

τιμαλφ|ής a. precious; ~ή (s.n.pl.) jewellery.

τιμάριθμος s.m. cost-of-living (index).

τιμάριον s.n. fief.

τιμή s.f. honour; price; value.

τίμημα s.n. price; value.

τιμητικός a. honorary; doing honour (to).

τίμι|ος a. honest; honourable; precious; ~ος σταυρός or ~ο ξύλο Holy Cross.

τιμοκατάλογος s.m. price-list.

τιμολόγιον s.n. invoice.

τιμόνι s.n. rudder; tiller; wheel; steering-wheel; handle-bars. ~έρης s.m. steersman.

τιμ|ώ v.t. honour, do honour to. ~ώμαι v.i. cost.

τιμωρ|ώ v.t. punish. ~ία s.f. punishment.

τίναγμα s.n. shaking; jerk, start.

τινάζ|ω v.t. shake; hurl; flap (wings);

~ω στόν αέρα blow up. ~ομαι v.i. jump (up), start; brush (something off) one's clothes.

τίποτ|α, ~ε pron. any, anything; (after neg.) nothing; ~α! don't mention it; άλλο ~ε very much (so).

τιποτένιος a. insignificant; worthless.

τιράντες s.f.pl. braces.

τιρμπουσόν s.n. corkscrew. [F. tirebouchon]

τίς pron. who?

τις pron. some, someone, one.

τίτλ|ος s.m. title. ~οφορώ v.t. entitle (name).

τμήμα s.n. portion, section; department; police-station.

τμηματάρχης s.m. head of department.

τμηματικώς adv. a bit at a time.

τό article & pron. n. the; it.

τοιοῦτ|ος pron. such; (fam.) homosexual. ~οτρόπως adv. thus, in such a way.

τοιχογραφία s.f. fresco.

τοιχοκόλλησις s.f. bill-posting.

τοῖχος s.m. wall.

τοίχωμα s.n. (inner) wall (of vessel, bodily organ).

τοκετός s.m. childbirth.

τοκίζω v.t. lend (money) at interest.

τοκογλύφος s.m. usurer.

τόκ|ος s.m. (fin.) interest. ~ομερίδιον s.n. dividend coupon.

τόλμη s.f. boldness; effrontery. ~ρός a. bold, daring.

τολμώ v.i. dare.

τολύπη s.f. lump (of raw wool); (fig.) flake (of snow); puff (of smoke).

τομάρι s.n. hide, skin.

τομάτα s.f. tomato.

τομεύς s.m. incisor; sector.

τομή s.f. cut, incision; section (diagram).

τόμος s.m. volume (book).

τονίζω v.t. accent; accentuate, stress; set to music.

τονισμός s.m. accentuation.

τόννος s.m. 1. ton. 2. tunny.

τόν|ος s.m. tone; (fig.) force, vigour; μιλώ μέ ~ο speak sharply; δίνω ~ο σέ liven up; (gram.) accent; (mus.) tone (interval), key.

τον|ώνω v.t. invigorate, liven up. ~ωτικός a. bracing, tonic.

τοξεύω v.t. shoot with bow.

τοξικ|ός a. toxic; poisonous. ~ομανής s.m.f. drug-addict.

τόξ|ον *s.n.* bow (*weapon*); arc, arch, curve; οὐράνιον ~ον rainbow; (*mus.*) bow. ~**οειδής** *a.* arched, curved. ~**ότης** *s.m.* archer.

τοπ(ε)ίον *s.n.* landscape; site, spot.

τόπι *s.n.* (*child's*) ball; bolt (*of cloth*); cannon (-ball).

τοπικ|ός *a.* local. ~**ισμός** *s.m.* localism.

τοπιογραφία *s.f.* landscape painting.

τοπογραφία *s.f.* topography.

τοποθεσία *s.f.* situation, site, spot.

τοποθετ|ῶ *v.t.* place, put, post; (*fin.*) invest. ~**ησις** *s.f.* placing, disposition; investment.

τόπ|ος *s.m.* piece of ground, place, site; country; room (*space*); πιάνω ~ο take up room *or* have effect *or* come in useful; ἔμεινε στὸν ~ο he died on the spot; ἀφήνω στὸν ~ο kill instantaneously; δίνω ~ο τῆς ὀργῆς give way (*in argument*); (*math.*) locus.

τοπούζι *s.n.* club; (*fig.*) stiff as a poker.

τοπωνυμία *s.f.* place-name.

τορν|εύω *v.t.* turn (*on lathe*); (*fig.*) give elegant shape to. ~**ευτής** *s.m.* turner. ~**ευτός** *a.* well-turned.

τόρνος *s.m.* lathe.

τορπίλλ|η *s.f.* torpedo. ~**ίζω** *v.t.* torpedo. ~**οβόλον** *s.n.* torpedo-boat.

τος *pron.* he; νά ~ here he is.

τοσάκις *adv.* so many times.

τόσο(ν) *adv.* so (much); ~ . . . ὅσο(ν) as (much) . . . as *or* both . . . and; ὄχι καὶ ~ not very much.

τόσ|ος *pron.* of such size *or* quantity; so much, so many; ~ος δά very small *or* little; ἄλλοι ~οι as many again; κάθε ~ο every so often; ἑκατὸν ~α a hundred odd.

τοσοῦτ|ος *pron.* of such size *or* quantity; ἐν ~ῳ all the same; ~ῳ μᾶλλον with all the more reason.

τότε *adv.* then (*at that time*); in that case; ~ πού when.

τουαλέττα *s.f.* toilet; woman's formal dress; dressing-room; dressing-table; cloak-room; lavatory.

τοῦβλο *s.n.* brick; (*fig.*) blockhead.

τουλάχιστον *adv.* at least.

τούλι *s.n.* tulle.

τουλούμ|ι *s.n.* skin (*receptacle*); βρέχει μὲ τὸ ~ι it is raining cats and dogs; τὸν ἔκανα ~ι I gave him a good hiding. ~**ήσιος** *a.* (*cheese*) prepared in skin.

τουλούμπα *s.f.* 1. pump. 2. sort of oriental cake.

τουλούπα *s.f.* see **τολύπη**.

τουλ(ου)πάνι *s.n.* muslin (kerchief).

τούμπ|α *s.f.* ~ 1. somersault, fall; (*fam.*) κάνω ~ες kowtow. 2. mound.

τούμπανο *s.n.* drum; (*fam.*) τό κάνω ~ blab the secret; θά σέ κάνω ~ I will give you a hiding.

τουμπάρω *v.t. & i.* overturn; inveigle. (*v.i.*) overturn.

τουμπελέκι *s.n.* small drum.

τουναντίον *adv.* on the contrary.

τουπέ *s.n.* (*fam.*) cheek; boldness. [F. *toupet*]

τουρισμός *s.m.* tourism.

τουρίστ|ας, ~**ής** *s.m.* tourist.

Τούρκ|α, ~**άλα**, ~**ισσα** *s.f.* Turkish woman.

τουρκεύω *v.i.* become a Turk; (*fig.*) become enraged.

Τουρκία *s.f.* Turkey.

τούρκικ|ος, ~**ός** *a.* Turkish.

τουρκοκρατία *s.f.* Turkish domination (*of Greece*).

τουρκομερίτης *s.m.* (*Greek*) from Turkey.

Τοῦρκος *s.m.* Turk; Mohammedan; (*fig.*) γίνομαι ~ become enraged.

τούρλα *s.f.* mound; (*adv.*) heaped up.

τουρλώ|νω *v.t.* heap up; cause to bulge out. ~**τός** *a.* heaped up; rounded and protruding.

τουρνέ *s.f.* (*theatrical*) tour. [F. *tournée*]

τουρσί *s.n.* pickle.

τούρτα *s.f.* gateau, layer-cake.

τουρτουρίζω *v.i.* shiver.

τουτέστι *adv.* that is, namely.

τοῦτος *pron.* this (one).

τοῦφα *s.f.* tuft, clump.

τουφέκ|ι *s.n.* rifle, musket. ~**ιά** *s.f.* gun-shot. ~**ίζω** *v.t.* shoot.

τράβαλα *s.n.pl.* troubles, fuss.

τράβηγμα *s.n.* pulling, pull, tug; drawing (*of liquid*).

τραβηξιά *s.f.* sip; pull (*at pipe, etc.*); *see also* **τράβηγμα**.

τραβ|ῶ *v.t. & i.* 1. pull, drag, draw; ~ῶ τὸ δρόμο μου go one's own way. 2. draw (*weapon, money, liquid, lot, etc.*); (*fam.*) τό ~άει he drinks. 3. absorb, take up (*liquid, exports, etc.*). 4. fire (*shot*), fetch (*blow*). 5. reach speed *or* distance of. 6. attract; δὲν μὲ ~άει it does not appeal to me. 7. call for, want; ὁ καιρὸς ~άει πανωφόρι the weather calls for an overcoat; ἡ καρδιά μου ~άει τσιγάρο I feel like a cigarette.

8. endure, go through. (v.i.) 9. make or head for; move on. 10. last, drag on. 11. draw (of chimney, pipe). ~ιέμαι v.i. withdraw, cease to take part; be in demand (of goods); δὲν ~ιέται it is unendurable; (fam.) ~ηγμένος drunk; ~ηγμένος ἀπὸ τὰ μαλλιά far-fetched.

τραγανίζω v.t. crunch.

τραγαν|ός a. crisp, firm (to the teeth). ~ό s.n. cartilage.

τράγειος a. goat's.

τραγέλαφος s.m. incongruous situation or thing, mix-up.

τραγήσιος a. goat's.

τραγί s.n. kid.

τραγικός a. tragic; a tragic poet.

τράγος s.m. goat.

τραγούδημα s.n. singing.

τραγούδ|ι s.n. song. ~ιστής s.m. singer. ~ιστός a. sung; melodious (voice). ~ῶ v.t. & i. sing.

τραγωδ|ία s.f. tragedy. ~ός s.m.f. tragic actor or actress.

τραῖνο s.n. (railway) train.

τράκ s.n. stage fright. [F. trac]

τρακάρ|ω v.t. & i. collide (with); meet unexpectedly; (fam.) touch (person) for (loan). ~ισμα s.n. collision; surprise meeting.

τρακατρούκα s.f. fire-cracker.

τράκ|ο s.n., ~ος s.m. collision; (fig.) attack, blow.

τρακτέρ s.n. (farm) tractor. [F. tracteur]

τράμ, ~βάϊ s.n. tram. [E. tramway]

τραμουντάνα s.f. north wind.

τραμπαλίζομαι v.i. see-saw; rock up and down.

τραμπούκος s.m. (taker of) petty bribe; rapscallion.

τραν|ός a. clear, plain; large, great, important. ~εύω v.i. grow, increase.

τράνταγμα s.n. jolting, shaking; jolt, start.

τραντάζω v.t. jolt, shake; fetch (blow).

τρανταχτός a. (fig.) spectacular, on a big scale.

τράπεζα s.f. 1. table; ἁγία ~ altar. 2. (fin.) bank.

τραπεζαρία s.f. dining-room (suite).

τραπέζι s.n. table; στρώνω ~ lay the table; τοὺς εἴχαμε ~ we had them to dinner.

τραπέζιον s.n. (small) table; trapeze; (geom.) trapezium.

τραπεζίτης s.m. 1. banker. 2. molar.

τραπεζιτικός a. bank, banking; a bank employee.

τραπεζογραμμάτιον s.n. banknote.

τραπεζομάντηλο s.n. tablecloth.

τραπεζώνω v.t. entertain to dinner.

τράπουλα s.f. pack (of cards).

τράτα s.f. 1. seine; fishing-boat using this. 2. a cyclic dance.

τραταμέντ|ο s.n. refreshment (offered to guest); κάνω τὰ ~α stand treat.

τρατάρω v.t & i. offer or pay for (refreshment).

τράτο s.n. (sufficient) time, room, or material.

τραυλ|ός a. a stammerer. ~ίζω v.i. stammer.

τραῦμα s.n. wound, injury; trauma. ~τίας s.m. wounded person, casualty. ~τίζω v.t. wound, injure.

τραχανᾶς s.m. sort of (home-made) noodles.

τραχεία s.f. trachea.

τραχέως adv. roughly, abruptly.

τραχηλιά s.f. collaret, ruff; bib.

τράχηλος s.m. neck.

τραχύνω v.t. & i. make or become rough.

τραχύς a. rough, hard; tough (meat); harsh, abrupt.

τρεῖς a. three; ~ κι' ὁ κοῦκος very few.

τρέλλα s.f. madness; folly; eccentricity; (fam.) anything delightful.

τρελλαίν|ω v.t. drive mad. ~ομαι v.i. go mad; be driven mad; (with γιά) be mad on.

τρελλοκομεῖο s.n. madhouse.

τρελλός a. mad; a lunatic; crazy; mischievous (child).

τρεμο|σβήνω, ~φέγγω v.i. flicker, glimmer.

τρεμούλ|α s.f. trembling, shivering; fright. ~ιάζω v.i. tremble, shiver.

τρέμω v.i. tremble, shake, quiver.

τρέξιμ|ο s.n. running; ~ατα (pl.) running here and there, activity.

τρέπ|ω v.t. turn, convert; ~ω εἰς φυγήν put to flight. ~ομαι v.i. turn (to).

τρέφω v.t. nourish, feed, nurture; grow (beard); cherish (hope); (v.i.) ἔθρεψε ἡ πληγή the wound has healed.

τρεχάλα s.f. running; (adv.) at the run.

τρεχάματα s.n.pl. running here and there, activity.

τρεχ|άμενος, ~ούμενος a. running.

τρεχαντήρι s.n. small sailing-boat.

τρεχᾶτος a. running (of persons).

τρέχ|ω v.i. & t. run; hasten, hurry; go round (all over the place); wander; flow; run, leak, τί ~ει; what is going on? (v.t.) run, make (person) run; ἡ πληγή ~ει πύον the wound is running with pus.

τρέχ|ων a. current; τὰ ~οντα happenings, events.

τρία num. three.

τριάδα s.f. trinity; trio.

τρίαινα s.f. trident.

τριάκοντα num. thirty.

τριακόσιοι a. three hundred.

τριακοστός a. thirtieth.

τριανδρία s.f. triumvirate.

τριάντα num. thirty.

τριαντάφυλλο s.n. rose.

τριάρι s.n. figure 3; three (at cards).

τριάς s.f. trinity; trio.

τριατατικός a. post-office worker.

τριβέλι s.n. drill, auger; (fam.) importunate chatterer.

τριβή s.f. friction, rubbing; wear; (fig.) practice, experience.

τρίβολος s.m. caltrop.

τρίβ|ω v.t. rub; polish; grate. ~ομαι v.i. crumble; show signs of wear; (fig.) acquire experience.

τρίγλυφ|ον s.n. ~ος s.m. triglyph.

τριγμός s.m. creak(ing), squeak(ing); grinding (of teeth).

τριγυρ|ίζω, ~νῶ v.i. & t. go or wander around. (v.t.) go all over (premises, district); surround; (fig.) run after, lay siege to.

τριγυρίστρα s.f. 1. whitlow. 2. gadabout (woman).

τριγύρω adv. (all) around.

τριγωνικός a. triangular.

τριγωνομετρία s.f. trigonometry.

τρίγωνον s.n. 1. triangle. 2. sort of cake.

τρίγωνος a. three-cornered.

τρίδιπλος a. triple, threefold.

τρίδυμα s.n.pl. triplets.

τριετής a. triennial; three years old; third-year.

τρίζω v.i. & t. creak, squeak. (v.t.) grind (teeth); (fam.) τοῦ 'τριξα τά δόντια I spoke to him threateningly.

τριήρης s.f. trireme.

τρικαντό s.n. three-cornered hat.

τρικλίζω v.i. stagger.

τρικλοποδιά s.f. tripping up; (fig.) piece of trickery.

τρίκλωνος a. three-ply (thread).

τρικούβερτος a. three-decked; (fig.) terrific (jollification or row).

τρικυμ|ία s.f. storm (at sea). ~ιώδης a. stormy.

τρίκωχο s.n. three-cornered hat.

τρίλλια s.f. (mus.) trill.

τριμελής a. with three members.

τριμερής a. tripartite.

τρι|μηνία s.f., ~μηνο s.n. quarter (three months); a quarter's pay or rent.

τρίμην|ος, ~ιαῖος a. for or of three months, quarterly.

τρίμμα s.n. fragment, crumb.

τριμμένος a. showing signs of wear; polished; grated.

τρίξιμο s.n. see τριγμός.

τρίπατος a. three-storied.

τριπλάσι|ος a. triple, threefold. ~άζω v.t. treble.

τριπλ|ός, ~οῦς a. triple, threefold.

τριποδίζω v.t. trot.

τρί|πους s.m., ~ποδο s.n. tripod, trestle, easel; ὡς ἀπὸ ~ποδος ex cathedra.

τρίπτυχον s.n. triptych.

τρίς adv. thrice.

τρισάγιο(ν) s.n. a canticle; a prayer for the dead.

τρίσβαθα s.n.pl. depths.

τρισδιάστατος a. three-dimensional.

τρισέγγονο s.n. great-great-grandchild.

τρισκατάρατος a. thrice-cursed; the devil.

τρίστρατο s.n. three-cross-roads.

τριτεύω v.i. come third.

τρίτη s.f. 1. Tuesday. 2. (mus.) third.

τρίτον 1. s.n. third (portion). 2. adv. thirdly.

τρίτος a. third; third party.

τριτώνω v.i. & t. happen or repeat for third time.

τρίφτης s.m. grater.

τριφύλλι s.n. clover.

τρίχ|α s.f. a hair, bristle; coat, fur (of animal); στὴν ~a spick and span; παρὰ (or ἀπό) ~a νὰ πνιγῶ I was almost drowned. (fam.) ~ες (pl.) nonsense, lies.

τριχιά s.f. rope.

τριχοειδής a. capillary.

τρί|χρους, ~χρωμος a. tricolour.

τρίχωμα s.n. coat, fur (of animal); hair (on body).

τριχωτός a. hairy.

τρίψιμο s.n. rubbing, friction; polishing; grating.

Τριώδιον *s.n.* three weeks of Carnival (*before Lent*).

τρίωρος *a.* lasting three hours.

τρολές *s.m.* (*overhead*) trolley.

τρόλλεϋ *s.n.* trolley-bus [E. *trolley*]

τρόμαγμα *s.n.* a fright.

τρομάζω *v.t. & i.* frighten; become frightened; (*with νά*) have one's work cut out (*to*).

τρομακτικός *a.* frightening; (*fig.*) terrific.

τρομάρα *s.f.* fright, terror; (*fam.*) ~ σου bless you! (*in surprise or indignation*).

τρομερός *a.* frightful, terrible; (*fig.*) terrific, amazing.

τρομοκρατ|ῶ *v.t.* terrorize. ~ία *s.f.* terrorism; (reign of) terror.

τρόμος *s.m.* fright, terror; trembling.

τρόμπα *s.f.* pump; ~ μαρίνα loud-hailer.

τρομπέτα *s.f.* trumpet.

τρομπόνι *s.n.* trombone.

τρόπαι|ον *s.n.* trophy; ~α (*pl.*) triumph. ~ούχος *a.* triumphant.

τροπάριον *s.n.* (*eccl.*) a hymn; (*fig.*) (*same old*) refrain.

τροπή *s.f.* turn (*change of direction or circumstance*); conversion; solstice.

τροπικ|ός *a.* 1. tropic(al); οἱ ~οί tropics. 2. (*gram.*) of manner.

τρόπις *s.f.* keel.

τροπολογία *s.f.* amendment.

τροποποίησις *s.f.* modification.

τρόπ|ος *s.m.* way, manner, method; (*mus.*) mode; ~οι (*pl.*) manners; μὲ ~ο discreetly, surreptitiously; ~ον τινά somewhat; μὲ κάθε ~ο at all costs; ~ος τοῦ λέγειν (in a) manner of speaking; ἔχει τὸν ~ο του he is well off.

τρούλλ|ος *s.m.* dome. ~ωτός *a.* domed.

τρουμπ- see **τρομπ-**.

τροφαντός *a.* early (*vegetable*); plump.

τροφή *s.f.* food, nourishment; board.

τρόφιμα *s.n.pl.* food, victuals.

τρόφιμος *s.m.f.* inmate, boarder; (*fig.*) nursling.

τροφοδοσία *s.f.* provisioning (*of army, etc.*).

τροφοδότ|ης *s.m.* caterer, purveyor. ~ῶ *v.t.* feed, serve, keep supplied.

τροφός *s.f.* wet-nurse.

τροχάδην *adv.* at a run; quickly.

τροχαῖ|ος 1. *s.m.* trochee. 2. *a.* wheeled; ~ον ὑλικόν rolling-stock; ~α κίνησις wheeled traffic; ἡ ~α traffic police.

τροχαλία *s.f.* pulley.

τροχιά *s.f.* track, rut; railway track; orbit, trajectory.

τροχίζω *v.t.* grind (*knife*); (*fig.*) sharpen (*mental faculty*).

τροχιόδρομος *s.m.* tramway.

τρόχισμα *s.n.* grinding (*of knives*); (*fig.*) sharpening.

τροχονόμος *s.m.* traffic-policeman.

τροχοπέδη *s.f.* brake.

τροχοπέδιλον *s.n.* roller-skate.

τροχός *s.m.* wheel; grindstone.

τροχοφόρ|ος *a.* wheeled. ~ον *s.n.* vehicle; paddle-steamer.

τρυγητής *s.m.* grape-harvester; (*fam.*) September.

τρυγητός *s.m.* grape-harvest, vintage.

τρυγόνι *s.n.* turtle-dove.

τρύγος *s.m.* grape-harvest, vintage.

τρυγῶ *v.t.* gather (*grapes, honey*); (*fig.*) milk, exploit.

τρῦπα *s.f.* hole; κάνω μιὰ ~ στὸ νερό make vain effort.

τρυπ|άνι, ~ανον *s.n.* drill, auger. ~ανίζω *v.t.* drill hole in, pierce; (*med.*) trepan.

τρύπημα *s.n.* perforating, piercing; prick.

τρυπητ|ός *a.* perforated, with holes. ~ό *s.n.* strainer.

τρύπιος *a.* in holes.

τρυπητήρι *s.n.* awl, punch.

τρυπιοχέρης *a.* spendthrift.

τρυπῶ *v.t. & i.* make hole in, pierce; prick. (*v.i.*) prick; go into holes.

τρυπώνω *v.t. & i.* hide away; baste (*in sewing*). (*v.i.*) hide oneself; squeeze in.

τρυφερ|ός *a.* tender, affectionate; (*fam.*) ~όν ἥμισυ better half.

τρυφερότ|ης *s.f.* tenderness, affection; ~ητες (*pl.*) amorous behaviour.

τρυφηλός *a.* soft, unused to hardship; epicurean.

τρωγαλίζω *v.t.* gnaw.

τρώγλ|η *s.f.* hole, den; hovel. ~οδύτης *s.m.* troglodyte.

τρώ(γ)|ω *v.t.* eat, bite; μὲ ~ει it itches; spend, consume, squander; wear out, eat away; worry, nag, importune; beat, get the better of: suffer, undergo; (*fam.*) ~ω ξύλο catch it, get a beating; ~ω τὸν κόσμο move heaven and earth *or* search everywhere; ~ω τὸ κεφάλι μου be hoist with one's own petard; ~ω τὴ χυλόπιττα be rejected (*of suitor*); δὲν ~ει ἄχυρα he is no fool; τὸν ~ει ἡ μύτη (*or* ράχη) του he is asking for trouble; τὸν ~ει ἡ γλῶσσα του he is itching to blab. ~ομαι v.i. be eaten or eatable; (fig.) be passable; ~ονται they are at each other's throats; φαγώθηκε νά he was madly keen to.

τρωκτικόν s.n. rodent.

τρωικός a. Trojan.

τρωτ|ός a. vulnerable. ~όν s.n. short-coming.

τσάγαλο s.n. green almond.

τσαγγός a. rancid; (fam.) difficult, testy.

τσαγι|έρα s.f., ~ερό s.n. teapot.

τσαγκάρης s.m. shoemaker.

τσαγκαροδευτέρα s.f. (fam.) day off.

τσάι s.n. tea.

τσακάλι s.n. jackal.

τσακίζ|ω 1. v.t. & i. break, smash; (fig.) weaken, exhaust. (v.i.) be broken (in health); abate (of wind, etc.). ~ομαι v.i. make great efforts (to). 2. v.t. fold.

τσακίρικος a. (flecked) blue-green or grey-green (eyes).

τσακίρ-κέφι s.n. (fam.) slight inebriation.

τσάκιση s.f. crease (of trousers).

τσάκισμ|α s.n. breaking, smashing; ~ατα (pl.) coquettish airs; (fam.) νά πᾶς στά ~ατα go to the devil!

τσακμάκι s.n. tinder-box.

τσάκωμα s.n. catching; quarrelling.

τσακών|ω v.t. catch (in the act). ~ομαι v.i. quarrel.

τσαλαβουτῶ v.i. splash or flounder about; (fig.) do a slovenly job.

τσαλακώνω v.t. crease, crumple.

τσαλαπατῶ v.t. trample on.

τσαλίμι s.n. dexterous movement; (fig.) coquettish air.

τσάμι s.n. pine-tree.

τσάμικος s.m. sort of cyclic dance.

τσάμπα adv. see τζάμπα.

τσαμπί s.n. bunch (of grapes).

τσαμπουν|ίζω, ~ῶ v.i. whimper; prate.

τσάμπουρο s.n. grape-stalk.

τσανάκι s.n. shallow bowl; (fam.) scoundrel.

τσάντα s.f. handbag; brief-case; shopping-bag; satchel; game-bag.

τσαντίρι s.n. tent.

τσάπ|α s.f., ~ί s.n. hoe.

τσαπατσούλης a. slovenly (in one's work).

τσαπέλλα s.f. string of dried figs.

τσαρδάκ|α s.f., ~ι s.n. hut of dried branches.

τσάρκα s.f. (fig.) walk, stroll.

τσάρος s.m. tsar.

τσαρούχι s.n. rustic shoe with pompom.

τσάτρα πάτρα adv. after a fashion, stumblingly (esp. of speech).

τσατσάρα s.f. comb.

τσαχπινιά s.f. exercise of wiles, coquettishness.

τσέκ s.n. cheque. [E. cheque]

τσεκούρ|ι s.n. axe. ~ώνω v.t. cut with axe; (fam.) inflict severe penalty on; plough (in exam.).

τσέλιγκας s.m. chief shepherd.

τσεμπέρι s.n. kerchief.

τσέπ|η s.f. pocket; pocketful. ~ώνω v.t. pocket.

τσερβέλο s.n. brains, mind.

τσέρι s.n. cherry-brandy.

τσέρκι s.n. hoop.

τσέτουλα s.f. tally; (fam.) on tick.

τσευδίζω v.i. lisp; have speech defect.

τσευδός a. lisping.

τσιγαρίζ|ω v.t. fry lightly, brown; (fig.) ~ομαι μὲ τὸ ζουμί μου suffer privation.

τσιγάρ|ο s.n. cigarette. ~οθήκη s.f. cigarette-case or box. ~όχαρτο s.n. tissue paper.

τσιγγάνος s.m. gipsy.

τσιγγούνης a. stingy; a miser.

τσιγκέλι s.n. (meat) hook.

τσιγκλῶ v.t. goad.

τσίκνα s.f. smell of burnt meat or hair.

τσικν|ίζω v.t. & i. burn (in cooking); have a burnt smell; (fam.) τά ~ισαν they had a tiff.

τσικουδιά s.f. 1. terebinth. 2. sort of spirit.

τσιληπουρδῶ v.i. gallivant.

τσίμα adv. ~ ~ only just; on the very edge.

τσιμέντο s.n. cement; (fam.) ~ νά γίνει I couldn't care less.

τσιμουδιά s.f. (fam.) δέν ἔβγαλε ~ he kept mum; ~! not a word!

τσίμπημα s.n. prick, pinch, nip; bite, peck; bite of food.

τσιμπιά s.f. pinch.

τσιμπίδα s.f. tongs, forceps.

τσιμπίδ|ι s.n. tweezers; clothes-peg. ~άκι s.n. tweezers; hair-clip.

τσίμπλα s.f. (fam.) mucus of eyes.

τσιμπούκι s.n. tobacco-pipe.

τσιμπούρι s.n. tick (insect); (fig.) pest.

τσιμπούσι s.n. (fam.) spread, feast.

τσιμπῶ v.t. prick, pinch, nip; bite, peck; have a bite of (food); (fam.) make, pick up, cadge (small profit or perquisites); nab.

τσίνουρο s.n. eyelash.

τσινῶ v.i. kick, get restive.

τσίπα s.f. skin, crust, membrane; (fig.) (sense of) shame.

τσιπούρα s.f. gilthead (sea-fish).

τσίπουρο s.n. sort of spirit.

τσιράκι s.n. apprentice, boy; (fig.) ~ τοῦ πατέρα του another edition of his father.

τσιρίζω v.i. screech, squall.

τσιριμόνιες s.f.pl. assiduous attentiveness.

τσιρίσι s.n. glue.

τσίρκο s.n. circus.

τσίρλα s.f. (fam.) diarrhoea.

τσίρος s.m. dried mackerel; (fig.) very thin person.

τσιρότο s.n. sticking-plaster.

τσίτα adv. (fitting) very tight (of clothes); ~ ~ only just.

τσίτι s.n. calico.

τσιτσίδι adv. stark naked.

τσιτσιμπύρι s.n. ginger-beer.

τσιτσουρίζω v.i. & t. sizzle; (fig.) torment slowly.

τσιτ|ώνω v.t. stretch; (fam.) τά ~ωσε he died.

τσιφλίκι s.n. large country estate.

τσιφούτης s.m. skinflint.

τσίχλα s.f. thrush; (fam.) very thin person.

τσόκαρο s.n. wooden shoe; (fam.) vulgar woman.

τσοκολάτα s.f. chocolate.

τσολιᾶς s.m. evzone (soldier of kilted Gk. regiment).

τσο(μ)πάνης s.m. shepherd.

τσόντ|α s.f. piece (of cloth, etc.) joined on. ~άρω v.t. join on (a piece); (fig.) make up (remainder of sum required). .

τσουβάλι s.n. sack, sackful; sacking; (fam.) βάζω στό ~ trick.

τσουγκράν|α s.f. rake. ~ίζω v.t. scratch.

τσουγκρ|ίζω v.t. knock (against, together); clink (glasses); (fig.) τὰ ~ισαν they fell out.

τσούζω v.i. & t. sting, hurt; (make someone) smart; (fam.) τό ~ be given to drinking.

τσουκάλι s.n. earthen cooking-pot; chamber-pot.

τσουκνίδα s.f. nettle.

τσούλα s.f. loose-living or low-class woman.

τσουλάω v.i. & t. slide along; (v.t.) drag or trail along; push (vehicle).

τσουλῆς s.m. untidy person.

τσούλ|ι, ~άκι s.n. (door-) mat.

τσουλίστρα s.f. slide, chute.

τσουλούφι s.n. lock of hair, kiss-curl.

τσουράπι s.n. woollen sock.

τσουρέκι s.n. large bun.

τσοῦρμο s.n. crowd; crew.

τσουρουφλίζω v.t. singe.

τσουχτερός a. biting, stinging.

τσούχτρα s.f. jellyfish.

τσόφλι s.n. shell (of egg, nut); peel.

τσόχα s.f. thick woollen stuff; (fam.) slippery customer.

τυγχάνω v.i. & t. (happen to) be; ἔτυχε νά it happened that; (with gen.) enjoy, obtain.

τύλιγμα s.n. twisting, winding, coiling, wrapping.

τυλί|γω, ~σσω v.t. twist, wind, coil, wrap (up or round); (fam.) hook (victim).

τύλος s.m. callus.

τυλ|ώνω v.t. fill; (fam.) τήν ~ωσε he gorged himself.

τύμβ|ος s.m. grave, tomb. ~ωρύχος s.m. grave-robber.

τύμπανον s.n. drum; eardrum; tympanum.

τυπικόν s.n. (gram.) morphology.

τυπικός a. formal, conventional; typical.

τυπογράφ|ος s.m. printer. ~εῖον s.n. printing-press. ~ία s.f. printing.

τυποδεμένος a. careful of one's appearance.

τυποποίησις s.f. standardization.

τύπ|ος s.m. imprint, mark; mould; type, model; form, type, kind; (eccentric) character; type, print; the press; (math.) formula. ~οι (pl.) conventions, rules, form; γιὰ τὸν ~ο for form's sake.

τύπτω v.t. hit, strike.

τυπώνω v.t. print, imprint.

τύρανν|ος s.m. tyrant. ~ία s.f. tyranny; torment, harassment. ~ῶ v.i. & t. be a tyrant; torment, harass.

τυρί s.n. cheese.

τυρινή s.f. last week of Carnival.

τυροκομία s.f. cheese-making.

τυρόπηττα s.f. cheese-pie.

τυρός s.m. cheese.

τύρφη s.f. peat.

τυφεκ- see τουφεκ-.

τύφλα s.f. blindness; (fam.) opprobrious gesture with open palm; ~ στὸ μεθύσι blind drunk; ~ νἄχει αὐτὸ μπροστὰ στὸ δικό σου this one is far inferior to yours.

τυφλόμυγα s.f. blind man's buff.

τυφλοπόντικας s.m. mole (animal).

τυφλ|ός a. blind; (fig.) ~οῖς ὄμμασι with one's eyes shut.

τυφλοσ(ο)ύρτης s.m. foolproof aid or instructions; ready-reckoner.

τυφλών|ω v.t. blind; (fam.) make τύφλα at. ~ομαι v.i. become blind.

τυφλώττω v.i. be blind; (fig.) be blind or indifferent (to).

τυφοειδής a. ~ πυρετός typhoid fever.

τῦφος s.m. ἐξανθηματικὸς ~ typhus; (κοιλιακὸς) ~ typhoid fever.

τυφών s.m. cyclone.

τυχαίνω v.i. & t. (happen to) be; μοῦ ἔτυχε it fell to me; ἔτυχε νὰ λείπω I happened to be away; τὸν ἔτυχα στὸ δρόμο I met him in the street.

τυχαῖ|ος a. fortuitous, chance; δὲν εἶναι ~ος ἄνθρωπος he is no ordinary man. ~ως adv. by chance.

τυχάρπαστος a. one raised by stroke of fortune to power or wealth.

τυχερ|ός a. fortunate, lucky. ~ό s.n. fortune, destiny. ~ά s.n.pl. (fam.) casual profits, perks.

τύχη s.f. chance, fortune; fate; (good) luck; στὴν ~ at random.

τυχηρός a. see τυχερός.

τυχοδιώκτης s.m. adventurer.

τυχόν adv. by any chance; τὰ ~ ἔξοδα incidental expenses.

τυχών a. ὁ ~ the first comer, anybody; δὲν εἶναι ὁ ~ he is no ordinary person.

τύψις s.f. pang (of remorse), prick (of conscience).

τωόντι adv. really, in fact.

τώρα adv. now, at present; at once; just now; ἀπὸ ~ θὰ φύγεις; are you going already?

τωρινός a. present, present-day.

Υ

ὕαινα s.f. hyena.

ὑάκινθος s.m. hyacinth; jacinth.

ὑαλ- see γυαλ-.

ὑαλοπίναξ s.m. pane of glass.

ὕαλος s.f. (pane of) glass.

ὑαλουργία s.f. glass-making.

ὑαλόφρακτος a. glazed.

ὑαλώδης a. glassy; vitreous.

ὑάρδα s.f. yard (measure).

ὕβος s.m. hump.

ὑβρεολόγιον s.n. string of abuse.

ὑβρίζω v.t. & i. abuse, revile, swear (at).

ὕβρ|ις s.f. insult; oath, term of abuse; ~εις (pl.) abuse.

ὑβριστικός a. insulting, abusive.

ὑγεία, ὑγειά s.f. health.

ὑγειονομικός a. of health, sanitary (inspector, regulations, etc.).

ὑγιαίνω v.i. be in good health.

ὑγιεινός a. healthy (good for health).

ὑγιής a. healthy (enjoying good health); (fig.) sound.

ὑγραίνω v.t. moisten.

ὑγρασία s.f. moisture, damp(ness).

ὑγρ|ός a. liquid; moist, damp. ~όν s.n. liquid, fluid. ~οποιῶ v.t. liquefy.

ὑδαρής a. aqueous, watery; (fig.) insipid.

ὕδατα s.n.pl. waters.

ὑδαταγωγός s.m. water-conduit.

ὑδατάνθραξ s.m. carbohydrate.

ὑδατογραφία s.f. watercolour.

ὑδατοπτώσεις s.f.pl. waterfalls.

ὑδατοστεγής a. water-tight.

ὑδατοφράκτης s.m. dam, weir.

ὑδραγωγεῖον s.n. aqueduct.

ὑδραντλία s.f. water-pump.

ὑδράργυρος s.m. mercury.

ὑδρατμός s.m. vapour.

ὑδραυλικ|ός a. hydraulic; a plumber. ~ή s.f. hydraulics.

ὑδρ|εύομαι v.i. be supplied with water. ~ευσις s.f. water-supply.

ὑδρία s.f. pitcher.

ὑδρόβιος a. aquatic.

ὑδρόγειος s.f. terrestrial globe.

ὑδρογόνον s.n. hydrogen.

ὑδρογραφία s.f. hydrography.

ὑδροηλεκτρικός a. hydroelectric.

ὑδροκέφαλος a. hydrocephalous.

ὑδροκίνητος a. water-driven.

ὑδροκυάνιον s.n. prussic acid.

ὑδρολήπτης s.m. water-consumer.

ὑδρόμυλος s.m. water-mill.

ὑδρονομεύς s.m. turncock; water-key.

ὑδροπλάνον s.n. seaplane.

ὑδρορρόη s.f. gutter (of roof).

ὑδροστάθμη s.f. water-level.

ὑδροστατικός a. hydrostatic.

ὑδροστρόβιλος s.m. whirlpool; (water) turbine.

ὑδροσωλήν s.m. water-conduit.

ὑδροφοβία s.f. hydrophobia.

ὑδροφόρος *a.* water-carrying.
ὑδροφράκτης *s.m.* dam, weir.
ὑδροχαρής *a.* water-loving.
ὑδροχλωρικός *a.* hydrochloric.
ὑδρόχρωμα *s.n.* whitewash.
ὑδρόψυκτος *a.* water-cooled.
ὕδρ|ωψ *s.m.*, ~ωπικία *s.f.* dropsy.
ὕδωρ *s.n.* water.
ὑελ- *see* ὑαλ-.
ὑετός *s.m.* downpour.
υἱικός *a.* filial.
υἱοθε|σία, ~τησις *s.f.* adoption. ~τῶ *v.t.* adopt.
υἱός *s.m.* son.
ὑλακ|ή *s.f.* bark, barking. ~τῶ *v.i.* bark.
ὕλη *s.f.* matter, substance, material; pus.
ὑλικ|ός *a.* material. ~όν *s.n.* material, stuff; ingredient.
ὑλισμός *s.m.* materialism.
ὑλιστ|ής *s.m.* materialist. ~ικός *a.* materialistic.
ὑλοτομία *s.f.* tree-felling.
ὑμεῖς *pron.* you.
ὑμέναιος *s.m.* wedlock.
ὑμέτερος *pron.* your, yours.
ὑμήν *s.m.* (*anat.*) membrane.
ὕμν|ος *s.m.* hymn, anthem. ~ητής *s.m.* eulogist, celebrator. ~ῶ *v.t.* hymn, celebrate.
ὑνί *s.n.* ploughshare.
ὑπαγορ|εύω *v.t.* dictate. ~ευσις *s.f.* dictation; dictate.
ὑπάγ|ω 1. *v.i.* go. 2. *v.t.* class, count, bring (*under heading, jurisdiction, etc.*). ~ομαι *v.i.* (*with* εἰς) belong to, come under.
ὑπαίθριος *a.* open-air, outdoor.
ὕπαιθρ|ος *a.* ἡ ~ος the country (*as opposed to towns*); τὸ ~ον the open air.
ὑπαινιγμός *s.m.* hint.
ὑπαινίσσομαι *v.t.* hint at.
ὑπαίτιος *a.* responsible, guilty.
ὑπακοή *s.f.* obedience.
ὑπάκουος *a.* obedient.
ὑπακούω *v.t. & i.* obey.
ὑπάλληλος *s.m.f.* employee, clerk, shop-assistant; official; δημόσιος ~ civil servant.
ὑπαναχωρῶ *v.i.* withdraw discreetly; go back on promise.
ὑπανδρεία *s.f.* marriage, wedlock.
ὑπανδρεύω *v.t. see* παντρεύω.
ὕπανδρος *a.* married.
ὑπάνθρωπος *s.m.* sub-human person.

ὑπαξιωματικός *s.m.* non-commissioned officer.
Ὑπαπαντή *s.f.* Candlemas.
ὑπαρκτός *a.* existent.
ὕπαρξις *s.f.* existence; (a) being.
ὑπαρχ|ή *s.f.* ἐξ ~ῆς from the beginning.
ὑπαρχηγός *s.m.* second-in-command.
ὕπαρχος *s.m.* (*naut.*) second-in-command (*of warship*).
ὑπάρχ|ω *v.i.* exist, be; ~ει there is; τὰ ~οντά μου my possessions.
ὑπασπιστής *s.m.* aide-de-camp; (*mil.*) adjutant.
ὕπατος 1. *a.* highest. 2. *s.m.* consul (*Roman or French Republican*).
ὑπέδαφος *s.n.* subsoil.
ὑπείκω *v.i.* give way (*to instincts, force, etc.*).
ὑπεισέρχομαι *v.i.* creep in.
ὑπεκμισθώνω *v.t.* sublet.
ὑπεκ|φεύγω *v.t. & i.* escape, dodge. ~φυγή *s.f.* escape; evasion, subterfuge.
ὑπενθυμίζω *v.t.* remind (*person*) of, call to mind.
ὑπενοικιάζω *v.t.* grant *or* hold sublease of.
ὑπεξαίρεσις *s.f.* misappropriation.
ὑπέρ *prep.* 1. (*with acc.*) over, above. 2. (*with gen.*) for, on behalf of; τὰ ~ καὶ τὰ κατά pros and cons.
ὑπερ- *denotes* 1. over, very much. 2. on behalf of.
ὑπεράγαν *adv.* too (much).
ὑπεραιμία *s.f.* (*med.*) congestion.
ὑπεραμύνομαι *v.t.* (*with gen.*) defend, fight for.
ὑπεράνθρωπος *a.* superhuman; (*s.m.*) a superman.
ὑπεράνω *prep.* (*with gen.*) over, above.
ὑπεράριθμος *a.* supernumerary.
ὑπερασπίζ|ω, ~ομαι *v.t.* defend.
ὑπεράσπισις *s.f.* defence.
ὑπεραστικός *a.* long-distance (*telephone, bus-service, etc.*).
ὑπερβαίνω *v.t.* cross, surmount; surpass, exceed.
ὑπερβαλλόντως *adv.* exceedingly; too.
ὑπερβάλλω *v.t.* surpass, exceed; exaggerate.
ὑπέρβασις *s.f.* exceeding, overstepping.
ὑπερβολ|ή *s.f.* excess; exaggeration; (*geom.*) hyperbola. ~ικός *a.* excessive; exaggerated; (given to) exaggerating.
ὑπέργηρ|ος, ~ως *a.* extremely aged.
ὑπερδιέγερσις *s.f.* over-excitement.
ὑπερέντασις *s.f.* over-strain.
ὑπερευαίσθητος *a.* over-sensitive.
ὑπερέχω *v.t.* (*with gen.*) excel, exceed.

ὑπερῆλιξ *s.m.f.* elderly person.

ὑπερήφαν|ος *a.* proud. ~εια *s.f.* pride. ~εύομαι *v.i.* be proud (*of*); grow proud.

ὑπερθεματίζω *v.i.* bid higher; (*fig.*) go one better.

ὑπερθετικός *a.* superlative.

ὑπερίπταμαι *v.i.* & *t.* (*with gen.*) fly over.

ὑπερισχύω *v.i.* & *t.* (*with gen.*) prevail (over); overcome, beat.

ὑπεριώδης *a.* ultra-violet.

ὑπερκέρασις *s.f.* (*mil.*) outflanking.

ὑπερκόπωσις *s.f.* overwork.

ὑπέρμαχος *s.m.f.* champion.

ὑπέρμετρος *a.* excessive.

ὑπερνικῶ *v.t.* overcome.

ὑπέρογκος *a.* enormous; inordinate.

ὑπεροπλία *s.f.* superiority in arms.

ὑπεροπτικός *a.* haughty.

ὑπέροχ|ος *a.* excellent, superb. ~ή *s.f.* superiority.

ὑπεροψία *s.f.* haughtiness.

ὑπερπέραν *s.n.* the beyond, life after death.

ὑπερπηδῶ *v.t.* overleap, surmount.

ὑπερπόντιος *a.* overseas.

ὑπέρποτε *adv.* more than ever.

ὑπεροιτισμός *s.m.* intensive feeding.

ὑπερσυντέλικος *a.* (*gram.*) pluperfect.

ὑπέρτασις *s.f.* high blood-pressure.

ὑπέρτατος *a.* highest, supreme.

ὑπέρτερ|ος *a.* (*with gen.*) superior to. ~ῶ *v.t.* excel, surpass.

ὑπερτιμ|ῶ *v.t.* overestimate; raise price of. ~ησις *s.f.* overestimation; rise in price.

ὑπερτροφία *s.f.* (*med.*) hypertrophy.

ὑπέρυθρ|ος *a.* reddish; ~οι ἀκτίνες infra-red rays.

ὑπερύψηλος *a.* very high.

ὑπερυψ|ῶ *v.t.* exalt; (*fig.*) καὶ ~οῦται more than enough.

ὑπερφαλάγγισις *s.f.* (*mil.*) outflanking.

ὑπερφίαλος *a.* overweening.

ὑπερφυσικός *a.* supernatural; (*fig.*) extraordinary.

ὑπερώα *s.f.* palate.

ὑπερωκεάνιον *s.n.* liner.

ὑπερῶον *-s.n.* attic, loft; gallery (*of theatre*).

ὑπερωρία *s.f.* overtime.

ὑπεύθυνος *a.* responsible, accountable.

ὑπέχω *v.t.* bear, be under; ~ λόγον be accountable.

ὑπήκο|ος 1. *a.* obedient. 2. *s.m.f.* subject (*member of state*). ~ότης *s.f.* nationality.

ὑπήνεμος *a.* sheltered from wind; (*naut.*) leeward.

ὑπηρεσία *s.f.* service, duty, function; domestic servant(s); εἶμαι τῆς ~s be on duty.

ὑπηρεσιακ|ός *a.* pertaining to one's official duties; ~ή κυβέρνησις caretaker government.

ὑπηρέτ|ης *s.m.* servant. ~ρια *s.f.* maid.

ὑπηρετῶ *v.i.* & *t.* serve; do one's (*military*) service.

ὑπναλέος *a.* drowsy, half-asleep.

ὑπναρᾶς *s.m.* one who loves sleeping.

ὑπνηλία *s.f.* inordinate desire for sleep.

ὑπνοβάτης *s.m.* sleepwalker.

ὕπνος *s.m.* sleep.

ὕπνωσις *s.f.* hypnosis.

ὑπνωτ|ίζω *v.t.* hypnotize. ~ισμός *s.m.* hypnotism.

ὑπνωτικόν *s.f.* soporific (*drug*).

ὑπνώττω *v.i.* slumber; (*fig.*) be inactive.

ὑπό *prep.* 1. (*with acc.*) below, beneath, under. 2. (*with gen.*) by (*agent*).

ὑπ(ο)- *denotes* under, secretly, slightly.

ὑπόβαθρον *s.n.* pedestal, plinth.

ὑποβάλλω *v.t.* submit, present; subject, put (*to expense, torture, etc.*); suggest.

ὑποβαστάζω *v.t.* support, hold up.

ὑποβιβάζω *v.t.* lower, decrease; degrade, demote; do less than justice to.

ὑποβλέπω *v.t.* eye (*with distrust or envy*); cast glances at.

ὑποβλητικός *a.* evocative.

ὑποβοηθῶ *v.t.* support, back up.

ὑποβολεύς *s.m.* prompter.

ὑποβολή *s.f.* submission, presentation; suggestion, prompting.

ὑποβολιμαῖος *a.* spurious; not one's own (*opinion, etc.*).

ὑποβόσκω *v.i.* smoulder.

ὑποβρύχιον *s.n.* submarine; (*fam.*) sort of sweet.

ὑπογεγραμμένη *s.f.* (*gram.*) iota subscript.

ὑπόγει|ος *a.* underground. ~ον *s.n.* basement, cellar.

ὑπόγλυκος *a.* slightly sweet.

ὑπογραμμίζω *v.t.* underline.

ὑπογραμμός *s.m.* τύπος καὶ ~ model, exemplary specimen (*of*).

ὑπογραφή *s.f.* signature, signing.

ὑπογράφω *v.t.* sign; (*fig.*) approve.

ὑπογράψας *s.m.* signatory.

ὑποδαυλίζω *v.t.* poke (*fire*); (*fig.*) foment.

ὑποδεέστερος *a.* inferior.

ὑπόδειγμα *s.n.* model, specimen. ∼τικός *a.* exemplary.

ὑποδεικνύω *v.t.* point out; suggest, propose.

ὑπόδειξις *s.f.* indication; suggestion.

ὑποδεκάμετρον *s.n.* decimetre; measuring rule.

ὑποδέχομαι *v.t.* receive, greet.

ὑποδηλῶ *v.t.* contain a hint of, convey.

ὑπόδημα *s.n.* boot, shoe. ∼τοποιείον *s.n.* shoemaker's.

ὑπόδησις *s.f.* (supplying with *or* wearing of) foot-gear.

ὑποδιαιρ|ῶ *v.t.* subdivide. ∼εσις *s.f.* subdivision.

ὑποδιαστολή *s.f.* (*math.*) decimal point.

ὑποδιευθυντής *s.m.* assistant director, vice-principal, *etc.*

ὑπόδικος *a.* (*person*) under trial.

ὑποδόριος *a.* subcutaneous.

ὑπόδουλ|ος *a.* enslaved. ∼ώνω *v.t.* subjugate.

ὑποδοχή *s.f.* reception.

ὑποδύομαι *v.t.* play role of.

ὑποζύγιον *s.n.* beast of burden.

ὑποθάλπω *v.t.* foment; protect, support (*esp. secretly*).

ὑπόθεμα *s.n.* (*med.*) suppository.

ὑπόθεσις *s.f.* hypothesis, supposition; matter, affair, business, case; subject, theme.

ὑποθετικός *a.* hypothetical, supposed; fictitious; (*gram.*) conditional.

ὑποθέτω *v.t. & i.* suppose, presume.

ὑποθήκ|η *s.f.* mortgage. ∼εύω *v.t.* mortgage. ∼οφυλακείον *s.n.* mortgage registry.

ὑποκαθιστῶ *v.t.* replace (*take place of, exchange for something else*).

ὑποκάμισον *s.n.* shirt.

ὑποκατάστασις *s.f.* replacement.

ὑποκατάστημα *s.n.* branch office *or* shop.

ὑποκάτω *prep.* (*with gen.*) underneath.

ὑπόκειμαι *v.i.* be subject *or* liable (*to*).

ὑποκείμεν|ον *s.n.* subject; (*pej.*) person, individual. ∼ικός *a.* subjective.

ὑποκινῶ *v.t.* stir up, incite.

ὑποκλέπτω *v.t.* purloin, appropriate.

ὑπο|κλίνομαι *v.i.* bow. ∼κλισις *s.f.* bow.

ὑποκόμης *s.m.* viscount.

ὑποκόπανος *s.m.* butt (*of weapon*).

ὑποκοριστικόν *s.n.* diminutive.

ὑπόκοσμος *s.m.* underworld (*social*).

ὑποκρίνομαι *v.t. & i.* act, play (role of), personate. (*v.i.*) dissemble.

ὑποκρισία *s.f.* hypocrisy.

ὑπόκρισις *s.f.* 1. acting of part. 2. dissembling.

ὑποκριτής *s.m.* 1. actor. 2. hypocrite.

ὑποκριτικός *a.* hypocritical.

ὑπόκρουσις *s.f.* (*mus.*) accompaniment.

ὑποκύπτω *v.i.* bend, give way, succumb.

ὑπόκωφος *a.* dull, muffled (*sound*).

ὑπόλειμμα *s.n.* remainder, remnant.

ὑπολείπομαι *v.i.* remain over; be inferior, come after.

ὑπόληψις *s.f.* regard, esteem.

ὑπολογ|ίζω *v.t.* estimate, reckon; take into account, attach importance to. ∼ισμός *s.m.* calculation, estimate; ἐξ ∼ισμοῦ with ulterior motive.

ὑπόλογος *a.* responsible, accountable.

ὑπόλοιπ|ος *a.* remaining, rest (of). ∼ον *s.n.* remainder, balance.

ὑπολοχαγός *s.m.* (*mil.*) lieutenant.

ὑπομένω *v.i. & t.* endure.

ὑπομιμνήσκω *v.t.* remind (*person*) of.

ὑπομισθώνω *v.t.* hold sublease of.

ὑπόμνημα *s.n.* memorandum; ∼τα (*pl.*) commentary.

ὑπόμνησις *s.f.* reminder.

ὑπομοίραρχος *s.m.* lieutenant of gendarmerie.

ὑπομον|ή *s.f.* patience. ∼εύω *v.i.* be patient. ∼ητικός *a.* patient.

ὑποναύαρχος *s.m.* (*naut.*) rear-admiral.

ὑπόνοια *s.f.* suspicion.

ὑπονομεύω *v.t.* undermine.

ὑπόνομος *s.m.f.* sewer; blasting charge; (*mil.*) mine.

ὑπονο|ῶ *v.t.* imply, hint at; ∼είται it is understood.

ὑποπίπτω *v.i.* (*with* εἰς) fall into (*error, etc.*); come to (*one's notice*).

ὑποπλοίαρχος *s.m.* (*naut.*) lieutenant; first mate.

ὑποπόδιον *s.n.* footstool.

ὑποπροϊόν *s.n.* by-product.

ὑποπρόξενος *s.m.* vice-consul.

ὑποπτεύομαι *v.t. & i.* suspect.

ὕποπτος *a.* suspect, suspicious.

ὑποσημείωσις *s.f.* footnote.

ὑποσιτισμός *s.m.* under-nourishment.

ὑποσκάπτω *v.t.* undermine.

ὑποσκελίζω *v.t.* trip up; supplant.

ὑποσμηναγός *s.m.* (*aero.*) flight-lieutenant.

ὑποστάθμη *s.f.* dregs.

ὑπόστασις *s.f.* existence; foundation (*in fact*); (*med.*) hypostasis.

ὑποστατικόν *s.n.* landed property.

ὑπόστεγον s.n. shed, hangar; shelter.
ὑποστέλλω v.t. strike (flag, etc.); reduce (speed).
ὑποστήριγμα s.n. support (that which supports).
ὑποστηρίζω v.t. support; back; maintain, assert.
ὑποστήριξις s.f. support; backing.
ὑποστράτηγος s.m. (mil.) major-general.
ὑπόστρωμα s.n. 1. substratum. 2. saddle-cloth.
ὑποσυνείδητον s.n. subconscious.
ὑπόσχεσις s.f. promise.
ὑπόσχομαι v.t. & i. promise.
ὑποταγή s.f. submission, obedience.
ὑποτακτικ|ός a. obedient; a servant. ~ή s.f. (gram.) subjunctive.
ὑπότασις s.f. low blood-pressure.
ὑποτάσσ|ω v.t. bring into subjection. ~ομαι v.i. submit.
ὑποτείνουσα s.f. (geom.) hypotenuse.
ὑποτελής a. subordinate, vassal.
ὑποτίθεμαι v.i. be supposed.
ὑποτιμ|ῶ v.t. underestimate; reduce price of. ~ησις s.f. underestimation; reduction in price.
ὑποτονθορύζω v.t. & i. murmur, hum.
ὑποτροπή s.f. relapse.
ὑποτροφία s.f. bursary, scholarship.
ὑποτυπώδης a. sketchy, not fully developed.
ὕπουλος a. underhand, shifty.
ὑπουργεῖον s.n. ministry (of state).
ὑπουργικ|ός a. ministerial; ~ὸν συμβούλιον cabinet.
ὑπουργία s.f. ministry (term of office).
ὑπουργός s.m. minister.
ὑποφαινόμενος a. ὁ ~ the undersigned; (fam.) yours truly.
ὑποφερτός a. bearable; passable.
ὑποφέρω v.t. & i. bear, endure, go through; suffer, feel pain.
ὑποφώσκω v.i. dawn.
ὑποχείριος a. under the thumb or power of (with gen.).
ὑποχθόνιος a. subterranean, infernal.
ὑποχονδρία s.f. hypochondria.
ὑπόχρεος a. obliged (in duty or gratitude).
ὑποχρεώνω v.t. oblige (bind or gratify).
ὑποχρέωσις s.f. obligation.
ὑποχρεωτικός a. obligatory; obliging.
ὑποχώρησις s.f. retreat, giving way; subsidence.
ὑποχωρῶ v.i. retreat, give way; abate, subside.

ὑποψήφι|ος a. aspirant; a candidate or applicant. ~ότης s.f. candidature, application.
ὑποψί|α s.f. suspicion. ~άζομαι v.i. suspect.
ὕπτιος a. supine, on one's back.
ὑπώρεια s.f. foot of mountain.
ὕσκα s.f. tinder.
ὕστατος a. last.
ὕστερα adv. after(wards), then, later on; furthermore; (prep.) ~ ἀπό after.
ὑστέρημα s.n. one's inadequately small savings.
ὑστερ|ία s.f., ~ισμός s.m. hysteria. ~ικός a. hysterical.
ὑστερ(ι)νός a. later, last.
ὑστεροβουλία s.f. ulterior motive.
ὑστερόγραφον s.n. postscript.
ὕστερον 1. adv. see ὕστερα. 2. s.n. after-birth.
ὕστ|ερος a. later; inferior; ἐκ τῶν ~έρων looking back (after event).
ὑστερῶ v.i. come after, be inferior.
ὑφ- see ὑπο-.
ὑφάδι s.n. weft.
ὑφαίνω v.t. weave.
ὕφαλα s.n.pl. part of ship's hull below water-line.
ὕφαλος s.f. reef, shoal.
ὕφανσις s.f. weaving; weave.
ὑφαντός a. woven.
ὑφαντουργία s.f. textile industry.
ὑφαρπάζω v.t. obtain by trickery.
ὕφασμα s.n. cloth, material; ~τα (pl.) textiles.
ὕφεσις s.f. abatement; (barometric) depression; (mus.) flat.
ὑφή s.f. texture.
ὑφηγητής s.m. university lecturer.
ὑφήλιος s.f. earth, globe.
ὑφίστ|αμαι v.t. & i. undergo, suffer. (v.i.) exist, be in force. ~άμενος s.m. subordinate.
ὕφος s.n. style; air, tone.
ὑφυπουργός s.m. under-secretary.
ὑψηλ|ός a. high, tall; (fig.) lofty, great; ~ὴ Πύλη Sublime Porte. ~ότης s.f. Highness.
ὑψηλόφρων a. 1. magnanimous. 2. arrogant.
ὑψικάμινος s.f. blast-furnace.
ὕψιλον s.n. the letter Υ.
ὑψίπεδον s.n. plateau.
ὕψιστος a. highest; the All-highest.
ὑψίφωνος s.f. soprano.
ὑψόμετρον s.n. altitude.

ὕψ|ος s.n. height; ἐξ ~ους from on high; (mus.) pitch.

ὕψωμα s.n. height (high ground).

ὑψωμός s.m. raising; rise (in price).

ὕψωσις s.f. raising, elevation; rise (in price).

ὑψώνω v.t. raise.

Φ

φάβα s.f. yellow pea; pease-pudding.

φαγάνα s.f. dredger; (fam.) insatiable person or machine.

φαγᾶς s.m. glutton.

φαγγρί s.n. sea-bream.

φαγγρίζω v.i. see φεγγρίζω.

φαγέδαινα s.f. canker.

φαγιάντζα s.f. faience; serving-dish.

φαγητόν s.n. meal, dish, food to eat.

φαγί s.n. food to eat.

φαγκότο s.n. (mus.) bassoon.

φαγοπότι s.n. eating and drinking, carousal.

φαγούρα s.f. itch, itching.

φάγωμα s.n. 1. corrosion, wearing away; part so affected. 2. wrangling.

φαγωμάρα s.f. 1. itching. 2. wrangling.

φαγωμένος a. eaten; worn away; εἶμαι ~ I have eaten.

φαγώσιμ|ος a. eatable; ~α (s.n.pl.) provisions.

φαειν|ός a. brilliant; ἡλίου ~ότερον clear as daylight; ~ή ἰδέα brainwave.

φαΐ s.n. food to eat.

φαιδρ|ός a. merry, gay; (fam.) laughable. ~ύνω v.t. cheer, gladden.

φαίνομαι v.i. appear, be visible; seem, look, be evident; prove, show oneself (to be).

φαινομενικῶς adv. seemingly.

φαινόμεν|ον s.n. phenomenon; prodigy; κατὰ τὰ ~α to all appearances.

φαιός a. grey; darkish.

φάκα s.f. mouse-trap.

φάκελλος s.m. envelope; file, dossier.

φακή s.f. lentil(s).

φακίδα s.f. freckle.

φακιόλι s.n. kerchief.

φακίρης s.m. fakir.

φακός s.m. lens; magnifying glass.

φάλαγξ s.f. phalanx; (mil.) column.

φάλαινα s.f. whale.

φαλάκρ|α s.f. baldness; bald patch.

~αίνω v.i. go bald. ~ός a. bald; bare (of mountain).

φαλ(λ)ίρω v.i.&t. go or make bankrupt.

φαλλός s.m. phallus.

φαλμπαλᾶς s.m. see φραμπαλᾶς.

φαλτσέτα s.f. shoemaker's knife.

φάλτσ|ο s.n. wrong note; (fig.) mistake. ~άρω v.i. be out of tune; (fig.) err.

φαμ|ίλια, ~ελιά s.f. family. ~ελίτης s.m. family man.

φάμπρικ|α s.f. factory; (fam.) scheme, dodge. ~άρω v.t. manufacture; (fig.) fabricate, concoct.

φανάρι s.n. 1. lamp, torch, lantern; headlamp; lighthouse; (fig.) κρατῶ τὸ ~ abet secret lovers. 2. hanging food-safe.

Φαναριώτης s.m. Phanariot.

φαναρτζῆς s.m. lamp-maker; tinsmith.

φανατίζω v.t. make fanatical.

φανατικός a. fanatical; a fanatic.

φανατισμός s.m. fanaticism.

φανέλλα s.f. flannel; vest.

φανερ|ός a. clear, obvious. ~ώνω v.t. reveal, show.

φανός s.m. lamp, lantern.

φαντάζομαι v.t. & i. imagine, suppose, think; grow conceited.

φαντάζω v.i. make an effect, show up well; look glamorous.

φαντάρος s.m. foot-soldier.

φαντασία s.f. imagination; fantasy; conceit (pride); (mus.) fantasia.

φαντασιοκόπος a. a dreamer.

φαντασιοπληξία s.f. extravagant idea; whim, caprice.

φαντασιώδης a. imaginary; imaginative; beyond imagination.

φάντασμα s.n. ghost.

φαντασμαγορία s.f. phantasmagoria.

φαντασμένος a. vainglorious.

φανταστικός a. imaginary; fantastic.

φανταχτερός a. showy, striking.

φάντης s.m. knave (cards).

φανφαρόνος s.m. braggart.

φάπα s.f. slap, cuff.

φάρα s.f. (pej.) race, breed.

φάρ|αγξ s.f. ~άγγι s.n. gorge, ravine.

φαράσι s.n. dustpan.

φαρδαίνω v.t. & i. make or become wider; stretch.

φάρδος s.n. width, breadth.

φαρδ|ύς a. wide, broad; ~ιά-πλατιά sprawling.

φαρέτρα s.f. quiver.

φαρί s.n. steed.

φαρμακεῖον s.n. chemist's; (fam.) place where one gets swindled.

φαρμακέμπορος s.m. wholesale druggist.

φαρμακερός a. poisonous; (fig.) biting.

φαρμάκι s.n. poison; (fig.) anything bitter (coffee, grief, cold, etc.).

φαρμακίλα s.f. bitter taste; (fig.) grief.

φαρμακομύτης s.m. venomous person.

φάρμακον s.n. drug, medicine.

φαρμακοποιός s.m. pharmacist, chemist.

φαρμακώνω v.t. poison; (fig.) grieve; taste bitter to.

φαρμπαλάς s.m. see φραμπαλάς.

φάρος s.m. lighthouse, beacon.

φάρσα s.f. farce; practical joke.

φάρυγξ s.m. pharynx.

φαρφουρί s.n. porcelain.

φασαρία s.f. disturbance, to-do; fuss, bother.

φασιανός s.m. pheasant.

φάσις s.f. phase.

φασιστικός a. fascist.

φάσκελο s.n. see μούντζα.

φασκιά s.f. swaddling-band.

φασκόμηλο s.n. sort of aromatic herb.

φάσκω v.i. ~ καὶ ἀντιφάσκω say now one thing now the opposite.

φάσμα s.n. 1. ghost, spectre. 2. spectrum.

φασματοσκόπιον s.n. spectroscope.

φασ|όλι, ~ούλι s.n. haricot bean.

φασο(υ)λάδα s.f. bean soup.

φασο(υ)λάκια s.f. green beans.

φασουλῆς s.m. Punch (puppet).

φάτνη s.f. manger.

φατνίον s.n. (anat.) alveolus.

φατρί|α s.f. faction. ~άζω v.i. form factions.

φάτσα s.f. face; front; (adv.) face to face.

φαυλόβιος a. living a depraved life.

φαυλοκρατία s.f. corruption (esp. in politics).

φαῦλος a. depraved; ~ κύκλος vicious circle.

φαφλατάς s.m. jabberer.

φαφούτης a. toothless.

Φεβρουάριος s.m. February.

φεγγάρι s.n. moon; ~α ~α at certain periods.

φεγγίτης s.m. skylight, fanlight.

φέγγος s.n. light.

φεγγοβολῶ v.i. give brilliant light.

φεγγρίζω v.i. be semi-transparent; (fig.) grow very thin.

φέγγ|ω v.i. 1. shine; ~ει it is daylight; ἔφεξε day dawned; (fam.) μοῦ 'φεξε I had unexpected good fortune. 2. See φεγγρίζω.

φείδομαι v.t. (with gen.) spare (abstain from hurting); be sparing or frugal of.

φειδώ s.f. thrift. ~λεύομαι v.i. be stingy. ~λός a. thrifty, sparing; stingy.

φελί s.n. finger-shaped piece (of food).

φελλός s.m. cork; (fam.) trivial person.

φέλπα s.f. velveteen.

φενάκη s.f. wig; (fig.) deceit.

φέουδ|ον s.n. fief. ~αρχικός a. feudal.

φερέγγυος a. solvent.

φέρελπις a. promising; (young) hopeful.

φερετζές s.m. Moslem woman's veil.

φέρετρον s.n. coffin.

φερέφωνον s.n. (fig.) one who echoes the views of another.

φερμάνι s.n. firman (order from Sultan).

φερμάρω 1. v.t. gaze at. 2. v.t. & i. stop (esp. of vehicle).

φέρμελη s.f. embroidered waistcoat.

φερμένος a. arrived, brought.

φερμουάρ s.n. (zip) fastener. [F. fermoir]

φέρνω v.t. & i. see φέρω.

φέρσιμο s.n. behaviour.

φέρ|ω v.t. & i. carry, bear; wear; bring, fetch; bring about, occasion; bring forward, produce; ~ω ἀντιρρήσεις raise objections; τόφερε ὁ λόγος the subject came up; ὁ λόγος τὸ ~νει in a manner of speaking; ~νω (with gen. or σέ) be somewhat like, have a suggestion of; ~ εἰπεῖν for example; ~ε νὰ δοῦμε let us see. ~ομαι v.i. behave; be reputed or considered.

φέσι s.n. fez; (fam.) γίνομαι ~ get drunk.

φέτα s.f. 1. slice. 2. sort of white cheese.

φέτ|ος adv. this year. ~ινός a. this year's.

φετφᾶς s.m. arbitrary ruling.

φεῦ int. alas.

φευγ|άλα s.f., ~ιό s.n. (precipitate) flight.

φευγαλέος a. fleeting.

φευγατίζω v.t. help to escape.

φευγάτος a. gone, departed.

φεύγω v.i. & t. leave, depart, go away; escape, fly. (v.t.) run away from; ὅπου φύγη φύγη said of one who takes to his heels.

φευκτέος a. to be avoided.

φήμ|η s.f. rumour; reputation, repute; fame. ~ίζομαι v.i. be famous.

φηρίκι *s.n.* sort of apple.

φθά|νω *v.i. & t.* be enough; arrive, draw near; become established *or* recognized; (*with* σέ) reach, reach the point (*of*), be reduced (*to*); ~νει νά provided that; νὰ μὴ ~σω on my head be it! λέει ὅτι ~ση he says whatever comes into his head. (*v.t.*) reach, catch up with; come up to, equal; δὲν τὸν ἔφτασα he was before my time.

φθαρτός *a.* perishable.

φθείρ *s.m.f.* louse.

φθείρ|ω *v.t.* damage, spoil, impair; corrupt. ~ομαι *v.i.* wear out; (*fig.*) lose prestige.

φθην- *see* **φτην-**.

φθινόπωρον *s.n.* autumn.

φθίνω *v.i.* wane, draw to a close; decline, waste away.

φθίσ|ις *s.f.* consumption. ~ικός *a.* consumptive.

φθόγγ|ος *s.m.* (*vocal*) sound; (*mus.*) note. ~όσημον *s.n.* (*mus.*) (*written*) note.

φθόν|ος *s.m.* (*malicious*) envy. ~ερός *a.* envious. ~ῶ *v.t.* be envious of.

φθορά *s.f.* damage, destruction, wear and tear.

φθορεύς *s.m.* destroyer; corrupter.

φθορισμός *s.m.* fluorescence.

φῖ *s.n.* the letter Φ.

φιάλη *s.f.* bottle.

φιγούρ|α *s.f.* (*mus. & dance*) figure; court card; (*fig.*) κάνω ~α cut a (fine) figure. ~άρω *v.i.* figure, appear; cut a fine figure; pose (*as*).

φιγουρίνι *s.n.* book of fashion-plates.

φιδές *s.m.* vermicelli.

φίδ|ι *s.n.* snake; βγάζω τὸ ~ι ἀπὸ τὴν τρύπα pull the chestnuts out of the fire. ~ωτός *a.* winding; snaky.

φίλαθλος *a.* interested in sports (*as spectator*).

φιλαλήθης *a.* truthful.

φιλάνθρωπος *s.m.f.* philanthropist.

φιλαράκος *s.m.* (*fam.*) beau; scamp, fine friend.

φιλάργυρος *a.* miserly; a miser.

φιλάρεσκος *a.* coquettish.

φιλαρμονική *s.f.* (*mus.*) band.

φιλαρχία *s.f.* love of power.

φιλάσθενος *a.* delicate, sickly.

φιλαυτία *s.f.* egoism.

φιλέκδικος *a.* vindictive.

φιλελεύθ|ερος *a.* liberty-loving; a Liberal; κόμμα τῶν ~έρων Liberal Party. ~ερισμός *s.m.* liberalism.

φιλέλλην *s.m.f.* philhellene.

φιλ|ενάδα, ~ηνάδα *s.f.* girl *or* woman friend; (*fam.*) mistress.

φίλεργος *a.* fond of work, industrious.

φίλερις *a.* quarrelsome.

φιλές *s.m.* (hair-) net.

φιλέτο *s.n.* 1. fillet (*meat*). 2. piping (*cloth*); narrow band (*decorative*).

φιλεύω *v.t.* (*with double acc.*) give (*present*) to (*person*); treat to.

φίλη *s.f.* friend.

φιλήδονος *a.* sensual; a voluptuary.

φίλημα *s.n.* kiss.

φιλήσυχος *a.* peace-loving.

φιλί *s.n.* kiss.

φιλία *s.f.* friendship.

φιλικ|ός *a.* friendly; friend's; member of ~ὴ Ἑταιρεία (*secret society for Gk. independence under Turks*).

φιλιππικός *s.m.* philippic.

φίλιππος *s.m.f.* horse-lover; (*fam.*) race-goer.

φιλιώνω *v.t. & i.* reconcile (*estranged persons*); become reconciled, make it up.

φιλιστρίνι *s.n.* porthole.

φίλμ *s.n.* film (*cinema, photographic*). [E.]

φίλντισι *s.n.* ivory; (*fam.*) mother-of-pearl.

φιλόδικος *a.* litigious.

φιλόδοξ|ος *a.* ambitious. ~ῶ *v.i. & t.* be ambitious; aspire to.

φιλοδώρημα *s.n.* tip, gratuity.

φιλοζωία *s.f.* love of one's own life; poltroonery.

φιλόκαλος *a.* with a taste for the beautiful.

φιλοκατήγορος *a.* censorious.

φιλοκερδής *a.* greedy of gain.

φιλολογία *s.f.* literature; philology; (*fam.*) mere words.

φιλομαθής *a.* eager to learn.

φιλομειδής *a.* smiling, cheerful.

φιλόμουσος *a.* a lover of music *or* the arts.

φιλόν|(ε)ικ|ος *a.* quarrelsome. ~ία *s.f.* quarrelling; quarrel. ~ῶ *v.i.* quarrel.

φιλόξεν|ος *a.* hospitable. ~ία *s.f.* hospitality. ~ῶ *v.t.* entertain, give hospitality to; find room for.

φιλοπαίγμων *a.* given to joking.

φιλοπατρία *s.f.* love of one's country.

φιλοπόλεμος *a.* bellicose.

φιλόπον|ος *a.* fond of work, industrious. ~ῶ *v.t.* prepare with zealous care.

φιλοπράγμων *a.* meddlesome, inquisitive.

φιλοπρόοδος *a.* progressive.

φίλος *a. & s.m.* dear; friendly; friend.

φιλόσοφ|ος *s.m.f.* philosopher. ~**ία** *s.f.* philosophy. ~**ικός** *a.* philosophic(al).

φιλόστοργος *a.* loving.

φιλοτελισμός *s.m.* philately.

φιλοτέχνημα *s.n.* work of art.

φιλότεχνος *a.* an art-lover.

φιλοτιμία *s.f. see* **φιλότιμο**. κάνω τὴν ἀνάγκη ~ make a virtue of necessity.

φιλότιμο *s.n.* one's honour, pride, dignity *or* face.

φιλότιμος *a.* having a sense of φιλότιμο; ambitious to excel; obliging; generous. **φιλοτιμ|ῶ** *v.t.* put (*person*) on his mettle. ~**οῦμαι** *v.i.* make it a point of honour.

φιλοφρόνη|μα *s.n.*, ~**σις** *s.f.* compliment.

φιλόφρων *a.* courteous, attentive.

φίλτατος *a.* dearest.

φίλτρον *s.n.* 1. philtre; (*parental*) love. 2. filter.

φιλύποπτος *a.* mistrustful.

φιλύρα *s.f.* lime-tree.

φιλῶ *v.t.* kiss.

φιμ|ώνω *v.t.* muzzle, gag. ~**ωτρον** *s.n.* muzzle.

φίνος *a.* fine (*of quality, feeling, manners*).

φιντάν|ι *s.n.* young plant. ~**άκι** *s.n.* (*adolescent*) girl.

φιόγκος *s.m.* bow (*ribbon*).

φιρίκι *s.n.* sort of apple.

φίρμα *s.f.* firm; trade-name; (*fam.*) (one who has made) a reputation.

φίσα·*s.f.* slip (*for filing*); chip (*for gambling*).

φίσκα *adv.* full to overflowing.

φιστίκι *s.n.* pistachio-nut; ~ ἀράπικο monkey-nut.

φιτίλι *s.n.* wick, fuse; braid, piping; τοῦ βάζω ~α I irritate *or* inflame him *or* egg him on.

φκ(ε)ιάνω *v.t. & i. see* **φτιάνω**.

φκυάρι *s.n.* shovel, spade.

φλαμούρι *s.n.* lime-wood; infusion of lime-blossom.

φλάμπουρο *s.n.* pennon.

φλάουτο *s.n.* flute.

φλέβα *s.f.* vein; lode; (*fig.*) talent.

Φλεβάρης *s.m.* (*fam.*) February.

φλέγμα *s.n.* phlegm, mucus; (*fig.*) phlegm. ~**τικός** *a.* phlegmatic.

φλεγμονή *s.f.* inflammation.

φλέγ|ομαι *v.i.* burn, be ablaze; ~**ον** ζήτημα burning question.

φλέμα *s.n.* phlegm, mucus.

φλέρτ *s.n.* flirtation; person one flirts with. [E. *flirt*]. ~**άρω** *v.i. & t.* flirt (with).

φλέψ *s.f.* vein; lode.

φληναφῶ *v.i.* prate.

φλιτζάνι *s.n.* cup; cupful.

φλόγα *s.f.* flame; (*fig.*) fire, passion.

φλογέρα *s.f.* shepherd's pipe.

φλογερός *a.* flaming; (*fig.*) passionate.

φλογίζω *v.t.* inflame.

φλογοβόλον *s.n.* (*mil.*) flame-thrower.

φλόγωσις *s.f.* inflammation.

φλοιός *s.m.* peel, rind, skin; shell; bark; crust (*of earth*).

φλοῖσβος *s.m.* lapping (*of waves*).

φλοκάτ|α, ~**η** *s.f.* peasant's thick blanket *or* cape.

φλόκος *s.m.* (*naut.*) jib.

φλομώνω *v.t. & i.* stupefy; (*fig.*) fill with noxious smell *or* smoke; (*v.i.*) grow pale.

φλόξ *s.f. see* **φλόγα**.

φλούδ|α *s.f.*, ~**ι** *s.n. see* **φλοιός**.

φλουρί *s.n.* gold florin.

φλύαρ|ος *a.* loquacious. ~**ία** *s.f.* loquacity, chatter. ~**ῶ** *v.i.* chatter, gossip.

φλύκταινα *s.f.* blister; pustule.

φλυτζάνι *s.n.* cup, cupful.

φοβᾶμαι *v.t. & i. see* **φοβοῦμαι**.

φοβέρα *s.f.* threat.

φοβερίζω *v.t.* threaten.

φοβερός *a.* frightful; terrific, amazing.

φόβητρον *s.n.* scarecrow; bogy.

φοβητσιάρης *a.* timorous.

φοβία *s.f.* phobia.

φοβίζω *v.t.* frighten; threaten.

φόβος *s.m.* fear.

φοβοῦμαι *v.t. & i.* fear, be afraid (of).

φόδρα *s.f.* lining.

φοινίκι *s.n.* sort of cake.

φοίν|ιξ *s.m.*, ~**ικιά** *s.f.* palm-tree.

φοιτ|ῶ *v.i.* (*with* εἰς) frequent; be a student. ~**ησις** *s.f.* attendance at a course of study. ~**ητής** *s.m.* student.

φόλα *s.f.* 1. dog-poison. 2. patch on a shoe.

φολίς *s.f.* scale (*of fish, etc.*).

φον|εύς, ~**ιᾶς** *s.m.* murderer.

φονεύω *v.t.* murder.

φόν|ος *s.m.*, ~**ικό** *s.n.* murder.

φόντο *s.n.* bottom, essential character; background; capital (*funds*); (*fig.*) moral *or* intellectual worth.

φόρα 1. *s.f.* way, impetus; force.

2. *adv.* βγάζω (στή *or* στά) ~ (*fig.*) bring into the open.

φορά *s.f.* force; way, impetus; direction (*of wind, current, events*); time (*occasion*); ἄλλη ~ some other time; ἄλλη μιά ~ once more; μιά ~ once; βλάκας μιά ~ a fool and no mistake.

φοράδα *s.f.* mare.

φορατζής *s.m.* tax-collector.

φορβάς *s.f.* mare.

φορβή *s.f.* fodder.

φορείον *s.n.* stretcher.

φόρεμα *s.n.* (wearing of) a dress.

φορεσιά *s.f.* suit of clothes; attire.

φορεύς *s.m.* carrier, bearer.

φορητός *a.* portable.

φόρμα *s.f.* 1. form, shape; mould, caketin, *etc.*; (*fig.*) σὲ ~ in good form, fit. 2. form, document. 3. overall.

φοροδιαφυγή *s.f.* tax-evasion.

φορολογ|ία *s.f.* taxation. ~ῶ *v.t.* tax; ~ούμενος a taxpayer.

φόρος *s.m.* tax, duty.

φορτηγ|ός *a.* freight-carrying. ~όν *s.n.* lorry; cargo-vessel.

φορτίζω *v.t.* charge (*with electricity*).

φορτικός *a.* importunate, pestering.

φορτίον *s.n.* cargo, load, freight; burden.

φορτοεκφορτωτής *s.m.* stevedore.

φόρτος *s.m.* (*fig.*) heavy load.

φορτσάρω *v.t. & i.* force (*lock, voice, etc.*); intensify. (*v.i.*) strengthen (*of wind*).

φόρτωμα *s.n.* loading; load; (*fig.*) burden, trial (*of persons*).

φορτών|ω *v.t. & i.* load (with); take on cargo. ~ομαι *v.t.* pester.

φορτωτική *s.f.* bill of lading.

φορ|ῶ *v.t.* wear; put on; τοῦ ~εσα τὰ παπούτσια I put his shoes on (*for him*); ~εμένα ροῦχα worn clothing.

φουβού *s.f.* charcoal stove; brazier.

φουγάρο *s.n.* tall chimney, funnel.

φουκαράς *s.m.* (*fam.*) poor chap.

φούμαρα *s.n.pl.* big words; castles in the air.

φουμάρω *v.t. & i.* (*fam.*) smoke.

φοῦμος *s.m.* soot; lamp-black.

φούντα *s.f.* tassel.

φουντάρω *v.t. & i.* sink (*ship*); (*v.i.*) drop anchor; sink.

φουντούκι *s.n.* hazel-nut.

φουντώνω *v.i. & t.* grow bushy; spread, grow in extent *or* intensity; (*v.t.*) make (*hair, dress*) puffed *or* bouffant.

φουντωτός *a.* bushy.

φούξια *s.f.* fuchsia.

φούρια *s.f.* impetuous haste.

φούρκ|α *s.f.* 1. gallows. 2. (*indignant*) anger; τόν ἔχω ~a I am furious with him. ~ίζω *v.t.* 1. hang. 2. infuriate.

φουρκέτα *s.f.* hairpin.

φουρνάρ|ης *s.m.* baker. ~ικο *s.n.* bakery.

φουρνέλο *s.n.* grid of cooking-stove; blasting-charge.

φουρνιά *s.f.* ovenful; (*fig.*) batch.

φοῦρνος *s.m.* oven; bakery.

φουρτούνα *s.f.* storm, rough sea; (*fig.*) tribulation.

φούσκα *s.f.* bladder; (*toy*) balloon; blister; bubble.

φουσκάλα *s.f.* blister; bubble.

φουσκί *s.n.* manure.

φουσκοδεντριά *s.f.* rising of sap.

φουσκοθαλασσιά *s.f.* swell (*of sea*).

φουσκώ|νω *v.t. & i.* swell, inflate, fill with air; pump up (*tyre*); (*fig.*) exaggerate; annoy. (*v.i.*) swell up, become inflated; rise (*of dough*); bulge; puff, pant; (*fig.*) puff oneself up; ~μένος swollen, bulging.

φουσκωτός *a.* curved; puffed, bouffant (*of dress, hair*).

φούστα *s.f.* skirt.

φουστανέλλα *s.f.* kilted skirt (*Gk. national costume*).

φουστάνι *s.n.* (*woman's*) dress.

φουφούλα *s.f.* (hanging portion of) breeches (*Gk. islanders' costume*).

φούχτα *s.f.* palm of hand; handful.

φραγγέλιον *s.n.* whip.

φραγκεύω *v.i.* become a Catholic.

Φραγκ|ιά *s.f.* Western Europe. ~ικος *a.* Frankish; Catholic; West European. ~ος *s.m.* Frank; Catholic.

φράγκο *s.n.* franc; (*fam.*) drachma.

φραγκοκρατία *s.f.* Frankish domination (*of Greece*).

φραγκολεβαντίνος *s.m.* Levantine.

φραγκοπαναγιά *s.f.* (*fam.*) person affecting prudishness *or* innocence.

φραγκόπαππας *s.m.* Catholic priest.

φραγκοστάφυλο *s.n.* redcurrant.

φραγκόσυκο *s.n.* prickly pear.

φραγκοχιώτικα *s.n.pl.* system of writing Gk. with Roman alphabet (*formerly used in Chios, etc.*).

φράγμα *s.n.* barrier; barrage, dam.

φραγμός *s.m.* barrier (*abstract*); (*mil.*) barrage.

φράζω *v.t. & i.* enclose, fence; obstruct, block; stop up; become stopped up.

φράκο *s.n.* evening-dress suit.
φραμπαλάς *s.m.* furbelow.
φράντζα *s.f.* fringe.
φραντζόλα *s.f.* long loaf.
φράξιμο *s.n.* enclosing; blockage.
φράουλα *s.f.* strawberry; sort of grape.
φράπα *s.f.* sort of (*large*) citrus fruit.
φράσ|ις *s.f.* phrase. ∼εολογία *s.f.* phraseology.
φράχτης *s.m.* fence, hedge.
φρέαρ *s.n.* well.
φρεγ|άς, ∼άδα *s.f.* frigate; (*fam.*) fine figure of a woman.
φρέν|α *s.n.pl.*, ∼ες *s.f.pl.* reason, wits; έξω ∼ῶν beside oneself (*with anger*); inconceivable.
φρενιάζω *v.t. & i.* make *or* become furious; (*fam.*) indulge wildly (*in*).
φρενῖτις *s.f.* delirium, frenzy; madness.
φρέν|ο *s.n.* brake (*of wheels*). ∼άρω *v.i.* brake.
φρενο|βλαβής, ∼παθής *a.* mentally deranged.
φρενοκομεῖον *s.n.* lunatic asylum.
φρενολογία *s.f.* alienism.
φρεσκάδα *s.f.* freshness; coolness.
φρεσκάρω *v.t. & i.* freshen; give a new look to.
φρέσκο *s.n.* 1. fresco. 2. coolness (*of temperature*). 3. (*fam.*) στό ∼ in quod.
φρέσκος *a.* fresh, new (*recent, not stale*); cool.
φρικαλέ|ος *a.* frightful. ∼ότης *s.f.* atrocity.
φρίκη *s.f.* horror; (*int.*) frightful!
φρικίασις *s.f.* shuddering.
φρικιῶ *v.i.* shudder.
φρικ|τός, ∼ώδης *a.* horrible, frightful.
φρίσσω *v.i.* ripple; shudder; be horrified.
φρόκαλ|ο *s.n.* rubbish; broom. ∼ῶ *v.t.* sweep (*with broom*).
φρόνημα *s.n.* morale; ∼τα (*pl.*) convictions (*esp. political*).
φρονηματίζω *v.t.* impart prudence *or* moderation to.
φρόνησις *s.f.* prudence, good sense.
φρονιμάδα *s.f.* good behaviour; prudence, good sense.
φρονιμεύω *v.i. & t.* settle *or* sober down.
φρονιμίτης *s.m.* wisdom-tooth.
φρόνιμ|ος *a.* sensible; well-behaved, good; virtuous. (*int.*) ∼α behave!
φροντ|ίζω *v.t. & i.* look after, take care of; (*with γιά*) see about; θὰ ∼ίσω I will see to it.

φροντ|ίς, ∼ίδα *s.f.* care, charge, concern; ∼ίδες (*pl.*) things to see to.
φροντιστήριον *s.n.* tutorial establishment, crammer's.
φρονῶ *v.i. & t.* think, believe.
φροῦδος *a.* vain, unavailing.
φρουρά *s.f.* guard; garrison.
φρούριον *s.n.* fort, fortress.
φρουρός *s.m.* guard, sentry; (*fig.*) guardian.
φρουρῶ *v.t.* guard, watch.
φροῦτο *s.n.* fruit.
φρυάττω *v.i.* be enraged.
φρύγανα *s.n.pl.* dry brushwood (*for fire*).
φρυγανιά *s.f.* piece of toast; fried bread with syrup or sugar.
φρύδι *s.n.* eyebrow.
φταίξιμο *s.n.* fault, blame.
φταίχτης *s.m.* person to blame, culprit.
φταίω *v.i.* be to blame.
φτάνω *v.i. & t.* see φθάνω.
φτειάνω *v.t. & i.* see φτιάνω.
φτελιά *s.f.* elm.
φτενός *a.* thin, slim.
φτέρη *s.f.* fern.
φτέρνα *s.f.* heel.
φτερν|ίζομαι *v.i.* sneeze. ∼ισμα *s.n.* sneeze, sneezing.
φτερό *s.n.* feather; wing; feather-duster; mudguard.
φτερούγ|α *s.f.* wing. ∼ίζω *v.i.* flutter.
φτην|ός *a.* cheap. ∼αίνω *v.t. & i.* make *or* become cheaper. ∼εια *s.f.* cheapness.
φτιά(χ)ν|ω *v.t. & i.* arrange, put right; make, have made; do; τί ∼εις; how are you? μοῦ τὴν ἔφτιαξε he played me a trick; τὰ ∼ω μέ start an affair with *or* make it up with. (*v.i.*) improve (in appearance). ∼ομαι *v.i.* make up (*one's face*); φτιαγμένος made (up); looking better.
φτιασίδ|ι *s.n.* cosmetic; make-up. ∼ώνομαι *v.i.* make up.
φτιαχτός *a.* artificial, affected.
φτού *int.* symbolic of spitting in disgust or to avert evil eye.
φτουρῶ *v.i.* last, be enough to go round (*of food*).
φτυάρι *s.n.* shovel, spade.
φτύνω *v.t. & i.* spit (on).
φτυσιά *s.f.* (clot of) spittle.
φτύσιμο *s.n.* spitting.
φτυστός *a.* (*fam.*) ∼ ὁ πατέρας του the very spit of his father.

φτωχαίνω *v.t. & i.* make *or* become poor.

φτώχεια *s.f.* poverty.

φτωχικ|ός *a.* poor (*in quality*). ~ό *s.n.* (*fam.*) one's humble home.

φτωχός *a.* poor.

φυγαδεύω *v.t.* help to escape.

φυγάς *s.m.f.* runaway, fugitive.

φυγή *s.f.* flight (*running away*).

φυγόδικος *s.m.f.* (*law*) defaulter.

φυγόκεντρος *a.* centrifugal.

φυγόμαχος *a.* unwilling to fight.

φυγόπονος *a.* unwilling to work; a shirker.

φυγόστρατος *a.* a shirker of military service.

φύκια *s.n.pl.* seaweed.

φυλάγ|ω *v.t.* guard, watch over; protect, look after; keep, set aside; lie in wait for. ~ομαι *v.i.* be careful, take precautions.

φύλακας *s.m.* keeper, guard, watchman.

φυλακείον *s.n.* guard-house; watchman's hut.

φυλακ|ή *s.f.* prison. ~ίζω *v.t.* imprison. ~ισμένος *s.m.* prisoner.

φύλαξ *s.m.* see φύλακας.

φυλά(σσ)ω *v.t.* see φυλάγω.

φυλαχτό *s.n.* talisman.

φυλ|ή *s.f.* race, tribe. ~αρχος *s.m.* headman of tribe. ~ετικός *a.* racial, tribal.

φυλλάδα *s.f.* booklet.

φυλλάδιον *s.n.* pamphlet; part, instalment (*of book*).

φυλλοκάρδια *s.n.pl.* depths of one's heart.

φυλλομετρῶ *v.t.* leaf through (*book*).

φύλλον *s.n.* leaf; petal; sheet (*paper, metal, pastry*); page; leaf (*of door, table, shutter, etc.*); ~ πορείας marching orders; (*fam.*) playing-card, newspaper.

φυλλοξήρα *s.f.* phylloxera.

φυλλορροῶ *v.i.* shed leaves; (*fig.*) fade (*of hopes*).

φύλλωμα *s.n.* foliage.

φῦλον *s.n.* 1. sex. 2. race.

φυματικός *a.* consumptive.

φυματίωσις *s.f.* tuberculosis.

φύομαι *v.i.* grow, be found (*of plants*).

φύρ|α *s.f.* shrinkage, loss of weight. ~αίνω *v.i.* shrink, lose weight.

φύραμα *s.n.* paste; (*pej.*) stuff, quality (*of character*).

φύρδην *adv.* ~ μίγδην higgledy-piggledy.

φυρός *a.* deficient in weight; shrunken.

φυσαλ(λ)ίς *s.f.* bubble; blister.

φυσαρμόνικα *s.f.* accordion; mouth-organ.

φυσέκι *s.n.* cartridge; cartridge-shaped packet of coins.

φυσερό *s.n.* bellows; (*fam.*) (*hand*) fan.

φύση *s.f. see* φύσις.

φύσημα *s.n.* blowing; puff; (*fig.*) παίρνω ~ depart hurriedly.

φυσίγγιον *s.n.* cartridge.

φῦσιγξ *s.f.* ampoule (*for serum*).

φυσικ|ά *s.n.pl.*, ~ή *s.f.* physics.

φυσικό *s.n.* habit.

φυσικ|ός *a.* natural; physical; a physicist. ~ά *adv.* naturally. ~ότης *s.f.* naturalness.

φυσιογνωμία *s.f.* cast of features, face; appearance; personality (*well-known person*).

φυσιοδίφης *s.m.* naturalist.

φυσιολάτρης *s.m.* lover of nature.

φυσιολογ|ία *s.f.* physiology. ~ικός *a.* physiological; (*fig.*) normal, healthy.

φύσ|ις *s.f.* nature; ~ει by nature.

φυσομανῶ *v.i.* rage.

φυσ|ῶ *v.t. & i.* blow (out). (*v.i.*) puff, blow; ~άει it is windy; (*fam.*) τὸ ~άει he has money; τὸ ~άει καὶ δὲν κρυώνει he cannot get over his chagrin.

φυτεία *s.f.* plantation; vegetation.

φυτ|εύω *v.t.* plant, implant. ~ε(υ)μα *s.n.* planting. ~ευτός *a.* cultivated (*of plants*).

φυτικός *a.* vegetable.

φυτοζωῶ *v.i.* live penuriously, barely exist; languish (*of trade, etc.*).

φυτοκομία *s.f.* horticulture.

φυτολογία *s.f.* botany.

φυτόν *s.n.* plant.

φύτρα *s.f.* plumule; (*fig.*) lineage.

φυτρώνω *v.i.* grow, come up (*of plants*).

φυτώριον *s.n.* nursery, seed-bed.

φώκια *s.f.* seal (*animal*).

φωλ|εά, ~ιά *s.f.* nest, lair, burrow. ~ιάζω *v.i.* nestle.

φωνάζω *v.i. & t.* shout, call (out), summon.

φωνακλᾶς *s.m.* one who talks loudly.

φωνασκῶ *v.i.* bawl.

φωνή *s.f.* voice; cry, shout.

φωνῆεν *s.n.* vowel.

φωνητικ|ός *a.* vocal; phonetic. ~ή *s.f.* phonetics.

φωνοληψία *s.f.* recording (*mechanical*).

φωρῶμαι *v.i.* be caught in the act; be shown up.

φῶς *s.n.* light; (*fig.*) (*faculty of*) sight; money; ~ φανάρι clear as daylight. φῶτα (*pl.*) lights; (*fig.*) knowledge, wisdom; Epiphany.

φωστήρ(ας) *s.m.* (*fig.*) luminary.

φωσφόρος *s.m.* phosphorus.

φωταγωγ|ῶ *v.t.* illuminate. ~ός *s.m.* light-well.

φωταέριον *s.n.* gas.

φωταψία *s.f.* illumination.

φωτεινός *a.* light, bright; lucid.

φωτιά *s.f.* fire; (*smoker's*) light; (*fig.*) great heat; anger; quickness; expensiveness.

φωτίζ|ω *v.i. & t.* shine (on), give light (to), light; enlighten; ~ει dawn breaks.

φώτιση *s.f.* enlightenment.

φωτισμός *s.m.* lighting.

φωτοβολία *s.f.* radiation, shining.

φωτοβολίς *s.f.* (*mil.*) flare.

φωτογενής *a.* photogenic.

φωτογραφία *s.f.* photograph; photography.

φωτογραφικ|ός *a.* photographic; ~ή μηχανή camera. ~ή *s.f.* photography.

φωτογράφος *s.m.* photographer.

φωτόμετρον *s.n.* light-meter.

φωτοσκίασις *s.f.* shading.

φωτοστέφανος *s.m.* halo.

φωτοχυσία *s.f.* flood of light.

Χ

χαβάγια *s.f.* Hawaiian-style song (*to guitar*).

χαβάνι *s.n.* brass mortar.

χαβᾶς *s.m.* tune.

χαβιάρι *s.n.* caviar.

χαβούζα *s.f.* cistern.

χάβρα *s.f.* synagogue; (*fig.*) uproar.

χαγιάτι *s.n.* upper gallery round courtyard.

χαδ- *see* χαϊδ-.

χαζεύω *v.i.* gape; idle away one's time.

χάζι *s.n.* pleasure, amusement; τό κάνω ~ it amuses me.

χαζός *a.* stupid.

χαϊβάνι *s.n.* beast; (*fig.*) ass.

χάϊδεμα *s.n.* caressing.

χαϊδευτικός *a.* caressing; affectionate.

χαϊδ|εύω *v.t.* caress, stroke, pat; pet, spoil; cajole. ~εύομαι *v.i.* desire caresses *or* attention; nuzzle, rub (*against*). ~εμένος spoilt.

χάϊδι *s.n.* caress; ~α (*pl.*) petting, cajolery.

χαϊδιάρης *a.* fond of being petted.

χαϊδιάρικος *a.* caressing; fond of being petted.

χαϊδολογ|ῶ *v.t.* caress repeatedly. ~ιέμαι *v.i. see* χαϊδεύομαι.

χαίνω *v.i.* gape (*of wound, abyss, etc.*).

χαιρέκακος *a.* malevolent.

χαιρετ|ίζω, ~ῶ *v.t.* greet; salute.

χαιρέτισ|μα, *s.n.*, ~μός *s.m.* greeting, salutation. ~μός (*ceremonial*) salute.

χαίρ|ω *v.i.* be glad; ~ετε *greeting on arrival or departure*; ~ω ἄκρας ὑγείας enjoy the best of health. ~ομαι *v.i. & t.* be glad; enjoy; ἔλα νά χαρῆς do please come! νά τό ~εσαι I wish you joy of it.

χαίτη *s.f.* mane.

χακί *s.n.* khaki.

χαλάζι *s.n.* hail.

χαλαζίας *s.m.* quartz.

χαλάλι *adv.* (*fam.*) ~ τά λεφτά I do not grudge the money; ~ σου you are welcome to it, you deserve it.

χαλαρ|ός *a.* loose, slack. ~ώνω *v.t.* loosen, relax.

χάλασμα *s.n.* destruction, demolition; a ruin.

χαλασμένος *a.* rotten, gone bad, decayed; broken, out of order; damaged, spoilt; seduced.

χαλασμός *s.m.* destruction; (*fig.*) ~(κόσμου) disaster; great upheaval, storm, crowd *or* excitement.

χαλάστρα *s.f.* μοῦ ἔκαναν ~ they spoilt my plans *or* cramped my style.

χαλβ|ᾶς *s.m.* halva (*sweetmeat*); (*fam.*) weak-willed person. ~αδόπιττα *s.f.* sort of nougat.

χαλεπός *a.* difficult.

χαλές *s.m.* privy; (*fam.*) ragamuffin.

χάλ|ι *s.n.*, ~ια (*pl.*) wretched *or* disreputable state.

χαλί *s.n.* carpet, rug.

χαλίκι *s.n.* gravel.

χαλιμ|ά *s.f.* παραμύθια τῆς ~ᾶς Arabian Nights.

χαλιν|άρι *s.n.*, ~ός *s.m.* bridle, bit. ~αγωγῶ *v.t.* lead by bridle; (*fig.*) curb.

χαλκᾶς *s.m.* ring, link.

χαλκεῖον *s.n.* coppersmith's forge; (*fig.*) place where lies are concocted.

χαλκεύω *v.t.* make out of copper; (*fig.*) concoct (*lies, etc.*).

χαλκιᾶς *s.m.* coppersmith.

χάλκ|ινος, ~οῦς a. copper.

χαλκογραφία s.f. copperplate engraving.

χαλκομανία s.f. transfer (design).

χαλκός s.m. copper.

χάλκωμα s.n. copper utensil. ~τᾶς s.m. coppersmith.

χαλνῶ v.t. & i. see χαλῶ.

χαλύβδινος a. steel.

χάλυψ s.m. steel.

χαλ|ῶ v.t. & i. spoil; break (put out of order); break off (agreement); spend (money); wear out; reduce quality of; pull down (building); undo (coiffure, knitting, etc.); change (banknote); seduce; ~ῶ τὸν κόσμο kick up a row, move heaven and earth. (v.i.) deteriorate, spoil; go bad; get out of order; lose one's looks; ~άει ὁ κόσμος there is a great to-do; δὲν ~ασε ὁ κόσμος things are not so serious.

χαμάδα s.f. ripe olive fallen from tree.

χαμαί adv. to or on the ground.

χαμαιλέων s.m. chameleon.

χαμαιτυπεῖον s.n. brothel.

χαμάλ|ης s.m. porter; (fam.) lout. ~ίκι s.n. toilsome labour.

χαμάμ s.n. Turkish bath.

χαμέν|ος a. lost; the loser (at cards); scatterbrained, good-for-nothing; ~ο κορμί wastrel; τὰ ἔχω ~α be confused or at a loss or weak in the head; πῆγε ~ο or στὰ ~α it was a wasted effort.

χαμερπής a. servile, crawling.

χαμηλός a. low.

χαμηλοφώνως adv. in a low voice.

χαμηλώνω v.t. & i. lower, bring down; become lower.

χαμίνι s.n. street urchin.

χαμόγελ|ο s.n. smile. ~ῶ v.i. smile.

χαμό|δεντρο, ~κλαδο s.n. shrub.

χαμο|μήλι, ~μηλο s.n. camomile (tea).

χαμός s.m. loss.

χάμου adv. see χάμω.

χάμουρα s.n.pl. harness.

χαμπάρ|ι s.n. (piece of) news; παίρνω ~ι get wind of, notice. ~ίζω v.t. & i. take notice of; (with ἀπό) know or understand about.

χάμω adv. to or on the ground.

χάνδαξ s.m. ditch, trench.

χάνι s.n. country inn; caravanserai.

χανούμ(ισσα) s.f. Turkish lady.

χανσενικός s.m. leper.

χαντάκ|ι s.n. ditch, trench. ~ώνω v.t. (fig.) ruin (effect of).

χαντζάρι s.n. short sword.

χάντρα s.f. bead.

χάν|ω v.t. & i. lose; miss (opportunity); τὰ ~ω get confused or embarrassed, lose one's head or wits; ~ω τὰ νερά μου feel a fish out of water. ~ομαι v.i. get lost, lose one's way, disappear; bother, waste one's time; (fam.) νὰ χαθῆς to hell with you! (also jocular); χάσου out of my sight! (see χαμένος).

χάος s.n. chaos.

χάπι s.n. pill.

χαρ|ά s.f. joy, pleasure;~ὰ θεοῦ a delight; (fam.) wedding; μιὰ ~ά very well, splendidly; γειὰ ~ά greeting; ~ὰ στὸ πρᾶμα (ironic) wonderful! στὶς ~ές σας to your marriage!

χάραγμα s.n. engraving, incision; ruling (of lines).

χαράδρα s.f. ravine.

χαράζ|ω I. v.t. see χαράσσω. 2. v.i. ~ει dawn breaks.

χάρακας s.m. ruler (implement).

χαράκι s.n. ruled line (in copy-book, etc.).

χαρακιά s.f. scratch, mark (on surface); groove, rifling; (ruled) line.

χαρακτήρ s.m. character. ~ίζω v.t. characterize, qualify.

χαρακτηριστικ|ός a. characteristic. ~ά s.n.pl. (person's) features.

χαράκτ|ης s.m. engraver. ~ική s.f. (art of) engraving.

χαράκωμα s.n. ruling (of lines); trench.

χαρακών|ω v.t. rule (lines). ~ομαι v.i. take shelter.

χάρ|αμα s.n. ~άματα (pl.) dawn.

χαραμάδα s.f. chink, crack.

χαραματιά s.f. chink, crack; scratch, mark (on surface).

χαράμ|ι adv. (fam.) to no purpose. ~ίζω v.t. waste, spend in vain.

χάραξις s.f. engraving, incision; marking out (of road, etc.).

χαράσσω v.t. engrave; rule (lines); write, trace; mark out (road, etc.).

χαράτσ|ι s.n. poll-tax (under Turks); (fig.) burdensome levy. ~ώνω v.t. (fam.) extract contribution from.

χαραυγή s.f. daybreak.

χάρβαλο s.n. a ruin.

χαρέμι s.n. harem.

χάρη s.f. charm, attractiveness; good point, advantage; favour, service; gratitude; ~ σὲ σένα thanks to you; λόγου ~ for example; ἀφίνω (μιὰ) ~ allow for a bit extra.

χαρίεις *a.* charming.

χαριεντίζομαι *v.i.* be in flirtatious *or* bantering mood; turn on the charm.

χαρίζ|ω *v.t.* give, make a present of; remit (*penalty, debt*); (*fam.*) δέν ~ω κάστανα stand no nonsense; (*v.i.*) σοῦ ~ει it flatters you (*of dress*). ~ομαι *v.i.* (*with σέ*) treat with favour *or* indulgence.

χάρ|ις *s.f.* grace, charm; pardon; ~ις εἰς thanks to; ~ιν (*with gen.*) for (the sake of); παραδείγματος ~ιν for example; πρὸς ~ιν σου for your sake.

χάρισμα *s.n.* gift; accomplishment; (*adv.*) for nothing, free.

χαριστικ|ός *a.* partial (*biased*); ~ὴ βολή coup de grâce.

χαριτόβρυτος *a.* full of charm.

χαριτολογῶ *v.i.* say witty things.

χαριτωμένος *a.* charming.

χάρμα *s.n.* (*source of*) delight, joy; ~ ἰδέσθαι a joy to behold.

χαρμάνι *s.n.* blend.

χαρμόσυνος *a.* glad, joyful (*news, bells, etc.*).

χαροκόπος *a.* pleasure-loving.

χάρος *s.m.* Death.

χαρούμενος *a.* merry, happy.

χαρούπι *s.n.* carob.

χαρταετός *s.m.* kite.

χαρτένιος *a.* paper.

χαρτζιλίκι *s.n.* pocket-money.

χάρτης *s.m.* paper; map; ~ ὑγείας toilet-paper.

χαρτί *s.n.* paper; (*playing*) card; (*fam.*) card-playing; ~ καὶ καλαμάρι word for word, in detail.

χάρτινος *a.* paper.

χαρτόδετος *a.* paper-bound.

χαρτοκλέφτης *s.m.* card-sharper.

χαρτοκοπτήρ(ας) *s.m.* paper-knife.

χαρτόνι *s.n.* cardboard.

χαρτονόμισμα *s.n.* paper currency; banknote.

χαρτο|παίκτης *s.m.* gambler. ~παιξία *s.f.* gambling.

χαρτοπόλεμος *s.m.* (battle of) confetti.

χαρτοπώλης *s.m.* stationer.

χαρτ|ορρίχτρα, ~οῦ *s.f.* fortune-teller (*with cards*).

χαρτόσημον *s.n.* stamp (*on document*); stamped paper.

χαρτοφυλάκιον *s.n.* brief-case; (*fig.*) portfolio (*ministry*).

χαρτοφύλαξ *s.m.* brief-case.

χαρτωσιά *s.f.* hand, trick (*at cards*);

(*fam.*) δέν πιάνει ~ μπροστά σου he cannot be compared with you.

χαρωπός *a.* cheerful, gay.

χασάπ|ης *s.m.* butcher. ~ικο *s.n.* butcher's shop. ~ικος *s.m.* sort of cyclic dance.

χασές *s.m.* cotton fabric.

χάση *s.f.* waning (*of moon*); στὴ ~ κα στὴ φέξη every now and then.

χάσιμο *s.n.* loss.

χασίσι *s.n.* hashish.

χάσκω *v.i.* gape (open).

χάσμα *s.n.* chasm; gap, void.

χασμούρημα *s.n.* yawn, yawning.

χασμ|ουριέμαι, ~ῶμαι *v.i.* yawn.

χασμωδία *s.f.* hiatus.

χασομερ|ῶ *v.i. & t.* waste time, loiter; cause to waste time.

χασούρα *s.f.* loss.

χαστούκι *s.n.* slap (*on face*).

χατζῆς *s.m.* hadji, pilgrim.

χατίρι *s.n.* favour, service; γιὰ τὸ ~ του for his sake.

χαυλιόδους *s.m.* tusk.

χαῦνος *a.* languid.

χαφιές *s.m.* (*fam.*) nark.

χάφτω *v.t.* gulp down; (*fig.*) swallow, believe.

χάχαν|ο *s.n.* noisy laugh. ~ίζω *v.i.* cackle with laughter.

χάχας *s.m.* simpleton.

χά χά χά *int. representing laughter.*

χαχόλικος *a.* (*fam.*) sloppy, ill-fitting (*of clothes*).

χαψιά *s.f.* gulp, mouthful.

χαώδης *a.* chaotic.

χέζ|ω *v.i. & t.* (*fam.*) defecate (on); (*fig.*) consign to the devil. ~ομαι *v.i.* (*fig.*) be in a funk; χέστηκα I could not care less.

χείλι *s.n.* lip.

χειλικός *a.* labial.

χείλος *s.n.* lip; rim (*of vessel*); (*fig.*) brink.

χειμαδιό *s.n.* winter quarters (*for sheep*).

χειμάζομαι *v.i.* suffer hardships (of winter).

χείμαρρος *s.m.* torrent (-bed).

χειμερινός *a.* winter.

χειμών|(ας) *s.m.* winter. ~ιάζει *v.i.* winter comes on. ~ιάτικος *a.* winter; wintry.

χείρ *s.f.* hand.

χειραγωγῶ *v.t.* lead by the hand.

χειράμαξα *s.f.* hand-barrow.

χειραφετῶ *v.t.* manumit; emancipate.

χειραψία *s.f.* handshake.

χειρίζομαι v.t. handle, manage, operate.

χειρισμός s.m. handling, management; (act of) manœuvring.

χειριστήρια s.n.pl. controls (of machine).

χειριστής s.m. operator.

χείριστος a. worst.

χειροβομβίς s.f. hand-grenade.

χειρόγραφον s.n. manuscript.

χειροδικία s.f. taking law into one's own hands.

χειροκίνητος a. worked by hand.

χειροκροτ|ῶ v.t. & i. applaud, clap. ~ημα s.n. applause.

χειρόκτιον s.n. glove, gauntlet.

χειρόμακτρον s.n. towel, napkin.

χειρομαντεία s.f. palmistry.

χειρονομ|ία s.f. gesture; gesticulation; νὰ λείπουν οἱ ~ίες paws off!

χειροπέδη s.f. handcuff.

χειροπιαστός a. palpable.

χειροπόδαρα adv. hand and foot.

χειροποίητος a. hand-made.

χειρότερ|ος a. worse; ὁ ~ος worst. ~α adv. worse. ~εύω v.t. & i. make or become worse.

χειροτεχνία s.f. handicraft.

χειροτονία s.f. ordination.

χειρουργικ|ός a. surgical. ~ή s.f. surgery.

χειρουργός s.m. surgeon.

χειροφίλημα s.n. hand-kissing.

χειρωνακτικός a. manual.

χέλι s.n. eel.

χελιδ|ών s.f., ~όνι s.n. swallow.

χελών|α, ~η s.f. tortoise, turtle.

χέρι s.n. hand; arm; handle; coat (of paint, etc.), going-over, treatment (washing, wiping, etc.); ~ ~ hand-in-hand; ~ (μὲ) ~ quickly, direct; βάζω ἕνα ~ lend a hand; βάζω ~ lay hands (on), fondle (amorously); βάζω στὸ ~ trick into giving; ἀπὸ πρῶτο ~ at first hand; ἔρχομαι στὰ ~α come to blows. χερικό s.n. κάνω ~ make a start; βάζω ~ lay hands on, start abusing; καλὸ ~ good luck.

χερόβολο s.n. sheaf, armful.

χερούλι s.n. handle.

χερσαῖος a. living on land; continental (climate).

χερσόνησος s.f. peninsula.

χέρσος a. uncultivated, fallow.

χέσιμο s.n. (fam.) defecation; (fig.) funk.

χηλή s.f. cloven hoof.

χημ|εία s.f. chemistry. ~ικός a. chemical; a chemist (scientist).

χήνα s.f. goose.

χήρ|α s.f. widow. ~εύω v.i. be widowed; (fig.) be vacant (of post).

χῆρος s.m. widower.

χθές adv. yesterday.

χθεσινός a. yesterday's; recent.

χθόνιος a. infernal (gods).

χῖ s.n. the letter Χ.

χιαστί adv. crosswise.

χίλια num. a thousand.

χιλιάρ|α, ~ικη s.f. bottle of 2½ okas capacity.

χιλιάρικο s.n. thousand-drachma, etc., note.

χιλι|άς, ~άδα s.f. thousand.

χιλιετία s.f. millennium.

χιλιόγραμμον s.n. kilogram.

χίλι|οι a. a thousand; (fig.) ~α δύο a hundred and one.

χιλιόμετρον s.n. kilometre.

χιλιοστημόριον s.n. thousandth part; insignificant amount.

χιλιοστ|όν, ~όμετρον s.n. millimetre.

χιλιοστός a. thousandth.

χίμαιρα s.f. chimera.

χιμπαντζῆς s.m. chimpanzee.

χιονᾶτος a. snow-white.

χιόν|ι s.n. snow. ~ιά s.f. snowy weather; snowball. ~ίζει v.i. it snows.

χιονίστρα s.f. chilblain.

χιονοδρομία s.f. ski-ing.

χιονόνερο s.n. sleet.

χιονοστιβάς s.f. avalanche.

χιούμορ s.n. humour. [E.]. ~ιστικός a. humorous.

χιτών s.n. robe, tunic; (anat.) cornea.

χιτώνιον s.n. (mil.) tunic.

χιών s.f. snow.

χλαίν|α, ~η s.f. (mil.) greatcoat.

χλαμύς s.f. mantle.

χλευ|άζω v.t. mock, deride. ~αστικός a. mocking, derisive.

χλιαίνω v.t. & i. make or become slightly warm.

χλιαρ|ός a. tepid.

χλιδή s.f. luxury.

χλιμιντρ|ίζω, ~ῶ v.i. neigh, whinny.

χλό|η s.f. grass, lawn; verdure. ~ερός a. verdant.

χλωμ|ός a. pale, pallid, wan. ~άδα s.f. pallor. ~ιάζω v.i. grow pale.

χλώριον s.n. chlorine.

χλωρίς s.f. flora.

χλωρός a. green, freshly cut; freshly made (cheese).

χλωροφόρμιον s.n. chloroform.

χλωροφύλλη *s.f.* chlorophyll.

χνότα *s.n.pl.* breath.

χνούδ|ι *s.n.* down, fluff, pile. ~ωτός *a.* downy, plushy.

χοάνη *s.f.* crucible; funnel, hŏrn.

χόβολη *s.f.* embers.

χοιρίδιον *s.m.* young pig.

χοιρινό *s.n.* pork.

χοιρομέρι *s.n.* ham.

χοῖρος *s.m.* pig.

χολέρα *s.f.* cholera.

χολ|ή *s.f.* bile. ~ιάζω *v.t.* & *i.* annoy; get annoyed.

χολόλιθος *s.m.* gall-stone.

χολοσκάνω *v.t.* & *i.* upset, exasperate; get upset *or* exasperated.

χολῶ *v.t.* anger.

χονδρικός *a.* wholesale.

χονδροειδής *a.* coarse, clumsy, boorish.

χόνδρος *s.m.* gristle, cartilage.

χονδρός *a.* thick, coarse, fat; unrefined, vulgar, rude.

χοντραίνω *v.t.* & *i.* make *or* become thicker *or* fatter; τὰ ~ use offensive language.

χοντροκέφαλος *a.* pig-headed; thick-headed.

χοντροκοπιά *s.f.* clumsy piece of work.

χοντρομπαλᾶς *s.m.* (*fam.*) very fat man.

χοντρόπετσος *a.* thick-skinned.

χόντρος *s.n.* thickness, fatness.

χοντρός *a.* 1. *see* χονδρός. 2. exaggerated.

χορδ|ή *s.f.* (*mus.*) string; (*anat.*) cord. ~ίζω *v.t.* tune, wind up.

χορεία *s.f.* group, body.

χορευτ|ής *s.m.* dancer. ~ικός *a.* with *or* for dancing.

χορεύω *v.i.* & *t.* dance; dance with; τὸν ~ στὸ ταψί I lead him a dance; (*fig.*) (*v.i.*) shake, toss, tremble.

χορηγ|ῶ *v.t.* provide, grant. ~ησις *s.f.* provision, granting. ~ός *s.m.* giver, provider.

χορογραφία *s.f.* choreography.

χοροδιδάσκαλος *s.m.* dancing-master.

χοροεσπερίς *s.f.* ball, dance.

χοροπηδῶ *v.i.* gambol, jump about.

χορός *s.m.* dance; chorus, choir.

χορταίνω *v.i.* & *t.* have one's fill (of); get tired of; satisfy, provide abundantly *or* excessively with.

χορτάρι *s.n.* grass. ~άζω *v.i.* get covered with grass.

χορταρικό *s.n.* vegetable.

χορτασμός *s.m.* satiety.

χορταστικός *a.* filling, substantial.

χορτᾶτος *a.* satisfied (*having had enough*).

χόρτ|ον *s.n.* grass; ~α (*pl.*) green vegetables.

χορτοφάγος *a.* vegetarian.

χορωδία *s.f.* chorus, choir.

χότζας *s.m.* Turkish priest, muezzin.

χουβαρντᾶς *s.m.* (*fam.*) liberal *or* generous person.

χουγιάζω *v.t.* shoo away.

χουζούρι *s.n.* ease, idleness.

χούϊ *s.n.* (bad) habit; knack.

χουλιάρι *s.n.* spoon; (*fam.*) a gossip.

χουνί *s.n. see* χωνί.

χουρμᾶς *s.m.* date (*fruit*).

χοῦς *s.m.* dust, earth.

χούφτ|α *s.f.* palm of hand; handful. ~ιά *s.f.* handful. ~ιάζω, ~ώνω *v.t.* grab.

χούφταλο *s.n.* (*fam.*) very old person.

χουχουλίζω *v.t.* blow on (*for warmth*).

χοχλακίζω *v.i.* boil, bubble.

χράμι *s.n.* hand-woven rug *or* blanket.

χρεία *s.f.* necessity, need; (*fam.*) privy.

χρειάζομαι *v.t.* & *i.* need, require; be necessary; (*fam.*) τά ~ become scared.

χρειώδης *a.* necessary.

χρεμετίζω *v.i.* neigh, whinny.

χρεόγραφον *s.n.* (*fin.*) bond, security.

χρεοκοπ|ία *s.f.* bankruptcy. ~ῶ *v.i.* go bankrupt, fail.

χρεολυσία *s.f.* amortization.

χρέος *s.n.* debt; obligation.

χρεοστάσιον *s.n.* moratorium.

χρεών|ω *v.t.* debit. ~ομαι *v.i.* incur debts.

χρεώστης *s.m.* debtor.

χρεωστῶ *v.i.* & *t. see* χρωστῶ.

χρῆμα *s.n.*, ~τα (*pl.*) money.

χρηματ|ίζω *v.i.* ἐ~ισε δήμαρχος he served as mayor. ~ίζομαι *v.i.* take bribes.

χρηματικός *a.* of money, pecuniary.

χρηματιστήριον *s.n.* stock exchange.

χρηματιστής *s.m.* (*fin.*) broker.

χρηματοδοτῶ *v.t.* finance.

χρηματοκιβώτιον *s.n.* safe.

χρησιμεύω *v.i.* be of use, serve.

χρησιμοποι|ῶ *v.t.* use. ~ησις *s.f.* use, utilization.

χρήσιμ|ος *a.* useful. ~ότης *s.f.* use, usefulness.

χρῆσ|ις *s.f.* use, enjoyment; ἐν ~ει in use; πρὸς ~ιν for the use (*of*); (*fin.*) financial year.

χρησμός *s.m.* oracle.

χρηστοήθης *a.* moral, upright.

χρηστομάθεια *s.f.* anthology of edifying passages.

χρηστός *a.* good (*virtuous*).

χρῖσμα *s.n.* chrism; anointing; (*fig.*) adoption as party candidate.

χριστιανικός *a.* Christian.

χριστιανισμός *s.m.* Christianity.

χριστιανός *s.m.* Christian; (*fam.*) chap (*esp. in expostulation*).

χριστιανοσύνη *s.f.* Christendom.

Χριστός *s.m.* Christ.

Χριστούγεννα *s.n.pl.* Christmas.

χρίω *v.t.* anoint; plaster.

χροιά *s.f.* complexion, colour, shade.

χρονιά *s.f.* year.

χρονιάτικο *s.n.* a year's payment.

χρονίζω *v.i.* take a long time, drag on; become chronic; become one year old; be one year dead.

χρονικογράφος *s.m.* chronicler.

χρονικ|όν *s.n.* chronicle; ~ά (*pl.*) annals.

χρονικός *a.* of time, temporal.

χρόνιος *a.* of ancient origin; chronic.

χρονογράφημα *s.n.* topical comment (*in newspaper*).

χρονογράφος *s.m.* writer of χρονογράφημα.

χρονολογ|ία *s.f.* date; chronology; era. ~οῦμαι *v.i.* date (*from*).

χρονόμετρον *s.n.* chronometer; metronome.

χρόν|ος *s.m.* 1. (*pl.* οἱ ~οι) time (*duration*); (*gram.*) tense, quanitity. 2. (*pl.* οἱ ~οι, τὰ ~ια) year; πρὸ ~ων years ago; τοῦ ~ου next year; ~ια πολλά many happy returns! κακό ~ο νἄχει bad luck to him! πόσω(ν) ~ῶν εἶναι how old is he?

χρονοτριβῶ *v.i.* waste time, dawdle.

χρυσαλλίς *s.f.* chrysalis.

χρυσάνθεμον *s.n.* chrysanthemum.

χρυσάφ|ι *s.n.* gold. ~ής *a.* the colour of gold. ~ικά *s.n.pl.* jewellery.

χρυσή *s.f.* (*med.*) jaundice.

χρυσίζω *v.i.* shine like gold.

χρυσικός *s.m.* goldsmith.

χρυσίον *s.n.* money.

χρυσοθήρας *s.m.* gold-digger.

χρυσόμαλλ|ος *a.* golden-haired; ~ον δέρας golden fleece.

χρυσός 1. *s.m.* gold. 2. *a.* gold, golden; (*fig.*) good-hearted, lovable.

χρυσοῦς *a.* gold, golden.

χρυσοχό|ος *s.m.* goldsmith; jeweller. ~εῖον *s.n.* jeweller's.

χρυσόψαρο *s.n.* goldfish.

χρυσώνω *v.t.* gild.

χρυσωρυχεῖον *s.n.* gold-mine.

χρῶμα *s.n.* colour; paint; suit (*in cards*).

χρωματίζω *v.t.* colour, paint; (*fig.*) give colour *or* expression to; attach (*political*) label to.

χρωματικός *a.* (*mus.*) chromatic.

χρωματισμός *s.m.* colouring, colour.

χρωματιστός *a.* coloured.

χρώμιον *s.n.* chromium.

χρωστήρ *s.m.* paint-brush.

χρωστικός *a.* colouring.

χρωστῶ *v.i. & t.* be in debt, owe; be obliged, must; (*fam.*) ~ τῆς Μιχαλοῦς be dotty.

χταπόδι *s.n.* octopus.

χτένι *s.n.* comb; rake.

χτενίζω *v.t.* comb; dress (*person's*) hair; (*fig.*) polish up (*speech, etc.*).

χτένισμα *s.n.* combing; hairstyle; (*fig.*) polishing up.

χτές *adv.* yesterday.

χτεσινός *a.* yesterday's; recent.

χτῆμα *s.n.* (*landed*) property.

χτίζω *v.t.* build; found (*city*); wall in.

χτικιό *s.n.* (*fam.*) tuberculosis; (*fig.*) torment, trial.

χτίριο *s.n.* building.

χτίσιμο *s.n.* (*act of*) building.

χτίστης *s.m.* bricklayer.

χτύπημα *s.n.* blow, stroke, knock; bruise; shock; (*act of*) beating *or* knocking.

χτυπητό *s.n.* roughcast.

χτυπητός *a.* beaten (*egg, etc.*); gaudy, loud; pointed (*hint, etc.*).

χτυποκάρδι *s.n.* throbbing of the heart.

χτύπος *s.m.* knock, beat, tick.

χτυπ|ῶ *v.t. & i.* knock (at), beat, strike, ring; clap (*hands*), stamp (*feet*); beat (*time*); beat up (*eggs*); attack; hit, wound; kill (*game*); bid for (*at auction*). (*v.i.*) strike, ring, sound (*of clock, bell, etc.*); beat, throb; knock against something, hurt oneself; ~άει ἄσχημα it looks *or* sounds bad; ~άει ἡ πόρτα there is a knock at the door; μοῦ ~άει στὰ νεῦρα it gets on my nerves. ~ιέμαι *v.i.* beat one's breast; come to blows.

χυδαΐζω *v.i.* use extreme form of demotic Gk.

χυδαιολογῶ *v.i.* speak vulgarly.

χυδαῖ|ος *a.* vulgar, crude. ~ότης *s.f.* vulgarity.

χυλόπιττα *s.f.* sort of macaroni; (*fam.*) τρώω τή ~ be rejected (*of suitor*).

χυλ|ός *s.m.* pap, chyle. ~ώνω *v.i.* form creamy consistency.

χύμα *s.n.* (*used as a. & adv.*) in confusion; loose (*not in package*); on draught; (*fam.*) τοῦ τά εἶπα ~ I told him straight out.

χυμ|ός *s.m.* sap, juice. ~ώδης *a.* juicy.

χυμ|ίζω, ~ῶ *v.i.* rush, swoop.

χύν|ω *v.t.* pour (out), shed, spill; cast (*metal*); ~ω ἐξάνθημα come out in rash; ~ ω λάδι στή φωτιά add fuel to the flames. ~ομαι *v.i.* pour (out), spill over; flow out; (*fig.*) rush, swoop.

χύσιμο *s.n.* pouring, shedding, spilling; casting.

χυτήριον *s.n.* foundry.

χυτός *a.* cast (*of metal*); scattered; loose (*of hair*); (*fig.*) well-proportioned (*of limbs*); fitting like a glove (*of clothes*).

χυτοσίδηρος *s.m.* cast iron.

χύτρα *s.f.* earthen *or* metal cooking-pot.

χώλ *s.n.* hall. [E. *hall*]

χωλ|ός *a.* lame. ~αίνω *v.i.* be lame, limp; (*fig.*) make slow progress.

χῶμα *s.n.* soil, earth; dust; ground. ~τινος, ~τένιος *a.* earthen, clay.

χώνευσις *s.f.* digestion; smelting.

χωνευτήριον *s.n.* crucible, melting-pot.

χωνευτικός *a.* digestible.

χωνευτός *a.* concealed (*of wiring, plumbing*).

χωνεύω *v.t. & i.* digest; smelt; (*fam.*) δὲν τὸν ~ I cannot stand him. (*v.i.*) be half spent *or* decomposed (*of fire, food being cooked, etc.*).

χωνί *s.n.* funnel, horn; cornet (*paper-bag, ice-cream*).

χών|ω *v.t.* thrust, stuff, stick (*into*); bury; hide. ~ομαι *v.i.* squeeze in; hide; (*fam.*) stick one's nose in.

χώρα *s.f.* country, land; chief town *or* village of locality; (*anat.*) region; λαμβάνω ~ν take place.

χωρατ|ό *s.n.* joke, pleasantry. ~ατζῆς *s.m.* joker. ~εύω *v.i.* joke.

χωράφι *s.n.* field.

χωρητικότης *s.f.* capacity; tonnage.

χώρια *adv.* separately, apart; (*prep.*) apart from, not counting.

χωριανός *a.* (fellow) villager.

χωριάτης *s.m.* peasant, countryman; (*fig.*) boor.

χωριάτικος *a.* peasant, country; boorish.

χωρίζ|ω *v.t. & i.* separate, part, divide;

divorce. (*v.i.*) get divorced; ~ω μέ part from. ~ομαι (*v.t.*) part from. (*v.i.*) part.

χωρικ|ός I. *a.* village, country. 2. *s.m.* peasant, villager. 3. *a.* ~ὰ ὕδατα territorial waters.

χωρι|ό *s.n.* village; (*fam.*) home-town; κάνομε ~ό we get on well together; γίναμε ἀπὸ δυὸ ~ά we quarrelled.

χωρίον *s.n.* I. village. 2. passage (*in book*).

χωρίς *adv. & prep.* (*with acc.*) without; not counting; ~ ἄλλο without fail; (*fam.*) μὲ ~ without.

χώρισμα *s.n.* sorting, division (*act*); partition (*structure*), compartment, pigeon-hole.

χωρισμένος *a.* divided; divorced.

χωρισμός *s.m.* separation, parting; division; sorting; divorce.

χωριστά *adv.* separately, apart; (*prep.*) not counting.

χωριστικός *a.* separatist.

χωριστός *a.* separate, apart.

χωρίστρα *s.f.* parting (*of hair*).

χῶρος *s.m.* space, room.

χωροφύλ|αξ *s.m.* gendarme. ~ακή *s.f.* gendarmerie.

χωρῶ *v.i.* advance.

χωρ|ῶ, ~άω *v.i. & t.* fit *or* go (*into*), find room enough; δὲν ~εῖ ἀμφιβολία there is no room for doubt; δὲν μοῦ ~άει τὸ καπέλλο the hat is too small for me. (*v.t.*) hold, contain, have room for; δὲν τὸ ~άει ὁ νοῦς μου it passes my understanding.

χώσιμο *s.n.* thrusting, sticking (in).

χωστός *a.* sunk, deep-set.

Ψ

ψάθ|α *s.f.* straw, cane; rush mat; (*wide-brimmed*) straw hat; (*fig.*) στὴν ~α in penury. ~άκι *s.n.* (*man's*) boater. ~ινος *a.* straw.

ψαλίδα *s.f.* shears.

ψαλίδ|ι *s.n.* scissors; curling-tongs. ~ίζω *v.t.* cut, clip. ~ωτός *a.* swallow-tailed.

ψάλλω *v.t. & i.* sing, chant.

ψαλμ|ός *s.m.* psalm. ~ωδία *s.f.* (chanting of) psalms; (*fam.*) monotonous recital.

ψαλτήριον *s.n.* psalter.

ψάλτης s.m. chorister, singer.

ψαμμίασις s.f. (med.) gravel.

ψάξιμο s.n. searching.

ψαράδικ|ος a. fisherman's. ~ο s.n. fishing-boat; fishmonger's.

ψαραίνω v.i. turn grey.

ψαράς s.m. fisherman; fishmonger.

ψάρε(υ)μα s.n. fishing.

ψαρεύω v.i. & t. fish (for); sound, pump (for information).

ψαρής a. grey-haired; a grey (horse).

ψάρι s.n. fish.

ψαρόβαρκα s.f. fishing-boat.

ψαροκόκκαλο s.n. fish-bone; herring-bone (pattern).

ψαρόκολλα s.f. fish-glue.

ψαρονέφρι s.n. fillet (meat).

ψαροπούλα s.f. fishing-boat.

ψαρός a. grey, grizzled.

ψαῦσις s.f. touching, feeling (action).

ψαύω v.t. touch, feel.

ψαχνό s.n. lean meat (without bone); (fam.) βαρᾶτε στό ~ shoot to kill!

ψάχν|ω v.t. & i. search (for). ~ομαι v.i. search one's pockets.

ψαχουλεύω v.i. search, grope.

ψέγ|ω v.t. blame, reprehend. ~άδι s.n. fault, defect.

ψεῖρ|α s.f. louse. ~ιάζω v.i. become lousy. ~ίζω v.t. rid of lice; (fam.) rob.

ψεκ|άζω v.t. spray. ~αστήρ s.m. spray, vaporizer.

ψελλίζω v.i. & t. stammer.

ψέλνω v.t. sing (hymns); (fam.) τὸν ἔψαλα I scolded him.

ψέμα s.n. lie; (fam.) τελείωσαν (or σώθηκαν) τὰ ~τα things are beginning to move in earnest; μὲ τὰ ~τα with very small outlay (but to good effect).

ψές adv. yesterday.

ψευδαίσθησις s.f. illusion.

ψευδάργυρος s.m. zinc.

ψευδής a. false; artificial, sham.

ψευδίζω v.i. lisp; have speech defect.

ψευδολογῶ v.i. tell lies.

ψεύδομαι v.i.i. lie.

ψευδομάρτ|υς s.m.f. false witness. ~υρῶ v.i. give false evidence.

ψευδορκ|ία s.f. perjury. ~ῶ v.i. commit perjury.

ψεῦδος s.n. lie, falsehood.

ψευδός a. lisping.

ψευδώνυμον s.n. pseudonym.

ψεῦμα s.n. lie.

ψεύ(σ)της s.m. liar.

ψευτιά s.f. lie, falsehood.

ψευτίζω v.t. lower quality of (goods).

ψεύτικος a. false, sham, artificial; inferior (in quality).

ψευτοφυλλάδα s.f. lying newspaper; (fig.) liar.

ψῆγμα s.n. filings, dust (of metal).

ψήκτρα s.f. brush.

ψηλαφ|ῶ v.t. & i. feel, finger; grope (for); feel one's way. ~ητός a. palpable; (fig.) obvious.

ψηλομύτης a. supercilious.

ψηλ|ός a. high, tall; ~ό καπέλλο top-hat. ~ά adv. high (up).

ψήλωμα s.n. high ground, elevation; growing taller.

ψηλώνω v.t. & i. make or grow higher or taller.

ψήν|ω v.t. bake, roast; cook; (fig.) torment; (fam.) persuade; τὰ ψήσανε they are having an affair. ~ομαι v.i. (fig.) get very hot; ripen; become broken in (to).

ψησιά s.f. potful, panful (in cooking).

ψήσιμο s.n. baking, roasting; cooking.

ψησταριά s.f. apparatus for barbecue.

ψηστικά s.n.pl. fee for cooking in public oven.

ψητ|ός a. roast, baked, grilled. ~ό s.n. roast or grilled meat; (fig.) heart of the matter.

ψηφιδωτόν s.n. mosaic.

ψηφίζω v.i. & t. vote (for).

ψηφίον s.n. (numerical) figure; (alphabetic) letter.

ψήφισμα s.n. resolution (by vote).

ψηφοδέλτιον s.n. ballot-paper.

ψηφοδόχος s.f. ballot-box.

ψηφοθηρῶ v.i. solicit votes.

ψῆφος s.m.f. vote; ἀναλογικὴ ~ proportional representation; μέλαινα ~ black ball.

ψηφοφορία s.f. voting; θέτω εἰς ~ν put to the vote.

ψηφῶ v.t. heed, respect.

ψῖ s.n. the letter Ψ.

ψίαθος s.m. straw, cane.

ψίδι s.n. vamp (of shoe).

ψίθυρ|ος s.m. whisper, murmur. ~ίζω v.i. & t. whisper, murmur. ~ισμα s.n., ~ισμός s.m. whispering, murmuring.

ψιλά s.n.pl. (small) change; (fig.) money.

ψιλαίνω v.t. make thinner; raise pitch of (voice).

ψιλή s.f. (gram.) smooth breathing.

ψιλικ|ά s.n.pl. haberdashery; small wares. ~ατζήδικο s.n. haberdasher's.
ψιλικό s.n. (fam.) money.
ψιλολογῶ v.t. examine minutely.
ψιλορωτῶ v.t. ask (person) many details.
ψιλ|ός a. thin, fine; ~ὰ γράμματα small print; shrill; light (armour).
ψιλοτραγουδῶ v.i. & t. hum.
ψιμάρι s.n. late-born lamb; (fig.) easy prey.
ψιμύθιον s.n. make-up (cosmetic).
ψιττακ|ός s.m. parrot. ~ίζω v.t. parrot.
ψίχα s.f. crumb (soft part of loaf); edible part of nut; pith; (fig.) morsel.
ψιχάλ|α s.f. drizzle; rain-drop. ~ίζει v.i. it drizzles.
ψίχ|αλο, ~ουλο s.n. crumb.
ψιχίον s.n. crumb.
ψιψίνα s.f. (fam.) pussy-cat.
ψιψιρίζω v.t. examine minutely.
ψόγος s.m. blame, reprehension.
ψουν- see ψων-.
ψοφίμι s.n. putrefying carcass; ~α (pl.) carrion.
ψόφιος a. dead (of animals); (fig.) exhausted; without vitality, spineless; ~ στὴν κούραση dog-tired.
ψοφολογῶ v.i. (fam.) (pej.) sleep.
ψόφος s.m. 1. dull noise. 2. death; (fam.) biting cold.
ψοφῶ v.i. die (of animals); (fig.) ~ γιά long for, be mad on.
ψυγεῖον s.n. refrigerator; radiator (of motor).
ψυκτικός a. cooling, refrigerating.
ψύλλ|ος s.m. flea; (fam.) γιὰ ~ου πήδημα at the least provocation, for the merest trifle.
ψῦξις s.f. refrigeration; chill.
ψυχαγωγ|ία s.f. recreation, diversion. ~ικός a. recreational.
ψυχανάλυσις s.f. psycho-analysis.
ψυχαρισμός s.m. linguistic doctrine of Psycharis (1854-1929), viz. advocacy of extreme demotic Gk.
ψυχή s.f. soul; heart; energy, spirit, courage; butterfly; μοῦ ἔβγαλε τὴν ~ he exasperated or exhausted me.
ψυχίατρ|ος s.m. psychiatrist. ~εῖον s.n. mental hospital. ~ική s.f. psychiatry.
ψυχικάρης a. compassionate.
ψυχικό s.n. (act of) charity; alms.
ψυχικ|ός a. psychical; psychic; ~ή διάθεσις humour; ~ὸς κόσμος one's moral resources; ~ὴ ὀδύνη (law) mental distress (as ground for damages).

ψυχογιός s.m. adopted son; boy (servant).
ψυχοκόρη s.f. adopted daughter.
ψυχολόγ|ος s.m. psychologist. ~ία s.f. psychology. ~ικός a. psychological.
ψυχολογ|ῶ v.t. read soul or mind of; ~ημένος done with psychological insight.
ψυχομαχῶ v.i. be in the throes of death.
ψυχοπαθής a. a psychopath.
ψυχοπαίδι s.n. adopted child.
ψυχοπόνια s.f. compassion.
ψυχόρμητον s.n. instinct.
ψυχορραγῶ v.i. be in the throes of death.
ψῦχος s.n. cold.
ψυχοσάββατο s.n. All Souls' Day.
ψυχοσύνθεσις s.f. one's psychological make-up.
ψύχρα s.f. chilly weather.
ψύχραιμ|ος a. cold-blooded (offish, etc.); cool, composed. ~ία s.f. sangfroid, composure.
ψυχραίν|ω v.i. & t. get cold (of weather); (v.t.) make cold. ~ομαι v.i. cool off (of feelings).
ψυχρολουσία s.f. cold shower or douche; (fam.) dressing-down.
ψυχρ|ός a. cold. ~ότης s.f. coldness.
ψυχρούλα s.f. freshness (of weather).
ψύχω v.t. freeze, cool, make cold.
ψύχωσις s.f. psychosis; (fam.) mania, complex.
ψωμ|ᾶς s.m. baker. ~άδικο s.n. bakery.
ψωμ|ί s.n. bread; loaf. ~άκι s.n. roll or piece of bread.
ψωμοζήτης s.m. mendicant.
ψωμοζῶ v.i. eke out one's existence.
ψωμοτύρι s.n. bread and cheese.
ψωμώνω v.i. develop well, fill out.
ψωνίζω v.t. & i. buy; do shopping; (fam.) get hold of, fish up (person); catch (cold, etc.); τήν ~ become queer or crazy.
ψώνι|ο s.n. thing bought; ~α (pl.) purchases, shopping; (fam.) ἔχω ~ο have a craze (for); εἶναι ~ο he is a queer fish.
ψώρα s.f. scabies, mange; (fig.) a pest (person).
ψωριάζω v.i. become mangy.
ψωριάρης a. mangy; (fig.) skinny, poverty-stricken, beggarly.
ψωρίασις s.f. (med.) psoriasis.
ψωριῶ v.i. have scabies or mange.
ψωροκώσταινα s.f. (fam.) poverty-stricken Greece.
ψωροπερηφάνεια s.f. pretensions not befitting one's poor condition.

ω

ῶ *int.* of surprise, alarm, *etc.*
ὡάριον *s.n.* ovum.
ῶδε *adv.* 1. thus. 2. here.
ὠδεῖον *s.n.* school of music.
ὠδή *s.f.* ode.
ὠδικ|ός *a.* singing. ~ή *s.f.* singing (lesson).
ὠδῖνες *s.f.pl.* pangs of childbirth.
ὠθῶ|ῶ *v.t.* push, impel. ~ησις *s.f.* pushing, impulsion.
ὠιμέ(να) *int.* alas!
ὠκεανός *s.m.* ocean.
ὠκύπους *a.* fleet-footed.
ὠλένη *s.f.* (*anat.*) forearm.
ὠμέγα *s.n.* the letter Ω.
ὠμοπλάτη *s.f.* shoulder-blade.
ὄμορφος *a.* see ὄμορφος.
ὦμος *s.m.* shoulder.
ὠμός *a.* 1. raw. 2. hard, cruel. 3. slow, spineless (*person*).
ὠμότ|ης *s.f.* cruelty; ~ητες (*pl.*) atrocities.
ὤν *v.i.* (*participle*) being.
ὤνια *s.n.pl.* provisions, goods.
ὠοειδής *a.* oval.
ὠοθήκη *s.f.* ovary.
ὠόν *s.n.* egg.
ὠοτόκος *a.* oviparous.
ὥρ|α *s.f.* hour; time; μὲ τὴν ~α by the hour; ~α μὲ τὴν ~α at any moment; ~ες ~ες now and then; μὲ τὶς ~ες for hours; ἦρθε στὴν (*or* μὲ τὴν) ~α του he came punctually *or* (*ironic*) late; εἶναι μὲ τὶς ~ες του he has his moods; εἶναι στὴν ~α της she is about to give birth; (*πάνω*) στὴν ~α at the very moment, just at the right (*or* wrong) moment; τῆς ~ας fresh, (*cooked*) to order; τῆς κακιᾶς ~ας of poor quality.
ὡραῖα *adv.* beautifully, well; (*int.*) good, very well.
ὡραιοπαθής *a.* in love with beauty.
ὡραῖ|ος *a.* beautiful, handsome; fine, good. ~ότης *s.f.* beauty.
ὡράριον *s.n.* (*employee's*) hours of work.
ὡριαῖος *a.* hourly; lasting an hour.

ὡριμάζω *v.i.* ripen, mature.
ὠρίμανσις *s.f.* ripening.
ὥριμ|ος *a.* ripe, mature. ~ότης *s.f.* ripeness, maturity.
ὥριος *a.* beautiful.
ὡρισμέν|ος *a.* fixed, determined; certain (*unspecified*). ~ως *adv.* definitely.
ὡροδείκτης *s.m.* hour-hand.
ὡρολόγιον *s.n.* clock, watch; ἡλιακὸν ~ sundial; time-table (*of work*); (*eccl.*) breviary.
ὡρολογοποιός *s.m.* watchmaker.
ὡροσκόπιον *s.n.* horoscope.
ὡρυγή *s.f.* howl, howling.
ὠρύομαι *v.i.* howl.
ὥς 1. *prep.* (*with acc.*) until, up to, as far as. 2. *conj.* ~ ὅτου (*νά*) until. 3. *adv.* (*with numbers*) about.
ὡς 1. *adv.* as, like, such as. 2. *conj.* as, while, as soon as. 3. *see* ὥς.
ὡσάν *adv.* like, as, as if.
ὡσαύτως *adv.* also, likewise.
ὡσότου *conj.* until, by the time.
ὥσπερ *adv.* like, as.
ὥσπου *conj.* until, by the time.
ὥστε *conj.* so, accordingly, consequently; that (*as result*); οὕτως ~ in such a way as to.
ὡστόσο *adv.* yet, however; meanwhile.
ὠτακουστ|ῶ *v.i.* eavesdrop. ~ής *s.m.* eavesdropper.
ὠτίον *s.n.* ear.
ὠτομοτρίς *s.f.* rail motor-car. [F. *automotrice*]
ὠτορινολαρυγγολόγος *s.m.* ear-nose-and-throat specialist.
ὠφέλεια *s.f.* benefit, good, profit (*general*); εἶδα ~ I benefited.
ὠφέλημα *s.n.* benefit, good, profit (*particular*).
ὠφέλιμος *a.* beneficial, useful, of service.
ὠφελ|ῶ *v.t.* benefit, do good to, help. ~οῦμαι *v.i.* benefit, profit.
ὤχ, ὤχου *int.* of pain or distress.
ὤχρα *s.f.* ochre.
ὠχριῶ *v.i.* become pale; (*fig.*) pale (*to insignificance*).
ὠχρ|ός *a.* pale, pallid; (*fig.*) faint, indistinct. ~ότης *s.f.* pallor.